Handbook of Research on AI and Machine Learning Applications in Customer Support and Analytics

Md Shamim Hossain
Hajee Mohammad Danesh Science and Technology University, Bangladesh

Ree Chan Ho
Taylor's University, Malaysia

Goran Trajkovski
Western Governors University, USA

A volume in the Advances in Business Information
Systems and Analytics (ABISA) Book Series

Published in the United States of America by
IGI Global
Business Science Reference (an imprint of IGI Global)
701 E. Chocolate Avenue
Hershey PA, USA 17033
Tel: 717-533-8845
Fax: 717-533-8661
E-mail: cust@igi-global.com
Web site: http://www.igi-global.com

Library of Congress Cataloging-in-Publication Data

Names: Hossain, Md Shamim, 1986- editor. | Ho, Ree C., 1986- editor. |
  Trajkovski, Goran, 1972- editor.
Title: Handbook of research on AI and machine learning applications in customer
  support and analytics / edited by Md Shamim Hossain, Ree Chan Ho, Goran
  Trajkovski.
Description: Hershey, PA : Business Science Reference, [2023] | Includes
  bibliographical references and index. | Summary: "The Handbook of Research on
  AI and Machine Learning Applications in Customer Support and Analytics
  explores various artificial intelligence and machine learning models and
  methods for business applications, as well as algorithmic approaches for
  customer support and analytics in a variety of fields and applications
  in the modern data-driven era where data is arriving in greater variety
  and with more velocity. This book is ideal for marketing professionals,
  managers, business owners, researchers, practitioners, academicians,
  instructors, university libraries, and students, and covers topics such
  as artificial intelligence, machine learning, supervised learning,
  unsupervised learning, deep learning, customer sentiment analysis,
  customer emotional analysis, natural language processing, data mining,
  neural networks, ensemble learning, business analytics and analytical
  geared toward"-- Provided by publisher.
Identifiers: LCCN 2022049409 (print) | LCCN 2022049410 (ebook) | ISBN
  9781668471050 (hardcover) | ISBN 9781668471074 (ebook)
Subjects: LCSH: Consumers--Research. | Consumer behavior--Data processing.
  | Artificial intelligence--Marketing applications.
Classification: LCC HF5415.32 .A39 2023 (print) | LCC HF5415.32 (ebook) |
  DDC 658.8/342028563--dc23/eng/20230117
LC record available at https://lccn.loc.gov/2022049409
LC ebook record available at https://lccn.loc.gov/2022049410

This book is published in the IGI Global book series Advances in Business Information Systems and Analytics (ABISA) (ISSN: 2327-3275; eISSN: 2327-3283)

British Cataloguing in Publication Data
A Cataloguing in Publication record for this book is available from the British Library.

For electronic access to this publication, please contact: eresources@igi-global.com.

Advances in Business Information Systems and Analytics (ABISA) Book Series

Madjid Tavana
La Salle University, USA

ISSN:2327-3275
EISSN:2327-3283

Mission

The successful development and management of information systems and business analytics is crucial to the success of an organization. New technological developments and methods for data analysis have allowed organizations to not only improve their processes and allow for greater productivity, but have also provided businesses with a venue through which to cut costs, plan for the future, and maintain competitive advantage in the information age.

The **Advances in Business Information Systems and Analytics (ABISA) Book Series** aims to present diverse and timely research in the development, deployment, and management of business information systems and business analytics for continued organizational development and improved business value.

Coverage

- Business Systems Engineering
- Data Governance
- Data Management
- Information Logistics
- Business Process Management
- Business Intelligence
- Strategic Information Systems
- Business Models
- Data Analytics
- Data Strategy

IGI Global is currently accepting manuscripts for publication within this series. To submit a proposal for a volume in this series, please contact our Acquisition Editors at Acquisitions@igi-global.com or visit: http://www.igi-global.com/publish/.

Titles in this Series

For a list of additional titles in this series, please visit:
http://www.igi-global.com/book-series/advances-business-information-systems-analytics/37155

Building Secure Business Models Through Blockchain Technology Tactics, Methods, Limitations, and Performance
Shweta Dewangan (ICFAI University, Raipur, India) Sapna Singh Kshatri (Shri Shankaracharya Institute of Professional Management and Technology, India) Astha Bhanot (Princess Nourah Bint Abdulrahman University, Saudi Arabia) and Mushtaq Ahmed Shah (Lovely Professional University, India)
Business Science Reference • ©2023 • 283pp • H/C (ISBN: 9781668478080) • US $250.00

Enhancing Business Communications and Collaboration Through Data Science Applications
Nuno Geada (ISCTE - University Institute of Lisbon, Portugal) and George Leal Jamil (Informações em Rede Consultoria e Treinamento, Brazil)
Business Science Reference • ©2023 • 262pp • H/C (ISBN: 9781668467862) • US $270.00

Revolutionizing Business Practices Through Artificial Intelligence and Data-Rich Environments
Manisha Gupta (Sharda University, India) Deergha Sharma (The NorthCap University, India) and Himani Gupta (Jagannath International Management School, India)
Business Science Reference • ©2022 • 300pp • H/C (ISBN: 9781668449509) • US $250.00

AI-Driven Intelligent Models for Business Excellence
Samala Nagaraj (Woxsen University, India) and Korupalli V. Rajesh Kumar (Woxsen University, India)
Business Science Reference • ©2023 • 267pp • H/C (ISBN: 9781668442463) • US $250.00

Handbook of Research on Foundations and Applications of Intelligent Business Analytics
Zhaohao Sun (Papua New Guinea University of Technology, Papua New Guinea) and Zhiyou Wu (Chongqing Normal University, China)
Business Science Reference • ©2022 • 425pp • H/C (ISBN: 9781799890164) • US $325.00

Utilizing Blockchain Technologies in Manufacturing and Logistics Management
S. B. Goyal (City University, Malaysia) Nijalingappa Pradeep (Bapuji Institute of Engineering and Technology, India) Piyush Kumar Shukla (University Institute of Technology RGPV, India) Mangesh M. Ghonge (Sandip Institute of Technology and Research Centre, India) and Renjith V. Ravi (MEA Engineering College, India)
Business Science Reference • ©2022 • 290pp • H/C (ISBN: 9781799886976) • US $250.00

701 East Chocolate Avenue, Hershey, PA 17033, USA
Tel: 717-533-8845 x100 • Fax: 717-533-8661
E-Mail: cust@igi-global.com • www.igi-global.com

List of Contributors

Abresham, Abu Eyaz / *Hajee Mohammad Danesh Science and Technology University, Bangladesh* 300

Al Noman, Md Abdullah / *Hajee Mohammad Danesh Science and Technology University, Bangladesh* 342

Aouiche, Abdelaziz / *Independent Researcher, Algeria* 128

Banga, Manu / *GLA University, India* 276

Bokhare, Anuja / *Symbiosis Institute of Computer Studies and Research, Symbiosis International University (Deemed), India* 248

Boulaaras, Zineb / *Larbi Tebessi University, Algeria* 128

Chafaa, Kheireddine / *Independent Researcher, Algeria* 128

Chatterjee, Kingshuk / *Government College of Engineering and Ceramic Technology, India* 113

Dahiya, Omdev / *Lovely Professional University, India* 342

Dey, Paramita / *Government College of Engineering and Ceramic Technology, India* 113

Duraipandy, Jeyabharathi / *Sri Krishna College of Technology, India* 183

George, Soumya / *St. George's College Aruvithura, India* 362

Gopal R. / *Bharathiar University, India* 325

Gupta, Ankur / *Vaish College of Engineering, India* 160

Gupta, Swati / *K.R. Mangalam University, India* 90

Gurram, Rajender / *GF, USA* 1

Ho, Ree Chan / *Taylor's University, Malaysia* 17

Hossain, Md Shamim / *Hajee Mohammad Danesh Science and Technology University, Bangladesh* 300, 342

Indiramma M. / *BMS College of Engineering, India* 227

Kesavaraja D. / *Dr. Sivanthi Aditanar College of Engineering, India* 183

Kumar, Kulamala Vinod / *Siksha 'O' Anusandhan (Deemed), India* 248

Kumar, Nitin / *K.R. Mangalam University, India* 90

Kumar, Rohit / *K.R. Mangalam University, India* 90

Leow, Nelvin XeChung / *Taylor's University, Malaysia* 17

Madhuri J. / *Bangalore Institute of Technology, India* 227

Manikandan K. / *Vellore Institute of Technology, India* 160

Napoleon D. / *Bharathiar University, India* 325

Pramanik, Sabyasachi / *Haldia Institute of Technology, India* 160

Pranto, Asif Jaied / *Hajee Mohammad Danesh Science and Technology University, Bangladesh* 300

Pretorius, André / *Stellenbosch University, South Africa* 56

Rahman, Md Raisur / *Hajee Mohammad Danesh Science and Technology University, Bangladesh* 300

Rahman, Md. Mahafuzur / *Hajee Mohammad Danesh Science and Technology University, Bangladesh* 300

Rao, Madhuri / *Symbiosis Institute of Computer Studies and Research, Symbiosis International University (Deemed), India* 248

Saharan, Naveen / *Fidelity Investments, India* 1

Sakib, S M Nazmuz / *International MBA Institute, School of Business and Trade, Dhaka International University, Bangladesh* 37, 202

Sasireka D. / *SRM Institute of Science and Technology, India* 183

Senapati, Ankit / *Siksha 'O' Anusandhan (Deemed), India* 248

Sharma, Yuvraj / *GF, India* 1

Sherly Alphonse A. / *Vellore Institute of Technology, Chennai, India* 183

Solavande, Vivek Dadasaheb / *Bharati Vidyapeeth (Deemed), India* 160

Talukdar, Suryansh Bhaskar / *Vellore Institute of Technology, India* 160

Talukdar, Veera / *RNB Global University, India* 160

Thakur, Uma Khemchand / *Jhulelal Institute of Technology, Nagpur, India* 80

Veeraiah, Vivek / *Adichunchanagiri University, India* 160

Vijarania, Meenu / *K.R. Mangalam University, India* 90

Table of Contents

Preface.. xix

Section 1
Customer Analytics

Chapter 1
Adoption of Churn Recognition System to Predict Customer Churn: A Study With Respect to
Semiconductor Supply Chain... 1
    Yuvraj Sharma, GF, India
    Rajender Gurram, GF, USA
    Naveen Saharan, Fidelity Investments, India

Chapter 2
Examining Customer Behavior Towards the Use of Contextual Commerce Powered by Artificial
Intelligence 17
    Ree Chan Ho, Taylor's University, Malaysia
    Nelvin XeChung Leow, Taylor's University, Malaysia

Chapter 3
Artificial Intelligence Model for Analyzing the Buying Patterns of Customers.................................. 37
    S M Nazmuz Sakib, International MBA Institute, School of Business and Trade, Dhaka
        International University, Bangladesh

Chapter 4
A Pedagogy to Support Learning Analytics: A Case for a Specific Higher Education Institution....... 56
    André Pretorius, Stellenbosch University, South Africa

Chapter 5
The Role of Machine Learning in Customer Experience 80
    Uma Khemchand Thakur, Jhulelal Institute of Technology, Nagpur, India

Chapter 6

Mall Customer Segmentation Engine Through Clustering Analysis 90
  Meenu Vijarania, K.R. Mangalam University, India
  Nitin Kumar, K.R. Mangalam University, India
  Rohit Kumar, K.R. Mangalam University, India
  Swati Gupta, K.R. Mangalam University, India

Section 2
Machine Learning for Optimization

Chapter 7

Application of Machine Learning for Optimization 113
  Paramita Dey, Government College of Engineering and Ceramic Technology, India
  Kingshuk Chatterjee, Government College of Engineering and Ceramic Technology, India

Chapter 8

Approval of Artificial Intelligence and Machine Learning Models to Solve Problems in Nonlinear
Active Suspension Systems 128
  Zineb Boulaaras, Larbi Tebessi University, Algeria
  Abdelaziz Aouiche, Independent Researcher, Algeria
  Kheireddine Chafaa, Independent Researcher, Algeria

Chapter 9

Machine Learning Frameworks in Carpooling 160
  Vivek Veeraiah, Adichunchanagiri University, India
  Veera Talukdar, RNB Global University, India
  Manikandan K., Vellore Institute of Technology, India
  Suryansh Bhaskar Talukdar, Vellore Institute of Technology, India
  Vivek Dadasaheb Solavande, Bharati Vidyapeeth (Deemed), India
  Sabyasachi Pramanik, Haldia Institute of Technology, India
  Ankur Gupta, Vaish College of Engineering, India

Chapter 10

Smart ATM With Tracking of Criminals Using Novel Di-Pattern and C-LDP (Combined Local
Directional Pattern) 183
  Jeyabharathi Duraipandy, Sri Krishna College of Technology, India
  Sherly Alphonse A., Vellore Institute of Technology, Chennai, India
  Sasireka D., SRM Institute of Science and Technology, India
  Kesavaraja D., Dr. Sivanthi Aditanar College of Engineering, India

Section 3
Predictive Analytics

Chapter 11
Restaurant Sales Prediction Using Machine Learning..202
    S M Nazmuz Sakib, International MBA Institute, School of Business and Trade, Dhaka
        International University, Bangladesh

Chapter 12
Big Data Analytics-Based Agro Advisory System for Crop Recommendation Using Spark
Platform..227
    Madhuri J., Bangalore Institute of Technology, India
    Indiramma M., BMS College of Engineering, India

Chapter 13
Clearance Date Prediction Using Machine Learning Techniques 248
    Madhuri Rao, Symbiosis Institute of Computer Studies and Research, Symbiosis
        International University (Deemed), India
    Ankit Senapati, Siksha 'O' Anusandhan (Deemed), India
    Kulamala Vinod Kumar, Siksha 'O' Anusandhan (Deemed), India
    Anuja Bokhare, Symbiosis Institute of Computer Studies and Research, Symbiosis
        International University (Deemed), India

Chapter 14
Predicting Healthcare Readmissions Using Artificial Intelligence...276
    Manu Banga, GLA University, India

Section 4
Artificial Intelligence in Customer Support

Chapter 15
AI and Machine Learning Applications to Enhance Customer Support 300
    Md Shamim Hossain, Hajee Mohammad Danesh Science and Technology University, Bangladesh
    Md. Mahafuzur Rahman, Hajee Mohammad Danesh Science and Technology University,
        Bangladesh
    Abu Eyaz Abresham, Hajee Mohammad Danesh Science and Technology University, Bangladesh
    Asif Jaied Pranto, Hajee Mohammad Danesh Science and Technology University, Bangladesh
    Md Raisur Rahman, Hajee Mohammad Danesh Science and Technology University, Bangladesh

Chapter 16
Customer Face-Detecting Artificial Intelligence With People Search Social Site Algorithm for
Product Encroachment in Supermarkets: Business Development With Customer Perspective AI
Technology...325
    Napoleon D., Bharathiar University, India
    Gopal R., Bharathiar University, India

Chapter 17
User Sentiment Prediction and Analysis for Payment App Reviews Using Supervised and
Unsupervised Machine Learning Approaches 342
    Md Shamim Hossain, Hajee Mohammad Danesh Science and Technology University, Bangladesh
    Omdev Dahiya, Lovely Professional University, India
    Md Abdullah Al Noman, Hajee Mohammad Danesh Science and Technology University,
        Bangladesh

Chapter 18
Sequence Graph-Based Query Auto-Suggestion (SGQAS) 362
    Soumya George, St. George's College Aruvithura, India

Compilation of References 381

About the Contributors 415

Index 421

Detailed Table of Contents

Preface...xix

Section 1
Customer Analytics

Chapter 1
Adoption of Churn Recognition System to Predict Customer Churn: A Study With Respect to
Semiconductor Supply Chain..1
    Yuvraj Sharma, GF, India
    Rajender Gurram, GF, USA
    Naveen Saharan, Fidelity Investments, India

In the cutthroat competitive arena, it is a very challenging task for any enterprise to make a balance between retaining its existing loyal customers and attracting new customers. It is a tedious task to find the right segment of active customers and understand the reason behind churn numbers. It is said that it is five times more costly to attract new customers as compared to retaining existing customers. The main aim of this chapter is to understand the customer churn application, which is one of the most useful applications of AI and ML in the customer analytics domain. Researchers further studied the most significant factors affecting customer behavior and responsible for increasing the customer churn rate. The study mainly targeted the semiconductor supply chain industry, which is one of the most complex industries and foundation of advanced technology and penetrated the walks of human life.

Chapter 2
Examining Customer Behavior Towards the Use of Contextual Commerce Powered by Artificial
Intelligence...17
    Ree Chan Ho, Taylor's University, Malaysia
    Nelvin XeChung Leow, Taylor's University, Malaysia

The integration of artificial intelligence into electronic commerce has revolutionized consumer behavior due to its capability in supporting cutting-edge features for conducting business online. It pertains to contextual commerce that facilitates customers to connect and buy goods wherever they are. This study aimed to examine the influence of artificial intelligence applications on the operations of contextual commerce. The conceptual framework was based on the UTAUT theory. The sample was the users of contextual commerce who were familiar with its usage. An online questionnaire was used to collect the data, and variance-based structured equation modeling was applied for data analysis. The four technological acceptance constructs derived from UTAUT were tested and confirmed as antecedents for contextual commerce. Furthermore, the inclusion of brand anthropomorphism as the antecedent was also supported. The empirical findings of the study explain the consumer attitude toward the significant use of artificial intelligence in contextual commerce.

Chapter 3
Artificial Intelligence Model for Analyzing the Buying Patterns of Customers...................................37
    S M Nazmuz Sakib, International MBA Institute, School of Business and Trade, Dhaka
       International University, Bangladesh

This study aims to incorporate artificial intelligence (AI) for analyzing buying patterns of customers and different factors that are playing its role by discovering the important factors that contribute towards changing patterns. In order to study, a survey has been conducted for this analysis. Selected dataset consists of four attributes (i.e., gender, age, estimated salary, and purchase). These factors are used as input to AI model. The dataset consists of 400 members. Eighty percent of the data has been used for the purpose of training, and the data used for testing purpose is 20%. Experimental results have shown that that model has achieved 90% accuracy. It means AI has contributed a lot towards changing behaviors and approach of the customers during online shopping.

Chapter 4
A Pedagogy to Support Learning Analytics: A Case for a Specific Higher Education Institution.......56
    André Pretorius, Stellenbosch University, South Africa

Learning analytics (LA) is a contemporary field of research with advances in machine learning that enables the user to draw conclusions about current teaching and learning based on indicators deduced from historical datasets. The need existed for an understanding of the fundamental grounding principles on which the institutional pedagogy is based. Therefore, the theoretical grounding for the implementation of a virtual learning environment that conforms to good educational practice and can inform a LA reference framework with the aim of identifying at-risk students is established. A gap existed in the institution to implement LA that identify at-risk students. The methodology that was used was a mixed method design science methodology to establish the historical philosophical grounding, linking it to modern teaching practice, establishing best practice through an institutional case study, and defining an appropriate pedagogy. It concludes with a description of a pedagogical model suited to LA, the result of the application of the pedagogy as a case study.

Chapter 5
The Role of Machine Learning in Customer Experience 80
    Uma Khemchand Thakur, Jhulelal Institute of Technology, Nagpur, India

Machine learning is a subtype of artificial intelligence in which computers use algorithms to learn from data and discover patterns, a capacity that businesses may exploit in various ways to improve customer service. Machine learning (ML) is improving nearly every function and process automation by enabling operational optimisation. As a result, it improves customer service, speeds up work, lessens errors, and improves accuracy. Customer service is one area of the company that might benefit from machine learning. Natural language processing and sentiment analysis are two technologies that can help businesses better understand how to respond to consumer comments and queries.

Chapter 6

Mall Customer Segmentation Engine Through Clustering Analysis 90

Meenu Vijarania, K.R. Mangalam University, India

Nitin Kumar, K.R. Mangalam University, India

Rohit Kumar, K.R. Mangalam University, India

Swati Gupta, K.R. Mangalam University, India

Finding related information within a cluster is done using a technique called clustering. The dataset cluster uses the data's maximum and minimum values to group together similar data. Clustering is a process in which matter has been split into groups and grouped based on a rule to maximize within-group similarity and minimize between-group difference likeness. In this chapter, the authors examine and contrast the various group analysis techniques and algorithms employed by Rapid Miner. Multiple clustering methods have been developed. In the chapter, two types of clustering for algorithms are analyzed. One area of mall patrons was evaluated. The data set is used with Rapid Miner tools to determine the proper cluster.

Section 2
Machine Learning for Optimization

Chapter 7

Application of Machine Learning for Optimization 113

Paramita Dey, Government College of Engineering and Ceramic Technology, India

Kingshuk Chatterjee, Government College of Engineering and Ceramic Technology, India

This chapter reviews the literature on machine learning and presents regularly used machine learning algorithms in an optimization framework. The interaction between learning algorithm and optimization shell are scrutinized. Methodologies that increase the scalability and efficiency are discussed. Optimizations strategies are predominant in customer support analytics. Optimization schedule basically endeavours to discover the greatest or least of a job, like the objective work, by creating a calculation that methodically chooses input values from a permitted set and computes the esteem of the work. Machine learning favours less-complex calculations that work in sensible computational time. Any side from data fitting, there are various optimization problems and optimization algorithms, and machine learning can ease the solution. In addition, many methods extensively used for the analytics of customer support have been proposed in optimization problems over the last few decades to obtain optimal resolution. Pros and cons of these models and future research directions have been shown.

Chapter 8

Approval of Artificial Intelligence and Machine Learning Models to Solve Problems in Nonlinear
Active Suspension Systems.. 128

Zineb Boulaaras, Larbi Tebessi University, Algeria

Abdelaziz Aouiche, Independent Researcher, Algeria

Kheireddine Chafaa, Independent Researcher, Algeria

In this chapter, the authors used a comparative study between passive and active suspension of quarter car models with deference intelligent controllers. This study aims to obtain an active suspension that adapts to all types of roads, especially rough and slippery ones, and absorbs shocks resulting from road vibrations, which gives more comfort to passengers and the driver. The results have proven that FOPID gave better results than PID in all types of road testing. The concerns related to the proposed chapter are that the car makers have a fear of the Fractional-Order controller FOPID to the difficulty of achieving it in the industrial field because of the difficulty of its mathematical equations and its high cost.

Chapter 9
Machine Learning Frameworks in Carpooling 160
    Vivek Veeraiah, Adichunchanagiri University, India
    Veera Talukdar, RNB Global University, India
    Manikandan K., Vellore Institute of Technology, India
    Suryansh Bhaskar Talukdar, Vellore Institute of Technology, India
    Vivek Dadasaheb Solavande, Bharati Vidyapeeth (Deemed), India
    Sabyasachi Pramanik, Haldia Institute of Technology, India
    Ankur Gupta, Vaish College of Engineering, India

Due to the development in human population and their requirements, the vehicular population on the globe is increasing day by day in the medium of public transportation. As a result, carpooling comes into play, with the fundamental notion being to share personal automobile space among persons travelling similar paths. Smart carpooling, car sharing, and ridesharing are other terms for the same thing. From a socioeconomic and environmental standpoint, the major task is to develop sustainable transportation. The success of carpooling should be measured in terms of cost, stress-free driving, traffic reduction, and air pollution reduction in the transportation solution system. The major challenge here is to assist vehicle users in gaining access to and picking an appropriate cost-effective transportation option based on their environmental footprint, matching his or her requirements, preferences, and legal limits, and determining the optimum route via specified areas.

Chapter 10
Smart ATM With Tracking of Criminals Using Novel Di-Pattern and C-LDP (Combined Local
Directional Pattern)... 183
    Jeyabharathi Duraipandy, Sri Krishna College of Technology, India
    Sherly Alphonse A., Vellore Institute of Technology, Chennai, India
    Sasireka D., SRM Institute of Science and Technology, India
    Kesavaraja D., Dr. Sivanthi Aditanar College of Engineering, India

Automated teller machine (ATM) surveillance system is a smart system based on image processing that incorporates various sensors and machine learning algorithms to continuously monitor its surroundings for suspicious activities like physical attack. To prevent these attacks, there is a need to find the criminal immediately and save the person's life. In this chapter, two ways are followed to detect the criminals. The first one is weapon detection; the second one is criminal facial identification. A novel magnitude-based feature extraction technique creates the magnitude pattern for the image using Di-Pattern (DiP). Di-Pattern utilizes both horizontal and vertical derivatives to create a unique feature vector of the objects. Based on thresholding, weapons are detected. Once weapon detection as well as facial identification is done, it gives the alert. This system makes its effective usage in the remote locations where threatening is more, thus providing security. The proposed method achieves better accuracy than the other existing methods.

Section 3
Predictive Analytics

Chapter 11

Restaurant Sales Prediction Using Machine Learning..202

S M Nazmuz Sakib, International MBA Institute, School of Business and Trade, Dhaka
    International University, Bangladesh

In general, the revenue forecast, offer information, and the weather gauge setting will record an accurate estimate of any restaurant's future revenue. The turnover is significantly focused on the need of the customers. Either way, the performance has transformed over the past couple of years with the presentation of huge amounts of information and calculations during the time taken to gain the upper hand. It is fundamental to learn and understand the importance of the information that will be used in any business process. Again, climate forecasting can be done alongside business expectations with the organization.

Chapter 12

Big Data Analytics-Based Agro Advisory System for Crop Recommendation Using Spark
Platform...227

Madhuri J., Bangalore Institute of Technology, India
Indiramma M., BMS College of Engineering, India

The advancements in science and technology have led to the generation of colossal data in the agricultural sector as a result of which has entered the world of big data. Big data analytics is the solution to store and analyze such large amounts of data to improve productivity in agricultural practices. Hence, the purpose of this research work is to develop a big data recommendation framework that enables farmers to choose the right crops considering the location-specific parameters. The location-specific weather parameters, soil parameters crop characteristics, and demand for the agricultural product in the previous years are considered in the work. The proposed recommendation model is based on the Spark framework that accepts the soil data in real-time analyses along with weather and pricing data by applying artificial neural networks and suggesting a suitable crop for the field conditions. The chapter prioritizes developing an application useful for farmers, agriculture officers, and researchers to provide efficient crop recommendations.

Chapter 13

Clearance Date Prediction Using Machine Learning Techniques 248

Madhuri Rao, Symbiosis Institute of Computer Studies and Research, Symbiosis
    International University (Deemed), India
Ankit Senapati, Siksha 'O' Anusandhan (Deemed), India
Kulamala Vinod Kumar, Siksha 'O' Anusandhan (Deemed), India
Anuja Bokhare, Symbiosis Institute of Computer Studies and Research, Symbiosis
    International University (Deemed), India

Machine learning is the cutting-edge technology in today's corporate world, making it the first choice for prediction or calculated suggestions relying on heavy amount of data. As companies are evolving towards technological advancement, they are trying to gather as much statistical knowledge as possible regarding their customers and trying to analyze and use that knowledge towards the firm's growth. Machine learning being the top-most of its genre provides the pathway to all of those technological achievements like predictions, statistical analysis, success rate of each customer companies, etc. Machine learning techniques such as linear regression (LR), XGBoost, random forest, and decision tree can be useful for the prediction problems. Here in this work, the authors use data pre-processing and feature selection before applying these machine learning models for predicting the clearance due date.

Chapter 14

Predicting Healthcare Readmissions Using Artificial Intelligence... 276
Manu Banga, GLA University, India

Hospital readmission systems increase the efficiency of initial treatment at hospitals. This chapter proposes a novel prediction model for identifying risk factors using machine learning techniques, and the proposed model is tested using 10-fold cross-validation for generalization and finds hidden patterns in the diagnosis, medications, lab test results, and basic characteristics of patients related to readmissions. This model predicts a statistically problem solving using searching patterns. Based on the findings of this study, for the given dataset, pruning dataset manifested the most accurate prediction of readmissions to the hospital with 94.8% accuracy for patients admitted in a year.

Section 4
Artificial Intelligence in Customer Support

Chapter 15

AI and Machine Learning Applications to Enhance Customer Support 300
Md Shamim Hossain, Hajee Mohammad Danesh Science and Technology University, Bangladesh
Md. Mahafuzur Rahman, Hajee Mohammad Danesh Science and Technology University, Bangladesh
Abu Eyaz Abresham, Hajee Mohammad Danesh Science and Technology University, Bangladesh
Asif Jaied Pranto, Hajee Mohammad Danesh Science and Technology University, Bangladesh
Md Raisur Rahman, Hajee Mohammad Danesh Science and Technology University, Bangladesh

The aim of this study is to investigate the applications of machine learning (ML) and artificial intelligence (AI) techniques in customer support and to make recommendations for future research directions. Based on that, this study analyzed the articles linked to both AI and ML in customer service published on various scientific platforms using a systematic literature review methodology. The findings suggested that different types of AI and ML approaches are helpful for organizations in providing improved customer support and service for different sub-issues in different dimensions (integrated product service offerings, word of mouth, service excellence, and self-service technology) of customer support. The current study also provides businesses with helpful knowledge about how AI and ML technologies may be used to enhance customer service. Practitioners might also get advice from the current study on the need for further crucial measures and improvements.

Chapter 16
Customer Face-Detecting Artificial Intelligence With People Search Social Site Algorithm for
Product Encroachment in Supermarkets: Business Development With Customer Perspective AI
Technology.. 325

Napoleon D., Bharathiar University, India
Gopal R., Bharathiar University, India

This chapter explores the use of an artificial intelligence system-based product suggestion in supermarkets. This is a great way for supermarkets to increase their sales and profitability. The proposed preprocess is to take a picture of the customer at the entrance, and the AI algorithm does the facial recognition with people search in the social sites like Facebook, Amazon, Flipkart, etc. Thus, the result of the search will be classified as what the customer has recently searched for and what his or her favorite and frequent shopping items are get popped up as results. Supermarkets will hold a display board using that system and will automatically do a price slash for the customers' products, which are extracted from their social site data. This helps customers and supermarkets using this technology increase the sales, and the customers will have an opportunity to get preferred goods at a discounted price.

Chapter 17
User Sentiment Prediction and Analysis for Payment App Reviews Using Supervised and
Unsupervised Machine Learning Approaches 342

Md Shamim Hossain, Hajee Mohammad Danesh Science and Technology University, Bangladesh
Omdev Dahiya, Lovely Professional University, India
Md Abdullah Al Noman, Hajee Mohammad Danesh Science and Technology University,
*   Bangladesh*

Businesses must be aware of customer sentiment in order to provide the best customer service. Instead of using cash or a credit card, a user can use a payment app on a mobile device to pay for a variety of services and digital or physical goods, which is becoming increasingly popular around the world. The goal of this study is to evaluate and predict user sentiment for payment apps using supervised and unsupervised machine learning (ML) approaches. For the study's data, Google Play Store reviews of the PayPal and Google Pay apps were gathered. Following cleaning, the filtered summary sentences were assessed for positive, neutral, or negative feelings using two unsupervised and five supervised machine learning approaches. According to the findings of the current study, the majority of customer reviews for payment apps were positive, with the average number of words with negative sentiment being higher. Furthermore, recent research found that, while all ML approaches can correctly classify review text into sentiment classes, logistic regression outperforms them in terms of accuracy.

Chapter 18
Sequence Graph-Based Query Auto-Suggestion (SGQAS) 362
  Soumya George, St. George's College Aruvithura, India

Query autosuggestion or auto-completion is a query prediction service that returns suggested queries for text-based queries when users type in the search box. It is a search-assistant feature of almost all search engines that helps users complete the queries without typing the entire search query. The process of query auto-suggestion typically involves analyzing the user's partial query and generating a list of suggestions based on factors such as popular search terms, the user's search history, and the search context. The suggestions are then displayed to the user in real-time, often in a drop-down menu or other interface types, allowing them to select and refine their search query easily. This chapter proposes a content-based query auto-suggestion using a graph-based word sequence representation of documents using a knowledge graph. It uses the whole sequence of all entered query terms to retrieve the names of all nodes connected to the end node of the entered path sequence of query terms to provide user suggestion queries.

Compilation of References 381

About the Contributors 415

Index 421

Preface

Artificial Intelligence (AI) and Machine Learning (ML) have rapidly advanced and revolutionized numerous industries, including customer support and analytics in recent years. These technologies have gained popularity due to their ability to process vast amounts of data and provide insights that enhance customer experiences and optimize business operations. Customer-facing businesses have particularly experienced significant impacts from AI and ML, transforming customer support, analytics, and experience.

This book, titled *Handbook of Research on AI and Machine Learning Applications in Customer Support and Analytics*, explores the diverse applications of AI and ML in these domains. In the modern data-driven era, AI and ML technologies that allow computers to mimic intelligent human behavior are essential for organizations to achieve business excellence. The ability of AI and ML to extract useful information from raw data is in high demand than ever, especially for customer support and analytics.

The book investigates the applications of AI and ML and how they can be implemented to enhance customer support and analytics at various levels of organizations. It covers topics such as artificial intelligence, machine learning, supervised learning, customer sentiment analysis, data mining, customer analytics, optimization strategies, predictive analytics, AI-based product suggestion, query auto-suggestion, and business analytics. This book is ideal for marketing professionals, managers, business owners, researchers, practitioners, academicians, instructors, university libraries, and students.

Overall, *Handbook of Research on AI and Machine Learning Applications in Customer Support and Analytics* provides readers with a comprehensive overview of how AI and ML are being used in different fields to improve customer support and analytics. The book is divided into four sections (Section 1: "Customer Analytics," Section 2: "Machine Learning for Optimization," Section 3: "Predictive Analytics," and Section 4: "Artificial Intelligence in Customer Support"), each with its own unique perspective on the applications and implications of AI and ML, this book is an essential resource for anyone interested in understanding the role of these technologies in enhancing customer experiences and optimizing business operations:

Section 1 explores various aspects of customer analytics, starting with the adoption of churn recognition systems to predict customer churn in the semiconductor supply chain industry. It further delves into examining the influence of AI applications on the operations of contextual commerce and its impact on consumer behavior. The section also presents a study that incorporates AI for analyzing buying patterns of customers to understand the different factors that contribute to changing patterns. In addition, the section discusses the implementation of a virtual learning environment that conforms to good educational practice and can inform a Learning Analytics (LA) reference framework with the aim of identifying at-risk students. Also, the role of machine learning in improving customer service and enhancing customer experience is explored. The last chapter of this section delves into the use of clustering analysis in customer segmentation for malls. Overall, this section provides insights into the importance of customer analytics, the integration of AI and ML in the field, and how it can be utilized to better understand customer behavior and improve overall business strategies.

The second section of this book is dedicated to exploring the application of machine learning for optimization. This section starts by reviewing the literature on machine learning and optimization and presents commonly used machine learning algorithms in an optimization framework. The interaction between learning algorithms and optimization shells is scrutinized, and methodologies that increase scalability and efficiency are discussed. Optimization strategies are becoming increasingly predominant in customer support analytics, as optimization schedules are used to discover the maximum or minimum value of a job, such as the objective function, by systematically selecting input values from a permitted set and computing the value of the function. Machine learning algorithms can make this process more efficient by favoring less complex algorithms that work within a reasonable computational time. Besides data fitting, machine learning can also help solve various optimization problems and optimization algorithms. Many methods that have been extensively used for customer support analytics have been proposed in optimization problems over the last few decades to obtain optimal solutions. The pros and cons of these models and future research directions are also discussed in this section. In addition, this section investigates the application of machine learning models in addressing challenges within specialized domains, such as developing active suspension systems in cars and implementing carpooling frameworks. The associated opportunities and obstacles are examined, and the potential advantages of utilizing machine learning techniques in these contexts are analyzed. Lastly, the section presents a sophisticated smart ATM surveillance system that employs image processing and machine learning algorithms to identify suspicious behavior, particularly physical attacks. This system is designed to enhance ATM security by employing advanced surveillance methods. Overall, this section aims to provide insights into the diverse range of optimization problems that can be addressed using machine learning and how machine learning can be used to improve efficiency and scalability in these problems.

Section 3 explores various topics related to Predictive Analytics. Predictive Analytics involves using data, statistical algorithms, and machine learning techniques to identify the likelihood of future outcomes based on historical data. One chapter in this section discusses using machine learning to predict restaurant sales based on factors such as weather and offers. Another chapter focuses on developing a Big Data recommendation framework for crop selection in agriculture using the Spark platform. Another chapter explores the use of machine learning techniques such as Linear Regression, XGBoost, Random Forest, and Decision Tree to predict clearance due dates in companies. The final chapter in this section discusses the use of machine learning techniques to predict healthcare readmissions using patient data. Overall, this section highlights the diverse applications of predictive analytics and how machine learning can be leveraged to make accurate predictions in a wide range of industries.

The world of customer support is evolving with the integration of Artificial Intelligence and Machine Learning technologies. Section 4 delves into the applications of AI and ML techniques in enhancing customer support. This section consists of several chapters that cover a range of topics such as AI-based product suggestion, user sentiment prediction, and query auto-suggestion. The aim of this section is to provide readers with a comprehensive understanding of the various AI and ML techniques that can be utilized to improve customer support and service. The chapters in this section analyze the articles published on various scientific platforms and present the findings of their research.

The proposed applications of AI and ML in customer support not only benefit organizations but also provide better experiences to customers. It helps in resolving issues faster, predicting customer behavior, and providing personalized services, among others. By implementing these technologies, businesses can improve their customer satisfaction and ultimately increase their profitability. We hope that this section will provide valuable insights to both practitioners and researchers, and inspire them to explore new avenues for the implementation of AI and ML in customer support.

We would like to express our gratitude to our team of authors, who have contributed their time, expertise, and insights to make this book a reality. We hope that this book will inspire further research and innovation in the field of AI and ML and help organizations achieve business excellence through data-driven decision-making.

In conclusion, we believe that this book will be a valuable addition to the existing literature on AI and ML in customer support and analytics. We invite readers to explore the diverse applications of AI and ML in these domains and discover the potential of these technologies to transform their organizations.

THE SOLUTIONS

The solutions presented in this book offer practical applications of AI and ML in customer support and analytics, as well as other fields. By leveraging the power of AI and ML, businesses can gain insights into their customers' behavior, preferences, and needs, and tailor their strategies accordingly. These solutions can help businesses improve customer satisfaction, increase revenue, and streamline their operations. Moreover, the solutions presented in this book can also help address some of the challenges businesses face in customer support and analytics. For example, the adoption of churn recognition systems can help businesses identify customers who are at risk of leaving and take proactive steps to retain them. Similarly, the use of AI and ML in healthcare can help reduce readmissions and improve patient outcomes, while the use of these techniques in agriculture can help optimize crop yields and reduce waste. Overall, the solutions presented in this book highlight the potential of AI and ML to transform businesses and industries, as well as the importance of continued research and development in these fields. By staying up-to-date with the latest developments in AI and ML, businesses and researchers can continue to innovate and improve their products and services, ultimately benefiting both customers and society as a whole.

Md Shamim Hossain
Hajee Mohammad Danesh Science and Technology University, Bangladesh

Ree Chan Ho
Taylor's University, Malaysia

Goran Trajkovski
Western Governors University, USA

Section 1
Customer Analytics

Chapter 1
Adoption of Churn Recognition System to Predict Customer Churn:
A Study With Respect to Semiconductor Supply Chain

Yuvraj Sharma
https://orcid.org/0000-0002-7015-422X
GF, India

Rajender Gurram
GF, USA

Naveen Saharan
https://orcid.org/0009-0004-5529-4912
Fidelity Investments, India

ABSTRACT

In the cutthroat competitive arena, it is a very challenging task for any enterprise to make a balance between retaining its existing loyal customers and attracting new customers. It is a tedious task to find the right segment of active customers and understand the reason behind churn numbers. It is said that it is five times more costly to attract new customers as compared to retaining existing customers. The main aim of this chapter is to understand the customer churn application, which is one of the most useful applications of AI and ML in the customer analytics domain. Researchers further studied the most significant factors affecting customer behavior and responsible for increasing the customer churn rate. The study mainly targeted the semiconductor supply chain industry, which is one of the most complex industries and foundation of advanced technology and penetrated the walks of human life.

DOI: 10.4018/978-1-6684-7105-0.ch001

INTRODUCTION

In the data driven era, Artificial Intelligence (AI) and Machine Learning (ML) techniques can play a crucial role in terms of extracting useful business information from raw data. Customer Segmentation, Behavior modeling, fraud detection, sentiment analysis, customer churn analytics, predicting customer wallet shares and understanding of customer loyalty are different use cases of AI and ML in customer support and analytics domain. Nowadays, it is very easy for any organization to collect and analyze vast amounts of data related to customer purchase, demographic, social media, supply chain performance issues, customer preference and reviews data. These data can help organizations to understand customer behavior to some extent and help to see a clear picture of the target audience including customers suppliers and academic world. In academic world, students, researchers and scholars can understand use case of AI and ML and its implications on day-to-day business activities.

By using raw data, firms can better understand about customers 360 visibility, check spending patterns and predict future behaviors of customers. Similarly, companies would be able to collect supplier related information in an appropriate manner. There are different organizations across the world including H20.ai, Odaia, Predicted Layer, Rulex, Tizamo which incorporated Artificial Intelligence to businesses for developing smart churn prediction applications. For business leaders, managers, researchers, practitioners and academician, this study could be useful in term of understand use case of AI/ML and its roles in data-driven decision-making in their respective areas. By evaluating methodologies, students belong to various universities and institutes would be able to get familiar with AI and ML applications from data science perspectives.

The overall problem talks about churn which means customers who stop using products & services of a firm due to certain reasons. Many enterprises across the world are facing customer churn problems and it is very difficult for them to make the right balance between customer satisfaction and revenue. In modern arena, artificial Intelligence based techniques could be beneficial for the companies to manage large amounts of customers data and understand their behavior in an appropriate manner (Sullivan, 2022). By adopting these advanced techniques, firms belong to various industries including finance & banking, retail, marketing and telecom etc. would be able to solve the problem of churn which is not good for any business. Today, many businesses are emphasizing the root cause why customers might leave in future (Alboukaey, Joukhadar & Ghneim, 2020). It is a tedious job to find the right segment of active customers and understand the reason behind churn numbers.

It is said that it is five times more costly to attract new customers as compared to retaining existing customers. In the big data era, mostly companies are more emphasizing on deliberate churners that bring more profit to business. Further, the chapter explores customer trends and identifies factors which are responsible for churn. The data has been collected from secondary data sources such as books, published journals, previous research papers and articles related to churn analytic to better understand the appropriate use of ML algorithms in customer support and analytics domain. The present study emphasizes the implications of machine learning models that can predict customer churn based on available data and help firms to take appropriate action. Researchers studied how different types of Machine learning algorithms including Logistic regression, Random Forest and Gradient boosted tree algorithms could be applied for classifying churned customers in the semiconductor supply chain industry. Confusion matrix, Recall, and AUC evaluation metrics could be useful to measure the performance of the ML models.

The present chapter has been written to target semiconductor supply chain industry which is one of the most complex industries to understand root causes behind churns and application of AI and ML to tackle those challenges. Across all major industries including media and entertainments, telecommunication, manufacturing, transportations and personal health and hygiene, semiconductors are used as foundations of advanced technology products. However, the results of the paper could be taken as reference by various companies belonging to telecom, marketing, semiconductor and supply chain and banking to identify high risk churned customers and develop win back strategies to retain existing profitable customers and reduce cost of maintaining customers.

BACKGROUND AND PROBLEM

As per the study conducted by Brain & Company, by increasing 5% retention rates, companies can enhance their profits by 25% to 95%. In the study, it is identified that 80% revenue is generated from 20% customers. According to McKinsey (2022), the global semiconductor market is strongly growing in 2021 and revenue will increase by 20% and reach $590 billion. It is expected that rising demand for electric vehicles, the expansion of 5G and remote working will boost the performance of the sector up to 2030. During the Post Covid Pandemic era, shortage of chip supply and supply chain performance issues became bottleneck problems and created significant disruption across all major industries (McKinsey, 2022). Semiconductor supply chain industry is struggling to meet chip shortage demand and failed to prioritize the specific requirements of its customers worldwide.

Lund et al. (2019) explored that automation, AI and additive manufacturing can reduce global goods trade and improve productivity and retain production. Supply chain performance issues are very critical for the industry in terms of customer retention. As per the study done by Nitesh and Chawla (2021), chip shortage, global transportation, shortage of shipping containers, premium pricing by air cargo, country specific & international laws are main semiconductor supply chain related issues that highly influence customer retention. From the result of the analysis, it is observed that there is strong correlation between retention of customers and supply chain inefficiencies (Nitesh & Chawla, 2021). It is a classic example of imbalance between demand/supply and talented manpower required to meet that demand in the semiconductor industry. It is estimated that companies across industries will face a shortage of 90,000 skilled technicians and 300,000 engineers by 2030.

From the studies, semiconductor companies are facing a lot of challenges related to talent retention and acquisitions which can affect the health of organizations and bet on the industry futures (McKinsey, 2022). Along with ongoing supply/demand related issues such as financial expectations, operational expectations, growth product and expectations, firms are facing challenges related to attracting, developing, and retaining skilled talent that can deliver quality products to meet changing demand of customers across the world (Foster & Gardner, 2022). In these circumstances, AI, and ML enabled techniques such as sentimental analysis, collaborative planning using cloud, IoT, mobility and customer analytics could be helpful for the semiconductor supply chain industry to understand sentiments of their customers and overcome issues which they are facing during pandemic and post pandemic era. In addition, the implication of AI enabled customer churn application could be seen in terms of reducing churn rates, increasing customer satisfaction, and enhancing corporate revenue (Naz, Shoaib & Shahzad, 2018).

There may be certain reasons such as high charges, talented manpower shortage, poor customer service, supply chain insufficiencies issues, getting better offers from competitors and some unknown facts that increase customer churn. Due to this, it is very difficult for organizations to make the right balance between customer satisfaction and profit margin. However, by adopting machine learning techniques, management of firms could be able to detect customer churn in advance (Madhani, 2019). By analyzing customers complaints, monitoring usages, and analyzing business rivals' offers, customer analytics teams could be able to enhance customer retention rate. Besides Artificial Intelligence, Internet of Things, data centers, Wireless technologies, automotive and strong bonding between auto manufacturers and semiconductor companies will continue to fuel growth and gaining momentum (Baghersad, Zobel, Lowry, & Chatterjee, 2022). However, in order to mitigate supply chain related issues, organizations are investing huge amounts of money in building new manufacturing plants and research. In such circumstances, AI & ML based applications could be helpful for the companies belonging to the supply chain domain to gain detailed insights into the end-to-end process and boost up the performance of any organization against their competitors.

OBJECTIVES OF THE STUDY

Many enterprises across the world are facing customer churn related problems and it is very difficult for them to make a balance between customer satisfaction and revenue. Researchers tried to explore customer churn analytics, which is one of the most crucial applications of AI and ML can be used to discover insights and improve decision making process in overall business.

1. What are the most significant factors affecting customer behavior and responsible for increasing the customer churn rate in the semiconductor supply chain?

2. How could firms effectively build a churn recognition system to predict customer churn rate?

3. What are the recommended interventions that can help enterprises to improve customer retention by implementing AI- and ML-based applications?

Literature Review

There are multiple use cases of churn prediction systems in different industries including retail market, marketing, telecommunication, financial institutions, human resource management and software as service provider. This section of the article provides detailed information about customer churn which is one of the most useful applications of AI and ML to predicting customer churn. Further researchers provided detailed information about consumer behavior and its impact on churn and identified various factors which are responsible for the churn in the semiconductor supply chain. The overall customer churn problem talks about churn which means customers who stop using products and services of a firm due to certain reasons.

Churners can be classified into different categories including voluntary and involuntary. Involuntary churn customers can be defined as customers who stopped using services due to fraud, no payment of bills and do not want firm services anymore. On the other hand, identification of voluntary customers is very difficult because it is again classified into two classes: incident churners who change their decisions due to change in financial position and location, and deliberate churners are those churners who change their mindsets due to change in technology and price (Arenas & Coulibaly 2022). In the big data era, mostly companies belonging to the semiconductor supply chain industry are more emphasizing on deliberate churners that bring more profit to business. It is very important to solve the problem of churn because it is not good for any business, and it holds true for any industry.

According to Clootrack (2022), customer buying behavior directly affects customers and its understanding is essential for any organization to analyze the success for its current products and planning for new product launches. Consumers and processes that they are using to choose products and services are studied under consumer behavior. Personal factors including demographics (age, gender, and culture), social factors (education level, social media, income, family, and friends) and psychological factors that influence consumer behavior (Clootrack, 2022). Behavior of customers is changing due to the changing in disposable income, live style, technology, trends, and fashion etc. It is identified that customer differentiation is used in marketing to classify customers based on their needs and wants to differ from other groups. It also helps companies to expand the width and breadth of their services.

From the past studies, it is identified that proper understanding of consumer behavior not only helps companies to attract new customers but also to retain existing loyal customers with them in the long run (Clootrack, 2022). Hence, it can be said that there is a direct relationship between customer behavior and churn because if a company is unable to understand consumer needs, then they will stop using firm services. Hence, it is very essential for the companies to understand customer behavior that helps them to solve the problem of churn which is not good for any business. Outcome of delayed deliveries could be seen in the form of dropping revenue and customer satisfaction in the semiconductor supply chain industry. Besides that, a study of consumer behavior not only helps marketers to create effective marketing campaigns but also motivates them to make repeat purchases (Gouda & Saranga, 2018).

Understanding consumer behavior allows companies to effectively utilize their resources and build production strategy in such a way that will save marketing and warehouse costs. In addition, a study of consumer behavior analysis will help enterprises belonging to different sectors to find out answers to some questions such as why customers are switching to competitor brands, what influences customers to buy products and what gaps customers identified in the existing products as compared to other competitors etc.

FACTORS AFFECTING CUSTOMER CHURN

From the past studies done by multiple researchers, it has been identified that the customer churning process is influenced by various factors including negative customer experience, supply chain inefficiencies, low quality of customer support, customer preference change, financial issues, switching to competitors and services that did not meet customer needs, etc. (Ullah et al., 2019) conducted a study to know the factors which are responsible behind customer attrition and proposed a churn prediction model to identify churn customers. (Pamina, et al., 2019) developed a customer churn prediction model using binary classification algorithm to recognize the telecom segment customers who are about to churn.

Customer Expectation and Lack of Communication

According to the study of commbox (2022), 42% of customers discontinue their services due to poor customer service. In addition, a lack of continued communication and building a weak communication attribute can also lead to an enhanced customer churn. In the modern data-driven digital era, customer expectation is very high, and they expect personalized experience. Attract the wrong audience who are not genuinely interested in products and services causing high churning rates. It is identified that lack of awareness about competitors, their strategies, their pricing, and failure to recognize them on time could be other important factors that enhance churn of the customers (commbox, 2022). Customer Satisfaction and Service Quality is considered as an important factor.

Customer Satisfaction and Service Quality

Ramesh, Emlyn & Vijayakumar (2021) presented extensive solutions to determine the factors that influence customer churns. They proposed Artificial Neural Networks and Random Forest Algorithms to identify crucial factors and achieve better levels of performance. From the result of study, it is cleared that customer satisfaction and service quality factors highly influence customer churn. Patil et al. (2022) identified customer satisfaction is one of the most crucial factors that cause companies to lose customers and impact revenue of industries. Customer satisfaction in global supply chain industry play an important role in term of better understanding of customers and their requirements. Responsiveness, innovation & digitization, integration of various stakeholders, supply chain analytics, customer centric culture and end to end visibility are crucial factors in supply chain that influence customer satisfaction.

Researchers developed Machine learning models to analyze churn rate in Banking and Telecom departments. ANN, KNN, SVM, Naïve Bayes and Logistic Regression Model were implemented on datasets. From the result, it is found that Random Forest technique gave higher accuracy 87.05% on the banking dataset and for telecom dataset, ANN obtained the highest accuracy of 81.93%. Customer churning process is influenced by various factors such as customer demographic data, payment information, employee interactions with customers, quality of service, purchase history, payment mode, complaint data and quick query resolution process adopted by organizations (Tien et al., 2019). Besides that, quality, customer service, continuous interaction and price are crucial factors that can help companies to predict behavior of the customers.

Switching Costs

According to Mhizha and Zvitambo (2018), switching costs can play an important role in retaining customers. It could be monetary, effort based, time based and psychological. They identified that accessibility, technology, service, and lack of customer-oriented strategies can affect churn. Based on the conceptual framework designed, it can be said that switching cost and dissatisfaction with the firm services are cited as the major reasons (Mhizha & Zvitambo, 2018). In order to retain existing customers, companies are emphasizing towards various elements including convenience, emotional, exit fees and time based. It is identified that many companies are charging exit fees from their customers while they are leaving for ex. administrative fees for closing an account. In addition, if closing time takes more time when switch from one brand and lot of paperwork involve then customer will think prior to switch another brand. Researchers identified the relationship between switching costs and customer churn. They said that when switching costs will be high then customer attrition will be low (Batra et al., 2018). In data driven era, from the past studies, it is observed that attracting new and retaining existing talent is very challenging task for any organization.

Attracting and Retaining Talent

Researchers' studies that the customer churning process in the Semiconductor supply chain sector is highly influenced by various factors including attracting and retaining skilled manpower, chip shortage, digital transformation, flexible/adaptable supply chain and potential disruption to supply chains. These issues occur as threats for companies in cutthroat competitive business arena. Weaker retention policies and gaps between organizations' thinking and customer demand are responsible for weakening the bond between firms and its customers (Park & Heo, 2020).

From the past studies, it is clear that semiconductor players fare badly to measure sentiment of their employees as compared to big tech and automotive competitors. Work life balance, challenges across culture, and diversity, career development, and right compensation related factors directly influenced the workforce of the semiconductor industry. These factors impact could be seen on attracting, retaining, and exciting customers around the world (McKinsey, 2022). However, selection of appropriate factors can also affect performance of the model in the era of big data. Appropriate product, time, and locations can play a significant role.

Appropriate Product, Time, and Locations

It is observed that product specification, price, customer services, terms and on-time delivery are most important factors which affect buying decisions of customers and distributors. In addition, order lead time, on time delivery gaps and fulfillment requirements are other constraints which can influence target delivery of products and services to customers in the semiconductor supply chain. According to McKinsey report (2018), it is essential for semiconductor companies to effective use of the right product, right time, and right locations metric in a proper manner. In addition, better inventory management, improving forecasting efficiency, vendor management and invaluable assistance that meet customers' expectations (McKinsey, 2018).

CHURN PROBLEM MAPPED WITH ML METHODOLOGIES ACROSS INDUSTRIES

From the results of comprehensive studies, it can be said that customer churn is an interesting problem because it will bring huge losses to the profits. It is observed that factors affecting churn in the different industries are relatively scattered and not much emphasized on high value customers bringing profits to the company. It is studied that innovative machine learning solutions could be beneficial for companies in terms of real-time decision-making processes, improving visibility into supplier base and driving real-time decision-making process to boost customer retention. Scholars studied different types of machine learning algorithms used across various industries and proposed churn recognition systems which could be suitable for the semiconductor supply chain industry (Delgado & Mills, 2020).

Further researchers explained how customer retention issues could be mapped with innovative AI and ML techniques to monitor supply chain related issues and step by step implementation of customer churn application into semiconductor supply chain industry. After getting data from source, several steps could be performed such as data exploration, visualization, feature importance, feature engineering, setting a baseline, splitting data (train & test), applying various machine learning models and hyper parameter tuning for improving performance of those models etc. It is observed that logistic regression could be applied on a dataset if researchers are looking for churn probability (Esmaeilian et al., 2020). Similarly, decision tree algorithms can be applied to classify upcoming system spends and streamlines the operations of the company in an appropriate manner.

Jain et al. (2021) conducted a study on churn prediction. They used Deep learning CNN algorithm for the purpose of feature extraction and predicting customer churn. They emphasized ensemble learning and stacking techniques for proposing churn prediction model. It is a combination of four different ML algorithms including Logistic Regression, Decision Tree, XGboost and Native based. From the experimental results, it shows that the proposed model has 96.12% accuracy and state of the art churn recognition systems. Ahmad, Jafar and Aljoumaa developed a churn prediction model using machine learning algorithms to predict customers who are most likely to churn. Spark environment was used and different classification techniques including Decision tree, Random Forest and XGboost were applied. It has been observed that the XGboost algorithm gave best results and obtained a high Area under curve (AUC) value 93.3%. Ullah et al. (2019) identified the factors which are responsible for customer attrition and further, they proposed a churn prediction model to identify churn customers.

Random Forest Algorithm has been implemented for classifying correct instances and K mean clustering was used for creating the segments of churning customer's data in order to provide group-based retention offers. Accuracy, precision, recall and roc evaluation metrics were used to measure performance of proposed churn prediction model. (Pamina et al., 2019) developed a customer churn prediction model using binary classification algorithm to recognize the telecom segment customers who are about to churn. From the experiment, it is observed that the Decision Tree algorithm performed well as compared to all others models with the highest recall value.

Measure Performance of ML Models

Customer churn rate business metric can be defined as the percentage of customers who are terminating their relationship with an enterprise in a specific time period. Different types of metrics are used by companies to check how accurately a model is performing to predict outcome. Accuracy is a good metric for measuring the performance of a machine learning model. However, presence of outliers and imbalance dataset can affect performance of the models. Hence, it can be said that this metric is not very suitable for the current business scenario (De Martini, 2021). If data is imbalanced then other performance metrics including confusion metric, F1 score, recall and ROC could be used to predict churners more accurately.

F1 – Score is also known as recall and harmonic mean of precision. It is used generally when False Negative and False Positive are more important than True Positive and True Negative. It is useful when imbalance classes present in a dataset. However, it is less interpretable as compared to precision and recall. Recall is also referred to as 'Sensitivity' and this ratio is calculated on the basis of correctly predicted positive class out of total actual positive class (TP and FN). When the cost of false negative is low and the cost of false negative is high, then this ratio is used. Precision can be calculated on the basis of correctly predicted positive class out of all total positive classes (TP and FP). When the cost of a false positive is very high and the cost of a false negative is low, it is better to use recall as an evaluation metric. Confusion metrics can be used to compare between actual and prediction made by the model. With help of performance metrics, analyst would be able to calculate the number of correct and incorrect predictions (Park & Heo, 2020).

True Positive (TP) presents the number of predicted positive results that are actual positive in the validation data. True Negative (TN) presents the number of predicted negative results that are actual negative in the validation data. False Positive (FP) is used When results are actual negative in the validation data, but it calculates the number of predicted positive results (Delgado & Mills, 2020). False Negative (FN) is calculated when the results under TP show the number of predicted negative results that are actual positive in the validation data. Receiver Operating Characteristic (ROC) curve presents the rate of FP against the rate of TP over a graph. Each point in the ROC curve represents a sensitivity pair for a particular decision threshold. If the curve is a straight line, it means that the model is not trained at all. The higher diagonal value indicates that the model will work well for detecting churned customers.

Here researchers' main motive is to find positive class or predicting the churned customers. Recall can be applied to calculate actual positives identified by a model and if the model gives a decent score for predicting customer churned, researchers accept the model and if it will get a bad recall score it means the model failed for detecting churned customers in an appropriate manner.

SOLUTIONS RELEVANT TO CURRENT PROBLEM

In the present article, researchers went through various strategies proposed by previous researchers to solve customer churn issues and propose the best techniques used for churn prediction in the semiconductor supply chain industry. Exploratory data analysis could be used to discover patterns into available data. From the review of literature, it is observed that machine and deep learning approaches are frequently used for predicting customer churn across various industries. The current problem comes under binary classification that will help management of firms to figure out which customers stayed, and which ones churned (Foster & Gardner, 2022).

Based on available data, different types of classification approaches could be applied such as logistic regression, support vector machine, decision tree, random forest etc. for discovering underlying reasons behind customer churn. Further, researcher emphasizes on identifying the relationship between dependent variable (churn) and independent variables. Positive relationships will show higher probability of leaving customers and negative relationships indicate customers less likely to churn (Lund et al., 2019). However, results of past studies shows that most powerful models including deep learning, boosting and LSTM based approaches could also be used for analyzing the churn data. In addition, time series domain models like ARIMA could be used if researchers have up to two years of customer information.

Hence, from the review of literature and studies conducted in the past, it can be said that classification algorithms such as Logistic Regression, SVM, Decision tree, Random Forest and XGboost etc. are given best results and can help management of the companies to identify factors that are responsible for customer churn. However, selection of appropriate factors can also affect performance of the model in the era of big data.

DEVELOPMENT OF CHURN RECOGNITION SYSTEM

This section of the article explores how end-to-end customer churn analysis is carried out in the semiconductor supply chain sector, what types of processes involved, methods to build recognition systems and challenges associated while carrying out the analysis in a proper manner. Developing a churn recognition system begins with understanding the scope and depth of the problem that are trying to solve (Park & Heo, 2020). While building a prediction system, it is essential for the customer analytics team to properly frame the problem and get the answers to several questions such as what kinds of data available for use, how this system is going to be used and what outcome stakeholders are expecting from this ML enabled system etc. Further, Key performance indicators (KPI) are defined to measure the performance or success of the project. After setting the performance indicators, service level agreement will be defined to accomplish the goal within stipulated time.

Moreover, recommended churn recognition systems could be beneficial for various sectors such telecom, retail, banking and marketing etc. Besides that, identify pain points and risky customers are main advantages of implementing churn prediction system. In Telecom sector various companies including AT&T, Vodafone and T-Mobile are already implementing ML based solutions for reducing churn rate in a highly competitive market. From the failure case of American retailer Toy R, it is clear that companies can't ignore insights provided by AI/ML enabled systems in data driven era. Similarly, retail-based firms are also emphasizing towards measuring and reducing churn rate to understand customer buying patterns. Banking and Financial organizations can be used churn prediction system for the purpose of launching of several ads and forecast churn with high accuracy.

WORKFLOW TO PREDICT CUSTOMER CHURN RATE

After specifying the problem, data could be collected from various sources. The Semiconductor supply chain industry is dynamic and vibrant. Digital transformation, changes in demand of customers, supply chain inefficiencies, local & internal laws and globalization are encouraging customers not to stick with a single firm. Companies can collect customer churn data from different sources. First party data which is the most valuable and trusted data source that can be directly collected based on company and customer interactions (Sullivan, 2022). SAP CRM, Oracle NetSuite, Salesforce, Zendesk CRM, ZOHO CRM and Microsoft Dynamics 365 platforms are adopted by different industries to collect and manage huge amounts of customer data. Second party data is collected from a partner or collaborator when companies do not directly deal with customers. Apart from that, firms can collect data from their websites, campaigns, surveys, and social media.

Preprocessing of data is done after collecting a large amount of customer demographic, transaction, and intermediate records. The next task is to preprocess that messy data. Data could be scattered at different places, for processing of the data it is essential that data might be extracted and converted into a single format. Data warehouses could be created and different operations such as extract, transform and load (ETL) operations can be performed. A selection of an ideal tool is highly dependent on a base of common criteria including use case, budget, capabilities, data source supportability and technical latency etc.

SAS Data Management, Hadoop, AWS Glue, Azure Data Factory, Google Data Flow, Talend open studio, IBM data stage and oracle data integrator tools are usually adopted by most of the organizations to perform operations (Bisong, 2019). SQL, Python and Java are most common languages also used for building ETL tools. In this phase, the customer analytics team can check dimensions of the data, missing value, outliers and consistent values. It is observed that raw data must be organized before being fetched to the model. In addition, highly unstable values and empty cells will affect the outcome of the prediction. Hence, prior to building any model, it is essential to treat missing values, deletion of empty columns and conversion string values to mathematical values. For example, If the Date column is missing values, then it will be replaced by the last date of the month and other continuous variables missing value replaced by 0.

Data Exploration is the first step of analyzing data is to read and store data in proper format. It is observed that the dataset has many columns and rows records. At the beginning of EDA, the analytics team emphasized understanding as much as information about data, discovering patterns and identifying anomalies to better perform further evaluations. Explaining the features include dependent (target) variables might have two classes and the churn prediction problem can be classified into a binary class classification problem. The category "0" will indicate the customer did not leave the company and "1" will indicate that customers decided to terminate the relationship and leave services of the firm (Vartak & Madden, 2018).

Independent variables could be customer demographic data, supply chain related issues, average revenue per customer, average revenue per unit, consumption level rate, interaction with the firm, and quality of service-related factors. Selection of right attributes, data labeling and dealing with imbalanced data are main problems associated with the customer data. Exploratory Data Analysis and Feature Extraction steps could be performed in this stage. This section of the chapter can be divided into multiple subsections to better understand data, discover patterns, and check any assumptions before performing further analysis.

From the results of comprehensive studies, it can be said that customer churn is an interesting problem because it will bring huge losses to the profits. It is observed that factors affecting churn are relatively scattered and not much emphasized on high value customers bringing profits to the company. In the present case, scholars have gone through various strategies proposed by scholars to solve customer churn issues across different industries and select the best techniques that could be used for churn prediction in the semiconductor supply chain sector. It is found that exploratory data analysis is the most important and time-consuming task, but it is very beneficial to discover patterns into available data which lead to solving business problems (Gouda & Saranga, 2020).

Different types of visualizations and numerical summaries of the data could be used to better understand the surface-level of the data. Statistical and numerical methods could be adopted to draw inference about the data with help of images, plots, charts, and graphs etc. Feature engineering can help to derive new variables. For example, use product/services from the firm in two consecutive months (Madhani, 2019). It can help researchers to identify if this reveals any trend in customer churn data. For easier manipulation of data, all the columns should be converted to the same numeric data type. If the dataset is not balanced for example, the count of churners is much less than the count of non-churners. Analytics team will treat outliers by down sampling the majority class. As per the definition of high value customers, there is a need to select 70th percentile and above records.

Machine Learning Model Development and Error Analysis

This section provides detailed information about how machine learning models could be applied on a churn dataset and explores different stages which are applied prior to building any ML models. The current problem comes under binary classification that will help management of companies to figure out which customers stayed, and which ones churned. Researchers try to explore stages which would generally follow prior to building a churn recognition system in the semiconductor supply chain industry.

Normalization is applied prior to building any machine learning model. It is essential to normalize data which ensures that all features are on similar scales. Data Scientist will rescale real-valued numeric attributes into a 0 to 1 range. Dataset will be split into two parts (Pavlyshenko, 2018). The training set will be used in creating a model and the testing step will be used to evaluate the model. Stratified shuffle split approach could be used to split the data into train (0.70) and test set (0.30). It ensures that both the training and the testing sets have the same percentage of minority class.

By using the SMOTE algorithm, oversampling of training data is done. The analytics team could be to prevent the classifier getting too biased towards the majority sample. SMOTE will help to up sample the minority class so that the dataset has a 50-50 share of majority and minority classes. The up sampling will create synthetic data points in the minority class. Note, up sampling is done only on the training data. However, researchers are not going to modify the test set in any way (Sullivan, 2022). Predictive modeling is used to predict which of the customers will churn or not. Therefore, this is a supervised classification problem to be trained with algorithms defined below. Analysis first starts with a logistic regression model because it is a standard industry algorithm that is commonly used in practice. Analytics team can set parameter class weights to be balanced which ensures that the loss in misclassifying samples in the minority class is more than the majority class. In other words, the model does not overfit the majority class. It is observed that roc_auc is a good scoring measure in cross validation for imbalanced classes.

Logistic regression model with L1 regularization would be applied to overcome chance of model overfit/underfit. Further, Area Under ROC value could be compared against Random Model AUC value (0.5). If the model value is greater than the random model, then it can be said that the model will give the best result and perform well. Decision tree algorithm is preferred for solving Classification problems and it contains tree type structure. Branches represent the decision rules, internal nodes represent the features of a dataset, and each leaf node represents the outcome. If there is a gap between train & test accuracy, then it can be said that there is a chance of overfit. Random Forest is an ensemble learning method which contains several decision trees to provide solutions to complex problems. It handles missing values very well and is more accurate as compared to decision trees (Pavlyshenko,2018).

Apart from customer churn, random forest techniques could be applied in other business areas such as credit worthiness of loan applicants in banks, diagnosis patients in healthcare, identify potential markets for stocks and predict the preference of the customers in the ecommerce domain. ROC_AUC is a good measure for class imbalance and could be used to measure performance of the model. XGBoost uses sophisticated algorithms to handle irregularities in the data. In this case, boosting algorithm could be helpful to tackle the class imbalance and give better results as compared to the other classifiers (Esmaeilian, Sarkis, Lewis, & Behdad, 2020). Hyper parameter tuning can be done to ensure that the model does not overfit the majority class. If AUC value is good, then it can be said that there is not much difference between train & test datasets accuracy. Hence, it can be said that there is no chance of overfitting.

After applying different models, the analytics team can perform comparisons between different models based on different business metrics. From the past studies, it is clear that if AUC value will be higher than model performance will be better. It can easily distinguish between the positive and negative classes. On the basis of the performance metric, it can be said that which model did a better job of classifying the positive class in the dataset. Essentially, this would mean that the model should have high sensitivity and high accuracy. The specificity is less of a concern for this problem. However, the XGBoost model is also quite good when the company wants even better accuracy and low specificity. In this case, the company does not want to bother too many users in the non-churn group with promotional offers.

With help of error analysis, the analytics team can try to understand how good the models are in correctly detecting the churn vs not churn customers? With the help of a confusion matrix, Type 1 and Type 2 errors could be calculated. The Type 1 Error Rate or False Positive Rate of any model should be less for the best model as compared to other ML models. It is important to keep the Type 1 error rate to be low, so that churn customers are not incorrectly classified as non-churn customers. Hence, Type 1 error is detected meaning there is a need for Cleaning of data and fixing the output (Bisong, 2019). Ideally, Type 2 Error Rate or False negative Rate should be less. It is important to keep the Type 2 error rate to be low, so that non-churn customers are not incorrectly classified as churn customers. From the result of previous studies, it is found that Logistic regression is performed well in many cases because it is less prone to overfitting. However, it can be overfit in high dimensional datasets. Regularization (L1 and L2) techniques could be used to avoid overfitting problems.

The probabilities resulting from this approach are well-calibrated (Pavlyshenko, 2018). However, some constraints associated with logistic regression model. It will perform well when the dataset is linearly separable and easier to implement, interpret and very efficient to train. Non-linear problems cannot be solved using the logistic regression technique. Therefore, transforming these non-linear problems to linear may a time be challenging and a wastage of time. High dimensional datasets lead to the model being over-fit. It is likely to have trouble capturing complex relationships.

Robustness of the model check can be checked based on different parameters. The analytics team can check if the model is robust or not. For a model to be good, AUC value should be greater than 0.70. If the most influential predictors of the model have a very high weight in the overall prediction, this is often a sign of target leakage. Typically, this can be done by looking at the data-generating process of that feature (Vartak & Madden, 2018). Model deployment could be performed after training the model with actual data. Hyper parameters are fine-tuned before the model is deployed into production. The model can be deployed as an embedded application, mobile application, and web services (Flask or Django) are exposed to the real world. In addition, Streamlit, Docker and Kubernetes could be used to deploy machine learning models. With help of reports, it could be identified that KPI is achieved or not because business goals are bounded with these business insights.

IMPLICATION OF CHURN RECOGNITION SYSTEM

The implications of the churn recognition system could be seen in the form of identifying causes of churn, understanding factors which are responsible for customer churn and preparing strategies to reduce churn through targeted proactive retention. However, there are some challenges associated with the implementation of the churn recognition system in the semiconductor supply chain such that data mining and traditional statistical models are highly dependent on historical data and depend on human behaviors which are not bound by any rules. By developing various models and comparing their performance in a particular situation, companies would be able to identify the best approaches as per their business. By engaging customers, companies would be able to develop retention strategies and roll out operational strategies in an appropriate manner. Its impact could be seen in form of huge saving to business and keeping customers engaged.

Conclusion and Suggestions

From the past two years, economic resiliency is seen across different industries, and it is very necessary for companies to quickly normalize and summarize complex customer data that will make churn recognition systems more successful. It is found that growth of semiconductors is only possible when the supply chain is truly supported by blockchains, AI and ML, IoT and connectivity (5G/6G). The study concluded various factors such that customer expectation, lack of communication, supply chain inefficiencies, low quality of customer support, demographic data, payment information, weaker retention policies and gap between organizations think and customer demand, chip shortage and attracting and retaining talent which are the most significant factors responsible for increasing the customer churn rate across semiconductor supply chain. After that, researchers explored various phases of the proposed system that is required to build a churn recognition system and predict customer churn rate.

After comparing results of different Machine learning algorithms and previous studies results, it is identified that Logistic regression machine learning model could be the best model because it did not suffer from overfitting to the training data or data leakage and maintain consistent performance on unseen data. However, results of the study could be taken as reference by other industries such as Marketing, Telecom, Finance & Banking etc. to identify high risk churned customers and develop win back strategies to retain existing profitable customers and reduce cost of maintaining customers. It was found that AI and ML enabled churn recognition systems can help companies to enhance visibility and transparency into the system.

Future Research Directions

The study would be helpful for all industries and different types of people such as students, marketers, scholars, and entrepreneurs to understand the factors responsible for customer churn and explore how AI enabled churn recognition systems could be implemented in semiconductor supply chains. In addition, it is observed that the customer churn issue was addressed by many researchers but still there is no standard approach which addresses all issues related to customer churn accurately in the semiconductor supply chain industry. Hence, it can be said that there is still scope of improvement in the model which could be achieved by overcoming supply chain related issues, predicting human behavior, and making a balance between attracting and retaining skilled talent.

REFERENCES

Alboukaey, N., Joukhadar, A., & Ghneim, N. (2020). Dynamic behavior-based churn prediction in mobile telecom. *Expert Systems with Applications*, *162*, 113779. doi:10.1016/j.eswa.2020.113779

Arenas, G., & Coulibaly, S. (2022). *A New Dawn for Global Value Chain Participation in the Philippines*. Academic Press.

Baghersad, M., Zobel, C. W., Lowry, P. B., & Chatterjee, S. (2022). The roles of prior experience and the location on the severity of supply chain disruptions. *International Journal of Production Research*, *60*(16), 5051–5070. doi:10.1080/00207543.2021.1948136

Batra, G., Nolde, K., Santhanam, N., & Vrijen, R. (2018). *Right product, right time, right location: Quantifying the semiconductor supply chain*. McKinsey & Company.

Bisong, E. (2019). *Building machine learning and deep learning models on Google cloud platform: A comprehensive guide for beginners*. Apress. doi:10.1007/978-1-4842-4470-8

De Martini, F. (2021). *Supply chains and disruptive events: An inventory management system perspective*. Academic Press.

Delgado, M., & Mills, K. G. (2020). The supply chain economy: A new industry categorization for understanding innovation in services. *Research Policy*, *49*(8), 104039. doi:10.1016/j.respol.2020.104039

Esmaeilian, B., Sarkis, J., Lewis, K., & Behdad, S. (2020). Blockchain for the future of sustainable supply chain management in Industry 4.0. *Resources, Conservation and Recycling, 163*, 105064. doi:10.1016/j.resconrec.2020.105064

Foster, S. T., & Gardner, J. W. (2022). *Managing quality: Integrating the supply chain.* John Wiley & Sons.

Gouda, S. K., & Saranga, H. (2018). Sustainable supply chains for supply chain sustainability: Impact of sustainability efforts on supply chain risk. *International Journal of Production Research, 56*(17), 5820–5835. doi:10.1080/00207543.2018.1456695

KPMG. (2022). *Global Semiconductor industry outlook 2022.* KPMG.

Lund, S., Manyika, J., Woetzel, J., Bughin, J., & Krishnan, M. (2019). *Globalization in transition: The future of trade and value chains.* Academic Press.

Madhani, P. M. (2019). Strategic supply chain management for enhancing competitive advantages: Developing business value added framework. *International Journal of Value Chain Management, 10*(4), 316–338. doi:10.1504/IJVCM.2019.103270

McKinsey. (2018). *Right product, right time, and right location: Quantifying the semiconductor supply chain.* Author.

McKinsey. (2022). *How Semiconductors makers can turn a talent challenge into competitive advantage.* Author.

Naz, N. A., Shoaib, U., & Shahzad Sarfraz, M. (2018). A review on customer churn prediction data mining modeling techniques. *Indian Journal of Science and Technology, 11*(27), 1–27. doi:10.17485/ijst/2018/v11i27/121478

Nitesh, M., & Chawla, A. (2021). *Semiconductors Supply Chain Model.* https://www.google.com/url?sa=t&rct=j&q=&esrc=s&source=web&cd=&cad=rja&uact=8&ved=2ahUKEwi_jcPT5LX9AhVkRmwGHY47CZEQFnoECAkQAQ&url=https%3A%2F%2Fwww.birlasoft.com%2Farticles%2Fdigital-supply-chain-resilience-semiconductor-industry&usg=AOvVaw1NrCRKJ-n2XHOo-nbJxjUK

Pamina. (2019). Inferring machine learning based parameter estimation for telecom churn prediction. In *International Conference on Computational Vision and Bio Inspired Computing* (pp. 257-267). Springer.

Park, C., & Heo, W. (2020). Review of the changing electricity industry value chain in the ICT convergence era. *Journal of Cleaner Production, 258*, 120743. doi:10.1016/j.jclepro.2020.120743

Pavlyshenko, B. (2018). Using stacking approaches for machine learning models. In *2018 IEEE Second International Conference on Data Stream Mining & Processing (DSMP)* (pp. 255-258). IEEE. 10.1109/DSMP.2018.8478522

Sullivan, E. (2022). Understanding from machine learning models. *The British Journal for the Philosophy of Science.*

Tien, N. H., Anh, D. B. H., & Thuc, T. D. (2019). *Global supply chain and logistics management. Dehli.* Academic Publications.

Ullah, Raza, B., Malik, A. K., Imran, M., Islam, S. U., & Kim, S. W. (2019). A churn prediction model using random forest: Analysis of machine learning techniques for churn prediction and factor identification in the telecom sector. *IEEE Access : Practical Innovations, Open Solutions*, *7*, 60134–60149. doi:10.1109/ACCESS.2019.2914999

Vartak, M., & Madden, S. (2018). Modeldb: Opportunities and challenges in managing machine learning models. *IEEE Data Eng. Bull.*, *41*(4), 16–25.

KEY TERMS AND DEFINITIONS

AI: It is simulation of human intelligence and related to building machines capable of performing human tasks.

Churn: Customers who stop using products and services of a firm due to certain reasons.

Logistic Regression: It is classification algorithm and used to predict customer will churn or not churn.

ML: Without being explicitly programmed, it allows systems to learn and improve from experience.

Chapter 2
Examining Customer Behavior Towards the Use of Contextual Commerce Powered by Artificial Intelligence

Ree Chan Ho
Taylor's University, Malaysia

Nelvin XeChung Leow
Taylor's University, Malaysia

ABSTRACT

The integration of artificial intelligence into electronic commerce has revolutionized consumer behavior due to its capability in supporting cutting-edge features for conducting business online. It pertains to contextual commerce that facilitates customers to connect and buy goods wherever they are. This study aimed to examine the influence of artificial intelligence applications on the operations of contextual commerce. The conceptual framework was based on the UTAUT theory. The sample was the users of contextual commerce who were familiar with its usage. An online questionnaire was used to collect the data, and variance-based structured equation modeling was applied for data analysis. The four technological acceptance constructs derived from UTAUT were tested and confirmed as antecedents for contextual commerce. Furthermore, the inclusion of brand anthropomorphism as the antecedent was also supported. The empirical findings of the study explain the consumer attitude toward the significant use of artificial intelligence in contextual commerce.

INTRODUCTION

The advancement of artificial intelligence is influencing us in many aspects of our life (Javaid et al., 2022). The business world jumped on this bandwagon effect to gain its benefits (Enholm et al., 2022; Loureiro et al., 2021; Sestino & De Mauro, 2022). What makes it effective is its use by businesses in

DOI: 10.4018/978-1-6684-7105-0.ch002

achieving business performance. The advancement of AI keeps growing with the development of neural networks, machine learning, and deep learning (Kraus et al., 2020; Naim, 2022; Shaikh et al., 2022). The direct impact of artificial intelligence usage on business performance (Wamba-Taguimdje et al., 2020). The current literature has an abundance of studies relating the use of artificial intelligence with business operations (Di Vaio et al., 2020; Lee et al., 2019; Rana et al., 2022). Electronic commerce was no exception with the integration of artificial intelligence into its operations. Many of them are integrated with tools engineered by advanced use of predictive data analytics in different industries. For example, hospitality (Mariani, 2019), supply chain management (Gunasekaran et al., 2017), and fashion retailing (Shi et al., 2020).

Electronic commerce is becoming the main platform of business transactions in the post-Corvid era(Li et al., 2021). One of the new waves is contextual commerce (González et al., 2021). Contextual commerce refers to customers who would make purchases while conducting non-shopping activities, such as jogging, and watching drama. In another word, it means buying in context. While it is still a new concept to many, it has been progressing to be the new online initiative for many firms that are tapping on its potential to reach out the ever-demanding customers. It is about a new online experience for consumers moving away from merely buying goods. This suits the trend of on-demand-oriented customers who choose products they need and purchase instantly and without any hassle while they are working on their other tasks. With the increasing use of AI, consumers are enjoying many useful functionalities embedded in online shopping apps. such as electronic product fulfillment (Zhang et al., 2021), smart tourism (Samara et al., 2020), and e-chatbot (Moriuchi et al., 2021).

The implementation of contextual commerce has been highly supported by online retailers. It brings about the innovative idea of engaging the customers more deeply. Similarly, consumers are expected to enjoy the "on-the-move" features in providing more convenience to their shopping experience (Ho, 2022). However, there is little coverage of the literature on the new and innovative features of electronic commerce. The current literature on electronic commerce is highly devoted to customer acceptance, consumer needs, and functionalities (Rosário & Raimundo, 2021). With contextual commerce, many features are controlled by systems intelligence and automation (Khrais, 2020). The shopping journey is highly driven by artificial intelligence. Therefore, the acceptance of the consumers in this avenue is lacking and warrants further exploration.

The rollout of this new electronic commerce initiative depends heavily on technology. Hence, the application of the unified theory of acceptance and use of technology (UTAUT) as the theoretical framework is relevant. Furthermore, UTAUT is proven to have predictive inference in many online shopping applications, such as e-payment (Soomro, 2019), social commerce (Sarker et al., 2020), and mobile commerce (Marinković et al., 2020). In order to fully paint the picture of contextual commerce, anthropomorphism is proposed as the variable to provide the explanatory power for the artificial intelligence influence. Anthropomorphism represents the need for human-like artificial components (Epley et al., 2007). It could serve as the antecedent for the adoption of the consumer toward the likelihood to use contextual commerce explained by UTAUT variables. The consumer acceptance of contextual commerce is highly related to anthropomorphism features. The inclusion of the many related online shopping functions is driven by automated and complex procedures handled by artificial intelligence (Chen et al., 2021). Hence, the requirement of anthropomorphism in validating the use of contextual commerce is expected to enhance the consumer's shopping experience.

The main objective of this study was to investigate the features of artificial intelligence and its influence on the usage of contextual commerce by consumers. It aimed to uncover the AI-related precursor for the technology acceptance variables rooted in UTAUT theory for the adoption of contextual commerce. Therefore, anthropomorphism was hypothesized as antecedent and further exerted its influence on contextual commerce usage. Combined with the other four main variables of UTAUT, i.e. performance expectancy, effort expectancy, social influence, and facilitating conditions. The study provides a theoretical model for further understanding customer behavior with their involvement in contextual commerce. Therefore, it offers new insight into the application of artificial intelligence in contextual electronic commerce.

LITERATURE REVIEW

Contextual Commerce

The world is experiencing a massive shift to the digital-driven economy with online activities and sales growing exponentially in the Corvid-19 era (Rosenbaum & Russell-Bennett, 2020). With new and innovative ways of electronic commerce to support the omnichannel shopping experience (Chang & Li, 2022; Huré et al., 2017). Among all, contextual commerce is changing the way consumers perform the way to buy and pay for purchases (González et al., 2021). In another word, it refers to buying in context. It means the consumers would engage in the buying process while they are doing their daily activities. The purchase can be instantaneously, and no waiting is required as contextual commerce triggers the customers to get involved in engaging with the retailers in the buying and payment transactions. Retailers are enjoying the benefits to secure the opportunity to showcase the products the consumers intend to buy when they are in the right moment. At the same time, the retailers would also provide product assistance or even messages to influence the consumers to purchase via dynamic messages (Grewal et al., 2022). The retailers could reach the consumers in various channels instead of the push products approach but catch the eyes of consumers through the contents of the consumers they are interested in.

Artificial Intelligence

The integration of artificial intelligence into electronic commerce has revolutionized consumer behavior due to its capability in supporting innovative features for conducting business online (Haenlein et al., 2019; Quan & Sanderson, 2018). Artificial intelligence consists of machine learning, natural language processing, dynamic messaging, and etc., that incorporated into various shopping aspects (Pillai et al., 2020). It applies to contextual commerce that facilitates customers to connect and purchase goods in their desired context ubiquitously. Contextual commerce depends on a plethora of advanced technologies. It needs various kinds of technologies to support the consumer shopping journey in as many devices they use, everywhere and at any time possible. This includes augmented and virtual reality, the internet of things, automatic speech recognition, natural language processing, and data analytics (Seshia et al., 2022). Among all these technologies, artificial intelligence is critical to omnichannel for electronic commerce (Cheah et al., 2020). The many tools that consumers possess, either in the workplace, home, or places they visited are gathering the data on daily activities.

Different types of artificial intelligence are used to provide a predictive mechanism for retailers to know about consumer preferences and needs. This permits the retailers to anticipate the kinds of product listings following the requirements of the consumers. For instance, adaptive neural networks could instantly deliver the right product information based on consumer shopping behavior (Cai et al., 2020). Natural language processing is ideal to understand consumer needs and support with the right product usage information and recommendations (Liu et al., 2021). Furthermore, machine learning is required in contextual commerce to analyze large churns of data and to provide specific insights of consumer needs based on market trends and consumer demographic changes (Kratsch et al., 2021). Deep learning, another branch of artificial intelligence, learned from customer data to generate highly personalized content desired by consumers (Guan et al., 2019). It can also influence the customer who intends to abandon the shopping cart with attractive content from abandoned it.

UTAUT Theory

The rapid development and exponential growth of online business transactions have led to the deployment of new and innovative features in electronic commerce. Existing literature has an abundance of studies devoted to the new ways of doing online business and many of them were based on the theoretical stances of the Unified Theory of Acceptance and Use of Technology (UTAUT) (Erjavec & Manfreda, 2022; Ikumoro & Jawad, 2019). It has the predictive power in examining both the technological and behavioral aspects of new and innovative deployment (Ho & Song, 2023; Hu et al., 2020). It has influenced many electronic commerce studies (Ahn et al., 2019). The integration of artificial intelligence features into contextual commerce falls into this arena of study. Chong (2013) investigated mobile commerce powered by neural networks to support the integration of artificial intelligence with shopping functions. Therefore, the study adopts it as the underpinning theoretical framework to explore further.

Figure 1. Conceptual framework

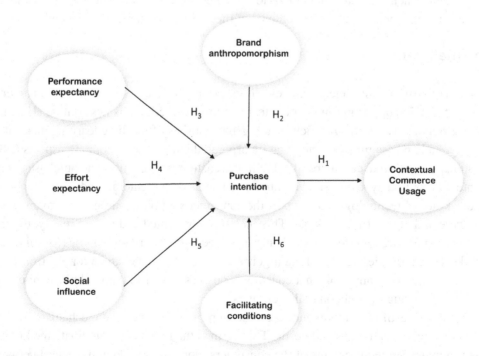

Figure 1 shows the conceptual framework of this study. There are five main determinants of UTAUT, namely performance expectancy, effort expectancy, social influence, and facilitating conditions. They are posited as the antecedents in influencing consumer adoption of contextual commerce which is supported heavily by artificial intelligence.

Use Behavior in Contextual Commerce

The main dependent variable of this study is the purchase intention which represents the use behavior of consumers. Purchase intention is denoted as the willingness of the consumers to buy the products or services (Meskaran et al., 2013). In other words, it suggests that there is a high possibility for consumers to purchase goods or services in the future from the same channel (Ho, 2019). Consumers are likely to buy from the same channel if they have a stronger purchase intention (De Cannière et al., 2010). With the convenience of buying products as the consumers could do at anywhere and anytime promised by contextual commerce, the intention to purchase is expected to be high. The consumers can instantly engage in the buying process, like browsing the product listings, and make payments directly while they are doing the diary work and chores. Furthermore, the customers would also receive dynamic messages generated by artificial intelligence from the retailers to provide further shopping assistance and product information. In this study, the purchase intention was posited to exert influence on the adoption of this new shopping channel. Hence, the following hypothesis was formed:

H_1: Purchase intention positively results in the use of contextual commerce.

Brand Anthropomorphism

With plenty of artificial elements in business technologies today, anthropomorphism plays an important role in getting humans to enjoy the benefits of the deployment of technology. In short, humanize the business process for consumers to relate and engage well with the retailers. Brand anthropomorphism refers to the act of anthropomorphism to transform a brand with human-like attributes to enhance the likelihood of customer closer engagement with the brand. The existing literature has witnessed the increase of brand anthropomorphism in the arena of consumer behavior (Aggarwal & McGill, 2012; Guido & Peluso, 2015; Rauschnabel & Ahuvia, 2014). The rise was attributed to the enormous growth of the use of electronic commerce after the Corvid-19 era. The increasing demand for customer interaction with brands heightened the need for closer interaction and frequent communication for both sellers and customers (Azar et al., 2016). Hence, the current published works have devoted attention paid to brand anthropomorphism. Khenfer et al. (2020) have examined the requirement of customer empowerment for a better understanding of consumer preference. Furthermore, the impression of a brand can behave like humans for improved customer and seller interaction (Kim & Kramer, 2015). In addition, Ali et al. (2021) indicated that brand anthropomorphism and brand love combined have a direct linkage to brand loyalty. The same result is supported by a study conducted by (Kaya et al., 2019) that the importance of the anthropomorphized human elements is key to lead to customer retention. Hence, brand anthropomorphism is proposed in this study for its influence on purchase intention with the following hypothesis:

H_2: Brand anthropomorphism positively results in the purchase intention of contextual commerce.

Performance Expectancy

Performance expectancy is one of the five main determinants under the UTAUT theory. It refers to the expectation of the customers for the new implementation or technologies to perform and complete the tasks as promised (Oh et al., 2009). The notion of performance expectancy has been confirmed as critical to influencing the adoption of many previous business innovations (Engotoit et al., 2016; Jaradat & Al Rababaa, 2013). Ryu and Fortenberry (2021) examined the importance of the performance expectancy of US consumers towards the omnichannel shopping platform. The new features or functionalities are deployed to make the processes work to achieve better performance. With many benefits brought by artificial intelligence initiatives, the use of contextual commerce as one of the new transaction channels is highly anticipated (Cai & Lo, 2020). In addition, the ubiquitous features in placing the purchase gained from the convenience of the contextual commerce would be much helpful to the consumers. Hence, the following hypothesis was suggested:

H_3: Performance expectancy positively results in purchase intention of contextual commerce.

Effort Expectancy

Effort expectancy means the expected time, energy, and learning efforts needed to work on the activities or tasks (Alraja et al., 2016). In this study, this notion is regarded as consumer expectation of how much effort is required to purchase products or services under contextual commerce. The current literature has a great list of research exploring the need for effort expectancy to use many different types of shopping channels (Alkhunaizan & Love, 2012; Lai & Lai, 2014). Rahi et al. (2019) investigated the mediating role of effort expectancy to improve e-service quality. In general, effort expectancy served as a key driver in getting the customers' attention to adopt the new shopping initiatives (Pappas et al., 2014). Consumers need to devote time and effort to learning to use and familiar with the shopping processes and systems prepared by the retailers. Their absorptive capacity to learn new processes is critical for their usage benefits (Ho & Chua, 2015). The effort expectancy is expected to be higher with the use of machine learning in the customer support of contextual commerce. Furthermore, it can further improve customer support with the deployment of robotics technology to handle customer calls, email correspondence, and live chat. Therefore, the high level of effort expectancy is envisaged to have a direct impact on molding the higher purchase intention for contextual commerce. Hence, the following hypothesis is developed ad listed as follows:

H_4: Effort expectancy positively results in purchase intention of contextual commerce.

Social Influence

Social influence is an important notion in UTAUT viewing from the social perspective. It means the influence of people who are close to us in affecting our decision to act (Book & Tanford, 2019). This is natural for consumers to secure guidance from acquaintances whom they think are competent in the tasks they intended to carry out. Their influence could be intensified or higher if they are from family members and close friends. Electronic commerce is transformed into many varieties of platforms such as social commerce, live selling, social selling, etc. The importance of socially connected consumers is obvious in these types of channels via consumer socialization process (Ho & Teo, 2022; Hu et al., 2019). Social influence has been validated as one main factor in generating sales (Kim & Kim, 2018)

The consumers gained more comprehensive product knowledge from their peers with more use of social media by business (Ho & Amin, 2022). Hence, with more advanced functionalities in artificial intelligence in managing the large set of social media data and interpreting it to predict consumer buying patterns, product needs, and consumer behavior. For instance, Facebook's DeepText system serves as a deep learning mechanism to analyze its customer data. This applies to the customers using contextual commerce when they approach their social network contact or refer to other social media posts about the brands they are interested in before they committed to purchase. Therefore, the role of social influence is equally critical and hence it is worth investigation. The following hypothesis is then developed:

H$_5$: Social influence positively results in purchase intention of contextual commerce.

Facilitating Conditions

Facilitating conditions are defined as the infrastructure needed to ensure the use of a system in a proper manner (Peñarroja et al., 2019). This includes both the physical components and soft skills required to provide the processes and procedures for the users. The importance of facilitating conditions in supporting many business operations is presented in the extant literature (Chowdhury et al., 2014; Ho & Amin, 2019). Having said that, it is validated as one major factor for the successful implementation of various types of electronic commerce channels (Yang & Forney, 2013). Yahia et al. (2018) further confirmed the need of facilitating conditions of social media to drive the adoption of social commerce. Just like other electronic commerce platforms, technology components, particularly infrastructure of internet is critical for contextual commerce as well. The increasing use of many types of artificial intelligence in contextual commerce is necessary to optimize the customer experience. However, the acceptance of the customer remains an untapped area to be explored further. Therefore, we propose the following hypothesis:

H$_6$: Facilitating conditions positively results in purchase intention of contextual commerce.

RESEARCH METHODOLOGY

Sample Design

The respondents for this study were active online shoppers in Malaysia who were familiar with and experienced in the use of contextual commerce. They were approached and joined to participate in the questionnaire. Firstly, they were filtered and needed to answer a qualification question to confirm they had purchased products with contextual commerce. Hence, a total of 205 respondents were validated and formed the sample of this study. Table 1 is the descriptive statistics about the sample.

Survey Design

The questionnaire was the instrument used to collect the data for this study. It was divided into 2 sections. Section 1 contains general information about the study and the requested demographic information from the respondents. Section 2 was the questions related to the conceptual framework of the study. Item measurements for the main constructs were adapted from the established items used in past studies. We measured brand anthropomorphism with the scale sourced from Rauschnabel and Ahuvia (2014). The item measuring the main constructs of UTAUT was adapted from Venkatesh et al. (2011). Items

Table 1. Descriptive statistics of the sample

	Category	Frequency	Percentage
Sex	Male	101	49.3%
	Female	104	50.7%
Age	18 – 29	108	52.7%
	30 – 39	61	29.8%
	40 – 49	20	9.8%
	50 – 59	15	7.3%
	Above 60	1	0.5%
Job category	Student	57	27.8%
	Employed for wages	102	49.8%
	Self-employed	43	20.9%
	Homemaker	3	1.5%
No. of year use of contextual commerce	1	124	60.5%
	2 – 3	75	36.6%
	> 3	6	2.9%
Frequency online purchase per month	1	65	31.7%
	1 – 3	133	64.9%
	> 3	7	3.4%

Table 2. Item measurement design of the questionnaire

Construct	Scale	Source
Brand anthropomorphism	BRA1: Brand and the products seem to have good and own free will. BRA2: Brand and the products seem to experience positive emotions. BRA3: Brand and the products seem to have their own positive consciousness.	Rauschnabel & Ahuvia (2014)
Contextual commerce use	CCU1: I have used contextual commerce to purchase online products. CCU2: I have used contextual commerce to shop for products from different online retailers. CCU3: I have used different kinds of contextual commerce for online shopping.	Chopdar et al. (2018)
Effort expectancy	EFE1: It is easy to learn how to use contextual commerce. EFE2: Interacting with contextual commerce is clear and easy to understand. EFE3: Contextual commerce is easy to use.	Venkatesh et al., 2011
Facilitating condition	FAC1: I had no difficulty in finding and using contextual commerce. FAC2: I had no difficulty in customizing the contextual commerce for my use. FAC3: Overall, contextual commerce has good performance.	Venkatesh et al., 2011
Performance expectancy	PEX1: Contextual commerce can be useful in managing my online shopping. PEX2: Contextual commerce can be valuable to my online shopping. PEX3: Contextual commerce can be advantageous in better managing my online shopping.	Venkatesh et al., 2011
Purchase intention	PUI1: I intend to buy products or services from contextual commerce PUI2.If somebody asks me for advice on buying a product or service, I will recommend products or services from contextual commerce PUI3.In the future, I will buy products or services from contextual commerce.	Thomas et al., 2019
Social influence	SOI1: I want to use contextual commerce because my friends do so. SOI2: Using contextual commerce reflects my personality to other people. SOI3: According to people who are important to me, I should use contextual commerce.	Venkatesh et al., 2011

relating to purchase intention were the work of Thomas et al. (2019), while the use of contextual commerce was obtained from Chopdar et al. (2018). Refers to Table 2 for the item measurement design of the questionnaire.

Data Analysis

The study employed 2-stage structured equation modeling which included exploratory and confirmatory factor analyses. It was selected based on the premise that we have a list of latent variables separated into two levels under the conceptual framework of the study. With that, the inter-relationship of multiple constructs could be examined and tested the associated hypotheses. Therefore, SmartPLS was the main inferential statistics software to discover the significance of the paths from the conceptual model.

Measurement Model

The validity and reliability tests were applied to examine the measurement model. The composite reliability (CR) and its related average variance extracted (AVE) were calculated to test the measurement model. The results were relevant and met the acceptance level. It implied that convergent validity was

Table 3. Summary results for the measurement model

Variable	Scale	Loadings	CR	Cronbach Alpha	AVE
Brand anthropomorphism	BRA1	0.841	0.957	0.801	0.735
	BRA2	0.870	-	-	-
	BRA3	0.834	-	-	-
Contextual commerce use	CCU1	0.832	0.832	0.822	0.673
	CCU2	0.860	-	-	-
	CCU3	0.822	-	-	-
Effort expectancy	EFE1	0.746	0.925	0.814	0.747
	EFE2	0.865	-	-	-
	EFE3	0.804	-	-	-
Facilitating conditions	FAC1	0.882	0.868	0.791	0.688
	FAC2	0.804	-	-	-
	FAC3	0.822	-	-	-
Performance expectancy	PEX1	0.797	0.905	0.887	0.749
	PEX2	0.841	-	-	-
	PEX3	0.876	-	-	-
Purchase intention	PUI1	0.858	0.917	0.800	0.704
	PUI2	0.815	-	-	-
	PUI3	0.808	-	-	-
Social influence	SOI1	0.805	0.836	0.870	0.697
	SOI2	0.816	-	-	-
	SOI3	0.828	-	-	-

attained. Furthermore, Cronbach's alpha for each of the variables used was higher than the optimum value of 0.7. Hence, the model achieved the required internal consistency. Table 3 depicts the summary test result of the measurement model.

As for the discriminant validity, Heterotrait-Monotrait (HTMT) method was applied in this study and its results were depicted in Table 4. Therefore, the model was able to attain discriminant validity. After all, the reliability and validity tests conducted demonstrated the goodness of the measurement model for this study.

Table 4. Discriminant validity: Heterotrait-Monotrait ratio of correlations (HTMT)

Constructs	1	2	3	4	5	6	7
1. Brand anthropomorphism							
2. Contextual commerce use	0.715						
3. Effort expectancy	0.616	0.733					
4. Facilitating conditions	0.688	0.630	0.781				
5. Performance expectancy	0.783	0.754	0.680	0.664			
6. Purchase intention	0.776	0.763	0.742	0.633	0.764		
7. Social influence	0.881	0.657	0.639	0.794	0.602	0.679	

Structural Model

The bootstrapping method was used to test the structural model for re-sampling purposes. The standard error, t score, and p value were calculated and altogether were able to validate the structural model. Table 5 depicts the goodness of the structural model for this study.

Table 5. The test results of structural model

Hypothesis	Beta	Std. Error	t-Value	p-Value
H_1: PUI → CCU	0.374	0.054	2.349	0.000
H_2: BRA → PUI	0.270	0.011	3.836	0.000
H_3: PEX → PUI	0.425	0.062	5.756	0.000
H_4: EFE → PUI	0.238	0.084	5.226	0.000
H_5: SOI → PUI	0.246	0.082	3.298	0.000
H_6: FAC → PUI	0.225	0.083	2.737	0.005

Following that, a blindfolding procedure was conducted to calculate the R^2 value for the dependent variables as shown in Table 6. Both R^2 and Q^2 values met the threshold required to validate the structural model. Purchase intention's R^2 value was 0.38. Contextual commerce usage has its R^2 at 0.48. Hence, the scores indicated that the main determinants of this study sufficiently explain the variance needed. The Q^2 score for other variables was gained with the use of the Stone-Geisser sample reuse technique.

Table 6. Blindfolding results

Construct	R²	Q²
Brand anthropomorphism	-	0.231
Contextual commerce usage	0.483	0.328
Performance expectancy	-	0.352
Effort expectancy	-	0.243
Social influence	-	0.290
Facilitating conditions	-	0.181
Purchase intention	0.379	0.315

The Q^2 score for performance expectancy was 0.352, followed by 0.243 for effort expectancy, 0.290 for social influence, 0.181 for facilitating conditions, and 0.315 for purchase intention respectively.

Hypotheses Testing

Hypotheses for the model were further examined with the use of path analysis. Hence, the list of hypotheses was valid and accepted accordingly. Table 7 recorded the test results for the structural model.

Table 7. The result of hypothesis testing

Hypothesis	Path	Decision
H_1	PUI → CCU	Supported
H_2	BRA → PUI	Supported
H_3	PEX → PUI	Supported
H_4	EFE → PUI	Supported
H_5	SOI → PUI	Supported
H_6	FAC → PUI	Supported

The list of the test results can be summarized as follows. The path of performance expectancy was accepted with t-value = 5.756 and p value =0. The path of effort expectancy with t-value =5.226, p-value =0. The test results for contextual commerce usage were t-value =3.836, and p-value =0. Also, social influence obtained t-value =3.298, and p-value =0, and facilitating condition was supported with a t-value =2.737, and p-value =0. Hence, all the hypotheses of the conceptual framework were supported significantly as depicted in Table 7 which validated the structural model.

CONCLUSION

The purpose of this study was to examine the application of artificial intelligence on the consumer acceptance of contextual commerce. It investigated and validated the antecedents influenced by artificial intelligence features. The main determinants were derived from the UTAUT theory. This includes performance expectancy, effort expectancy, social influence, and facilitating conditions and they were confirmed as influential in the adoption by the consumers. Furthermore, the need for brand anthropomorphism was tested as one of the key antecedents in relating the integration of artificial intelligence and contextual commerce. This provides a theoretical model to understand customer behavior and involvement in contextual commerce. Hence, a new insight was shed into the usefulness of artificial intelligence in supporting contextual commerce.

Theoretical Contribution

This study applied the UTAUT theory as the main theoretical basis to discover consumer behavior with the use of artificial intelligence in contextual commerce. It extends the theory with the inclusion of brand anthropomorphism as the additional variable to explain the features brought forward by the artificial intelligence elements. The major variables from UTAUT were included to provide a solid foundation to drive the research. All the variables were supported and hence it shed new light on the adoption theory with the integration of artificial intelligence and context commerce. Among all variables, performance expectancy offered higher predictive power based on the result obtained from this study. This is followed by effort expectancy, social influence, and facilitating condition was weaker when compared to the rest of the variables. The results are consistent with studies on consumer acceptance of other major electronic commerce channels under the purview of UTAUT theory (Puriwat & Tripopsakul, 2021). Facilitating conditions were validated as less influential. A similar finding was shown in other studies (Al-Qeisi et al., 2015; Tusyanah et al., 2021). It explains facilitating conditions were least critical in the eyes of the consumers. The result was due to the competency of many consumers who are familiar with and have been exposed to the use of internet applications (Mannan et al., 2019). It is noted that most electronic commerce applications were user-friendly, and it would not take a long time for consumers to learn and use them effectively. The significance of brand anthropomorphism was confirmed by this study. It is a fact that consumers are receptive to communicating with a human-like brand because it resembles more toward an actual human being. This led to the expected closer interaction and boosted consumer engagement with relationship support from brands (Ho & Cheng, 2020).

In a nutshell, this study was validated as the extended UTAUT theory in explaining brand anthropomorphism to explain the use of artificial intelligence for contextual commerce. Therefore, it shed new light on the theoretical discourse to understand consumer behavior who are presented with artificial intelligence driven shopping options that allow them to purchase while they are carrying out their daily activities. Hence, this extended theoretical framework could offer a theoretical explanation for an increasing demand of consumers who would choose to buy in context at their convenience.

Practical Contribution

The burgeoning application of artificial intelligence is prevalent in the business world. It is unstoppable in making business applications to learn and carry out human-like tasks. Contextual commerce offers the convenience to do shopping ubiquitously and is gaining momentum with its integration with artificial intelligence capabilities. Businesses venturing into this new electronic commerce platform will have to be equipped with the related resources and strategies to manage it successfully (Sestino & De Mauro, 2022). The need to adjust and integrate the more personalised demands of the buying in-context consumers from contextual commerce. Hence, the use of advanced artificial intelligence tools is critical. For instance, the application of natural language processing to assist in interpreting consumer requests and fully understanding them. It would avoid mistakes in providing incorrect products or solutions to the customers. Furthermore, a new development in machine learning offers innovative customer support with a comprehensive learning algorithm. Personalized support or product recommendations can be unique only to the actual need of each customer (Bang & Wojdynski, 2016). In short, the customer centricity focused strategy should be designed and implemented to provide a much more enjoyable customer shopping experience and directly fulfill the shopping needs.

Limitation and Future Direction

The study has its limitations although it offers novel implications for the impact of artificial intelligence on electronic commerce. The current study focuses on the overall evaluation of the customers from a general perspective. The shopping experience generally can be divided into a few main stages, i.e. pre-purchase, during the purchase, and finally after-sale service (Frasquet et al., 2015). Hence, it was a cross-sectional approach that overlooked the full shopping journey. This limitation affects the causal effect needed and reduces the generalizability of the implications gained from this study. It is anticipated that it can be extended into various stages of contextual commerce for future research works. In addition, contextual commerce is subject to the loss of customer confidentiality and privacy due to its need for open data sharing during its operations (Kim et al., 2021). Hence, it is suggested that customer privacy requires further investigation. Customer impulsive purchase is another area worth exploring in the future in view of the overly easy shopping benefits derived from contextual commerce.

REFERENCES

Aggarwal, P., & McGill, A. L. (2012). When brands seem human, do humans act like brands? Automatic behavioral priming effects of brand anthropomorphism. *The Journal of Consumer Research*, *39*(2), 307–323. doi:10.1086/662614

Ahn, S., Jo, W., & Chung, D. (2019). Factors Affecting Users to Adopt Voice Shopping: Empirical Evidence from the UTAUT Model. *Journal of Technology Innovation*, *27*(4), 111–144. doi:10.14386/SIME.2019.27.4.111

Al-Qeisi, K., Dennis, C., & Abbad, M. (2015). How viable is the UTAUT model in a non-Western context? *International Business Research*, *8*(2), 204–219. doi:10.5539/ibr.v8n2p204

Ali, F., Dogan, S., Amin, M., Hussain, K., & Ryu, K. (2021). Brand anthropomorphism, love and defense: Does attitude towards social distancing matter? *Service Industries Journal*, *41*(1-2), 58–83. doi:10.1080/02642069.2020.1867542

Alkhunaizan, A., & Love, S. (2012). What drives mobile commerce? An empirical evaluation of the revised UTAUT model. *International Journal of Management and Marketing Academy*, *2*(1), 82–99.

Alraja, M. N., Hammami, S., Chikhi, B., & Fekir, S. (2016). The influence of effort and performance expectancy on employees to adopt e-government: Evidence from Oman. *International Review of Management and Marketing*, *6*(4), 930–934.

Azar, S. L., Machado, J. C., Vacas-de-Carvalho, L., & Mendes, A. (2016). Motivations to interact with brands on Facebook–Towards a typology of consumer–brand interactions. *Journal of Brand Management*, *23*(2), 153–178. doi:10.1057/bm.2016.3

Bang, H., & Wojdynski, B. W. (2016). Tracking users' visual attention and responses to personalized advertising based on task cognitive demand. *Computers in Human Behavior*, *55*, 867–876. doi:10.1016/j.chb.2015.10.025

Book, L. A., & Tanford, S. (2019). Measuring social influence from online traveler reviews. *Journal of Hospitality and Tourism Insights*, *3*(1), 54–72. doi:10.1108/JHTI-06-2019-0080

Cai, X., Qian, Y., Bai, Q., & Liu, W. (2020). Exploration on the financing risks of enterprise supply chain using Back Propagation neural network. *Journal of Computational and Applied Mathematics*, *367*, 112457. doi:10.1016/j.cam.2019.112457

Cai, Y.-J., & Lo, C. K. (2020). Omni-channel management in the new retailing era: A systematic review and future research agenda. *International Journal of Production Economics*, *229*, 107729. doi:10.1016/j.ijpe.2020.107729

Chang, Y. P., & Li, J. (2022). Seamless experience in the context of omnichannel shopping: Scale development and empirical validation. *Journal of Retailing and Consumer Services*, *64*, 102800. doi:10.1016/j.jretconser.2021.102800

Cheah, J.-H., Lim, X.-J., Ting, H., Liu, Y., & Quach, S. (2020). Are privacy concerns still relevant? Revisiting consumer behaviour in omnichannel retailing. *Journal of Retailing and Consumer Services*, *102242*. Advance online publication. doi:10.1016/j.jretconser.2020.102242

Chen, S., Wei, H., Ran, Y., Li, Q., & Meng, L. (2021). Waiting for a download: The effect of congruency between anthropomorphic cues and shopping motivation on consumer patience. *Psychology and Marketing*, *38*(12), 2327–2338. doi:10.1002/mar.21564

Chong, A. Y.-L. (2013). Predicting m-commerce adoption determinants: A neural network approach. *Expert Systems with Applications*, *40*(2), 523–530. doi:10.1016/j.eswa.2012.07.068

Chopdar, P. K., Korfiatis, N., Sivakumar, V., & Lytras, M. D. (2018). Mobile shopping apps adoption and perceived risks: A cross-country perspective utilizing the Unified Theory of Acceptance and Use of Technology. *Computers in Human Behavior*, *86*, 109–128. doi:10.1016/j.chb.2018.04.017

Chowdhury, I. R., Patro, S., Venugopal, P., & Israel, D. (2014). A study on consumer adoption of technology-facilitated services. *Journal of Services Marketing*, *28*(6), 471–483. doi:10.1108/JSM-04-2013-0095

De Cannière, M. H., De Pelsmacker, P., & Geuens, M. (2010). Relationship quality and purchase intention and behavior: The moderating impact of relationship strength. *Journal of Business and Psychology*, *25*(1), 87–98. doi:10.100710869-009-9127-z

Di Vaio, A., Palladino, R., Hassan, R., & Escobar, O. (2020). Artificial intelligence and business models in the sustainable development goals perspective: A systematic literature review. *Journal of Business Research*, *121*, 283–314. doi:10.1016/j.jbusres.2020.08.019

Engotoit, B., Kituyi, G. M., & Moya, M. B. (2016). Influence of performance expectancy on commercial farmers' intention to use mobile-based communication technologies for agricultural market information dissemination in Uganda. *Journal of Systems and Information Technology*, *18*(4), 346–363. doi:10.1108/JSIT-06-2016-0037

Enholm, I. M., Papagiannidis, E., Mikalef, P., & Krogstie, J. (2022). Artificial intelligence and business value: A literature review. *Information Systems Frontiers*, *24*(5), 1709–1734. doi:10.100710796-021-10186-w

Epley, N., Waytz, A., & Cacioppo, J. T. (2007). On seeing human: A three-factor theory of anthropomorphism. *Psychological Review*, *114*(4), 864–886. doi:10.1037/0033-295X.114.4.864 PMID:17907867

Erjavec, J., & Manfreda, A. (2022). Online shopping adoption during COVID-19 and social isolation: Extending the UTAUT model with herd behavior. *Journal of Retailing and Consumer Services*, *65*, 102867. doi:10.1016/j.jretconser.2021.102867

Frasquet, M., Mollá, A., & Ruiz, E. (2015). Identifying patterns in channel usage across the search, purchase and post-sales stages of shopping. *Electronic Commerce Research and Applications*, *14*(6), 654–665. doi:10.1016/j.elerap.2015.10.002

González, E. M., Meyer, J.-H., & Toldos, M. P. (2021). What women want? How contextual product displays influence women's online shopping behavior. *Journal of Business Research*, *123*, 625–641. doi:10.1016/j.jbusres.2020.10.002

Grewal, D., Herhausen, D., Ludwig, S., & Ordenes, F. V. (2022). The future of digital communication research: Considering dynamics and multimodality. *Journal of Retailing*, *98*(2), 224–240. doi:10.1016/j.jretai.2021.01.007

Guan, Y., Wei, Q., & Chen, G. (2019). Deep learning based personalized recommendation with multiview information integration. *Decision Support Systems*, *118*, 58–69. doi:10.1016/j.dss.2019.01.003

Guido, G., & Peluso, A. M. (2015). Brand anthropomorphism: Conceptualization, measurement, and impact on brand personality and loyalty. *Journal of Brand Management*, *22*(1), 1–19. doi:10.1057/bm.2014.40

Gunasekaran, A., Papadopoulos, T., Dubey, R., Wamba, S. F., Childe, S. J., Hazen, B., & Akter, S. (2017). Big data and predictive analytics for supply chain and organizational performance. *Journal of Business Research*, *70*, 308–317. doi:10.1016/j.jbusres.2016.08.004

Haenlein, M., Kaplan, A., Tan, C.-W., & Zhang, P. (2019). Artificial intelligence (AI) and management analytics. *Journal of Management Analytics*, *6*(4), 341–343. doi:10.1080/23270012.2019.1699876

Ho, R. C. (2019). The outcome expectations of promocode in mobile shopping apps: an integrative behavioral and social cognitive perspective. *Proceedings of the 2019 3rd International Conference on E-commerce, E-Business and E-Government*.10.1145/3340017.3340028

Ho, R. C. (2022). Unearthing Customer Engagement in Mobile Wallet Usage: A Uses and Gratifications Perspective. In *Handbook of Research on Social Impacts of E-Payment and Blockchain Technology* (pp. 392-408). IGI Global. 10.1145/3340017.3340028

Ho, R. C., & Amin, M. (2019). What drives the adoption of smart travel planning apps? The relationship between experiential consumption and mobile app acceptance. *KnE Social Sciences*, 22–41.

Ho, R. C., & Amin, M. (2022). Exploring the role of commitment in potential absorptive capacity and its impact on new financial product knowledge: A social media banking perspective. *Journal of Financial Services Marketing*, 1–14. doi:10.105741264-022-00168-7

Ho, R. C., & Cheng, R. (2020). The impact of relationship quality and social support on social media users' selling intention. *International Journal of Internet Marketing and Advertising*, *14*(4), 433–453. doi:10.1504/IJIMA.2020.111051

Ho, R. C., & Chua, H. K. (2015). The influence of mobile learning on learner's absorptive capacity: a case of bring-your-own-device (BYOD) learning environment. *Taylor's 7th Teaching and Learning Conference 2014 Proceedings*.

Ho, R. C., & Song, B. L. (2023). User Acceptance Towards Non-Fungible Token (NFT) as the FinTech for Investment Management in the Metaverse. In *Strategies and Opportunities for Technology in the Metaverse World* (pp. 59-77). IGI Global.

Ho, R. C., & Teo, T. C. (2022). Consumer Socialization Process for the Highly Connected Customers: The Use of Instagram to Gain Product Knowledge. In Research Anthology on Social Media Advertising and Building Consumer Relationships (pp. 657-674). IGI Global.

Hu, S., Laxman, K., & Lee, K. (2020). Exploring factors affecting academics' adoption of emerging mobile technologies-an extended UTAUT perspective. *Education and Information Technologies*, *25*(5), 4615–4635. doi:10.100710639-020-10171-x

Hu, X., Chen, X., & Davison, R. M. (2019). Social support, source credibility, social influence, and impulsive purchase behavior in social commerce. *International Journal of Electronic Commerce*, *23*(3), 297–327. doi:10.1080/10864415.2019.1619905

Huré, E., Picot-Coupey, K., & Ackermann, C.-L. (2017). Understanding omni-channel shopping value: A mixed-method study. *Journal of Retailing and Consumer Services*, *39*, 314–330. doi:10.1016/j.jret-conser.2017.08.011

Ikumoro, A. O., & Jawad, M. S. (2019). Intention to use intelligent conversational agents in e-commerce among Malaysian SMEs: An integrated conceptual framework based on tri-theories including unified theory of acceptance, use of technology (UTAUT), and TOE. *International Journal of Academic Research in Business & Social Sciences*, *9*(11), 205–235. doi:10.6007/IJARBSS/v9-i11/6544

Jaradat, M.-I. R. M., & Al Rababaa, M. S. (2013). Assessing key factor that influence on the acceptance of mobile commerce based on modified UTAUT. *International Journal of Business and Management*, *8*(23), 102–112. doi:10.5539/ijbm.v8n23p102

Javaid, M., Haleem, A., Singh, R. P., & Suman, R. (2022). Artificial intelligence applications for industry 4.0: A literature-based study. *Journal of Industrial Integration and Management*, *7*(01), 83–111. doi:10.1142/S2424862221300040

Khenfer, J., Shepherd, S., & Trendel, O. (2020). Customer empowerment in the face of perceived Incompetence: Effect on preference for anthropomorphized brands. *Journal of Business Research*, *118*, 1–11. doi:10.1016/j.jbusres.2020.06.010

Khrais, L. T. (2020). Role of artificial intelligence in shaping consumer demand in E-commerce. *Future Internet*, *12*(12), 226. doi:10.3390/fi12120226

Kim, H. C., & Kramer, T. (2015). Do materialists prefer the "brand-as-servant"? The interactive effect of anthropomorphized brand roles and materialism on consumer responses. *The Journal of Consumer Research*, *42*(2), 284–299. doi:10.1093/jcr/ucv015

Kim, N., & Kim, W. (2018). Do your social media lead you to make social deal purchases? Consumer-generated social referrals for sales via social commerce. *International Journal of Information Management*, *39*, 38–48. doi:10.1016/j.ijinfomgt.2017.10.006

Kim, Y., Wang, Q., & Roh, T. (2021). Do information and service quality affect perceived privacy protection, satisfaction, and loyalty? Evidence from a Chinese O2O-based mobile shopping application. *Telematics and Informatics*, *56*, 101483. doi:10.1016/j.tele.2020.101483

Kratsch, W., Manderscheid, J., Röglinger, M., & Seyfried, J. (2021). Machine learning in business process monitoring: A comparison of deep learning and classical approaches used for outcome prediction. *Business & Information Systems Engineering*, *63*(3), 261–276. doi:10.100712599-020-00645-0

Kraus, M., Feuerriegel, S., & Oztekin, A. (2020). Deep learning in business analytics and operations research: Models, applications and managerial implications. *European Journal of Operational Research*, *281*(3), 628–641. doi:10.1016/j.ejor.2019.09.018

Lai, I. K., & Lai, D. C. (2014). User acceptance of mobile commerce: An empirical study in Macau. *International Journal of Systems Science*, *45*(6), 1321–1331. doi:10.1080/00207721.2012.761471

Lee, J., Suh, T., Roy, D., & Baucus, M. (2019). Emerging technology and business model innovation: The case of artificial intelligence. *Journal of Open Innovation*, *5*(3), 44. doi:10.3390/joitmc5030044

Li, H., Hu, Q., Zhao, G., & Li, B. (2021). The co-evolution of knowledge management and business model transformation in the post-COVID-19 era: Insights based on Chinese e-commerce companies. *Journal of Knowledge Management*, *26*(6), 1113–1123. doi:10.1108/JKM-03-2021-0177

Liu, X., Shin, H., & Burns, A. C. (2021). Examining the impact of luxury brand's social media marketing on customer engagement: Using big data analytics and natural language processing. *Journal of Business Research*, *125*, 815–826. doi:10.1016/j.jbusres.2019.04.042

Loureiro, S. M. C., Guerreiro, J., & Tussyadiah, I. (2021). Artificial intelligence in business: State of the art and future research agenda. *Journal of Business Research*, *129*, 911–926. doi:10.1016/j.jbusres.2020.11.001

Mannan, M., Ahamed, R., & Zaman, S. B. (2019). Consumers' willingness to purchase online mental health services. *Journal of Services Marketing, 33*(5), 557–571. doi:10.1108/JSM-05-2018-0163

Mariani, M. (2019). Big data and analytics in tourism and hospitality: A perspective article. *Tourism Review, 75*(1), 299–303. doi:10.1108/TR-06-2019-0259

Marinković, V., Đorđević, A., & Kalinić, Z. (2020). The moderating effects of gender on customer satisfaction and continuance intention in mobile commerce: A UTAUT-based perspective. *Technology Analysis and Strategic Management, 32*(3), 306–318. doi:10.1080/09537325.2019.1655537

Meskaran, F., Ismail, Z., & Shanmugam, B. (2013). Online purchase intention: Effects of trust and security perception. *Australian Journal of Basic and Applied Sciences, 7*(6), 307–315.

Moriuchi, E., Landers, V. M., Colton, D., & Hair, N. (2021). Engagement with chatbots versus augmented reality interactive technology in e-commerce. *Journal of Strategic Marketing, 29*(5), 375–389. doi:10.1080/0965254X.2020.1740766

Naim, A. (2022). E-learning engagement through convolution neural networks in business education. *European Journal of Innovation in Nonformal Education, 2*(2), 497–501.

Oh, S., Lehto, X. Y., & Park, J. (2009). Travelers' intent to use mobile technologies as a function of effort and performance expectancy. *Journal of Hospitality Marketing & Management, 18*(8), 765–781. doi:10.1080/19368620903235795

Pappas, I. O., Pateli, A. G., Giannakos, M. N., & Chrissikopoulos, V. (2014). Moderating effects of online shopping experience on customer satisfaction and repurchase intentions. *International Journal of Retail & Distribution Management, 42*(3), 187–204. doi:10.1108/IJRDM-03-2012-0034

Peñarroja, V., Sánchez, J., Gamero, N., Orengo, V., & Zornoza, A. M. (2019). The influence of organisational facilitating conditions and technology acceptance factors on the effectiveness of virtual communities of practice. *Behaviour & Information Technology, 38*(8), 845–857. doi:10.1080/0144929X.2018.1564070

Pillai, R., Sivathanu, B., & Dwivedi, Y. K. (2020). Shopping intention at AI-powered automated retail stores (AIPARS). *Journal of Retailing and Consumer Services, 57*, 102207. doi:10.1016/j.jretconser.2020.102207

Puriwat, W., & Tripopsakul, S. (2021). Explaining social Media adoption for a business purpose: An application of the UTAUT model. *Sustainability, 13*(4), 2082. doi:10.3390u13042082

Quan, X. I., & Sanderson, J. (2018). Understanding the artificial intelligence business ecosystem. *IEEE Engineering Management Review, 46*(4), 22–25. doi:10.1109/EMR.2018.2882430

Rahi, S., Mansour, M. M. O., Alghizzawi, M., & Alnaser, F. M. (2019). Integration of UTAUT model in internet banking adoption context: The mediating role of performance expectancy and effort expectancy. *Journal of Research in Interactive Marketing, 13*(3), 411–435. doi:10.1108/JRIM-02-2018-0032

Rana, N. P., Chatterjee, S., Dwivedi, Y. K., & Akter, S. (2022). Understanding dark side of artificial intelligence (AI) integrated business analytics: Assessing firm's operational inefficiency and competitiveness. *European Journal of Information Systems, 31*(3), 364–387. doi:10.1080/0960085X.2021.1955628

Rauschnabel, P. A., & Ahuvia, A. C. (2014). You're so lovable: Anthropomorphism and brand love. *Journal of Brand Management, 21*(5), 372–395. doi:10.1057/bm.2014.14

Rosário, A., & Raimundo, R. (2021). Consumer Marketing Strategy and E-Commerce in the Last Decade: A Literature Review. *Journal of Theoretical and Applied Electronic Commerce Research, 16*(7), 3003–3024. doi:10.3390/jtaer16070164

Rosenbaum, M. S., & Russell-Bennett, R. (2020). service research in the new (post-COVID) marketplace. *Journal of Services Marketing, 34*(5), 1–5. doi:10.1108/JSM-06-2020-0220

Ryu, J. S., & Fortenberry, S. (2021). Performance Expectancy and Effort Expectancy in Omnichannel Retailing. *The Journal of Industrial Distribution & Business, 12*(4), 27–34.

Samara, D., Magnisalis, I., & Peristeras, V. (2020). Artificial intelligence and big data in tourism: A systematic literature review. *Journal of Hospitality and Tourism Technology, 11*(2), 343–367. doi:10.1108/JHTT-12-2018-0118

Sarker, P., Hughes, D. L., & Dwivedi, Y. K. (2020). Extension of META-UTAUT for examining consumer adoption of social commerce: Towards a conceptual model. In *Advances in digital marketing and eCommerce* (pp. 122–129). Springer. doi:10.1007/978-3-030-47595-6_16

Seshia, S. A., Sadigh, D., & Sastry, S. S. (2022). Toward verified artificial intelligence. *Communications of the ACM, 65*(7), 46–55. doi:10.1145/3503914

Sestino, A., & De Mauro, A. (2022). Leveraging artificial intelligence in business: Implications, applications and methods. *Technology Analysis and Strategic Management, 34*(1), 16–29. doi:10.1080/09537325.2021.1883583

Shaikh, A. A., Lakshmi, K. S., Tongkachok, K., Alanya-Beltran, J., Ramirez-Asis, E., & Perez-Falcon, J. (2022). Empirical analysis in analysing the major factors of machine learning in enhancing the e-business through structural equation modelling (SEM) approach. *International Journal of System Assurance Engineering and Management, 13*(1), 681–689. doi:10.100713198-021-01590-1

Shi, Y., Wang, T., & Alwan, L. C. (2020). Analytics for cross-border e-commerce: Inventory risk management of an online fashion retailer. *Decision Sciences, 51*(6), 1347–1376. doi:10.1111/deci.12429

Soomro, Y. A. (2019). Understanding the adoption of sadad e-payments: UTAUT combined with religiosity as moderator. *International Journal of E-Business Research, 15*(1), 55–74. doi:10.4018/IJEBR.2019010104

Thomas, M.-J., Wirtz, B. W., & Weyerer, J. C. (2019). Determinants of Online Review Credibility and Its Impacts On Consumers' Purchase Intention. *Journal of Electronic Commerce Research, 20*(1), 1–20.

Tusyanah, T., Wahyudin, A., & Khafid, M. (2021). Analyzing factors affecting the behavioral intention to use e-wallet with the UTAUT model with experience as moderating variable. *The Journal of Economic Education, 10*(1), 113–123.

Venkatesh, V., Thong, J. Y., Chan, F. K., Hu, P. J. H., & Brown, S. A. (2011). Extending the two-stage information systems continuance model: Incorporating UTAUT predictors and the role of context. *Information Systems Journal, 21*(6), 527–555. doi:10.1111/j.1365-2575.2011.00373.x

Wamba-Taguimdje, S.-L., Wamba, S. F., Kamdjoug, J. R. K., & Wanko, C. E. T. (2020). Influence of artificial intelligence (AI) on firm performance: The business value of AI-based transformation projects. *Business Process Management Journal, 26*(7), 1893–1924. doi:10.1108/BPMJ-10-2019-0411

Yahia, I. B., Al-Neama, N., & Kerbache, L. (2018). Investigating the drivers for social commerce in social media platforms: Importance of trust, social support and the platform perceived usage. *Journal of Retailing and Consumer Services, 41*, 11–19. doi:10.1016/j.jretconser.2017.10.021

Yang, K., & Forney, J. C. (2013). The moderating role of consumer technology anxiety in mobile shopping adoption: Differential effects of facilitating conditions and social influences. *Journal of Electronic Commerce Research, 14*(4), 334.

Zhang, D., Pee, L., & Cui, L. (2021). Artificial intelligence in E-commerce fulfillment: A case study of resource orchestration at Alibaba's Smart Warehouse. *International Journal of Information Management, 57*, 102304. doi:10.1016/j.ijinfomgt.2020.102304

KEY TERMS AND DEFINITIONS

Artificial Intelligence: Machine ability to conduct activities typically needing human intelligence with the support of machine learning, natural language processing, dynamic messaging, and other elements.

Brand Anthropomorphism: The act of anthropomorphism to transform a brand with human-like attributes to enhance customer engagement with the brand.

Contextual Commerce: It refers to customers who would make purchases while conducting non-shopping activities, such as jogging, and watching drama.

Effort Expectancy: The effort dedicated to familiarizing and learning to use technologies or tools.

Facilitating Conditions: The infrastructure and facilities supporting the operations of technology deployment.

Performance Expectancy: The expected task accomplishment with the use of technologies or tools.

Self-Efficacy: Self-assurance of own abilities in conducting a behavior or task to completion.

Social Influence: The affection and support from other people while conducting a task and behavior.

Chapter 3
Artificial Intelligence Model for Analyzing the Buying Patterns of Customers

S M Nazmuz Sakib
https://orcid.org/0000-0001-9310-3014
International MBA Institute, School of Business and Trade, Dhaka International University, Bangladesh

ABSTRACT

This study aims to incorporate artificial intelligence (AI) for analyzing buying patterns of customers and different factors that are playing its role by discovering the important factors that contribute towards changing patterns. In order to study, a survey has been conducted for this analysis. Selected dataset consists of four attributes (i.e., gender, age, estimated salary, and purchase). These factors are used as input to AI model. The dataset consists of 400 members. Eighty percent of the data has been used for the purpose of training, and the data used for testing purpose is 20%. Experimental results have shown that that model has achieved 90% accuracy. It means AI has contributed a lot towards changing behaviors and approach of the customers during online shopping.

INTRODUCTION

This comparative study aims to incorporate the role of artificial intelligence in the changing buying pattern of consumers, and the role of digital spaces in this changing behavior. It has been witnessed that consumer behaviors have been fully transformed in this decade. Marketing trends and sense have been changed and fully transformed. Advertising plays an important role in influencing the targeted audience. But this process of changing trends was not at so much pace, certain events happen in the last three years that help to fully transform consumer behavior. COVID-19 was one of the reasons that fully transformed consumer behavior.

Social restrictions and measures taken for the safety of individuals during the COVID-19 pandemic have brought about the improvement of new propensities (JagdishSheth, 2020), and the countries'

DOI: 10.4018/978-1-6684-7105-0.ch003

economy has gone through critical changes all over the world. The quick reaction that was expected for COVID-19 required the utilization of advanced innovations in all parts of life (Shreshth, Shikhar, Rakesh, & Sukhpal, 2020) and, to protect, individuals all around the world have rehearsed preventive conduct. People's self-efficacy and seen force might be utilized to follow and evaluate conduct changes. The COVID-19 pandemic established an extraordinary climate where people and organizations quickly took on digitalization: embracing computerized advances can help with keeping social separation. During the COVID-19 pandemic, advanced and social media assumed a significant part in connecting with purchasers (Noel & Kieran, 2020). Because of COVID-19, the commitment of buyers to social media has risen (Raouf, 2021).

But social media advertisement is considered very effective and reliable in terms of effectiveness and budget. This way of communication has effective customers reach and millions of people all over the world have a presence on different types of social media platforms. Social media advertisement has got so much height currently in this country and overall globally. There are some key advantages of social media advertisements: First, it influence rate is high on customers. Second, it has reached a large audience and it can also reach the targeted audience. Third, it creates a strong impact and influences them to purchase a product and make a decision effectively. Effectiveness is very important in social media advertisement, this helps to grow and survive.

Client commitment alludes to the cycles, techniques, and advances used to keep up with consistent correspondence with customers through all conceivable touchpoints. Client commitment is utilized by advertisers to catch the consideration of clients by providing them with important information. All through the client experience, advertisers intend to keep their items and administrations at the focal point of the buyer's brain. Social media is one of the most impressive stages for purchaser collaboration. Clients ought to have the option to utilize social media to draw in with organizations. Clients who are content with the items and administrations will make presents by sharing them on social media. Business associations might utilize offensive purchaser criticism on social media platforms to go through a change in their current items and administrations (Yogesh, Elvira, Laurie, & Jamie, 2021). In this era of the world, brilliant showcasing is the standard. Artificial intelligence is one of the growing areas which has a huge influence on changing patterns. Artificial intelligence (AI) can be utilized by advertisers to accelerate smart showcasing (Arnaud, Vijay, & Yean, 2020). Organizations may likewise screen buyer audits on social media to make altered limited time lobbies for every client to change over them, and checking purchaser conduct on social media could assist with expanding transformation rates (Sameh & Ozgur, 2020). Computerized advances are changing the plans of action. Artificial intelligence empowered computerized stage assists the organizations in engaging the customers (Raghu & Praveen). The advanced insurgency has made the business environment more pitiless. Artificial intelligence further develops business intelligence and execution. Research is expected to decide the effect of social media client commitment on transformation rates. Shopping experience change through social media is a persistent interaction rather than a one-time event. The swapping scale of clients shows their buying expectations.

But there is a difference in order to understand the connection between transformation rate and buyer purchasing goals. Effect of technology on daily life is enormous (Mohammad & Nastaran, 2021). In moral promoting rehearses, the permeability of social media sites is basic. Computer-based intelligence and expanded reality (AR) give two amazing open doors and difficulties to firms. Organizations use AI to foresee customer conduct as purchasers move to internet shopping platforms to buy goods and services (Rajasshrie, Brijesh, & Yogesh, 2020). A study to measure the impact of AI and digital technologies on social media and customer engagement is missing.(Emmanuel & Taiwo, 2020). Therefore, artificial intelligence can be utilized in the engagement of customers through social media platforms that are indeed customized for every client. Organizations are seeking after business intelligence bits of knowledge to draw in customers on social media platforms. In the present digitalized time, the commercial center has changed into a market space. Customers' conduct on computerized stages is additionally being checked by advertisers. All things considered, purchasers burn through 5-6h daily on social media sites. Advertisers require AI technology to screen buyer conduct in the advanced domain. Artificial intelligence applications permit advertisers to understand and break down customer conduct while moreover giving customized client information bases (Shu-Hui, 2020).

Computerized ad is turning out to be more costly, even though their presentation is declining. Rather than barraging all customers with computerized commercials on social media, publicists should screen their customers' buying propensities and keep up with records (Fast et al., 2020). Publicists might utilize AI to channel likely clients from social media clients, considering more customized advertisements. For great client cooperation, advertisers should focus on customized promoting collaboration on computerized and social media. Information-driven client commitment is the need of the hour, and it tends to be constructed utilizing a machine learning model. This minimal expense information-driven buyer commitment can support change rates.

Eleonora and Alessandro (2018) contrived a system to think about customer behavior during online shopping and offline shopping. They featured that on account of internet shopping upsides of conduct have a more prominent impact. Clients' purchasing conduct and intention are changing because of the Internet of Things, which is furnished with advanced technology and AI. Advertisers endeavor to boost deals volume in the computerized time by focusing on buyers in advanced and social media stages. Since disappointed purchasers can rapidly speak more loudly through different social media stages, organizations actually must treat shopper objections cautiously. There is a requirement for an investigation into how shoppers' conduct is changing because of the advanced interruption climate.

The computerized and AI upsets have tremendously affected purchasing conduct, and customers' shopping propensities have changed through digitalization (Emmanuel & Taiwo, 2020). Artificial intelligence is upsetting organizations and rethinking new creative business models, and the capacity of people to settle on choices is improved by AI-empowered frameworks. The utilization of computerized and AI technology is being driven by the developing requirement for data and information (Raouf, 2021). The developing headway of AI advancements gives huge open doors to advertisers and could be utilized to build the shopper's repurchase goals by drawing in them. As an outcome, a review is expected to evaluate the impact of AI and advanced technology on the fulfillment determined during on the web connection and purchasing and further advancement of repurchase expectations.

BACKGROUND

The retail industry has been undergoing significant changes in recent years due to the emergence of e-commerce and increased competition among businesses. As a result, understanding customer buying patterns has become more critical than ever for retailers to remain competitive and profitable. In this context, the current trend in the retail industry is to leverage the power of data analytics to gain insights into customer behavior, preferences, and needs. Retailers are collecting vast amounts of data from various sources, such as online transactions, social media, and customer feedback, to better understand their customers and provide them with personalized shopping experiences. The traditional method of manual data analysis is no longer sufficient to handle the vast amounts of data generated by retailers. This is where Artificial Intelligence (AI) comes into play. AI can analyze large datasets quickly and accurately, providing valuable insights into customer buying patterns. The importance of this study lies in its ability to develop an AI model that can analyze customer buying patterns and provide insights to retailers. The proposed AI model can help retailers optimize their inventory, pricing, and marketing strategies based on the insights gained from customer buying patterns. For instance, the model can identify which products are frequently purchased together, which customers are likely to make repeat purchases, and which products are likely to be popular in the future. This information can help retailers tailor their product offerings to meet the needs of their customers, resulting in increased sales and profitability. In conclusion, the retail industry is currently experiencing a trend of using data analytics and AI to gain insights into customer behavior. This study is significant because it demonstrates the potential of AI technologies in the retail industry and highlights the importance of leveraging data-driven approaches to remain competitive in a rapidly changing market. By analyzing customer buying patterns, retailers can gain valuable insights that can help them optimize their operations, improve customer satisfaction, and increase sales and profitability.

LITERATURE REVIEW

Role of AI in Online Marketing

Most of the organizations use AI and other innovations to connect with their clients. Social media platform stages furnished with AIs are utilized to change over the guests into clients (Anita & Kumar, 2016). Computer-based intelligence depends on machine learning model driven by large information (Rameshwar, Gunase, & Stephen, 2020). Computer-based intelligence's capacity in promoting is to further develop crusade advancement, work on content showcasing productivity, increment transformation rate enhancement, assess design investigation, estimate deals and embrace fruitful market division (Miller, 2019). Computer-based intelligence helps with foreseeing and furnishing buyers. The tools available like Google Analytics, Google Adwords, and web search tool advancement are probably the most well-known AI strategies. The proficiency of the substance is estimated utilizing Google Analytics. It monitors what data clients are seeing and sharing, surveys the adequacy of sites in light of their substance, and offers thorough insights regarding the site clients. It gives helpful data that aid the detailing of an ideal technique. Advertisers might utilize Google Analytics to decipher and investigate the aftereffects of their sites (Miller, 2019). Google Adwords is a computerized advertisement administration run by Google. It helps in the advancement of web promotions that focus on a huge crowd. Watchwords are the reinforcement of Adwords. For Google Adwords, watchword research and offer are significant. It is likewise viewed as compensation for each snap promoting effort. One more fundamental technique for internet advertising is site design improvement: this upholds the improvement of site rankings and works on the consistency and amount of traffic to sites. Off-page streamlining and on-page improvement are the two fundamental parts of website improvement. Advertisers utilized backlinks to produce traffic on sites in off-page streamlining, while they utilized the substance of the sites to create more traffic on the sites in on-page improvement Computer-based intelligence speeds up advanced change by improving troublesome development (Rajasshrie & Sivathanu, 2020).

Social Media Engagement Through Social Media Platforms

Social media engagement measures sharing, likes, and remarks of general society towards certain online business drives in web-based social media by firms. Individuals today generally use Facebook, Instagram and Twitter as the three most well-known social media locales. These stages have their singular ways for clients to communicate their sentiments as remarks/audits against certain posts, and this can be estimated by utilizing business examination devices to create experiences for business choices. Client commitment is named as the conduct of clients towards an association and is characterized as a fantastic and genuinely joined connection between an organization and its clients: clients are persistently being connected with by firms. The essential goal of client commitment is to persuade clients to make motivational buys and is subsequently a fundamental component of a business crusade. If the objective of firms is lined up with clients, then, at that point, client commitment has a positive effect on the general execution of the organization. Client commitment alludes to a client's mental state as it connects with their eco-innovative and intuitive experience with firms on social media. Clients can now get data all the more effectively through social media. Through web-based audits, social media permits organizations to look into their buyers' preferences and inclinations (Kannan, 2017). Advanced change has completely changed the worth creation process.

Utilizing social media to connect with consumers is a difficult assignment. It requires a careful comprehension of the objective business sectors, top-notch content, and a thoroughly examined approach. To arrive at customers via online media stages, advertisers should initially comprehend their objective crowd (Eleonora & Alessandro, 2018). Understanding the necessities and wants of consumers and adjusting publicizing and missions to address those issues and assumptions produces online media traffic. As well as monitoring consumers via online media, it is likewise essential to react to them quickly: it has a decent impression on consumers (Mohammad & Nastaran, 2021). Associations should stay in contact with their allies every day. Following the presentation of advanced promotion via online media stages, the organization can utilize opinion analysis to screen client surveys and input. Opinion analysis aids the recognizable proof of the substance that is frequently requested to consumers, as well as the updating of content. It can be seen from Table 1 that customers are involved on these platforms.

Table 1. Customers engagement on platforms

User-ID	Gender	Age	Estimated Salary	Purchase
1	Male	19	19000	0
2	Female	35	20000	0
3	Male	26	26000	0
4	Female	27	43000	1

Conversion of Purchase From Social Media Platforms

The conversion rate estimates the viability of internet showcasing. It is the proportion of objective conversion isolated by the all-out number of traffic visited on the advanced promotion or sites. It helps in working out the profit from a computerized publicizing effort. The achievement of an advanced ad can be estimated utilizing key execution pointers. Assuming the transformation rate is low, it demonstrates that the web-based promoting program is incapable, and it should be overhauled. The essential objective of advanced social media promotion is to expand income. The utilization of fitting catchphrases is basic for the change rates (Noel & Kieran, 2020), and their determination in content assists with diminishing the skip rate. Just producing on the web traffic doesn't help the association until the guests are not changing over. A similar advanced commercial might have different change rates on various computerized and online media stages; this additionally assists with assessing the reasonably advanced stage for online advancement exercises. Suitable strategies are expected to energize the clients and convert them: moment transformation is unimaginable. Consequently, associations need to connect with clients and afterward attempt to change over them through viable computerized promoting strategies. Compelling and proficient client commitment is pivotal for expanding the transformation rate via web-based media sites (Linda, 2019). It can be seen from the Table 2 purchase column shows that customers have purchased.

Table 2. Conversion of customers from platforms

User-ID	Gender	Age	Estimated Salary	Purchase
1	Male	23	19000	1
2	Female	43	20000	1
3	Female	26	26000	1
4	Female	21	43000	1

Customer Satisfaction

The level of consumer loyalty decides the consistency of the connection between consumers and organizations. Clients' requests have been raised because of proceeded with mechanical development. Firms plan to include clients in their computerized experience by satisfying their necessities and wants to accomplish these assumptions. In examination of customary advertising, computerized and web-based promoting is more affordable yet more muddled. Interpersonal interaction may likewise be utilized to convey input. Individuals use web-based media to post both productive and negative comments on labor and products. These remarks are seen by many individuals and fundamentally affect the association with whom the items and administrations have a place. Client service additionally serves to measure up to the assumptions of the clients. Positive client experience helps the association to hold them and improve the repurchase aims of the clients; this builds the change rate. Negative remarks additionally empower the organizations to know where they are missing and assist them with working on their procedures (Xia, Hyunju, & Alvin, 2021).

To enhance customer loyalty in the digital age, organizations need to adopt a holistic approach that considers both the rational and emotional aspects of customer behavior. Loyalty programs are one of the tools that can help organizations achieve this goal, but they need to be designed and executed with care and innovation. According to McKinsey partner Jess Huang, loyalty programs should be based on four key principles:

Put Consumers First: Loyalty programs should be tailored to the needs and preferences of different customer segments, rather than offering a one-size-fits-all solution. They should also provide value beyond discounts and rewards, such as personalized recommendations, exclusive access, or social recognition.

Define Clear Objectives: Loyalty programs should have a clear purpose and align with the organization's overall strategy and goals. They should also be measurable and trackable, using data and analytics to evaluate their performance and impact.

Leverage Data and Technology: Loyalty programs should use data and technology to create a seamless and engaging customer experience across channels. They should also use predictive analytics to anticipate customer behavior and preferences, and offer relevant and timely offers and communications.

Innovate and Differentiate: Loyalty programs should not be static or complacent, but constantly evolve and adapt to changing customer needs and expectations. They should also seek to differentiate themselves from competitors by offering unique benefits or features that create a lasting impression.

By following these principles, organizations can create loyalty programs that not only increase customer retention and spending, but also enhance customer satisfaction and advocacy. Loyalty programs can also help organizations collect valuable data and insights that can inform their marketing strategies and decisions. In addition, loyalty programs can help organizations communicate their values and purpose to customers, which can increase their trust and loyalty in the long term. Therefore, loyalty programs are not just a transactional tool, but a strategic asset that can help organizations build lasting relationships with customers in the digital age.

Customer Retentions

Customer repurchase aims are helped by consumer loyalty. Clients utilize social media widely to acquire item-related data, and organizations utilize online media sites to support the changing pace of their clients. Client maintenance is urgent for holding existing clients and convincing them to repurchase. Clients that are fulfilled post positive remarks web-based media stages, affecting the web-based local area. Digital consumers are a very compelling mechanism for web-based media buzz advertising. Holding existing clients is substantially less costly than drawing in new ones. Thus, associations put forth a purposeful attempt to draw in their unwavering clients by giving them added administrations.

Further developing the client's repurchase expectation is basic in the web-based media market. It brings about bringing down the complete expense of advanced promotion while as yet expanding the profit from the venture.

Hypothesis Development

The progressive changes in AI advancements essentially affect the behavior of clients. The arising AI advancements give an intuitive customized experience in the excursion of clients via web-based media sites. Web-based media sites are changing the shopping conditions in an alternate culture to satisfy the assumptions of the clients (Noel & Kieran, 2020). Computer-based intelligence advances for web-based media advertising can impact what's more anticipate the conduct of clients and gives an expansive extent of appropriate investigation capacity to web-based media clients as far as sense-production, independent direction, and understanding age that help to draw in the clients. Computer-based intelligence is acquiring a complete change the advertising exercises. Computer-based intelligence assists with social affairs and breaks down the data at an inner mind level.

Computer-based intelligence works on an organization's ability to draw in clients using online media sites (Rameshwar, Gunase, & Stephen, 2020). Utilizing web-based media sites could improve the powerful data handling of an association and aggregate applicable data to enhance social media smoothness. Drawing in clients via online media produces more data that is an important understanding for the organizations. Web-based media overcomes any barrier between firms and clients (Rajasshrie, Brijesh, & Yogesh, 2020), however radical data created through online media is awkward for advertisers. To conquer this issue, advertisers need the help of AI innovation to investigate information successfully, lessening the techno-stress of the salesman who employments web-based media sites to build deals volume. A mechanized mining framework for data gathered through online media improves the productivity of web-based media advertisers. Appropriate comprehension of AI innovation could work on the effectiveness of deals on the board. Advertisers utilize online media sites to connect with clients and investigate the created information through AI innovation.

The techno-stress of the salesman who employments web-based media sites to build deals volume. A mechanized mining framework for data gathered through online media improves the productivity of web-based media advertisers. Appropriate comprehension of AI innovation could work on the effectiveness of deals on the board. Advertisers utilize online media sites to connect with clients and investigate the created information through AI innovation.

Some of the benefits and challenges of using AI for social media data analysis are:

- **Benefits:**
  - AI can help marketers process and analyze large amounts of data more efficiently and accurately. This can help them gain valuable insights into their audience's sentiment, preferences, needs, and behaviors. For example, Symanto is a tool that can help marketers understand the sentiment of social media posts, comments, and reviews.
  - AI can help marketers personalize and customize their content and offers for each user. This can help them increase their engagement and conversion rates. For example, Netflix uses AI to recommend movies and shows based on each user's preferences and viewing habits.
  - AI can help marketers optimize and automate their content and campaigns across various platforms and channels. This can help them save time and money and improve their performance and ROI. For example, Google Ads uses AI to optimize ad performance based on various factors, such as keywords, location, device, time of day, and user intent.
  - AI can help marketers track and compare their social media performance against that of their competitors. This can help them identify their strengths and weaknesses and adjust their strategies accordingly. For example, Iconosquare is a tool that can help marketers track social media growth and get social analytics to improve engagement with followers.
- **Challenges:**
  - AI can pose ethical issues and data privacy concerns for marketers and users. Marketers need to ensure that they use AI in a responsible and transparent way that respects the rights and interests of their users. They also need to comply with the relevant data protection regulations and standards in their markets. For example, the General Data Protection Regulation (GDPR) in the European Union requires marketers to obtain consent from users before collecting and processing their personal data.

- AI can require human oversight and quality control for marketers. Marketers need to monitor and evaluate their AI applications regularly and ensure that they are accurate, reliable, and consistent. They also need to correct any errors or biases that may arise from the AI algorithms or data sources. For example, some AI applications may generate inappropriate or offensive content that may harm the brand reputation or user experience.
- AI can create new skills and competencies for marketers. Marketers need to keep up with the latest developments and trends in AI technology and learn how to use it effectively for their social media marketing goals. They also need to collaborate with other professionals, such as data scientists, developers, or designers, who can help them implement and improve their AI applications.

By using AI for social media data analysis, marketers can enhance their social media marketing strategies and outcomes. However, they also need to be aware of the potential risks and challenges of using AI and adopt best practices to overcome them.

AI Deployment Affects User Engagement

Implementation of AI technology via social media sites draws in clients and converts them into consumers. Web-based media changes the approach to carrying on with work in advanced stages. It is one of the main advanced media, and a web-based media crusade upheld by AI can increment also further develop local area connections and upgrade the transformation rate. Connection, transformation, and sharing input are on the whole conceivable on interpersonal interaction sites, bringing about quicker data exchange. Organizations can draw in clients through online media promoting endeavors (JagdishSheth, 2020). Responsiveness and change are the two significant types of client commitment that fundamentally affect computerized showcasing. Discussions via online media impact clients and rouse them to buy an item. Responsiveness addresses customer cooperation with show publicizing on friendly media sites (Linda, 2019). Information base showcasing is the vital reason for carrying out simulated intelligence innovation to decipher the information. Simulated intelligence innovation gives an edge in the investigation of the social and social ramifications of online media sites, and it can resolve the difficulties of investigating large information. Clients' purchasing inclinations have changed because of Internet shopping, what's more, they visit web-based shopping sites for an assortment of reasons.

As an outcome, it is attractive for advertisers to configure consumers' standards of conduct on digital stages altogether to foresee future deals. (Sameh & Ozgur, 2020) made a system that portrays the connection among sites and change rates; sites that are easy to use can further develop change rates. Digitalization is vital for maintaining a business effectively in the 21st century. Organizations are focusing on customization of advertising via web-based media for a potential portion of consumers. It is urgent to focus on the advanced change to comprehend the purchasing conduct of consumers who utilization web-based media sites. Simulated intelligence improves the capacities of advanced advertisers to build the transformation pace of clients via online media sites.

Artificial intelligence (AI) is a powerful tool that can help marketers optimize their digital marketing campaigns and achieve higher conversion rates. Conversion rate is the percentage of users who take a desired action after interacting with a digital asset, such as an email, a website, or an ad. A higher conversion rate means more customers, more revenue, and more return on investment (ROI) for marketers.

AI can enhance digital marketing in various ways, such as:

Personalizing Content and Offers: AI can analyze large amounts of data from various sources, such as customer profiles, browsing histories, purchase behaviors, and social media interactions, to create personalized and relevant content and offers for each customer. For example, Netflix uses AI to recommend movies and shows based on each user's preferences and viewing habits.

Segmenting and Targeting Customers: AI can help marketers identify and segment customers based on their characteristics, needs, interests, and behaviors. This can help marketers tailor their messages and strategies to different customer segments and target them more effectively. For example, Spotify uses AI to create personalized playlists for each user based on their music tastes and listening patterns2.

Optimizing Ad Placement and Bidding: AI can help marketers automate and optimize their ad placement and bidding strategies across various platforms and channels. AI can also help marketers test and evaluate different ad variations and formats to find the most effective ones. For example, Google Ads uses AI to optimize ad performance based on various factors, such as keywords, location, device, time of day, and user intent.

Enhancing Customer Experience and Engagement: AI can help marketers improve the customer experience and engagement across the customer journey. AI can also help marketers provide timely and responsive customer service and support through chatbots, voice assistants, and other conversational agents. For example, Sephora uses AI to provide virtual makeup try-ons and beauty advice to its customers through its app2.

By using AI in digital marketing, marketers can increase their conversion rates by delivering more personalized, relevant, and engaging content and offers to their customers. AI can also help marketers save time and money by automating and optimizing various tasks and processes. However, AI is not a magic solution that can guarantee success. Marketers still need to have a clear understanding of their goals, objectives, metrics, and customers. They also need to monitor and evaluate their AI applications regularly and ensure that they are ethical, transparent, and compliant with data privacy regulations.

AI Deployment Has a Positive Relationship With Conversion

The development of virtual correspondence via web-based media has changed the method of correspondence. Web-based media stages affect clients' buy aims through the hypothesis of socialization. The socialization interaction of clients via web-based media impacts the disposition of novices and altogether affects the change rate. Online media is quickly turning into a showcasing apparatus to impact consumers, furthermore, internet business organizations are building solid groups of computerized advertisers to draw in consumers and persuade consumers towards motivation buying. Most organizations use AI instruments to build the per-derivability of clients via web-based media (Xia, Hyunju, & Alvin, 2021), and the digital commitment of consumers is likewise exceptionally subject to online media. Social media sites make state-of-the-art data accessible to clients and can impact them and convert them into clients. It is gainful for advertisers to plan a suitable web-based media limited time procedure to connect with clients for significant stretches, really at that time will organizations get a positive result. Online media gives a market space where purchasers and merchants cooperate. Web-based media sites enable clients what's more innovation empowers consumers to sift through messages and do a similar analysis of various items. Online media clients share the data, pictures also limited-time data that advantages firms. The progression of innovation on friendly media improves the worth creation for business houses. Clients sharing data on friendly media increment deal volumes through advanced media (Sameh & Ozgur, 2020).

The emergence of virtual communication through social media has revolutionized the way businesses communicate with their consumers. Social media platforms have a significant impact on consumers' purchase intentions through the process of socialization. The socialization process of consumers through social media affects their attitude towards the product or service and significantly influences the conversion rate. With the rapid growth of e-commerce, companies are building strong teams of digital marketers to engage consumers and persuade them towards impulsive buying. AI tools are widely used by businesses to increase the predictability of consumers through social media. Digital engagement of consumers is also highly dependent on social media. Therefore, it is beneficial for marketers to design an appropriate social media promotional strategy to engage consumers for extended periods.

With the increase in the use of social media, businesses have access to real-time data that provides valuable insights into consumer behavior. The proliferation of social media sites has created a market space where buyers and sellers interact, enabling businesses to improve their value creation. Social media users share information, images, and promotional information that benefits firms. The advancement of technology on social media enhances the value creation for businesses, increasing sales volumes through digital media. Studies have shown that social media users who share information about a product or service have a higher likelihood of making a purchase than those who do not.

Furthermore, social media platforms are constantly evolving, and businesses need to stay up-to-date with the latest trends and features to maximize their marketing efforts. Social media algorithms are constantly changing, making it essential for businesses to adapt their marketing strategies accordingly. To stay ahead of the competition, businesses need to leverage the latest social media tools and features, such as live video streaming, augmented reality, and chatbots.

One of the latest trends in social media marketing is the use of influencer marketing. Influencer marketing involves partnering with individuals who have a significant social media following to promote a product or service. Influencer marketing has become increasingly popular in recent years, and studies have shown that it can be highly effective in driving sales and increasing brand awareness. Many businesses are partnering with micro-influencers, who have smaller followings but higher engagement rates, to promote their products or services.

Another trend in social media marketing is the use of social listening tools. Social listening involves monitoring social media platforms for mentions of a brand or product and using that information to improve marketing efforts. Social listening tools allow businesses to gain insights into customer sentiment and behavior, enabling them to adjust their marketing strategies accordingly.

AI Deployment Has a Positive Effect on User Engagement and Conversion Rate

A customer's experience is significant for any association. On the online platforms, clients experience an innovation intervened shopping venture. In the advanced space, online media is molding another climate that incorporates physical and virtual items. Drawing in clients also giving a one-of-a-kind encounter via online media is vital for advertisers. Organizations are zeroing in on the arrangement of significant worth added suggestions to create an ideal client experience in the computerized world. Virtual advancements have a critical sway on clients' insight. Security issues are urgent for clients who like to buy items and administrations through computerized media and web-based media assumes an indispensable part in looking for consistency to coordinate clients' insight. It is imperative for advertisers to comprehend the effect of advanced innovations on clients' experiences (Rajasshrie, Brijesh, & Yogesh, 2020).

Digitalization promoting credits have a U-formed relationship with clients' web-based surveys that differ as per their segment profile. Positive remarks affect the mental course of different clients, at last honing the affecting force of the web networks. Different client commitment practices are normal for various client fragments:

Customers' commitment is basic in the advanced age. Advertisers need to foster solid web-based media investigation to comprehend the division of consumers.

AI Deployment Has a Positive Effect on Satisfying Experience

A web-based online buying experience is complicated and serious. Organizations need to give quality items and remarkable administrations to consumers, assisting with holding consumers and making clients devotion. Notwithstanding the nature of items, convenient conveyance impacts consumers' fulfillment levels (Raghu & Praveen), and consumers' apparent worth has a critical positive effect on repurchase aims. Advertisers should deal with moving along the inherent traits of the computerized stage to improve consumers' repurchase expectation. Consumer loyalty decidedly affects client responsibility and client trust; nonetheless, this doesn't imply that fulfilled clients generally have positive repurchase expectations. Web-based buying is changing the purchasing conduct aim of consumers. The nature of the virtual space draws in clients and upgrades consumer loyalty. Repurchase aim depends on client situated hypotheses, for instance, decadent and utilitarian qualities have a positive association with purchase again and again. The sped-up utilization of online interacting platforms has created broad data that is extremely valuable for organizations that could remove this information to frame a fitting on the web advertising system to hold existing clients. In light of AI, a prescient methodology supports the mining of online substances. Moreover, saw trust influences the apparent handiness of the repurchase goal, going about as an intervening variable between saw values what's more client repurchase expectation. Keeping a decent standing and improving customers esteem after a first buy is basic for organizations. Fulfilled clients become steadfast clients and repurchase.

With the increasing prevalence of e-commerce, online shopping experiences have become complex and serious. In today's world, customers expect not only quality products but also exceptional services that help build loyalty. The importance of timely delivery cannot be ignored, as it has a significant impact on customer satisfaction levels. According to a study by Raghu and Praveen, timely delivery is the key to retaining customers and creating customer loyalty.

However, it is not just the quality of products and services that drive customer loyalty. The perceived value of the products also plays a crucial role in repurchase intentions. In this digital era, marketers need to leverage the inherent characteristics of the digital platform to improve repurchase intentions. Customer satisfaction positively influences customer commitment and trust. But customer satisfaction does not always guarantee positive repurchase intentions.

The emergence of online platforms has changed consumer behavior and purchasing intentions. The quality of the virtual space can attract customers and enhance customer satisfaction, which in turn can lead to repurchase intentions. Decadent and utilitarian values have a positive association with repurchasing intentions. The widespread use of online platforms has generated a wealth of data that businesses can use to develop appropriate online marketing strategies to retain existing customers.

AI has enabled a predictive approach to extract useful insights from online content. This can help companies to better understand their customers and tailor their marketing strategies accordingly. Furthermore, perceived trust has a significant influence on the perceived usefulness of the repurchase intention, acting as a mediating variable between perceived values and customer repurchase intentions. Maintaining a good reputation and enhancing customer value after the first purchase is crucial for businesses. Satisfied customers are more likely to become loyal customers and make repeat purchases.

Recent data shows that the e-commerce market has continued to grow rapidly, with online sales expected to reach $4.9 trillion by 2025. This trend has been driven by the increasing adoption of smartphones and the internet, as well as the convenience and flexibility of online shopping. In addition, the COVID-19 pandemic has accelerated the shift to online shopping, as consumers have been forced to avoid physical stores due to lockdowns and social distancing requirements.

With the rise of AI and machine learning, businesses can now leverage customer data to gain deeper insights into their customers' behavior and preferences. By analyzing data such as browsing history, search queries, and purchase history, companies can gain a better understanding of their customers' needs and tailor their marketing strategies accordingly. This can help to improve customer satisfaction, loyalty, and retention.

The integration of AI and chatbots has also improved the online shopping experience for customers. Chatbots can help customers find products and provide personalized recommendations based on their preferences and browsing history. This can help to enhance the customer experience and build customer loyalty.

RESEARCH METHODOLOGY

A statistical survey has been conducted in order to get better understanding that how artificial intelligence contributing towards the changing buying pattern of customers.

Data-Set Details

After getting data, data-set has been divided into different attributes. This data contain four columns; Age, gender, estimated salary and purchased. The column age contains the age of persons, because for some products age is very important. The column gender tells about the person either male or female. The third column contains the estimated salary of the person. Salary is very important factor in determining either person will buy specific product or not. The fourth column contains information about purchased or not purchased product. Purchased product has been represented with the help of 1 and not-purchased with the help of 0. This is our dependent variable. Dataset consists of 400 entries. The ranges of age has been explained through Figure 1 and range of estimated salary has been shown through Figure 2.

Methodology

Artificial intelligence model has been used for the measuring the effectiveness of AI deployment on social media network ads, which helps to figure out how different factors play important role in purchasing of any product. Preprocessing, architecture and post-processing are three major steps in artificial intelligence research methodology. In the first step, data has been collected from the reliable website. In this step, the collected data has been normalized and redundant and irrelevant information has been eliminated in order to get results. In the second step, using back propagation approach relationship between inputs

Figure 1. Distribution of age

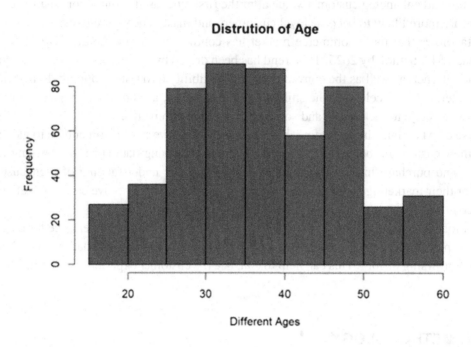

Figure 2. Distribution of estimated salaries

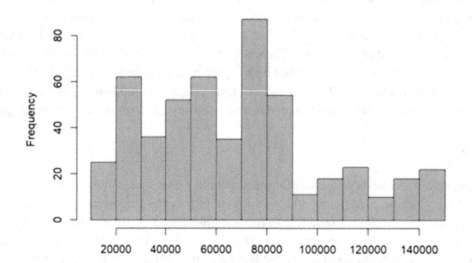

and outputs has been built. In the last step, reverse processing of the first step is done to get an idea that expected outcome has been achieved.

In this methodology, this basic algorithm Artificial intelligence has been used to adjust the values such that it produces the expected output for the given output of data. The 80% of the data collected from 400 respondents has been used for the training purpose and remaining 20% of the data has been used for testing the model.

RESULTS

The results obtained from this study has been shown in the Figure 3 (shows the error for the validation data using the model trained for number of epochs) and Figure 4 (shows the accuracy for the validation data using model trained for the number of epochs). The results have shown that validation data has shown good accuracy. The results have shown that social media advertisement can affect the purchase of products which is based on gender, age and estimated salary. This has given justification that during the process of social media advertisement, the factors of age, salary and gender are very important. Through these contributing factors, social media marketers can take advantage of users' demographic information and can target their ads respectively.

Figure 3. Model loss

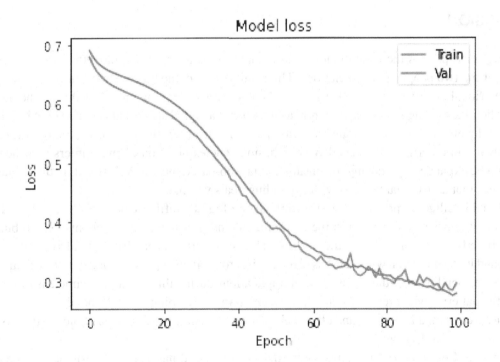

Figure 4. Model accuracy

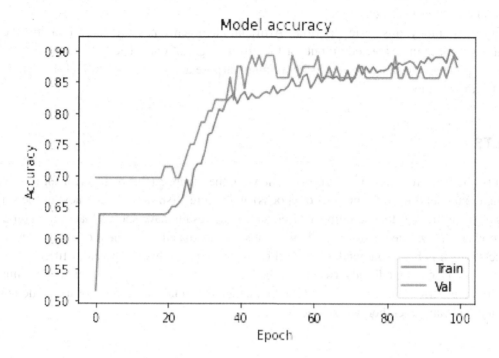

DISCUSSION

This study incorporates the presumptions that computerized interruption altogether affects the social conduct of the two people and associations. The result of this comparative study shows that conveying AI has a critical positive sway on change and client's commitment via online media. In the advanced period, clients are changing themselves from a customer to a digital space that is fueled by AI. This study estimated the effect of AI on the transformation pace of consumers through online media stages. Also, from drawing in clients, AI impacts drive purchasing. The exploration likewise infers that the change rate could be expanded by drawing in consumers via web-based media. Web-based media is one of the main stages that assist organizations with expanding deals volume.

Artificial intelligence prepared web-based media profoundly infiltrate people's lives. Computerized innovation assumes a positive part in the commitment and transformation of clients, which builds the internet-based deals volume all over the world. Chabot's and virtual specialists upheld by Artificial intelligence, and its combination with web-based media, improve client experience and have a critical positive effect on the social parts of the clients. Social implications during this era of pandemic has motivated to change the patterns, who presently really like to buy items by keeping up with social separation. Along these lines, social media websites and other web-based platforms give a superior choice to the customers for commitment and buying.

The result of this comparative study shows that conveying AI has a critical positive sway on change and client's commitment via online media. In the advanced period, clients are changing themselves from a customer to a digital space that is fueled by AI. This study estimated the effect of AI on the transformation pace of consumers through online media stages. Also, from drawing in clients, AI impacts drive purchasing . The exploration likewise infers that the change rate could be expanded by drawing in consumers via web-based media. Web-based media is one of the main stages that assist organizations with expanding deals volume.

One of the ways that AI can enhance social media engagement and conversion is by generating captivating and relevant content for different platforms and audiences. AI can use natural language processing and generation to create catchy headlines, captions, hashtags, and calls to action that can attract and persuade users to click, share, or buy. For example, ClevrAI is a tool that can help marketers create social media posts and other copy with ease using AI. Another example is Edyzoo, a tool that can help marketers generate persuasive ad copy using ChatGPT.

Another way that AI can improve social media engagement and conversion is by analyzing and optimizing the performance of different content and campaigns. AI can use data analytics and machine learning to measure the impact of various factors, such as keywords, images, videos, timing, frequency, and audience segments, on the engagement and conversion rates. AI can also provide recommendations and guidance on how to improve the content and campaigns based on the data insights. For example, Iconosquare is a tool that can help marketers track social media growth and get social analytics to improve engagement with followers.

A third way that AI can boost social media engagement and conversion is by personalizing and customizing the content and offers for each user. AI can use data mining and recommender systems to understand the preferences, interests, needs, and behaviors of each user and provide them with content and offers that match their profile and intent. AI can also use chatbots and voice assistants to interact with users in a natural and conversational way and provide them with relevant information, support, or guidance. For example, Sephora uses AI to provide virtual makeup try-ons and beauty advice to its customers through its app.

By using these methods, AI can help marketers create more engaging and converting social media content and campaigns that can increase their sales volume and ROI. However, marketers should also be aware of the potential challenges and risks of using AI in social media marketing, such as ethical issues, data privacy concerns, human oversight, and quality control.

CONCLUSION

In this review paper, a relationship between AI and clients' commitment via web-based media is useful for transformation has been presented. The pandemic has changed clients' social and personal conduct standards; they are turning out to be more reliant upon computerized stages to buy items and administrations. The significant center is to build the change rate by connecting with clients via online media. Sending AI connects with consumers as well as impacts clients towards driving purchasing. Online media is a savvy apparatus for advertising. The expanded spotlight on AI and online media has captivated consumers and expanded deals volume in the online business. Because of the change, consumers' normal devotion increments. Fulfilled clients are as yet devoted and have plans to purchase from the organization once more. Consumers' motivation to re-purchase is estimated from their level of fulfillment. This encourage their aims to buy once more. With regards to purchasing choices, individuals are progressively going to computerized and web-based media. Simulated intelligence and web-based media zero in on giving enormous open doors. Purchaser fulfillment is basic in persuading them to make rehash buys.

REFERENCES

Anita, P., & Kumar, V. (2016). Customer engagement: the construct, antecedents, and consequences. *Journal of the Academy of Marketing Science*, 294-316.

Arnaud, D. B., Vijay, V., & Yean, S. B. (2020, August 20). Artificial Intelligence and Marketing: Pitfalls and Opportunities. *Journal of Interactive Marketing*, *51*, 91–105. doi:10.1016/j.intmar.2020.04.007

Eleonora, P., & Alessandro, G. (2018). Shopping as a "networked experience": An emerging framework in the retail industry. *International Journal of Retail & Distribution Management*, *46*(7), 690–704. Advance online publication. doi:10.1108/IJRDM-01-2018-0024

Emmanuel, M., & Taiwo, O. S. (2020). The implications of artificial intelligence on the digital marketing of financial services to vulnerable customers. *Australasian Marketing Journal*, *29*(3). Advance online publication. 10.1016%2Fj.ausmj.2020.05.003

Linda, D. (2019). Developing business customer engagement through social media engagement-platforms: An integrative S-D logic/RBV-informed model. *Industrial Marketing Management*, *81*, 89–98. Advance online publication. doi:10.1016/j.indmarman.2017.11.016

Miller, T. (2019). Explanation in artificial intelligence: Insights from the social sciences. *Artificial Intelligence*, *267*, 1–38. Advance online publication. doi:10.1016/j.artint.2018.07.007

Mohammad, S., & Nastaran, H. (2021). How human users engage with consumer robots? A dual model of psychological ownership and trust to explain post-adoption behaviours. *Computers in Human Behavior*, *117*, 106660. Advance online publication. doi:10.1016/j.chb.2020.106660

Noel, C., & Kieran, C. (2020). Normalising the "new normal": Changing tech-driven work practices under pandemic time pressure. *International Journal of Information Management*, *55*, 102186. Advance online publication. doi:10.1016/j.ijinfomgt.2020.102186 PMID:32836643

Raghu, N. C., & Praveen, G. (2022, March 29). Emerging trends in digital transformation: A bibliometric analysis. *Benchmarking*, *29*(4), 1069–1112. Advance online publication. doi:10.1108/BIJ-01-2021-0009

Rajasshrie, P., Brijesh, S., & Yogesh, K. D. (2020). Shopping intention at AI-powered automated retail stores (AIPARS). *Journal of Retailing and Consumer Services*, *57*, 102207. Advance online publication. doi:10.1016/j.jretconser.2020.102207

Rajasshrie, P. B., & Sivathanu, Y. K. (2020). Shopping intention at AI-powered automated retail stores (AIPARS). *Journal of Retailing and Consumer Services*, *57*, 102207. Advance online publication. doi:10.1016/j.jretconser.2020.102207

Rameshwar, D. (2020, August). Big data analytics and artificial intelligence pathway to operational performance under the effects of entrepreneurial orientation and environmental dynamism: A study of manufacturing organisations. *International Journal of Production Economics*, *226*, 107599. Advance online publication. doi:10.1016/j.ijpe.2019.107599

Raouf, A. (2021). Demystifying the effects of perceived risk and fear on customer engagement, co-creation and revisit intention during COVID-19: A protection motivation theory approach. *Journal of Destination Marketing & Management*, *20*, 100564. Advance online publication. doi:10.1016/j.jdmm.2021.100564

Sameh, A.-N., & Ozgur, T. (2020). A comparative assessment of sentiment analysis and star ratings for consumer reviews. *International Journal of Information Management*, *54*, 102132. Advance online publication. doi:10.1016/j.ijinfomgt.2020.102132

Sheth, J. (2020). Impact of Covid-19 on consumer behavior: Will the old habits return or die? *Journal of Business Research*, *117*, 280–283. Advance online publication. doi:10.1016/j.jbusres.2020.05.059 PMID:32536735

Shreshth, T., Shikhar, T., Rakesh, T., & Sukhpal, S. G. (2020). Predicting the growth and trend of COVID-19 pandemic using machine learning and cloud computing. *Internet of Things*, *11*, 100222. Advance online publication. doi:10.1016/j.iot.2020.100222

Shu-Hui, C. (2020). Co-creating social media agility to build strong customer-firm relationships. *Industrial Marketing Management*, *84*, 202–211. Advance online publication. doi:10.1016/j.indmarman.2019.06.012

Xia, L., Hyunju, S., & Alvin, C. (2021, March). Examining the impact of luxury brand's social media marketing on customer engagement: Using big data analytics and natural language processing. *Journal of Business Research*, *125*, 815–826. Advance online publication. doi:10.1016/j.jbusres.2019.04.042

Yogesh, K. D., Elvira, I. D., Laurie, H., & Jamie, C. (2021). Setting the future of digital and social media marketing research: Perspectives and research propositions. *International Journal of Information Management*, *59*, 102168. Advance online publication. doi:10.1016/j.ijinfomgt.2020.102168

Chapter 4

A Pedagogy to Support Learning Analytics:
A Case for a Specific Higher Education Institution

André Pretorius

iD https://orcid.org/0000-0002-5814-0466

Stellenbosch University, South Africa

ABSTRACT

Learning analytics (LA) is a contemporary field of research with advances in machine learning that enables the user to draw conclusions about current teaching and learning based on indicators deduced from historical datasets. The need existed for an understanding of the fundamental grounding principles on which the institutional pedagogy is based. Therefore, the theoretical grounding for the implementation of a virtual learning environment that conforms to good educational practice and can inform a LA reference framework with the aim of identifying at-risk students is established. A gap existed in the institution to implement LA that identify at-risk students. The methodology that was used was a mixed method design science methodology to establish the historical philosophical grounding, linking it to modern teaching practice, establishing best practice through an institutional case study, and defining an appropriate pedagogy. It concludes with a description of a pedagogical model suited to LA, the result of the application of the pedagogy as a case study.

INTRODUCTION

Learning analytics (LA) is a relatively new field of application in the Analytics domain. Its main aim is to analyse teaching and learning (T&L) data from various sources to provide users with insights towards improving T&L. One of these T&L improvements is a greater focus on student success and more accurate methods of limiting student failure. This process starts with the identification of students at risk of failure (so-called "at-risk" students) through a prediction methodology which commonly falls within the knowl-

DOI: 10.4018/978-1-6684-7105-0.ch004

edge sphere of Artificial Intelligence (AI), more specifically Machine Learning (ML). In contemporary information systems, the supporting platform for this is provided by an LA information system (LAIS) that relies on an underlying virtual learning environment (VLE), which in turn uses T&L data from a learning management system (LMS). This chapter focuses on providing the theoretical grounding for the implementation of a VLE that conforms to good educational practice and can adequately inform a learning analytics (LA) reference framework with the aim of identifying at-risk students. This research was necessitated by the need for an understanding of the fundamental grounding principles on which the institutional pedagogy is based to define an appropriate pedagogy to support LA. There exists a gap in the institution to implement LA that can help to identify at-risk students. However, before an effective LA system can be implemented, the supporting pedagogy must be in place. This required an extensive exploratory study of the theoretical background for the pedagogy which is lacking as the philosophy of teaching is outdated. The methodology that was followed was a mixed method design science methodology which focused on firstly establishing the historical philosophical grounding, secondly linking it to modern teaching practice, thirdly establishing best practice through an institutional case study and lastly defining an appropriate pedagogy. The chapter is divided into specific key concepts that aim to provide a background study to key concepts and provide input into the research objectives. These concepts are a definition of education and learning, background to teaching philosophy which includes a look at major T&L philosophies and theories of schooling. It ends with a description of a pedagogical model suited to LA that was the result of extensive institutional application of the pedagogy as a case study. The objectives of this chapter are (1) to define education and learning in the context of the institution, (2) to establish an appropriate teaching and learning philosophy for the institution as background to the pedagogy that would support LA, and (3) to define a pedagogy model to support LA in the institution.

DEFINITIONS OF EDUCATION AND LEARNING

Definition of Education

One true philosophy of education exists, not simply a matter of opinion but a scientific theory, just as there is a clear distinction between knowledge and opinion (Adler, 1942). Individual or group experiences do not reflect theory as these are mere opinions based on practical means, which do not fall within the realm of theory (Brooke & Frazer, 2013). Philosophy is a purely theoretical field based on logic and, although deductions can be made from the principles of a particular philosophy and applied to a practical field, these do not contribute to the theory of philosophy (Machan, 2011). Experiences and practicalities fall within the ambit of policy, not philosophy (Adler, 1942). These practical aspects and divisions should form the scope of an educational philosophy.

Definition of Learning

"Learning" is perhaps best defined in a description of its aims. Learning aims to acquire those virtues which may be universal or acceptable to society (Power, 1996). Therefore, education's purpose is to instil these virtues in the student. The nature and extent of knowledge have been debated since Socrates' dialogues in ancient Greek philosophy. In modern society these virtues, among others, have become the grounding and reason for teaching philosophies (McEwan, 2011). Later in this chapter various teaching philosophies are briefly discussed as the foundation for current teaching practice.

Teaching and Learning Philosophy

In evaluating which teaching and learning model is most suitable, one must establish the fundamental principles of education (Brooke & Frazer, 2013). Teaching and learning models are numerous. Therefore, to decide on the most suitable, one must investigate its epistemology (that we can know and how we can know it) and ontology (what kinds of things exist) (Kirillov, Fadeeva, & Fadeev, 2016). The field of educational philosophy addresses these fundamentals within philosophy. This serves as a starting point to describe the origins of the eventual teaching and learning model that is applied in this study.

Criteria for Philosophical Inquiry

"Philosophy" from Greek, translates as the love ("philo") of wisdom ("sophia") (Boldyguin, 2013). The goal of philosophical logic is to distinguish truth from falsity (Machan, 2011). This means that it should be possible to derive first principles of education that forms the basis to clearly define a valid educational doctrine. Adler (1942) showed that these criteria effectively prove the validity of the first principles of an education philosophy which in turn is further used to trace a clear path through the various historical educational approaches to an effective modern approach which may be applied to the current research problem.

The criteria for this philosophical inquiry can be traced back some 2000 years to the major schools of philosophical logic of Plato, Aristotle, and Zeno (Power, 1996). These schools developed expansive rules of logic, also called axioms and syllogisms, which are briefly explained as follows. The methodology to arrive at the fundamentals of logical thought were remarkably similar to patterns followed in arriving at mathematical axioms (Devlin, 1997). The logically convincing argument that proves mathematical theorems and axioms follows a distinct process, namely:

Observation → abstraction → understanding → description → proof

This method dominated the Greeks' approach to all knowledge creation for centuries. Aristotle and Zeno used this method to derive their Organon and Stoic reasoning, respectively. Both these schools of logic were based on patterns of language and, although initially in dialectic form, it was later converted to symbolic form, in much the same fashion as mathematics (Devlin, 1997; Bobzien, 2006).

The Need for a Philosophy of Education

Western philosophy as a knowledge domain has numerous real-word applications, ranging from applications in "knowledge and certainty, to being and reality, language and meaning, mind and body, self and freedom, God and religion, morality and good life, ethics, state and governance, beauty and art, and life and its meaning" (Cottingham, 2020, p. 5). Kirilov, Fadeeva and Fadeev (2016), Machan (Machan, 2011) and Ongaro (2017) classifies philosophy into Metaphysics, Epistemology, Logic, Ethics, and Aesthetics. Power (1996) elaborates on the origins of each based on its purposes as described below.

The Inspirational Purpose

The inspirational purpose of education as a "utopian" view of an ideal society in which education achieves our envisioned goals (Power, 1996). Two classical philosophy literatures that best exemplifies this is Plato's (427 – 348 B.C.) *Republic* and Jean Jacques Rousseau's (1712 – 1778) *Émile*. Plato elaborated in detail on the need for education that would empower the state's citizens and warned of the eventual decline of any state that neglects to develop its citizens' talents through education (Jowett, 2016). Power conceded that educational philosophy without considerations for practical implementation is futile. Power advised that both inductive and deductive logic should be used to derive first principles of education and devise working educational practice (Power, 1996).

The Analytical Purpose

Education philosophy, as all other philosophies, must have the primary purpose of defining the truth before acting (Power, 1990). Power described the Socratic method as a relentless search for fundamental meaning through interpretation of dialogue. The analytic method for philosophy can be inductive or deductive, which is highlighted in Frances Bacon's *The Advancement of Learning* (Spedding, 2010). Devlin (Goodbye, Descartes, 1997) argued that such philosophical methods, referred to as linguistic analysis (induction through syllogism) or logical empiricism (deduction through observation) should be the primary methods to analyse our educational practice as grounded by educational philosophy.

The Prescriptive Purpose

Adler (1942) contended that educational philosophy must describe the ends and means in education. Ends are defined as the ultimate or first principles of education, both "absolute and universal" for all humans, whilst the means in general are secondary principles (Adler, In defence of the philosophy of education, 1942). Furthermore, Power (1990) expounded that the role of educational philosophy is never to prescribe methodology or to define specific approaches to teaching. Educational philosophy has its place in education as the origin of educational policy which, in turn, should define and describe how educational practice should be undertaken as a pedagogical model (Power, 1990).

The Investigative Purpose

Although education philosophy is to inform policy, not prescribe practice, it does, however, investigate and interrogate policy and practice (Power, 1990). The eventual aim of philosophy is to either justify or to reconstruct policy and practice based on the fundamental principles set by philosophical truths (Adler, In defence of the philosophy of education, 1942). Jowett (2016) explained that the Socratic method was prime example of this investigative approach of philosophy; an approach that would never accept any statement not satisfactorily proven to be truthful.

First Principles of Philosophy of Education

The philosophy of education forms a sub-category of philosophy but all other subcategories of philosophy inform the philosophy of education, making it impossible to trace the origins of educational philosophy to a singular branch of philosophy. However, the fundamental principles (or first principles) of education can in fact be traced (Livingston, McClain, & DeSpain, 1995). These principles are either self-evident or demonstrably proven through inductive or deductive reasoning (Adler, 1942, p. 10). For brevity, only those propositions of the sixteen first principles of philosophy that apply to teaching are listed below:

- *"Only man can know intellectually, and man has free will."*
- *"Habit is modification of a human power resulting from its rational and free exercise."*
- *"The good is convertible with being."*
- *"The good of any imperfect thing consists in the actualisation of its potencies."*
- *"In the case of human powers, the actualisation of potency is good only if it conforms to natural tendency of that power to its own perfection."*

These first principles of the philosophy of education underpin the major educational philosophies and should inform educational policy and practice (Adler, 1942).

Major Philosophies of Education

Ancient Educational Philosophies

Discourse about best approaches towards teaching and learning (T&L) has occurred since earliest times. Ancient Greek philosophers, Aristotle and Plato wrote about their individual philosophies towards teaching, and their seemingly contrasting views are still argued today as primarily a matter of methodology of instruction (instructionist) versus teaching as a continuation of relationship building between students, teachers, and society (connectivist) (McPherran, 2013). This extended into disagreement about what should be taught, i.e., vocational skills vs life skills, and which approach should be followed, i.e., training vs education (McEwan, 2011).

Humanism is viewed as the origin of modern philosophies of education and can be traced back to Ancient Greece, Rome, and early Christian empires (Power, 1990). Arguably the most influential scholar of the time was Socrates whose *eros* teaching method was the foundation for his philosophical teachings, which was also the foundation of most other Greek schools (Hull, 2002). Eros required a very personal relationship between student and teacher in which the affection for the teacher would translate to an affection for the knowledge and a knowledge acquisition process through dialogue and rhetoric (Jowett, 2016).

The ancient era of educational philosophy culminated in the early Christian empire's contribution to the field, called Religious Humanism. Christian schooling was eager to eliminate all references to paganism that pervaded Greek education. It valued rhetoric, logic, and grammar but ancient literature was excluded for being paganistic. A teaching programme aimed at producing citizens able to serve the state, church and themselves moved away from rhetoric and dialect as teaching outcomes towards mastery of basic skills in writing, reading and arithmetic. The seven liberal arts (grammar, arithmetic, logic, rhetoric, geometry, music, and astronomy) formed the mainstream of Christian education, which all students had to pass before accessing divine learning (Power, 1990). Religious Humanism was followed by Classical Humanism in the Middle Ages after the restoration of education and liberal arts following the dark ages. The works of John of Salisbury (1110? -1180) in *Metalogicon*, Erasmus (1469-1536) and Philip Melanchthon (1497-1560) were instrumental in establishing pre-modern educational philosophy and curriculum (Power, 1990).

Following on the ancient era of education philosophy, pre-modern, modern philosophies and contemporary philosophies evolved, forming the basis for various theories of schooling.

Pre-Modern Philosophies of Education

Religious Realism

Amos Comenius (1592 – 1670) was a religious teacher whose approach was characterised by the tenet that "learning begins with those experiences that make an impression on the senses" (Power, 1990, p. 49). The sensory impression of the world that surrounded the student was deemed most important, implying that the school should present the world as it was, and not an idealised environment. This also implied that girls and boys should be taught in the same classroom and that vernacular language should be used (Power, 1996).

Educational Empiricism

School programmes that focused on current content presented in a practical manner to empower people for the work environment was advocated by John Locke (1632 – 1704). These programmes evolved from Comenius' work and extended to experiential learning in which knowledge had to be founded on empirical data (Power, 1996).

Romantic Naturalism

In the fictional world of Jean Jacques Rousseau's *Emile*, all children were subjected to a highly passive education, with sensory deprivation the aim. Rousseau contrasted this with a highly sensory and experiential learning environment of Emile and warned the reader of the danger of education in which the masses are deprived of contextualised learning that would create social misfits. Rousseau's France and the world beyond did not value broad-based education to all children. Education was the privilege of the rich and upper class. Rousseau would not see his theories actualised in his lifetime, but the ideas of a liberated education individualised for each person was still an ideal in modern education (McEwan, 2011).

National Education

In the 1700s, European nations realised the benefits of creating school systems that catered for the needs of the state. It would find value in controlling citizenships through strict propagandistic subject matter and political alignment. Additionally, it required the formalisation of educational philosophy of the state through a scientific method. Johann Herbart (1776 – 1841), in his *Science of Education*, prescribed a curriculum of personal, social, and political morality aimed at achieving education for the state (McPherran, 2013).

Modern Education Philosophies

Colonial and National Education

Colonial rule in the new worlds dictated the use of national education as primary philosophy. But, due to the remoteness of these regions, emphasis was on mastery of practical skills for settlers to be self-sufficient. Francis Bacon's *The Advancement of Learning* was commonly referenced as guide to ministers and religious zealots who were primarily employed as tutors (Spedding, 2010). The building of schools and educational policy were national priorities to promote national interests (McPherran, 2013).

Common Schools

Thomas Jefferson's (1743-1826) efforts to democratise teaching into a universal education system that was open to all, with a focus on civic education rather than secular motives, was only partially realised in the common school crusade of the mid 1800s in American history. In the late 1800s, however, his ideals were perverted by the aristocracy into an educational system that served the purpose of subjugating the citizens to prevent anarchy and unruliness in their new, fragile republic (Power, 1990).

Progressive Education

With the advent of the industrial revolution and the liberation of the sciences and arts, a new approach to teaching was required. Strictly speaking, this falls within the realm of educational practice and not educational philosophy, but its current relevance rests in that this period was the infant of a later educational philosophy, pragmatism. The focus of progressive education was on education of social and personal growth, liberal in nature and student-centred but with the aim of cultivating new thinking in emerging fields (Brooke & Frazer, 2013).

Contemporary Education Philosophies

Idealism

Idealism, essentially based on Platonic thinking regarding the nature of knowledge and its origins, postulated that knowledge requires the presence of human sense to validate its existence. This philosophy was famously encapsulated in the statement by René Descartes (1596 – 1650): "*[Cogito, ergo sum]*; I think, therefore I am" (Power, 1990). It required spiritual realm to form part of the teaching syllabus but assumes that human natural abilities and free choice must be fostered. The educational practice focused on first developing human character before human abilities and social skills. The teacher's role was that of educational environment builder and developing the student's natural abilities (Brooke & Frazer, 2013).

Realism

Realism demanded scientific and empirical proof of knowledge which makes the physical world independent of the existence of knowledge. It aimed to prove the universality of the scientific knowledge. Various forms of realism exist, starting with Aristotle's Realism, continuing to this day as the major scientific philosophy. Realism accepted that human behaviour was also governed by scientific rules, but reality may differ depending on the observer's view. Realistic education focussed on preparing the student for life. It placed a high premium on discovery of new knowledge whilst acknowledging that the teacher's role must be to aid learning of existing knowledge (Brooke & Frazer, 2013).

Religious-Rational Humanism

Religious-rational Humanism followed the basic tenet of human reasoning as the basis for education. It proposed that humans living in a material world can, through proper reasoning and religious grounding, arrive at sound knowledge and truth (Brooke & Frazer, 2013; Butler, 1968; Maritain, 1938). This philosophy placed the student in the centre of learning as agents and recipients of learning. It placed high value in teaching social responsibility with the basic subjects of liberal education as grounding. The teacher was seen as the keeper of knowledge, of truth and moral values to be imparted upon students. The teaching of religion in school, although sectarian, was not advocated (Power, 1996).

Pragmatism

Perhaps the best-known founders of pragmatism, John Dewey, described pragmatism as "empirical naturalism" (Dewey, 1938). His approach was that philosophy was not in itself truth, but represents the search of truth through scientific methods. The philosophical positions acknowledge that human knowledge evolves in the physical reality, relative to other knowledge in the experiences of humans (Power, 1996). It viewed education inseparable from personal experience, with no difference between liberal or vocational education. The teacher was seen as a facilitator to guide the student in discovering knowledge through learning-by-doing.

Existentialism_

This philosophy placed emphasis on fulfilment of personal goals and freedom with responsibility. It presupposed that knowledge could be found through an inward journey of truth and discovery of one's own destiny (Satre, 1956). Harper best described the influence of this philosophy of education as: "Education can point the way or ways to both happiness and good character; it cannot prescribe or enforce. Education was the journey, not the end of the journey" (Harper, 1955). This perspective best describes the influence of Existentialism on education, but this philosophy never elaborated on its views of education (McPherran, 2013).

Analytics (Linguistic Analysis and Logical Positivism)

Analytics (not to be confused with modern Analytics which focus on the analysis of large datasets) was the culmination of modern philosophy into a pragmatic approach to philosophy based on scientific method in the analysis of language (linguistics) and mathematics (logic) (Power, 1996). The most notable proponents of each were George Edward Moore (1873 – 1958) and Bertrand Russel (1872 – 1970). The implication on philosophy was described as an indoctrination to establish scientific truth after which alternate truths were encouraged through peer teaching (McPherran, 2013).

Theories of Schooling

The numerous philosophies of education are not necessarily limited to these mentioned in this study, and new philosophies will inevitably arise in the future. The question therefore arises as to what was the function of these philosophies in the contemporary teaching environment? As mentioned earlier in this chapter, one must find a bridge between practice and theory to transform philosophy for it to be usable in the classroom. The theories of schooling attempts to bridge that gap between theoretical philosophies of education and the actual practice of teaching and learning (Power, 1990).

Essentialism

Essentialism evolved in the 1930s as a conservative teaching approach that focussed on traditional class-room activities. This philosophy was grounded in the belief that the American society was conservative in nature and therefor no need exists to challenge the status quo. Schools' main function was to instil these norms and values so that students may become responsible citizens. Teaching was to transmit knowledge that was rarely questioned or inspected for truthfulness and correctness. Absolute knowledge may not be questioned, and the learner's sole responsibility was to absorb such knowledge to fit the educational mould (Sadker & Zittleman, 2016). A high premium was placed on progression of students through achievement levels and on the principle of mastery of different levels of complexity in maths, physics, history, and language theory (Harmon & Jones, 2005).

Teaching was teacher-centred and allows for very little student originality of thought. It required student exploration or initiative, because knowledge was contained in the teacher who transmits this onto the student. Achievement was the only measure of success and of student ability (McPherran, 2013). This approach had high hopes of producing highly responsible members of society who have the essential skills and knowledge to function as effective citizens. It assumed that these skills could be transmitted through repetition and role-modelling. Very little emphasis on originality produced a very apt worker force, yet stifled artistic creativity. One could argue that it created the foundation for future conflict, as the moral and ethical capacity to evaluate state actions are not present at critical times (Kirillov, Fadeeva, & Fadeev, 2016).

Progressivism

John Dewey (1859-1952) was the first proponent of this approach which places a high premium on social reform whilst maintaining strong fundamentals of science. It encouraged self-development and individualism in the learning of the student. It was seen as progressive in an established academic environment founded on essentialist views. Dewey developed this teaching philosophy at the University of Chicago in the 1920s, based on a revolutionary new approach to teaching research using experimentation to verify his theories (Pring, 2013). His theories are summarised in his own words:

"We may, I think, discover certain common principles amid the variety of progressive schools now existing." (Dewey, 1938, p. 2). Philosophically, Dewey believed that learning best took place through our interaction with our environment. The learner was the master of her or his environment but must embrace the entropy evident in nature. Through our ability to think independently, we may solve the problems in our society and effectively bring about change in our own thinking, i.e., learning took place (Pring, 2013)

Dewey's method revolved around a "method of recitation" by teachers. The method involved five distinct steps—"preparation, presentation, comparison, generalization, and application" (Dewey, 1938, p. 2). Dewey was a proponent of the Platonic concept of teaching which required the teacher to also be a healer, who proposed that learning cannot happen without mutual affection (or love) between teacher and pupil (McEwan, 2011). It was also based on the principles of "learning by doing" and "learning through play" – a radical approach at the time. Problem solving was emphasised as fundamental skill for every student to be able to navigate the challenges of change. A prominent teaching theory in this field was experiential learning that provides an effective "interface between student learning styles and the institutional learning environment" (Kolb & Kolb, 2005, p. 193).

Perennialism

The Oxford dictionary describes "Perennial" as meaning "enduring, apparently for an infinite time" (i.e., "everlasting"). Similarly, Perennialism argued that knowledge was universal and depends on founding principles which are enduring and true for eternity. It required that education should focus on these ideas. Students should strive to become true intellectuals who can argue the merits of statements based on fundamental truths. Furthermore, all modern knowledge stands on the shoulders of previous knowledge and therefor the study in all fields should teach this to its students. Ancient philosopher-teachers were strong proponents of the ideas of perennialism and required the dialectic and deductive reasoning to be grounded in founding principles. Plato described this Socratic method in his dialogues, whilst Aristotle formalised this in his syllogisms (Harmon & Jones, 2005). Perennialism left little room for student preference in subject choice; the student voice remained silent as the teacher preference in methodology dictated classroom activities. It also argued against institutions of higher education becoming training grounds for students' future careers (Livingston, McClain, & DeSpain, 1995).

More recently, Hutchins argued for a return to the founding knowledge in the American educational system: "Textbooks have probably done as much to degrade the American intelligence as any single force." (Hutchins, 1945, p. 78).

Existentialism

Existentialism as a relatively modern philosophy, born from the minds of Soren Kierkegaard and Friedrich Nietzsche in the 1800s, rejected traditional philosophy and strongly emphasised the individual creating her or his own reality. Similarly, in the existential philosophy of education, the traditional teaching philosophies were rejected, and the student was placed in the centre of her or his own learning. Furthermore, students' understanding of themselves took precedence over knowledge, and students had the freedom to choose their own educational path and content. The teacher, on the other hand, helped the student to discover her or his own essence with broad curricular statements meant to guide, rather than prescribe learning. Creativity was encouraged through artistic expression rather than prescribed procedural methodologies commonly found in vocational training and the sciences (Jaarsma, Kinaschuk, & Xing, 2016). All existential teaching needs to encourage exploration by students and teachers. It requires the freedom to express new-found knowledge inside and outside the classroom. The teacher still had an important role in teaching through their use of religious and other texts (Power, Philosophy of education, 1990).

Behaviourism

In contrast to existentialism, behaviourism postulated that human behaviour can be modified through reward and punishment. It followed therefore that human behaviour was entirely determined by its external environment. Originating in the 1900s from the work of Ivan Pavlov and John Watson, behaviourism required positive reinforcement of students to learn new behaviour. It relied on scientific knowledge in a rigid world of set rules and facts which can only be determined by observation of the individual's reaction to stimuli. Human perceptions of morals and the environment are guided by these stimuli (Sadker & Zittleman, 2016).

Behaviourism was a field of philosophy that has its roots in Darwinian evolution (Tabane, 2016). It moved from the premise that only observable behaviours provide an objective measure of learning that has taken place. Additionally, the focus was on changing behaviour and learning new patterns of behaviour through repetition (Tabane, 2016). Major contributions to this field include the well-known Ivan Petrovich Pavlov's Behaviourist Learning Theory (1904), John B. Watson's application of Pavlov's theory to humans (1930), Edward L. Thorndike's Conditioning (1930) and Burrhus F. Skinner's conditioning, reinforcement, punishment, and motivation (1950) (Meyer, Moore, & Viljoen, 1989).

The behaviourist school assigned high value to empirical scientific evidence and the making of predictions based on such evidence. In the schooling system, this translated into the concepts "conditioning" and "reinforcement" which are directed at modifying the students' behaviour, thus demonstrating that learning had taken place. This typical behaviourist classroom was one where objectives of learning with clearly stated outcomes are linked to changed behaviour in students (Power, 1996). Assessment was done on a set of specific competencies that the students must demonstrate. Assessment thus requires a high level of technical design skills to measure the set outcomes effectively. The role of the student was analogous to clay in the potter's hand, a passively complying participant in acceptable behaviour as conditions for their intended vocation, whilst the teacher was held accountable for the student's learning through strictly controlled processes (Blumberg, 2013).

Cognitivism

Cognitive theories of learning refer to those focused on understanding the mental processes of learning, searching for reasons for different learning experiences (Omidire, 2017). Various reasons for differing learning experiences may exist, which include varying perceptions; different levels of reasoning; varying levels of problem-solving; language processing skills; memory capacity; and differing levels of information processing (Omidire, 2017). These reasons were investigated in cognitive psychology, which focussed on describing learning through an understanding of the mind and experimental evidence of mental functions (Matsumoto, 2009).

Major contributors to this theory included Jean Piaget (cognitive development theory), Jerome Bruner (theory of cognitive growth), L.S. Vygotsky (sociocultural theory) and D.P. Ausubel (advance organisers). One of the most widely accepted outputs from this theory was Bloom's taxonomy of learning framework (Bloom, 1956). His taxonomy classified the cognitive processes from the most basic (knowledge recall) to most complex (evaluation of knowledge) (see Figure 1). It was useful to note that not only did it classify the learning goals that needs to be achieved in terms of complexity, but also the process of building knowledge in the student (Omidire, 2017). Especially helpful to both student and lecturer, it classified learning styles that explains what the cognitive cues are that facilitate learning in an individual. The student should therefore be aware of his/her learning style preferences, whilst the lecturer should accommodate the learning styles in curriculum design and teaching interventions (McPherran, 2013).

Constructivism

Carl Rogers (1969) stated that "individuals exist in a continually changing world of experience in which they are the centre" (Rogers, 1951, p. 2. Ch9). Constructivist theories of learning are based on the concept that knowledge of the student is built on the student's prior knowledge (Ganga & Maphalala, 2016). This implies that the teacher must gauge the student's prior knowledge to design learning activities that build on this prior knowledge. It also challenges the behaviourist approach that knowledge exists elsewhere (i.e., in the teacher) and needs to be transferred onto the student (McEwan, 2011). Different styles of

Figure 1. Bloom's revised taxonomy
Source: Omidire (2017)

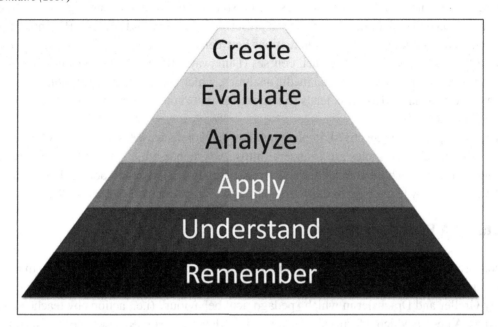

teaching that are relevant today originated in this theory. Such styles include cooperative learning, blended learning, problem-based learning, discovery learning (expository learning), scaffolding, proximal learning, communities of practice, jigsaw learning, case study learning, spiral reflective learning, and project learning (Bates, 2015). Notably, although these are major teaching approaches, they are also classified as learning approaches, implying that the teaching focus was on the building of knowledge by the learner based on her or his existing, own knowledge (Taylor & Maor, 2000).

Constructivists believe that knowledge was essentially subjective in nature, constructed from our perceptions and mutually agreed upon conventions (Bates, 2015, p. 54). Modern technologies, like the LMS, have made it possible to implement virtual environments where such interactive learning was the cornerstone of the success of students (Khoza, 2018). A modern example of a technological implementation of constructivism is the so-called eXtended-Massive Open Online Course (xMOOC) platform. These platforms allow for large student groups to use online guided, semi-facilitated and synchronous/asynchronous delivery in highly structured courses that allow student groups to collaborate online. Students structure their learning and have many opportunities to learn from one another through online forums, discussion groups, group work, peer learning and teacher guided activities (Bates, 2015). Some current examples of providers include edX and Khan Academy.

Connectivism

Connectivism, a contemporary teaching methodology, finds its roots in the idealist and existentialist teaching philosophies. It postulates that knowledge cannot be constructed for the student, and that sense-making of knowledge was a process that happens through the interactions of students with others and the environment. Knowledge is therefore not finite and discreet, as set out by the teacher, but must be explored and expanded as the course progresses (Kop, 2011).

Connectivism relies on four major activities for learning to take place. These are aggregation, remixing, repurposing, and feeding forward. The emphasis is on students defining the learning space and content through interaction and collaboration, rather than prescriptive lectures and content (Ravenscroft, 2011). These activities rely on intensive social interactions between students, and traditional classrooms often do not have the resources to facilitate such courses (Dunaway, 2011). Connectivist courses are social media reliant and require extensive social media analytics, which are not readily available to educational institutions (McPherran, 2013). This leads to knowledge that remains current and useful for decision making (Goldie, 2016).

Modern examples of connectivist implementation are connected-Massive Open Online Courses (cMOOC). Two notable examples are Coursera (https://www.coursera.org/) and FutureLearn (https://www.futurelearn.com/). These courses are less structured, allow students to define their own learning path and build the knowledge base in the course through mutual interaction (Bates, 2015).

Case Study: A Pedagogy Model

It is evident from Drachsler and Kalz (2016) that the pedagogical model used in teaching must support the capturing of data for the LA system. This approach is supported in the LA and pedagogy framework defined by Greller and Drachsler in which "pedagogical behaviour" (i.e., actions by teachers/students) feed into the LA design which informs the defining of "pedagogical consequences" (i.e., learning design adjustments) and feeds back into pedagogical behaviour again (Greller & Drachsler, 2012). In this study the working prototype would be in the form of a VLE that would provide data for the LA model which in turn would provide feedback for learner and teacher. However, the limited scope of this study excludes the demonstration and evaluation phases of the DSRM.

Classroom Approach

From the previous sections, the following general approach was deduced as best suited to the specific needs of the teaching environment. In the relatively new field of LA research regarding which pedagogical approach is best supported by LA is relatively neglected (Greller & Drachsler, 2012). However, the behaviourist-instructivist approach is most frequently used successfully to implement and test LA systems (Pardo & Kloos, 2011). Generally, this approach requires self-directed learning, facilitates a high degree of interactivity, offers continuous feedback, uses a blended teaching approach and utilises a guiding structure. It also requires continuous progress assessment and requires some collaboration between students in the learning process, determined by their personal cognitive style (Enss, 93; Marrs & Benton, 2009; Biggs, 1996). Separate knowing (SK) refers to evaluating knowledge in an "objective, analytical, and detached manner" (Marrs & Benton, 2009, p. 58), whilst connected knowing (CK) refers to a relational approach that involves the "discovery of a personal connection between the individual and the thing, event, person, or concept under consideration" (Marrs & Benton, 2009, p. 58). The faculty, due to the nature of its student body (either residential or distance), have aligned with the Stellenbosch University approach (Center for Teaching and Learning (CTL), 2013) of blended learning and in some cases hybrid learning. This approach is characterised by:

- **Self-Directedness.** Students are to a large extent expected to accept responsibility for their learning. This means that the set outcomes of the course need to be reached to a large extent at their own pace, yet with measurable milestones (SU, 2017).
- **High Degree of Interactivity.** The need to supplement content with additional resources that would help to facilitate deeper understanding is required, as the teacher acts as facilitator of learning. Facilitation of learning implies a high degree of individualised attention to students' specific needs which can be accomplished through e-content. Besides obvious advantages, such as time saving for the teacher, a bank of re-usable content and improved learning through learner-customised structures, interactivity would also enable the concept of "teacherbots" (Bayne, 2015).
- **Continuous Feedback.** This is essential for teacher and student as a continuous feedback loop must be achieved to ensure that student progress was monitored for diagnostic and remedial actions (SU, 2017). Supported by the research of Gibbs (1988) and Knight (2020) which describes a continuous feedback process in six steps to ensure continuous improvement in learning and teaching. These are (1) a description of the learning activity, (2) a description of the student's feelings, (3) an evaluation of the student's impressions of the activity, (4) a sense-making exercise of the student's interpretation, (5) concluding deductions of what needs to improve, and (6) a plan to implement improvements which was returned back into the feedback loop (Gibbs, 1988) .
- **Collaboration Between Students and Teacher.** Students are bound to feel the effects of isolation due to the individualised nature of teaching. It is therefore imperative that activities that require collaboration between students, yet in which the voice of the teacher is also heard, are created (SU, 2017).

These general characteristics that the approach should adhere to is the starting point for the specific pedagogical approach described in the next section.

Institutional Pedagogical Approach

Several imperatives for the future delivery of learning in the faculty were identified from the annual institutional strategic planning for 2020 – 23 (SA Military Academy, 2019). These imperatives necessitate a change in pedagogy and delivery of the content of the faculty to address future HE needs. These imperatives include:

- The need to deliver the same content to residential and distance students, with an adaption to the pedagogy for distance students (Khoza & Van Zyl, 2015).
- A new approach was required to address the increased time constraints on class time and reduced resources (staff, facilities, and funds) (SA Military Academy, 2019).
- The need to deliver content to current and potential new clients in the Massive Open Online Course (MOOC) format (SA Military Academy, 2019).
- The generation and use of data to improve learning, teaching, and course results. This would also enable the implementation of an LA platform to assist in the above (SU, 2017).

The inclusion of these imperatives in the solution can be achieved in the pedagogy by using specific tools and interactions (SU, 2017), the most notable described below.

Blended Learning (BL) and Hybrid Learning (HL)

Traditional face-to-face classrooms have been supplemented progressively with computer-based and e-learning. Initially, these were simply sporadically used by a minority of technologically inclined or young at heart, educationally speaking, lecturers as classroom multimedia tools. But, CBE and e-learning have since evolved to become a mainstream category of teaching which encompasses a wide range of teaching approaches called BL, a mix of face-to-face (synchronous) classes with technology aids and online resources (Bates, 2015). This methodology has in some cases produced significant improvement in student performance (Means, 2009). Additionally, significant improvements in efficiency can be achieved through synchronous and asynchronous activities to optimise time (Bates, 2015). HL is the progression of BL to a campus characterised by fully online synchronous and asynchronous classes and resources. Hybrid learning is especially useful in the fully distance education environment (Bates, 2015).

The Flipped Classroom

Flumefelt and Green (2013) describes a "new" teaching approach that may be used to identify at-risk students effectively. The flipped learning (FL) approach is described as an effective method to "flip" traditional lecture time into time for higher level learning engagements (Enfield, 2013). It is part of the BL class of teaching approaches. This approach allows more time for students to process knowledge through teacher and peer engagement. Additionally, it allows for more time for remedial interventions of at-risk students. It is an ideal approach for technology support, as VLEs allow for a high level of individualisation and customization (Flumerfelt & Green, 2013). Jovanović et al. (2016a) demonstrated that the FL approach can support all learning strategies of students effectively, and even help improve learner results. FL requires that learners maintain a high level of engagement before, during and after scheduled teacher contact sessions (Lage, Platt, & Tregua, 2000) which is an ideal enabler for the generation of sufficient LA data for analysis (Mirriahi & Lorenzo Vigentini, 2017). Birkenkrahe and Kjellin (2015) found that student interaction and engagement maybe improved through the FL approach. Bruff (2019) described the FL process as a blended approach which uses "computer-mediated" activities to engage students in a highly structured environment by using self-regulated activities before, during and after synchronous contact sessions. The process is illustrated in Figure 2.

Figure 2. The flipped classroom approach
Source: Bruff (2019)

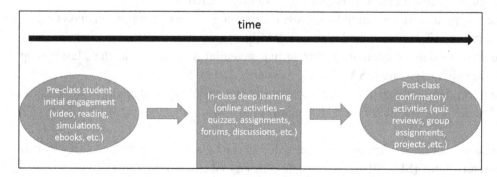

Adam et al. (2020) provided a list of ways in which flipped learning can increase the efficiency of teaching. These are summarised below.

- Increased student engagement with content from class and additional sources using quizzes, interactive content, problem solving and other activities.
- Real time feedback to students by teachers, tutors, teacher-bots, or peers.
- Including marks for participation in class and out of class activities in final student grades.
- Having in-class learning environments which are highly structured and well-planned.
- Having data and analytics play a vital part in informing teaching activities and learning design.
- Scaffolding through mastery of concepts, outcomes or objectives to improve student performance.
- Building highly incentivised activities for mastery, participation and progression into the course structure.

Gauging Student Self-Efficacy and Affective Responses

The direct relationship between student perceptions of course quality, affective indicators and motivation have a direct influence on student success (Berg, 2005). Therefore, a model to gauge students' level of satisfaction and motivation must be devised. This includes students' ongoing perceptions of quality, lecturer proficiency, level of support and students' level of motivation throughout the course. It is of course difficult to gauge this continuously, and time-consuming, but a realistic methodology would be to gauge levels at specific intervals. Students need to engage in a reflective practice cycle as part of a feedback portfolio to the teacher (Wise A., Vytasek, Hausknecht, & Zhao, 2016). This is especially useful in developing students' self-regulation in improving their learning (Roll & Winne, 2015). The reflective cycle has three phases: preparatory phase, the task completion phase, and an assessment phase (Miller, 2015).

Progress Tracking

Progress tracking should provide for the needs of teacher and learner to track progress for diagnostic, remedial and motivational purposes effectively (Nagy, 2016). Several tools on the Moodle and other platforms are available to facilitate progress tracking, which include a progress bar and completion graph. Additional tools that could supplement progress tracking are gamification and experience point plugins, both of which serve as indicators of effort and participation, yet also serve as motivational tools (De Raadt, 2021).

A Model to Provide Data for LA Prediction

The requirement for such a model would be to provide descriptive, diagnostic, and predictive analytics of at-risk students. It would also have to provide the teacher with real-time monitoring capabilities based on pre-defined at-risk indicators. Typical indicators from practice include task completion rate (You, 2016), level of participation and engagement (Phillips, Maor, Preston, & Cumming-Potvin, 2012), milestone results and overall results (You, 2016), VLE activity usage (Agudo-Peregrina, Iglesias-Pradas, Conde-González, & Hernández-García, 2014), time on task (Cerezo, Sanchez-Santill, Paule-Ruiz, & Núñez, 2016), formative and summative assessment results (Strang, 2017), to name a few. It is clear from research that each course may have different indicators of success, and therefore also of at-risk students. These different indicators are influenced by students' preferences, their educational and social backgrounds, and various other factors, but may also be influenced by poor learning design or pedagogy (Hansen, Emin, Wasson, Mor, & Rodriguez-Triana, 2013). The proposed model should make provision for a comprehensive list of indicators from literature and empirical studies and case data from diagnostics to indicate suitable indicators of at-risk students. This will feed into dynamic redesign of learning content and the adaptation of pedagogy, and will assist ultimately in at-risk student identification (Bakharia, et al., 2016).

Learning Design and LA Alignment

A model is needed to include the pedagogic elements from the previous section as part of the learning design and LA design process to make provision for specific interventions. The model for Student Tuning (Wise A., Vytasek, Hausknecht, & Zhao, 2016) and Align Design Framework (Wise & Vytasek, 2017) discussed in this section addresses the requirements for alignment. Reflective practice (continuous feedback) is a keystone to the use of LA as part of self-regulated learning (Winne, 2017). Students need inputs from metacognitive monitoring of their learning behaviour to accomplish self-regulation (Roll & Winne, 2015). Winne (2017) further asserts that one of the biggest stumbling blocks to successful self-directed learning is either students' lack of discipline to monitor their own progress, or the lack of student progress monitoring by facilitators. To address this, Wise, et. al. (2016) introduced the Student Tuning Model to align the LA system with self-reflective and self-regulated learning (see Figure 3).

Figure 3. A model student tuning
Source: Wise (2014)

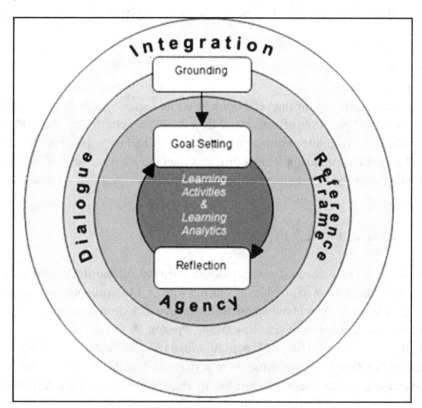

In pursuing the implementation of LA to support teaching and learning, a pedagogical model is required to suit not only the learning and teaching environment, but also one that will meet the requirements of LA. In turn, LA data will hopefully support redesign of teaching, which will result in a continuous feedback loop in the tradition of design science methodology (Laurillard, 2013b). Wise et al. describes this cyclical process in their Align Design Framework (Wise A., Vytasek, Hausknecht, & Zhao, 2016) captured in Figure 4. The figure illustrates the relationship between the four principles of the design framework.

Figure 4. The align design framework
Source: Wise (2016)

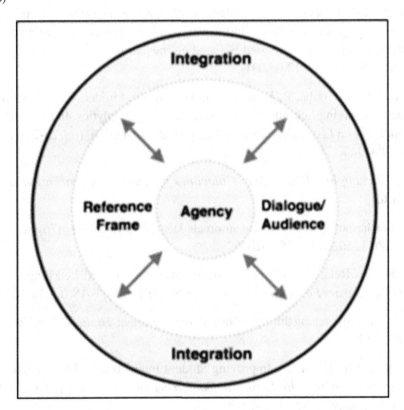

CONCLUSION

In this chapter, the origins of education philosophy were investigated. This investigation led to prominent modern education philosophies and schooling theories. Several implementations of teaching pedagogy were implemented at the institution as a case study leading to meaningful feedback and analysis of best practice. It is concluded that the behaviourist philosophy with an instructivist teaching approach would be best suited for the faculty to support LA. A specific pedagogic model was proposed to support this approach and to identify at-risk students using an LA system.

REFERENCES

Adam, M., Bonch, D., Fisher, D., Klemmer, S., McFarland, D., Noor, M., . . . Campbell, J. (2020). *Flipped Classroom Field Guide*. https://www.coursera.org/lecture/university-teaching/flipped -learning-rKwAE

Adler, M. (1942). In defence of the philosophy of education. In N. Henry (Ed.), *The Fortyfirst Yearbook of the National Society for the Study of Education* (pp. 197–249). Public School Publishing Company.

Adler, M. (1984). *The Paideia Program*. Institute of Philosophical Research.

Agudo-Peregrina, A., Iglesias-Pradas, S., Conde-González, M., & Hernández-García, A. (2014). Can we predict success from log data in VLEs? Classification of interactions for learning analytics and their relation with performance in VLE-supported F2F and online learning. *Computers in Human Behavior*, *31*, 542–550. doi:10.1016/j.chb.2013.05.031

Bakharia, A., Corrin, L., de Barba, P., Kennedy, G., Gaševi, D., Mulder, R., ... Lockyer, L. (2016). A Conceptual Framework linking Learning Design with Learning Analytics. In *Proceedings of the Sixth International Conference on Learning Analytics & Knowledge (LAK '16)* (pp. 25-29). New York: ACM. 10.1145/2883851.2883944

Bates, A. (2015). *Teaching in a Digital Age: Guidelines for Designing Teaching and Learning*. Tony Bates Associates Ltd.

Bayne, S. (2015). Teacherbot: Interventions in automated teaching. *Teaching in Higher Education*, *20*(4), 455–467. doi:10.1080/13562517.2015.1020783

Berg, C. (2005). Factors Related to Observed Attitude Change Toward Learning Chemistry Among University Students. *Chemistry Education Research and Practice*, *6*(1), 1–18. doi:10.1039/B4RP90001D

Biggs, J. (1996). Enhancing teaching through constructive alignment. *Higher Education*, *32*(3), 347–364. doi:10.1007/BF00138871

Birkenkrahe, M., & Kjellin, H. (2015). Improving Student Interaction and Engagement in the Flipped Classroom. In *Proceedings of the 14th European Conference on e-Learning (ECEL 2015)* (pp. 73-79). Curran Associates, Inc. doi:978-1-5108-1431-8

Bloom, B. (1956). *A taxonomy of educational objectives*. Longman, Green & Co.

Blumberg, P. (2013). *Assessing and Improving Your Teaching : Strategies and Rubrics for Faculty Growth and Student Learning*. Jossey-Bass Higher and Adult Education Series.

Bobzien, S. (2006). Stoic Logic. In M. de Grazia & S. Wells (Eds.), *Cambridge Companions Online* (pp. 85–123). doi:10.1017/CCOL0521650941

Boldyguin, G. (2013). On The Meaning of the Word "Philosophy"(on History of the Word). *Journal of Siberian Federal University*, *11*, 1599–1609.

Brooke, C., & Frazer, E. (Eds.). (2013). *Ideas of Education: Philosophy and Politics from Plato to Dewey*. Routledge, ProQuest Ebook Central. doi:10.4324/9780203817544

Bruff, D. (2019). *Intentional Tech: Principles to Guide the Use of Educational Technology in College Teaching (Teaching and Learning in Higher Education)* (1st ed.). West Virginia University Press.

Butler, J. (1968). *Four philososophies add their practice in education and religion.* Harper & Row Publishers, Inc.

Center for Teaching and Learning (CTL). (2013). *Strategy for Teaching and Learning 2014 - 2018.* Retrieved from University of Stellenbosch: www.sun.ac.za/ctl

Cerezo, R., Sanchez-Santill, M., Paule-Ruiz, M., & Núnez, J. (2016). Students' LMS interaction patterns and their relationship with achievement: A case study in higher education. *Computers & Education, 96,* 42–54. doi:10.1016/j.compedu.2016.02.006

Cottingham, J. (2020). *Western Philosophy: An Anthology* (3rd ed.). Blackwell Publishing.

De Raadt, M. (2021). *Progress Bar.* Retrieved 7 7, 2021, from Moodle: https://moodle.org/plugins/block_progress

Devlin, K. (1997). *Goodbye, Descartes.* John Wiley and Sons, Inc.

Dewey, J. (1938). *Experience and education.* Macmillan.

Drachsler, H., & Kalz, M. (2016). The MOOC and learning analytics innovation cycle (MOLAC): A reflective summary of ongoing research and its challenges. *Journal of Computer Assisted Learning, 32*(3), 281–290. doi:10.1111/jcal.12135

Dunaway, M. (2011). Connectivism Learning theory and pedagogical practice for networked information landscapes. *Emerald Insight, 39*(4), 675–685.

Enfield, J. (2013). Looking at the impact of the flipped classroom model of instruction on undergraduate multimedia students at CSUN. *TechTrends, 57*(6), 14–27. doi:10.100711528-013-0698-1

Enss, C. (1993, February). Integrating separate and connected knowing: The experiential learning model. *Teaching of Psychology, 20*(1), 7–13. doi:10.120715328023top2001_2

Flumerfelt, S., & Green, G. (2013). Using Lean in the Flipped Classroom for At Risk Students. *Journal of Educational Technology & Society, 16*(1), 356–366.

Ganga, E., & Maphalala, M. (2016). Contributions of Constructivism to Teaching and Learning. In Teaching and Learning Strategies in South Africa (pp. 43 - 54). Cheriton House, UK: Cengage.

Gibbs, G. (1988). *Learning by Doing: A Guide to Teaching and Learning Methods.* Oxford Further Education Unit.

Goldie, J. (2016). Connectivism: A knowledge learning theory for the digital age? *Medical Teacher, 38*(10), 1064–1069. doi:10.3109/0142159X.2016.1173661 PMID:27128290

Greller, W., & Drachsler, H. (2012). Translating Learning into Numbers: A Generic Framework for Learning Analytics. *Journal of Educational Technology & Society, 15*(3), 42–57.

Hansen, C., Emin, V., Wasson, B., Mor, Y., & Rodriguez-Triana, M. (2013). *Towards an Integrated Model of Teacher Inquiry into Student Learning, Learning Design and Learning Analytics*. Paphos, Cyprus: EC-TEL 2013 - 8th European Conference, on Technology Enhanced Learning. doi:10.1007/978-3-642-40814-4 73

Harmon, D., & Jones, T. (2005). *Elementary Education: A Reference Handbook (Contemporary Education Issues)* (1st ed.). ABC-CLIO.

Harper, R. (1955). *Significance of Existence and Recognition for Education. In 54th Yearbook of the National Society for the Study of Education*. University of Chicago Press.

Hull, K. (2002). Eros and Education: The Role of Desire in Teaching and Learning. *The NEA Higher Education Journal*, 19 - 32.

Hutchins, R. (1945). *The Higher Learning in America*. Transaction Publishers.

Jaarsma, A., Kinaschuk, K., & Xing, L. (2016). Kierkegaard, Despair and the Possibility of Education: Teaching Existentialism Existentially. *Studies in Philosophy and Education, 35*(5), 445–461. doi:10.100711217-015-9488-x

Jovanović, J., Gašević, D., Dawson, S., Pardo, A., & Mirriahi, N. (2016a). Learning Analytics to Unveil Learning Strategies in a Flipped Classroom. *The Internet and Higher Education, 33*, 74–85. doi:10.1016/j.iheduc.2017.02.001

Jowett, B. (2016). *The Dialogues of Plato, Volumes 1 - 3*. Eternal Sun Books.

Khoza, L. (2018). Reflection: Usage of the Learning Management System at the Faculty of Military Science. In *International Conference on e-Learning* (pp. 161-170). Kidmore End: Academic Conferences International Limited.

Khoza, L., & Van Zyl, G. (2015). Disparity: Threat or opportunity to distance education throughput at the South African Military Academy. *Scientia Militaria. South African Journal of Military Studies, 43*(2), 151–173. doi:10.5787/43-2-1128

Kirillov, N., Fadeeva, V., & Fadeev, V. (2016). Modern philosophy of education. *Web of Conferences, 28.* 10.1051hsconf/20162801034

Knight, S. (2020). Augmenting Assessment with Learning Analytics. In M. Bearman, P. Dawson, R. Ajjawi, J. Tai, & D. Boud (Eds.), *Re-imagining University Assessment in a Digital World. The Enabling Power of Assessment* (Vol. 7). Springer. doi:10.1007/978-3-030-41956-1_10

Kolb, A., & Kolb, D. (2005). Learning Styles and Learning Spaces: Enhancing Experiential Learning in Higher Education. *Academy of Management Learning & Education, 4*(2), 193–212. doi:10.5465/amle.2005.17268566

Kop, R. (2011). The challenges to connectivist learning on open online networks: Learning experiences during a massive open online course. *International Review of Research in Open and Distance Learning, 12*(3), 19. doi:10.19173/irrodl.v12i3.882

Lage, M., Platt, G., & Tregua, M. (2000). Inverting the classroom: A gateway to creating an inclusive learning environment. *The Journal of Economic Education, 31*(1), 30–43. doi:10.1080/00220480009596759

Laurillard, D. (2013b). *The teacher as action researcher: Building Pedagogical Patterns for Learning and Technology*. Routledge.

Livingston, M., McClain, B., & DeSpain, B. (1995). Assessing the consistency between teachers' philosophies and educational goals. *Education, 116*(1), 124.

Machan, T. (2011). Truth in Philosophy. *Libertarian Papers, Academic OneFile, 3*. Retrieved 07 22, 2019, from http://link.galegroup.com/apps/doc/A280387350/AONE?u=27uos&sid=AONE&xid=201e249e

Maritain, J. (1938). *True humanism*. Charles Scribner's Sons.

Marrs, H., & Benton, S. (2009). Relationships between Separate and Connected Knowing and Approaches to Learning. *Sex Roles, 60*(1-2), 57–66. doi:10.100711199-008-9510-7

Matsumoto, D. (2009). *The Cambridge dictionary of psychology*. Cambridge University Press.

McEwan, H. (2011). Narrative Reflection in the Philosophy of Teaching: Genealogies and Portraits. *Journal of Philosophy of Education, 45*(1), 125–140. doi:10.1111/j.1467-9752.2010.00783.x

McPherran, M. (2013). Socrates, Plato, erôs, and liberal education. In C. Brooke, E. Frazer, C. Brooke, & E. Frazer (Eds.), *Ideas of Education: Philosophy and Politics from Plato to Dewey* (pp. 6–19). Routledge.

Means, B. e. (2009). *Evaluation of Evidence-Based Practices in Online Learning: A Meta-Analysis and Review of Online Learning Studies Washington*. US Department of Education.

Meyer, W., Moore, C., & Viljoen, H. (1989). *Personality Theories - from Freud to Frankl*. Lexicon.

Mirriahi, N., & Lorenzo Vigentini, L. (2017). Analytics of Learner Video Use. In C. Lang, G. Siemens, A. Wise, & D. Gasevic (Eds.), *Handbook of Learning Analytics* (pp. 251–267). Society for Learning Analytics Research. doi:10.18608/hla17.022

Nagy, R. (2016). Tracking and visualizing student effort: Evolution of a practical analytics tool for staff and student engagement. *Journal of Learning Analytics, 3*(2), 165–193. doi:10.18608/jla.2016.32.8

Omidire, M. (2017). Contributions of Cognitive Theories to Teaching and Learning Strategies. In M. Maphalana (Ed.), Teaching and Learning Startegies in South Africa (pp. 27 - 42). Cheriton House, UK: Cengage.

Ongaro, E. (2017). *Philosophy and Public Administration: An Introduction*. Northampton, MA: Edward Elgar Publishing Limited, ProQuest Ebook Central. Retrieved July 22, 2019, from https://ebookcentral.proquest.com/lib/sun/detail.action?docID=4980439

Pardo, A., & Kloos, C. D. (2011). Stepping out of the box: Towards analytics outside the learning management system. In *Proceedings of the 1st International Conference on Learning Analytics and Knowledge* (pp. 163–167). New York, NY: ACM. 10.1145/2090116.2090142

Patzig, G. (1968). What is an Aristotelian Syllogism? In *Aristotle's Theory of the Syllogism. Synthese Library (Monographs on Epistemology, Logic, Methodology, Philosophy of Science, Sociology of Science and of Knowledge, and on the Mathematical Methods of Social and Behavioral Sciences)* (Vol. 16). Springer. doi:10.1007/978-94-017-0787-9_1

Phillips, R., Maor, D., Preston, G., & Cumming-Potvin, W. (2012). Exploring Learning Analytics as Indicators of Study Behaviour. In T. Amiel, & B. Wilson (Ed.), *Proceedings of EdMedia 2012—World Conference on Educational Media and Technology* (pp. 286-286). Association for the Advancement of Computing in Education (AACE).

Power, E. (1990). *Philosophy of education.* Waveland Press.

Power, E. (1996). *Educational philosophy: A history from the ancient world to modern America.* Garland Publishing, Inc.

Pring, R. (2013). John Dewey: Saviour of American education or worse than Hitler? In C. Brooke & E. Frazer (Eds.), *Ideas of Education: Philosophy and Politics from Plato to Dewey* (pp. 267–284). Routledge.

Ravenscroft, A. (2011). Dialogue and Connectivism: A New Approach to Understanding and Promoting Dialogue-Rich Networked Learning. *International Review of Research in Open and Distance Learning, 12*(3), 139. doi:10.19173/irrodl.v12i3.934

Rogers, C. (1951). *Client Centred Therapy.* Hachette.

Roll, I., & Winne, P. H. (2015). Understanding, evaluating, and supporting self-regulated learning using learning analytics. *Journal of Learning Analytics, 2*(1), 7–12. doi:10.18608/jla.2015.21.2

Rousseau, J.-J. (1979). *Emile: Or, On education.* Basic Book.

SA Military Academy. (2019). *Annual Performance Plan 2019. Saldanha, RSA.* SA Military Academy.

Sadker, D., & Zittleman, K. (2016). *Teacher-Centered Philosophies. Teachers, Schools, and Society: A Brief Introduction to Education.* McGraw Hill.

Satre, J. (1956). *Being and nothingness* (H. Barnes, Trans.). Philosophical Library.

Spedding, E. (2010). Advancement of Learning. In *The Works of Francis Bacon* (pp. 1857–1870). London: Bartleby.com. Retrieved 6 11, 2019, from https://www.bartleby.com/br/193.html

Strang, K. (2017). Beyond engagement analytics: Which online mixed-data factors predict student learning outcomes? *Education and Information Technologies, 22*(3), 917–937. doi:10.100710639-016-9464-2

SU. (2017). *SU strategy for teaching and learning 2017-2021.* Retrieved Oct 6, 2021, from https://www.sun.ac.za/english/learning-teaching/ctl/Documents/SU%20TL%20Strategy.pdf

Tabane, R. (2016). Contributions of Behaviourist Theories to Teaching and Learning. In M. Maphalala (Ed.), Teaching and Learning Strategies in South Africa (pp. 13 - 26). Cheriton House: Cengage.

Taylor, P., & Maor, D. (2000). Assessing the efficacy of online teaching with the Constructivist On-Line Learning Environment Survey. In A. Herrmann, & M. Kulski (Ed.), *Flexible Futures in Tertiary Teaching. Proceedings of the 9th Annual Teaching Learning Forum.* Curtin University of Technology.

Winne, P. H. (2017). A cognitive and metacognitive analysis of self-regulated learning. In P. Alexander, D. Schunk, & J. Greene (Eds.), *Handbook of selfregulation of learning and performance* (pp. 15–32). Routledge. doi:10.4324/9781315697048-3

Wise, A., & Vytasek, J. (2017). Learning Analytics Implementation. In C. Lang, G. Siemens, A. Wise, & D. Gasevic (Eds.), Handbook of Learning Analytics (pp. 151 - 160). New York: Society of Learning Analytics Research. doi:10.18608/hla17

Wise, A., Vytasek, J., Hausknecht, S., & Zhao, Y. (2016). Developing Learning Analytics Design Knowledge in the "Middle Space": The Student Tuning Model and Align Design Framework for Learning Analytics Use. *Online Learning*, *20*(2), 155–182. doi:10.24059/olj.v20i2.783

You, J. (2016). Identifying significant indicators using LMS data to predict course achievement in online learning. *Internet and Higher Education*, *29*, 23–30. doi:10.1016/j.iheduc.2015.11.003

Chapter 5
The Role of Machine Learning in Customer Experience

Uma Khemchand Thakur
Jhulelal Institute of Technology, Nagpur, India

ABSTRACT

Machine learning is a subtype of artificial intelligence in which computers use algorithms to learn from data and discover patterns, a capacity that businesses may exploit in various ways to improve customer service. Machine learning (ML) is improving nearly every function and process automation by enabling operational optimisation. As a result, it improves customer service, speeds up work, lessens errors, and improves accuracy. Customer service is one area of the company that might benefit from machine learning. Natural language processing and sentiment analysis are two technologies that can help businesses better understand how to respond to consumer comments and queries.

INTRODUCTION

In the field of artificial intelligence, a computer mimics human behaviour. Computers are becoming smarter these days. To compete successfully in the market in today's corporate environment, offering good customer service is more important than ever. Machine learning-enhanced technology is one of the best ways to support these endeavours. Machine learning addresses the question of how to build computers that improve automatically through experience (Jordan & Mitchell, 2015). The convergence of computer science and statistics, as well as the foundation of artificial intelligence and data science, make it one of the technical domains with the fastest growth rates today. Machine learning has enormous potential for reducing the cost of goods and services, accelerating company operations, and improving customer service. In current period of extraordinary technical advancement, it is acknowledged as one of the most significant application areas, and adoption is accelerating across practically all industries. Customer experience refers "to the total of all experiences the customer has with the business, based on all interactions and thoughts about the business" (Rajkhowa, n.d.). It is stated that about 95% of all interactions with customers will take place through mediums supported by artificial intelligence by 2025 (Vangie, n.d.).

DOI: 10.4018/978-1-6684-7105-0.ch005

Figure 1. Key attributes of customer experience

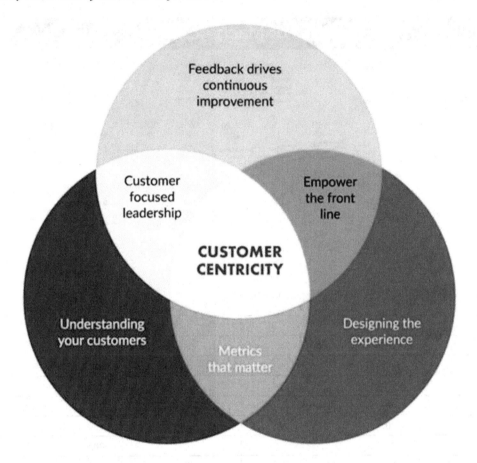

Google Cloud Services and Amazon Web Services provide access to machine learning, which is a reasonable choice. Machine learning algorithms may identify when a customer needs assistance when making a purchase on an eCommerce website, allowing the deal to go through smoothly. As a result, it enhances both the entire consumer experience and sales. Programs can record prior customer encounters and learn from them using machine learning. As a result, businesses are continually enhancing their capacity for providing customer service. Over time, algorithms are improved while maintaining a high standard of customer support. In comparison to retraining human personnel, this is far more practical and beneficial. Machine learning is therefore a crucial tool for providing better customer service at all levels, from enhancing overall security to providing highly individualised levels of help.

There is no doubting that machine learning already has a significant impact on the consumer experience. And other analysts believe that the possibilities are much more promising.

Even while they are helpful, chatbots and virtual assistants, for instance, have not yet realised their full potential. Currently, a few chatbot and virtual assistant replies are incorrect. Sometimes they are unable to respond to some inquiries or are unable to understand certain queries. Chatbots and virtual assistants can have a wide range of replies in their database and a better understanding of facts as machine learning continues to advance.

Figure 2. Examples of machine learning in customer experience

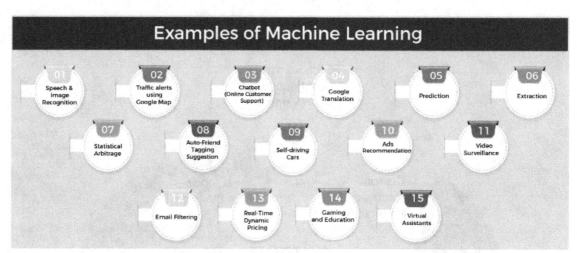

Table 1. Evolution of machine learning

Year	ML Usage in Business
2010	5%
2011	7%
2012	10%
2013	12%
2014	15%
2015	20%
2016	25%
2017	50%
2018	65%

Customers are only as happy as their interactions with the companies they do business with. Organizations must adapt to technology advancements; it is not a choice. a must to stay up with trends, update systems, and catch up to the customer base that is technologically educated. Although customer engagement and communication mediums have changed, the fundamental factor that determines whether a client is satisfied with the way their complaint was handled by customer service is emotional and empathetic communication. While allowing businesses to contact more people and penetrate the consumer market more deeply, AI has also given consumers more options, accessibility, convenience, and tailored service. As consumers and businesses transition to a technologically advanced era; an emotional intelligence and empathy communication experience. While marketers say that it is difficult to replicate personal human interaction with customers while using digital technologies, consumers feel that organizations are struggling in trying to create such experiences (Kevin, 2017).

Figure 3. Prediction of future with the usage of artificial intelligence in customer experience

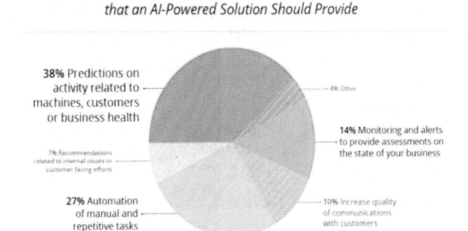

The Most Important Benefit
that an AI-Powered Solution Should Provide

38% Predictions on activity related to machines, customers or business health

4% Other

7% Recommendations related to internal issues or customer facing efforts

14% Monitoring and alerts to provide assessments on the state of your business

27% Automation of manual and repetitive tasks

10% Increase quality of communications with customers

Outlook on Artificial Intelligence in the Enterprise 2016 *Presented by Narrative Science in partnership with National Business Research Institute*

Rationale for the Study

Attaran and Deb (2018) state that Fraud detection is another area where machine learning is being absorbed. Fraud detection is being used increasingly often. Fraud is no longer committed by individuals; rather, it is now committed by automated systems, such as a bot that purchases all of the event tickets so that scalpers may resell them. By creating a bot that reacts to debates automatically, criminals may quickly enter social media. Real-time bot detection and blocking is far more difficult. However, ML makes it feasible.

In his research article, Thomas Davenport (2020) offered a framework for understanding AI's impact, particularly on how it affects marketing tactics and consumer behaviour. In his opinion, AI will be more effective if it supplements human managers rather than replacing them in the near and medium term.

Neha Soni (2019) explains how AI is affecting business, covering everything from innovation to future changes in business structures. She outlines the two key elements that have made AI the foundational technology for excessive automation. She also discusses the idea of "AI Divide" and "The Dark Side of AI."

Cline et al. (2017) declare that in order to predict future quantitative results, predictive customer service analytics uses information from previous customer service interactions. Quantifiable statistics are needed in order to continually enhance customer service. Therefore, machine learning tools enhance support metrics with a predictive component. Businesses who offer customer service and want to deliver better experiences could gain a lot from having these insights. Additionally, machine learning is used to fuel consumer recommendation engines, which enhance the client experience and provide customised experiences. For instance, Amazon and Walmart employ recommendation algorithms to personalise and expedite the purchasing process.

Figure 4. Sub-branches of machine learning

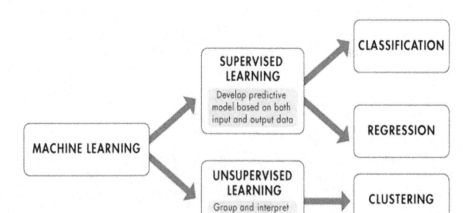

Materials and Methods

In order to get accurate results, the descriptive research methodology was adopted in this study. The current study gives a thorough overview of how machine learning affects the consumer experience. To produce a meaningful knowledge of the pertinent work on customer experience, with supporting evidences, the relevant study was located, classified, summarised, evaluated, and synthesised in accordance with the established principles. It is feasible to study trends in the use of related topics thanks to the amount of data on the Internet.

Many sectors require machine learning systems that can prove they can satisfy customer expectations (Dhaoui et al., 2017). Machine learning is essential for keeping an eye on the business environment, identifying customer demands, and putting the right solutions in place. The gap between client needs and the availability of efficient or high-quality services is thus filled. The business climate changes significantly as a result of ML's opening up of new prospects. For instance, it results in big data trends and improved product design to suit customers' wants and preferences. E-commerce has profited the most from the expanding application of machine learning to enhance the effectiveness and quality of services. ML helps to lessen problems that might develop as a result of errors made by humans (Doshi et al.,). Therefore, machine learning is a key aspect in the development and success of e-commerce. Internet marketing, With ML systems, e-commerce can handle electronic payments and take control of the logistics involved in sending goods to customers.

Companies have realised that it might be challenging to match clients constantly shifting expectations. As a result, companies are coming up with plans to maintain their competitiveness by offering more than simply what clients desire. More clients will be drawn to a business that looks to be easing the discomfort involved in buying procedures. Based on data about the market and the rivals, this kind of business employs machine learning to develop a model that increases efficiency. Furthermore, the use of ML guarantees that the information provided is accurate and customised in order to interact with the target audience in the most efficient manner. As a consequence, ML will increase the offer's relevance, boosting customer interest and engagement.

E-commerce has changed how businesses communicate with their customers and business partners. The information and communication technology (ICT) sector has advanced at a rate that has caused the global e-commerce market to grow at an unheard-of rate. Studies predict that worldwide e-commerce revenues will hit $4.2 trillion in 2020 and $6.5 trillion in 2023. Businesses now have access to a vast amount of data on these transactions because to the rise in the number of transactions taking place on e-commerce platforms. Utilizing this data will enhance user experience and customer satisfaction. Big Data Analytics (BDA), Data Mining, Machine Learning (ML), and Artificial Intelligence (AI) are the techniques being utilised to extract information from the data that may be used to improve the User Experience through suggestions, dynamic pricing, search results that are optimised, etc.

Self-driving automobiles are one of ML's most useful uses. The development of self-driving automobiles, like those being produced by Tesla, depends heavily on machine learning. Hardware maker NVIDIA now has the most advanced artificial intelligence on the market, and it is built on an unsupervised learning algorithm. The model uses deep learning and collects information from each of its drivers and vehicles. It uses Internet of Things sensors that are both internal and external. Organizations may now carry out tasks on a scale and in a way that was previously unthinkable thanks to machine learning (Lemley et al., 2017). In addition, data is essential to the operation of any organisation. Decisions based on data are increasingly determining whether a business stays competitive or slips further behind. Machine learning

Table 2. Intelligent agent: Functions, characteristics, and models

Functions	Characteristics	Models
Reasoning functions search for the best rational action in response to a state. An agent maintains a belief state that represents which states of the world are currently possible. From the belief state and a transition model, the agent can predict how the world might evolve in the next time step. Observables and a sensing function allow the agent to update the belief state.	• Deterministic - belief states are determined by logical formulas. • Probabilistic - belief states are quantified as likely or unlikely	Boolean logic; Temporal models such as hidden Markov models, Kalman filters and dynamic Bayesian networks (special cases are hidden Markov models and Kalman filters); Multiple object tracking by nearest-neighbour filter and Hungarian algorithm.
Decision-making: the maximization of expected utility in episodic or sequential decision problems.	• Logical agent cannot deal with uncertainty and conflicting goals; • Goal-based agent deals with binary distinction between good (goal) and bad (non-goal) states • Decision-theoretic (utility and probabilistic theory) agent can make decisions based on what it believes and what it wants with continuous measure of outcome quality	Decision networks, decision-theoretic expert system, multiple agents (game theory), Markov decision process, dynamic Bayesian network.
Optimization (planning) is devising a plan of action to achieve goal. Optimization finds the best hypothesis within action space.	• Search-based problem-solving, Logical agent; • Constrained optimization • Constrained optimization	Hill climbing and simulated annealing for local search, convex optimization and linear programming for continuous spaces, backward (regression) and forward (progression) state-space search, graphs
Learning function is acquiring knowledge based on the observed states after applying the action. Learning improves reasoning by enriching the knowledge or experience used in reasoning function.	• Supervised learning with labelled data • Unsupervised learning with unlabelled data • Reinforcement learning based on maximizing a cumulative reward with taken actions	Regression, K-nearest neighbour, support vector machine, Bayesian network; Clustering, principal component analysis; Markov decision process, Q-learning, game theory.

has the ability to reveal the value of consumer and corporate data and provide businesses the tools they need to make decisions that will keep them competitive (Marr, 2019).

Results and Discussion

The results of the studies illustrate critical facets of the idea of machine learning use in the customer experience. In order to provide a thorough understanding of the role of machine learning in meeting consumer requirements in the business sector, this research has sought to provide a critical summary of the key ideas of applying machine learning to improve client services and gadgets. As a result of the study, it has been discovered that machine learning has achieved great success in a number of scientific fields, including computer vision, computer graphics, natural language processing, speech recognition, decision-making, and intelligent control. It is true that people make decisions, not robots, but ML provides trustworthy data and knowledge that facilitates this process.

Figure 5. Benefits of AI in customer service

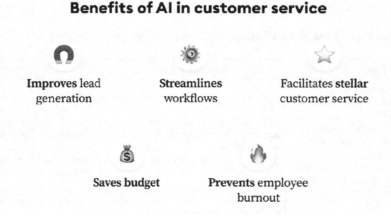

Benefits of AI in customer service

Improves lead generation

Streamlines workflows

Facilitates stellar customer service

Saves budget

Prevents employee burnout

Limitations of the Study

Even though the results were satisfying, several limitations were encountered throughout the study. First and foremost, there has been less research done in this area because of the small number of articles and research papers available for this study.

Machine learning's lack of repeatability is a complicated and expanding problem made worse by a lack of open source code and model testing procedures. New models are created in research laboratories and promptly implemented in practical applications. However, even if the models are created to incorporate the most recent scientific advancements, they could not function in actual situations.

The knowledge gap of the customer service executive is a significant barrier to providing excellent customer service. This results in partial problem resolution and erroneous problem identification. As one might assume, one executive cannot be familiar with all of a company's systems and procedures. Customers are unhappy because customer support representatives lack knowledge.

Nowadays, it's getting harder and harder to tell reality from fiction in machine learning. You must assess the issues you hope to resolve before choosing which AI platform to employ. The tasks that are carried out manually every day and have a fixed output are the simplest to automate. Prior to automation, complicated procedures need more examination. While machine learning may undoubtedly aid in the automation of some processes, not all automation issues require it.

Machine learning and deep analytics are still relatively young fields of study. As a result, there aren't enough qualified workers to manage and provide analytical information for machine learning. Expertise in a particular field and in-depth understanding of science, technology, and mathematics are frequently required for data scientists. Paying high compensation when hiring will be necessary since these workers are frequently in demand and are aware of their value. Additionally, as many managed service providers have a list of qualified data scientists available at all times, you may ask them for assistance with staffing.

RECOMMENDATIONS

We recommend the following for the thorough development and promotion of new technologies for artificial intelligence and machine learning customer experience based on the study mentioned above:

significantly raise the bar for customer service provided by artificial intelligence. The foundation of the consumer resistance is the fact that the quality of the artificial intelligence customer service is currently inferior to the traditional real-human customer service, even though customers do not yet feel negative toward the artificial intelligence customer service itself. Therefore, a complete update of relevant technology and an improvement in service quality are a necessary need and direction for the sector.

Use machine learning to gradually and methodically replace conventional real-human customer support. Customer service has changed as a result of the development and marketing of artificial intelligence.

Due to advancements in technology, several companies have decided to adopt machine learning customer service in place of their conventional real-human customer care. The retailer could have acted too quickly in this process and switched from the initial real-human customer care to machine learning customer service. However, it is challenging for customers to satisfy their demands because of the current subpar quality of artificial intelligence and machine learning customer service and the absence of conventional real-human customer care as a support. First, let machine learning and artificial intelligence serve as a crucial complement to traditional real-human customer service. Next, gradually integrate traditional real-human customer service into artificial intelligence customer service. Finally, traditional real-human customer service will be entirely replaced by machine learning and artificial intelligence customer service. Only a small portion of real-human service can currently be replaced by machine learning.

We must improve the marketing of commercial applications of machine learning customer experience if we want to promote machine learning customer service generally. Artificial intelligence is not only a cutting-edge technology in the twenty-first century, but it is also unavoidably where technology will go in the future. The public's cooperation is essential to the industry's progress. Customers cooperation and understanding are also necessary for the growth of machine learning customer service. The public will be better able to grasp how machine learning is used in customer service and will be less resistant to the use of artificial intelligence in the customer experience thanks to the growth and inevitable trend of popular science artificial intelligence.

CONCLUSION

In summary, we can conclude the following main study conclusions:

Artificial intelligence and machine learning customer service is being utilised extensively in the sector and is well-liked by the general public. More than 92.3% of customers have interacted with artificial intelligence customer care. At present, consumers generally accept artificial intelligence customer service because of its 24-hour service capabilities, more neutral and objective positions, and the future development trends that it represents (Xin & Den, n.d.).

It has been observed that machine learning is a key factor in the growth and success of e-commerce. Network marketing, electronic payments, and management of the logistics involved in product delivery to clients are all made possible by ML systems in e-commerce. Additionally, machine learning analyses consumer data in order to forecast behavioural trends and patterns. For instance, machine learning algorithms may be able to determine when a consumer needs assistance when making a purchase on an eCommerce website, guaranteeing that they can successfully complete the transaction. It thus increases consumer happiness and sales.

From improving overall security to giving highly customised advice, machine learning is a crucial tool for delivering improved customer services at all levels. Business owners all across the world use machine learning to market their goods and services more successfully, handle customer questions more swiftly, and find potential leads.

REFERENCES

Attaran, M., & Deb, P. (2018). Machine learning: The new 'big thing' for competitive advantage. *International Journal of Knowledge Engineering and Data Mining.*, *5*(4), 277–305. doi:10.1504/IJKEDM.2018.095523

Cline, B., Niculescu, R. S., Huffman, D., & Deckel, B. (2017). Predictive maintenance applications for machine learning. In *2017 annual reliability and maintainability symposium (RAMS)* (pp. 1-7). IEEE. 10.1109/RAM.2017.7889679

Davenport, T., Guha, A., Grewal, D., & Bressgott, T. (2020). How artificial intelligence will change the future of marketing. *Journal of the Academy of Marketing Science, 48*(1), 24-42.

Dhaoui, C., Webster, C. M., & Tan, L. P. (2017, September 11). Social media sentiment analysis: Lexicon versus machine learning. *Journal of Consumer Marketing*, *34*(6), 480–488. doi:10.1108/JCM-03-2017-2141

Doshi, R., Apthorpe, N., & Feamster, N. (2018). Machine learning ddos detection for consumer internet of things devices. In *2018 IEEE Security and Privacy Workshops (SPW)* (pp. 29-35). IEEE.

Jordan, M. I., & Mitchell, T. M. (2015). Machine learning: Trends, perspectives, and prospects. *Sci (NY)*, *349*(6245), 255–260. doi:10.1126cience.aaa8415 PMID:26185243

Kevin, L. (2017). *Mark Cuban Says This Is Where the World's First Trillionaires Will Emerge.* https://fortune.com/2017/03/14/mark-cuban-sxsw-first-trillionaire-ai/

Lemley, J., Bazrafkan, S., & Corcoran, P. (2017, March 15). Deep Learning for Consumer Devices and Services: Pushing the limits for machine learning, artificial intelligence, and computer vision. *IEEE Consumer Electronics Magazine.*, 6(2), 48–56. doi:10.1109/MCE.2016.2640698

Marr, B. (2019). *Artificial intelligence in practice: How 50 successful companies used AI and machine learning to solve problems.* John Wiley & Sons.

Rajkhowa, B. (n.d.). *Impact of Artificial Intelligence on Customer Experience.* Retrieved from: https://www.ijrte.org/wp-content/uploads/papers/v9i2/B3727079220.pdf

Soni, N., Sharma, E. K., Singh, N., & Kapoor, A. (2019). Impact of Artificial Intelligence on Businesses: From Research, Innovation, Market Deployment to Future Shifts in Business Models. *Journal of Business Research.*

Vangie, B. (n.d.). What is customer experience. *Webopedia.* https://www.webopedia.com/TERM/C/customer_experience.html

Xin, H., & Den, Z. (n.d.). *Research on Artificial Intelligence Customer Service on Consumer Attitude and Its Impact during Online Shopping.* Academic Press.

Chapter 6
Mall Customer Segmentation Engine Through Clustering Analysis

Meenu Vijarania
K.R. Mangalam University, India

Nitin Kumar
K.R. Mangalam University, India

Rohit Kumar
K.R. Mangalam University, India

Swati Gupta
K.R. Mangalam University, India

ABSTRACT

Finding related information within a cluster is done using a technique called clustering. The dataset cluster uses the data's maximum and minimum values to group together similar data. Clustering is a process in which matter has been split into groups and grouped based on a rule to maximize within-group similarity and minimize between-group difference likeness. In this chapter, the authors examine and contrast the various group analysis techniques and algorithms employed by Rapid Miner. Multiple clustering methods have been developed. In the chapter, two types of clustering for algorithms are analyzed. One area of mall patrons was evaluated. The data set is used with Rapid Miner tools to determine the proper cluster.

INTRODUCTION

It is necessary to have great shopping experiences to reach customer satisfaction because shopping is a part of consumers' lives and is changing all the time. The statistics used to analyze customer behavior are older. The logical and emotional context was studied in 1950. Multiple studies in shopping clas-

DOI: 10.4018/978-1-6684-7105-0.ch006

sification are put out, shaping a variety of inputs into various forms, shopping motivation, specifically, and utilitarianism. Variations rely on the features that the articles represent. The items are grouped or collected according to a set of rules that amplifies intra-class closeness and reduces proximity between classes. The organization of information is originally divided into groups based on information comparability (e.g., using clusters), and a lot denotes the typically small number of groups. There are many integrated techniques offered, including classification, regression, population, girds, based, advanced data, and fundamental integration. Integration includes segmenting larger data sets and grouping them appropriately. These are clustering algorithms as well. In this study, we only discuss two approaches that use related objects as their bases for measuring the distances between them. The process of clustering entails analyzing a subset, selecting a feature to cluster, and choosing, and pre-processing it for use with another method. The three main attribute ideas for the object are to be pointed tree dimension spaces using a room and representation clustering, so the object's points are moved to a two-dimensional space (like a room) and representation clustering is typically made to be less hard. Incremental clustering and irresponsibility about the record request, highest dimensional, accountable, clustered under limitations, and simplicity.

Figure 1. Clustering algorithms

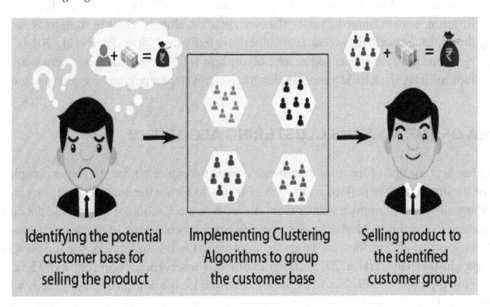

LITERATURE SURVEY

Data Mining classification is primarily used as a supervised learning process, with a small amount of unsupervised learning (some bunch models area unit for both). Large data sets are sorted through data mining to find patterns and relationships that may be used in data analysis to assist solve business challenges. Businesses can foresee future trends and make more educated business decisions thanks to data mining techniques and tools. Bunch's objective is descriptive, while the classification's objective is prophetic. The new teams are a unit of interest in themselves, and their evaluation is essential, as the aim of the bunch is to discover a completely new set of classes. However, since the teams must replicate a reference set of categories, a significant portion of the assessment in classification tasks occurs outside of the teams. The expanding body of scholarship analyses often occurring economic data. The most crucial task is the one that needs to be focused on to finish in the allotted time. (Clustering of Information) Given a data structure D (information lattice D), divide its columns (records) into sets C1–Ck so that the lines (records) in each group are "comparable." We purposely used a loose description here because bunching allows for a variety of similarities; some are not clearly stated in closed structures for comparison work. In the aspects of advancement issues that speak to group participation of information focuses, which can be often characterized as a bunching issue, the target study builds a sound scientific quantification of intergroup likeness as far as these factors. According to Ijaz (2021), customers are segmented by decision-makers using a variety of factors. Age, gender, family, education level, and income are the most basic and widely used demographic segmentation factors. The other main factors that are employed for segmentation include socio-cultural, geographic, psychographic, and behavioral variables. Vivek (2018) provided a quick summary of the numerous clustering algorithms categorized under dividing, hierarchical, density, grid-based, and model-based algorithms while also taking into account Big Data features including size, noise, dimensionality, algorithm calculations, and cluster structure. Investigated the need for client segmentation utilizing clustering methods as the primary CRM feature. The benefits and drawbacks of the two most popular clustering methods, hierarchical K-Means, and hierarchical clustering were examined. Finally, the concept of developing a hybrid strategy is addressed by combining the two tactics with the potential to outperform individual ideas (Patel et al., 2014). To cluster steel industry clients, fuzzy c-means and genetic algorithms were combined. Customers were separated into two groups utilizing the LRFM variables (length, recency, frequency, and monetary value) method.

THE IDEA OF THE K-MEANS CLUSTERING ALGORITHM

Clustering has become one of the most common methods for exploring data to gain a complete understanding of its structure. It is defined as the job of trying to locate the subtitles and subgroups in the data set. Many subgroups comprise similar data. A cluster is a collection of aggregated data points that communicate some qualities. Market basket analysis employs clustering to segment customers based on their behaviors and transactions. Based on the information in the data describing the objects or their relationships, cluster analysis (Hsu, 2015) classifies objects (observations, occurrences). The intention is for the things in a group to be distinct from (or unconnected to) the objects in other groups while being similar (or related) to one another. The "better" or more distinct the clustering, the greater the similarity (or homogeneity) inside a group and the larger the difference across groups. In many applications, clusters are not effectively separated from one another and the notion of what makes up a cluster is not clear. However, most cluster analyses aim to classify the data into non-overlapping groups, therefore. To better understand Figures 1a through 1b, which show fifteen points and three distinct ways they can be grouped into clusters, illustrate the difficulties in defining what exactly qualifies as a cluster. The most logical interpretation of the structure of these points, if clusters may be nested, is that there are two clusters, each one of which has three subclusters of both. Though the two larger clusters' division into three smaller ones may be just a quirk of the human visual system. Finally, it might not be absurd to assert the points from four groups. As a result, we want to emphasize once more that there is no clear definition of what a cluster is, and that the best description will vary depending on the type of data and the desired outcomes. The basic idea behind clustering is to classify each data point into a specific group. Data points that are of the same group should exhibit similar features, while data points of different groups exhibit dissimilar properties and features.

K-means is an entire clustering algorithm, every unit is accurately assigned to one cluster set of the k-mean. K-means needs to stand for Clustering is the most popular and simplest Machine Learning algorithm, and it utilizes an iterative approach to dividing up the dataset into different "k" numbers of predefined and non-overlapping subgroups, for each data point belonging to only one subgroup based on their comparable qualities. The process will begin to choose how many clusters we want from our dataset for different clustering algorithms. So, we'll refer to the value of k as. These k values are supposed smallest integers like as many as 2, 3, or 4, but they can be big. Therefore, we go back and decide which values of k will be chosen from the available possibilities.

Figure 2. K-means clustering process

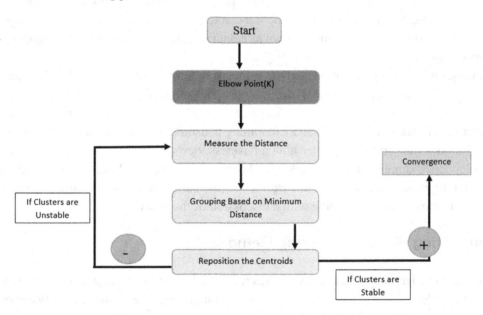

Challenges of Performing Analysis

Customer segmentation analysis has several obvious advantages, which are obvious. Retailers who have a better awareness of their customer base may deploy resources more effectively to gather and analyze pertinent data to increase revenues.

For many merchants, getting to the stage of performing high-level consumer segmentation analysis is more challenging than first assumed. Many merchants might have the legal right to the data needed to undertake the study, but they lack the tools to access it easily or staff members who are qualified to utilize-analyze it. The largest barrier to smaller companies performing such research is likely a lack of qualified employees or technology to handle the required volume of data. This sort of research has become more accessible because to the rise of open-source computer languages like R and Python, but it still requires merchants to have a programmer on their team who is proficient in one of those languages.

Furthermore, some shops are merely ignorant of the scope of their data collecting or are not yet motivated to explore it. Nonetheless, statisticians who have not completely embraced consumer segmentation analysis probably do so out of a lack of financial means. They may not have the time, resources, or manpower to carry out the study. The purpose of this work is to demonstrate how easily and effectively this extensive analysis may be carried out. Retailers do not use consumer segmentation analysis for another, more subtle, but no less important, reason: it is too difficult to comprehend. High-level consumer segmentation analysis demands significantly more accurate knowledge of machine learning and the mathematics that characterize how the algorithms function than conventional demographic segmentation or RFM analysis. Moreover, programmers and data analysts are not well-suited to do marketing responsibilities, and conventional marketing analysts lack the arithmetic and programming abilities required to integrate customer segmentation research using machine learning approaches.

This creates a further problem because it turns a typical marketing task—segmenting customers based on their purchasing patterns—into a pure programming task. As a result, the marketing team lacks the necessary skills to code the task themselves, and the programming team lacks the marketing expertise to interpret the results. As a result, a hybrid function that requires expertise in marketing, programming, and business is required. This position is known as a data scientist or information specialist in contemporary workplaces.

In summary, customer segmentation analysis is the act of attempting to comprehend a client base by segmenting it. Even though conventional analysts have had some success with RFM or demographic analysis, these models simply lack the technology capacity to offer deep insight into more precise information about the clients. On the other hand, combining consumer segmentation research with machine learning techniques may completely alter how a business views their data. As a result, merchants are looking for low-cost, simple solutions to adopt and convey the usage of clustering to segment their client base. After a thorough introduction to customer segmentation analysis, it is time to examine a few clustering techniques before concluding with a discussion of the study.

Clustering Using Machine Learning Methods

While many machine learning applications, such as regression and classification, concentrate on predicting the result or value of an instance, they do not try to comprehend the similarities between examples; rather, they only look at the relationship between instances and their respective outputs. So, the focus must shift from supervised machine learning to unsupervised machine learning when looking for algorithms or approaches that compare features of instances.

Whether or not the instances used to train the model in the training data have their goal value determines whether a method belongs to supervised or unsupervised machine learning. In every instance of supervised machine learning training, instances are coupled with a goal value, which, depending on the situation, may be either a scalar or a vector. Unsupervised machine learning, on the other hand, works with input that isn't matched with a goal value. It can be beneficial to look at these differences through an example to order to explain them clearly, as well as some commonalities.

Consider a retailer with a store that has been operating for more than a year and is interested in looking at their data to better understand their consumers and forecast how much they will spend on their next visit. The owner uses their prior purchases to forecast the worth of their next ticket by making an educated prediction based on those prior purchases. This is an example of supervised machine learning since it incorporates prediction as well as the results of prior data and their outcomes (the tickets themselves). To be more precise, this kind of technique is known as regression since the owner is probably attempting to forecast the monetary amount the buyer will spend.

The owner, on the other hand, chooses to examine some customer data that has been gathered to determine if there are any larger patterns or similarities amongst the consumers in to order to better understand them. This is an example of unsupervised machine learning since the data and method have no obvious target value or conclusion. This is a better illustration of clustering.

In machine learning words, clustering is an unsupervised technique that divides instances into groups based on their similarities. Simply said, clustering is a method of visualizing or analysing data by focusing on the natural groups or segments that distinguish data instances.

Similarity Measures

A clustering algorithm's success depends on its capacity to select the appropriate similarity measure before grouping. Yet, selecting the optimum similarity measure necessitates a thorough understanding of what similarity is and how it may be quantitatively defined.

In data science, similarity is mostly a function of distance; the closer two instances' values are to one another, the more similar they will be.

Determining the distance between two instances is easier to define in certain situations than others. The clustering technique would account for the variations between the instances and group them based on those if a data scientist were to cluster instances based purely on one numerical attribute (Tikmani et al., 2015).

The distance between features is a little difficult if the data scientist takes into account two features. Instead of focusing just on the variations between the cases. Considering the distance in Euclid between examples x and y:

$$\text{distance}(x, y) = \sqrt{(x_1 - y_1)^2 + (x_2 - y_2)^2} \tag{1}$$

The Pythagorean Theorem and the notion that a straight line always connects any two locations in Euclidean geometry serve as the foundation for this formula. Using the method above, the length of the single direction in this situation is determined. Yet now is a good moment to pause and assess certain perceptions and drivers of what is happening.

It was first required to identify the link between similarity and distance to order to figure out how to compare how similar two instances are. The reasonable relationship to construct in most situations is an inverted relationship, which is what is done in this study.

Determining the distance between two instances is the next need. The basic Euclidean Distance Formula is the obvious distance measure to employ with numerical data, such as the data in this project or the instances before it. The fact that are interested in grouping numerical data makes this the most obvious way to estimate distance. The straightforward numerical concept offered here begins to deviate from conceptions of similarity in other situations, such as Natural Language Processing.

Yet, the crucial issue is that determining similarity between two instances requires at least two considerations:

As previously mentioned, this project uses the Euclidean Distance to specify the separation between two instances. The two examples above discuss distance on a one- or two-dimensional level, but the data for this project comprises considerably more than two aspects, necessitating an expansion of the intuition that underpinned lower-dimensional thinking to higher dimensions.

It turns out that the distance formula takes on a more uniform appearance when expanded into n features:

$$\text{distance}\left(x, y\right) = \sqrt{\sum_{i=0}^{n}(x_i - y_i)^2} \tag{2}$$

$$\text{distance}\left(x, y\right) = \sum_{i=0}^{n}(x_i - y_i)^2 \tag{3}$$

The distance formula may be used to describe clustering in academic texts or publications without the square root indication.

When it comes to minimizing the distance, finding the minimum of a squared distance or the square root of some squared distance provides the same minimum. This is a technique for conserving processing power in the actual clustering procedure.

Once similarity has been discussed, it is reasonable to start looking at two alternative clustering procedures. Both were utilized in the context of this project, making it essential to contrast the two methods in this study since doing so offers a broader understanding of how various forms of clustering might be applied in various scenarios.

Application

A common unsupervised learning approach used in machine learning is K-means clustering, which divides a dataset into groups depending on how similar the data points are to one another. With its ease of use and effectiveness, the technique is one of the most used clustering algorithms in a variety of applications. Here are some common applications of K-means clustering in machine learning:

Customer Segmentation: Customers can be divided into groups based on their buying habits, demographics, or other factors using K-means clustering. This might assist organizations in focusing their marketing efforts on particular client segments.

Image Segmentation: Using K-means clustering, photos may be divided into sections based on their colour, texture, or other attributes. Applications involving image processing and computer vision can benefit from this.

Anomaly Detection: When a dataset contains anomalies or outliers that do not fit into any of the clusters, K-means clustering can be utilised to find them. This can be helpful in spotting fraud, locating faulty goods, or seeing data problems.

Text Clustering: Text documents can be grouped using K-means clustering depending on how similar their contents are. Applications for document categorization, topic modeling, and information retrieval can all benefit from this.

Recommender Systems: Based on a user's past behavior or interests, K-means clustering can be used to suggest goods or services to them.

Natural Language Processing: K-means clustering allows for topic modeling and sentiment analysis by grouping documents or text data according to their content.

Document Clustering: Based on their content, related papers can be grouped using K-means clustering. Information retrieval and document organization may both benefit from this.

Bioinformatics: Bioinformatics can utilize K-means clustering to group genes or proteins according to their expression patterns or other characteristics. This can be used to find illness biomarkers or forecast medication effectiveness.

K-means clustering is a flexible technique that has a wide range of uses in machine learning and other fields.

Difference Between K-Means and X-Means

A dataset may be divided into groups of related observations using the clustering algorithms K-means and X-means. The method K-means and X-means choose the ideal number of clusters in a dataset is their primary distinction from one another.

K-means is a centroid-based clustering technique that needs the user to predetermine the K-cluster count. After initializing K cluster centroids, the method iteratively assigns each observation to the closest centroid, changes the centroid position depending on the mean of the assigned observations, and then finishes. Until the centroid positions no longer fluctuate considerably or the maximum number of iterations has been achieved, this procedure continues.

The number of clusters in a dataset is automatically determined by X-means, an extension of K-means. In order to achieve a certain goal, such as a minimum reduction in within-cluster variance or a maximum number of clusters, X-means repeatedly divides clusters into subclusters. The algorithm compares the goodness of fit of the K-means clustering algorithm with K clusters to the K+1 clusters iteratively starting with the K=1 cluster. The method divides the cluster into two subclusters and continues the process for each subcluster if the inclusion of an additional cluster significantly lowers the within-cluster variance.

In conclusion, X-means is a more sophisticated and adaptable algorithm that can automatically determine the ideal number of clusters and handle clusters of different shapes and sizes, whereas K-means is a simpler and faster algorithm that requires the user to specify the number of clusters in advance.

In conclusion, X-means automatically identifies the ideal number of clusters by repeatedly dividing clusters into subclusters, in contrast to K-means, which needs the user to choose the number of clusters in advance.

Advantages

A common unsupervised learning approach used in machine learning, K-means clustering divides a dataset into k groups depending on how similar the data points are to one another. The ease and effectiveness with which K-means clustering can cluster huge datasets are one of its key benefits. The following are some benefits of K-means clustering:

Simplicity: K-means is a popular method for novices in machine learning since it is straightforward and simple to comprehend.

Scalability: K-means clustering is an efficient technique that handles big datasets with ease. The time complexity of the algorithm scales linearly with the number of data points and clusters. It can therefore handle datasets with millions of data points with ease.

Flexibility: In many different fields, such as image segmentation, natural language processing, and customer segmentation, among others, K-means may be used to cluster data.

Interpretability: K-means clustering is helpful for exploratory data analysis since the findings are simple to understand and show.

Ease of Implementation: K-means clustering is a straightforward and uncomplicated technique with few input parameters. The parameters of the algorithm may be adjusted to get the desired results and are simple to comprehend.

Fast Convergence: K-means clustering is a rapid technique that gets to the endpoint quickly. Because of this, it is appropriate for real-time applications where speedy results are required.

Robustness: The robust method K-means assigns points to the closest cluster centroid in order to manage noisy and missing data.

Handles Noisy Data: K-means clustering can manage outliers and missing values in the data and is resistant to noise.

Efficiency: K-means is computationally effective and can converge on a solution quite rapidly.

K-means is a helpful and adaptable clustering technique that may be used to solve a range of machine-learning issues.

Disadvantages

A common unsupervised learning approach called K-means clustering seeks to divide a given dataset into K groups depending on how similar the data points are to one another. It does, however, have a unique set of restrictions and downsides, just like every other algorithm. The following are some of the primary drawbacks of k-means clustering:

Sensitivity to Initial Conditions: The initial random distribution of centroids has an impact on the K-means algorithm's performance and can provide various results. As a result, it is less trustworthy than certain other clustering techniques.

Sensitivity to Outliers: Data outliers can have an impact on the clustering results since K-means clustering is sensitive to them. Inaccurate clustering might result from outliers skewing the centroids' positions.

Dependency on Initial Centroids: The initial placements of the centroids have a significant impact on the quality of the clustering results. Poor clustering outcomes may stem from careless initial position selection.

Limited to Euclidean Distance: The Euclidean distance metric is the only one available for K-means clustering, which may not be suitable for all sorts of data. For instance, Euclidean distance may not make sense and result in inaccurate clustering if the data contains categorical characteristics.

Assumes Spherical Clusters: K-means clustering makes the spherical and equal variance assumptions, which could not hold true for all datasets.

Difficulty in Choosing the Optimal K: There is no certain way to establish the ideal value of K (the number of clusters), hence choosing the optimal value might be difficult. Finding the best K, which might vary depending on the value of K, takes both testing and domain expertise.

Does Not Work Well With Non-Linear Data: K-means clustering is a linear technique, therefore non-linear data does not respond well to it. K-means clustering might not be able to capture complicated non-linear relationships in the data, leading to erroneous clustering results.

Determination of the Number of Clusters: Finding the ideal number of clusters can be difficult since the number of clusters in a dataset is not always known in advance. Inappropriate K selection might produce unsatisfactory clustering results.

Not Suitable for Non-Spherical Data: K-means clustering works best with well-separated data and clusters that are nearly the same size and presupposes that the clusters are spherical. It is not suitable for data with varied densities or unusual shapes.

Outliers Can Impact Clustering Results: Outliers in the dataset might have a detrimental effect on the clustering outcomes since the algorithm may allocate these points to a cluster, which results in less-than-ideal cluster assignments.

Scalability: Due to the high computing cost of the technique and the exponentially increasing runtime with dataset size, K-means clustering does not scale well for big datasets.

Lack of Flexibility: Given that K-means clustering is a rigid technique, datasets with complicated structures or where the clusters are not clearly defined may not be appropriate candidates.

Biased Towards Equal-Sized Clusters: When working with datasets that naturally have an uneven distribution of samples among various clusters, K-means clustering's attempt to produce clusters of equal size might be troublesome.

No Guarantees on Global Optimality: As a local optimization process, K-means clustering cannot be guaranteed to converge to the global optimum. As a result, the algorithm's output might not always be the greatest answer to the situation at hand.

METHODOLOGY

The goal of the vector quantization technique known as "k-means clustering" is to divide n observations into k clusters, with each observation belonging to the cluster that has the closest mean (also known as the cluster centroid or cluster centers). As a result, the data space is divided into Voronoi cells. The

Figure 3. K-means clustering

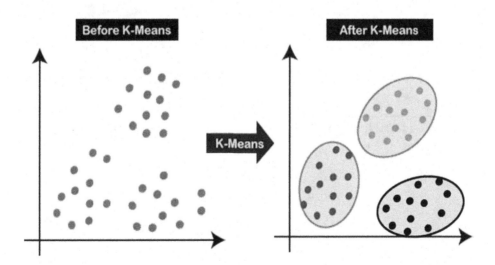

geometric median is the only one that minimizes Euclidean distances; Although regular Euclidean distances would be the more difficult Weber problem, k-means clustering reduces within-cluster variations (squared Euclidean distances). For instance, k-medians and k-medoids can be used to find better Euclidean solutions. Although the problem is computationally challenging (NP-hard), effective heuristic algorithms rapidly reach a local optimum. An iterative refining technique used by these is often analogous to the expectation-maximization procedure for mixtures of Gaussian distributions using both k-means and Gaussian mixture modeling. Both employ cluster centers to represent the data; however, the Gaussian mixture model allows for a variety of cluster shapes, whereas k-means clustering tends to find clusters with similar spatial extent.

It is an iterative technique that splits an unlabeled dataset into k distinct clusters, with each dataset only belonging to one group that shares characteristics with the others. In machine learning or data science, clustering issues are resolved using the unsupervised learning algorithm K-Means Clustering (Potharaju et al., 2017). The unlabeled dataset is divided into various clusters with the help of the unsupervised learning algorithm K-Means Clustering. It allows us to categorize the data into diverse groups and offers a workable technique for quickly and accurately determining the groups in the unlabeled dataset without the need for any training.

Figure 4. Before and after k-means clustering

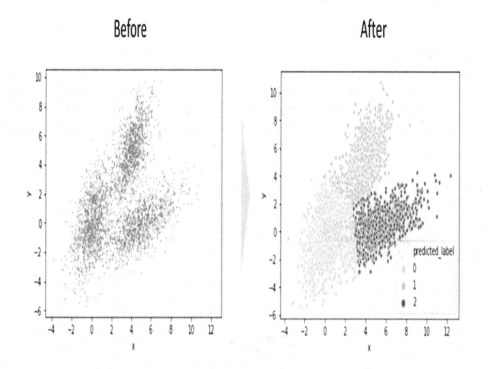

The Working Ideology of the Mall Customer Segmentation Engine

The Outcome of Clustering Analysis Represented Through Visualization Techniques

Depending on the primary data set, the procedures used for the cluster that was affected. Most significant is this comparable function represented by the data set. Imagine that the graph depicts the typical amount of money that a customer will spend while inputting. It is difficult to know something during a slow sequence using genuine measures like the geometer metric. Instead, alternative metrics such as layout variation or structure to similarity must be used. Integration of pedestrian items is crucial in situations requiring extensive understanding.

Figure 5. The cluster that was affected

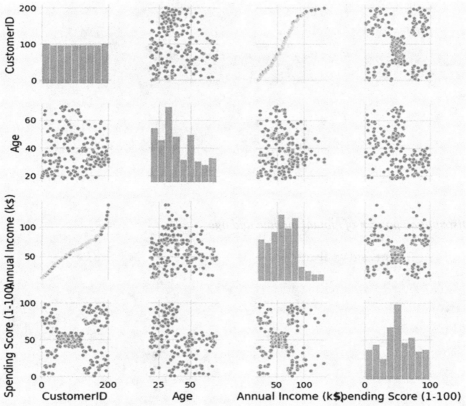

The gender distribution in the mall is depicted in the pie chart above. Interestingly, women hold the majority with a share of 56%, while men have a portion of 44%. This is a significant disparity, especially considering that men outnumber women in terms of population.

In the above Plots, we can see the Distribution Pattern of Annual Income and Age, by looking at the plots, we can infer one thing few people earn more than 100 US Dollars. Most people make between $50 and $75 each week. Additionally, we may say that the lowest income is about $20.

Figure 6. Pie chart shows gender gap

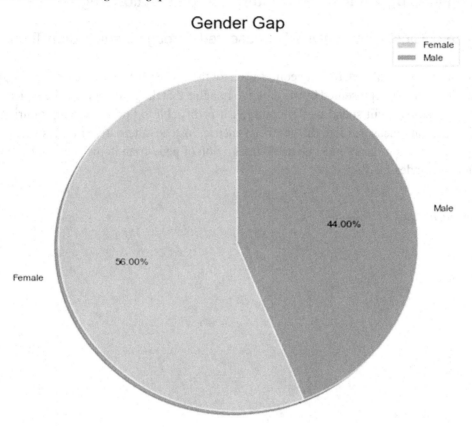

Figure 7. Distribution pattern of annual income and age

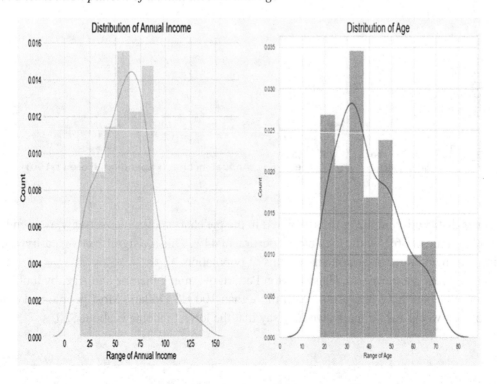

Forming an opinion about the clients.

The mall's most frequent patrons are often between the ages of 30-35. The age group of seniors, however, visits the mall the least frequently. There are fewer young people than middle-aged people.

Figure 8. Distribution of age

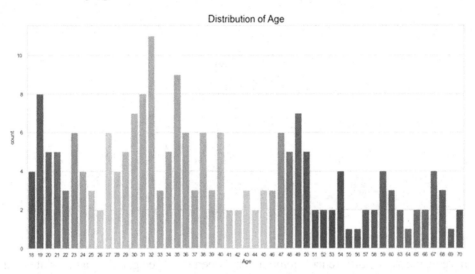

For a greater understanding of the Visitor's Age Group at the Mall, this graph displays a more interactive chart on the distribution of each age group there. Observing the graph above- Although the age range of 27 to 39 is common, there is no discernible pattern; instead, we can only identify group-level patterns, such as the older age groups is less common than the younger ones. Interesting fact: The number of mall visitors between the ages of 18 and 67 is equal. People who are 55, 56, 69, and 64 years old rarely visit malls. Most mall visitors are 32 and older.

Figure 9. Gender and spending score comparison

According to a bivariate analysis of spending scores by gender, most males have spending scores between $25k and $70k, whereas most females have spending scores between $35k and $75k. which once more emphasizes the fact that women lead in shopping.

Figure 10. Representation of gender vs. annual income

To once more visualize the differences in income between the three genders, a bivariate analysis was performed between gender and annual income. Males get paid more frequently than females in general. However, when it comes to having a low annual income, the proportion of men and women is equal.

Figure 11. Distribution of spending score

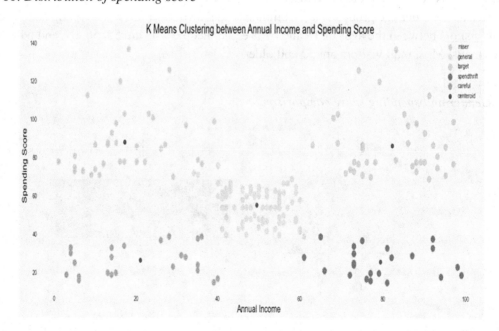

From the standpoint of the mall, this is the Most Important Chart since it is crucial to have a general intuition and understanding of the Spending Score of Visitors to the Mall. 23

On a broad scale, we may say that many customers have spending scores between 35 and 60. It is interesting to see that customers have scores of I am Spending and 99 Spending, demonstrating how the mall serves a wide range of clients with various demands and requirements.

The graph above displays the relationships between the various characteristics of the Mall Customer Segmentation Dataset, this heat map shows the features that are most strongly connected with orange colour and the least strongly correlated with yellow colour.

Figure 12. Spending score vs. annual income

This Clustering Analysis provides us with a clear understanding of the various mall segments. Based on their annual income and spending score, there are five consumer segments: Miser, General, Target, Spendthrift, and Careful. These are the greatest factors/attributes to identify a customer's section in a mall.

I have grouped the consumers into four categories: Usual Customers, Priority Customers, Senior Citizen Target Customers, and Young Target Customers, based on my intuition from the above clustering plot between the age of the customers and their related spending scores. Then, after receiving the data, we can design alternative marketing tactics and policies by them to maximize client spending scores at the mall.

Figure 13. Four distinct categories namely usual customers

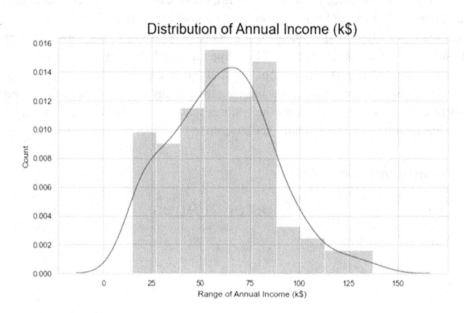

RESULTS AND DISCUSSIONS

Mall Customer data is an interesting dataset that has hypothetical customer data. have information about our clients and must categorize them into diverse groups based on that information.

The data is interesting. Let us look at the data distribution. Now correlate the data.

Figure 14. Most of the annual income falls between 50K to 85K

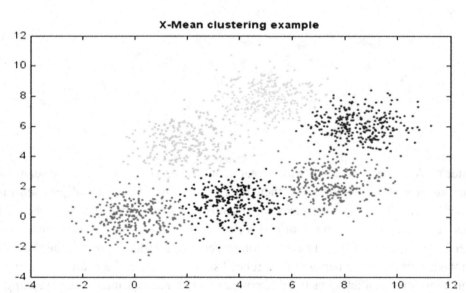

Weakness of K-Means and the Need for X-Means

Data is grouped into several clusters or groups through the process of clustering, to achieve the highest level of similarity between data inside a cluster and the lowest amount of similarity between clusters. For metric data, K-means has long been the workhorse (Ozan 2018).

The K-Means algorithm's flaw in this instance is how to determine the initial cluster Centre point. This is due to the lack of a method utilized to choose and establish the cluster Centre point.

K-means is a well-liked clustering technique that is frequently used in data analysis and machine learning. The X-means method is a variation that fixes some of its flaws, although it still has significant shortcomings that restrict its use in specific circumstances.

The sensitivity of K-means to the initial selection of centroids is one of its key drawbacks. K-means can converge to a less-than-ideal solution, which cannot correctly reflect the underlying data structure, depending on where the centroids are first placed. This problem is addressed by the X-means technique, which increases the accuracy of the clustering findings by automatically calculating the initial centroids and the number of clusters.

The assumption that there is an equal amount of variation in each data dimension is another drawback of K-means. When the data contains distinct variances in several dimensions, this assumption may result in subpar clustering results. This problem is addressed by the X-means technique, which permits each cluster to have its own covariance matrix, better capturing the structure of the data.

In conclusion, K-means is a strong clustering technique, but its sensitivity to the beginning conditions and assumption of equal variance may restrict its usefulness in some circumstances. By automatically estimating the number of clusters and accounting for various deviations in each dimension of the data, the X-means method corrects these flaws.

Figure 15. K-means clustering

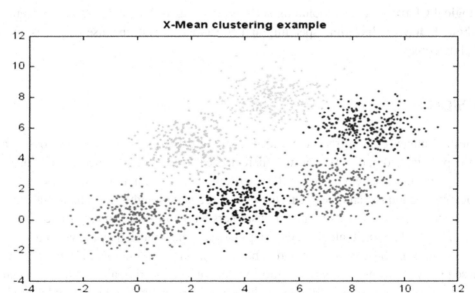

Explanation of X-Means

Following each K-means run, X-means takes over and determines locally which portion of the currently existing centroids should split to get a better fit.

For a given value of k, the X-Means method uses the K-Means algorithm (Improve-params), and cluster splitting (Improve-structure) is used to maximize the value of k following the Information Criterion. Using this strategy, the actual value of K is estimated in an unmonitored way that only depends on the data set. Kmax and Kmin are the upper and lower limits of what X might be. Recognize that X = Xmin denotes the first step of the X-means grouping, which involves finding the initial structure and centroid. The projected structure is divided into two groups, and in the subsequent phase, each cluster in each group is treated as the parent cluster.

The X-Means clustering technique, which is an enhanced version of K-Means, aims to automatically count the number of clusters based on BIC values. The X-Means algorithm comes into play after each K-Means iteration, choosing locally which subset of the existing centroids should divide themselves to match the data more closely. The splitting decision is made by computing the Bayesian Information Criterion (BIC).

Utilizing K Means Clustering, Segmenting Customers

One of the main uses for K means clustering is the segmentation of consumers to gain a deeper understanding of them, which might then be used to boost the company's income. The interest area is separated from the background using the unsupervised K-Means clustering approach. The given data is clustered or divided into K clusters or sections based on the K-centroids.

The following are the most typical ways that businesses divide up their clientele:

Demographic Data: Including gender, age, marital status, family situation, income, and employment.

Geographical Data: Varies depending on the company's scope. If a business is localized, this information may apply to towns or counties. For bigger businesses, it could refer to a customer's home city, state, or even nation.

Psychological Characteristics: Including social status, way of life, and personality features.

Data About Behavior: Including spending and consumption patterns, use of goods and services, and intended outcomes.

CONCLUSION

The study of the findings demonstrates the effectiveness of the K-means method without using a comparison of the principal components. Because there are fewer instances of uncorrected cluster objects, the X-means approach is a better choice for class clustering. As a result, the paper's results are x, which denotes efficient functioning, and the clustering of the tree is thoroughly explained. Various shopping centers are currently making efforts to attract customers who will spend money there. To average out consumer spending and divide it into distinct groups based on how much they are willing to spend when they reach a certain age, the x-means method is best. X- means a step in the direction of a quick inner loop for these pricey algorithms. One of the most widely used clustering algorithms, K means clustering is frequently used by practitioners to begin clustering assignments to gain an understanding of the dataset's structure. Data points are organized using K means into discrete, non-overlapping groupings. One of the main uses for K means clustering is the segmentation of consumers to gain a deeper understanding of them, which might then be used to boost the company's income. The main goals of current CAD model clustering research have been to improve shape representations and assess how well these shape measures can be retrieved using Precision-Recall and E-measures. These measurements presuppose that the data's classification in its ground truth is known from the start. Like how objects in CAD datasets have been clustered using clustering techniques, the efficiency of the clustering has only been evaluated using purity or entropy measurements.

REFERENCES

Adomavicius, G., & Tuzhilin, A. (2010). Context-aware recommender systems. In *Recommender systems handbook* (pp. 217–253). Springer US.

Bramer, M. (2007). *Principles of data mining* (Vol. 180). Springer.

Choudhury, T., Kumar, V., & Nigam, D. (2015). Intelligent classification & clustering of lung & oral cancer through decision tree & genetic algorithm. *International Journal of Advanced Research in Computer Science and Software Engineering*, 5(12), 501–510.

Choudhury, T., Kumar, V., & Nigam, D. (2015). An innovative and automatic lung and oral cancer classification using soft computing techniques. *International Journal of Computer Science & Mobile Computing*, 4(12), 313–323.

Engle, R. F., & Russell, J. R. (1997). Forecasting the frequency of changes in quoted foreign exchange prices with the autoregressive conditional duration model. *Journal of Empirical Finance*, 4(2-3), 187–212. doi:10.1016/S0927-5398(97)00006-6

Ezenkwu, C. P., & Ozuomba, S. (2015). *Application of K-Means Algorithm for Efficient Customer Segmentation: A Strategy for Targeted Customer Services*. Academic Press.

Ezenkwu, C. P., Ozuomba, S., & Kalu, C. (2015). Application of K-Means algorithm for efficient customer segmentation: A strategy for targeted customer services. *International Journal of Advanced Research in Artificial Intelligence*, 4(10), 40–44.

Fayyad, U. M., Reina, C., & Bradley, P. S. (1998, August). Initialization of Iterative Refinement Clustering Algorithms. In KDD (pp. 194-198). Academic Press.

Fraley, C., & Raftery, A. E. (2002). Model-based clustering, discriminant analysis, and density estimation. *Journal of the American Statistical Association*, 97(458), 611–631. doi:10.1198/016214502760047131

Gupta, S., Vijarania, M., & Udbhav, M. (2023). A Machine Learning Approach for Predicting Price of Used Cars and Power Demand Forecasting to Conserve Non-renewable Energy Sources. In *Renewable Energy Optimization, Planning and Control: Proceedings of ICRTE 2022* (pp. 301-310). Singapore: Springer Nature Singapore. 10.1007/978-981-19-8963-6_27

Hsu, D. (2015). Comparison of integrated clustering methods for accurate and stable prediction of building energy consumption data. *Applied Energy, 160*, 153-163.

Ijaz, M. U. (2021). Analysis of Clustering Algorithms for Mall. *International Journal of Wireless Communications and Mobile Computing, 8*(2), 39.

Jain, A. K. (2010). Data clustering: 50 years beyond K-means. *Pattern Recognition Letters, 31*(8), 651–666. doi:10.1016/j.patrec.2009.09.011

Kanungo, T., Mount, D. M., Netanyahu, N. S., Piatko, C. D., Silverman, R., & Wu, A. Y. (2002). An efficient k-means clustering algorithm: Analysis and implementation. *IEEE Transactions on Pattern Analysis and Machine Intelligence, 24*(7), 881–892. doi:10.1109/TPAMI.2002.1017616

Kettani, O., Ramdani, F., & Tadili, B. (2014). An agglomerative clustering method for large data sets. *International Journal of Computers and Applications, 92*(14).

Kushwaha, D. Y., & Prajapati, D. (2008). *Customer segmentation using K-means algorithm.* 8th Semester Student of B. tech in Computer Science and Engineering.

Moore, A. (2001). *K-means and Hierarchical Clustering.* Academic Press.

Ozan, Ş. (2018, September). A case study on customer segmentation by using machine learning methods. In *2018 International Conference on Artificial Intelligence and Data Processing (IDAP)* (pp. 1-6). IEEE. 10.1109/IDAP.2018.8620892

Patel, D., Modi, R., & Sarvakar, K. (2014). A comparative study of clustering data mining: Techniques and research challenges. *International Journal of Latest Technology in Engineering, Management & Applied Sciences, 3*(9), 67–70.

Popat, S. K., & Emmanuel, M. (2014). Review and comparative study of clustering techniques. *International Journal of Computer Science and Information Technologies, 5*(1), 805–812.

Potharaju, S. P., & Sreedevi, M. (2017). A Novel Clustering Based Candidate Feature Selection Framework Using Correlation Coefficient for Improving Classification Performance. *Journal of Engineering Science & Technology Review, 10*(6), 38–43. doi:10.25103/jestr.106.06

Potharaju, S. P., Sreedevi, M., & Amiripalli, S. S. (2019). An ensemble feature selection framework of sonar targets using symmetrical uncertainty and multi-layer perceptron (su-mlp). In *Cognitive Informatics and Soft Computing: Proceeding of CISC 2017* (pp. 247-256). Springer Singapore.

Potharaju, S. P., Sreedevi, M., Ande, V. K., & Tirandasu, R. K. (2019). Data mining approach for accelerating the classification accuracy of cardiotocography. *Clinical Epidemiology and Global Health, 7*(2), 160–164. doi:10.1016/j.cegh.2018.03.004

Rastogi, M., Vijarania, D., & Goel, D. (2022). *Role of Machine Learning in Healthcare Sector.* Neha.

Sajana, T., Rani, C. S., & Narayana, K. V. (2016). A survey on clustering techniques for big data mining. *Indian Journal of Science and Technology, 9*(3), 1–12. doi:10.17485/ijst/2016/v9i3/75971

Sari, J. N., Nugroho, L. E., Ferdiana, R., & Santosa, P. I. (2016). Review on customer segmentation technique on ecommerce. *Advanced Science Letters, 22*(10), 3018–3022. doi:10.1166/asl.2016.7985

Sculley, D. (2010, April). Web-scale k-means clustering. In *Proceedings of the 19th international conference on world wide web* (pp. 1177-1178). 10.1145/1772690.1772862

Selim, S. Z., & Ismail, M. A. (1984). K-means-type algorithms: A generalized convergence theorem and characterization of local optimality. *IEEE Transactions on Pattern Analysis and Machine Intelligence*, *PAMI-6*(1), 81–87. doi:10.1109/TPAMI.1984.4767478 PMID:21869168

Snekha, C. S., & Birok, R. (2013). Real Time Object Tracking Using Different Mean Shift Techniques–a Review. *International Journal of Soft Computing and Engineering*.

Thakur, R., & Workman, L. (2016). Customer portfolio management (CPM) for improved customer relationship management (CRM): Are your customers platinum, gold, silver, or bronze? *Journal of Business Research*, *69*(10), 4095–4102. doi:10.1016/j.jbusres.2016.03.042

Tikmani, J., Tiwari, S., & Khedkar, S. (2015). An Approach to Customer Classification using k-means. *International Journal of Innovative Research in Computer and Communication Engineering*, *3*(11).

Trivedi, A., Rai, P., DuVall, S. L., & Daumé, H. III. (2010, October). Exploiting tag and word correlations for improved webpage clustering. In *Proceedings of the 2nd international workshop on Search and mining user-generated contents* (pp. 3-12). 10.1145/1871985.1871989

Vijarania, M., Gambhir, A., Sehrawat, D., & Gupta, S. (2022). Prediction of Movie Success Using Sentimental Analysis and Data Mining. In *Applications of Computational Science in Artificial Intelligence* (pp. 174–189). IGI Global. doi:10.4018/978-1-7998-9012-6.ch008

Vijarania, M., Udbhav, M., Gupta, S., Kumar, R., & Agarwal, A. (2023). Global Cost of Living in Different Geographical Areas Using the Concept of NLP. In Handbook of Research on Applications of AI, Digital Twin, and Internet of Things for Sustainable Development (pp. 419-436). IGI Global. doi:10.4018/978-1-6684-6821-0.ch024

Vivek, S. (2018). *Clustering algorithms for customer segmentation*. Academic Press.

Windler, K., Jüttner, U., Michel, S., Maklan, S., & Macdonald, E. K. (2017). Identifying the right solution customers: A managerial methodology. *Industrial Marketing Management*, *60*, 173–186. doi:10.1016/j.indmarman.2016.03.004

Section 2
Machine Learning for Optimization

Chapter 7
Application of Machine Learning for Optimization

Paramita Dey

🆔 https://orcid.org/0000-0003-1306-0929

Government College of Engineering and Ceramic Technology, India

Kingshuk Chatterjee

Government College of Engineering and Ceramic Technology, India

ABSTRACT

This chapter reviews the literature on machine learning and presents regularly used machine learning algorithms in an optimization framework. The interaction between learning algorithm and optimization shell are scrutinized. Methodologies that increase the scalability and efficiency are discussed. Optimizations strategies are predominant in customer support analytics. Optimization schedule basically endeavours to discover the greatest or least of a job, like the objective work, by creating a calculation that methodically chooses input values from a permitted set and computes the esteem of the work. Machine learning favours less-complex calculations that work in sensible computational time. Any side from data fitting, there are various optimization problems and optimization algorithms, and machine learning can ease the solution. In addition, many methods extensively used for the analytics of customer support have been proposed in optimization problems over the last few decades to obtain optimal resolution. Pros and cons of these models and future research directions have been shown.

INTRODUCTION

The pursuit to make intelligent machines that can coordinate and conceivably rival people in thinking and settling on savvy choices returns to at minimum the beginning of the improvement of the computerized registering in the last part of the 1950s (Bennett and Mangasarian, 1993). The objective is to empower the machines to fill complex problem roles by gaining from the previous encounters and afterward taking care of the perplexing issues under conditions that are fluctuating from the past perceptions. Machine learning is quickly developing, with numerous hypothetical logical advances and applications in an as-

DOI: 10.4018/978-1-6684-7105-0.ch007

sortment of fields. Analysts have concentrated on improvement as a significant piece of Artificial Intelligence. The common purpose is to delegate machines to accomplish the cognitive functions by learning from the past occurrences and then solving the complex problems under the state of affairs and different forms of the past consideration. The optimization calculation is built upon an emphasis conspire that proceeds to select the modern input values so that the most extreme or least of the objective work is accomplished (Rousu et al, 2006). Driven by the exponential growth of computing techniques and the data collection and a wide range of practical applications, machine learning is now a strategically important area in the field of optimization algorithm method (Nemhauser and Wolsey, 1999). The recognizable proof of the basic plan, design factors, which are dominatingly changed during the advancement cycle of mathematical optimization process and programming model, is the initial phase in forming an optimization problem (Rousu et al, 2006). In Data fitting, optimization algorithm is built upon a cycle plot that proceeds to pick out latest input values so that the most extreme or least value of the proficient objective data functions. Many new algorithmic, theoretical, mathematical and computational benefaction of optimization have been proposed to decipher several data function problems in utilization of Machine Learning mechanism (Flaxman et al, 2005). Artificial Intelligence depends on the improvement of a model that gives the fruitful result when given a particular information. The heuristic method has been initiated further supple and systematic structured than the deterministic viewpoint. Though the obtained data solution quality ineffective or not guaranteed (Flaxman et al, 2005).

Machine learning approaches have been increasingly prominent in the optimization methodologies in recent years. To help machine learning algorithms discover faster answers, several optimization strategies have been developed. The gradient descent approach, for example, is a common optimization technique for quickly finding the optimal weight sets. The goal of this book chapter is to include both the original research papers and review papers on many disciplines of machine learning applications, with an emphasis on the optimization approaches and optimization algorithms for the time-series data analytics. Optimization methodologies take part in a dominant role in machine learning projects as well as adapting the learning algorithms for training of datasets. The step of preparing the data before fitting the model and the step of adjusting the selected model are also called optimization problems. In fact, the entire predictive modelling approaches can be seen as one big optimization problem as a whole. In this chapter, we show the interaction between machine learning and optimization method and also we examine how many types of algorithm have in optimization technique and how they are related to each other. Both the methodologies play a crucial role in customer support analytics, especially in E-commerce websites.

There are some brief applications where machine learning algorithms are used and optimization techniques plays an important role to optimize the solutions.

- **ChatGPT:** ChatGPT is an applications/bot of a class of machine learning based on the Natural Language Processing models known as LLM (Large Language Model). LLMs collects huge quantities of text data as repository and infer relationships between words to generate an elaborated text. These models have grown over the last few years as we've seen advancements in the computational and storage power. LLMs increase their capability as the size of their input datasets and parameter space increase. The most basic training of language models involves predicting a word in a sequence of words. Most commonly, this is observed as either next-token-prediction or masked-language-modelling. From the user feedback using Reinforcement learning and optimization techniques, the output is improved.

- **E-Commerce Customer Services:** E-commerce cite use customer feedback and process the data for future improvement. Net promoter score, Customer satisfaction score, Customer effort score, Customer churn rate are the different parameters which indicates the customer satisfaction. Generally it involves large scale of data and strategies for large scale data analytics. Different machine learning and deep learning methods are used to analysis and prediction of customer data which also involves optimizations techniques. In today's digital age, marketers need not narrow their feedback systems into one media, but they have to use a plethora of communication medium available to engage their customers. This is what a multiplatform or omni-platform strategy is concerned of. Both multi and omni- platform involve servicing and supporting customers across several digital platforms. It depends on where the targeted customers are communicated. If targeted customers are avid Instagram users, then it will have to service and support them on Instagram in order to keep them satisfied. Likewise, if targeted customers are avid users of Facebook, then providers have to be accessible on that platform. Blending different communication media so as to provide the customers with options for how they would like to interact with a brand or product. According to the study, over 35% of customers expect to be able to contact the same customer service representative on any media. Therefore there is a huge scope of artificial intelligence in this area and machine learning using optimization can be the most efficient paradigm to achieve the goal.

- **Storage:** In warehouse RFID tags are extensively used as the IOT (Internet of Things) tools to locate the product. Since IoT data is among the most significant sources of the raw data, approaches and techniques will provide a considerable contribution to making IoT applications more intelligent and automated. Analytics of IOT data is the combination of different scientific fields that uses data mining, machine learning, optimization techniques and other techniques to predict patterns and new insights from the collected data. These techniques include a broad range of algorithms and paradigms which applicable in this particular domains. The process of getting insights from the data in that particular areas involves defining data types such as volume, variety, and velocity; data models such as neural networks and deep networks, classification, and clustering methods, and applying efficient optimization techniques that best suited with the characteristics of collected data. The steps towards the processing of data involves the following steps: as collected data is generated from the different sources with the specific data types, it is important to adopt or develop algorithms that can handle the characteristics of the data . Generally RDBMS or structured database like SQL (Structured query language). Therefore NSQL database like MongoDB can be used for that purpose. Secondly, the large number of resources that is RFID data that generated in real-time are not without the problem of scale and velocity. Real time data analysis require more efficient optimization techniques for reducing time complexity. Moreover, finding the best data model that fits the collected information is one of the most important issues for the output characteristics and analysis of the IoT data. These issues have opened a vast number of opportunities in expanding new developments of machine learning analysis of large scale data. Big data, which is characterised as the high-volume, high-velocity, and high variety data that demands cost-effective, innovative forms of information processing that enable enhanced insight, decision making, and process automation for the storage and warehouse.

Rest of the chapter is organised as following sections. Section 2 describes the interaction between machine learning and optimization problem. In this section we describe the preliminaries or basics of Machine Learning and optimization methodologies. We describe some optimization algorithm that very much use now days and we draw the table of optimization problem. Section 3 presents the recent research work in this research area in the tabular manner for easy reference of the recent works. Section 4 represents optimization techniques using machine learning. Section 5 concludes the chapter.

INTERCONNECTION BETWEEN MACHINE LEARNING AND OPTIMIZATION

The interconnection between the machine learning and optimization is one of the utmost prime expansions in latest data processing computational data retrieval. Optimization approaches and conceptualization are demonstrate to be crucial in fabricate algorithms to pull out the vital information from the enormous data. Machine learning is a rapidly spreading area and it generates a modern idea of optimization (Shivaswamy et al, 2006).

Machine Learning Preliminaries

Machine learning is a software layout field, and its goal is to create programs that allow learning to do things yourself through learning algorithms and methods. Such algorithms include neural network processing and pattern matching, genetic algorithms and rule-based learning. Machine learning often has the powerful statistical elements. Machine learning (ML) is a building and understanding procedure that 'learn' and improve data performance and working well on some model tasks. It is the fragment of Artificial Intelligence. Machine-learning algorithms construct a model depend on selected sample data, called as training-data, for the purpose of making decisions and forecast without being completely model programmed. The algorithms of Machine Learning are utilized in a large variety of implementation namely in computer vision, medicine and speech recognition.

Machine Learning as a review is an overall approach to inferring that a similar label has been applied to an exploration field, as well regarding its principle object the way in which the machines can further develop their undertaking execution, to various classes of procedures to anticipate the relationship among data factors including neural-organizations and even to the individual models that ML professionals fabricate utilizing these strategies. There are two types of machine learning models: supervised and unsupervised learning (Dolan and More, 2002).

Supervised Learning

Supervised learning is the most common type of machine learning algorithms. It uses a known dataset (called the training dataset) to train an algorithm with a known set of input data (called features) and known responses to make predictions. The training dataset includes labelled input data that pair with desired outputs or response values. From it, the supervised learning algorithm seeks to create a model by discovering the relationships between the features and output data and then makes predictions of the response values for a new dataset.

In supervised learning, for each observation of predictor measures, a response measurement is available, and the goal is to construct a model that reliably predicts the response of future observations. Supervised learning is a machine learning technique that uses labelled data to train a model. In supervised learning, we can use both input x and output y, and the target is to grasp a function (*f*) that approximates the relationship between the input and its output with reasonable error. Prediction accuracy is evaluated using a loss function $L(f(x), y)$ that computes a measure of the distance between the predicted output and the actual output (Rifkin and Klautau, 2004). In this learning, the model must find a matching function that matches the input variable (*x*) with the output variable (*y*)$y=f(x)$.

Some standard supervised algorithms includes the following techniques:

Classification: This is used for categorical response values, where the data can be separated into specific classes. A binary classification model has two classes whereas in a multiclass classification model there are several classes. Common classification algorithms include Logistic regression, Support vector machines (SVM), Neural networks, Naïve Bayes classifier, Decision trees, Discriminant analysis, K-Nearest neighbors (kNN), Ensemble Classification, Generalized Additive Model (GAM).

Regression: It is used for numerical continuous-response values for prediction of the outputs. Some popularly used regression algorithms include Linear regression, Non-linear regression, Generalized linear models, Decision trees, Neural networks, Gaussian Process Regression, Support Vector Machine Regression, Ensemble Regression.

Unsupervised Learning

In contrast, unsupervised learning is a technique for training a machine to use unclassified or unlabelled data. This means that we cannot provide training data and the machine has to learn on its own.

Machines must be able to classify data in the absence of prior knowledge of the statistics and evidence data. The idea is to set out a machine an enormous amount of different data and learn from that data to get previously unknown information and discover hidden patterns. Therefore, unsupervised learning algorithms do not necessarily produce specific results. Rather, it defines what is different or interesting to a given data set.

In unsupervised learning knowledge of makes use of gadget gaining knowledge of algorithms to investigate and cluster unlabelled records sets. These algorithms find out hidden styles in records without the want for human intervention (it is unsupervised).

A mainstay is to contemplate when explore a model is the complexity of the model. Learning very intricate models, this can arouse over fitting. This means having a model that fits well to the training data but does not generalize to other data.

Unsupervised learning is a type of machine learning algorithm used to draw inferences from datasets without human intervention, in contrast to supervised learning where labels are provided along with the data. The most common unsupervised learning method is cluster analysis, which applies clustering methods to explore data and find hidden patterns or groupings in data. There are several clustering algorithms as follow: Hierarchical clustering: builds a multilevel hierarchy of clusters by creating a cluster tree, k-Means and k-medoids clustering: partitions data into k distinct clusters based on distance, Gaussian mixture models: models clusters as a mixture of multivariate normal density components, Density-based spatial clustering (DBSCAN): groups points that are close to each other in areas of high density, keeping track of outliers in low density regions, Self-organizing maps: uses neural networks that learn the topology and distribution of the data, Spectral clustering: graph-based clustering that can handle arbitrary non-convex shapes

Other methods that apply unsupervised learning include semi-supervised learning and unsupervised feature ranking. Semi-supervised learning reduces the need for labelled data in supervised learning. Clustering applied to the whole data set establishes similarity between labelled and unlabelled data, and labels are propagated to previously unlabelled and similar cluster members. Unsupervised feature ranking assigns scores to features without a given prediction target or response.

Unsupervised learning is typically applied before supervised learning, to identify features in exploratory data analysis, and establish classes based on groupings. k-means and hierarchical clustering are most commonly used unsupervised learning. Unsupervised learning or clustering is also used as a tool for compress large scale data. Unsupervised feature ranking is available to apply distance-based clustering more efficiently to large data sets.

Ensemble Learning

Ensemble learning is a general meta-approach to machine learning that seeks better predictive performance by combining the predictions from multiple models. Although there are a seemingly unlimited number of ensembles that one can develop for the predictive modelling problem, there are three methods that dominate the field of ensemble learning. The three main classes of ensemble learning methods are bagging, stacking, and boosting. Bagging involves fitting many decision trees on different samples of the same dataset and averaging the predictions. Stacking involves fitting many different models types on the same data and using another model to learn how to best combine the predictions. Boosting involves adding ensemble members sequentially that correct the predictions made by prior models and outputs a weighted average of the predictions.

In Bagging, we are varying of the training data used to fit each ensemble member, which, in turn, results in skilful but different models. The steps in the methodology are: at first bootstrap the samples of the training dataset, then unpruned the decision trees for fit the sample data and in the third stage, voting or averaging of the predictions generates the final output after bagging. Many popular ensemble algorithms are based on this approach, including: Bagged Decision Trees (canonical bagging), Random Forest and Extra Trees.

Stacked Generalization, or stacking for short, is an ensemble method that seeks a diverse group of members by varying the model types fit on the training data and using a model to combine predictions. Stacking has its own nomenclature where ensemble members are referred to as level-0 models and the model that is used to combine the predictions is referred to as a level-1 model. The two-level hierarchy of models is the most common approach, although more layers of models can be used. For example, instead of a single level-1 model, one can have 3 or 5 level-1 models and a single level-2 model that combines the predictions of level-1 models in order to make a prediction. Any machine learning model can be used to aggregate the predictions, although it is common to use a linear model, such as linear regression for regression and logistic regression for binary classification. This encourages the complexity of the model to reside at the lower-level ensemble member models and simple models to learn how to harness the variety of predictions made. We can summarize the key elements of stacking as follows: training dataset remins unchanged, different machine learning algorithms for each ensemble member are used, machine learning model to learn how to best combine predictions to derive the optimum solution.

Diversity comes from the different machine learning models used as ensemble members. In this scenario, it is desirable to use a suite of models that are learned or constructed in very different ways, ensuring that they make different assumptions and, in turn, have less correlated prediction errors. Many popular ensemble algorithms are based on this approach, including: Stacked Models (canonical stacking), Blending, Super Ensemble.

Boosting is an ensemble method that seeks to change the training data to focus attention on examples that previous fit models on the training dataset have gotten wrong. The key property of boosting ensembles is the idea of correcting prediction errors. The models are fit and added to the ensemble sequentially such that the second model attempts to correct the predictions of the first model, the third corrects the second model, and so on. This typically involves the use of very simple decision trees that only make a single or a few decisions, referred to in boosting as weak learners. The predictions of the weak learners are combined using simple voting or averaging, although the contributions are weighed proportional to their performance or capability. The objective is to develop a single strong-learner from different purpose-built weak-learners. Generally, the training dataset is left unchanged and instead, the learning algorithm is modified to pay more attention to specific examples (rows of data) based on whether they have been predicted correctly or incorrectly by previously added ensemble members. For example, the rows of data can be weighed to indicate the amount of focus a learning algorithm must give while learning the model. Now all methodologies can be summarised as the key elements of boosting as follows: at first bias training data toward those instances that are hard to predict. Then iteratively add ensemble members to correct predictions of prior models. Finally combine all predictions using a weighted average of models to generate the strong prediction.

The idea of combining many weak learners into strong learners was first proposed theoretically and many algorithms were proposed with little success. It was not until the Adaptive Boosting (AdaBoost) algorithm was developed that boosting was demonstrated as an effective ensemble method. After Ada-Boost, several boosting methods have been developed and some, like stochastic gradient boosting, may be among the most effective techniques for classification and regression on tabular (structured) data. To summarize, several popular ensemble algorithms are proposed based on this approach, like AdaBoost (canonical boosting), Gradient Boosting Machines, Stochastic Gradient Boosting (XGBoost and similar).

Optimization Preliminaries

The optimization process expand in the particular machine-learning area are distinct that can be simulate the progress of mainstream optimization methods. Continuous mathematical function optimization, in which the input data contentions to the functional boundaries are genuine esteemed numeric qualities, for example floating point values is the most common kind of optimization-problem issued in Machine Learning. An optimization algorithm is a process that compares numerous solutions iteratively until an optimum or satisfying one is identified. (Saman et al, 2020). The purpose of the optimization problem is to find a collection of inputs that produces a maximum or minimal function evaluation. This complex problem lies at the heart of many machine learning techniques, from fitting logistic regression models to training artificial neural networks. Optimization-methods are preliminary a mathematical concept. As, mathematical problems, they are mathematically well-defined, meaning that given limitless processing power and time, there is some answer that can be produced and proved to be error free. Optimization is a set of apparatus for finding the elements of set D that minimize the function f. All machine learning problems can be summarized in this format, as are many problems that have nothing to do with machine learning. We know that for NP-hard optimization problem polynomial time calculations is impossible (when P=NP). In addition, a total whole set identification arrangement for expansive discrete-optimization issue occurrences is regularly not conceivable with the existing computing innovation. Subsequently, much exertion has been coordinated towards creating proficient heuristic calculations to discover near-optimal arrangements in a sensible sum of computing time.

In this table we divide optimization problem in two categories Convex and Non-convex. The fundamental difference of these major two optimizations is that only one optimal-solution has in convex optimization and no feasible-solution is the problem so we can say it is globally optimized and significantly easier than non –convex problem.

In non-convex optimization we can say there are many local optimal points. It is also harder for smooth and simple function and it is very time consuming to deal with any problem. Convex optimization is used in classification of multiclass; we can say it is model or data fitting. We are handle easily derivative or differentiable convex optimization problem. If we take the derivative of convex problem it gives us significant first order data or information. Here some algorithms are a) conjugate gradient and b) Gradient Descent. When optimization problem's goal is convex function $(f_l(x))$ then we say that it is convex optimization and the inequality function f_a are convex and the equality function g_b are join or affine (Jason, 2021).

Minimize x $(f_l(x)$ (convex function)

$f_a(x) \leq 0$ (convex set)

$g_b(x)=0$ (join or affine)

When we allow the constrained convex function, it can be equality or inequality constraints or mixed. We can optimized and construct the loss function predicted on some metrics. In constrained function within a greater range, the chosen variable can only take on particular values and a function is minimized or maximised based upon constraints, we can say this function is objective function. There are various types of optimization algorithms that are commonly deployed nowadays. A list of optimization algorithms are listed below:

Deterministic Algorithms Optimization

They follow particular guidelines while moving from one resolution to the next. These methods have been effectively used to a variety of engineering design challenges in the past.Optimization functions are parameters it encode the layout of deterministic algorithm in computational steps and formulate the algorithm selected in this algorithms family. The constraint of the optimization problem ensures the convergence of the algorithm to solve the problem under consideration (Boyd and Vandenberghe, 2004).

Stochastic Algorithms Optimization

Stochastic algorithms are probabilistic in nature translation rules. Stochastic optimization is that type of method for maximizing or minimizing objective-function when the stochastic issues are considered. Stochastic optimization calculations have a wide run of applications in factual issues. The stochastic gradient method is a fair-minded assess of the genuine slope. This optimization strategy diminishes the overhaul time for managing with huge numbers of tests and expels a certain sum of computational repetition and theoretical redundancy (Vapnik, 2013). Over the past few decades, these strategies have been proposed for the designing, computer science, commerce and insights as basic instruments. Stochastic optimization plays a vital part within the investigation, plan, and execution of advanced frameworks.

Gradient Descent Optimization

The gradient descent strategy is the foremost well-known optimization strategy. The thought of this strategy is to update the factors iteratively within the inverse of gradients of the objective function. With each upgrade, this strategy identifies the target output and slowly merge to the ideal value of the objective work. The gradient approach produces a basic calculation comprising of slope and projection step. For the course of models considered, the projection requires arrangement of energetic program or organizes stream models for which very productive calculations exist. The strategy is regularized by early ceasing (Ming et al, 2012).

Conjugate Gradient Optimization

The conjugate-gradient approach is utilized for understanding huge scale straight frameworks of conditions and nonlinear enhancement issues. The first-order strategies have a moderate merging speed. Though, the second-order strategies are heavy-resource method. Conjugate gradient enhancement is a middle calculation, which combines the points of interest of first-order data whereas guaranteeing the meeting speeds of high-order strategies (James et al, 2013).

Derivate-Free Optimization

Derivative-free heuristic optimization Coordinate descent is a typical method. There is a classification of mathematical programs based on the types of goals and constraints. There are now many variations of math programs: linear, quadratic, semi-deterministic, semi-infinite, integer, non-linear, objective, geometric, fractional, etc. For example, linear programs have linear goals and linear constraints. There are potentially hundreds of common optimization algorithms to choose from, as well as tens of algorithms in popular scientific code libraries. It might be difficult to decide which algorithms to utilise for a specific optimization issue because of this (Alexander et al, 2011).

There are now many variations of the math programs: linear, quadratic, semi-deterministic, semi-infinite, integer, non-linear, objective, geometric, fractional, etc. For example, linear programs have linear goals and linear constraints.

There are potentially hundreds of common optimization algorithms to choose from, as well as tens of algorithms in popular scientific code libraries. It might be difficult to decide which algorithms to utilise for a specific optimization issue because of this.

For a few optimization issues, we see this algorithm can continuously be drawn nearer through a slope since the objective-function derivative may not necessarily differentiable on that gradient or slope and sometimes it isn't easy to determine.

This is often where derivative free optimization algorithm comes into the mind and we know that optimization pick out a heuristic algorithm strategies that worked well in machine-learning application instead of determines efficient or precise-answer.

Zeroth Order Optimization

Zeroth Arrange optimization is a successful and reasonable strategy for assessing the unfavourable effect of significant instruction and machine learning frameworks. Optimizing the Zeroth-Order can be a subset of gradient or slope free optimization that's built totally different action and indication in machine learning applications. Apparatuses for optimizing Zeroth-order function are basically first-order gradient-free counterparts. Utilizing derivation free function slope calculations, Zeroth Arrange approximates add up to stochastic-gradient (Mitsos et al, 2018).

In addition, we must include convexity plays a crucial part within the design of optimization calculations (Suvritsrav et al, 2011). Usually generally due to the truth that it is much less demanding to analyse and test calculations in such a context (Saman et al, 2020). In other words, in case the calculation performs ineffectively indeed within the curved setting, regularly we ought to not trust to see incredible comes about something else. Besides, indeed in spite of the fact that the optimization issues in profound learning are for the most part non-convex, they regularly display a few properties of raised ones close nearby local minima. To summarize, alluring properties of an optimization calculation from the ML viewpoint are 1) versatility to expansive problems, 2) great execution in hone in terms of execution times and memory requirements, 3) great generalization. It is difficult to write all algorithms together in one review but we try to summarize the most of the algorithm and we find the interplay of ml and optimization model.

The expression "optimization" alludes to a technique for assessing the information boundaries or contentions to a mathematical function that function outcome in the insignificant or greatest result. Here a reaction size is to be had for every remark of predictor measurements and the purpose is to fit a version that as it should be predicts the reaction of destiny observations (Barreno et al, 2010).

In machine learning, optimization refers to the process of obtaining a minimal (or maximum) value or a collection of optimum parameter values for a given function. This function is known as an objective function in the field of mathematical programming, and it is closely related to many aspects of optimization theory, such as mathematical analysis and numerical approaches.

Expert knowledge has been employed in the field of optimization since antiquity, but it wasn't until the 19th century that mathematics was applied to practical problems. In many disciplines of research and engineering, the quest for increased efficiency and productivity has propelled the development of mathematical optimization (Agarwal et al, 2010).

They build slight changes to the problems models and allowing for the creating strong new approaches like Multi-kernel technique, graph-based clustering, and structured learning and ranking approaches are developed.

The algorithm arises for dividing the minor problems into some convex sub problem which is easy to solve. Neural network researchers testing, inspecting back propagation and exploring several unconstrained nonlinear-programming approaches.

RECENT RESEARCH WORK

This chapter presents the related work where machine learning and optimization problems are interconnected. Table 1 presents the work in Tabular form

Table 1. Recent research work with the focus area

Author and Year	Focus
Bennet and Mangasarian, 1993	This paper describe about the Bilinear-program. It finishes in a limited number of steps at a point meeting a required optimality constraint or at a global minimum if it has a vertex solution.
Nemhauser and Wolsey, 1999	Authors discussed about integer and combinatorial optimization frame work. This gives an idea of the machine learning's versatility in the field of combinatorial Optimization.
Dolan and More, 2002	This review discussed on benchmark of the optimization software and the key technological concerns addressed the analysis and interpretation of the data provided by the benchmarking process.
Fung and Mangasarian, 2004	This paper is focussing on linear-programming implementation of SVM (Support-Vector-Machines) classifiers and the approach is also capable of dealing with the situations involving a high number of data points and does not necessitate the use of specialist linear programming software.
Rifkin and Klautau, 2004	Authors discussed about multiclass classification and the training–set contains data points associated with distinct classes and construct function.
Boyd and Vandenberghe, 2004	Authors chronicled comprehensive description about the convex optimization.
Flaxman et al, 2005	In this paper author proposes an approach where general convex optimization structure must pick a single point (from a possible set) and make a cost equal to the following function's value on that point.
Shivaswamy et al, 2006	Author proposes a new 2nd order cone-program expression and design robust and favourable classifiers which can control unpredictability in every observations.
Rousu et al, 2006	Authors represent an algorithm of kernel based that is made for text classification and is easily workable for thousands of training data set.
Agarwal et al, 2010	Authors introduce about Bandit-Convex Optimization and the multi-point Bandit setting, it is a unique example of convex optimization.
Barreno et al, 2010	Authors describes about machine learning's capacity to quickly advance to changing and multiple circumstances has made a difference it ended up a crucial appliance for security of computers.
Ming et al., 2012	Authors present the latest improvement of deterministic strategies for executing the signomial programming issues and non-linear programming issues.
James et al., 2013	Authors proposed a formulation that is based on optimizing concept within an algorithm of parameterized-family and state the steps of the algorithm.
Jason, 2021	Authors describes the use of stochastic-optimization methods in optimization algorithm or in objective function and as a part of local search procedure.
Ioffe and Szegedy, 2015	Authors draw equality form of making normalization a portion of the show model-architecture and performing normalization method for every training mini batch data. This acknowledges utilizing higher learning-rates.

OPTIMIZATION IN A MACHINE LEARNING PROBLEM

In addition to adapting learning algorithm to the training dataset, optimization is an important aspect of a machine learning project. The process of preparing data before fitting a model and adjusting a model that has been chosen may both be presented as optimization problems. In fact, a predictive modelling project as a whole may be viewed as a huge optimization issue. We use optimization methodologies to solve the challenges like optimizing a production schedule, maximizing the projected return on a product portfolio while maintaining a reasonable level of the risk, and evaluating strategic investment initiatives.

A mathematical model is created that represents the real world as an abstraction. An objective function decision variables (the levers we can pull), and limitations make up the system. A solver is an optimization method that determines the ideal levers to pull for a particular model and data collection

Neural Network in Optimization Algorithm

Model weights are the function inputs, which are optimization issues that need an iterative global search procedure. We can see that each approach makes various assumptions about the mapping function's shape, which has an impact on the sort of optimization issue that has to be addressed. We can also see that the default optimization algorithm used by each machine learning algorithm is not random; it represents the most efficient algorithm for solving the specific optimization problem posed by the algorithm, such as stochastic gradient descent instead of a genetic algorithm for neural nets. Deviating from these defaults necessitates justification

Combinatorial Optimization

Combinatorial-optimization is the methods of finding maxima and minima of objective function of discrete domain but substantial configuration volume (N dimensional continuous area).

Some common combinatorial-optimization problems examples are:

- **The Traveling Salesman Problem (TSP):** Considering the (x_i, y_i) positions of Nth distinct cities, Find the shortest path that passes through each city precisely once.

Given a set of cities and the distance between every pair of cities, the problem is to find the shortest possible route that visits every city exactly once and returns to the starting point. Note the difference between Hamiltonian Cycle and TSP. The Hamiltonian cycle problem is to find if there exists a tour that visits every city exactly once. Here we know that Hamiltonian Tour exists (because the graph is complete) and in fact, many such tours exist, the problem is to find a minimum weight Hamiltonian Cycle.

- **Bin-Packing:** The bin packing problem is an optimization problem, in which items of different sizes must be packed into a finite number of bins or containers, each of with a fixed given capacity, in a way that minimizes the number of bins used. Considering a set of Nth objects each having a distinct size s_{ij}, fit into as one or two bins (each of size B_i) as feasible.

Graph Neural Network in Combinatorial Optimization Problem

Several combinatorial-optimization approaches can be expressed in the term of constraint-satisfaction problems. Data presented in the form of graph neural network (GNN) design architecture for figure out optimization methods. The generic architecture performs well for binary satisfaction problems. Unsupervised training is adequate for relatively micro instances and derive networks accomplish well on larger occurrences (10 times large scale) of the dataset. We can use techniques of optimization to test on a number of challenges, as well as Max Cut problem and Max-independent Set problem. Despite its general nature, we can state that this technique matches or outperforms most semi-definite and also greedy programming problem that based on optimization algorithms, and in certain cases, even exceeds state-of-the-art heuristics problems for specific situations (Rifkin, 2004).

In various applications, such as e-commerce, e-business, social networks sites, and biological network; graphs have been widely needed to demonstrate complex data sets. For graph-based systems, efficient and effective graph data processing is critical using conventional optimization techniques. However, the majority of graph analysis activities are NP-hard combinatorial optimization (CO) issues. Machine learning (ML) has recently received a lot of attention for its ability to tackle graph-based CO challenges.

CONCLUSION

In this chapter, we inspect few of the regularly utilized optimization strategies. Optimization is important to find a feasible solution for any analytics problem. Separated from these, there are numerous other strategies. Machine learning methods were used to inform clinical decision using a variety of approaches, algorithms, statistical software, and validation strategies. The issue of optimization for Machine learning doesn't conclusion here since not all issues come beneath discrete or convex or high order optimization. We know that Non-convex optimization is one of the troubles in all optimization problems. If we convert the non-convex optimization into a curved optimization then the issue solved, and after we utilize the convex optimization strategy. Research on optimization and machine learning is drawing attention due to the widespread application of optimization in many areas such as mathematical planning, game theory, prediction, control systems, operations management, and finance. Machine Learning is interested in understanding and creating intelligent agents that work intelligently and "learn" from the experience and knowledge gained through problem solving. The popularity of machine learning techniques for implementing them has increased significantly over the last decade as they can be applied to a variety of issues in many application domains. The other is to utilize a few uncommon optimization strategies such as gradient descent, stochastic gradient descent, substituting minimization, maximization calculation and deterministic optimization and its variations. Optimization is a useful tool in some machine learning algorithms and models because it allows machine learning mechanisms to work in an optimized way. More specifically, optimization seeks to find the best element or value that satisfies a given set of objective functions limit. This value ensures that the system is functioning optimally. Since machine learning requires learning that the entire model works, optimization is paramount to allowing the model to be trained and trained efficiently. In short, much of the machine learning literature relies on fine-tuning parameters by solving established optimization problems. Stated the quick advancement in computing automation and technology over the last few decades, huge optimization assumption and algorithms have been offered to resolve different types of real-world computational-functions. For that reason, to allow a systematic review of the remaining literature is opposition that motivates the study of optimization approaches and algorithms, especially for that the area of optimization has expand and progress rapidly. Multiple machine learning approaches can be used, the software estimation strategy must be clearly outlined, and both internal and external affirmation must be performed to ensure that patient care actions are based on the highest quality substantiation. Ensemble approaches comprising many machine learning techniques should be widely used in research topic. This tasks initial analysis and technique for continuous optimization and survey of advancement in machine learning application. Deterministic, convex and nonlinear programming in problems of optimization and discrete optimization are found. All these algorithms can be used in automated customer support analytics for finding an optimum solution using machine learning.

REFERENCES

Agarwal, A., Dekel, O., & Xiao, L. (2010). Optimal algorithms for online convex optimization with multi-point bandit feedback. *Proceedings of the annual Conference on Learning Theory.*

Barreno, M., Nelson, B., Joseph, A. D., & Doug Tygar, J. (2010). The security of machine learning. *Machine Learning, 81*(2), 121–148. doi:10.100710994-010-5188-5

Bennett, K. P., & Mangasarian, O. L. (1993). Bilinear separation of two sets in n-space. *Computational Optimization and Applications, 2*(3), 207–227. doi:10.1007/BF01299449

Boyd, S., & Vandenberghe, L. (2004). *Convex Optimization.* Cambridge University Press. doi:10.1017/CBO9780511804441

Brownly, J. (2021). A Gentle Introduction to Stochastic Optimization Algorithms. *Optimization.*

Dolan, E., & More, J. (2002). Benchmarking optimization software with performance profiles. *Mathematical Programming, 91*(2), 201–213. doi:10.1007101070100263

Flaxman, A. D., Kalai, A. T., & McHanan, H. B. (2005). Online convex optimization in the bandit setting: gradient descent without a gradient. *ACM-SIAM Symposium on Discrete Algorithms (SODA).*

Fung, G. M., & Mangasarian, O. (2004). A Feature Selection Newton Method for Support Vector Machine Classification. *Computational Optimization and Applications, 28*(2), 185–202. doi:10.1023/B:COAP.0000026884.66338.df

Ioffe, S., & Szegedy, C. (2015). Batch normalization: accelerating deep network training by reducing internal covariate shift. *ICML'15: Proceedings of the 32nd International Conference on International Conference on Machine Learning, 37,* 448–456.

James, G., Witten, D., Hastie, T., & Tibshirani, R. (2013). *An Introduction to Statistical Learning* (Vol. 112). Springer. doi:10.1007/978-1-4614-7138-7

Lin, Tsai, & Yu. (2012). A Review Of Deterministic Optimization Methods in Engineering and Management. Mathematical Problems in Engineering.

Maroufpoor, S., & Bozorg-Haddad, O. (2020). Stochastic optimization. Handbook of Probabilistic Models.

Mitsos, A., Najman, J., & Kevrekidis, I. G. (2018). Optimal deterministic algorithm generation. *Journal of Global Optimization, 71*(4), 891–913. doi:10.100710898-018-0611-8

Nemhauser, G., & Wolsey, L. (1999). *Integer and Combinatorial Optimization.* Wiley.

Nikolaev & Jacobson. (2011). Using Markov chains to analyze the effectiveness of local search algorithms. *Discrete Optimization, 8*(2), 160-173.

Rifkin, R., & Klautau, A. (2004). Defences of one-vs-all classification. *Journal of Machine Learning Research, 5*(Jan), 101–141.

Rousu, J., Saunders, C., Szedmak, S., & Shawe-Taylor, J. (2006). Kernel-based learning of Hierarchical multilabel classification models. *Journal of Machine Learning Research, 7,* 1601–1626.

Shivaswamy, P. K., Bhattacharyya, C., & Smola, A. J. (2006). Second order cone programming approaches for handling missing and uncertain data. *Journal of Machine Learning Research*, 7, 1283–1314.

Suvritsra, Nowozin, & Wright. (2011). Optimization for Machine Learning. MIT Press.

Vapnik, V. (2013). *The Nature of Statistical Learning Theory*. Springer Science & Business Media.

Chapter 8

Approval of Artificial Intelligence and Machine Learning Models to Solve Problems in Nonlinear Active Suspension Systems

Zineb Boulaaras

https://orcid.org/0000-0002-2404-3051

Larbi Tebessi University, Algeria

Abdelaziz Aouiche

Independent Researcher, Algeria

Kheireddine Chafaa

Independent Researcher, Algeria

ABSTRACT

In this chapter, the authors used a comparative study between passive and active suspension of quarter car models with deference intelligent controllers. This study aims to obtain an active suspension that adapts to all types of roads, especially rough and slippery ones, and absorbs shocks resulting from road vibrations, which gives more comfort to passengers and the driver. The results have proven that FOPID gave better results than PID in all types of road testing. The concerns related to the proposed chapter are that the car makers have a fear of the Fractional-Order controller FOPID to the difficulty of achieving it in the industrial field because of the difficulty of its mathematical equations and its high cost.

DOI: 10.4018/978-1-6684-7105-0.ch008

INTRODUCTION

The suspension of cars is discussed in this chapter connection the cars motion and ride feature of vehicles. The authors were used a two degree of freedom (2DOF) of quarter car model because is simple but sufficiently detailed to capture many of the key suspension performance tradeoffs. Such as ride quality (represented by suspension deflection), and packaging (represent by suspension stroke), also known as the rattle space (Ulsoy, Deng, & Calanakci, 2012). The active suspension system is a type of suspension on a car. In general, Suspension is a system for controlling the vertical motion of a vehicle's wheels for the car's body structure rather than passive suspension provided by springs, and dampers, where the motion is determined by the road surface. Active suspension is divided into two classes: real active suspension and semi-adaptive suspension only varies shock absorber finesse to match changing road or dynamic conditions active suspension uses some type of actuator to raise and lower the chassis independently (Saintilan & Shelley, 2013), and (Applegard & Wellstead, 1995).

These technologies allow car manufactures to achieve a greater degree of ride quality and car handling by keeping the tires perpendicular to the road allow a batter traction for the car and control it (Lin & Kanellakopoulos, 1997; Tseng & Hrovat, 2015; Huang, 2015).

Figure 1. Demonstration of the active suspension system of a car
Source: Riduan et al. (2018)

The vehicle contacts the ground through the spring and damper in the suspension system, as in Figure 2. To achieve the same level of stability as the skyhook theory, the vehicle must contact the ground-contacting the spring, and the imaginary line with the damper. Theoretically, if the damping coefficient reaches an infinite value, the vehicle will not vibrate (Sun, Zhao, & Li, 2014).

Figure 2. Quarter car suspension model
Source: Ignatius et al. (2016)

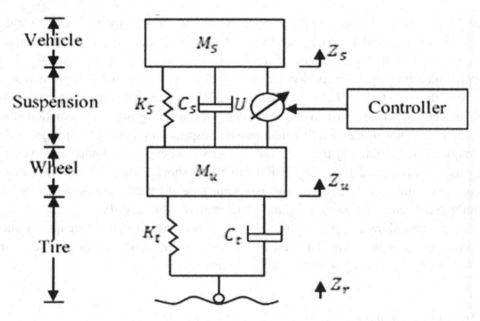

Active suspension is the first to be offered, and it uses separate actuators that can exert independent force on the suspension to improve characteristics and performance of car. The defects of this design are high cost, added complication and mass of the apparatus, and the need for frequent maintenance on some implementation. Maintenance can require specialized tools, and some problems can be difficult to diagnose (Dan & Sun, 2018) and (Mohammadi & Ganjefar, 2017). In this chapter, the authors study the model of an active suspension of quarter car, and applied two types of controllers:

- The first one is a proportional Integral Derivative Controller (PID).
- The second one is a Fractional-Order PID (FOPID).

For adjust these controllers the researches used Artificial neural Network and optimization methods.

BACKGROUND

Suspension design for automobiles has traditionally been a compromise between the three opposing criteria of road handling load-bearing and occupant comfort. The suspension system must support the vehicle, provide directional control during maneuvering and provide effective occupant/cargo isolation from road disturbance. Good ride comfort requires a soft suspension, while sensitivity to applied loads requires a hard suspension (Venhovens, Knaap, & der, 1995). Good handling requires a suspension setup somewhere in between the two, because of these conflicting demands, suspension design must be a compromise, determined largely by the type one must independently determine for load-carrying characteristics, handling, and ride quality (Kashem, Nagarajah, & Eklesabi, 2018).

A passive suspension can store energy through a spring and dissipate it through a damper. Their parameters are generally fixed and selected to achieve a certain level of corresponding road holding, load bearing, and comfort. An active suspension system can store, dissipate and introduce energy into the system. It may change its parameters depending on the operating conditions and can know other than the deflection to which the passive system is limited (Erjavec & Thompson, 2014). An active suspension has become the focus of attention for researchers and car manufacturers, so they study various controls that give good results in car stability and passenger comfort. In reference (Barr and Ray 1996) the authors controlled of an active suspension system using fuzzy logic and linear quadratic Gaussian, the objective of this research was to design, simulate, and test a fuzzy logic controller for active vehicle suspension. First, the basic information of a two-degree-of-freedom quarter-car suspension model followed by fuzzy logic console design was examined. Simulations were completed using Matlab and Simulink. For comparison purposes, passive feedback and linear-squared (LQG) active feedback were also simulated. The three suspensions were subjected to a random input of linear power spectral density and random white noise. For both entries, the Fuzzy Logic suspension showed superior ride characteristics when compared to LQG and passive suspension; none of the active suspension controls showed improvements in road handling. In Ghazaly et al. (2016), the main objective of this research is to develop a sports model of the active suspension system that is exposed to road excitation and controlled by using H technology for a quarter of the car model to improve ride comfort and road handling. The comparison between passive and active suspension systems is made using graded, sinusoidal, and random road profiles. The performance of the H∞ controller is compared to the passive suspension system. It has been found that body acceleration, suspension deflection and tire deflection using H∞ active suspension are better than passive suspension. In Anh (2020), the researchers focused on analysis, evaluation, comparison and two controllers were implemented: a PID controller and an LQR controller for an active suspension system. Research results showed that when the vehicle is equipped with an active suspension system, the displacement values and inflated block acceleration is greatly improved. Besides, the controller supports PID for body optimization acceleration, LQR controller support to optimize body displacement. The reference Wang et al. (2020) the authors developed a new type of active turbulence denial control to improve the ride comfort of all-vehicle suspension systems while taking into account suspension non-linearity and engine saturation. The proposed controller combines active disturbance rejection control with fuzzy slip mode control and is called active disturbance rejection control in fuzzy slip mode. To validate the mathematical model of the system and analyze the performance of the controller, a virtual prototype was constructed where the simulation results show better performance of the active perturbation rejection control in the fuzzy slip pattern compared to the current active perturbation rejection control.

MAIN FOCUS OF CHAPTER

Issues, Controversies, Problems

This chapter aims to study active suspension and compare it with passive suspension, by studying them on different types of difficult and rough roads, controlling it by applying artificial intelligence, and reaching a suspension that gives better stability to the car and comfort for the driver and passengers.

MATHEMATICAL MODEL OF QUARTER CAR MODEL FOR AN ACTIVE SUSPENSION

The dynamics of a real car have important nonlinear characteristics they include air spring and, damper. The quarter-car model of a vehicle is illustrated in Figure 3. The model is consisting of a sprung mass and wheels connected by a primary suspension system. The air spring is placed between the body of the car and the vehicle that includes it. When an active suspension system is applied, the active forces are produced by motors (Ahmed, Hazlina, & Rashid, 2016).

Figure 3. Components a quarter car model for an active suspension system
Source: Liu et al. (2019)

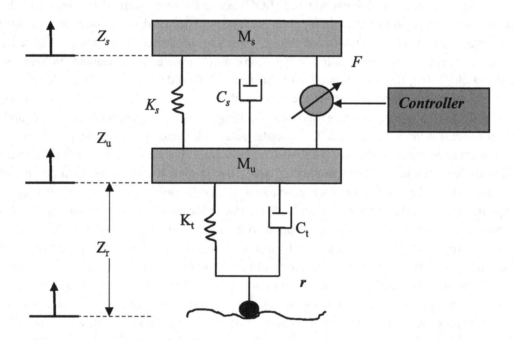

With F is Actuator Force, M_s Sprung mass, M_u Unsprung mass, K_s, K_t is Spring of suspension system, and Spring of wheel and tire, C_s, C_t is Demper of suspension and wheel, Z_s, Z_u, and Z_r is Body Displacement, wheel displacement, and r Vertical position of the road profile (TurnIip & Panggbean, 2020).

In this research a 2-DOF model is used to test the performance of the quarter car model, and. An active suspension system is shown in Figure 3. The assumption simulation parameters are mentioned in Table 1. The main equations of motion that is considered in the mathematical model in equation 1 (Izadkhah, Nouri, & Nikoobin, 2020):

The equations of motion for the quarter car model are shown in equations 1 (Zha et al., 2022):

Table 1. Description and numeric Parameters of quarter-car model (Yar & Shi, 2013)

Parameters	Description	Values	Unit
M_s	Body Mass (Sprung Mass)	972.2	Kg
M_u	Suspension Mass (Unspring Mass)	113.6	Kg
K_s	Spring of suspension system	42,719.6	N/m
K_t	Spring of wheel and tire	101,115	N/m
C_s	Damping of suspension system	1,095	N.s/m
C_t	Damping of wheel and tire	14.6	N.s/m

$$\begin{cases} M_s \ddot{Z}_s = -K_s\left(Z_s - Z_u\right) - C_s\left(\dot{Z}_s - \dot{Z}_u\right) + F \\ M_u \ddot{Z}_u = K_s\left(Z_s - Z_u\right) + C_s\left(\dot{Z}_s - \dot{Z}_u\right) - K_t\left(Z_u - Z_r\right) - C_t\left(\dot{Z}_u - \dot{Z}_r\right) - F \end{cases} \quad (1)$$

The dynamics of the quarter car model are defined in a state-space format [24]:

$$\begin{cases} \dot{Z} = AZ + BF + GZ_r \\ y = CZ + DF + EZ_r \end{cases} \quad (2)$$

So, we can get state space from as below:

$$\begin{cases} Z_1 = \dot{Z}_s \\ Z_2 = Z_s \\ Z_3 = \dot{Z}_u \\ Z_4 = Z_u \end{cases} \rightarrow \dot{Z}_1 = \begin{cases} -\dfrac{C_S}{M_S}Z_1 - \dfrac{K_S}{M_S}Z_2 + \dfrac{C_S}{M_S}Z_3 + \dfrac{K_S}{M_S}Z_4 + \dfrac{1}{M_S}F \\ \dot{Z}_2 = Z_1 \\ \dot{Z}_3 = \dfrac{C_S}{M_u}Z_1 + \dfrac{K_S}{M_u}Z_2 - \dfrac{\left(C_S + C_t\right)}{M_u}Z_3 - \dfrac{\left(K_S + K_t\right)}{Mu}Z_4 + \dfrac{K_t}{M_u}Z_r + \dfrac{C_t}{M_u}\dot{Z}_r - \dfrac{1}{M_u}F \\ \dot{Z}_4 = Z_3 \end{cases} \quad (3)$$

Since, the vertical velocity of road profile is very small, we can neglect it, the equation of variable becomes:

$$\dot{Z}_3 = \dfrac{C_s}{M_u}Z_1 + \dfrac{K_s}{M_u}Z_2 - \dfrac{\left(C_s + C_t\right)}{M_u}Z_3 - \dfrac{\left(K_s + K_t\right)}{M_u}Z_4 + \dfrac{K_t}{M_u}Z_r - \dfrac{1}{M_u}F \quad (4)$$

The state vectors, input, and output matrices are defined as:
Inputs System

$$\underbrace{\begin{bmatrix} \dot{Z}_1 \\ \dot{Z}_2 \\ \dot{Z}_3 \\ \dot{Z}_4 \end{bmatrix}}_{\dot{Z}} = \underbrace{\begin{bmatrix} -\dfrac{C_s}{M_s} & -\dfrac{K_s}{M_s} & \dfrac{C_s}{M_s} & \dfrac{K_s}{M_s} \\ 1 & 0 & 0 & 0 \\ \dfrac{C_s}{M_u} & \dfrac{K_s}{M_u} & \dfrac{(C_s + C_t)}{M_u} & \dfrac{(K_s + K_t)}{M_u} \\ 0 & 0 & 1 & 0 \end{bmatrix}}_{A} \begin{bmatrix} Z_1 \\ Z_2 \\ Z_3 \\ Z_4 \end{bmatrix} + \underbrace{\begin{bmatrix} \dfrac{1}{M_s} \\ 0 \\ -\dfrac{1}{M_u} \\ 0 \end{bmatrix}}_{B} F + \underbrace{\begin{bmatrix} 0 \\ 0 \\ \dfrac{K_t}{M_u} \\ 0 \end{bmatrix}}_{G} Z_r \tag{5}$$

Outputs System

$$y = \begin{bmatrix} Z_s \\ \dot{Z}_s \\ \ddot{Z}_s \\ Z_s - Z_u \end{bmatrix} = \underbrace{\begin{bmatrix} 0 & 1 & 0 & 0 \\ 1 & 0 & 0 & 0 \\ -\dfrac{C_s}{M_s} & -\dfrac{K_s}{M_s} & \dfrac{C_s}{M_s} & \dfrac{K_s}{M_s} \\ 0 & 1 & 0 & -1 \end{bmatrix}}_{C} \begin{bmatrix} Z_1 \\ Z_2 \\ Z_3 \\ Z_4 \end{bmatrix} + \underbrace{\begin{bmatrix} 0 \\ 0 \\ \dfrac{1}{M_s} \\ 0 \end{bmatrix}}_{D} F + \underbrace{\begin{bmatrix} 0 \\ 0 \\ 0 \\ 0 \end{bmatrix}}_{E} Z_r \tag{6}$$

CONTROLLERS DESIGN

The objective of control system design is to construct a system that has a desirable response to standard inputs. So, in this work the goal of control is to give the required dynamic behavior of car under road variations, in this section, the design of selected and proposed controllers will present (Nise, 2020).

Proportional-Integral- Derivative (PID)

A proportional-integrated-derived controller (PID controller or three terminal controllers) is a control loop mechanism that uses feedback that is widely used in industrial control systems and a variety of other applications that require continuously adjusted control. The PID controller continuously computes the error value e (t), where e (t) is the difference between the desired set point (SP) and the measured process variable (PV) and applies a correction based on the proportionality, integral, and derivative terms (denoted by P, I, and D respectively) (Wang L., 2020). In industrial field, the PID automatically applies an accurate and responsive patch to the control function. An everyday example is a car's cruise control, where going up a hill will reduce speed if constant engine power is applied. The controller's PID algorithm restores the measured speed to the required speed with minimal delay and overshoot by increasing the motor's power output in a controlled method (Hammoodi, Flayyih, & Hamad, 2020). The first theoretical analysis and practical application of PID were in the field of automatic guidance systems for ships, which were developed from the early 1920s onwards. It was then used for automatic process control in the manufacturing industry, being widely implemented initially in pneumatic and then electronic control devices. Today the PID concept is used globally in applications that require precise and optimized automation control (Fellani & Gabaj, 2015).

The PID controller is mathematically represented as:

Figure 4. Design of PID controller
Source: Fellani and Gabaj (2015)

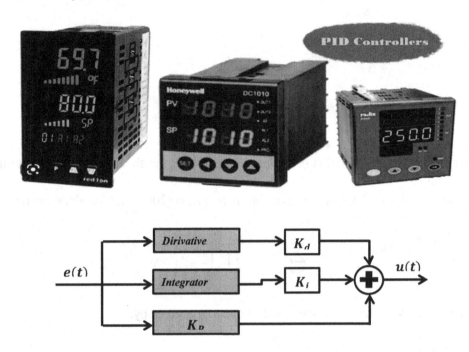

$$u(t) = K_p e(t) + K_i \int_0^t e(\tau) d\tau + K_d \frac{d}{dt} e(t) \tag{7}$$

Where: (K_p) is the proportional Gain, $(K_i = K_p / T_i)$ whereas (K_i) the integral Gain and (T_i) the integral time, $(K_d = K_p \times T_d)$ whereas (K_d) presents the derivative Gain and (T_d) derivative time.

Fractional-Order PID FOPID

Fractional Order Control (FOC) is a control theory that uses partial order integration as part of the control system design tools. The fractional calculus (FC) is used to improve and generalize control methods and strategies (Pandula & Antonio, 2011).

The basic idea of fractional-order controllers goes back to Alin Oustaloup, who developed the CRONE controller (Pondlubny, 1998). After him, Podlubny gave the idea of ($PI^\lambda D^\mu$) controller using Laplace transform to solve the following fractional-order differential equation (Reza & Abbs, 2011; Ma & Hori, 2004):

$$L\left[\alpha D_t^q f(t)\right] = s^q F(s) - \sum_{i=0}^{m} \left[D^{q-i-1} f(t)\right]_{t=0} \tag{8}$$

Where q is the fractional order which can be a complex number and α and t are the limits of the operation

The differential and integral operators can be generalized into one fundamental operator αD_t^q where:

$$aD_t^q = \begin{cases} \dfrac{d^q}{dt^q} & q > 0 \\[2mm] 1 & q = 0 \\[2mm] \int_a^t (d\tau)^{-q} & q < 0 \end{cases} \tag{9}$$

There are many definitions like that of Grunwald-Lenikover, but the most used is the definition of Riemann-Liouville.

The Grunwald-Lenikover definition is given in Ma and Hori (2004) and Mouleeswaran (2012) as:

$$aD_t^q f(t) = \frac{d^q f(t)}{d(t-a)^q} = \lim_{N \to \infty} \left[\frac{t-a}{N} \right]^{-q} \sum_{j=0}^{N-1} (-1)^j \binom{q}{j} f\left(t - j \left[\frac{t-a}{N} \right] \right) \tag{10}$$

The Rieman-Liouville definition is the simplest one to use given by:

$$aD_t^q f(t) = \frac{d^q f(t)}{d(t-a)^q} = \frac{1}{\Gamma(n-q)} \frac{d^n}{dt^n} \int_0^t (t-\tau)^{n-q-1} f(\tau) d\tau \tag{11}$$

With $\Gamma(z) = \int_0^\infty t^{z-1-t} e^{-t} dt$ (12)

The transfer function of $PI^\lambda D^\mu$ controller has the following form:

$$F_c(s) = \frac{U(s)}{E(s)} = K_p + K_i \frac{1}{s^\lambda} e(t) + K_d s^\mu e(t) \tag{13}$$

Where $F_c(s)$ is the Transfer Function of a controller, $\dfrac{1}{s^\lambda}$ is an integrator term, and s^μ is a derivation term, the control signal $u(t)$ can be expressed in the time domain as (Mouleeswaran, 2012):

$$u(t) = K_p e(t) + K_i D^\lambda e(t) + K_d D^\mu e(t) \tag{14}$$

ARTIFICIAL INTELLIGENT METHODS (AI)

(AI), is a computer-controlled digital robot to perform tasks commonly associated with intelligent beings. The term is always applied to the project of developing systems that have intellectual processes characteristic of humans, such as the ability to think about or learn from previous experiences. Since the development of the digital computer in the 1940s, it has been proven that computers can be programmed to perform extremely complex tasks such as discovering evidence for mathematical theories or playing chess. However, despite continuous advances in computer processing speed and memory capacity, there is still no software that can match the flexibility. humanity in broader fields or in tasks that require a lot of everyday knowledge. On the other hand, some programs have achieved levels of performance of human experts and professionals in performing certain tasks, so AI in this limited sense is found in applications as diverse as medical diagnostics, computer search engines, and voice or handwriting recognition (Winston, 1992).

Artificial Neural Networks

Neural networks (NNs) have been developed to simulate the human nervous system for machine learning tasks by manipulating the computational units in the learning model as human neurons. The big idea of neural networks is to create artificial intelligence by building machine for computational operations to simulate human nervous system, this is no simple task because the computational power of today's fastest computer is a fraction of the computational power of the human brain. Neural networks were developed soon after computers in the 1950s and 1960s where Rosenblatt's visualization algorithm was seen as the fundamental cornerstone of neural networks, causing Initial excitement about the prospects for artificial intelligence (Aggarwal, 2018). Artificial neural networks are inspired by the structure of biological neurons such as the human brain, it consists of a large number of neurons, and each cell has it can complete the complex task very quickly and a good sheet (JFeldman, 1998). The neuron consists of the ramifications of the cell body called the fasting contains a nucleus and branches connected to the

Figure 5. Biological neuron
Source: Islam and Jin (2019)

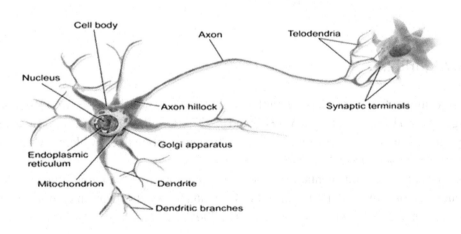

cell body to reserve signals from other neurons. The connection between the end of the nerve axis is called on the neutrino dendrites surrounding the synapse (a synapse is a communication unit between two neurons). When the overall signal is greater neurons are released (Hebb, 1993).

The artificial neural network is designed on the biological neural network. Like a biological neural network, ANN is a link between nodes, similar to neurons. Each neural network contains three critical components: node personality, network topology, and learning rules. The node character defines how information is processed by the node, the network structure determines the ways the nodes are organized and connected, and the learning rules define how weights are created and modified (Livingstone & al, 2008). The basic model of the node is shown in ANN in Figure 6. This process can be expressed as a mathematical model in the following form (Gowtham, 2022):

$$y = \left(\sum_{i=0}^{n} w_i x_i \pm T \right)$$

(14)

Where y is the output of the node, f is the transfer function, w_i is the weight of input x_i, and T is the threshold value. The transfer function has many forms. A nonlinear transfer function is more useful than linear ones (Tran & Hoang, 2016).

Figure 6. A basic model of a single node where x_i *= input,* w_i *= weight,* f *= transfer function,* y *= output*

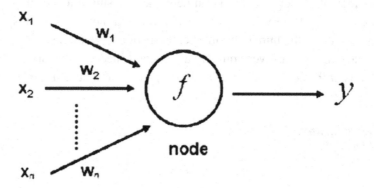

Genetic Algorithms

Genetic Algorithms (GAs) are adaptive methods used to solve search and optimization problems. The first to suggest the basic principle of GA is Holland in 1975 (Grollberg, 1989; Tandon & Randeep, 2011). Generally, this evolutionary algorithm (EV) gives many combinative problems whose mathematical formulations are difficult to realize (Kumar, 2018).

GA consists of three fundamental operators: reproduction, crossover, and mutation. The optimization by genetic algorithms encodes parameters as are binary models, then run recursively with the three operators in a random fashion (Jun-Yi, Jin, & Bing, 2005).

Figure 7. Diagram showing the steps of optimizing using genetic algorithms

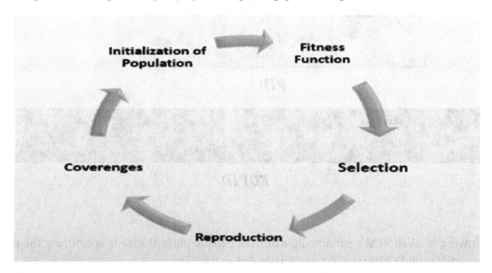

Genetic operators provide the basic search mechanism of the GA, the most usual operators are:

Reproduction: Is a basic operator of genetic algorithms, the basis of reproduction is copied into the next generation, according to the reproduction probability P_{ri} which is defined in Jayachitra and Vinodha (2015):

$$P_{ri} = F_i(\theta) / \sum_{i=1}^{P_i} F_i(\theta) \tag{16}$$

Where P_i is the population size.

Selection: The main goal is the selection of the chromosomes with the best qualities for integration in the next generation.

Crossover and Mutation: Crossover is the combination of chromosomes of two individuals. New chromosomes are created and integrated into the population. After the crossover part comes the step of mutation which uses random chromosome differences to generate new individuals (Herrero, Blasco, Martinez, & & Salcedo, 2002).

In this chapter the researches code the parameters of PID and FOPID and put them into one chromosome for each controller PID and FOPID respectively. The relation between the binary coding genes and the real parameters is shown in the equation (17):

$$X = min + (max - min) / (2^{10} - 1) \times b \tag{17}$$

Where *max* and min are Upper and Lower limits for parameters of our controllers, *b* is a binary value system (Meng & Baoye, 2007). Figure 8 presents the chromosomes of PID and FOPID after coding:

Figure 8. Chromosomes of controllers after coding

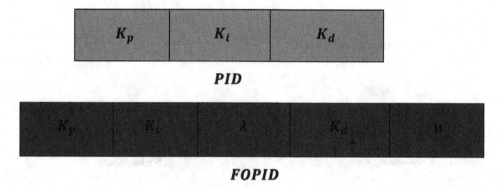

The following steps show the general algorithm of genetic algorithms for optimizing the parameters of controllers (PID and FOPID) (Ananatachaisilp & Lin, 2017):

Step 1: Initialize the parameter of the population with random solutions;
Step 2: Select the crossover, mutation, number of clusters;
Step 3: Define number of generations and determine the coding mode;
Step 4: Define and evaluate the value of the fitness function;
Step 5: Proceed with crossover and mutation operation and make up the new generation;
Step 6: Repeat step 02 until the best value is obtained.

The most important step in GA is a selection of an objective function (fitness) used to evaluate the suitability of each chromosome. The object function using in this work is shown in the following equation (Tandon, 2011):

$$J = \int_0^T t \left| e(t) \right| dt \tag{18}$$

Where t presents the time and e is the error to minimize, for that we use the fitness value to guide simulation in the best solution of the problem, as shown in the next equation (Tandon, 2011; Kramer, 2017):

$$Fitness\ Value = \frac{1}{J} \tag{19}$$

Particle Swarm Optimizations

In field of science, a particle Swarm Optimizations (PSO), is a computational method that optimizes a problem iteratively trying to improve a candidate solution with regard to a given measure of quality. It solves a problem by having a population of candidate solution here dubbed particles, and moving these particles around in the search space according to simple mathematical formula over the particle's position and velocity. Each particle's movement is influenced its local best-known position in the search-space, which are updated as better positions are found by other particles. This is expected to move the swarm toward the best solutions (Riccardo, James, & Tim, 2017).

Figure 9. Display the principle of particle swarm optimization

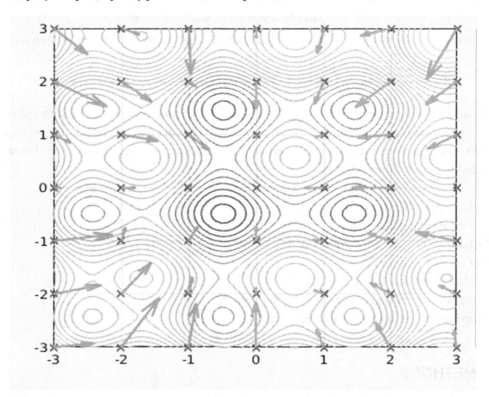

Particle swarm optimization is a technology inspired by the social behavior of birds and fish crowding. This technique was developed by Dr. Kenedy and Dr. Eberhart in 1995 (Kebdy & Russell, 1995). It makes to simultaneously search large region in the solution space of the optimized objective function (Raju & Reddy, 2016).

The PSO algorithm based on initializing n swarm of particles, who move in a j dimensional search space randomly in position and velocity (Joudhav & Vadnajacharya, 2012). It can obtain a high-quality solution in a shorter time, uses optimization particles that represent a potential solution to a problem. All particles looking for a certain velocity can be adjusted (Latha, Rajinikanth, & Surekha, 2013).

We can define the position X_i of ith particle of the swarm, and the velocity V_i of this particle at $(i+1)^{th}$ iteration as the following equations (Zhao, Zeng, Wang, & & Ji):

$$V_{ij}(i+1) = wV_{ij} + C_1 r_1 \left(Pbest_{ij} - X_{ij} \right) + C_2 r_2 \left(Gbest - X_{ij} \right) \tag{20}$$

With $X_{ij} = V_{ij} + X_{ij}$

$$w = w_{max}\left(\frac{iter}{maxiter}\right)\left(w_{max} - w_{min}\right) \tag{21}$$

Where $i = 1, 2, \ldots, n$, j is a search space, r_1 and r_2 are random numbers between $(0,1)$. C_1 and C_2 are correction factors (C_1 pulls each particle toward a local best position it called cognitive parameter, C_2 is a social parameter it pulls the particle toward a global best position, w_{max} is a final weight and w_{min} is an initial weight, *maxiter* is a maximum iteration number, *iter* is a current iteration number.

Object Function

Particle Swarm Optimization (PSO), like GA method it needs an objective function to improve which is the particle scaling function to minimize. To improve the parameters of PID and FOPID we used the fitness function mentioned in equation (19), the steps of the particle swarm algorithm is shown as follow (patrick, Idaumghar, & Julien, 2016):

Step 1: Define objective function;
Step 2: Define PSO parameters;
Step 3: Initialization of position and velocity;
Step 4: Define function Evolution;
Step 5: Update Pbest and Gbest;
Step 6: Compute velocity and position handling boundary;
Step 7: Stope while getting the best value.

TUNED METHODS

Adapt PID Control-Based Neural Networks

The Neural Network Control for automation and control technology, theory and as the twenty-first century types of networks for Artificial Neural Networks ((Ed) & Suzuki, 2013):

- Perceptron
- Feedforward Neural Network
- Multilayer Perceptron
- Convolutional Neural Network
- Recurrent Neural Network
- LSTM-Long Short-Term Memory
- Sequence to Sequence Models
- Modular Neural Network

This chapter based to method of Artificial Neural Network a method Multilayer Forword Network contains an output layer and an input layer, on or more hidden layer (Xu, Lai, Yu, & & Liu, 2013). The most topical in neural network structure and algorithm id the error backpropagation BP Neural Network, the Figure 10 show the diagram of BPANN (Ciba, Abghour, Moussaid, Omri, & Rida, 2018).

Figure 10. General structure of back-propagation neural network (BPNN)

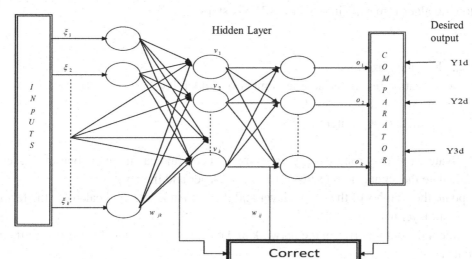

The function of the neurons for PID and FOPID is defined as follows:

$$\left\{ \begin{array}{l} P - neuron\ output = \sum_i input_i \\[2ex] I - neuron\ output = \int_0^t \sum_i input_i \\[2ex] D - neuron\ output = \frac{d}{dt} \sum_i input_i \end{array} \right. \tag{20}$$

$$\left\{ \begin{array}{l} P - neuron\ output = \sum_i input_i \\[2ex] I - neuron\ output = \int_0^t \sum_i input_i \\[2ex] D - neuron\ output = \frac{d}{dt} \sum_i input_i \\[2ex] \lambda - neuron\ output = \sum_i input_i \\[2ex] \eta - neuron\ output = \sum_i input_i \end{array} \right. \tag{21}$$

BPANN model used is described as follows:

$$F\left(x\right) = b_2 + w_2(f_A\left(b_1 + w_1 X\right)) \qquad (22)$$

The goal of Backpropagation algorithm is to adjust the weights to reduce the mean value of the Mean Square Error in all Neural Network confirmation samples (Gouravaraju, Narayan, Sauer, & Gautam, 2023), the flowing algorithm explain how the BPANN steps:

Step 1:

- Weight and bias initialization.
- Choose the activation functions and the number of hidden layers.
- Set the learning step and error threshold.
- Set the maximum number of iterations.

Step 2: Activate the perceptron by applying an input vector and calculate the output of each layer.

Step 3: Calculate the signal error terms of the output layer and the layers.

Step 4: Update the weights of the output layer and the hidden layers, and calculate the terms of the error for the output layer neurons.

Step 5: Reinfect the output error in the network and calculate the terms of the error for the neurons of the hidden layer.

Step 6: Adjust the parameters (weight) of the output layer and the hidden layer.

Step 7: If the condition on the error or the number of iterations is reached, go to Step 8, if not go back to Step 3 until the system stabilizes.

Step 8: End (Gouravaraju, Narayan, Sauer, & Gautam, 2023).

Figure 11 displays diagram on Simulink of tuned PID and FOPID controller by BP-Neural Network:

Figure 11. Structure of backpropagation neural network controller (PIDBPNN)

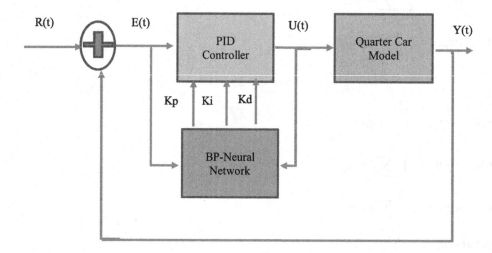

Figure 12. Structure of backpropagation neural network controller (FOPIDBPNN)

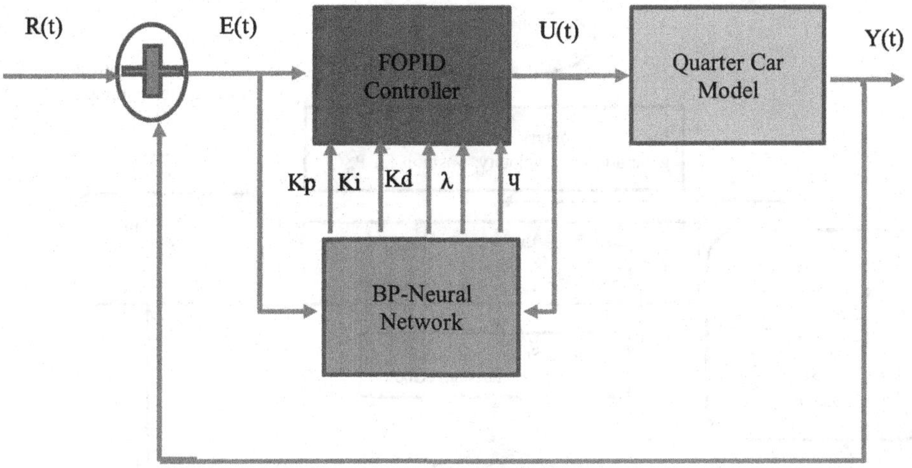

Adapt PID Control Using Optimization Methods

The GA and PSO algorithms are a research technique that achieves a compromise balance between the utilization of research space and the exploitation of the best solution (Sun, Cao, & Zhao, 2019). The Figure 12 display the diagram of an active suspension system of quarter car model designed with PID and FOPID controllers and Figure 13 illustrate the algorithm of PSO to adapt PID and FOPID Controllers:

Figure 13. Block diagram of an active suspension system using PID and FOPID controllers

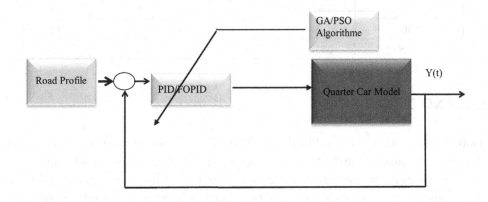

Figure 14. GA and PSO flow-short

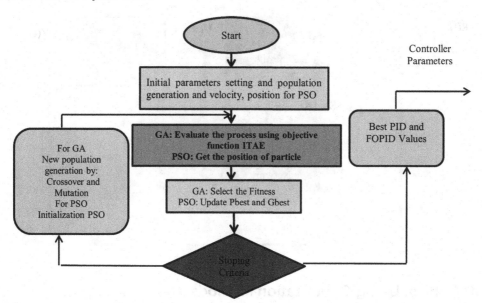

Table 2. Description the parameters PID and FOPID

Tuned Method		k_p	k_i	k_d	»	¼
PID	GA	10.400	0.091	5772.06	—	—
	PSO	24.50	0.081	8953.04	—	—
	ANN	8.502	0.3815	9853.1603	—	—
FOPID	GA	0.865	1.0968	6000	0.1	1
	PSO	0.950	0.800	10000	0.5	1
	ANN	0.950	0.811	12953.654	1.2	1

RESULTS AND DISCUSSION

The simulation results-based MATLAB/SIMULATION and illustrate it a comparative study between the passive and active suspension controlled by PID, and Fractional-Order adapt by intelligent methods.

In this section using the mathematical model of a quarter car suspension, and testing by three types of roads. The Simulation show the velocity of car, body acceleration for measured handling and ride comfort of driver and passengers, and the body displacement of the quarter car with suspension deflection.

The roads using in this study is step road input =1cm/s (Excavated Road); Bumpy Road (Sinusoidal input) =1cm/s, then Random input (Noisy Road) = 0.2 Noise Power, the Figure 15 show a different road using for testing an input of quarter car model.

Figure 15. (a) Step input road, (b) bumpy input road, (c) random input road

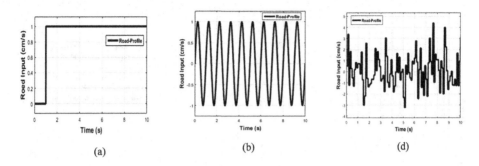

(a)	(b)	(d)

The performance of the suspension system in term of ride comfort and car stability will be show in Figure 16 to Figure 18 divided into (a), (b), (c), (d) for all testing road:

For Step Road Input

Figure 16a. Response for body displacement between passive and active suspension

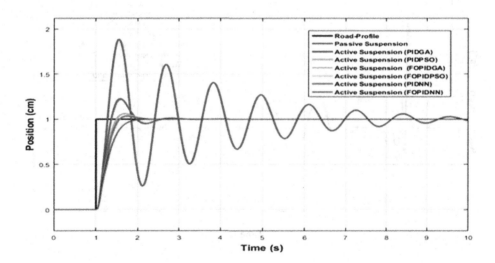

Figure 16b. Response for velocity between passive and active suspension

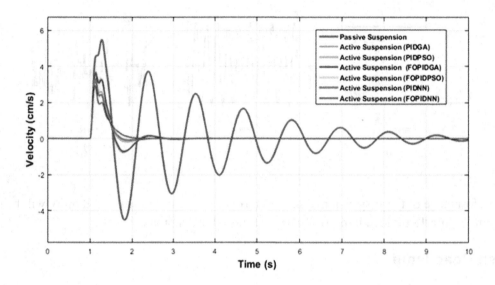

Figure 16c. Response for body acceleration between passive and active suspension

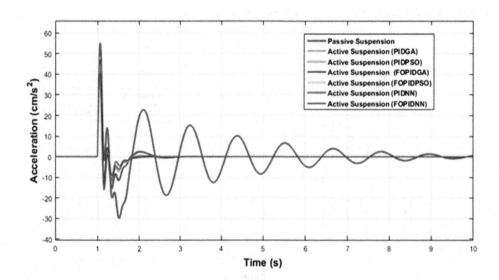

Figure 16d. Response for suspension deflection between passive and active suspension

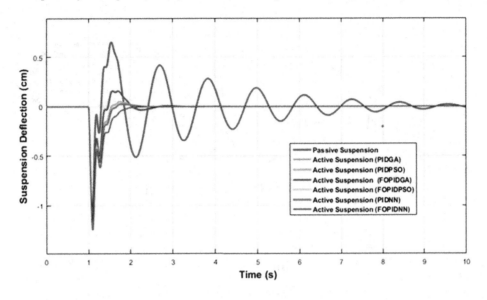

For Bumpy Road Input

Figure 17a. Response for body displacement between passive and active suspension

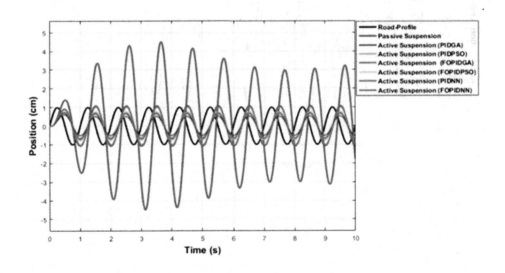

Figure 17b. Response for velocity between passive and active suspension

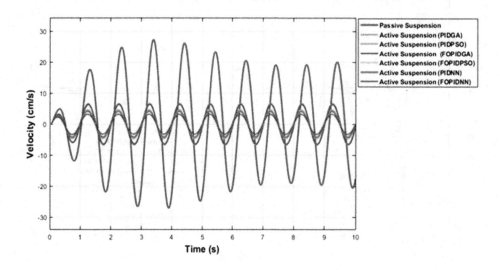

Figure 17c. Response for body acceleration between passive and active suspension

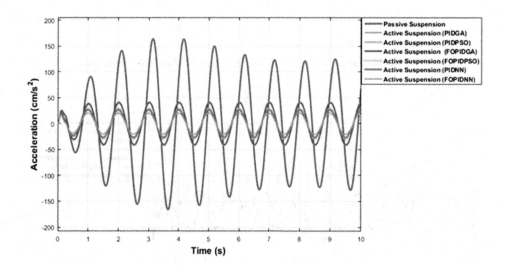

Figure 17d. Response for suspension deflection between passive and active suspension

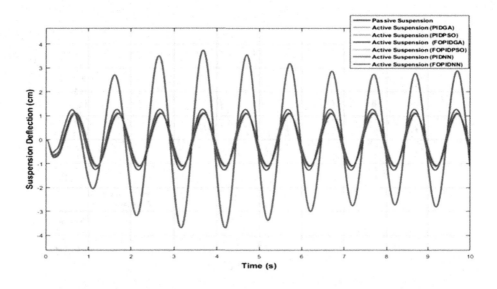

For Random Road Input

Figure 18a. Response for body displacement between passive and active suspension

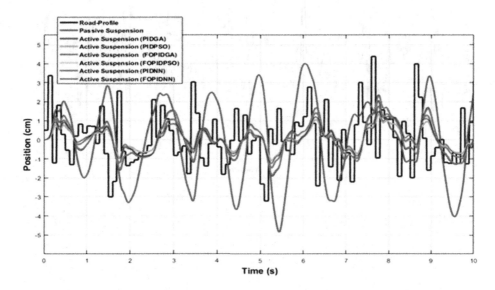

Figure 18b. Response for velocity between passive and active suspension

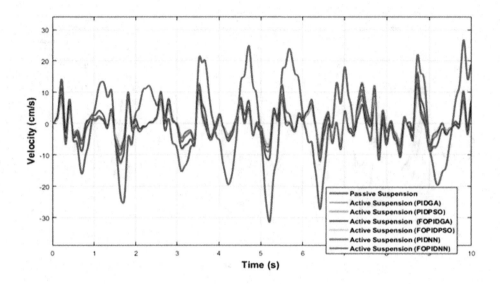

Figure 18c. Response for body acceleration between passive and active suspension

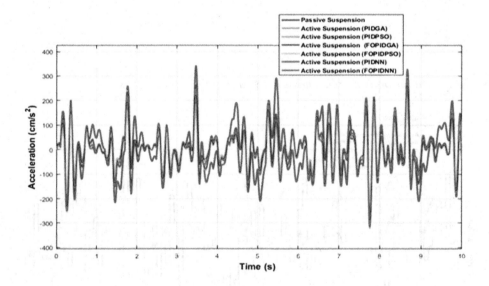

Figure 18d. Response for suspension deflection between passive and active suspension

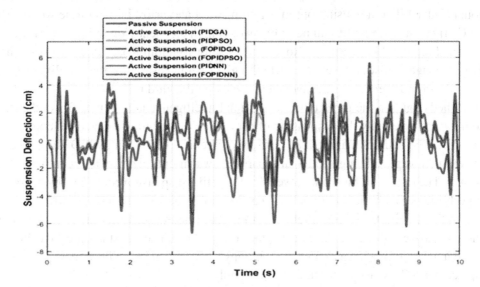

Active control of suspension system undergoing disturbance from all types of the roads, this study effective suppression of vibration of the sprung mass displacement, and an active suspension can be an avoid damaging the structure integrity of vehicles and improve service life of suspension system.

Table 2 shows Root Mean Sequard Error (RMS) (E. Shi, Oliveares, & Rosseel, 2020), of quarter car model for active suspension, and it based to comparative study between Passive suspension and Active suspension controlled by optimal PID and optimal FOPID.

$$RMSE(t) = \sqrt{\frac{1}{n}\sum_{i=0}^{n}\left(S_i(t) - O_i(t)\right)^2} \qquad (23)$$

Where O_i are the Observation, S_i Predictive Values of a variable, and n the number of observations available for analysis.

Table 3. Study RMS Error between Passive and Active Suspension of Quarter Car Model

	Road Profiles Technique Methods		Step Road Input	Sinusoidal Input (Bumpy Road)	Random Road Input
Study RMS Error Of Quarter Car Suspension	**Passive Suspension**		9.701e^{-01}	2.436	2.097
	Active Suspension	**PID** *GA*	8.808e^{-01}	6.330e^{-01}	8.298e^{-01}
		PID *PSO*	8.621e^{-01}	4.424e^{-01}	7.669e^{-01}
		PID *ANN*	8.580e^{-01}	6.055e^{-01}	8.117e^{-01}
		FOPID *GA*	8.794e^{-01}	3.972e^{-01}	6.200e^{-01}
		FOPID *PSO*	8.574e^{-01}	4.077e^{-01}	6.276e^{-01}
		FOPID *ANN*	8.448e^{-01}	3.171e^{-01}	5.393e^{-01}

Table 3 shows a comparison between passive and active suspension controlled by conventional PID and Fractional Order PID tuned using optimization method and artificial neural networks. The result proves the FOPID adjusted by artificial neural networks high efficiency on reduction error estimate of 13% for step road input, 98% for Bumpy Road, and 97% for Random Road. In conclusion, the FOPID tuned by Backpropagation Neural Network (BPNN) gives better results for the stability of the car, and better ride comfort for drivers and passengers, especially on the hard roads.

This work sheds light on the importance of artificial intelligence and its benefits in the field of the automotive industry, especially the suspension of cars. We used different methods to control the active suspension, where the authors manipulated conventional controllers such as PID and processed with smart methods such as genetic algorithms and particle swarm optimization and compared them with neural networks. The results of this work proved that the active suspension controlled by neural networks gave better performance than the traditional suspension and the active suspension controlled by PID and fractional-order PID (FOPID). The only problem is that, unlike neural networks, the controllers mentioned above are not expensive and the purchaser can benefit from them. Their cost is expensive, but Its results are impressive in terms of passenger comfort on bumpy roads and giving a faster car speed without any vehicle displacements. It is also environmentally friendly.

Many authors have made active suspension control using Artificial Neural networks their main concern and have many papers such as (Aela, Kenne, & Mintsa, 2022), (Liu, Zhu, Liu, Wang, & Tong, 2022), and, (Hamza & Yahia, 2023) these publications have proven that artificial intelligence in general and artificial neural networks, in particular, have played a major role in moving from an era in which cars depended on old and primitive technologies to an era in which smart and self-driving cars became more comfortable.

CONCLUSION

The automotive industry is one of the most developed sectors in recent years, and it has been characterized by continuous renewal and its ability to absorb technological development that includes all components of the car. And if today's car is equipped with technologies that adopt technologies that were known to aircraft decades ago, the car of tomorrow will be more technically advanced and will become a smart, self-driving machine that is connected to the Internet, relies on artificial intelligence to a large extent, and is non-polluting to the environment.

The basic function of the car as a transportation tool is no longer the only concern for car manufacturers today. Rather, they seek, in the context of employing technology, to develop a modern luxury lifestyle and make it a smart mobility machine that focuses on performance, comfort, and safety and enables the reduction of stress resulting from the daily commute. Future cars will contribute to providing the highest levels of comfort, luxury, and safety, and will reduce the risks of using the roads while reducing environmental pollution.

In the industrial field, the PID control is one of the oldest control strategies because of its very sampling of design, good performance including low percentage overshoot, and small setting time for showing industrial processes. Recently, the FOPID Controller appeared and caused a sensation in the industrial field, it is based on the Proportional, Integral, and Derivative parameters (with two additional parameters the order of fractional integral, and the order of fractional derivative. The result of this work proved effective in the FOPID tuned by intelligent methods especially Artificial Neural Networks, unlike PID.

In general, the design methods of classical PID controllers give similar results when the PSO algorithm, GA, or ANN is used, but when using the FOPID is better than the resultant optimal criteria when using conventional PID controllers. In other words, the FOPID controller gives better performance compared to the PID controller. However, in the industrial field especially the automobile industry, manufacturers tend to use PID in active suspension because it less expensive and there are many studies on it, unlike FOPID, which is still under study with a difficulty of its mathematical equations and its cost is very expensive.

REFERENCES

Aela, A., Kenne, J. P., & Mintsa, H. (2022). Adaptive neural Network and Nonlinear Electrohydraulic active suspension control system. *Journal of Vibration and Control, 28*(3-4), 243–259. doi:10.1177/1077546320975979

Aggarwal, C. C. (2018). *Neural Networks and Deep Learning.* Springer International Publishing AG.

Ahmed, M. I., Hazlina, M. Y., & Rashid, M. (2016). Mathematical Modeling and Control of Active Suspension System for a Quarter Car Railway vehicle. *Malaysian Journal of Mathematical Sciences, 10*, 227–241.

Ananatachaisilp, P., & Lin, Z. (2017). Fractional order PID control of rotor suspension by active magnetic bearings. In actuators. *Multidisciplinary Digital Publishing Institute, 6*(1), 4.

Anh, N. (2020). Control an Active Suspension System using PID and LQR Controller. *International Journal and Production Engineering Research and Development, 10*(3), 7003-12.

Applegard, M., & Wellstead, a. P. (1995). Active suspension: Same Background. *IEEE Proceedings-Control theory and Application, 14*(2), 123-128.

Barr, A. J., & Ray, A. J. (1996). Control of an active suspension using fuzzy logic. *Proceedings IEEE the International Fuzzy Systems, 1*, 42-48.

Ciba, Z., Abghour, N., Moussaid, K., Omri, A. E., & Rida, M. (2018). A novel Architecture Combined with Optimal Parameters for Back-Propagation Neural Network Applied to Anomaly Network Instrusion Detection. *Computers & Security, 75*, 36–58. doi:10.1016/j.cose.2018.01.023

Dan, H., & Sun, W. (2018). Nonlinear output feedback finite-time control for vehicle active suspension systems. *IEEE Transaction on Industrial Information, 15*(4), 2073–2082.

Suzuki, K. (Ed.). (2013). *Artificial Neural Networks. Architecture and applications.* B.D. Books on Demand.

Erjavec, J., & Thompson, R. (2014). *Automotive technology a systems approach.* Ongage Learning.

Feldman, M. A. (1998). *Computing with Structured Neural Networks.* Academic Press.

Fellani, M. A., & Gabaj, A. (2015). PID Controller Deign for Two Tanks Liquid Level Control System Using MATLAB. *Iranian Journal of Electrical and Computer Engineering, 5*(3), 436.

Ghazaly, N. M., Ahmed, A. E., Ali, A. S., & El-Jaber, G. (2016). H^∞ Control of An Active Suspension System for a Quarter Car Model. *International Journal of Vehicle Structures and System*, *8*(1). Advance online publication. doi:10.4273/ijvss.8.1.07

Gouravaraju, S., Narayan, J., Sauer, R. A., & Gautam, S. S. (2023). A Bayesian regularization-back-propagation neural network model for peeling computations. *The Journal of Adhesion*, *99*(1), 92–115. doi:10.1080/00218464.2021.2001335

Gowtham, K. J. (2022). A Study of Cellular neural networks with new vertex-edge topological indices. *Int. J. Open Problems Compt. Math*, *15*(3), 115–133.

Grollberg, D. (1989). *Genetic algorithms in search, optimization, and machine learning*. Addison-Wesley.

Hammoodi, S. J., Flayyih, K. S., & Hamad, A. (2020). Design and implementation Speed Control System of DC Motor Based PID Control and MATLAB/SIMULINK. *International Journal of Power Electronic and Drive Systems*, *11*(1), 127. doi:10.11591/ijpeds.v11.i1.pp127-134

Hamza, A., & Yahia, N. (2023). Artificial Nearal Networks Controller of Active Suspension for Ambulance based on ISO Standards. Proceedings of Institution of Mechanical Enginners, Part D. *Journal of Automobile*, *237*(1), 34–37. doi:10.1177/09544070221075456

Hebb, D. O. (1993). *The organization of behavior*. John Wiley & Sons.

Herrero, J. M., Blasco, X., Martinez, M., & Salcedo, J. V. (2002). Optimal pid tuning with genetic algorithms for nonlinear process models. *IF1AC Proceedings, 35*(1), 31-36.

Huang, Y., Na, J., Wu, X., Liu, X., & Guo, Y. (2015). Adaptive control of nonlinear uncertain active suspension system with prescribed performance. *ISA Transactions*, *54*, 145–155. doi:10.1016/j.isatra.2014.05.025 PMID:25034649

Ignatius, O., Obinalv, C. E., & Evboglai, a. M. (2016). Modeling Design and Simulation of Active suspension system PID Controller Using automated Tuning Technique. *Network and Complex Systems, 6*, 11-15.

Islam, M. G. C., & Jin, S. (2019). An Overview of Neural Network. *American Journal of Neural Networks and Applications*, *5*(1), 7–11. doi:10.11648/j.ajnna.20190501.12

Izadkhah, A., Nouri, K., & Nikoobin, A. (2020). Proportional Integral Derivative Control of Fractional-Order for a Quarter Car System. *Ram. J. Phys, 65*, 103.

Jayachitra, A., & Vinodha, R. (2015). Genetic algorithm based PID controller tuning approach for continuous stirred tank reactor. *Advances in Artificial Intelligence*, *2014*, 9–9.

Joudhav, A. M., & Vadnajacharya. (2012). Performance Verification of PID Controller in an Interconnected Power System Using Particle Swarm Optimization. *Energy Procedia*, *14*, 2075–2080. doi:10.1016/j.egypro.2011.12.1210

Jun-yi, C., Jin, L., & Bing, A. C. (2005). Optimization of fractional-order pid controllers based on genetic algorithms. *International conference on machine learning and cybernetics*, *9*, 5686-5689.

Kashem, S., Nagarajah, R., & Eklesabi, M. (2018). *Vehicle Suspension System and Electromagnetic Damper*. doi:10.1007/978-981-10-5478-5

Kebdy, J., & Russell, E. (1995). Particle Swarm Optimization. *Proceedings of ICNN95-International Conference on Neural Networks, 4.*

Kramer, O. (2017). *Genetic algorithms, genetic algorithm essential.* Springer.

Kumar, L., kumar, P., Satyajeet, & Narang, D. (2018). Tuning of fractional-order controllers using evolutionary optimization for pid tuned synchronous generator excitation system. *IFAC-PapersOnLine, 51*(4), 859–864. doi:10.1016/j.ifacol.2018.06.121

Latha, K., Rajinikanth, V., & Surekha, P. (2013). Pso-based PID Controller Design for a Class of Stable and Unstable Systems. *International Scholarly Research Notices.*

Lin, J. S., & Kanellakopoulos, I. (1997). Nonlineardesign of active suspension. *IEEE Control Systems Magazine*, 45–59.

Liu, L., Zhu, C., Liu, Y. J., Wang, R., & Tong, S. (2022). Performance Improvement of active susepnsion Constrained system via Neural Networks and Learning System. *IEEE Transactions on Neural Networks and Learning Systems.*

Liu, Y. J., Zeng, Q., Tong, S., Chen, C. L. P., & Liu, L. (2019). Adaptive Neural Network Control for Active Suspension Systems with Time-Varying Vertical Displacement and Speed Constraints. *IEEE Transactions on Industrial Electronics, 66*(12), 9458–9466. doi:10.1109/TIE.2019.2893847

Livingstone, J. D. (2008). *Artificial Neural Networks Methods and Applications.* Humana Press.

Ma, C., & Hori, Y. (2004). Fractional order control and its application of PI/SUP/SPL alpha //d. *Proceedings of the 4th International power electronics and motion control conference*, 1477-1482.

Meng, X. H., & Baoye, S. (2007). Fast genetic algorithms are used for pid parameters optimization. In *International conference on automation and logistics.* IEEE. 10.1109/ICAL.2007.4338930

Mohammadi, Y., & Ganjefar, S. (2017). Quarter Car Active Suspension system: Minimum time controller design using singular perturbation method. *International Journal of Control, Automation, and Systems, 15*(6), 2538–2550. doi:10.100712555-016-0608-3

Mouleeswaran, S. (2012). *Design and Development of PID Controller-Based Active Suspension System for Automobiles. PID Controller Design Approaches: Theory, Tuning and Application to Frontier Areas.* BoD–Books on Demand.

Nise, N. S. (2020). *Control System Engineering.* John Wiley and Sons.

Pandula, F., & Antonio, V. (2011). *Tuning Rules for Optimal PID and Fractional- Order PID Control.* Academic Press.

Patrick, S., Idaumghar, L., & Julien, A. L. (2016). *Swarm Intelligence-Based Optimization.* Berlin: Springer International Publishing AG.

Pondlubny. (1998). *Fractional differential equations.* Academic Press.

Raju, N. R., & Reddy, P. (2016). Robustness Study of Fractional Order PID Controller Optimized by Particle Swarm Optimization in AVR System. *Iranian Journal of Electrical and Computer Engineering, 6*, 2033–2040.

Reza, F. M., & Abbs, A. N. (2011). *On fractional-order pid design. Application of matlab in science and engineering*. Intech Open.

Riccardo, P., James, K., & Tim, B. (2017). *Particle Swarm Optimization Intelligence*. Academic Press.

Riduan, A. F., Tamaldin, N., Sudrajat, A., & Ahmad, A. F. (2018). Review on active suspension system. *SHS Web of Conferences, 54.*

Saintilan, D., & Shelley, M. J. (2013). Active suspension and their non-linear models. *Competes Rendus Physique, 4*(6), 497-517.

Shi, A. M., Oliveares, A., & Rosseel, A. Y. (2020). Assessing fit in Ordinal Factor Analysis Models: SRMR vs RMSEA Structural Equation Modeling. *A Multidisciplinary Journal, 27*(1), 1-15.

Sun, S., Cao, Z., Zhu, H., & Zhao, J. (2019). A Survey of Optimization Methods form a Machine Learning Perspective. *IEEE Transactions on Cybernetics, 50*(8), 3668–3681. doi:10.1109/TCYB.2019.2950779 PMID:31751262

Sun, W., Zhao, Y., & Li, J., L. Z. (2014). Active suspension control with frequency band constraints and actuator input delay. *IEEE Transactions on Industrial Electronics, 59*(01), 530–537.

Tandon, A. R. (2011). Genetic algorithm-based parameter tuning of PID controller for a composition control system. *International Journal of Engineering Science and Technology, 3*(8), 6705–6711.

Tandon, B., & Randeep, K. (2011). Genetic algorithm-based parameters tuning of pid controller for a composition control system. *International Journal of Engineering Science and Technology, 3*(8), 6707–6771.

Tran, T. H., & Hoang, N. D. (2016). Predicting Colonization Growth of Algae on Mortar Surface with Artificial Neural Network. *Journal of Computing in Civil Engineering, 30*(6), 04016030. doi:10.1061/(ASCE)CP.1943-5487.0000599

Tseng, H. E., & Hrovat, D. (2015). State of the art survey: Active and semi-active suspension control. *Vehicle System Dynamics, 53*(7), 1034–1062. doi:10.1080/00423114.2015.1037313

TurnIip, A., & Panggbean, J. H. (2020). Hybrid controller design-based magneto-rheological damper lookup table for quarter car suspension. *Int. J. Artif Intell, 18*(1), 193-206.

Ulsoy, A. G., Deng, H., & Calanakci, A. M. (2012). *Active Suspension, Automotive control systems*. Academic Press.

Venhovens, K. P. T., & der, a. A. (1995). *Delft active suspension (DAS)*. Academic Press.

Wang, H., Lu, Y., Tian, Y., & Christov, N. (2020). Fuzzy Sliding mode Based Active Disturbance Rejection Control for Active Engineers. Part D. *Journal of Automobile Engineering, 234*(2-3), 449–457. doi:10.1177/0954407019860626

Wang, L. (2020). *PID Control System Design and Automatic Tuning Using MATLAB/SIMULINK*. John Wily and Sons. doi:10.1002/9781119469414

Winston, P. H. (1992). *Artificial Intelligence Addison*. Westely Longman Publishing Co, Inc.

Xu, H., Lai, J. G., Yu, Z. H., & Liu, J. Y. (2013). Based on neural network PID controller design and simulation. *Advanced Materials Research*, *756*, 514–517. doi:10.4028/www.scientific.net/AMR.756-759.514

Liang, Y. J., & Wu, S. L. (2013). Optimal vibration control for tracked vehicle suspension systems. *Mathematical Problems in Engineering*, *2013*, 1–7. doi:10.1155/2013/178354

Zha, J., Nguyen, V., Su, B., Jiao, R. et al., "Performance of the Seat Suspension System Using Negative Stiffness Structure on Improving the Driver's Ride Comfort," SAE Int. J. Veh. Dyn., Stab., and NVH 6(2):135-146, 2022, https://doi.org/ doi:10.4271/10-06-02-0009

Zhao, L., Zeng, Z., Wang, Z., & Ji, C. (n.d.). PID control of vehicle active suspension based on particle Swarm optimization. Journal of Physics: Conference Series, 1748(3). doi:10.1088/1742-6596/1748/3/032028

KEY TERMS AND DEFINITIONS

Artificial Intelligence (AI): Is machine intelligence, as opposed to the intelligence exhibited by non-human creatures and humans, the ability to perceive, synthesize, and infer information. Speech recognition, computer vision, interlanguage translation, and various mappings of inputs are a few examples of activities where this is done.

Artificial Neural Networks (ANN): Computing systems inspired by the biological neural networks that make up animal brains are commonly referred to as neural networks (NNs) or neural nets. Artificial neurons, which are a set of interconnected units or nodes that loosely resemble the neurons in a biological brain, are the foundation of an ANN. Like the synapses in a human brain, each link has the ability to send a signal to neighboring neurons. An artificial neuron can signal neurons that are connected to it after processing signals that are sent to it. The output of each neuron is calculated by some non-linear function of the sum of its inputs, and the "signal" at a connection is a real number. Edges refer to the connections. The weight of neurons and edges often changes as learning progresses.

Body Motion: They are largely produced by cornering and braking motions and are known as bounce, pitch, and roll of the sprung mass.

Machine Learning (ML): The machine learning field is a branch of artificial intelligence (AI) that focuses on using data and algorithms to mimic how people learn, gradually increasing the accuracy of its predictions.

Ride Comfort: Is directly connected to the acceleration that road-riding passengers experience.

Road Handling: Is connected to the forces that the tires exert on the road.

Suspension Travel: Is used to describe the difference in relative displacement between the sprung and unsprung masses.

Two Degrees of Freedom: The term "two-degree-of-freedom systems" refers to some dynamic systems that need two independent coordinates, or degrees of freedom, to characterize their motion. The directions of the degrees of freedom may or may not line up.

Chapter 9
Machine Learning Frameworks in Carpooling

Vivek Veeraiah
Adichunchanagiri University, India

Vivek Dadasaheb Solavande
Bharati Vidyapeeth (Deemed), India

Veera Talukdar
iD https://orcid.org/0000-0002-9204-5825
RNB Global University, India

Sabyasachi Pramanik
iD https://orcid.org/0000-0002-9431-8751
Haldia Institute of Technology, India

Manikandan K.
Vellore Institute of Technology, India

Ankur Gupta
iD https://orcid.org/0000-0002-4651-5830
Vaish College of Engineering, India

Suryansh Bhaskar Talukdar
Vellore Institute of Technology, India

ABSTRACT

Due to the development in human population and their requirements, the vehicular population on the globe is increasing day by day in the medium of public transportation. As a result, carpooling comes into play, with the fundamental notion being to share personal automobile space among persons travelling similar paths. Smart carpooling, car sharing, and ridesharing are other terms for the same thing. From a socioeconomic and environmental standpoint, the major task is to develop sustainable transportation. The success of carpooling should be measured in terms of cost, stress-free driving, traffic reduction, and air pollution reduction in the transportation solution system. The major challenge here is to assist vehicle users in gaining access to and picking an appropriate cost-effective transportation option based on their environmental footprint, matching his or her requirements, preferences, and legal limits, and determining the optimum route via specified areas.

DOI: 10.4018/978-1-6684-7105-0.ch009

INTRODUCTION

In carpooling (Marcondes et al., 2021) framework which was found on client's summary along with path, a suggestion was made by us for a revolutionary approach, i.e., through which authorization is given to apply clustering (Dutta et al., 2021). In other words, three concluding results are prepared like: cluster of users through comparable routes, same user's profile and the users along with parallel route and their profile outline. Furthermore, we describe standardization of symbols and keywords related with travel sharing environment, i.e., carpooling. Use of K-Means (Jayasingh et al., 2022) for clustering users with connected profiles and working over very finicky part of clustering which is based on prior arrangement to combine clusters of user's trip so as to produce ultimate clusters that contain list of users who has some relationship with their profile outline and route.

Machine knowledge is considered to be as one of the major foundation of present information technology among all advance technology. Our demand for the sum of data is still increasing day-by-day and which should be obtainable in good quality. The reason for more smart data study is due to more persistent characteristics which is needed component for different technological purposes and that gives guarantees for good resolution. Due to the nature of explaining the trouble thoroughly through the science of machine learning (Pramanik et al., 2021) which provides help for the identification of problem with their solution. In machine learning an algorithm can be reproduced in diverse ways for a given crisis which depend on its communication along with its familiarity or surroundings or entered data. For this reason, it is initially necessary to adopt a learning medium through which algorithm accept the problem and its data. In real life only few learning models are present out of which some algorithm can encompass. Technique for organizing the machine learning algorithm is purely practical approach since it requires some force to think in relation to the effort made over data with the model used in training

Figure 1. Flow diagram of machine learning

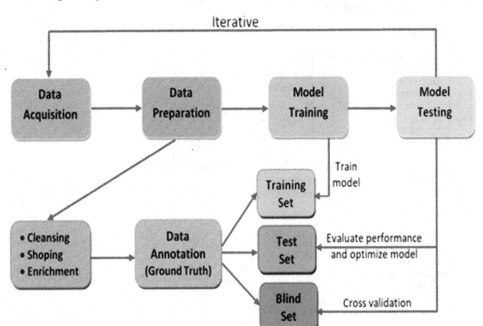

(Kaushik et al., 2021) process and then selecting the best one which support more appropriate prediction (Dushyant et al., 2022) to get the target result. Therefore special thanks to those application areas where machine learning can be facilitated with much more enthusiasm. In machine learning algorithm it is necessary to know the diverse learning styles with their diverse parts. These are:

Methodologies Used in Carpooling

Supervised Learning: In Supervised learning more emphasis is given over an objective function which is used for forecasting the values which indicate separate class feature that should be accepted or not. Machine learning algorithm is utilized for making predictions where application is static in nature but in case of supervised learning algorithm searches are made for best model by changing labels assigned to data points. This algorithm is responsible for ending changeable and that should be used to predict the staring, set of specified predictors that is sovereign variable. By using these set of variable, the basic purpose is produced which map input to wanted output. Here the training procedure will continue till the model accomplishes the stage of accurateness on the basis of training dataset. As a result of this complete procedure, it is helpful to decrease the time spend on physical review for significance and coding process. Some of the examples of supervised learning are: Artificial Neural Network (Pramanik et al., 2020), Regression (Fitzenberger et al., 2022), Decision Tree (Mohebbanaaz et al., 2022), KNN (Palimkar et al., 2022), Logistic Regression (Pidstrigach et al., 2022), SVM (Tanveer et al., 2022), and Naïve Bayes (Lalwani, 2022). So, in overall point of views which is divided into two different parts:

 Learning: It refers to learning of a model by means of learning data.

 Testing: It refers to testing of the model by utilizing unknown dataset for checking correctness of the model.

Figure 2. Supervised learning process

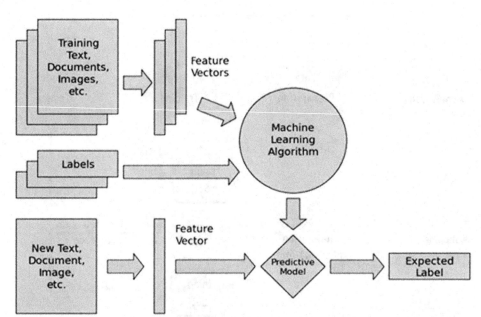

The above two parts are used repeatedly by using trial and error. This machine has capability to learn from his previous experience and also always trying to capture best promising acquaintance for making correct business decision like Markov Decision Process (Ullah et al., 2022). Here the machine has learned to select an achievement for maximizing the pay off. Here appropriate use of algorithm change its policy to learn well again and again in order to produce best judgment and makes more precision.

Unsupervised Learning: Through this learning process, learning of valuable information without characterized class, condition optimization, feedback signal or any past or previous information further than raw data which known as unsupervised learning. The learning algorithm has no unpredictable objective of approximation means there is no several label which are linked with data points i.e. training data class label is indefinite. Here the algorithm is use to organize the data into bunches for explaining the arrangement, i.e., data cluster use to disclose significant partition and hierarchy. It create easy and attractive look of the data that should be prepared for analysis. Some of the examples are K-Means (Libório et al., 2022), Fuzzy clustering (Trinh et al., 2022) and Hierarchical clustering (Karna, A., 2022). Entered data has neither label nor identified results. This particular model has capability to infer about the current situation from the present input dataset. It may remove broad rules, i.e., during a mathematical procedure; it may methodically reduce the dismissal.

Figure 3. Unsupervised learning process

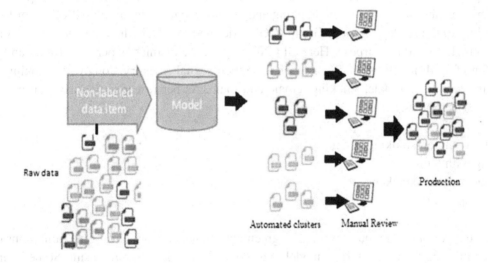

Reinforcement Learning: The basic purpose of this algorithm which used here is for making machine qualified enough to make explicit decision by itself. This algorithm has capability to make use of each data point and learn from them, so that later the machine can able to make superior decision in an environment where he trained.

Figure 4. Reinforcement learning process

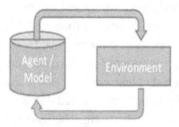

PROFILE MATCHING

In background of the carpooling social detachment features are not being explored by the researcher. Here before any ride comparison should be made among the people who have intention towards sharing of any ride as it's purely on the user to recognize whether a ride is very imperative for hearten or simply deny the demand for a ride. As per aforesaid, description about the ability of social remoteness like: gender, age, habits can be important factors of smolder for safekeeping or wellbeing in a ride. Here proposal is made to utilize time-space network flow method for expanding the model that can be second-hand for explaining problems of carpooling with pre- matching order. Pre-matching information require number of characteristics like: smoking or non-smoking and sexual category etc. for classification of final riders. According to the survey, Carpool Group (CG) is defined as CNG where the rider has no interest to offer a vehicle for riding purpose. Here all CNG request are distinct as per description and can be classified into four different types which depends on their sexual category along with smoking option: non-smoking female and male, smoking female and male. As per research classification of Carpool Group (CNG) as follows:

- Riding with non-smoking females
- Riding with females
- Riding with non-smokers
- Non supplicant

The above types of CNG request where an agreement is made in work have some limitations or little strain for composing the network flow model to discover final ride matching result. Some boundaries are specified when smoker requesting for journey with non-smoker then it will not match etc. (Orlane Moynat et al., 2022) planned social remoteness which calculates affiliation between riders. But, they merely compute the distance between rider's home and office. (Chen et al., 2022) present a figure of the model for socio-spatial network which provides information about commonly travelled route. This work is considered to be social network that provides a graph (Kutiel, 2017) whose nodes are referred to real-world people while edges referred to relationship between traveler with an anticipate query language which consists of graph traversal (Huang, S. 2019) process for accelerating formulation of queries more than network. This research work proposed for each participated user of social network (Pramanik et al., 2022) can be represented through their own property like: hobby, name, etc.

Figure 5. Relation between CNG type with request and vehicle type

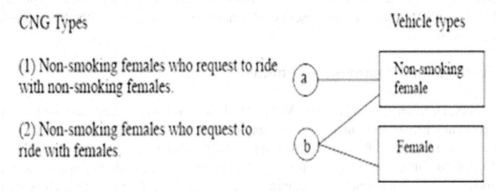

This research work suggests using little feature about user which may be measured through social network such as: sexual category, age of rider, hobbies and standing capability. Previous characteristic are very imperative for the situation of carpooling, because during for reputation, users can make their own status for other users. We propose an unlike come up for the situation of carpooling process. K-Means process is applied to find out related user according to any other attribute. This work, exclusively uses attributes that was preferred as per the survey and others were chosen according to reply of questionnaire.

CLUSTERING ENSEMBLE

By combining power of several individual clustering algorithms we can determine clustering ensemble. The main idea for clustering ensemble is to get confirmation about final clusters which provides better outcomes in some features such as sturdiness, inventiveness, calmness and scalability at last for some particular clustering algorithm also. Furthermore, it shows potential for adding clusters of diverse datasets, clusters of unlike feature of identically dataset and clusters for various algorithms. Clustering is usually necessitate meaning of resemblance of determine among description which is a harsh task devoid of previous facts about cluster figure. According to textual information present, clustering ensemble has conveyed enhancement in clusters results and this method is used in genuine area request like: video recovery, cluster testing and feature selection. Universally there are two steps in algorithm which is used for ensemble clustering: (i) store results for sovereign cluster which belongs to like or unlike clusters algorithm. (ii) Agreement utility use to find an ending partition. Consensus congregation defines the way through which dissimilar clusters can be mutual among them. There are little clustering ensemble approaches like: voting process, co-alliance based occupation, hyper graph splitting; limited fusion model etc. suggests new clustering ensemble algorithms, which based on voting, present relationship which corresponds to likeliness of cluster. This particular research suggest for agreement purpose which is known as RELABEL, this use K-Means for fabrication of cluster members and then introduce connection for unite cluster labels which are proposed engaging of management for the clustering ensemble practice. For getting extra enhancements on the cluster result, research suggest three kind of consensus function: the first will encourage comparison based calculation for partitioning and it is known as Cluster- based Similarity Partitioning Algorithm (CSPA) that believe connection between substances in the same cluster and use it for organizing to determine pair wise similarity. The second algorithm is known as Hyper

Graph Partitioning Algorithm (HGPA). At last the third algorithm is known as Meta-Clustering Algorithm (MCLA). HGPA algorithm uses Hyper Graph where vertex is matched with objective belonging to equivalent cluster.

Supervised Machine Learning Techniques

Neural Network, Decision Tree and Support Vector Machine used in supervised machine learning technique for providing help to learn high-level perception out of low-level image (Pramanik et al., 2020) feature. Such performances perform organizational processes with help of previously considered training dataset. Then for training of data, require both input and output which is already approved. Supervise learning method is taught through known training data, it can be useful for facilitating new data that is not found. The machine learning algorithm here predicts the uncertain image group, which is nothing more than a semantic view of the query image. As an alternative to the complete database there is a fit here at the bottom of the query image panel and in the query image. So the refund results are very clean.

Support Vector Machine (SVM)

SVM is a learning model which overseen an integrated learning algorithm which make analysis over data and then use it for classification. Classification refers to which class or data field is associated with types. The Learning classification is consider as a phenomenon of machine-supervise learning, which refer to the task for guessing an object out of branded training data. Training data for an image reconstruction development accurately modify place of image in accurate class. Here every class belongs to different type of image. SVM training protocols are structured in the model, where new instances are assigned to single group class or other. The depiction of examples in the genres in this model is done with clear intervals, which are promising.

Definition of SVM

The basic idea behind SVM is classification of input data for creating hyper plane in high dimensional space. Created hyper plane now represents sub-space that is one step less than its surrounding space. If there is a 3-dimensional gap, its hyper plane is 2 dimensional planes. Sufficient gap was achieved with largest detachment in training-data point which is closest for any class through hyper plane. Departure from created hyper plane to the closet data points is known as separation boundary. So simplicity in classifier is false because the range of the section is small. Main purpose of SVM engine to detect precision hyper-plane, which may prevent the range of the unit from being too large or increase when this level is met, or the judgment we may obtain in these situations may differ between the two classes, which is at last known as the ideal created hyper-plane. All identified support vectors perform vital job in learning process which is required for learning purposes because support vectors are classified as components of product database that, if disconnected then it may change separation among hyper-plane points in SVM training algorithm. Models starting in two classes have a maximum margin hyper-plane of a trained SVM and these models at the rim and rims known as support vectors or data points on the rating surface. The underlying reliability of the vector support machine assembly lies in erudition algorithms that create internal kernel products between support vector X and vector X from respiratory region, i.e., breathing space while the vector refers to small portion of output generated by study method while identified vector refers to the small part of the product of data extracted by learning method. Mapping process is used by SVM program for maintaining the computational load can be transferred to an innovative location, ensuring that point products can be calculated effortlessly, by declaring them based on the kernel function and calculating them substantially based on the kernel function. Now, the problem can be easily solved.

Figure 6. HP1 does not divide the class, HP2 does excluding through diminutive margin, HP3 divide with maximum margin

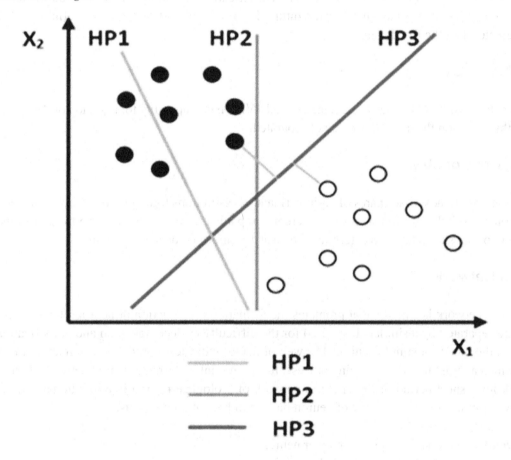

Method Used in SVM

Data classification is a broad authority of machine learning. It explores learning and construction of machine learning method which may train to perform data prediction. Let's face it - most brochures go straight into the tank. Different images (r- dimensional vector) are insert and we need to know if such points are differentiated though hyper plane (r-1). There are varieties of hyper plane that can capture data. But we must decide what is best for each divorce. Two important value functions: Graphical display that is not in the Donor Patter line instead of the highest level feature. Creating the optimal hyper plane to separate the shapes into the key size spaces obtained in first process.

Inputs: Group of training models, that is x1; x2; x3; xn and the output effect is y. In this we can see many features that we need.

Outputs: A weight group w, one for each element, is divided by lines predicting value of y. At this point, we utilize reduction force of reduction scale to reduce zero weight scale, the last few interacting with the determining factors in determining hyper plane. These non-zero weights communicate through support vector.

Advantages

SVM provides an excellent presentation of data classification in training. SVM provides better organization with better data management for the future. It does not provide a definitive definition of data. It is not greater than the fitted data.

Disadvantages

Different types of SVM classes are accepted but all SVMs have capability for rejection of the data points. So, in this situation the data points are not separated.

Applications of SVM

SVM often use to advertise shares of various financial institutions through forecasting. When comparing a concert suitable for the shares of different companies from the comparative field. So this finite judgment of the shares helps to determine the basis for informed decision making.

Neural Network

The neural network is a model that promotes the formation and function of neurobiological networks. They are separated by a similar shape used for the difficulty of decomposition and classification. It is based on the model of simple neuron. The web of neural indicates reproductive sign about the human brain which attempt to reflect learning process. It is commonly referred as neural network. Term neural network for a short period of time refer to network of biological neuron in a functional and unstable sensory system, respectively. Most of neuron has 3 numbers of components:

- **Dendrite:** It collects input from other neurons.
- **Soma:** It makes the first step unbalanced, i.e., non-linear processing.
- **Axon:** It looks like cable wire through which output signal is passed on to other neuron for spreading downward of processing chain.

However, Artificial Neural network (ANN) is the groups of artificial neuron which use continuous arithmetic computation model depend on connector that connects them.

The connective tissue made up of by two neurons is known as synapse. In ANN, there is a standard x_j that converts the spikes (short electric pulses). The rate x_j for all neuron which transmit signal to the neuron i is weighted through parameter w_{ij}. It can be said here that these weights are relating in terms of the practical application of j from first association. Here weight is known as 'synaptic efficacy'. The x_i effect of neuron i is an innocent element for input effect, wherever the number of input line changes to the neuron i and # are the base set at the threshold. In fact, neuron has three number of parameter - placement, entry and sole activation function.

Learning the sub-level definition of a set of correction images sent to the classical neural network creates link between low-level image definitions with that of high- level definition. It follows learning through instance rule and configured for detail application like:

- Pattern identification
- Data cataloguing

This kind of machine is called as cognition (computer model which is designed for representing the capability to understand as well as to select).

Advantages

An adaptive program is based on external or internal information flowing into a network that changes its structure.

Disadvantages

This requires an enormous amount of data which is extremely focused.

Applications

- Speech Recognition
- Vehicle Driving
- Text Writing and Fraud Detection.

Decision Tree

Decision tree uses a branching method to show the effects of a decision. Here internal or non-leaf node represent an unique characteristics where as all branch of the tree represent end of testing process, and leaf node or terminal node represent the class of detailed information, i.e. the final result after all calculations. In this tree the rules of the system are specified during the path which start from root node and ends at leaf node of the tree.

Supervised learning algorithm considered as a standard method which used for categorization. They work for clear and unchanging flexibility, i.e., incessant dependent variables. The decision tree methods generate the result model depend on the definite values of attribute in data. The results go into the tree structure until the end of the known record, i.e., for forecasting of decision. Decision Trees are taught in categorization of data and deterioration issues. They are often quick, accurate and highly desirable for machine learning. As per this algorithm, data is divided into more than one consistent set. This is done as per the important characteristics, which is very important to create as many groups as possible. Divide data into several heterogeneous groups using different strategies such as Gini in sequence gain, Chi- square, entropy.

Input: The purpose or conditions defined by the definition.
Output: Input value results.
Representation of the final tree:
Every interior node has quality for testing its attribute.

Every branch of decision tree is related to their attribute value that all the terminal node or leaf node give to the classification.

Figure 7. Decision tree for play tennis

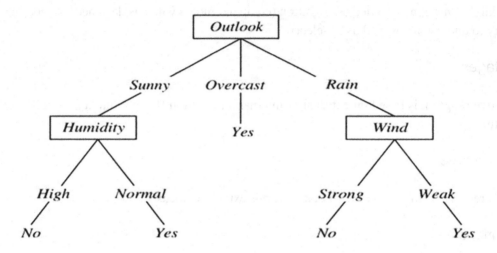

Types of Decision Trees Classification Trees

These trees are utilized for extracting dataset differently from unlike classes based on retort variables. These are used only when answer variables are not compromised nature.

Regression Trees

In this tree answer or objective variable is constant or mathematical where degenerative pressure is applied. These are mainly used in analytical types of problem. The various algorithms applicable in decision trees are:

Classification and Regression Trees (CART)

This is a kind of binary tree which helps in decision making. It is created by dividing a node which considered being parent node into exactly two numbers of child node, repetitively root node holds limited learning sample. CART algorithm identifies major variables and clears non-significant variables.

Iterative Dichotomiser (ID3)

The evaluation of the input attributes for this algorithm should be detached. ID3 finds the most constructive attributes in categorizing a particular group. Here the functional attribute is the one which gains largest information in it.

C 4.5

This algorithm has capability to handle unremitting properties. As per this algorithm, one of the data characteristics is selected at each node of the tree, which most proficiently divides the bunch of samples into two subgroups. The feature with the utmost standardized information benefit is selected to for decision making.

Naïve Bayes Classifier

Following Thomas Bayes expected theorem, this classification technique is developed which focused on Bayes' theorem. By referring to postulation of sovereignty among predictors', Naive Bayes classifies that association of a particular attribute in a class does not apply to any other quality standard. If a fruit is red, rounded and about 3 inches in diameter it is measured as an apple. Whether this interpretation is interdependent or a continuation of the other interpretation, this classification considers all the properties in order to independently provide the possibility of thinking that the fruit is an apple. It is simple for manufacturing of this model and particularly applicable for huge dataset with less effort. Through its simplest form, it includes complex advance methods for classification which works well unexpectedly.

Bayesian method clearly use Bayes' theorem for different problem like: classification and regression.

$$P(C \backslash X) = \frac{P(X \backslash C)P(C)}{P(X)} \tag{1}$$

$$Posterior = \frac{Likelihood \times Prior}{Evidence} \tag{2}$$

Bayesian Rule

The probability model permits us to acquire the skepticism about model in an honest manner by determining probability of consequences. In machine learning, the probability classifier is a classifier, when giving an example as input, can assign probability assignments over a group of classes, in spite of outputting only possible classes that the sample should fit.

Advantages

It has capability to solve analytic and exclusion type of problems.

It facilitates practical learning algorithm along with combine pre- introduction and experiential data.

It gives a valuable insight into recognizing and assessing multiple learning methods. It computes the apparent probabilities of hypothesis. This is serious for noise in entered data.

Applications

This type of classification is used as probabilistic learning method. Of these, almost everyone agrees and the most admired method of learning for catalogue text document.

Spam filtering is the excellent recognized application system. It primarily used for identification of spam emails. This spam filtering has evolved as a fashionable method for generating unsolicited spam email from formal email.

Combined with mutual filtration, Naive Bayes creates a hybrid switching method of filtration and prediction in resource allocation. So, this is considered to be very accurate, measurable and efficient technique.

Regression

Regression is a type of supervised learning method which follows categorization. It finds an association among few autonomous, i.e., known variable with many reliant type i.e. unknown variable. Degradation provide unrestricted incessant yield value stand on previously agreed entered value along with uncompromising yield charge of classification, Quadratic, cubic, power, logarithmic and many other functions obliged for finding the best guess for weakening cost. Accepted Regression algorithms are successively named as Logistic Weakening, Linear Regression, Stepwise Regression, Ridge Regression, Lasso Regression, Elastic net Regression and Polygonal Regression respectively.

Linear Regression Objective

It has been found that the association among an autonomous (forecaster (X)) and a needy (condition (Y)) can be changed by predicting the potential cost of the dependent relative. Uncomplicated regression use a self-reliant inconsistent and many expectations. The dependent variable is permanent and sovereign incompatibility with distinct or unremitting value. There is two types of regression model is present. One model is linear while the other model is non linear. In linear regression model direct line is use while in non linear regression model curled line associations among dependent relative and sovereign variable is used.

Working Process

Lay down the data of the time-reliant and sovereign variable value in disperse plot. The correspondence with the correlation coefficient index value from -1 to +1 of the disperse area is the most obligatory to diagrammatically recognize the association among the variable. The correlation coefficient corresponds to the power (strongest) of the interactions among the variable. The maximum contact coefficient cost of the slope in between .5 to .99 is the finest predictive meter of probability dependent variable. The preeminent t or successful regression line is desired to create a broad plan to forecast that forthcoming may change from precedent data.

Best Fitting Regression Line: A line or row with least number of distances from data point in the disperse plot is to identify the failure line or row. The failure line or row usually goes during the average of reliable and sovereign variable. Excess reserve data points are known as error term.

In Linear regression, these error terms can access on behalf of real-world data. The optimal degradation line or row is portrayed with assistance from Least-squares method.

Least-Squares Method: Here totaling made from square of dissimilarity among every data point to line or row. It is also known as the square error or mistake. There is a very small square error in the regression line. The best deterioration line would be detailed away from the past data area to imagine value of upcoming data. Few self- sufficient data value in disperse plot may be remote from ideal regression line or row. These data points are called as outliers. Occasionally far missing data point are less efficient than all data points in a horizontal line. It is also known as outlier observation/Outliers. Outliers should be avoided.

Residuals: The Residual helps to recognize whether there is a additive relationship between data is exist or not.

Extrapolation: Accessing data point exterior of occupied difficulty. Example: Adolescent kid and mass computation difficulty may use senior data point. These data point are called extrapolation which should be avoided.

Formula of regression line:

$F(x) = mx + b + e$ where, x = independent variable

$F(x)$ = dependent variable b = y-intercept

m = slope of line e = error term

Ordinary Least Square (OLS) is used for reducing error value is used with more potential for formula: Σ [Actual (y) – Predicted (y)]^2

Preparing Data for Linear Regression

The subsequent procedure for training where data will provide the finest predictive correctness.

Linear Assumption: It presumes that the reliant and sovereign variable is linear. Therefore in practice one popular data renovation method is used (example: log based transformation) along with linear data for better forecast.

Remove the Noise: Use data maintenance method to keep data soundless and outliers.

Remove Co-Linearity: To avoid being larger than fitting due to variables at the same time, make a pair-wise connection and move simultaneously.

Gaussian Distributions: Share Gaussian data to obtain calculations with greater reliability.

Rescale Inputs: Normalization or routine operations to get back contributory variables improve destructive reliability.

Advantages

- Optimal shows the linear link between variable dependence and independence with optimal results.
- It is a plain model which is simple to recognize.

Disadvantages

- Here output is expected in number only which has no relation to non-linear data. It is very responsive with outliers.

Data should be autonomous.

- Applications only in Real-Time environments
- It has the capability to study about engine presentation out of test data of vehicle.
- For climatic data investigation OLS weakening it is used.

Application of linear regression analysis is in research study over the market and also in buyer survey result.

Unsupervised Learning

K-Means, Clustering approaches, inherited algorithms are some unsupported machine learning method. The input data of this learning method are not categorized and there are no approved results. A model is fitted by subtracting adjacent structures from the enter data and extracting global rules. It can undergo an arithmetic practice to categorize data by systematically reducing or comparing unemployment. The basic idea of this model is for determining the data patterns or grouping. Here the specific objective properties of the data are missing and our interest is to travel around data to find some of their built-in configurations. In clustering method emphasis are given over to find out number of comparative groups within data which known as cluster. It makes groups by taking instances of data which are comparable with one another within a group and those who are different positions from one another is known as unlike cluster. Clustering is frequently referred as unofficial learning because class values are not specified and derived category group of data instances are not provided. This indicates a dilemma with getting unseen structures out of the labeled data. There are no metrics of outcomes which will escort the learning process. Image clustering is a learning process that has not been characterized. It categorizes the set of images, which should minimize the comparison between different clusters. The algorithms used for this purpose are apriori algorithm and K-Means algorithm.

K-Means Algorithm

K-Means algorithm belongs to divisional - clustering algorithm. Its main aim is to divide the agreed n explanation into K number of clusters. Here mean of every group is required to create and accordingly image is placed inside the cluster based on the mean that has smallest Euclidean detachment as well as image attribute vector. The K-Means clustering frequently cannot disconnect images with dissimilar concepts well sufficient is due to multifaceted distribution of image data. Clustering like weakening explains class of difficulty and group of methods. All the clustering methods are classified based on their characteristics in two different modeling approaches i.e. centroid-based and Hierarchical. K-means algorithm which is commonly accepted among all essentially comes underneath grouping of clustering in unconfirmed learning. K-Means is an unconfirmed algorithm through which clustering difficulties can be resolved. Here practice follows an uncomplicated and easy way to categorize specified dataset throughout convinced integer of clusters (take as K clusters). In each cluster data points are homogeneous i.e. uniform and heterogeneous i.e. diverse to peer groups. Let us set data points x1; x2;:::xn where x 1; x 2;:::x r is a vector in a re-valued space X r as well as at this point r represent

 i i R

 numeral for attribute of information. This algorithm partition participation of data has number of clusters where every cluster has its centroid. Here the value of k is required to provide through the user.

Cluster Formation in K-Means

Here k numbers of points are selected for designing of every cluster recognized as Centroid. Each data point formulates groups having contiguous centroids which mean k number of cluster. Locate every cluster's Centroid depend on the accessible members of the cluster. At this place we got new centroids. Since new centroids with us, now replicate step 2 and 3 operations. Discover contiguous detachment intended for every data points from fresh Centroid and try to make connection with newly obtained k-clusters. Repeat the procedure continuously until junction will not arrive i.e., centroids kept as fixed.

Figure 8. K-means clustering

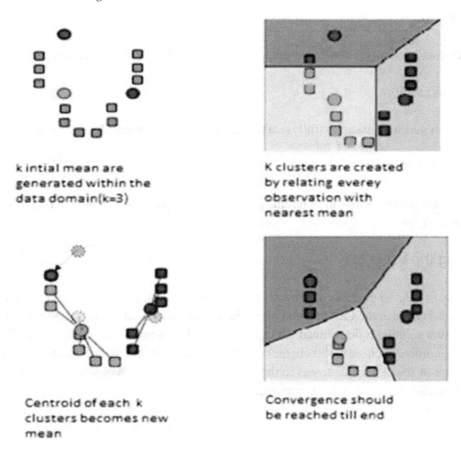

k intial mean are generated within the data domain(k=3)

K clusters are created by relating everey observation with nearest mean

Centroid of each k clusters becomes new mean

Convergence should be reached till end

K-Means or Hard C-Means Clustering is a partial technique used for making analysis over the data and treat data perceptions as objects that depend on locations and distance between dissimilar input data point. Apportioning object into basically unconnected clusters (K) ends up in such a design that the objects in each group are as conceivable to each other as can be imagined, although many of the other clusters can be considered.

ALGORITHM STEPS FOR K-MEANS CLUSTERING

Set

Fix the value of K as per the selection of required number of clusters.

Initialization

Select K number of starting point which will be used for estimation of cluster centroids. These are assigned as early starting values.

Classification

Exploring dataset's every point and then gives out its Centroid to its nearest cluster.

Centroid Calculation

After the dataset's each point successfully sent to cluster then new K centroids must required recalculating

Convergence Criteria

Step 3 and 4 should be repetitive until its cluster allocation digresses at any time or there is no thorough progress for centroids.

Determining the Value of K

In K-Means, every cluster contains their own Centroid. Sum of square values for cluster is fixed by square of discrepancies between the Centroid and every data point inside that same cluster. Sum of the square values for cluster solution is determined through addition of the sum of square values for all clusters. By increasing the number of clusters, this charge continues to decrease, but the condition is that we smoothly reduce the sum of the plot's uniqueness to the same value of K, after which it goes slowly, where best number of possible clusters can be determined.

Strength of K-Means

- Easy to recognize and feel.
- Efficient performance: Time complexity: (tkn) where n = number of data point

k = number of cluster, t = number of repetition. If both t and k are small then it is thought as linear algorithm.

Weakness of K-Means

This algorithm simply applies when significance is defined. The user must identify value of k.

This algorithm is responsive towards foreigners (data points which are situated distantly with respect to other data points).

It is easy to identify hyper-sphere clusters.

Fuzzy C-Mean Algorithm (FCM)

Fuzzy clustering algorithm used by this algorithm; Professor Jim Bestek urbanized this algorithm in the year 1981. The FCM algorithm divides data into different fuzzy group with values for certain individual criteria. Every data item in Fuzzy C-Mean Algorithm belongs to two or more cluster. Nevertheless, in hard clustering or non- fuzzy, data is treated as crisp cluster and exactly one Centroid is present for every data element. The result of FCM algorithm is number of centroids.

It is unusual compared to previously known and commonly used fuzzy clustering algorithm. It was originally planned by Dunn and expanded into Bestek's universal FCM clustering algorithm. The main reason for Fuzzy C-mean algorithm is to divide vector space of pattern point in different sub-space according to distance measure.

Advantages of FCM

- Implementation is straightforward
- Practically very strong behavior
- Application to multi-dimensional data
- Ability to model uncertainty within data

ALGORITHM STEP FOR FUZZY C-MEANS CLUSTERING

Here the objective is to hit c, where the value of c lies in between 2 to (n-1), then choose a value for parameter 'm' and subsequently set $U(0)$ partition matrix. Accordingly, as per this method, it is labeled as 'r', where $r = 0, 1, 2...$.

The algorithm is stated below:

Figure 9. Fuzzy c-mean algorithm

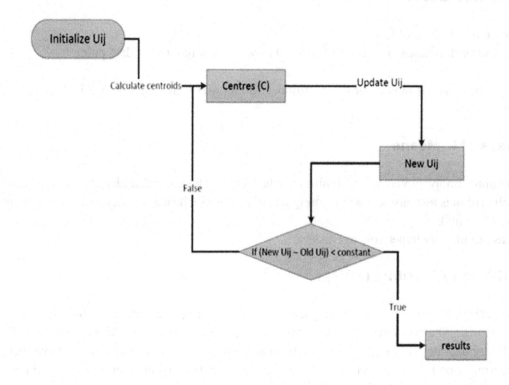

1. We are to compute the c center vector $\{V_{ij}\}$ for each step.

$$V_{ij} = \frac{\sum_{k=1}^{n}(\mu)_{ik}^{m}}{\sum_{k=1}^{n}(\mu)_{ij}^{m}} X_{kj} \tag{3}$$

2. Calculate the distance matrix D[c.n].

$$D_j = \left(\sum_{j=1}^{n}(x_{kj} - v_{ij})^2\right)1/2 \tag{4}$$

3. Update the partition matrix for the rth step, U(R) as

$$\mu_{ij}^{r-1} = \left(\frac{1}{\sum_{j=1}^{e}\left(\frac{d_{ik}^{r}}{d_{jk}^{r}}\right)^{2/m\_1}}\right) \tag{5}$$

Fast Fuzzy C-Means (FFCM) Clustering

The FFCM algorithm has some improvements over FCM. One of its main explanations is to minimize the volume of calculations through examining membership cost of each point and to reject these points with smaller sponsorship values than the entrance value. The resolution of the appropriate edge depends on the experimentations.

FFCM plan to reduce the degree of reserve counts of FCM by dispensation the space between data points and the center of a flanking cluster center for points, where the membership values are significantly higher than an edge, T, where the assumption for T is under 1 and more significant than 0. Right now, there is no strong reason to figure distance for points with partisanship values not as much as T since these merits do not critically enhance the results, only some distance estimates can be saved.

Feature Weighted Fuzzy C-Means Clustering

In cluster inspection, majority of existing algorithms realize that each feature of the example has a regular involvement in the cluster study. When thinking about many features that have different implications, the characteristic weight function seen as an unanticipated event of feature determination. That is, the quality of a motivation in the intermediate showing the content of that feature we call this value "feature weight".

```
Algorithm - Feature - Weighted Fuzzy C-Means
Input: Dataset
Output: Final fuzzy partition matrix Final center matrix
Final center matrix
Final feature-weight vector
Begin algorithm
Set number of clusters C, fuzzification exponent m and fuzzy partition matrix
Initialize Feature - Weight vector using normalized Term Variance
While (not achieve termination condition) Update the cluster centers
Calculate the distances
Update the fuzzy partition matrix
Update the elements in the feature-weight vector End while
End algorithm
```

Weighted Image Patch-Based Fuzzy C-Means Clustering

Image links are commonly used in image de-noising, mainly for non-local algorithms, using the proximity of data installed on image links to calculate image similarity. Importantly, image square-based de-noise techniques work better than relying on pixels because the image link has more data than the internal pixel, and the image properties can be depicted even more. The FCM-based image segmentation algorithm can improve the target work of each pixel used in the nucleus by replacing it with recording image patch, where all pixels are weighed with adaptability. Unlike other FCM-based algorithms, the FCM (WIPFCM) algorithm, based on unbiased image linking, sees each image patch as the primary unit, packaged instead of each pixel. In these ways, spatial compulsion is naturally mixed into the clustering process without penalty period.

Kernel-Based Fuzzy C-Means Clustering

Kernel FCM is an expanded form of technique suggest by Fuzzy C-Means clustering. Now, special input sources are being converted to more advance dimensional space for certain purposes. In an inventive space, models are more triumphant at being inaccessible or grouped. The Conservative Fuzzy C-Means algorithm uses the KFCM algorithm bit work as an alternative to the Euclidean separation on a commercial scale, for example, which is expected to outline high-dimensional space by partial dimension, thus creating a distinction between cluster points which can defeat the obstacle that customary FCM does not perform well in managing fuzzy cluster center.

CONCLUSION

The study is carried out with the help of the Spyder simulation toolbox. It is a strong scientific programming environment with open source capabilities that supports cross-platform integrated development environments. It has the potential to work with other open source software. The suggested carpooling system is analyzed based on the route and the quantity of passengers. In this experiment, three different routes for picking up people are available. The distances traversed by each route are 35 km, 37 km, and 30 km, respectively. The total number of passengers picked up on each route is 3, 3 and 2, respectively. Now, among the other routes, route no. 3 is chosen since it has the least distance. Finally, when picking up passengers in that route profile, a matching is created between the driver and the passenger, and corresponding people may be authorized for the same trip based on their resemblance. This experiment's findings may be improved in three ways. This study might be expanded to include a multi-hop car-sharing system (i.e. sharing a trip having more than one driver). Prior estimate of trip time may be done in order to improve the forecast of real voyage travel time. The integrative study of community networks, research excellence, and psychology are all emphasized in the development of a smart carpooling matching model.

REFERENCES

Chen, F., Nielsen, C. P., Wu, J., & Chen, X. (2022). Examining socio-spatial differentiation under housing reform and its implications for mobility in urban China. *Habitat International, 119*, 102498. doi:10.1016/j.habitatint.2021.102498

Dutta, S., Pramanik, S., & Bandyopadhyay, S. K. (2021). S. K. (2021) "Prediction of Weight Gain during COVID-19 for Avoiding Complication in Health. *International Journal of Medical Science and Current Research, 4*(3), 1042–1052.

Huang, S., Jiau, M., & Liu, Y. (2019, March). An Ant Path-Oriented Carpooling Allocation Approach to Optimize the Carpool Service Problem With Time Windows. *IEEE Systems Journal, 13*(1), 994–1005. doi:10.1109/JSYST.2018.2795255

Jayasingh, R. (2022). Speckle noise removal by SORAMA segmentation in Digital Image Processing to facilitate precise robotic surgery. *International Journal of Reliable and Quality E-Healthcare*, *11*(1), 1–19. Advance online publication. doi:10.4018/IJRQEH.295083

Karna, A., & Gibert, K. (2022). Automatic identification of the number of clusters in hierarchical clustering. *Neural Computing & Applications*, *34*(1), 119–134. doi:10.100700521-021-05873-3

Kutiel, G. (2017). Approximation Algorithms for the Maximum Carpool Matching Problem. In P. Weil (Ed.), Lecture Notes in Computer Science: Vol. 10304. *Computer Science – Theory and Applications. CSR 2017*. Springer. doi:10.1007/978-3-319-58747-9_19

Lalwani, P., Mishra, M. K., Chadha, J. S., & Sethi, P. (2022). Customer churn prediction system: A machine learning approach. *Computing*, *104*(2), 271–294. doi:10.100700607-021-00908-y

Libório, M. P., Martinuci, O., Machado, A. M. C., Lyrio, R. M., & Bernardes, P. (2022). Time–Space Analysis of Multidimensional Phenomena: A Composite Indicator of Social Exclusion Through k-Means. *Social Indicators Research*, *159*(2), 569–591. doi:10.100711205-021-02763-y

Marcondes, F. S., Durães, D., Gonçalves, F., Fonseca, J., Machado, J., & Novais, P. (2021). In-Vehicle Violence Detection in Carpooling: A Brief Survey Towards a General Surveillance System. In *Distributed Computing and Artificial Intelligence, 17th International Conference. DCAI 2020. Advances in Intelligent Systems and Computing* (vol. 1237). Springer. 10.1007/978-3-030-53036-5_23

Mohebbanaaz, K., Kumari, L. V. R., & Sai, Y. P. (2022). Classification of ECG beats using optimized decision tree and adaptive boosted optimized decision tree. *SIViP*, *16*(3), 695–703. doi:10.100711760-021-02009-x

Moynat, O., Volden, J., & Sahakian, M. (2022). How do COVID-19 lockdown practices relate to sustainable well-being? Lessons from Oslo and Geneva. *Sustainability: Science, Practice and Policy*, *18*(1), 309–324.

Palimkar, P., Bajaj, V., Mal, A. K., Shaw, R. N., & Ghosh, A. (2022). Unique Action Identifier by Using Magnetometer, Accelerometer and Gyroscope: KNN Approach. In M. Bianchini, V. Piuri, S. Das, & R. N. Shaw (Eds.), *Advanced Computing and Intelligent Technologies. Lecture Notes in Networks and Systems* (Vol. 218). Springer. doi:10.1007/978-981-16-2164-2_48

Pidstrigach, J., & Reich, S. (2022). Affine-Invariant Ensemble Transform Methods for Logistic Regression. *Foundations of Computational Mathematics*. Advance online publication. doi:10.100710208-022-09550-2

Pramanik, S., Galety, M. G., Samanta, D., & Joseph, N. P. (2022). Data Mining Approaches for Decision Support Systems. *3rd International Conference on Emerging Technologies in Data Mining and Information Security*.

Pramanik, S., & Ghosh, R. (2020). Intelligent Agent Facilitated e-Commerce. *Turkish Journal of Computer and Mathematics Education*, *11*(2), 906–913.

Pramanik, S., Sagayam, K. M., & Jena, O. P. (2021) Machine Learning Frameworks in Cancer Detection. ICCSRE 2021.

Pramanik, S., & Suresh Raja, S. (2020). A Secured Image Steganography using Genetic Algorithm. *Advances in Mathematics: Scientific Journal*, *9*(7), 4533–4541.

Trinh, C., Huynh, B., Bidaki, M., Rahmani, A. M., Hosseinzadeh, M., & Masdari, M. (2022). Optimized fuzzy clustering using moth-flame optimization algorithm in wireless sensor networks. *Artificial Intelligence Review*, *55*(3), 1915–1945. doi:10.100710462-021-09957-3

Ullah, I., Kim, C. M., Heo, J. S., & Han, Y.-H. (2022). An Energy-efficient Data Collection Scheme by Mobile Element based on Markov Decision Process for Wireless Sensor Networks. *Wireless Personal Communications*, *123*(3), 2283–2299. doi:10.100711277-021-09241-1

Chapter 10
Smart ATM With Tracking of Criminals Using Novel Di-Pattern and C-LDP (Combined Local Directional Pattern)

Jeyabharathi Duraipandy
Sri Krishna College of Technology, India

Sherly Alphonse A.
Vellore Institute of Technology, Chennai, India

Sasireka D.
SRM Institute of Science and Technology, India

Kesavaraja D.
iD https://orcid.org/0000-0002-5036-4238
Dr. Sivanthi Aditanar College of Engineering, India

ABSTRACT

Automated teller machine (ATM) surveillance system is a smart system based on image processing that incorporates various sensors and machine learning algorithms to continuously monitor its surroundings for suspicious activities like physical attack. To prevent these attacks, there is a need to find the criminal immediately and save the person's life. In this chapter, two ways are followed to detect the criminals. The first one is weapon detection; the second one is criminal facial identification. A novel magnitude-based feature extraction technique creates the magnitude pattern for the image using Di-Pattern (DiP). Di-Pattern utilizes both horizontal and vertical derivatives to create a unique feature vector of the objects. Based on thresholding, weapons are detected. Once weapon detection as well as facial identification is done, it gives the alert. This system makes its effective usage in the remote locations where threatening is more, thus providing security. The proposed method achieves better accuracy than the other existing methods.

DOI: 10.4018/978-1-6684-7105-0.ch010

Figure 1. Different attacks in ATM

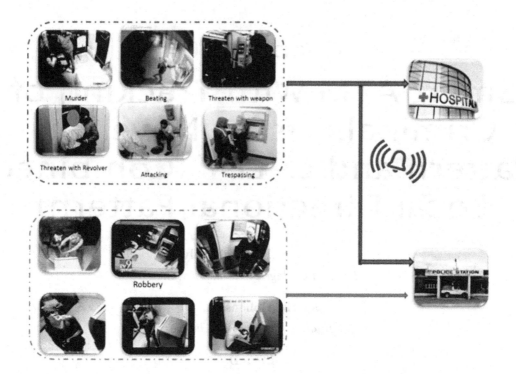

INTRODUCTION

Automated Teller Machines (ATM) offers much convenience to everyone in life due to their easy and readily available cash. Frauds related to the ATM are increasing day by day which is a serious issue. Some of the ATM issues are shown in Figure 1. ATM is equipped with surveillance monitor; criminals usually attack the customers and try to steal their wealth by occluding their faces. The thefts on ATMs are steadily rising and this is a serious problem for law enforcement and banking sectors. This paper mainly focusing on protection of customers inside the ATM using CCTV security cameras and emergency sirens.

In different security systems enabled in banks and ATM's, the automatic face recognition plays a major role in video surveillance. The alternate methods like finger print identification have major drawbacks like the need of co-operation of the suspect. The face recognition methods are overcoming those drawbacks and are more cost-effective. The face recognition applications play a major role in law enforcement. In most of the cases the photo database of the criminals maintained by the police are enough. But in certain situations when the photos are not available the sketch drawn through eye-witnesses come to a rescue. This work proposes an automatic detection of the criminals through such sketches with high accuracy (Benson & Perrett, 1991). Caricature is a special drawing of human faces which has the needed details of a human face. They represent the essential information. These caricatures can be used to recognize a human being. Bruce et al. (1992) have explained that the cartoons with shading and pigmentation details can also be well recognized by human beings. The computers can recognize the human beings using these sketches and cartoons at a better accuracy than the human beings. In most of the existing methods

184

the photos are converted to sketch before recognition (Tang & Wang, 2002; Wang & Tang, 2009). Then, a patch-by-patch comparison is made. In the proposed work there is no separate conversion of photo to sketch representation and no separate patch-by-patch comparison. A novel C-LDP algorithm is devised that converts the photo and sketch to a code image of less variation. The proposed algorithm also creates a feature vector that has a patch information for better accuracy. The use of ELM classifier enables faster and accurate classification.

The paper is structured as follows: Section 2 presents the concepts of the proposed work. The experimental results are given in Section 3. Finally, conclusion and future work are presented in Section 4.

PROPOSED WORK

The proposed system first classifies whether it's a weapon or not and the based on criminal database facial identification is done. If both are matched, it gives the alert to the nearby policy stations.

1. Weapon detection
2. Facial identification

Weapon Detection

Manual screening procedures for detecting concealed weapons such as handguns, knives, and explosives are common in controlled access settings like airports, entrances to sensitive buildings, and public events.

The detection of weapons concealed underneath a person's clothing is an important obstacle to the improvement of the security of the general public.

In case of ATM, the automatic detection of weapon is a most important one to save human lives. For weapon detection the proposed system introduces the feature descriptor Di-Pattern (DiP). That classify whether it is a weapon or not. If it a weapon then alert is given within a fraction of time.

Di-Pattern (DiP)

The working process of Di-Pattern (DiP) is shown in Figure 2. From the given image each objects are taken as 4×4 size of blocks. For each 4×4 size of blocks DiP generate the feature vector that utilize both horizontal and diagonal derivative of magnitude pattern. These two patterns are combined together to form Multiple Magnitude Pattern (MMP). Then find the magnitude patterns.

Finally construct the feature vector using the below formulas. The equation to create a magnitude pattern is given below. Two magnitude patterns are generated, one is based on the direction , . Another one is generated based on . Based on horizontal and vertical first order derivative, the magnitude patterns are generated. Edge values from horizontal and vertical point can be used to generate the unique pattern from each block of object. That's why the proposed work utilized the horizontal and vertical first order magnitude pattern to generate a feature vector.

$$I_0^1(g_1) = g_c + I_0^0 \tag{1}$$

Figure 2. DiP working process

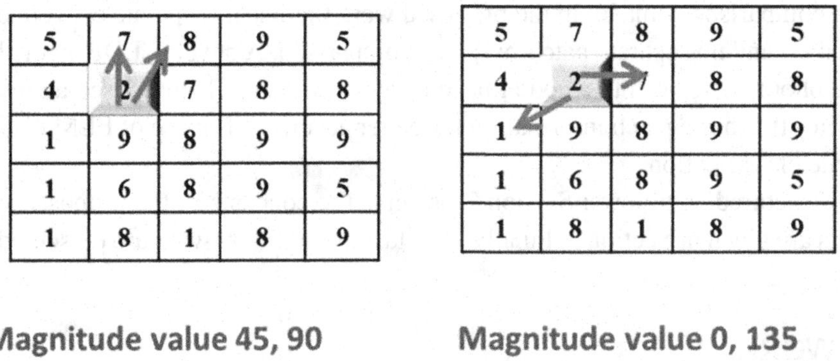

Magnitude value 45, 90   **Magnitude value 0, 135**

$$I_{45}^1(g_1)= g_c + I_{45}^0 \tag{2}$$

$$I_{90}^1(g_1)= g_c + I_{90}^0 \tag{3}$$

$$I_{135}^1(g_1)= g_c + I_{135}^0 \tag{4}$$

$$M_I^1(g_1)= \sqrt{I_{45}^1\left(g_p\right)^2 + I_{90}^1\left(g_p\right)^2} \tag{5}$$

$$M_I^1(g_2)= \sqrt{I_0^1\left(g_p\right)^2 + I_{135}^1\left(g_p\right)^2} \tag{6}$$

$$f_1\left(M_I^1\left(g_1\right) - M_I^1\left(g_1\right)\right)= f\left(x\right) = \begin{cases} 1, x \geq 0 \\ 0, x < 0 \end{cases} \tag{7}$$

$$F_{i=1\ldots n}\left(B\right) = \frac{1}{N*M}\sum_{i=1}^n f\left(x\right) \tag{8}$$

Where *n* is a number of block, *N*, *M*-row and column size of an object. *f(x)* is a magnitude pattern, g_c centre pixel.

Criminal Facial Identification

The proposed work is described in detail using the system architecture given in Figure 3. The proposed algorithm uses the images acquired using the surveillance camera implanted in the ATM. The images of the persons obtained using the camera are used for tracking the criminals. The face of the person using the ATM is compared with the sketch of the criminals stored in the database available with the police. If there is a match with the sketch, then the person using the ATM is detected as the suspect and security measures can be taken immediately. The detection process is done through our algorithm. The proposed work uses the sketch of the suspects available with the police dataset as the training data. The C-LDP (Combined Local Directional Pattern) is applied on the training data and a code image is obtained. Then, the C-LDP is applied on the facial image/photo obtained through the surveillance camera. Then, using Extreme Learning Machine (ELM) a comparison is done and if the code image of the facial image matches with the code image of the sketch in the dataset, the person currently using the ATM is detected as the suspect. This proposed work uses the facial images and the sketch images available in the CUHK Face Sketch (CUFS) dataset.

Figure 3. System architecture

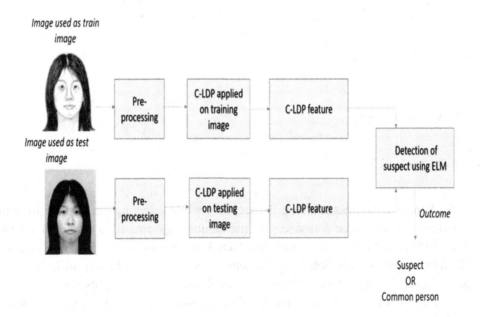

C-LDP Algorithm

The facial images are pre-processed before applying the edge detectors as in Figure 4. The facial images and the sketch images are converted to gray-scale images before applying C-LDP algorithm. The C-LDP algorithm uses the Canny edge detector, Kirsch masks and Sobel edge detector for the creation of code images from the facial image and the sketch of the facial image (Kirsch, 1971; Robinson, 1977; Vincent & Folorunso, 2009). The most prominent edges obtained using each edge detection technique is used for the creation of a code image from which a feature descriptor is obtained using the grid formation and histogram creation. The C-LDP algorithm creates three code images having prominent edges avoiding faint edges. Different edge detection algorithms work well under different conditions (Sherly Alphonse & Dharma, 2017a; Sherly Alphonse & Dharma, 2017b; Sherly Alphonse & Dharma, 2017c; Sherly Alphonse & Starvin, 2019). Therefore, this algorithm gets the advantages of the three edge detection techniques. The C-LDP feature represents the structure of the face eliminating the random noise. The eight directional kirsch masks are given as follows:

$$K_{,1} = [-3 \ -3 \ 5; \ -3 \ 0 \ 5; \ -3 \ -3 \ 5];$$

$$K_{,2} = [-3 \ 5, \ 5; \ -3 \ 0 \ 5; \ -3 \ -3 \ -3];$$

$$K_{,3} = = [\ 5 \ 5 \ 5; \ -3 \ 0 \ -3; \ -3 \ -3 \ -3];$$

$$K_{,4} = = [\ 5 \ 5 \ -3; \ 5 \ 0 \ -3; \ -3 \ -3 \ -3];$$

$$K_{,5} = = [\ 5 \ -3 \ -3; \ 5 \ 0 \ -3; \ 5 \ -3 \ -3];$$

$$K_{,6} = = [-3 \ -3 \ -3; \ 5 \ 0 \ -3; \ 5 \ 5 \ -3]; \qquad (9)$$

$$K_{,7} = = [-3 \ -3 \ -3; \ -3 \ 0 \ -3; \ 5 \ 5 \ 5];$$

$$K_{,8} = = [-3 \ -3 \ -3; \ -3 \ 0 \ 5; \ -3 \ 5 \ 5];$$

The presence of noise in the images affects the accuracy while detecting the suspects from the facial images and the sketch of the police database. The maximum responses filter out the noise present in the images and helps to get a feature descriptor unaffected by random noise. The Sobel edge detection method uses the following mask. The Sobel edge detector calculates the gradient from the images through computing the discrete differences among the rows and columns. A 3X3 neighbourhood is used for the calculations. The Sobel operator convolves the facial image integer filter. The eight directional masks for Sobel edge detection are given below:

$$S_{,1} = [1 \ 2 \ 1; \ 0 \ 0 \ 0; \ -1 \ -2 \ -1];$$

$$S_{,2} = [2 \ 1 \ 0; \ 1 \ 0 \ -1; \ 0 \ -1 \ -2];$$

$$S_{,3} = [1 \ 0 \ -1; \ 2 \ 0 \ -2; \ 1 \ 0 \ -1];$$

$S_{,4} = [0 -1 -2; 1\ 0 -1; 2\ 1\ 0];$

$S_{,5} = [-1 -2 -1; 0\ 0\ 0; 1\ 2\ 1];$

$S_{,6} = [-2 -1\ 0; -1\ 0\ 1; 0\ 1\ 2];$

$S_{,7} = [-1\ 0\ 1; -2\ 0\ 2; -1\ 0\ 1];$ (10)

$S_{,8} = [0\ 1\ 2; -1\ 0\ 1; -2 -1\ 0];$

The Prewitt edge detector uses the eight directional masks as follows. It's a conventional technique and uses the mask in eq. (11). It uses the first derivatives.

$P_{,1} = [1\ 1\ 1; 0\ 0\ 0; -1 -1 -1]$

$P_{,2} = [1\ 1\ 0; 1\ 0 -1; 0 -1 -1]$

$P_{,3} = [1\ 0 -1; 1\ 0 -1; 1\ 0 -1]$

$P_{,4} = [0 -1 -1; 1\ 0 -1; 1\ 1\ 0]$

$P_{,5} = [-1 -1 -1; 0\ 0\ 0; 1\ 1\ 1]$

$P_{,6} = [-1 -1\ 0; -1\ 0\ 1; 0\ 1\ 1]$ (11)

$P_{,7} = [-1\ 0\ 1; -1\ 0\ 1; -1\ 0\ 1]$

$P_{,8} = [0\ 1\ 1; -1\ 0\ 1; -1 -1\ 0]$

The grid formation before feature extraction helps in patch-by-patch comparison of the face images and the synthesized sketch.

Figure 4. Face-sketch images from dataset

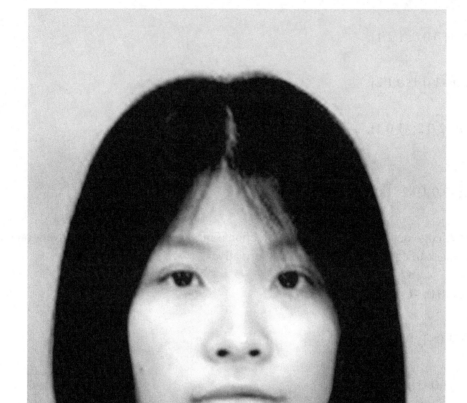

The maximum response-based code image $K(x, y)$ is created using Kirsch masks as in eq. (12).

$$K(x, y) = \max(RK_{\theta i}(x, y) \mid 0 \leq i \leq 7) \tag{12}$$

The maximum response-based code image $K(x, y)$ is created using Sobel edge detection masks as in eq. (13).

$$S(x, y) = \max(RS_{\theta i}(x, y) \mid 0 \leq i \leq 7) \tag{13}$$

The maximum response-based code image $P(x, y)$ is created using Prewitt masks as in eq. (14).

$$P(x, y) = \max(RP_{\theta i}(x, y) \mid 0 \leq i \leq 7) \tag{14}$$

Where $RK_{\theta i}$ is the response produced by each mask $K_{\theta i}, 0 \leq i \leq 7$, $RS_{\theta i}$ is the response produced by each mask $S_{\theta i}, 0 \leq i \leq 7$ and $RP_{\theta i}$ is the response produced by each mask $P_{\theta i}, 0 \leq i \leq 7$. The code images obtained through Kirsch masks, Sobel edge detection and Prewitt edge detection techniques are given as follows.

Figure 5. Code images obtained from testing images (sketch) using three edge detection techniques in C-LDP

Figure 6. Code images obtained from training images(photo) using three edge detection techniques in C-LDP

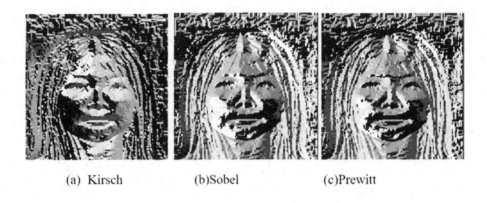

(a) Kirsch   (b)Sobel   (c)Prewitt

Figure 7. Feature vector formation from code images (for training images-photo)

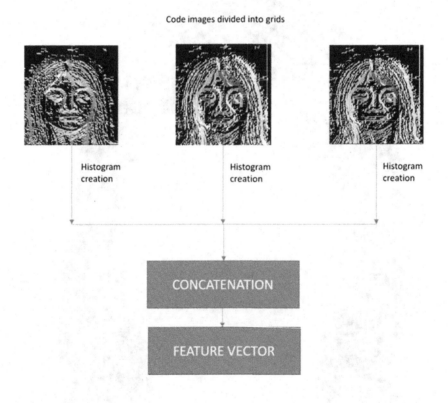

The

$$feature\ vector\_Kirsch = \left\langle H_{k1}, H_{k2} \ldots \ldots H_{kN} \right\rangle \tag{15}$$

where the code image obtained using Kirsch masks are divided into N number of equal sized grids and the histograms are calculated. The

$$feature\ vector\_Sobel = \left\langle H_{s1}, H_{s2} \ldots \ldots H_{sN} \right\rangle \tag{16}$$

where the code image obtained using Sobel masks are divided into N number of equal sized grids and the histograms are calculated. The

$$feature\ vector\_Prewitt = \left\langle H_{p1}, H_{p2} \ldots \ldots H_{pN} \right\rangle \tag{17}$$

where the code image obtained using Prewitt masks are divided into N number of equal sized grids and the histograms are calculated. The final feature vector is obtained using

$$feature\ vector_{Final} = \left\langle feature\ vector_{Kirsch}, feature\ vector_{Sobel}, feature\ vector\_Prewitt \right\rangle \tag{18}$$

The Extreme Learning Machine (ELM) with Radial Basis Function Kernel (RBF) is used for the classification purpose. The Extreme Learning Machine performs well for both binary classification and multi-classification. As the proposed work is a real-time application, it provides a rapid and accurate detection of the suspects compared to other classification algorithms. The feature vectors obtained for training(sketch) and testing(photo) images are given to ELM for the detection of suspects. The photos are classified as either a suspect or a common person.

IMPLEMENTATION

Dataset and Settings

CUHK Face Sketch database (CUFS) is a database that has a face-sketch combination of images. It has 188 faces chosen from the Chinese University of Hong Kong (CUHK) student database, 123 faces selected from the AR database, and 295 faces chosen from the XM2VTS database. Totally there are 606 faces in the database. For all the faces in the dataset there is a sketch drawn by an artist. The images are taken in frontal pose using neutral emotions of faces and normal illuminations (Martinez & Benavente, 1998; Messer et al., 1999).

Weapon Identification

Knives Images Database is taken for knife detection (http://kt.agh.edu.pl/~matiolanski/KnivesImages-Database/). The database is available on public. A database have two types of images: one is positive sample images, another one is negative sample images are required. Positive samples which contains images of knife in the hands of humans and negative samples i.e. image without knives were created.

The dataset contains 12866 images of which 3559 are positive samples and 9340 are negative samples. For efficient neural network training, it is required to have a greater number of negative samples compared to positive sample.

The accuracy of the result is measure using F-Score. The result is shown in Table 1. Experimental result of DiP pattern is shown in Figure 8. Proposed work accurately detect the weapons even in scaling changes and position changes in the frame.

Table 1. Average f-score value for proposed work

Proposed DiP	Knive Dataset	Gun Dataset (https://sci2s.ugr.es/weapons-detection)
Image 1	77.23	84.43
Image 2	76.78	79.12
Image 3	73.53	74.89
Image 4	92.78	82.18
Image 5	92.78	89.99
Image 6	84.78	87.92
Image 7	70.34	79.66
Image 8	98.45	95.67
Image 9	89.22	89.67
Image 10	85.20	88.47

Figure 8. Experimental result of proposed DiP for weapon dataset

Figure 9. Performance evaluation based on metric f-score on gun sequences

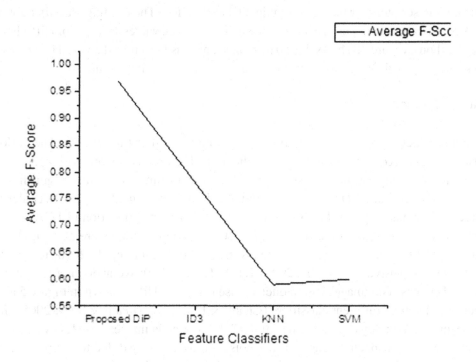

Figure 10. Performance evaluation based on metric f-score on gun sequences

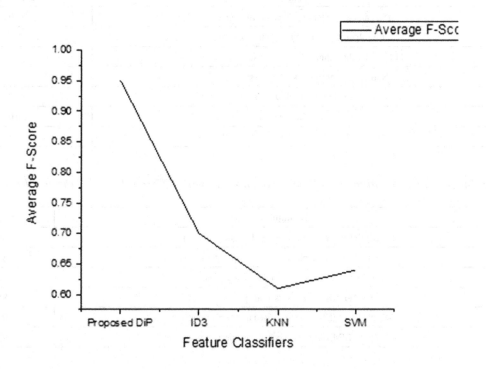

Figure 9 demonstrates the experimental results of the proposed feature descriptor along with other existing feature descriptors for the task of Object Classification. The existing classification techniques KNN, ID3, SVM are taken for performance analysis. The F-Score values are high for DiP when compared with other methods. Figure 10 shows the performance analysis for Knive dataset. The observation from the analysis is, proposed DiP perform well compared to other existing methods.

Facial Identification

The available images in the dataset are divided into training and testing images. The performance of the algorithm is analyzed using ten-fold cross-validation. The proposed work is compared with several approaches like PCA algorithm, Bayesian-face (Bayes) algorithm, Fisher-face algorithm, null-space LDA algorithm, dual-space LDA algorithm, and Random Sampling LDA (RSLDA) algorithm. Due to the large variation among the sketch and the photos, the direct application of PCA, Eigen face and other methods in literature do not achieve high accuracy. These methods are also highly sensitive to illumination variations and occlusions (Ahmed & Kabir, 2012; Jabid et al., 2010; Lyons et al., 1998; Ojala et al., 2002; Ojansivu & Heikkilä, 2008; Tan & Triggs, 2010; Weinberger et al., 2006). The proposed method creates code images with reduced noise using C-LDP as shown in Figure 5 and Figure 6. It has been verified with different classifiers (Chang & Lin, 2011; Huang & Siew, 2005; Huang et al., 2012; Recognition, n.d.; Suykens & Vandewalle, 1999). The code images have less variations resulting in high accuracy. This happens because of the noise removal achieved due to the prominent edge usage in C-LDP. The patch by patch comparison is achieved by grid formation before feature extraction

Table 2. Performance comparison with other algorithms

Technique	Accuracy (%)
PCA algorithm + Eigen Transformation	75.0
Bayes algorithm + Eigen Transformation	81.3
Fisher-face algorithm + Eigen Transformation	79.7
Null-space algorithm + LDA classifier	84.0
Dual-space algorithm + LDA classifier	88.7
RS algorithm + LDA classifier	90.0
C-LDP+RBF-ELM	93.5

Table 3. Suspect identification classification accuracies with different lighting, and occlusions

Technique	Accuracy (%)
C-LDP+RBF-SVM (sketch is used as query image)	85.6
C-LDP+RBF-SVM (photo is used as query image)	88.7
C-LDP+KNN (sketch is used as query image)	83.4
C-LDP+KNN (photo is used as query image)	85.8
C-LDP+RBF-ELM (sketch is used as query image))	92.3
C-LDP+RBF-ELM (photo is used as query image)	93.5

Table 4. Classification accuracies using different feature extraction methods

Technique	Accuracy (%)
DTP	89.7
LTP	87.2
LBP	78.1
Gabor	85.4
LD$_1$P	89.6
C-LDP	93.5
Human visual system	80.0

and using histograms adds additional performance. The algorithms used in (Belhumeur et al., 1997; Chen et al., 2000; Moghaddam & Pentland, 1997; Wang & Tang, 2004a; Wang & Tang, 2004b; Wang & Tang, 2006; Wiskott et al., 1997) like PCA, Eigen space, Null-space and Dual Space fail to capture the structure of the human face like the edges of the face and corners. C-LDP captures the structure and edge information of the face very well.

The proposed C-LDP methods performs better when combined with ELM than with SVM and KNN.

The photos are synthesized using different lighting variations, occlusions and pseudo photos are created to check the efficiency of the proposed algorithm. These photos are used in the experimentations and the classification accuracy is computed using different methods as in Table 3 and 4. The other feature extraction methods are not developing a code image with lesser variations between the testing and the training image. Hence C-LDP is successful than the other methods for feature extraction. Also, the patch by patch comparison in C-LDP using grid formation results in a better performance than the existing methods. Existing methods fail in creating a common code image from the sketch and the photo. They also do not have a patch-by-patch comparison. The proposed approach uses images of resolution 200×200 for the application of masks. The code images obtained are divided into grids of size 20×20. The histograms of size bin size 7 is created for each grid and a feature vector of size 700 is created for each code image. Therefore, the total size of the feature vector is 2100. In RBF-ELM, σ is chosen among $\{2^{12}, 2^7 ... 2^{-7}, 2^{-12}\}$. The regularization parameter P is chosen using the range $P = 10^l, l = -5, ..., 5$. The grid search technique and cross validation are initially applied on the feature vectors obtained using the sketches. Then, the optimum values are chosen in the classification of the feature vectors obtained from photos. Thus, the photos are identified as a suspect or common person.

A. Comparison With Human Visual System

In this experiment, a group of 50 students were allowed to use the sketches to choose the faces that matches from the available images in dataset. The time taken was very high when compared to our proposed technique. Also, the accuracy was only 80% which is very low when compared to our proposed technique.

Comparison

A.   Computational Complexity

Magnitude pattern is computed using proposed DiP pattern on every 4 × 4 region of image.

In that two computational operational is done on every 4 × 4 image region. In update step, 3 multiplications and 1 addition on each 4 x 4 image region is performed. Therefore, the computational complexity of the proposed method is O(3m)+O(n), where n is the number of frames in a video, m is the number of 4 × 4 image regions in one frame. This denotes that the proposed work can produce good results with much lower computational complexity. So, it is well suited for real time applications

B. Magnitude Pattern vs. Derivative Pattern

Magnitude patterns hold the vital information of each object. Compare to texture feature descriptor, Magnitude pattern generate a more concrete and unique feature.

CONCLUSION

A novel DiP pattern for weapon detection and a novel technique for criminal identification using the cameras in smart ATM has been proposed in this paper.

The C-LDP algorithm proposed in this paper analyzes the face structure and creates a code image for both photo and the sketch in the database. Then, the code images are matched using the ELM classifier. If a match is found then the identified person is a suspect/criminal. The proposed approach is tested on a dataset having images of both faces and sketches of 606 people. The proposed approach significantly performs better than the other current techniques.

REFERENCES

Ahmed, F., & Kabir, M. H. (2012) Directional ternary pattern (DTP) for facial expression recognition. In *IEEE International Conference on Consumer Electronics* (pp. 265-266). 10.1109/ICCE.2012.6161859

Belhumeur, P. N., Hespanda, J., & Kiregeman, D. (1997, July). Eigenfaces vs. Fisherfaces: Recognition Using Class Specific Linear Projection. *IEEE Transactions on Pattern Analysis and Machine Intelligence*, *19*(7), 711–720. doi:10.1109/34.598228

Benson, P. J., & Perrett, D. I. (1991). Perception and recognition of photographic quality facial caricatures: Implications for the recognition of natural images. *The European Journal of Cognitive Psychology*, *3*(1), 105–135. doi:10.1080/09541449108406222

Bruce, V., Hanna, E., Dench, N., Healy, P., & Burton, A. M. (1992). The importance of 'mass' in line drawings of faces. *Applied Cognitive Psychology*, *6*(7), 619–628. doi:10.1002/acp.2350060705

Chang, C. C., & Lin, C. J. (2011). LIBSVM: A library for support vector machines. *ACM Transactions on Intelligent Systems and Technology*, *2*(3), 27.

Chen, L., Liao, H., Ko, M., Lin, J., & Yu, G. (2000). A New Lda Based Face Recognition System which Can Solve the Small Sample Size Problem. *Pattern Recognition*, *33*(10), 1713–1726. doi:10.1016/S0031-3203(99)00139-9

Huang, G. B., & Siew, C. K. (2005). Extreme learning machine with randomly assigned RBF kernels. *Int J Inf Technol, 11*(1), 16–24.

Huang, G. B., Zhou, H., Ding, X., & Zhang, R. (2012). Extreme learning machine for regression and multiclass classification. Part B. *IEEE Transactions on Systems, Man, and Cybernetics, 42*(2), 513–529. doi:10.1109/TSMCB.2011.2168604 PMID:21984515

Jabid, T., Kabir, M. H., & Chae, O. (2010). Robust facial expression recognition based on local directional pattern. *ETRI Journal, 32*(5), 784–794. doi:10.4218/etrij.10.1510.0132

Kirsch, R. A. (1971). Computer determination of the constituent structure of biological images. *Computers and Biomedical Research, an International Journal, 4*(3), 315–328. doi:10.1016/0010-4809(71)90034-6 PMID:5562571

Lyons, M., Akamatsu, S., Kamachi, M., & Gyoba, J. (1998). Coding facial expressions with gabor wavelets. *Third IEEE International Conference on Automatic Face and Gesture Recognition*, 200-205. 10.1109/AFGR.1998.670949

Martinez, A. M., & Benavente, R. (1998). *The AR Face Database*. CVC Technical Report #24.

Messer, K., Matas, J., Kittler, J., Luettin, J., & Maitre, G. (1999). XM2VTSDB: the Extended of M2VTS Database. *Proceedings of International Conference on Audio- and Video-Based Person Authentication*, 72-77.

Moghaddam, B., & Pentland, A. (1997, July). Probabilistic Visual Learning for Object Recognition. *IEEE Transactions on Pattern Analysis and Machine Intelligence, 19*(7), 696–710. doi:10.1109/34.598227

Ojala, T., Pietikainen, M., & Maenpaa, T. (2002). Multiresolution gray-scale and rotation invariant texture classification with local binary patterns. *IEEE Transactions on Pattern Analysis and Machine Intelligence, 24*(7), 971–987. doi:10.1109/TPAMI.2002.1017623

Ojansivu, V., & Heikkilä, J. (2008). Blur insensitive texture classification using local phase quantization. *International conference on image and signal processing*, 236–243. 10.1007/978-3-540-69905-7_27

Recognition. (n.d.). In *Advanced Multimedia and Ubiquitous Engineering*. Springer.

Robinson, G. S. (1977, October 1). Edge detection by compass gradient masks. *Computer Graphics and Image Processing, 6*(5), 492–501. doi:10.1016/S0146-664X(77)80024-5

Sherly Alphonse, A., & Dharma, D. (2017a). Enhanced Gabor (E-Gabor), Hypersphere-based normalization and Pearson General Kernel-based discriminant analysis for dimension reduction and classification of facial emotions. *Expert Systems With Applications, 90*, 127-45.

Sherly Alphonse, A., & Dharma, D. (2017b). Novel directional patterns and a Generalized Supervised Dimension Reduction System (GSDRS) for facial emotion recognition. *Multimedia Tools and Applications*, 1-34.

Sherly Alphonse, A., & Dharma, D. (2017c). A novel Monogenic Directional Pattern (MDP) and pseudo-Voigt kernel for facilitating the identification of facial emotions. *Elsevier International Journal of Visual Communication and Image Representation, 49*, 457-470.

Sherly Alphonse, A., & Starvin, M.S. (2019). A novel Maximum and Minimum Response-based Gabor (MMRG) Feature Extraction method for Facial Expression Recognition. *Springer Multimedia Tools and Applications.*

Suykens, J. A., & Vandewalle, J. (1999). Least squares support vector machine classifiers. *Neural Processing Letters*, 9(3), 293–300. doi:10.1023/A:1018628609742

Tan, X., & Triggs, B. (2010). Enhanced local texture feature sets for face recognition under difficult lighting conditions. *IEEE Transactions on Image Processing*, 19(6), 1635–1650. doi:10.1109/TIP.2010.2042645 PMID:20172829

Tang, X., & Wang, X. (2002). *Face photo recognition using sketch.* Image Processing.

Vincent, O.R., & Folorunso, O. (2009). A descriptive algorithm for sobel image edge detection. In *Proceedings of Informing Science & IT Education Conference (InSITE)* (Vol. 40, pp. 97-107). California: Informing Science Institute.

Wang, X., & Tang, X. (2004a). Dual-Space Linear Discriminant Analysis for Face Recognition. *Proc. IEEE Int'l Conf. Computer Vision and Pattern Recognition.*

Wang, X., & Tang, X. (2004b). Random Sampling Lda for Face Recognition. *Proc. IEEE Int'l Conf. Computer Vision and Pattern Recognition.*

Wang, X., & Tang, X. (2006). Random Sampling for Subspace Face Recognition. *International Journal of Computer Vision*, 70(1), 91–104. doi:10.100711263-006-8098-z

Wang, X., & Tang, X. (2009). *Face Photo-Sketch Synthesis and Recognition. In IEEE Transactions on Pattern Analysis and Machine Intelligence* (Vol. 31). PAMI.

Weinberger, K. Q., Blitzer, J., & Saul, L. K. (2006). Distance metric learning for large margin nearest neighbor classification. *Advances in Neural Information Processing Systems*, 1473–1480.

Wiskott, L., Fellous, J., Kruger, N., & Malsburg, C. (1997, July). Face Recognition by Elastic Bunch Graph Matching. *IEEE Transactions on Pattern Analysis and Machine Intelligence*, 19(7), 775–779. doi:10.1109/34.598235

Section 3
Predictive Analytics

Chapter 11
Restaurant Sales Prediction Using Machine Learning

S M Nazmuz Sakib

https://orcid.org/0000-0001-9310-3014

International MBA Institute, School of Business and Trade, Dhaka International University, Bangladesh

ABSTRACT

In general, the revenue forecast, offer information, and the weather gauge setting will record an accurate estimate of any restaurant's future revenue. The turnover is significantly focused on the need of the customers. Either way, the performance has transformed over the past couple of years with the presentation of huge amounts of information and calculations during the time taken to gain the upper hand. It is fundamental to learn and understand the importance of the information that will be used in any business process. Again, climate forecasting can be done alongside business expectations with the organization.

INTRODUCTION

The use of Machine Learning, Deep Learning, and Artificial Intelligence has provided an effective approach to solve problems for the restaurant industry. Through research, it has been concluded that the use of these technologies can assist in predicting revenue and sales data for restaurants. This is done by analyzing different data sources and weather conditions to make precise predictions. Additionally, Machine Learning can help minimize human error and perform tasks more quickly. The use of different algorithms is important in creating an accurate prediction of revenue and sales for future years. The impact of weather on sales will also be evaluated in the study, and interactive machine learning algorithms will be utilized for accurate predictions. The results will be represented graphically for better understanding. Overall, Machine Learning is an effective approach to solve problems in the restaurant industry.

DOI: 10.4018/978-1-6684-7105-0.ch011

BACKGROUND

Different researchers have contributed toward development process based on machine learning techniques in our daily life routine activities. Sales predication based on weather forecasting with the help of machine learning concepts has being an effective approach to detail with. Machine learning has provided unique mechanism that can be utilized as an effective solution to deal with different real time problem.

Impact of Weather on Sales Prediction of Restaurants

This section previews the impact of weather on the sales prediction of different restaurants according to study conducted by different researchers.

Another effective mechanism that was utilized by Holmberg and Halldén (2018) in order to achieve forecasting or sales in restaurant based on the concepts of machine learning is considered as a one of the most appropriate techniques in the domain of restaurants. In the research study three different dataset were utilized for the purpose of experimentation based on three different cities. Whereas the data extraction was performed on the basis of SMHI concepts and data pre-processing process, correlation of features, standardization and normalization are involved in the implementation process. Further root means square error, extreme gradient boosting, model setup, final XG Boost model, LSTM neural network involves the setup of model and at last final LSTM model utilization were part of the implementation process. The most significant highlights while foreseeing the deals are plainly the highlights with respect to date, while the climate highlights has the least effect. This is for the most part valid for all restaurants, obviously there are eateries in which the climate highlights have a bigger effect than in others. The assessment and examination of the different eateries gave a thought of the assortment between the kinds of eateries and the absence of highlights in our models. All restaurants are accepted to be occasion subordinate, yet at different degrees. The occasion information, outer or inner, are relied upon to have a greater effect than the climate information by and large. Whereas evaluation of the implemented model was based on date features, weather features, features importance and selection, summer and weekday dataset.

According to different researches the fact was concluded that preferences of customer are based on season and weather which impact the commodity of sales generated by any restaurant. A study conducted by Abadi et al. (2016) which evaluate the system of TensorFlow which is considered as machine learning infrastructure based on large scale. The capability of the considered system lies on the evaluation of different parameter in Big dataset without any jurisdictions. The model for execution of TensorFlow flows a specific pattern to evaluate different state and computation of algorithms based on machine learning. The tensor model is capable of executing concurrent on multiple based on a subgraph of overlapping. while the element related to graph for dataflow were operated within different operators Tensor, operations, operations of stateful based on variables and stateful operations based on queues. While the following activities were involved within the methodology in the research study such as execution based on concurrent and partial, execution based on distributed manner and dynamic flow of controls. Cases studies of extensibility of the implemented model was carried out in the following way which can be illustrated as the following optimization and differentiation, training process of large models, tolerance of fault, synchronization based on coordination of replicas. The evaluation was performed through the following techniques which can be described as following single machine based on benchmark, synchronous microbenchmark replication, classification of images and modelling of language.

The impact created by weather over sales of restaurant were evaluated in a study proposed by Liu and Ichise (2017). The study specifically considers the supermarket chains in japan. The study briefly described the important prospective of encounter and LSTM which were part of the research methodology. The implementation of LSTM in the proposed study clarify the dependence of different factors related to sales over weather variations. While the prediction through LSTM utilize the factors of days, date, weather and sales for the purpose of prediction. The method of LSTM takes input in the takes in the input in the form of sequences. While the main analysis of LSTM was carried out in different layers and further analyzed under different layer for the autoencoding then the final output is obtained in a label. For evaluation of proposed model from 2012 to 2013 data relate to supermarket sales in Japan was utilized. For the comparison of performance based on the factor of accuracy was evaluated as compared to other traditional approaches of machine learning AdaBoost, LR, GBDT and SVM. While further evaluation of the proposed study was based on the factors of score of F-1, recall and precision. Through analysis the researcher concluded that proposed methodology outperforms in different factors as compared to other method and techniques based on machine learning.

Figure 1. Process of construction of features
Source: Meulstee et al. (2008)

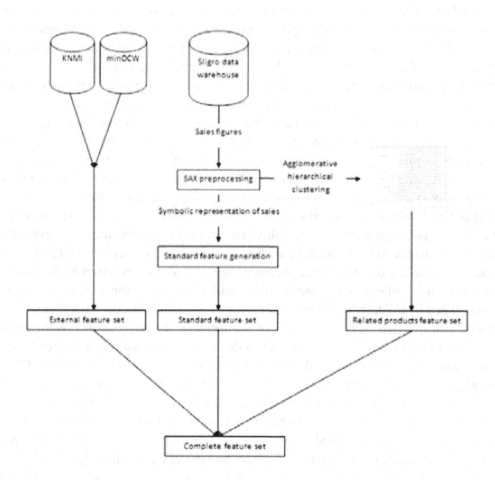

According to the business point of view prediction on sales provide an assumption based on previous record of business which can be used for create manifesto, effective business model and strategy which can provide effective results in terms of improvement. Through the research conducted by Meulstee and Pechenizkiy (2008) which emphasis on the prediction of sales while highlighting the aspects which were not utilized by any other researcher before. The research highlights the challenges faced during the prediction of food sales while considering the case study of food group company of Sligro. The research tends to implement the modern approach of ensemble learning which emphasized on the integration dynamically for the purpose better classification of different functionalities as per the requirement of the customer. Improvement in the sales through prediction was evaluated through analyzing different factors such as public holidays impact on sales, weather. Feature construction process in proposed study is illustrated in the Figure 2. While the experimentation was based on selection of targeted data and ensemble learning. Experimental analysis was based on the average of MSE, accuracy and absolute error. The researcher concluded that performance of ensemble approach of learning tends to surpass the performance of traditional algorithms utilized for prediction. Through implementation of ensemble technique, the researcher noticed that effective extraction of data over the impact of weather was noticed. The significant factor which was conclude from the research was that appropriate assignment of data related to public holiday and weather produce accurate prediction as compared to traditional approach implemented for this purpose.

Machine Learning Techniques for Prediction

This section briefly reviewed different machine learning techniques on the basis of supervised and unsupervised learning concepts for prediction.

Unsupervised Techniques

The effective implementation of unsupervised machine learning algorithms provides clear pattern and result when no specific categorization within the dataset exist. The capabilities of unsupervised algorithm rely on the cluster of datasets to evaluated different patterns within the dataset. A study proposed by Claypo and Jaiyen (2015) which implement the unsupervised algorithm of clustering through K-mean and selection of features through MRF which evaluates the reviews of restaurant based on Thailand. The study tends to cover the mining of opinion related to millions of reviews provided by customer to different restaurant in Thailand. The study focusses on attitude, opinion, emotions, evaluations and sentiments illustrated within the process of opinion mining in the proposed study through reviews of customer. Through different studies the fact was concluded that improvement in the services and food quality can be enhancement with the help of results concluded from mining of opinions. The study adapted the text processing through splitting the while mechanism into two parts in which the first part the reviews were transformed into token while further the next part involved the removal of those words which doesn't carry any specific meaning. The transformation of text was carried out in two part which were related to creation of keyword lists in the first part. Further the second part involved the creation of a formatted text file based in the format of numbers. The selection of features was carried through implementation based on optimization technique of Markov random field. The research implements the dataset of the trip advisor which consolidate the reviews of restaurant reviews. Further the clustering was performed through FCM, Hierarchical, SOM and K-means based factor of time and accuracy for the purpose of evaluation. Through experimentation the fact was conclude that computability of K-mean clustering surpasses the selection features mechanism of MRF in term of clustering.

Supervised Techniques

According to study proposed by Te et al. (2018) which implement the machine learning while utilizing the resources of web data services based on different restaurants data for the purpose of increasing the growth of the restaurant. Through this research, the data mining is performed on the large-scale data in order to achieve better pattern of policy and factor which may help the restaurant to increase their existing results in term of efficiency and accuracy. In the study the researcher implements the supervised algorithm based on machine learning in order to build pattern between data whereas comparison was considered another important feature of the study. The method involved for collection of data involved insurer data, web data based on central business names & trip advisor, open street map, swiss federal statistical office, swiss federal tax administration and fast food chains. Whereas the creation of label process and pre-processing of data were performed in a way such as growth label creation, input feature creation and construction of the growth model. whereas evaluation of the proposed study was based on the factor such as AUC, accuracy, sensitivity and specificity. Whereas random forest, multi-layer perception and logistic regression methods were utilized in the proposed study for the purpose of evaluation of the proposed model. Figure 1 shows the cooperate approach adapted by research for the linking of corporate data collection over the web samples. The research study was based in Switzerland, the researcher conclude that the results of the experimentation might have different outcomes over different regions.

Figure 2. Fast food chains

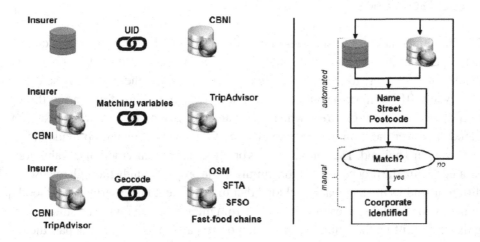

In domain of business, feedback and ratings are considered as interactive review from customers after utilizing the serves of business. Over the period of time different companies were able to perform effective as compared to its competitors after following the reviews and feedback of customers. In the domain of restaurant, in order to predict rating a study proposed by Kulkarni et al. (2019) address the idea by utilizing the concepts of algorithms based on machine learning for the purpose of prediction of rating. The proposed research utilized different machine learning techniques such as Decision Tree, Random Forest, XG Boost, Support Vector Machine, linear regression and ADA Boost in order to predict the rating of restaurants. Whereas evaluation prefer to follow the following parameter in order to utilize further for the process of prediction based on votes, area situated, cuisines, reviews and average cost for two people. Data pre-processing was performed on the data in order to filter or extraction of actual data instead of raw data. During the feature selection analysis following parameters were dropped form the dataset such as location, phone, address, review list and URL. Whereas exploratory data Analysis were further performed on distribution rate of restaurant, approximation of two people cost, rating based on online ordering, rating which deal with respect booking table, restaurant based on top rated and distribution based on online booking and ordering based rate and cost. Through experimentation it was concluded that accuracy rate of prediction of 83 percent was achieved through the utilization of ADA Boost technique.

According to survey conducted by Tsoumakas (2019) which tend to reviews different techniques of machine learning for prediction of sales in the domain of restaurant. The research tends to highlight the best approach which might be utilized in order to produce effective prediction based on the flow of data within the dataset. The evaluation of machine learning approaches and techniques of the accurate prediction of food sales are analysed through measurement of granularity within the temporal. The research highlights the perspective of output variables on the basis sales produce by each product while the weight was marked as another important entity toward development. While the evaluation of the experiment was based on the factor of accuracy which was based on the following measures such as MSE, RMSE, RRMSE, MAE, MAPE and MASE.

Effective Techniques for Prediction

The goal of every business is to achieve success in term of achieving the profit targets. According to research studies it is concluded that effective policy with the time should be adapted in order to achieve better and efficient outcomes. In the domain of restaurants business, the company has to follow different unique strategies in order to achieve better result in the shape of achieving the profit margins. The modern technology means it is concluded from different research that evaluation based on existing data of a successful business will provide different specific factor which were adapted by business in order to achieve successful. To deal with such scenario according to study proposed by Santhana Lakshmi and Bavishna (2020) which tend to analyse the existing data of restaurant using the modern technology in order to find out those factors which are actually responsible for increasing the sales so implementation of those factors might possibly boost the income of the restaurant. The study was carried under two different modules in order to figure out those factors which are responsible for increasing while evaluating through prediction modulation and analysis modulation. This study explores the monitoring of the restaurant system based on online system of delivery utilized for customer service along with those customers who directly approach restaurant for food. For the purpose of evaluation of the dataset Power BI and R Tool were utilized in order perform linear regression and other analysis on the dataset. Whereas following parameters were involved within the process of linear regression date, in dinner, take away, bulk order, diner, ambience, service, facilities, taste, Zomato, online, Zomato rating, swiggy, items, total, swiggy rating and diner rating were part of the evaluation of analysis and prediction modules. Through analysis it was found out that swiggy sales were the main reason behind success of the restaurant sales.

Classification of big data on the basis of sentiment analysis through implementation of apache spark were evaluated in the study conducted by Al-Saqqa et al. (2018). The study tends to highlight the correlation of different factor which are involved within the process of prediction. Evaluation the different corelated aspects on the basis of sentimental analysis was considered as one the significant factor of this conducted research. The proposed research not only briefly elaborated the significance of analysis based on sentiments, Apache Spark and big data. For the purpose of evaluation, the classifiers of SVM, LR and Naïve bayes were implemented under the command of environment setup in Spark. The research implements the dataset of reviews though amazon which were evaluated in the way such that over 2 M samples were evaluated within testing phase and over 1.8 M samples were evaluated within training phase. The pre-processing of dataset was carried out for cleansing of classifier and further preparation of classifiers. In the domain of the pre-processing certain review will null values were removed from the dataset and further separation based on characters were carried through implementation of tokenization within the research. Further the extraction feature in the research was based on conversion of textual data into vector of features. The researcher concluded that performance based on the factor of accuracy was provided through the implementation of SVM.

According to İşlek and Öğüdücü (2015) the forecasting process of demands related to a business company which tend to provide complete overview of product quality which meant to be purchased by customer. The paper focus on the utilization of effective model for forecasting in order to remove limitation during the whole process while achieving higher accuracy in terms of estimation or prediction. The adaptation of clustering of factor was perform through graph of bipartite process of clustering. Further the implementation of machine learning approach of Bayesian Network along with average moving model for the phase of hybrid forecasting. The involvement of direct supply chain, extended supply chain and ultimate supply chain within any organization was highlighted through the proposed research. The representation through the means of nodes and edge were handled through bipartite clustering of graph. For the assertions of conditional factor based on independence were represented graphically through the network of Bayesian. The methodology of the paper was conducted in the following manner such as construction of dataset, calculation of average moving values, construction of graph through bipartite, clustering through bipartite, implementation of machine learning and then the final result in the form of forecasting were achieved. For evaluation purpose dataset of companies of turkey were considered over the period of 2011 to 2013. The evaluation was based on the factor of MAPE for measurement of rate of error. The researcher concluded that effective improvement based on performance during forecasting was achieved through this research.

According to research conducted by Boyapati and Mummidi (2020) which evaluated different machine learning algorithms for the precise prediction. while the researcher tends to find those factors, which were responsible for effective increase in sales. The research performed the prediction through the implementation of simple linear regression, gradient boosting regression, support vector machine, random forest regression along with other supervised learning, unsupervised and reinforcement learning. The environment for experiment was based following tools and software for analysis such as python, NumPy, Pandas, Matplotlib, Sklearn, Seaborn. For the purpose of evaluation, a dataset containing 12 different attributes covering over 8523 instances was part of the research study. The study considered the following factors for purpose of finding correlation between data such as identifier, weight, Fat content, visibility, type, MRP related to items while as corresponding to outlet the following factors were evaluated such as type, sales, location, identifier and year in which the outlet is established. Data pre-processing process was carried out through encoding of values in categories and cross validation through stratified K-fold. While the evaluation of performance was based on the following factors such as score of accuracy, maximum error, absolute error based on mean values. For comparison of different algorithm, the evaluated was performed through calculation of average score of accuracy, average of absolute error mean value and average of maximum error. Through analysis the fact was concluded that the implementation of regression through random forest outcomes on the basis of different evaluation factor surpass other implement machine learning techniques and method.

Challenges During Sales Prediction

Another important aspect that can be considered as an important entity toward development of the restaurants can be illustrated on the basis of reviews. They are considered as one of the most efficient and effective tools to evaluate the performance of any restaurants whereas these tools can also utilize as an effective mechanism to introduce different policy based on the feedback of different customers. In this specific domain issues were further addressed by Hossain et al. (2017) which utilized the review of different customers and implement the machine learning techniques in order to achieve better performance based on sales of restaurant. For the purpose of experimentation, the research was based on the sample dataset embedded the review of people as Priyo dataset. Whereas over 50 selected restaurants were part of the dataset. Whereas the research utilized the tools of natural language toolkit for the process of pre-processing. Whereas the creating features involved review selection, tokenizing and part of speech tagging, selecting keyword and building classification model. whereas process of evaluation involved four different algorithms such as logistic regression, support vector machine, k nearest neighbour, and multinomial naïve Bayes, Whereas performance of the implemented model was based on the factor of Accuracy, TPR, TNR and AUC. Through this research the researcher concluded that the impact of review will provide unique mechanism to different restaurants to identify their market statistics.

The location of business point is also considered as a crucial entity toward business growth and development in a very short span of time. According to different research it was concluded that traffic situations around business point creates extra opportunities for business awareness in common people. Such scenarios were covered by the research proposed by Abrishami et al. (2017) which review the traffic situation around different business including restaurants in order to find out the result which are occurring due to this factor. The research covers the data of 100 business over the period of 1 year based on the traffic situation around the business. For the collection of AP Mac, Client Mac, Seen Epoch and RSSI were utilized in the process along with data processing was also based on these mentioned factors. For the evaluation of error and measurement of those error during forecasting MAE, RMSE and MAPE were utilized. Whereas the prediction model was based on the following factors such as function learning (based on weather, holidays, special event and location). While the evaluation of the proposed research the business was categorized into 6 different categories such as gym, coffee shop, restaurants, bar and barbershop. Whereas evaluation of the dataset was performed on different machine learning approaches such as utilization of python package sklearn in order to utilize the service of regression based on random forest, Libsvm in order to utilize the services of regression based on support vector machine along with predictor based on cloud services of Google. The experimentation process was divided into five different stages. Through experiment result it was concluded that's accuracy and performance of SVM in order to perform evaluation was effective and efficient as compared to other utilized techniques.

The study proposed by Aishwarya et al. (2020) address a critical issue related to restaurant management. The research emphasized on the technology means of which utilizes the services of learning based on concept of machine for the prediction of food demand. The idea behind this proposed research was to address and manage the food services with the passage of time and review them as per prediction. The main reason for conducting this research was to provide an effective and accurate mechanism which allows the management to plan their buying or export of ingredients in a mean while time. Whereas in the domain of restaurant we are pretty much aware of the most of the item have life based on short term period. The research also utilized the concepts of demand forecasting which emphasize on the estimation as per the demand of customer based on the data based in history. This research targets the quantity of ingredients based on the orders utilized against them while analysing them using the techniques and algorithms based on machine leaning. This research utilizes the services of linear regression, decision forest regression, Bayesian linear regression, support vector machine and XG Boost for the purpose of dealing with forecasting method. While the statistical method based on dataset was carried through stepwise method in the proposed study. Whereas forecasting based on the number of customers in the proposed research was carried in the following cases such as on track variable along with forecasting was performed via the following parameters such as number order, homepage featured, email for promotion, operation area, city code and region code. Through evaluation it was concluded that every utilized algorithm for the purpose of prediction shows similar result based on performance for forecasting.

Different issues are associated with the implementation of algorithms based on machine learning. The uncertainty within the signals will always overcome the financial aspects according to research conducted by Chen et al. (2018). The appropriate implementation of learning techniques based on machine learning will provide effective mechanism for encountering those strategies which might turn out to be disaster

Figure 3. Online Operation in CAPA
Zliobaite et al. (2009)

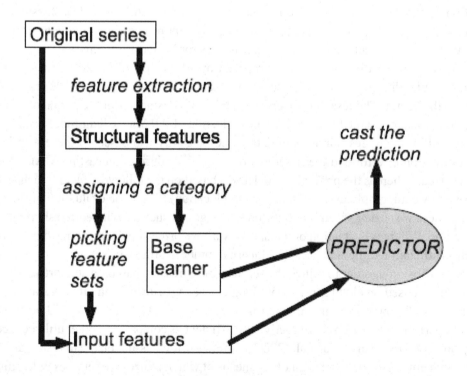

for business or damage the performance of business based on facts and figures. For establishment of system which is based on machine learning concepts which can further utilized in the management of financial aspect of any restaurant consumes a bit of time frame for the purpose of effective development of the ideal system. Different researcher has noticed that still some effective factor should be discovered in the domain of business in order to adapt the modern means of technology for effective performance according to Francis and Kusiak (2017). While the issues related to accuracy within the workflow of restaurant were notified as a serious lack of the system. Through effective implementation of algorithms based on artificial intelligence the accuracy on the any proposed system can be achieved.

We are familiar with the fact that for performing any specific task there are various number of ways evaluated on the basis of performance factor. Such a study which evaluated the performance of different techniques for prediction of sales and reviews were conducted by(Lasek et al. (2016). The study focusses on the method and techniques utilized for prediction of demand of customer and sales of restaurant. Along with evaluation of other proposed model the research tends to highlight the important aspect of forecasting of demand. The effective implementation of any prediction model can be possible through an effective management system of revenue which can adjust the prices of food as per the demand of the customer. For the purpose of prediction following parameter were utilized within the project such as time, weather, holiday, promotions, events, historical data, indicator of macroeconomics, competitive issues, websites, type of location, location of demographics. The research tends to highlight the performance of the following algorithms such as multiple regression, passion regression, model of Box-Jenkins or known as ARIMA, Holt winter and model based exponential smoothing, artificial neural network, Bayesian network and other hybrid models. The research highlights some associated rules of analysis based on the market basket. While the input, output, advantages and disadvantages related to above illustrated algorithm and techniques are part of the research paper.

In order to maintain the profitability of business and management of stock in the domain of business the company should undergo for predictions on time basic in order to evaluate statistics based on accuracy. The research study conducted by Žliobaite et al. (2009) tend to predict the sales based on content aware food. The approach of CAPA tend to selects the algorithm for predictions based on the historical sales properties presented in structural way. While the operation of online activity and offline activity were implemented in the CAPA through the means of decision support. Figure 3 illustrate the CAPA online operation. While the categorization of learning was based on the factors such as bottom up categorization which embedded the methodology of validation & training, and top down categorization. The data reside in the external and internal system are utilized in the process of forecasting which are furthermore utilized within features input space. For the purpose of evaluation Sligro group food industry case study was implemented which contain a data of six thousand products and 40 different outlets. The setup of experiments was based on the factor of bases predictor selection, categorization of learning, accuracies based on prediction. The researcher concluded that the most difficult encountered throughout the whole research was proper categorization for extracting accurate results.

MAIN FOCUS OF THE CHAPTER[1]

Overview of Analysis

In the past few year, the food delivery through online services is effectively adapted by customer. The preference of customer is changing form eating food at restaurant to ordering food through online services. The dataset comprises the data of restaurant based in Bangalore India for the purpose of analysis and evaluation. while the exploration of implemented model was based on the analysis of two different datasets. The dataset of order wise sales summary or OSS contain 45 different number of features and 33,401 number of rows embedded within it. The other dataset based on customer data of restaurant contain 10 different features and 28,16o number of rows were part of the dataset. For effective prediction specific features were cleaned from the dataset which was utilized though the implementation of data cleaning process in the dataset.

As a result of data cleaning, specifically 9 different features were extracted form overall 45 features of OSS dataset. Form the CDR dataset only 7 different features were extracted from the overall features. Through Table 1 the features selected form OSS dataset is illustrated. While the illustrated of cleaned features form CDR dataset are represented through Table 2.

Table 1. Data clean features form OSS dataset

Features No	Features Name in OSS Dataset
1	Cancellation
2	Delivery Time
3	Grand Total
4	Order Date
5	Order Source
6	Packaging Charge
7	Payment Mode
8	Pre-order
9	Restaurant Discount

Table 2. Data clean features form CDR dataset

Features No	Features Name in CDR Dataset
1	Phone No
2	Customer Name
3	Last transaction
4	Last transaction Days
5	Total orders
6	Revenue
7	Average Basket Size

The dataset of order wise sales summary was based on the information of sales related to the time period of year 2017 to 2018 comprises the details of sales generated while utilizing the online services. Different analysis was performed on the dataset in order to evaluate different trend and factor within the dataset while utilizing the concepts of machine learning. The correlation between number of customers utilizing different online food service is analysed under machine learning approach. The results concluded from the analysis is illustrated in Figure 4 which clear shows what significant number of users uses the service of Zomato and Swiggy. The effective services provided by Swiggy and Zomato are significantly trusted and utilized by customer all over the region.

Figure 4. Order placed by customers on different platforms

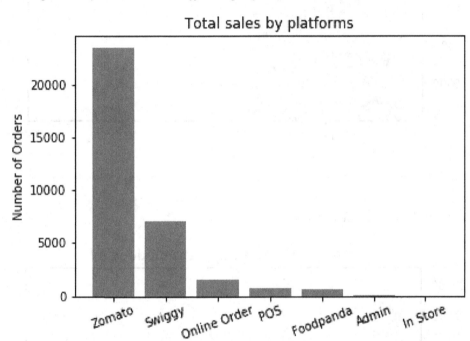

This study further evaluates another interesting fact which emphasized on the booking of pre-order for food by customer. This sort of feature is provided to customer to manage the food service for different schedule meetings and sittings. Figure 5 illustrated the usage of pre-order feature by different customers. Through analysis the fact was concluded that very low percentage of customer prefer to go for pre-order service. While most of the customers prefer not to go for the pre-ordering service because of different restriction are associated with the pre-order features of Swiggy, Zomato and other online services.

Online services have provided interactive platform to customers in terms of service, reliability and effective domain for helping customer. The mode of payment is also considered effective entity toward customer care and service. Figure 6 illustrated the different payment mode utilization for using the resources of any online food service. Through analysis the fact was concluded that most of the payment were performed through online banking services. Through analysis the fact was find out that 39 minutes average time for delivery is required for the delivery of food to the end customer.

Figure 5. Usage of pre-order service by customers

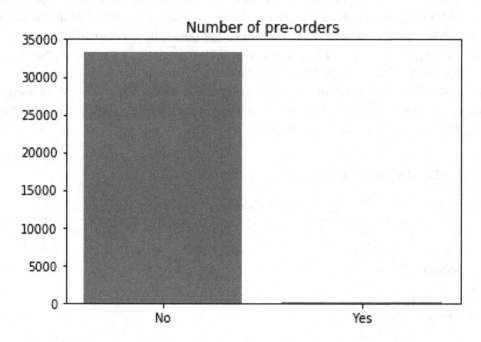

Figure 6. Usage of different mode of payments

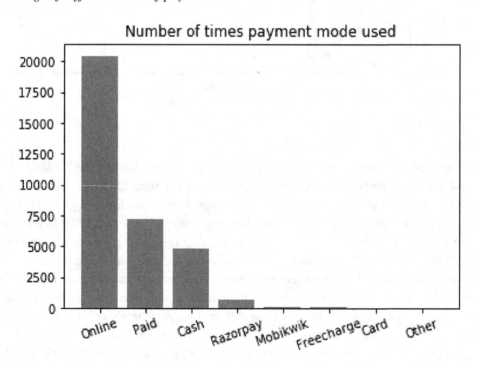

Impact of Weather on Orders and Daily Sales

The fact can be denied or prove wrong that condition of weather influences the orders and daily sales of restaurant. According to different research the fact was concluded that seasonal changes impose a significant variation within the order and daily sales of restaurant. While different factor of weather is also associate with human psychology which let them to order food through different restaurants. In order to perfectly organize the demand of customer according to weather different analysis should be conducted in order to carry some precautions while dealing with customer in different season changes. Through different research the fact was concluded that one the most significant part contribution is naturally provided by the factor of weather in order to improve the performance of restaurant.

The analysis based on the relation between impact of weather on sales is illustrated in Figure 7. On the other hand, other analysis, the relation between impact of weather on revenue generated on those sales is illustrated in Figure 8. Both the analysis will provide effective understanding over the impact of weather on sales of restaurant.

Figure 7. Impact of weather on count of sales in average

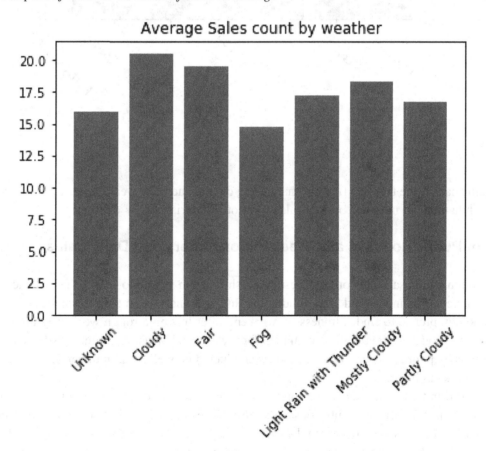

Figure 8. Impact of weather on cost of sales in average

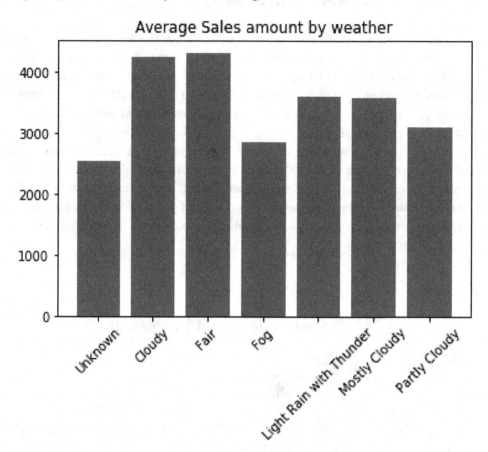

Through analysis the fact was find out that during cloudy and fairy weather most count of sales was noticed. While the least number count of sales was noticed during foggy weather.

Impact of Public Holidays and Weekend on Orders and Daily Sales

The fluctuation within sales and order of restaurant shifts from season to season. The impact of public holidays can be easily understood after conducting different analysis on the relevant relation. The human psychology prefers to find calmness on weekend after having a rough week they prefer to order food online to spend some quality time with their family and find pleasure in life. In order to completely understand the dept of the situation analysis was conducted between total number of sales against the number of weeks in Figure 9.

Figure 9 illustrates the impact of sales on the basis of days of week. Through this analysis it is concluded that the most significant number of sales were achieve during Sunday throughout the week. While the least number of sales were observed during Thursday throughout the week. It turns out to provide effective policies which can be adapted in order to deal with further more increase the sales.

Another interesting analysis was conducted over the different months of year 2017 and year 2018 against the total number of sales generated in those months shown in Figure 10. Through analysis the

Figure 9. Average sales based on days of the week

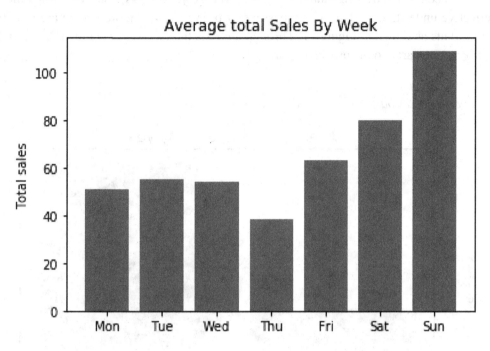

fact was find out over the years the greatest number of sales are generated in the month of September. The management team can use this opportunity to create remarkable profit margin if effective polices are implemented precisely. While the least number of sales were noticed in the month of February.

Figure 10. Average sales based on days of the month

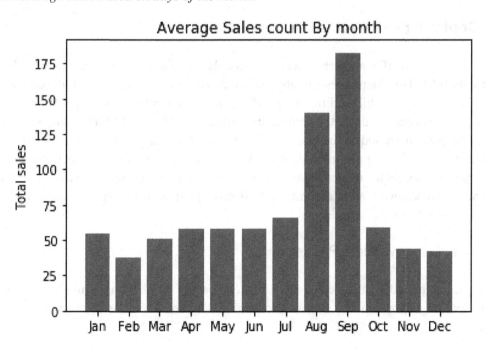

The Analysis conducted over the number of sales over the year shows effective result which tend to provide effective understanding that with a passage of time more and more people are preferring the food of restaurants as shown in Figure 11. Through analysis the fact was concluded that average sales increase 50% as compared to the previous year.

Figure 11. Average sales based on a yearly basis

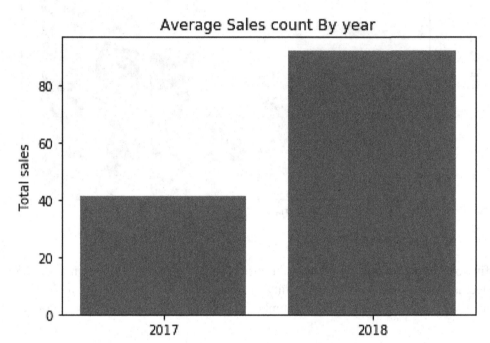

Issues, Controversies, Problems

The author(s) included different machine learning models to achieve the research goal of effective prediction of sales related to different restaurants. They aimed to figure out the impact of weather on orders and sales of restaurants and utilized different specific methods and techniques to extract data and features for prediction. They concluded that the performance achieved by LightGBM algorithm surpassed other implemented algorithms based on the basis of MAE score. However, the author(s) also expressed their interest in exploring other algorithms such as random forest, Naïve bayes, and other machine learning and deep learning models for implementation in the same domain of research. This indicates that the author(s) aimed to achieve a more accurate and effective prediction by experimenting with different machine learning models and techniques.

More Issues, Controversies, Problems

While the research provides valuable insights into the impact of weather on restaurant sales and the use of machine learning algorithms for revenue prediction, there are several research gaps that need to be addressed.

Figure 12. Methodology adapted in this study
Source: Awad and Khanna (2015)

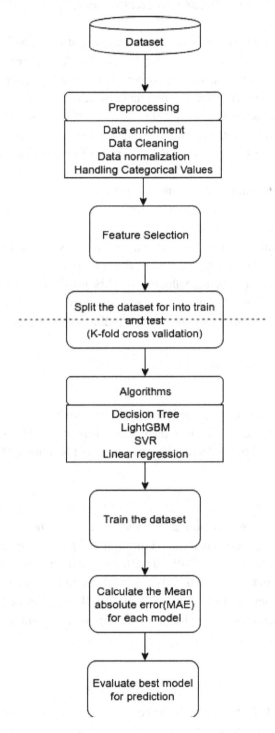

Firstly, the research does not address the potential influence of location on restaurant revenue. The restaurant industry is highly competitive, and different locations may have unique customer needs and preferences, which can affect sales.

Secondly, while the research mentions the importance of customer feedback, it does not explore the role of customer reviews and sentiment analysis in predicting restaurant revenue. Customer reviews can provide valuable information on the factors that drive customer satisfaction and dissatisfaction, which can help restaurants to improve their offerings and increase revenue.

Thirdly, the study only focuses on a few machine learning algorithms, and there is a need to explore the potential of other algorithms and deep learning models for revenue prediction. The use of more advanced algorithms and models can improve the accuracy of revenue predictions and provide a competitive advantage to restaurants.

Fourthly, the research only examines the impact of weather on restaurant sales, and there is a need to explore other external factors that can affect revenue, such as economic conditions, seasonal trends, and customer demographics.

Lastly, the research is limited to a specific region, and there is a need to conduct similar studies in different regions to determine the generalizability of the findings.

In summary, while the research provides valuable insights into the use of machine learning algorithms for revenue prediction and the impact of weather on restaurant sales, there are several research gaps that need to be addressed to provide a comprehensive understanding of the factors that drive restaurant revenue.

METHODOLOGY

In order to perform machine learning different methodologies can be adapted to effectively deal with the problem based in real time. In order to achieve the goals of this proposed research and objective behind this research are illustrated in Figure 12 according to Awad and Khanna (2015).

Data Pre-Processing

The complete exploration of dataset is elaborated in the Section 3 of the proposed study. The transforming of data into required information is performed through this part of the research. Pre-process of data is considered as technique of data mining utilized for turning data in raw to a more appropriate format. Removal of missing entries and bulk or null values is performed in this part of the research. while the process of normalization, enrichment and cleaning of data will be performed to trained the model while implementing algorithm based on machine learning. Technique of encoding based on the model of one hot is considered for this research.

Features Selection

The selection of those valuable features which can be related to our perspective of research and objective are extracted from the implementation of features selection. The removal of unnecessary features is also performed through this method. The performance was effective improved after the removal of unnecessary features. While the feature of mobile number was utilized as the entity for acquiring unique records.

The identification of customer for loyalty is performed through conducting analysis which validate the entity against their respective phone number.

K-Fold Cross Validation

The implementation of K-Fold cross validation during machine learning tend to provide effective implementation of data and provide a unique pattern which can easily be understandable. This method tends to split the data into number of K folds. In order to stopping the proposed system in terms of over training only twenty percent of the dataset was utilized in the testing period while eight percent of the dataset was evaluated in training of dataset. Along with effective generalization of the data was achieved through utilization of K-fold cross validation. While the evaluation at each level based on different folds shows effective performance during evaluation.

Evaluation and Models

Different algorithms were in this study evaluation period which was based on the following algorithms such as Linear Regression, Support Vector Regression, LightGBM and Decision Tree. After completely the pre-processing of data, selection of different features based on features selection and validation through the means of K-Fold cross validation the complete evaluation of performance along with model training process is considered as the final part of the proposed study. In order to achieve the aims of this proposed research which based on effective prediction for the daily basis sales and total numbers of orders different algorithms were implemented in the proposed study. The validation score turns out to check point which validate the different machine learning till no effective improvement can be observed till straight away two hundred round of time lapse. The evaluation of the proposed study was based on the MAE or Mean Absolute Error for every implemented model of machine learning which were SVR, LR, DT and LGBM. While the performance factor of every algorithm was based on the factor of MAE which will clearly help the researcher to find out the most effective algorithm that can be utilized for effective prediction of sales and orders.

SOLUTIONS AND RECOMMENDATIONS

Discussion and Results

The result obtained from evaluation of different machine learning algorithm is discussed in this section. The preference of the researcher lies in the meeting the mark up objective of the proposed research which emphasized on the prediction of the revenue which can totally generated on daily basis while which factor can be utilized in order to boost up the number of total sales. While prediction goals also emphasized on the order which can be placed on daily basis. The research implemented different well-known machine learning approaches for the purpose of training and testing of dataset. For evaluation of performance of different learning algorithms based on machines the factor of Mean absolute error is implemented. The programming language of Python was used for the coding scheme for different machine learning algorithms. While the execution of these program was performed on Jupiter notebook. The analysis on total order numbers turned out to be a comparison between different machine learning approaches on

Table 3. MAE value bases on daily basis total orders

Algorithm	Mean Absolute Error
Support Vector Regression	34.431
Light Gradient Boosting Machine	15.389
Linear Regression	17.845
Decision Tree	19.120

Table 4. MAE value bases on daily basis total sales

Algorithm	Mean Absolute Error
Support Vector Regression	10161.840
Light Gradient Boosting Machine	4119.150
Linear Regression	4329.010
Decision Tree	5878.30

the basis of factor of MAE shown in Table 3 which also calculate the performance of different machine learning algorithms.

Though evaluation of MAE score in Table 3 of different machine learning algorithms on total number of orders shows the fact that least number of MAE score is secured by algorithm of light Gradient Boosting machine. While the highest score was achieved by SVR during the evaluation of MAE. The main reason behind effective performance of LGBM lies in the fact the algorithm performs to compile data in categorical form which provide advantage as compared to other algorithms.

The analysis on total Sales turned out to be a comparison between different machine learning approaches on the basis of factor of MAE shown in Table 4. Through evaluation the fact was concluded that most satisfying and significantly less encountered were recorded under the implementation of LightGBM technique as compared to other technique. While the least performance in terms high mean absolute error was achieved by Support Vector Regression.

Through different evaluation in Section 3 of this research we concluded that cloudy or fair weather boost up the total number of sales and order which can be effectively taken as a vital opportunity to generate extra money in those condition. Foggy weather was turn out to be condition of weather in which customer feels unsecured to order food while introducing different interactive ideas to overcome this issue can be an interactive solution to these issues. Through different evaluation conducted on impact of public holidays on sales and order of restaurant interesting facts were find out. The most significant sales and orders were placed on Sunday which lead us to the fact that restaurant business and management cannot lose this vital opportunity to attract customer in the mean while time. while the least number of customers prefer to use the service of pre-orders. Through evaluation the fact was find out that Zomato is the most used food service used by different users in India. Another interesting analysis was related to extracting the loyal customer were part of this research. The researcher was able to fetch over five hundred top customers on the basis of their loyalty on score generated on the basis of revenue spend by these customers. Different features information related to these loyal customers were part of this evaluation.

CONCLUSION

The complete overview of the research will be elaborated in this part of this research. This research provided a complete overview of factors which are involved in the effective prediction of sales related to different restaurants. Through this work the effective understanding can be concluded the impact of weather on order and sales of restaurant can be figured out. Different machine learning concepts that can be adapted by different system in order to perform precise prediction is part of the research goals. The vast research provides effective approach to learn modern machine learning algorithms along with its implementation. Different specific method and techniques were imposed on dataset just for effective extraction of data and features in order to utilize those features for the purpose of prediction. While effective prediction was generated after analyzing the existing work based on the total number of sales generated on daily basis along with the total number of orders generated on daily basis. The research highlight majority of customer prefer to pay for expense of restaurant through online services. The greatest number of customers for purpose of online food delivery prefer to use the platform of Zomato. During Public Holiday, especially on Sunday's effective revenue was generated when a very large number of orders and sales are placed. Different algorithms based on machine learning were implemented for the purpose of prediction. Through different performance evaluation the fact was concluded that the performance achieved by LightGBM surpasses the prediction achieved by any other implemented algorithm on the basis of MAE score. The analysis also identified top first five hundred loyal customer on the base of revenue spend on these platforms. The opportunity will provide a more discount to those customers in order to provide much more effective service to valuable customers. The researcher looks up to other algorithms such as random forest, Naïve bayes and other machine learning and deep learning model for implementing in the same domain of research. Feedback provided by customer is the missing entity in the dataset which can turn out to be effectively improve the performance of any restaurants. In order to achieve effective visualization, the approach of Sentimental analysis should be deployed in the infrastructure for effective analysis.

REFERENCES

Abadi, M., Barham, P., Chen, J., Chen, Z., Davis, A., Dean, J., Devin, M., Ghemawat, S., Irving, G., & Isard, M. (2016). TensorFlow: A System for Large-Scale Machine Learning. In *12th USENIX Symposium on Operating Systems Design and Implementation (OSDI 16)* (pp. 265-283). USENIX.

Abrishami, S., Kumar, P., & Nienaber, W. (2017). Smart stores: A scalable foot traffic collection and prediction system. In *Industrial Conference on Data Mining*. Springer. 10.1007/978-3-319-62701-4_9

Aishwarya, Rao, Kumari, Mishra,& Rashmi. (2020). Food demand prediction using machine learning. *International Research Journal of Engineering and Technology*, *07*, 3672–3675.

Al-Saqqa, S., Al-Naymat, G., & Awajan, A. (2018). A large-scale sentiment data classification for online reviews under apache spark. *Procedia Computer Science*, *141*, 183–189. doi:10.1016/j.procs.2018.10.166

Awad, M., & Khanna, R. (2015). Support vector regression. In *Efficient Learning Machines* (pp. 67–80). Springer. doi:10.1007/978-1-4302-5990-9_4

Boyapati, S.N., & Mummidi, R. (2020). *Predicting sales using Machine Learning Techniques*. Academic Press.

Chen, T., Yin, H., Chen, H., Wu, L., Wang, H., Zhou, X., & Li, X. (2018). Tada: Trend alignment with dual-attention multi-task recurrent neural networks for sales prediction. In *2018 IEEE International Conference on Data Mining (ICDM)*. IEEE. 10.1109/ICDM.2018.00020

Claypo, N., & Jaiyen, S. (2015). Opinion mining for thai restaurant reviews using K-Means clustering and MRF feature selection. In *2015 7th International Conference on Knowledge and Smart Technology (KST)*. IEEE. 10.1109/KST.2015.7051469

Francis, H., & Kusiak, A. (2017). Prediction of engine demand with a data-driven approach. *Procedia Computer Science*, *103*, 28–35. doi:10.1016/j.procs.2017.01.005

Holmberg, M., & Halldén, P. (2018). *Machine Learning for Restaurant Sales Forecast*. Academic Press.

Hossain, F. T., Hossain, M. I., & Nawshin, S. (2017). *Machine learning based class level prediction of restaurant reviews. In 2017 IEEE Region 10 Humanitarian Technology Conference (R10-HTC)*. IEEE. doi:10.1109/R10-HTC.2017.8288989

İşlek, İ., & Öğüdücü, Ş. G. (2015). A retail demand forecasting model based on data mining techniques. In *2015 IEEE 24th International Symposium on Industrial Electronics (ISIE)*. IEEE. 10.1109/ISIE.2015.7281443

Kulkarni, A., Bhandari, D., & Bhoite, S. (2019). Restaurants Rating Prediction using Machine Learning Algorithms. *International Journal of Computer Applications Technology and Research, 8*(9), 375-378.

Lasek, A., Cercone, N., & Saunders, J. (2016). Restaurant sales and customer demand forecasting: Literature survey and categorization of methods. In *Smart City 360* (pp. 479–491). Springer. doi:10.1007/978-3-319-33681-7_40

Liu, X., & Ichise, R. (2017). Food sales prediction with meteorological data—a case study of a japanese chain supermarket. In *International Conference on Data Mining and Big Data*. Springer. 10.1007/978-3-319-61845-6_10

Meulstee, P., & Pechenizkiy, M. (2008). Food sales prediction: "If only it knew what we know". In *2008 IEEE International Conference on Data Mining Workshops*. IEEE. 10.1109/ICDMW.2008.128

Santhana Lakshmi, V., & Bavishna, A. (2020). Analyzing the Restaurant data to Predict the Best Mode of Income. *Sustainable Humanosphere*, *16*, 270–277.

Te, Y.-F., Müller, D., Wyder, S., & Pramono, D. (2018). Predicting the growth of restaurants using web data. *Economic and Social Development (Book of Proceedings)*, 237.

Tsoumakas, G. (2019). A survey of machine learning techniques for food sales prediction. *Artificial Intelligence Review*, *52*(1), 441–447. doi:10.100710462-018-9637-z

Žliobaite, I., Bakker, J., & Pechenizkiy, M. (2009). Towards context aware food sales prediction. In *2009 IEEE International Conference on Data Mining Workshops*. IEEE. 10.1109/ICDMW.2009.60

KEY TERMS AND DEFINITIONS

Absolute Error: It is the absolute value of the difference between predicted values and actual values in a dataset.

Accuracy: It is the percentage of correct predictions in a dataset.

Computer Science: The study of computing, programming, and computation in correspondence with computer systems.

Correlation: It is a statistical measure that indicates the degree of association between two variables.

Customer Data of Restaurant (CDR) Dataset: A dataset that contains information on the customers who have used the online services of a restaurant, such as their phone number, name, total orders, revenue generated, etc.

Customer Demographics: Refers to the characteristics of a customer base, such as age, gender, income, and education, which can impact their preferences and purchasing behavior.

Customer Feedback: Refers to the opinions and comments shared by customers about their experience with a restaurant. Customer reviews and sentiment analysis can provide valuable information on factors that drive customer satisfaction and dissatisfaction, which can help restaurants improve their offerings and increase revenue.

Data Cleaning: The process of identifying and removing or correcting errors, inconsistencies, and inaccuracies in a dataset in order to improve its quality and usefulness for analysis.

Data Pre-Processing: Refers to the technique of data mining utilized for turning raw data into a more appropriate format. This includes removing missing entries, null values, normalization, enrichment, and cleaning of data.

Dataset: A collection of data that can be analyzed and used for different purposes.

Decision Tree: Refers to a tree-shaped model used to make decisions, with each internal node representing a "test" on an attribute, and each leaf node representing a class label.

Deep Learning Models: Refers to a subset of machine learning algorithms that use artificial neural networks to model and solve complex problems.

Economic Conditions: Refers to the state of the economy, such as inflation, unemployment, and economic growth, which can impact consumer spending and restaurant sales.

Ensemble Learning: It is a machine learning technique that combines multiple models to improve the accuracy of predictions.

Extreme Gradient Boosting (XG Boost): It is a machine learning algorithm that uses decision trees to improve the accuracy of predictions.

Features Selection: Refers to the selection of valuable features related to the research perspective and objective. The removal of unnecessary features is also performed through this method.

Information Technology: The use of technology to store, process, transmit and retrieve information.

K-Fold Cross Validation: Refers to a method of splitting data into K folds to provide an effective implementation of data and provide a unique pattern that is easily understandable.

LightGBM: Refers to a gradient boosting framework that uses tree-based learning algorithms.

Linear Regression: Refers to a statistical approach for modeling the relationship between a dependent variable and one or more independent variables.

Location: Refers to the physical place of a restaurant and its influence on customer needs and preferences, which can affect sales.

Long Short-Term Memory (LSTM) Neural Network: It is a type of recurrent neural network that can learn long-term dependencies in sequential data.

Machine Learning Algorithms: Refers to a set of statistical models and techniques that enable computers to learn from data, identify patterns, and make predictions without being explicitly programmed.

Machine Learning: A subfield of Artificial Intelligence (AI) that enables systems to learn and improve from experience without being explicitly programmed.

Mean Squared Error (MSE): It is a measure of the difference between predicted values and actual values in a dataset, calculated as the average of the squared differences.

Mode of Payment: The method used by customers to make payment for the food they order online, such as online banking, credit/debit card, cash on delivery, etc.

Normalization: It is the process of scaling data to a range of 0 to 1, making it easier to compare and analyze.

Order Wise Sales Summary (OSS) Dataset: A dataset that contains information on the sales generated through online services during a certain time period. It includes different features related to the orders, such as order date, delivery time, payment mode, etc.

Pre-Order: A feature provided by online food delivery services that allows customers to book food in advance for a specific time or date.

Public Holidays and Weekend Impact on Sales: The influence of public holidays and weekends on the sales and orders of a restaurant, as customers may have more free time and prefer to order food online during these times.

Root Mean Square Error (RMSE): It is a measure of the difference between predicted values and actual values in a dataset.

Sales: The exchange of goods or services for money or other valuable consideration.

Sales Prediction: The process of forecasting future sales of a business based on historical sales data, market trends, and other relevant information.

Seasonal Trends: Refers to the recurring patterns of behavior, preferences, and activities that change with the seasons, which can impact restaurant sales.

Standardization: It is the process of transforming data to have a mean of zero and standard deviation of one, making it easier to compare and analyze.

Support Vector Regression: Refers to a machine learning algorithm used for regression analysis, which uses a subset of training points in the decision function.

TensorFlow: It is an open-source software library for dataflow and differentiable programming across a range of tasks. It is used for machine learning applications such as neural networks.

Weather Forecasting: It is the process of using scientific and mathematical techniques to predict atmospheric conditions for a particular location and time.

Weather Impact on Sales: The effect of weather conditions, such as rain, fog, or sunshine, on the number of orders and daily sales of a restaurant.

Chapter 12
Big Data Analytics–Based Agro Advisory System for Crop Recommendation Using Spark Platform

Madhuri J.
Bangalore Institute of Technology, India

Indiramma M.
BMS College of Engineering, India

ABSTRACT

The advancements in science and technology have led to the generation of colossal data in the agricultural sector as a result of which has entered the world of big data. Big data analytics is the solution to store and analyze such large amounts of data to improve productivity in agricultural practices. Hence, the purpose of this research work is to develop a big data recommendation framework that enables farmers to choose the right crops considering the location-specific parameters. The location-specific weather parameters, soil parameters crop characteristics, and demand for the agricultural product in the previous years are considered in the work. The proposed recommendation model is based on the Spark framework that accepts the soil data in real-time analyses along with weather and pricing data by applying artificial neural networks and suggesting a suitable crop for the field conditions. The chapter prioritizes developing an application useful for farmers, agriculture officers, and researchers to provide efficient crop recommendations.

INTRODUCTION

Unprecedented population growth and related socioeconomic challenges are associated with global food shortage (Slavin, 2016). It is estimated that by the year 2050 the world population would increase by 30%, which calls for accelerating food productivity by 70%. We need to address the requirements of

DOI: 10.4018/978-1-6684-7105-0.ch012

agriculture to feed a growing global population with a reduced environmental footprint while adapting to mitigate the effects of changing climate. The necessity to harness the increasing food demands has initiated several studies since early 2000 in the field of agriculture (Basso et al., 2001; Robert, 2002). Hence there is a critical need to increase innovations in the field of agriculture considering the different factors affecting food production.

Interaction with technology in the agricultural field plays a crucial role in providing affordable, nutritious food, feedstuff, and fibers to humankind with the looming challenges of climate change (Karimi et al., 2018). Although there is unquestionable progress in the use of technology in farming practices, it fails to deliver the equivalent impact globally. Most agricultural innovations fail to reach the intended end users thus failing to generate expected improvements in the farming sectors. Measures to reach more target users and add value by utilizing the improved quality of life of millions of farmers and consumers around the world are necessary. Innovations in the agricultural sector have to be driven by challenges of climate extremities, variable soil conditions, demand for the products, and the well-being of the end-users such as farmers and consumers. Technology can be conceptualized as a driver for successful innovation. The concept of precision agriculture, based on information technology, is an important step in agricultural innovation supporting site-specific crop management strategies based on observing multiple parameters such as climate, soil conditions, and developmental stages of plant and crop health. Precision agriculture leverages the technologies to analyze historical climate patterns, sensor data, and soil variability. With the introduction of Precision agriculture, traditional agriculture has been reformed by advanced Information and Communication Technologies (ICTs), eventually contributing to significant improvements in agricultural productivity and sustainability (Wolfert et al., 2017). Concerning this, agriculture systems utilize inputs from Global Information Systems (GIS), soil sensors, and physical measurements of the soil and emphasize utilizing inputs to provide a factual recommendation about crop management to the farmers.

The enormous amount of data indicates the need for large-scale collection, storage, preprocessing, modeling, and analysis of huge amounts of data coming from various heterogeneous sources. Compared with traditional datasets, massive unstructured data requires big data platforms which enable performing real-time data analysis. This helps us to acquire a better understanding of the hidden values in the data and hence encourages us to take up new challenges e.g., how to effectively organize and manage such datasets (Kshetri, 2014). Though big data analytics is a popular term in various industries such as banking, insurance, retail, and social networking, it is being introduced in the field of agriculture only recently (Lokers et al., 2016). Our goal in this paper is aimed at extend our knowledge about harnessing big data in the agricultural sector and the expected changes that are caused by big data developments. In this work, we are focusing on a case study of developing the recommendation model to enable the farmers to choose the suitable crop. The recommendation model considers the location-specific climate data, soil data, crop characteristics, and the pricing trend of the crop. The model makes use of the Apache Spark platform for big data analysis.

POTENTIAL OF BIG DATA ANALYTICS

Big data analytics comprises all the procedures and technologies required for knowledge discovery, including data extraction, transformation, loading, and analysis, as well as particular tools, methodologies, and approaches for delivering results to decision-makers (Osman, 2019). Big data analytics offers an opportunity to expand standard information extraction methodologies into new realms. This opportunity prompted researchers and technology vendors to create sophisticated platforms, frameworks, and algorithms to address the big data challenges.

Big Data Analytics Framework

The big data analytics framework can be divided into four segments, namely: Data collection, information extraction, data analysis, and data interpretation. Big Data Analytics frameworks are shown in Figure 1.

Figure 1. Big data analytics framework

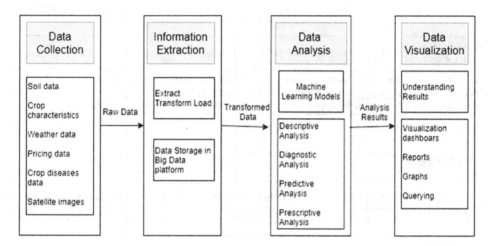

Data Collection

The primary phase in data analytics is considered data collection. The procedure of collecting, measuring, and evaluating correct insights for study using established approved procedures is known as data collection. Regardless of the subject of study, data collecting is usually the first and most significant phase in the research process. In agriculture, both structured and unstructured data are gathered from a variety of sources, including weather reports, soil conditions, satellite photos, and more. Open-source datasets available for agriculture analysis are listed in

Table 1. Open source data sets

Dataset	Description
Open Government Data (OGD) Platform India (Open Government Data (OGD) Platform India, n.d.)	A portal is a single point of access to information, documents, services, tools, and applications produced by the Government of India's ministries, departments, and organizations.
World Bank Open Data (World Bank Open Data, n.d.)	Maintains 2 million data resources and millions of Database Analyses, which includes a collection of time series data. Includes data about agricultural and rural development indicators across the globe.
Online Agricultural Marketing Information System (Home Page, n.d.)	Maintains pricing information about the selling prices of cereals, vegetables, and fruits in India
Bhoomi Geo Portal (Bhoomi NBSS&LUP Geo Portal, n.d.)	Contains information on the soil and site characteristics of India. Soil maps of 1:10000 scales depict the potential area of crops and cropping patterns.
India Meteorological Department (IMD, n.d.)	All India weather forecast data.
Arkansas Plant Diseases Database (Arkansas Plant Disease Database, n.d.)	Pathological (infectious) and non-pathological (physiological/environmental) diseases of agronomic row crops and horticultural crops are shown in these photos. Growers of the crops listed will find these images useful for identifying diseases.

Information Extraction

The information-extraction phase extracts only the data needed for analysis. Data is interpreted, integrated, mined, analyzed, cleansed, and stored in a data warehouse to obtain information (Adnan & Akbar, 2019).

Data Analysis

Data analysis is used to help people make better decisions. As agricultural data is both structured and unstructured, Big Data analytics helps in finding trends and analytics to utilize this information and gain farming insights (Mikalef et al., 2017).

Data Visualization

The graphical depiction of information and data is known as data visualization. Data visualization tools make it easy to examine and comprehend trends, outliers, and patterns in data by employing visual elements like charts, graphs, and maps. Data visualization is a technique that blends automated analysis with interactive elements. Visualizations enable analyzing, reasoning, and making decisions based on very vast and complicated data sets (Slavin, 2016). The benefits of data visualizations include:

- The ability to quickly absorb information, gain new insights and make better decisions;
- A better knowledge of what has to be done next to strengthen the organization;
- An improved ability to keep the audience's attention by providing information that they can understand;

- A simple means of disseminating information that increases the opportunity to share ideas with all parties involved;
- Machine learning is rapidly being used by businesses to analyze vast volumes of data that can be difficult to sort through, interpret, and explain. Visualization can help speed up this process and convey data patterns to the stakeholders in a way that they can understand.

The potential of the Big Data is in transforming the process driven agriculture into data driven agriculture. Process driven agriculture encourages the farmers to follow standard cropping methods, plant protection methods and strategies. With data driven agriculture based on past trends and patterns of weather, infestation, pesticide usage, fertilizer usage can be observed to plan farm management strategies. Big data combined with machine learning has the potential to derive useful results from agricultural data. Machine learning, in its broadest sense, refers to a set of modelling approaches or algorithms that can learn from data and make decisions without the need for human intervention, once the model is built. Big data and Machine learning applications in the field of agriculture include crop recommendation, crop yield prediction, crop disease identification, fertilizer management, irrigation management to name a few. Developing a crop recommendation system considering the location specific land and climate parameters benefits the farmers to make a suitable choice. The proposed crop recommendation system proposed in this chapter recommends the location specific crop along with their suitability classes. The proposed system classifies the experimental dataset into four classes: highly suitable (class 1), moderately suitable (class 2), marginally suitable (class 3), and not suitable (class 4). Class 1 and 2 agriculture sites might be used for crop cultivation in their current state, however, class 3 agriculture farms need to be further processed by applying sufficient manure before cultivating the crop, and class 4 agriculture land cannot be used for cultivation.

AN EFFECTIVE BIG DATA-BASED CROP RECOMMENDATION SYSTEM

The goal of our work is to construct a recommendation system with an efficient data analytic framework via which the farmer community can receive location-specific crop information. The suggested framework creates a recommendation system that considers soil physical qualities, climatic variables, and crop attributes to identify a suitable crop. Crop yields may be increased by selecting the correct crop suiting the conditions of each location. The recommendation system provides the options to choose the right crop for the farmers. It can also assists government agencies in devising appropriate land management methods to boost production and preserve soil fertility. The data pipeline of the recommendation system includes the actions that take the data from its sources, pre-process the data, build the machine learning model and reach the destination for storing the results. To build a framework that works in real-time, the proposed system utilizes Big Data platforms namely Apache Kafka, Apache Spark, and Elastic search to handle the data pipeline efficiently. The machine learning model is built with artificial neural networks to classify the recommended crops into its suitability classes. The crops considered for recommendation are Rice. Finger millet, Maize and Sugarcane.

Background Work

Agricultural Recommendation System

The difficulty faced by Indian farmers is that they do not select the appropriate crop for their land. They will see a significant drop in production as a result of this. Precision agriculture has been used to solve the farmers' dilemma. Precision agriculture is a contemporary agricultural approach that combines research data on soil properties, soil types, and crop production statistics to recommend the best crop to farmers based on their unique site conditions. This minimizes the number of times a crop is chosen incorrectly and increases production. (Pudumalar et al., 2017) addresses this challenge by offering a recommendation system based on a machine learning ensemble model. The Internet of Things (IoT) is considered a promising aspect of agriculture to provide access to farming information globally. (Veerachamy & Ramar, 2021) proposes an irrigation recommendation system based on IoT where the sensors installed in the farm collect the details of soil such as temperature, humidity, soil moisture, and wind speed. Based on these inputs and weather parameters the system recommends five types of irrigation alerts. The suitability of the crops is recommended using weather parameters (Fabregas, 2019).

Big Data Platforms Used

Apache Kafka

Apache Kafka is a high-performance, scalable, and long-lasting publish-subscribe messaging system. Apache Kafka is used to designing real-time data pipelines and streaming applications. Real-time streaming is used in a wide range of businesses and organizations for several purposes.

The major advantage of Kafka is its capacity to receive huge amounts of data in real-time with minimal latency while staying fault-tolerant and scalable. Kafka supports a high number of data streams for reading and writing (Apache Kafka, n.d.). It securely stores data streams in a cluster that is distributed, duplicated, and fault-tolerant. A replication factor of three is a standard production option, which means your data will always be duplicated three times. A producer sends messages to a Kafka topic (messaging queue). A topic can alternatively be thought of as a message category or a name for the feed where the messages are published.

Producer API and Consumer API are the two major libraries of Kafka. An application can use the Producer API to transmit a stream of records to Kafka topics. An application can use the Consumer API to subscribe to Kafka topics and process the stream of records. Kafka stream API has higher-level processing features for real-time event streams.

Apache Spark

Apache Spark is a distributed open-source processing solution for large data workloads. Data reuse is enabled by the generation of data frames, which is the extension of the Resilient Distributed Dataset (RDD) (Apache Spark, n.d.). Apache Spark (Lu et al., 2016) is in the limelight as it has enabled iterative machine learning jobs, interactive data analysis, and batch data analysis. The original design goal of Spark, which stands for "lightning-fast cluster computing platform," was to make data analysis faster and also to be able to develop programs quickly and easily (Triguero et al., 2016). Spark can be used for implementing distributed SQL, establishing data pipelines, importing data into a database, running Machine Learning algorithms, dealing with graphs or data streams, and much more. Spark can deal with both organized and unstructured data, such as CSV files and JSON files.

Figure 2. Apache Spark software stack

The components of spark include Spark SQL, Spark Streaming, MLlib, and GraphX. Spark Streaming is a Spark library that takes streaming data from Kafka and analyses it in real-time. MLlib is an efficient machine learning library that includes classification, regression, clustering, collaborative filtering, dimensionality reduction, and underlying optimization primitives, as well as common learning algorithms and utilities. Spark SQL is a structured data processing Spark module. It provides DataFrames as a programming abstraction and may also serve as a distributed SQL query engine. Spark SQL can be used to execute SQL queries. GraphX is a new element of

Spark for graphs and graph-parallel processing. GraphX adds a new Graph abstraction to the Spark RDD: a directed multigraph with attributes linked to each vertex and edge. Spark Core is the platform's fundamental general execution engine, on which all other features are built.

Apache HBase

HBase is a Hadoop Distributed File System (HDFS) based column-oriented non-relational database management system. HBase is a fault-tolerant storage system for sparse data sets, which is popular in many big data applications (Apache HBase, n.d.). The HBase system is built to scale linearly. It is similar to a typical database in that it consists of a collection of standard tables with rows and columns. The tables in HBase are ordered by row and it is a column-oriented database. Only column families, or key-value pairs, are defined in the table schema. A table can include several column families. Each column family can contain any number of columns. The values of subsequent columns are saved on the disc in a logical order.

Elasticsearch

Elasticsearch is a real-time full-text search and analytics open-source distributed database system. It's written in Java and has grown in popularity over the years, currently being widely utilized in many common or lesser-known search and data analysis uses of the Apache Lucene library. Elasticsearch receives raw data from several sources, such as logs, system metrics, and web applications. Users can conduct complex searches against their data and use aggregations to receive elaborate summaries of their data once it has been indexed in Elasticsearch. The following are some well-known websites or apps that use Elasticsearch: Stack Overflow (for queries based on geolocation), Wikipedia (for full-text search and suggestions), and GitHub (code searching) (Zamfir et al., 2019).

Proposed Framework

The proposed framework for the crop recommendation system is shown in Figure 3.

Figure 3. Crop recommendation model

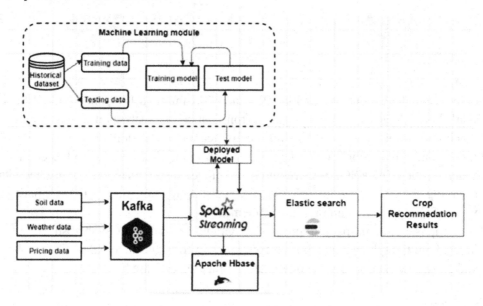

The proposed framework for the recommendation system is shown in Figure 5. It consists of four parts: data producer-consumer model, ML model, data storage, and UI for displaying results.

Data Collection

In this work, we focus on gathering datasets for the Doddaballapur (dist.) localities in Karnataka, India. The district is located at latitude 13^0 20' North and longitude 77^0 31' East. The data collection includes unique soil and climatic features for maize, finger millet, sugarcane, and rice crop requirements. Additional environmental factors namely precipitation, humidity, wind speed, sunlight hours, and Potential Evoporation Transpiration (PET) are considered in addition to typical meteorological parameters such as rainfall and temperature. Daily meteorological data From 2007 to 2017, for the site, was collected from the open government data platform, in India (Open Government Data (OGD) Platform India, n.d.). The land/ soil characteristics for this location are obtained from the National Bureau of Soil Survey and Soil Usage Planning (NBSS & LUP), Bengaluru (Bhoomi NBSS&LUP Geo Portal, n.d.).

Table 2. Attributes used in the recommendation system

	Dataset Parameter	Description
1	Minimum Temperature	Minimum temperature of the day.
2	Maximum Temperature	Maximum temperature of the day.
3	Sunshine hours	Measure of daytime duration
4	Potential Evapotranspiration	Calculated from Thornthwaite (Black, 2007) Quantity of evaporation happening in the region.
5	Soil texture	Texture of the soil 1. Clay 2. Loamy sand 3. Sandy loam 4. Sandy clay loam 5. Sandy
6	Soil pH	Acidity content measured in soil
7	Gravel code	Indicates particle size in the soil 1. Non-gravel if <15% of soil particles are coarse 2. Gravelly if 15-35% of soil particles are coarse)
8	Erosion code	Amount of topsoil carried away due to wind and water 1. Severe erosion 2. Moderate erosion 3. Slight erosion
9	Slope	Specifies the inclination of the soil surface relative to horizontal. It is indicated by the values 1 - 4. 1. Level to nearly level if the inclination is 0-1% 2. Very gently sloping if the inclination is 1-3% 3. Gently sloping if the inclination is 3-5% 4. Moderately sloping if the inclination is 5-10%
10	Depth	Specifies the support given by soil for shedding roots and absorption of water. It is indicated by the values 1 - 3. 1. Shallow if depth is 25-50 cm 2. Deep if depth is 100-150 cm 3. Very deep if depth is >150 cm
11	Mean temperature	Average temperature necessary for the crop
12	Soil drainage	Measures how excess water moves across, through or out of soil
13	Soil Potassium	Potassium present in soil
14	Soil Nitrogen	Nitrogen present in soil
15	Soil Phosphorus	Phosphorus present in soil
16	Length of growing period	Time taken by the crop to sprout and reach the harvest stage
17	Effective root depth	Distance of roots of a crop from the surface down into the ground

The soil dataset contains 17 soil physical property measurements and crop characteristics. Six qualities that are common and important for crops have been evaluated among these measures. Texture, soil pH, gravel code, erosion code, and water retention qualities such as slope and depth are all part of the soil data. The soil characteristics are critical for crop development. Soil efficiency has a direct impact on crop development, regardless of nutrient levels (Pudumalar et al., 2017). For each crop under investigation, the crop data include mean temperature, soil drainage, texture, depth, slope, and length of growth period (Naidu et al., 2006).

Four sets of crop data for rice, maize, sugarcane, and finger millet are considered as the experimental dataset. Categorical data makes up the majority of the dataset. One-hot encoding is used to transform categorical data into numerical form, which enables the implementation of machine learning algorithms easier.

Data Ingestion

Apache Kafka producer acquires the data from different data sources. Our proposed system consists of three topics soil, weather and prices. Messages under the same topic are stored under different partitions. The Kafka cluster is made up of several brokers, which are server nodes and the partitions of each topic are divided over these brokers. The topics from these partitions are subscribed to by the consumers. The producer is responsible for ensuring that the data is full and consistent until it is viewed by the consumer. The consumers of Kafka streaming data are Spark streaming and HBase.

Machine Learning Model

Spark streaming creates the data frames of the real-time data ingested from Apache Kafka. Apache Spark consists of the machine learning library- MLlib which runs on the data frames to provide the predictions. The machine learning model was built offline using the historical data of soil, weather, and pricing and is deployed to predict crop suitability recommendations. The algorithms used to build the model are Artificial Neural Networks (ArNN) and Decision tree. pyspark.MLLIB package facilitates running the deployed model on the streaming data frames. The machine learning model consists of four stages namely: 1) Data preprocessing, 2)Feature Selection, 3) Machine Learning algorithms, and 4) Evaluating Metrics for the results

1. Pre-processing is one of the most important phases to efficiently express data for the machine learning algorithm that has to be trained and tested. In our model, the missing values are identified and they are filled by the mean value of that attribute.
2. Feature Selection is used to determine the important features in the dataset. In the current paper, we are using a hybrid filter and wrapper method for feature selection (MJ & IM, 2022). The Pearson Correlation coefficient based filter method is combined with the backward elimination wrapper method to specify important features required for crop recommendation.
3. Machine learning algorithms

The classification algorithms used in this proposed system are

*   Multilayer perceptrons (MLP) are fully connected Artificial Neural Networks (ArNN). Neural networks learn from the representation of the training data and relate it to the output variable. It mainly consists of three layers namely the input layer, hidden layer, and output layer. Neural networks are trained based on their network topology, activation functions, and weight adjustments. The arrangement of neurons with connecting links and associated weights is the network topology. Activation functions that are applied along with the input define the output of that layer and avoid the linearity of the output. In ArNN, learning indicates the adjustments of weights as-

sociated with each link. A gradient descent algorithm is used to train the MLP. The following algorithm summarizes the gradient descent

1. Each training example is a pair of the form(x,t) where x is the vector of input values, t is the output values, ŋ is the learning rate
2. Initialize each weight w_i to a random value
3. Until the termination condition is met, Do,
    a. Initialize each Δw_i to zero.
    b. For each (x,t) in training examples, Do,
        i. Input instance x_i to the unit and compute the output o
        ii. If calculated o ^{1} t, For each linear weight wi, Do
            $\Delta wi \, _\neg \Delta wi + ŋ (t - o) xi$
    c. For every linear unit Do,
        $\Delta \, _\neg wi + \Delta wi$

Where ŋ is the learning rate (0.005), w_i is the weight across the connecting links between the layers. We have extended the gradient descent with optimization algorithms to find the optimal values for the neural network parameters (Wang et al., 2017).

Gradient Descent Optimization Algorithms

*   **Momentum Method:** This method considers the exponentially weighted average of gradients to accelerate the gradient descent to converge at local minima faster (Zhang, 2019).

$$Wt+1 = Wt - ŋmt$$

Where,

$$mt = \beta_{mt} - + (1 \, _{-\beta})[\delta L/\delta W]$$

m_t = gradients 1 at time t
m_{t-1} = gradients at time t-1
ŋ = Learning rate
Wt = weights at time t
Wt+1 = weights at time t+1
$\delta L/\delta W$ = change in loss function with reference to weight

*   Root Mean **Square Propagation (RMSProp)**

Adagrad optimizer calculates each parameter's stepsize by summing the partial derivatives seen so far during the search and then dividing this sum by the square root of the step size hyperparameter. But adagrad has the problem of slowing down during search in terms of small learning rates for each parameter. Hence the search could be stopped because reaching the minima. The RMSProp extends Adagrad so that monotonous learning rate declines are avoided (Mykel & Kochenderfer, 2019). RMSProp uses the moving average of the partial derivatives in order to calculate the learning rate for each parameter. It discards the partial derivative values from the extreme past and focuses on most recently seen convex.

$$W_{t+1} = W_t - \frac{\eta_t}{v_t + } \frac{\delta L}{\delta w_t} \quad (1)$$

Where,

$$v_t = \beta v_t + (1-\beta)\left[\frac{\beta L}{\beta w_t}\right]2 \quad (2)$$

Wt = weights at time t Wt+1 = weights at time t+1 αt = learning rate at time t ¶L = derivative of Loss Function

¶Wt = derivative of weights at time t

Vt = sum of square of past gradients. [i.e sum(¶L/¶Wt-1)] (Initially, Vt = 0)

β = Moving average parameter (const, 0.9)

ϵ = A small positive constant (10^{-8})

• **Adam Optimizer**

To provide a more optimized gradient descent, the Adam Optimizer builds on the strengths of the two previous methods momentum method and RMS prop method. When the global minima are reached, the gradient descent rate is controlled to minimize oscillations while taking sufficient steps to overcome the hurdles of local minima. By combining the above methods, the global minimum can be efficiently reached.

$$m_t = \beta_1 m_{t-1} + (1-\beta_1)\left[\frac{\beta L}{\beta W}\right] v_t = \beta_2 v_t + (1-\beta_2)[\frac{\beta L}{\beta W_t}]^2 \quad (3)$$

Adam optimizer corrects the problem of high oscillations while reaching global minima by computing bias-corrected m_t and v_t. Instead of normal weight parameters, we consider the bias corrected weight parameters, $\bar{m}$ t and $\bar{v}$ t. The general equation can be shown as,

$$W_{t+1} = W_t - m_t(\frac{\eta}{\sqrt{V_{t+\epsilon}}}) \quad (4)$$

where ϵ is the small value to avoid divide by zero error when $v_t = 0$

Every output unit summates its weighted input signal and the corresponding output signal is computed using the activation function as shown in the following equation:

$$(t) = (åh(t)WO + {}_B O) \tag{5}$$

Every neuron in the network has an activation function. RELU activation function is used for hidden units and the Softmax activation function is used in the output layer. RELU outputs zero for inputs lesser than zero and outputs one for inputs greater than zero. The Softmax activation function is applied to the output of the hidden layers to convert the scores into probability values that sum up to one.

Softmax activation function can be expressed as:

$$\sigma(z) = \frac{e^{z_j}}{\sum_{j=1}^{K} e^{z_j}} \tag{6}$$

Performance Metrics

The major objective of this component is to create a machine-learning model that achieves the best possible accuracy during the testing process. The performance parameters that are evaluated for classifier efficiency and performance are True positive (TP), true negative (TN), false positive (FP), and false negative (FN). These parameters can be determined from the counts of testing samples belonging to class 'C'. By identifying the number of correct predictions made from all the predictions, classification accuracy scores can be calculated as follows:

$$Accuracy = \frac{TP + TN}{TP + TN + FP + FN} \tag{7}$$

The ratio of predicted positive events to actual positive events is known as precision.

$$\mathrm{Pr}\,ecision = \frac{\sum_{i=0}^{n} TP}{\sum_{i=1}^{n} TP + FP} \tag{8}$$

During the result phase, the errors—Mean squared error (MSE) and root mean squared error (RMSE)—are also determined.

- The average of the squared differences between the actual and expected observation is represented by the Mean Square Error (MSE).

$$MSE = \frac{1}{N} \sum_{i-1}^{N} (So_i - Se_i)^2 \qquad (9)$$

where S_o is the original value and S_e is the expected value

- For a model whose main purpose is the prediction of values, it is important to know how close the predicted values are to the actual values. Because it has the same units as the output variable, RMSE is a useful indicator of the model's prediction accuracy. A lower RMSE number implies that the model is more accurate.

$$RMSE = \sqrt{\frac{1}{n}} \sum (So_1 - Se_i)^2 \qquad (10)$$

Data Storage and Indexing

Spark converts the streaming data into data frames and the data is stored in HBase. The results of the ML model, as well as the original data from the data source, are then saved in HBase. The recommendation output of the ML model is indexed with the Elasticsearch cluster.

The work steps can be summarized as follows:

Step 1: Users search for specified content through the User interface;
Step 2: If there is hit information in Elastic Search, go to Step 7, else go to Step 3
Step 3: The service issues the input through the message subscription module in Kafka;
Step 4: The Spark stream processing module receives the input;
Step 5: The Spark stream processing module processes it with deployed machine learning module;
Step 6: The Spark Stream processing module stores the input and output in the HBase storage;
Step 7: The Spark Stream processing module stores the processed data indexed with the field survey number in Elasticsearch;
Step 8: Return the crop recommendation to the User interface.

EXPERIMENTAL RESULTS

The suggested work is run on an Ubuntu 18.04 LTS platform with a Core i5 CPU and 8GB RAM. JDK 11, Scala 2.11.12, Apache Kafka 2.12, and Apache Spark 2.1.0 are utilized to create streaming processing in the system. *pyspark. streaming* and *pyspark. MLLIB* is the package to build the offline machine learning model and apply the deployed model on real-time data. HBase version 2.2.1 is used. First, the soil, and weather data of a particular location is collected and the price data for the crops are collected from different data sources cited in Table 3. The data retrieved is in the form of CSV files. Kafka was used to reading the data that was produced from soil characteristics, Weather parameters, and pricing details of the crops. Kafka uses a python producer script to stream the data saved in the CSV file as data streams into the analytics model in Spark. When this script is run, data from the CSV file is read and published into Kafka at regular intervals. This information is published under appropriate Kafka topics. The data ingested is used by Spark streaming to build the machine learning model using MLlib package.

The dataset available is in the form of categorical data. The categorical data is converted into the numerical form using one-hot-encoding that enables easy implementation of machine learning algorithms. In the course of developing the machine learning model, the dataset is deliberately split into the training set and testing set in the ratio of 70:30. The artificial neural network model consists of 17 input neurons which represent the different attributes in the dataset. The model was trained with the different number of hidden layers. The output layer consists of 4 neurons to represent suitability classes of rice, maize, finger millet, and sugarcane. Neural networks are trained with three, five, and seven hidden layers. Each neural network is trained for 50 epochs. The model is trained with a stochastic gradient descent algorithm and is evaluated with different optimization techniques namely the momentum method, RMSProp, and Adam optimizer. The performance of the model is shown in Table 3.

Table 3. Performance of artificial neural networks with different optimization algorithms

Performance of Artificial Neural Networks With Different Optimization Algorithms	
	Accuracy
Momentum Method	87.2
RMS Prop	89.1
Adam optimizer	91.3

Rectified Linear Unit (RELU) activation function was employed in the input layer and hidden layers. This model evaluates the probability of crops namely maize, finger millets, rice, and sugarcane, and ranks them in order of suitability. Therefore softmax function was used in the output layer.

The suggested model classifies the experimental dataset into four classes: highly suitable (class 1), moderately suitable (class 2), marginally suitable (class 3), and not suitable (class 4). Class 1 and 2 agriculture sites might be used for crop cultivation in their current state, however, class 3 agriculture farms need to be further processed by applying sufficient manure before cultivating the crop, and class 4 agriculture land cannot be used for cultivation.

One of the most important architectural parameters that influence the execution of ANN during the training and preparation of information for learning is the number of hidden layers and the number of epochs. In this regard, defining these parameters in advance has remained a challenge in machine learn-

Table 4. Performance metrics of ANN with 3 and 5 hidden layers iterated for 80 epoch

Performance Metrics	Performance of ANN With Three Hidden Layers	Performance of ANN With Five Hidden Layers
	Class 1 Class 2 Class 3 Class 4 Class 1 Class 2 Class 3 Class 4	
Accuracy	0.86 0.87 0.81 0.84	0.88 0.83 0.91 0.81
Precision	0.87 0.85 0.88 0.95	0.91 0.94 0.89 0.95
MSE	0.012 0.01 0.01 0.001	0.001 0.014 0.001 0.001
RMSE	0.26 0.27 0.26 0.26	0.04 0.03 0.041 0.02

ing research. In the proposed work ANN was implemented with 3, 5 hidden layers with 80 epochs for each. Table 4 describes the results obtained for each class using ANN.

Table 5. Performance metrics of decision tree

Performance Metrics	Decision Tree Classifier
	Class 1 Class 2 Class 3 Class 4
Accuracy	0.78 0.72 0.73 0.84
Precision	0.77 0.74 0.78 0.75
MSE	0.014 0.02 0.024 0.002
RMSE	0.28 0.37 0.26 0.26

Table 5 defines the performance metrics of decision tree classifier.

From the results, we can infer that performance of ANN with 5 hidden layers is better than the decision tree to forecast the suitability of the crops. Hence ANN can be used in the crop recommendation framework.

The crop suitability results are stored in the Elasticsearch cluster and are indexed to quickly access the results for the query posted through the web interface. The field survey numbers along with the longitude and latitude values of the location are considered as the index whose corresponding crop suitability is the document. Every index has the suitability for Rice, Maize, finger millet, and sugarcane.

Table 6. Elasticsearch index information

Index	Document
Survey no 77, 13° 20'N, 77° 31' E	Suitability of Rice: Class 3 Suitability of Finger millet: Class 2 Suitability of Maize: Class 2 Suitability of sugarcane: Class 3
Survey no 78, 13° 20'N, 77° 31' E	Suitability of Rice: Class 3 Suitability of Finger millet: Class 1 Suitability of Maize: Class 2 Suitability of sugarcane: Class 2

The sample of the Elasticsearch cluster is shown in Table 6.

The suggested model analyses the given agriculture area and delivers reliable results for sustainable agriculture development. As a result, this proposed model might be employed as a land suitability recommendation model to boost crop production for long-term agriculture development. The user interface developed requests the location and soil parameters as the input. The input form is as shown in Figure 4a. The output form shown in Figure 4b provides the crop suitability results.

Figure 4. Input form

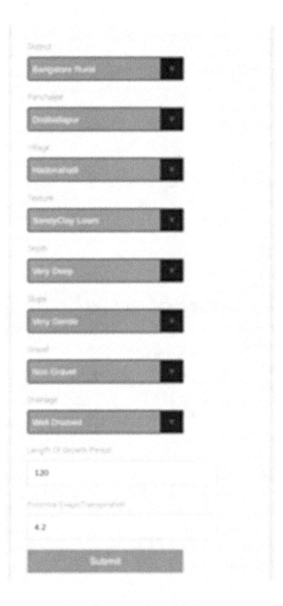

DISCUSSION

The classification results obtained as shown in Tables 4 and 5 are largely influenced by several performance parameters. For the multiclass classification dataset, the suggested study aggregates several performance parameters for the evaluation and assessment of ANN and Decision Tree. The performance of ANN is found to increase with the increase in the number of hidden layers. The MSE and RMSE are found to be low and decreasing. Furthermore, this leads to a better convergence of error, which in turn led to proper feature learning. The performance parameters discussed earlier such as accuracy, precision and others appear to follow a similar pattern. The performance of ANN with five hidden layers is found to be significantly better than that of ANN with three layers. However, because the number of hidden

Figure 5. Crop suitability output

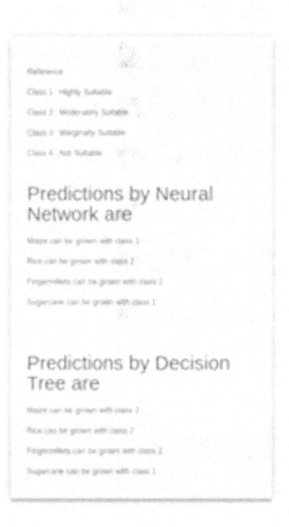

layers has increased architectural complexity, convergence optimization can be accomplished with fewer iterations. On observing the performance measures of ANN with five hidden layers, it is found to be providing better results than the Decision Tree.

Furthermore, given the current experimental methodology, slightly different results could be obtained because the biases and initial weights of the neural networks are generated at random. If an appropriate weight set is fixed at the start, similar settings may yield better outcomes. This argument may be supported towards the end of the neural network training process and gradient descent may not always ensure a near-ideal weight set.

In comparison to other approaches, the suggested model analyses the given agriculture area and produces better results for sustainable agricultural production. This methodology helps agriculturists assess their land effectively by providing a reliable decision on the appropriateness level of agricultural land in four different categories. As a result, this proposed model might be employed as a land appropriateness recommendation model to boost crop production for long-term agriculture development.

CONCLUSION

In this paper, we presented a real time crop recommendation model that was developed based on Apache Kafka, Apache Spark, and Elasticsearch. The recommendation model reads the streaming data of soil characteristics for location specific survey numbers, real-time weather data, and pricing details for the considered crops. The real time soil and weather data is received by Apache Kafka and passed to the Apache Spark consumer. Artificial neural networks and Decision tree learning algorithms were applied to the streaming soil, weather and crop price data to derive meaningful insights for crop recommendation. With the measured accuracy values, it was learned that the recommendation model created with ANN performs better with an accuracy of 89 percent compared to the Decision tree classifier with 77 percent accuracy. The recommended suitable crops corresponding to input are indexed in Elasticsearch to enable faster retrieval of results. The multiclass classification would provide real time results to ensure better crop yield. The suggested system can be expanded in the future to account for market demand, market infrastructure availability, projected profit, post-harvest storage, and processing technologies. This would result in a detailed crop recommendation based on geographical, environmental, and economic factors, resulting in an effective agricultural system.

REFERENCES

Adnan & Akbar. (2019). An analytical study of information extraction from unstructured and multidimensional big data. *J. Big Data, 6*(1), 1–38. doi:10.1186/S40537019-0254-8

Apache HBase. (n.d.). *Apache HBase™ Home*. https://hbase.apache.org/

Apache Kafka. (n.d.). https://kafka.apache.org/

SparkA. (n.d.). https://runawayhorse001.github.io/LearningApacheSpark/setup.html

Arkansas Plant Disease Database. (n.d.). https://www.uaex.edu/yard-garden/resource-library/diseases/

Basso, B., Ritchie, J. T., Pierce, F. J., Braga, R. P., & Jones, J. W. (2001, May). Spatial validation of crop models for precision agriculture. *Agricultural Systems, 68*(2), 97–112. doi:10.1016/S0308-521X(00)00063-9

Bhoomi NBSS&LUP Geo Portal. (n.d.). https://www.nbsslup.in/bhoomi/

Black, P. E. (2007, December). Revisiting the Thornthwaite and Mather water balance. *Journal of the American Water Resources Association, 43*(6), 1604–1605. doi:10.1111/j.1752-1688.2007.00132.x

Fabregas, A. C. (2019). Decision Tree Algorithm Applied in Suitability Assessment of Temporary Crops Based on Agrometeorological Forecasts. *Indian Journal of Science and Technology*, *12*(26), 1–7. doi:10.17485/ijst/2019/v12i26/145096

Home Page. (n.d.). https://www.krishimaratavahini.kar.nic.in/department.aspx

IMD. (n.d.). https://mausam.imd.gov.in/

Karimi, Karami, & Keshavarz. (2018). Climate change and agriculture: Impacts and adaptive responses in Iran. *Journal of Integrative Agriculture*, *17*(1), 1–15. . doi:10.1016/S2095-3119(17)61794-5

Kshetri, N. (2014, July). The emerging role of Big Data in key development issues: Opportunities, challenges, and concerns. *Big Data & Society*, *1*(2). Advance online publication. doi:10.1177/2053951714564227

Lokers, R., Knapen, R., Janssen, S., van Randen, Y., & Jansen, J. (2016, October). Analysis of Big Data technologies for use in agro-environmental science. *Environmental Modelling & Software*, *84*, 494–504. doi:10.1016/j.envsoft.2016.07.017

Lu, X., Shankar, D., Gugnani, S., & Panda, D. K. D. K. (2016). High-performance design of apache spark with RDMA and its benefits on various workloads. *Proc. - 2016 IEEE Int. Conf. Big Data*, 253–262. doi:10.1109/BigData.2016.7840611

MJ & IM. (2022). *Hybrid filter and wrapper methods based feature selection for crop recommendation.* . doi:10.1109/ICESIC53714.2022.9783542

Mikalef, Pappas, Krogstie, & Giannakos. (2017). Big data analytics capabilities: a systematic literature review and research agenda. *Inf. Syst. E-bus. Manag.*, *16*(3), 547–578. . doi:10.1007/s10257-017-0362-y

Mykel & Kochenderfer. (2019). *Algorithms for Optimization*. The MIT Press. Available: https://edu-bookpdf.com/computer/algorithms-for-optimization-the-mit-press.html

Naidu, L. G. K., Ramamurthy, V., & Challa, O. (2006). *Soil suitability criteria for major crops.* National Bureau of Soil Survey and Land Usage Planning. http://krishikosh.egranth.ac.in/displaybitstream?handle=1/2034266

Open Government Data (OGD) Platform India. (n.d.). https://data.gov.in/

Osman, A. M. S. (2019, February). A novel big data analytics framework for smart cities. *Future Generation Computer Systems*, *91*, 620–633. doi:10.1016/j.future.2018.06.046

Pudumalar, S., Ramanujam, E., Rajashree, R. H., Kavya, C., Kiruthika, T., & Nisha, J. (2017). Crop recommendation system for precision agriculture. *2016 8th International Conference on Advanced Computing, ICoAC 2016*, 32–36. 10.1109/ICoAC.2017.7951740

Robert, P. C. (2002, November). Precision agriculture: A challenge for crop nutrition management. *Plant and Soil*, *247*(1), 143–149. doi:10.1023/A:1021171514148

Slavin. (2016). Climate and famines: A historical reassessment. *Wiley Interdisciplinary Reviews: Climate Change*, *7*(3), 433–447. doi:10.1002/wcc.395

Triguero, I., Galar, M., Merino, D., Maillo, J., Bustince, H., & Herrera, F. (2016). Evolutionary under-sampling for extremely imbalanced big data classification under apache spark. *2016 IEEE Congr. Evol. Comput. CEC 2016*, 640–647. 10.1109/CEC.2016.7743853

Veerachamy, R., & Ramar, R. (2021, March). Agricultural Irrigation Recommendation and Alert (AIRA) system using optimization and machine learning in Hadoop for sustainable agriculture. *Environmental Science and Pollution Research International*, *2021*, 1–20. doi:10.100711356-021-13248-3 PMID:33788091

Wang, Z., Xie, P., Lai, C., Chen, X., Wu, X., Zeng, Z., & Li, J. (2017, January). Spatiotemporal variability of reference evapotranspiration and contributing climatic factors in China during 1961–2013. *Journal of Hydrology (Amsterdam)*, *544*, 97–108. doi:10.1016/j.jhydrol.2016.11.021

Wolfert, S., Ge, L., Verdouw, C., & Bogaardt, M. J. (2017). Big Data in Smart Farming – A review. *Agricultural Systems*, *153*, 69–80. doi:10.1016/j.agsy.2017.01.023

World Bank Open Data. (n.d.). https://data.worldbank.org/

Zamfir, V. A., Carabas, M., Carabas, C., & Tapus, N. (2019). Systems monitoring and big data analysis using the elasticsearch system. *Proc. - 2019 22nd Int. Conf. Control Syst. Comput. Sci. CSCS*, 188–193. 10.1109/CSCS.2019.00039

Zhang, J. (2019). Gradient Descent based Optimization Algorithms for Deep Learning Models Training. https://arxiv.org/abs/1903.0361410.1109/CSCS.2019.00039

Chapter 13
Clearance Date Prediction Using Machine Learning Techniques

Madhuri Rao

iD https://orcid.org/0000-0003-1976-0627

Symbiosis Institute of Computer Studies and Research, Symbiosis International University (Deemed), India

Ankit Senapati

Siksha 'O' Anusandhan (Deemed), India

Kulamala Vinod Kumar

Siksha 'O' Anusandhan (Deemed), India

Anuja Bokhare

Symbiosis Institute of Computer Studies and Research, Symbiosis International University (Deemed), India

ABSTRACT

Machine learning is the cutting-edge technology in today's corporate world, making it the first choice for prediction or calculated suggestions relying on heavy amount of data. As companies are evolving towards technological advancement, they are trying to gather as much statistical knowledge as possible regarding their customers and trying to analyze and use that knowledge towards the firm's growth. Machine learning being the top-most of its genre provides the pathway to all of those technological achievements like predictions, statistical analysis, success rate of each customer companies, etc. Machine learning techniques such as linear regression (LR), XGBoost, random forest, and decision tree can be useful for the prediction problems. Here in this work, the authors use data pre-processing and feature selection before applying these machine learning models for predicting the clearance due date.

DOI: 10.4018/978-1-6684-7105-0.ch013

INTRODUCTION

In the corporate world every product based companies have their own product and each of those companies have numerous number of client companies who buy or use their products. Many business's today are based on the model of Peer-to Peer (P2P) lending and investments (Fitzpatrick et al., 2021). Machine Learning have been explored in predicting loan defaulters (Song et al., 2023) and credit card defaulters (Arora et al., 2022), but can also be explored in predicting the financial performance of Peer-to-Peer entities in a business system.

For a corporate, understanding and assessing risks associated with its client companies is very crucial. The financial stability of an enterprise depends on how well it plans it monetary inflows and outflows. When any client company buys their product, an *INVOICE* or an official document is generated, which is to hold all the legal information regarding the transaction between two companies. It holds information such as name of the client, total transaction amount, due date, quantity of the products, document creation date, clear date etc. A typical invoice is a record that essentially provides a way to track the sell date of a product or service. The amount charged for the product and service is depicted in an invoice and can clearly mention customer's any outstanding balances. While auditing, invoices are of immense help as they take you to the source of income generation. On the other hand they also serve to mention accounts payable at the buyer's end.

There are some challenges in Invoice processing, when done manually. Large enterprises who are likely to deal with large number of invoices have to ensure that process of data entry is automatic and not done manually. Manual data entry could lead to human errors and is also time consuming. Products can also be tagged with sensors and with Internet of Things (IoT) movement of products within an organization and when in transit can be monitored. However often this service has additional charges and indeed this area of sensor tagged inventory is still in its nascent stage. Well there are chances that on an invoice data is misspelt or accidentally left null or void. Duplicate entries are also likely to happen. Processing of invoices is often done with software equipped with Optical Character Recognition (OCR) capabilities.

Nowadays, data can be the most valuable asset to a company. It depends upon how the company uses it to find out information regarding its clients, future growth, profits etc. Machine learning is the cutting edge technology which uses those data to provide meaningful results or conclusions which will be helpful in making analysis and taking fruitful decisions towards a company's growth (Hastie et al., 2009). (Zannin et al., 2020) develops a regularized logistic regression method to discriminate between potential good and bad borrowers in P2P systems. They consider data that is available at Loan Book of Lending (LC) which is retrieved from LC or Kaggle websites.

The Scope of Machine Learning in Invoice Processing

Machine learning techniques have gained quite a dominance in scenarios where unknowing the unknown is desired. Invoices processing has many challenges. Business are impacted if invoices contain incorrect data or if processed incorrectly. Machine learning techniques can be of potential help in following ways:

1. Classification of clients and customers based on data from invoices can be performed. A typical scenario would be knowing all the invoices generated with date of generation and amount details for a given customer or client. Sometimes it is important for a C-Suite official to foresee what transactions will be held in future as committed in an invoice. Many a times, simultaneous trans-

actions with respect to a given date is to be considered. Machine Learning Techniques like Linear Regression, Artificial Neural Network (ANN) could be explored in such cases.

2.   Duplicate Invoices are likely to be generated in an organization which sometimes have also led to payment being done twice. This can be avoided and be detected with Machine learning approaches.

3.   Often Businesses are dependent on how quick certain deals are accepted or not. For any organization this is a very risky situation. A machine learning model can be developed with all the aspects of invoices data. A system is thereby trained and tested to deal with new and unknown scenarios. The system can be useful is suggesting what can be done by exploring the new values in the search space.

4.   The other and quite interesting use of machine learning techniques is to explore its use in predicting the invoice payment. Based on details of the invoice, a ML model can predict possible inflow of funds in a given time period. This is very important for organizations that are in expanding stage. Sometimes, the nature of customers and their challenges can be distinguished based on these predictions. How well these predictions are made, is therefore very important. The chapter explores and discusses the use of machine learning techniques in due date prediction of clients as per data available in an invoice.

Objective

The objective of this work is to develop a machine learning model which will use a dataset created on the basis of all the invoices created per transaction with each client. It will try to predict the clearance date of each invoice amount which hasn't been paid yet using all the provided data on the dataset and the previous transaction details. It will help the organization to differentiate between the actual clearance date and predicted clear date which will help them figure out how accurate their prediction is and they can use this data to analyze their client companies. It will give them a broader understanding of which clients are more accurate with their payment and which of them are not, which client gives them more profits in terms of margin. Based on all the facts and analysis the company can take decisive actions like giving some rebate or offers to some clients in order to maintain a long term relationship, cutting out the some of the clients which are not so profitable for the company etc.

The chapter is organized as follows. In the next section some recent and related work is presented. Research questions are formulated in this section as well. Sections 4 discusses about the dataset and preprocessing techniques. The proposed machine learning models employed for the prediction problem taken here are explained in Section 5. The clearance date prediction using data from an invoice needs to be pre-processed before applying the machine learning models. Section 6 explains the Results and discusses its impact. Conclusion and future scope of work is finally presented.

BACKGROUND

Now a days, invoices in an organization are generated electronically and sent via emails or messaging applications. Gone are those days when invoices were printed and sent by post or delivered physically. (Schulz et al., 2009) have developed an invoice recognition software smartFIX which essentially was based image processing and image extraction techniques. Their intention was to gather all details from an invoice received as a hardcopy paper. Their minimized the scope of human error when reading and analyzing invoices was needed. Invoices are essentially very important in how business choices are made.

Gathering information from an invoice using Image processing technique is one aspect of research which has evolved over the years. Invoice generation is an automotive process in many organizations. A company usually would have a database storing all the invoices and all its details. This could be used analyzed timely in order understand business priorities and plan cash inflows and outflows. Understanding invoices in an over a period of time can help the top level management in how they deal with their potential customers and the ones currently engaged.

The current systems is essentially a database of invoices which is basically a dataset with null and duplicated values as well. A proper format is lacking and format of data is inconsistent. It does not contain a target column which is needed to be predicted. It is not a clean dataset upon which modeling techniques can be used to check error results. Prediction on this dataset will result in massive error results and far from being close to accurate (Alpaydin et al., 2016).

Clearance Date Prediction Methods From Invoices

Analysis made on the basis of the dataset is current form will be of no use because it will give us inaccurate results. Figure 1 in this section depicts the block diagram of the proposed system. The proposed system is to contain a clean dataset without any null and duplicated values. It contains proper format to show the data. A target column gets calculated in this dataset using previous data with the help of machine learning techniques. It is a clean dataset upon which various modeling techniques can be used. The performance of the techniques are then compared on the basis of their error results. Ultimately, the best technique is chosen for performing the prediction task. Prediction on this dataset now is likely to have more accurate results. We can make analysis on the basis of the prediction results to take necessary decisions (Jordon et al., 2015). Here the dataset is taken as input to the system. The first step is to preprocess the data, followed by processing of missing and duplicate values. The constants and quasi constants are then checked. We then split the data set into two halves, followed by feature selection and feature engineering. We then apply machine learning technique like Linear Regression (Seber et al., 2003), Decision Tree (Cherfi et al., 2018) Random Forest (Goel et al., 2017) and XGBoost (Chen et al., 2019). Testing and analysis based on error results is then performed and finally the target value is predicted.

The proposed model will produce a cleaner and better dataset. It will disregard all the information which are of no use or doesn't provide any relevance to the future analysis. This model will provide a pre-processing technique which will omit any highly correlated values, columns with constant values or same values. It will result in better analytical results. Any company using this model will get an understanding of how each of its customers add to the organization's profits. How much delay one customer does in terms of payment clearance, how quickly one company clears its dues. The model uses various modeling techniques such as random forest, linear regression, Decision tree etc. for making prediction based on the lower error scores (Kelleher et al., 2020; Ledesma et al., 2018). The modeling algorithm which gives exceptional results in terms of error scores compared to other algorithms has been used in this model to ensure close to accurate prediction results.

Figure 1. Block diagram of the proposed system

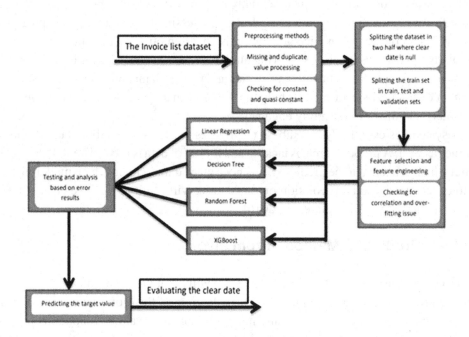

Problem Description and Solution Overview

The work considered in this chapter comprises of following steps as also explained with the help of Flow Diagram as depicted in Figure 2. The steps comprise of Pre-processing, Identification of Target column, Splitting of the dataset into Training, testing and validation, followed by Machine Learning modelling techniques. In this chapter four Machine learning techniques namely – Linear Regression, Random Forest, Decision Trees and XGBOOST are considered. Label encoding is then performed following which the target column is identified. The performance of evaluating the clearance date prediction is then presented.

The clearance due date prediction task is an imbalanced binary classification problem, where the target variable is an indication of whether or not a client has paid the due on the date as initially given in the invoice.

Research Questions

The department of any organization dealing with invoices needs to identify and know the answers for these questions:

R1: How successful are you in finding a given invoice from your invoice database system?
R2: Can key details of an invoice be extracted automatically?
R3: Can a staff based on his role access / approve/view any invoice from any location (mobile device/ online)?
R4: Are the invoices organized/ archived and how well is it used for audit trailing and budget planning?

Figure 2. Flow diagram of the proposed system

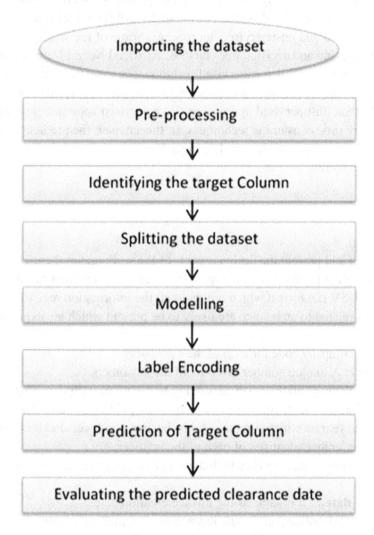

R5: Are invoices promptly processed and help in planning cash flows?

R6: Can you view early payments discounts, keep track of due dates and identify clients pattern of process payment?

R7: Can you predict good and bad clients based on how payment is cleared in current date and with respect to how it was done in past?

In this chapter, we explore these research questions essentially and propose to build a machine learning based model that can especially help in attaining R6 and R7.

Scope and Relevance of Machine Learning Techniques

Machine Learning is very useful in predictive modelling. Predictive analytics is based on dataset taken as input where historical and current data's relationship and trends help in giving new insights into behaviour and trends in the system under study. Outcomes can be predicted based on associated relationship of dependent and independent variables that affect a system. Broadly predictive analysis problems could be modelled using supervised and unsupervised approaches. Some of the widely explored supervised techniques are linear regression and decision trees models. Artificial Neural Network (ANN) are model that are unsupervised techniques. When supervised techniques are used in prediction problems, care should be taken for proper label of datasets. In many scenarios simple supervised techniques are effective in predicting outcomes than unsupervised approaches. Unsupervised approaches may explore a wider search space but are more time consuming techniques. In this chapter, the prediction problem taken is solved using supervised approaches such namely Linear Regression, Random Forest, Decision Trees and XGBOOST is also explored.

THE DATASET

In this section we explain and present the design aspects of the work undertaken. The dataset taken for study is available at Kaggle repository (). A company can use its own dataset of invoices list. The list essentially must be in a CSV file format which will hold all the information regarding that transaction. Essentially 16 attributes related to an invoice are likely to be present which are explained below:

1. **Business Code:** A company code for each of their accounts.
2. **Customer Number:** A unique number given to all the customers.
3. **Name Customer:** Name of all the customers doing transactions with the company.
4. **Clear Date:** The date on which every customer company paid its full due amount.
5. **Business Year:** The year on which company did its business and prepared accounting documents.
6. **Doc ID:** It is also an unique identifier of each of the invoices.
7. **Document Create Date:** The date on which the seller company created the invoice for the seller company.
8. **document_create_date.1:** It is same as the invoice creation date.
9. **Due in Date:** It is the deadline date for the buyer company to clear its dues.
10. **Invoice Currency:** It defines in which currency the buyer company needs to pay the total due amount.
11. **Document Type:** It defines which format the document has been created.
12. **Posting ID:** It defines whether the given document is an invoice or a deduction or accounting papers, etc. by its value.
13. **Baseline Create Date:** It is same as the invoice creation date but in a different format.
14. **Customer Payment Terms:** It defines the various payment conditions and terms upon which the transaction is being done and what offers and discounts are given based on its value or code.
15. **Invoice ID:** It defines each new document with a unique number.
16. **Is Open:** It informs about each invoice, whether that is still open or closed.

Figure 3 depicts the dataset taken with following attributes as explained above. The dataset considered in this work is taken from Kaggle (https://www.kaggle.com/datasets/ulrikthygepedersen/online-retail-dataset).

Figure 3. The dataset and its attributes

	business_code	cust_number	name_customer	clear_date	buisness_year	doc_id	posting_date	document_create_date	document_create_date.1	d
0	U001	0200315290	KWI in	2019-03-07 00:00:00	2019.0	1.928827e+09	2019-02-20	20190220	20190220	:
1	U001	0200769623	WAL-MAR foundation	2020-01-16 00:00:00	2020.0	1.930350e+09	2020-01-04	20200103	20200104	:
2	U001	0200820380	SMITH'S associates	2019-07-08 00:00:00	2019.0	1.929617e+09	2019-06-21	20190619	20190621	:
3	U001	0200769623	WAL-MAR corp	2019-03-22 00:00:00	2019.0	1.928943e+09	2019-03-12	20190311	20190312	:
4	U001	200230690	DECA in	2019-06-03 00:00:00	2019.0	1.929350e+09	2019-05-21	20190521	20190521	:
...										
49995	U001	0200726979	BJ'S us	NaN	2020.0	1.930709e+09	2020-03-27	20200326	20200327	:
49996	U001	CCCA02	KRAFT in	NaN	2020.0	1.930694e+09	2020-03-25	20200324	20200325	:
49997	U001	0200762301	C&S WH corporation	NaN	2020.0	1.930606e+09	2020-03-06	20200305	20200306	:
49998	U001	0100001196	DOLLAR	NaN	2020.0	1.930761e+09	2020-04-09	20200408	20200409	:
49999	U001	0200794332	COST systems	NaN	2020.0	1.930586e+09	2020-03-03	20200301	20200303	:

50000 rows × 18 columns

Figure 2 explains the various phases or steps undertaken during the execution of the program. Once the dataset is imported, pre-processing is performed. The target column is identified in the next step. Dataset is further spitted and is then modelled using machine learning techniques. After label encoding the target column is successfully identified and finally the prediction of clearance date is evaluated. After we import the dataset we will pre-process the dataset to achieve a clean dataset with no duplicates, null values, less correlated and with no constant features.

When the pre-processing is done, we will divide the dataset to design three different datasets. Whenever any new data gets loaded into the dataset, it will be equally distributed in these three sets so that the model can educate itself in terms of those new data and can perform better at its predictions.

1. **Training Set:** Which will hold more than 75% of the actual dataset. It will be used to train our model each time new data comes into the system.
2. **Testing Set:** It will contain half of the remaining 20-30% of data after getting divided from the training set and it will be used to test all the algorithms and test cases in this set.
3. **Validation Set:** It will contain the other half of the remaining data and all the modelling algorithms will be tested on this set to check the error scores to determine how well it performs and based on the data the prediction will take place.

In some cases like in Rao et al. (2022) the 70% of the dataset is used for training and 30% is used for testing. The performance of Machine learning models are dependent on the quality of the dataset primarily. Modelling is a process which is used to train our model from a machine learning algorithm to predict from the existing data and features making it useful for real life problems and provide valid results for business analysis. In this model we have used various modelling algorithms and test our model with different error scores. In machine learning errors help in deciding and choosing a best model from considered modelling algorithm based on how well learn is achieved and prediction accuracy for present data and on unseen data too as well.

The study proposed in this chapter needed an Intel Processor with 4GB RAM and 256 GB or Memory. Windows 10 or 11 operating system was used and Jupyter Notebook was using for developing the proposed algorithms

PRE-PROCESSING

The learning ability of a machine learning model is dependent on the quality of the data set used for training. Pre-processing is therefore a very important aspect of machine learning algorithms. Following measures are basically carried out in the dataset ta ken for study.

Null Values Are Taken Care of and Handled

Any dataset taken for study is likely to contain NULL and NaN values which it cannot resolve on its own. Sometimes the dataset is created by sensors and devices of Internet of Thongs type. When a value is not

Figure 4. Pre-processing of the dataset (removing duplicates, null values)

```
#checking the dataframe for any null values
data.isnull().sum()
```

```
business_code              0
cust_number                0
name_customer              0
clear_date              4819
buisness_year              0
doc_id                     0
posting_date               0
document_create_date       0
document_create_date.1     0
due_in_date                0
invoice_currency           0
document type              0
posting_id                 0
total_open_amount          0
baseline_create_date       0
cust_payment_terms         0
invoice_id                 3
isOpen                     0
dtype: int64
```

```
#dropinng every row containing the invoice_id column value as NULL
data = data.dropna(axis = 0, subset = ['invoice_id'])
```

```
#checking for any duplicate values from the dataframe
data.duplicated().sum()
```

```
0
```

```
#droping all the duplicated values
data = data.drop_duplicates(keep = 'first').reset_index()
data.duplicated().sum()
```

```
0
```

changing or if the value recorded for an attribute is zero, a NULL value may be recorded in the dataset. In some scenarios dropping rows and columns containing NULL values is a feasible approach. However this is not advisable when the dataset is small or has few attributes. In certain cases data imputation can be performed. In our study we have removed the rows and columns contacting null values. Imputation can be performed by creating customized functions where some probabilities of possible values could be considered, though at this point we have not explored. We have also removed rows containing duplicate values in our dataset, as sometimes the same record is entered twice by mistake or also when the systems is recovering from a fault or network failure.

Pre-processing the dataset is the first step and here we first try to remove duplicated values and null values as depicted in Figure 4.

Feature Selection

In a dataset, if a column has only one value for all the rows of a dataset then it is considered as a constant feature or column. As the values are same for all the rows, it doesn't add more weight towards a prediction model. Although it might affect the model's accuracy in terms of prediction as the model will only deal with same values again and again. In feature selection we actually remove the constant features by using Variance Threshold as 0, which says that the column which has the number unique values as 0%. It means 100% of that column values are same. Just like constant features, quasi constant features are similar to constant features as vast majority of their column value is same for almost all the rows in a dataset. So it doesn't add anything extra to a regression or classification model towards their better prediction results. In feature selection technique we will remove the quasi constant features by putting the Variance Threshold as 0.1, which means the columns which have 99.9% of all their values are same for all the rows in the dataset will be removed. The authors in Kumat et al. (2022) show how feature selection can actually impact the performance of a machine learning model. Essentially feature selection helps in reducing the dimensionality of the dataset and when appropriate features that have an impact on the output are considered, the overall time complexity is tremendously reduced. The learning ability of the machine learning model is often also enhanced when significant features in the domain of the dataset are given more weightage than considering all the attributes of the dataset. Particle Swarm Optimization based feature selection model was developed in Kumar et al. (2022) where the classification accuracy of the Machine learning Model was not degraded even when after reducing 75.15% of the features. Exploring such techniques for clearance due date prediction could also be explored at a later point of time.

Removing Highly Correlated Columns

The dataset may have values that are correlated strongly which impacts the performance of the algorithm. Hence we use heat map to check the highly correlated features and remove them accordingly as depicted in Figure 5.

From Figure 5 we can see that several columns are highly correlated such as document_create_month with baseline_create_month or due_in_month with posting_date_month etc. It is important therefore, to remove each one of these columns as they otherwise will impact the performance of the proposed model negatively. Removing the correlated features might lead to modelling to over-fitting. We have removed one of the correlated columns in order to reduce the margin of error because correlated features don't

Figure 5. Heat map for correlated features

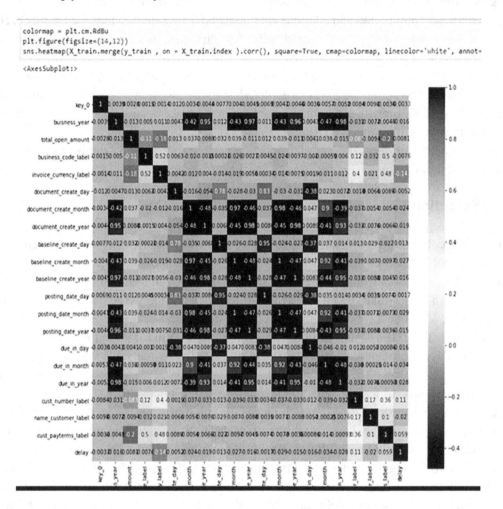

add anything special to the dataset but might increase the complexity of the algorithm, as is depicted in Figure 6.

We have removed one of the two correlated columns using the heat map so that all correlated columns having the correlation close to one or 1 will be eligible as highly correlated.

Label Encoding

In a dataset we will get all kinds of values including objects, date time, strings, numerical etc. In order to make it useful for modelling algorithms to perform error calculation, we need to make our dataset machine friendly. Label encoding helps convert all the distinct values of a column of all data types other than columns with numerical data types and labels them into machine level numerical format. It is one of the most important pre-processing steps for a prediction model. Figure 7 depicts the types of all the columns present in the training set before label encoding.

Figure 6. Removal of correlated features

```
In [480]: X_train, X_val, X_test = column_drop(['baseline_create_day'])
          X_train, X_val, X_test = column_drop(['baseline_create_month'])
          X_train, X_val, X_test = column_drop(['baseline_create_year'])

In [481]: X_train, X_val, X_test = column_drop(['document_create_month'])
          X_train, X_val, X_test = column_drop(['document_create_year'])

In [482]: X_train, X_val, X_test = column_drop(['posting_date_day'])
          X_train, X_val, X_test = column_drop(['posting_date_month'])
          X_train, X_val, X_test = column_drop(['posting_date_year'])
```

Figure 7. Data types of all the columns present in the training set before label encoding

```
X_train.dtypes

business_code                   object
cust_number                     object
name_customer                   object
posting_date            datetime64[ns]
document_create_date    datetime64[ns]
due_in_date             datetime64[ns]
baseline_create_date    datetime64[ns]
cust_payment_terms              object
buisness_year                    int64
total_open_amount              float64
dtype: object
```

Figure 8. Result of label encoding

```
X_train.dtypes

buisness_year                int64
total_open_amount          float64
business_code_label          int32
document_create_day          int64
document_create_month        int64
document_create_year         int64
baseline_create_day          int64
baseline_create_month        int64
baseline_create_year         int64
posting_date_day             int64
posting_date_month           int64
posting_date_year            int64
due_in_day                   int64
due_in_month                 int64
due_in_year                  int64
cust_number_label            int32
name_customer_label          int32
cust_payterms_label          int32
dtype: object
```

Figure 8 depicts the data types of all the columns after label encoding is performed. Label encoding helps convert all the distinct values of a column of all data types other than columns with numerical data types and labels them into machine level numerical format.

TESTING PROCESS

We will test the model on the basis of error scores using several modelling techniques. The modelling algorithms that have been used in this model are:

Linear Regression (LR)

LR is a method used to find the target variable or the dependent variable y with the combination of more than one independent variable x. It performs various regression tasks. It provides a linear relationship between x and y variables as depicted in Figure 9.

The equation for the Linear Regression is given as per Equation (1), (2), and (3).

$$y = a + bx \qquad (1)$$

Here a is the y-intercept and b is the slope of the line. We can determine a and b in this way.

$$a = \frac{\left(\sum y\right)\left(\sum x^2\right) - \left(\sum x\right)\left(\sum xy\right)}{n\left(\sum x^2\right) - \left(\sum x\right)^2} \qquad (2)$$

Figure 9. Graphical representation of linear regression

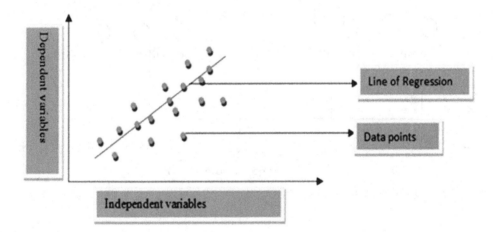

$$b = \frac{n\left(\sum xy\right) - \left(\sum x\right)\left(\sum y\right)}{n\left(\sum x^2\right) - \left(\sum x\right)^2} \qquad (3)$$

It is basically used to make predictions on continuous data such as sales, products etc.

Random Forest

Random Forest algorithm uses multiple decision trees to divide one initial dataset into a hierarchy of decision trees to train the model. Each tree then gives a result, out of which, it gives an optimal prediction value on the basis of majority of votes. It also helps to solve the over-fitting issue of decision tree algorithm. Figure 10 depicts as Random Forest.

Random Forest are used in following scenarios:

1. It performs classification, regression, prediction tasks.
2. It can handle large datasets.
3. It prevents the over-fitting issues of a dataset and enhances the accuracy.
4. It can also predict with fine accuracy even large portion of the data is missing. It uses a method called bagging. Bagging method basically uses variety of models rather than one model to create different training sets and out of all the results it chooses the result with majority of voting.

Figure 10. Graphical representation of random forest

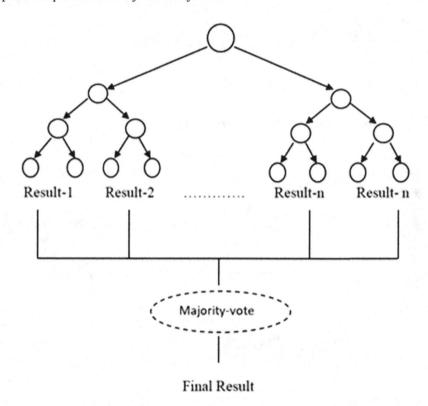

Decision Tree

Decision Tree algorithm uses one initial dataset to divide it into a tree based structure from where it can make the whole dataset into a tree based model until it has taken all values into account. It takes the leaves of that tree as resulted outputs and presents it as a prediction results. But it might run into some over-fitting issues which can be solved using Random forest algorithm. A graphical representation of a Decision Tree is depicted using Figure 11.

This algorithm is used to predict the target c values or columns in regression or classification models. There are two types of nodes in the decision tree.

1.   Decision node
2.   Leaf node

Figure 11. Graphical representation of decision tree

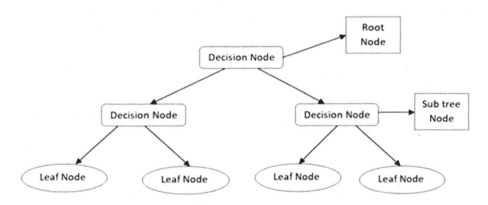

All the terminologies related to Decision tree are:

1.   **Root Node:** The decision tree starts from the root node and it divides the initial dataset into more than one sets.
2.   **Splitting:** It divides the sub nodes based on some conditions.
3.   **Leaf Node:** This is the final node which gives us the output.
4.   **Pruning:** It removes unwanted sub node from the decision tree.
5.   **Sub Tree:** It is the sub section of the decision tree.
6.   **Parent or Child Node:** The starting node is the Parent node and all the nodes that come under the starting node are sub nodes or child node.

But the problem with decision tree is, it often leads to model over-fitting which then results into bad prediction results. So we use random forest technique to avoid this issue.

XGBoost

It uses a framework called gradient boosting. It comprises of all the tree based algorithms and techniques like bagging, boosting, Decision tree algorithm and Random forest algorithm. It uses the random forest techniques to divide the dataset into multiple decision trees and then it uses gradient boosting to give an optimal prediction result. It uses the method Boosting. Boosting is an ensemble method which tries to build strong classifiers using weak classifiers. Figure 12 depicts XGBoost graphically.

It builds a model from the training data and then it tries to build another model by correcting the errors present in the first model. This process continues till it has reached its maximum capacity of creating models. After that it gives us a predicted result.

Suppose the model *F0* is the initial model to be used for prediction.

Its residual value will be *y-F0*.

Figure 12. Graphical representation of XGBoost

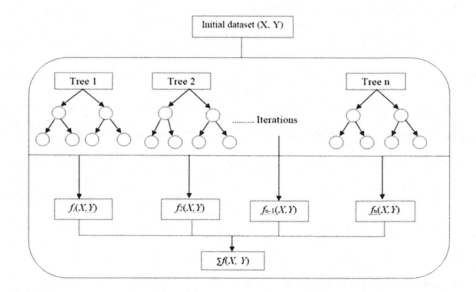

A new model *h1* will be built to fit the error value of *F0*.

The combination of both the *F0* and *h1* will produce a new boosted model *F1*. The Equations (3), (4), and (5) explain the same below mathematically:

$$F1(x) < -F0(X) + h1(x) \qquad (3)$$

After this a new model *F2* will get created the same as before:

$$F2(x) < -F1(X) + h2(x) \qquad (4)$$

After *n*th iteration the equation will follow as:

$$F_n(X) < -F_{n-1}(X) + h_n(x) \qquad (5)$$

RESULTS AND DISCUSSIONS

Invoices are very important for attaining financial process automation and when used wisely can help in identifying customer's patterns in financial behavior. This can be very useful for an organization in planning and venturing risk in certain cases. In this study we have taken an invoice dataset and performed pre-processing followed by feature selection, label encoding and removal of correlated values. Four machine learning model were developed to study the system. Results obtained are further analyzed with respect to how minimal error were obtained with each model. In machine learning errors are used to examine how accurately our model performs in terms of prediction on present data on the dataset and also on unseen data. The mean squared error has been used on this model to check the error score.

1.   1. **Mean Square Error:** The Mean Squared Error (MSE) is the simplest and most common loss function. To calculate the MSE, you take the difference between your model's predictions and the ground truth, square it, and average it out across the whole dataset. Let N be the number of samples we are trying to test. The MSE can be computed using Equation (6).

$$MSE = \frac{i}{N} \sum_{i=1}^{N} (y_i - \widehat{y_i})^2 \qquad (6)$$

2.   2. **R2/R squared Score:** The R2 score is a very important metric that is used to evaluate the performance of a regression-based machine learning model. It is pronounced as R squared and is also known as the coefficient of determination. It is the difference between the samples in the dataset and the predictions made by the model. The high value of R squared determines the less correlation between the dependent and independent features hence it represents a good prediction model. It can be calculated using the Equation (7).

$$R^2 = \frac{Explained\ Variation}{Total\ Varaiation} \qquad (7)$$

Random forest is the algorithm that has been chosen in order to make the prediction based on the error results.

Figure 13 depicts the heat map for correlation of columns after extracting the correlated features.

The accuracy and error scores of each modeling algorithm.

Figure 14 represents the code snippet of Linear Regression and Decision Tree and how checking the error scores and accuracy of training model is performed.

Figure 15 depicts the code snippet for checking the error scores and accuracy of training model using modeling algorithms like XGBoost and random forest.

Figure 16, Figure 17, Figure 18, and Figure 19 depict the scatter plot obtained for Liner Regression, XGBoost, Decision Tree and Random Forest Machine learning techniques based on actual and predicted values.

Figure 20 illustrates the code snippet for calculating MSE Test Error and R2 Test Error for the four machine learning techniques explored in this work.

Table 1 depicts the MSE and R2 Test error scores of Linear Regression, XGBoost, Decision Tree and Random Forest machine learning technique considered in this study. The data frame shows us the error results of all the algorithms used which gives us a better view at the scores. This is the graph of

Figure 13. Heat map

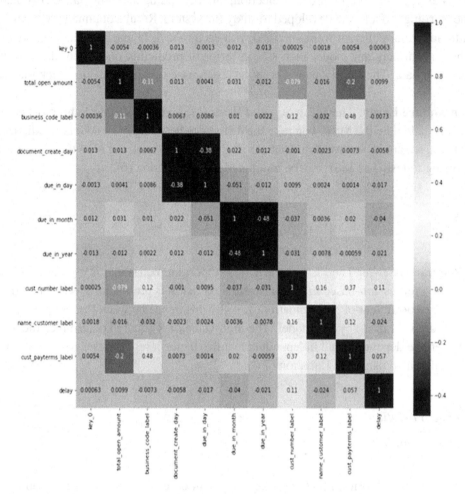

Figure 14. Linear regression and decision tree code snippet

Linear Regression

```
base_model = LinearRegression()
base_model.fit(X_train, y_train)

LinearRegression()

y_predict = base_model.predict(X_val)

MSE_LR = mean_squared_error(y_val, y_predict, squared=False)
MSE_LR

11.67156713905622

r2_LR = r2_score(y_test, y_predict)
r2_LR

-0.016473544218942315
```

Decision tree

```
regressor = DecisionTreeRegressor(random_state=0 , max_depth=5)

regressor.fit(X_train, y_train)

DecisionTreeRegressor(max_depth=5, random_state=0)

y_predict2 = regressor.predict(X_val)

MSE_DTR_train = mean_squared_error(y_test, y_predict2, squared=False)
MSE_DTR_train

10.248701828218236

r2_DTR = r2_score(y_test,y_predict2)
r2_DTR

-0.024558588108434698
```

Figure 15. Code snippet of XGBoost and random forest

XGBoost

```
boost = xgb.XGBRegressor()
boost.fit(X_train, y_train)

# Predicting the Validation Set Results
predicted = boost.predict(X_val)

MSE_XGB = mean_squared_error(y_val, predicted, squared=False)
MSE_XGB

13.457882545879663

r2_XGB = r2_score(y_test, predicted)
r2_XGB

-0.48546177955231173
```

Random Forest

```
forest = RandomForestRegressor()
forest.fit(X_train, y_train)

# Predicting the Validation Set Results
predicted2 = forest.predict(X_val)

MSE_RFR = mean_squared_error(y_test, predicted2, squared=False)
MSE_RFR

11.091727954997273

r2_RFR = r2_score(y_test, predicted2)
r2_RFR

-0.200044491253588697
```

Figure 16. Scatter plot of linear regression based on actual and predicted values

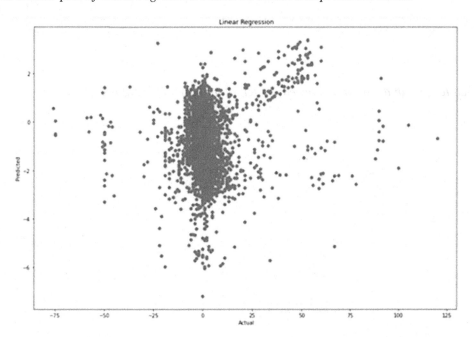

all four algorithms based on their error scores. Figure 21 depicts the bar graph of the error scores for all four machine learning models.

Figure 22 is a snapshot of the prediction result obtained for Random Forest model which is obtained in the target column as highlighted in this figure. The target column here is Prediction of Delay. Further Figure 23 depicts the output obtained for estimating the payment clearance date using the predicted target column which is the delay as depicted in Figure 22.

Finally, the dataset with the predicted payment clearance date is obtained as depicted in Figure 24.

Figure 17. Scatter plot of XGBoost based on actual and predicted values

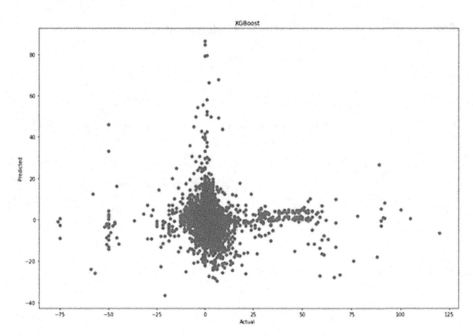

Figure 18. Scatter plot of decision tree based on actual and predicted values

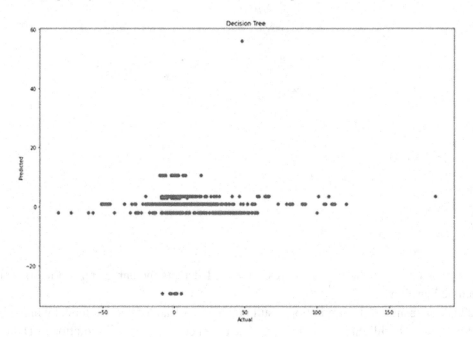

Figure 19. Scatter plot of random forest based on actual and predicted values

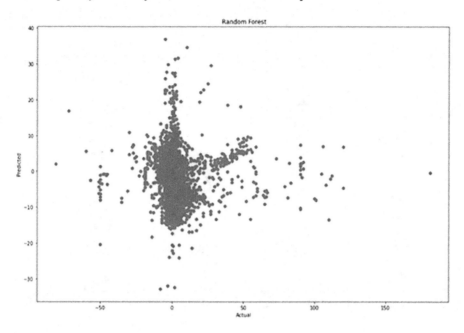

Figure 20. Code snippet to calculate MSE and R2 test errors

```
MSE_test_error=[MSE_LR,MSE_XGB,MSE_DTR,MSE_RFR]
R2_test_error=[r2_LR,r2_XGB,r2_DTR,r2_RFR]
col={'MSE Test Error':MSE_test_error,'R2 Test Error':R2_test_error}
models=['Linear Regression','XGB','Decision Tree','Random Forest']
df=pd.DataFrame(data=col,index=models)
df
```

Table 1. MSE test error and R2 test errors of the machine learning models

	MSE Test Error	**R2 Test Error**
Linear Regression	11.671567	-0.016474
XGB	13.457883	-0.485462
Decision Tree	8.254804	-0.024559
Random Forest	11.091728	-0.200045

Figure 21. Bar plot of all the modeling algorithms based on their error results

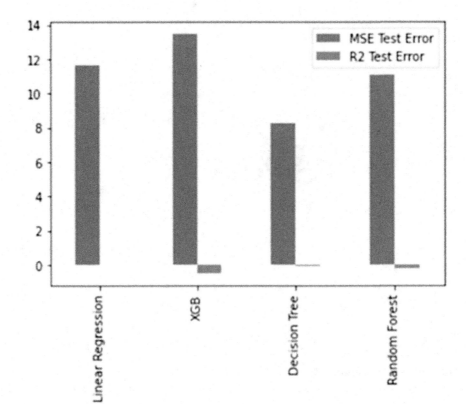

Figure 22. Predicting the target column using the random forest algorithm

```
final_result = forest.predict(real_test)

final_result = pd.Series(final_result, name = 'delay')

final = real_test.merge(final_result.astype(int), on = real_test.index)

final
```

nount	business_code_label	cust_number_label	name_customer_label	due_in_day	due_in_month	due_in_year	document_create_day	cust_payterms_label	delay
32.39	1	290	1209	26	4	2020	10	23	36
13.55	1	326	913	5	4	2020	21	14	41
13.07	1	276	920	15	3	2020	28	23	36
96.78	1	202	872	9	4	2020	25	10	48
87.79	1	7	59	14	3	2020	27	10	47
61.84	1	235	131	11	4	2020	26	10	51
51.51	1	495	573	29	4	2020	24	21	43
96.82	1	280	180	21	3	2020	5	14	42
27.95	1	1	323	24	4	2020	8	10	48
82.65	1	338	243	18	3	2020	1	12	47

Figure 24. The dataset with predicted payment clearance date

```
final_result = pd.merge(X_real_test, new_final, on = new_final.index)

final_result
```

	key_0	business_code	cust_number	name_customer	posting_date	document_create_date	due_in_date	baseline_create_date	cust_payment_terms	total_
0	0	U001	0200769623	WAL-MAR	2020-04-11	2020-04-10	2020-04-26	2020-04-11	NAH4	
1	1	U001	0200790107	ROU corporation	2020-03-21	2020-03-21	2020-04-05	2020-03-21	NAC6	
2	2	U001	0200759878	SA	2020-02-29	2020-02-28	2020-03-15	2020-02-29	NAH4	
3	3	U001	0200704045	RA corporation	2020-03-25	2020-03-25	2020-04-09	2020-03-25	NAA8	
4	4	U001	0100008001	ANHA foundation	2020-02-28	2020-02-27	2020-03-14	2020-02-28	NAA8	
...										
4814	4814	U001	0200726979	BJ'S us	2020-03-27	2020-03-26	2020-04-11	2020-03-27	NAA8	
4815	4815	U001	CCCA02	KRAFT in	2020-03-25	2020-03-24	2020-04-29	2020-03-25	NAG2	
4816	4816	U001	0200762301	C&S WH corporation	2020-03-06	2020-03-05	2020-03-21	2020-03-06	NAC6	
4817	4817	U001	0100001196	DOLLAR	2020-04-09	2020-04-08	2020-04-24	2020-04-09	NAA8	
4818	4818	U001	0200794332	COST systems	2020-03-03	2020-03-01	2020-03-18	2020-03-03	NAAX	

4819 rows × 11 columns

Figure 23. Prediction of payment clear date from the predicted target column

Calculating the clear_date

```
final['predicted_clear_date'] = final['due_in_date'] + pd.to_timedelta(final['delay'], unit = 'd')

final
```

number	name_customer	posting_date	document_create_date	due_in_date	baseline_create_date	cust_payment_terms	total_open_amount_y	predicted_clear_date
769623	WAL-MAR	2020-04-11	2020-04-10	2020-04-26	2020-04-11	NAH4	19132.39	2020-06-01
790107	ROU corporation	2020-03-21	2020-03-21	2020-04-05	2020-03-21	NAC6	91013.55	2020-05-16
759878	SA	2020-02-29	2020-02-28	2020-03-15	2020-02-29	NAH4	7713.07	2020-04-20
704045	RA corporation	2020-03-25	2020-03-25	2020-04-09	2020-03-25	NAA8	6696.78	2020-05-27
008001	ANHA foundation	2020-02-28	2020-02-27	2020-03-14	2020-02-28	NAA8	6987.79	2020-04-30
726979	BJ'S us	2020-03-27	2020-03-26	2020-04-11	2020-03-27	NAA8	261.84	2020-06-01
CCA02	KRAFT in	2020-03-25	2020-03-24	2020-04-29	2020-03-25	NAG2	14151.51	2020-06-11
762301	C&S WH corporation	2020-03-06	2020-03-05	2020-03-21	2020-03-06	NAC6	14898.82	2020-05-02
001196	DOLLAR	2020-04-09	2020-04-08	2020-04-24	2020-04-09	NAA8	5127.95	2020-06-11
794332	COST systems	2020-03-03	2020-03-01	2020-03-18	2020-03-03	NAAX	3382.65	2020-05-04

CONCLUDING REMARKS AND FUTURE DIRECTIONS

Any product based company using this model will get a close to accurate prediction results over the clearance date on the basis of which the company will take productive measurements. The rresultant dataset will produce a clean and more effective dataset which will clear out all the unnecessary information which comes with the initial invoice document. The predicted output is not the only output this model can produce. The output of the model will vary with time when new and unseen data will be introduced. New and more advanced pre-processing techniques can be applied to reduce the model over-fitting and in attaining a higher accuracy. Using different graphs for depiction and analysis of the data present in the dataset in terms of how it is behaving will help understand the model's performance. This shall also help in knowing its constraints that pose hindrance in attaining a higher potential that was possible. This proposed model will be helpful for service based companies in the future if used accordingly, where service based companies pick up projects from higher product based companies and invest their time, resources, people and money on it to complete the project and gain some profit from it.

There are possibilities of enhancing the performance of the proposed model by enhancing its rate of learning ability, reducing time and space complexity. There are other aspects related to invoice processing that can also be explored with machine learning approaches. The authors in Tang et al. (2020) develop a machine learning based system that can detect certain abnormal behaviors related to how invoices are processed in an organization. Some of these scenarios are as explained as follows:

Scenario 1: Invoices created electronically and saved on a cloud or a centralized server are prone to server counterfeiting. Sensitive data may be compromised and indeed new and not validated data may also get added.

Scenario 2: There may be multiple password attempts to the server for processing or viewing invoices. This could be case where an authorized user may be accessing the system.

Scenario 3: Some invoices may receive imbursements repeatedly.

Scenario 4: Invoice reimbursement may be fake and not real.

Scenario 5: A user to the system may believe that he is connected to the server where invoices are processed and saved, but the connection may be fake and actually connected to a hacked server or to a server of a competing business counterpart.

Scenario 6: A large number of invoices are issued in a short span of time by a given user having access to invoice processing.

Scenario 7: A large number of invoices of a large amount is issued in a short span by a given user having access to the invoice processing interface.

Scenario 8: Fake invoices are verified multiple number of times by a particular user having access to the invoice processing interface.

Scenario 9: Authentication attempts to the invoice processing interface failed multiple times for a particular user.

Scenario 10: Authentication attempts failed many times at a given system having access to the invoice processing interface.

Scenario 11: Approval of an invoice failed multiple times for a particular user is also a matter of utmost concern.

Scenario 12: Approval of more than one invoice failed for than once for a particular user accessing the system.

Scenario 13: Status of an invoice being updated multiple times.

Scenario 14: Authentication certificates failed in multiple instances.

The nature of such prediction is complex and exploring unsupervised learning techniques are very beneficial. Tools like TensorFlow (Abadi et al., 2016) could be used for developing systems where heterogeneous entities are involved.

Invoice processing and management of invoices is a very important aspect of how organization manage their businesses. With automation, this process may on one hand become easier but on the other hand is prone to issues as explained above. The invoice dataset available at the server of an organization can be used for analyzing how cash inflows and outflows happen over a period of time. Knowing which customers exercise good repayments and which do not can help in devising business strategies. In this chapter we have shown how machine learning techniques such as Linear Regression, Random Forest, Decision Trees and XGBoost can be explored. We have clearly outlined the steps to be undertaken for a machine learning problem. The code snippets depict how pre-processing, feature selection and removal of duplicate values can be done. India as a country is moving towards building a digital bridge across all sectors. The (https://einvoice1.gst.gov.in/) is a web portal where organizations can register their invoices electronically. The portal generates and returns a Unique Invoice Reference Number (URIN) which is digitally signed and also has a QR code. The government of a country can monitor and audit the invoices which are registered at a portal that is made available for its citizens. Many businesses that function online where products are sold and purchased online, invoices are electronically generated. A huge database is thus being created on a daily basis. The nature of how payments are made especially can be observed for trend analysis. Discounts can be offered for certain type of products by analysis the demand and supply of products as well. Machine Learning techniques can be a very viable solution for exploring new possibilities by analyzing invoices and how payments are made. There there are chances of anomalies and security issues which cannot be ignored.

REFERENCES

Abadi, M., Agarwal, A., Barham, P., Brevdo, E., & Zheng, X. (2016). *TensorFlow: large-Scale Machine Learning on Heterogeneous Distributed Systems*. https://einvoice1.gst.gov.in/

Alpaydin, E. (2016). *Machine learning: the new AI (The MIT press essential knowledge series)*. The MIT Press.

Arora, S., Bindra, S., Singh, S., & Nassa, V. N. (2022). Prediction of Credit card defaults through data analysis and machine learning techniques. *Materials Today: Proceedings*, *51*(part 1), 110–117. doi:10.1016/j.matpr.2021.04.588

Chen, T., He, T., Benesty, M., & Khotilvoich, V. (2019). *xgboost: eXtreme Gradient Boosting*. R package version 0.82.1

Cherfi, A., Kaouther, N., & Ferchichi, A. (2018). Very fast C4. 5 decision tree algorithm. *Applied Artificial Intelligence*, *32*(2), 119–137. doi:10.1080/08839514.2018.1447479

Fitzpatrick, T., & Mues, C. (2021). How can Lenders prosper? Comparing machine learning approaches to identify profitable Peer-to-Peer loan investments. *European Journal of Operational Research*, *294*(2), 711–722. doi:10.1016/j.ejor.2021.01.047

Goel, E., & Abhilasha, E. (2017). Random Forest: A Review. *International Journal of Advanced Research in Computer Science and Software Engineering*, *7*(1), 251–257. doi:10.23956/ijarcsse/V7I1/01113

Hastie, T., Tibshirani, R., & Friedman, J. (2009). *"The Elements of Statistical Learning", Data Mining, Inference, and Prediction* (2nd ed.). Springer Science & Business Media.

Jordan, M. I., & Mitchell, T. M. (2015). Machine learning: Trends, perspectives, and prospects. *Science*, *349*(6245), 255–260. doi:10.1126cience.aaa8415 PMID:26185243

Kelleher, J. D., Mac Namee, B., & D'arcy, A. (2020). *Fundamentals of machine learning for predictive data analytics: algorithms, worked examples, and case studies*. MIT Press.

Kumar, K. V., Kumari, P., Rao, M., & Mohapatra, D. P. (2022). Metaheuristic feature selection for software fault prediction. *Journal of Information & Optimization Sciences*, *43*(5), 1013–1020. doi:10.1080/02522667.2022.2103301

Kumar, V. K., Sharma, P. D., Rout, P., Vanit, A., Rao, M., & Mohapatra, D. (2022). Effect on Feature selection in Software Fault Prediction. In D. Mishra, R. Buyya, P. Mohapatra, & S. Patnaik (Eds.), *Intelligent and Cloud Computing. Smart Innovation, Systems and Technologies* (Vol. 286). Springer. doi:10.1007/978-981-16-9873-6_44

Ledesma, S., Ibarra-Manzano, M. A., Cabal-Yepez, E., Almanza-Ojeda, D. L., & Avina-Cervantes, J. G. (2018). Analysis of data sets with learning conflicts for machine learning. *IEEE Access : Practical Innovations, Open Solutions*, *6*, 45062–45070. doi:10.1109/ACCESS.2018.2865135

Rao, P., Pollayi, H., & Rao, M. (2022). Machine Learning based design of reinforced concrete shear walls subjected to earthquakes. *Journal of Physics: Conference Series*, *2327*(1), 4. doi:10.1088/1742-6596/2327/1/012068

Schulz, F., Ebbecke, M., Gillmann, M., Adrian, B., Agne, S., & Dengel, A. (2009). Seizing the Treasure: Transferring Knowledge in Invoice Analysis. *2009 10th International Conference on Document Analysis and Recognition*, 848-852. 10.1109/ICDAR.2009.47

Seber, G. A. F., & Lee, A. J. (2003). *Linear Regression Analysis*. Wiley Series. doi:10.1002/9780471722199

Song, Yu., Wang, Y., & Ye, X. (2023). Loan Default Prediction using a credit rating-specific and multi-objective ensemble learning scheme. Information Sciences, 629, 599-617.

Tang, P., Qiu, W., Huang, Z., Chen, S., Yan, M., Lian, H., & Li, Z. (2020). Anomaly Detection in electronic invoice systems based on machine learning. *Information Sciences*, *535*, 172–186. doi:10.1016/j.ins.2020.03.089

Zannin, L. (2020). Combining multiple probability predictions in the presence of class imbalance to discriminate between potential bad and good borrowers in peer-to-peer lending market. *Journal of Behavioral and Experimental Finance*, *25*, 100272. doi:10.1016/j.jbef.2020.100272

APPENDIX: PREPROCESSING THE LOST DATA FOR SOME CONSTANT OR DUPLICATED FEATURES

```
real_test.isna().sum()
#drop the clear date column as we are going to predict it
real_test.drop(['clear_date'], axis = 1,inplace = True)
X_real_test =
real_test[['business_code','cust_number','name_customer','posting_
date','document_cre
te_date','due_in_date',
'baseline_create_date','cust_payment_terms','total_open_amount']].copy()
```

Chapter 14
Predicting Healthcare Readmissions Using Artificial Intelligence

Manu Banga

ⓘ https://orcid.org/0000-0002-6764-5634

GLA University, India

ABSTRACT

Hospital readmission systems increase the efficiency of initial treatment at hospitals. This chapter proposes a novel prediction model for identifying risk factors using machine learning techniques, and the proposed model is tested using 10-fold cross-validation for generalization and finds hidden patterns in the diagnosis, medications, lab test results, and basic characteristics of patients related to readmissions. This model predicts a statistically problem solving using searching patterns. Based on the findings of this study, for the given dataset, pruning dataset manifested the most accurate prediction of readmissions to the hospital with 94.8% accuracy for patients admitted in a year.

INTRODUCTION

Prevention is better than cure, Benjamin Franklin's famous aphorism, is worth recalling at this troubling time for healthcare and the economy especially in Covid-19 pandemic (Abdel et al., 2021). There are various schemes sponsored by Indian government under flagship Ayushman Bharat National Health Protection Mission (AB-NHPM) hybrid of two major health initiatives, namely Health and wellness Centres (HWC) and National Health Protection Scheme (NHPM). This research explores the effectiveness of preventive care models using Intelligent Healthcare System to predict early hospital readmission in Indian healthcare system. In this research study, a novel Intelligent Software System for preventive care is proposed for reducing hospital readmission by machine learning analytics techniques on patients of high and low-risk categories using just-in-time deduction. The just-in-time (JIT) analytics not only ensure best readmission quality, but also handles patient's readmission by identifying and prioritizing them according to medical aid needed so patients with higher comorbidities can be given better medi-

DOI: 10.4018/978-1-6684-7105-0.ch014

cal facility based on their past medical history like lab tests, medicines thereby enhancing reliability of the intelligent software system. Intelligent Software System (ISS) comprises programs, methodologies, rules and related documentation and research that empower the client to collaborate with a computer, its equipment i.e. hardware, or perform errands. It comprises 4 V's and suffices the first V (Volume) of Big Data. The speed of healthcare data created from patient encounters and patient monitors are increasing, in and out of the clinic - second V (Velocity). Over 80 percentage of medical data resides in unstructured formats, such as doctors' notes, images, and charts from monitoring instruments – third V (Variety) and Fourth V (Veracity) deals with unsure or vague data. Most healthcare data from clinic and hospital records is afflicted with errors, as while entering data, technicians frequently attach research to the wrong person's record or copy research incorrectly. This section provides the context of the study research and its aim and objectives. It then demonstrates the significance of this research. Thus, the role played by the intelligent system is appreciated in the healthcare industry as Intelligent Software System can handle huge volumes of data, the amount of research with respect to the capacity for its storage and management in patient readmission cases.

BACKGROUND

Indian Healthcare system needs major reinvention based on income levels difference, ageing population, rising health awareness and positive outlook towards preventive healthcare are expected to increase demand of healthcare services in near future (Abdelrahman et al., 2020) thus making healthcare industry a critical and fastest growing industry in India with expectation to touch $280 billion in 2025. With the unscheduled dawn of the digital era and massive growth in healthcare, the vast amount of data can be anticipated from different health science data sources including data from patient electronic records, claims system, lab test results, pharmacy, social media, drug research, gene sequencing, home monitoring mobile apps etc. This data is called Big Data and Big data analytics can possibly change the way healthcare providers utilize modern innovations to extract knowledge from their medical data repositories and settle on educated choices. The new trend of medical data digitization is leading to an optimum model change in the healthcare industry As a result the healthcare industry is experiencing an increment in sheer volume of data regarding unpredictability, timeliness and diversity. Successfully acquiring and effectively analyzing a variety of healthcare data for a long period of time can shed light on a significant number of approaching healthcare challenges as and connected to Aarogya Setu and this requires identifying high-risk patients at the time of discharge from hospital.

Human body is a big source of Big Data. Data increases and moves faster than healthcare organizations can ingest it. Collecting this important data and analyzing it for clinical and advanced investigation is critical to enhancing healthcare and outcomes. Instead of looking at "Bigness", look for "Smartness" in data. In India, even if digitization of medical records is in its infancy stage (Forestiero et al., 2018). In today's research age, healthcare is transforming from assessment-based decisions to informed decisions based on data and analytics (Gravili et al., 2018).

The current research study deals with volume, variety and veracity of data. Due to privacy issues, this study could not access millions of instances but still thousands of real instances makes this reliable and efficient consisting of noisy, inconsistent, missing values in heterogeneous data. India, a developing country, with mammoth population, faces various problems in the field of healthcare in the form of huge expenditures, meeting the needs of the poor people, accessibility to the hospitals, medical research

Figure 1. Four dimensions of big data in designing intelligent software system for Indian healthcare

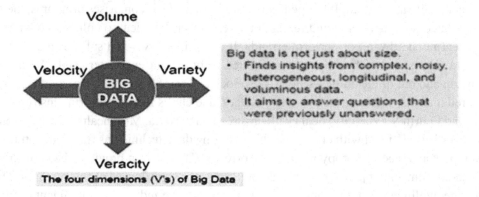

Figure 2. Depicts human body as a big data

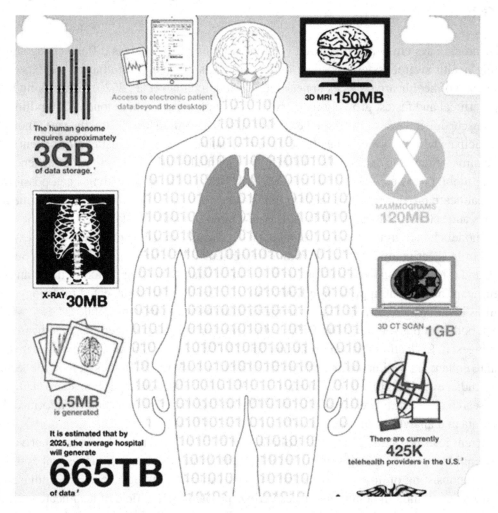

especially when an epidemic such as dengue or malaria spreads (Khanra et al., 2020). Operational efficiencies in Indian Healthcare can be improved by capturing every single detail about a patient to form a complete view which will help to predict and prevent an existing condition or disease from escalating and plan responses to disease epidemics. Unraveling the "Big Data" related complexities can give useful research in designing intelligent health care system by using data efficiently and effectively, it can provide some quick returns with respect to predicting spread of epidemic preventive healthcare, and fraud management (Babu et al., 2017) which will significantly lower healthcare costs. Thus, this study has performed various pre-processing techniques on the data to make it more accurate and reliable.

Figure 3. Shows use of big data in Indian healthcare scenario

MAIN FOCUS OF THE CHAPTER

Intelligent Healthcare System discovers trends in readmission data of various departments, thereby predicting and assessing readmission rate. Organizations utilize multiple methods to examine their data to predict future events. Intelligent Healthcare System is a combination of statistical analysis and various data mining techniques such as association, classification, clustering and pattern matching. It comprises exploration and preparation of data, defining an intelligent system and follows its process.

In development of Intelligent Healthcare System various authors carried primarily on Prescriptive Analytics using Descriptive Analytics, Diagnostic Analytics and Predictive Analytics and proposed a framework for healthcare industry of real time patients using Support Vector Machines. He achieved good accuracy but biased datasets resulted in false predictions (Abdel et al., 2021). For dealing with ambiguous biased datasets framework for COVID prediction proposed using personality traits. They conducted comprehensive study of Qatar and accessed various healthcare arising due to COVID-19 (Abdelrahman et al., 2020). Eminent researchers proposed system for Hospital Infrastructure Management

Figure 4. Shows stages in developing intelligent system

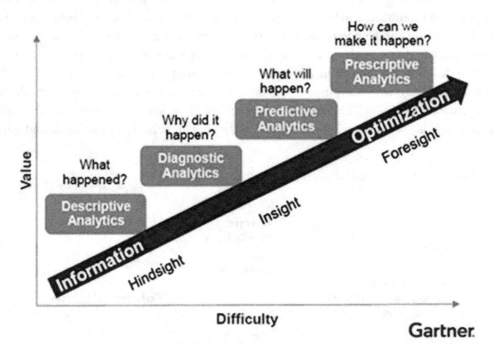

System. They conducted survey for designing comprehensive system covering multi-specialty domains (Babar et al. 2016). Some researchers designed diagnostic analytics system for heart failure readmission case as heart patient's readmission based on pulmonary infection using Naïve Bayes Theorem. They achieved 71% accuracy in probability assessment (Babu et al., 2017). Researchers carried out extrinsic survey on various reasons for hospital readmission between year 2016 to 2020 and novel method based on hybrid approach of extracting relevant feature selection was proposed for a recurring deterioration of patients with comorbidities (Bossen et al., 2020). Following the sequence of readmission proposed a real time system for tracking nosocomial disease. They intelligently collaborated doctor on call with a patient message (Cheng et al., 2018). Researchers extensively applied big data analytics on diabetes patients and achieved invariably same accuracy on multiple datasets (De Silva et al., 2015). As data is highly skewed some researchers applied distributed and parallel algorithms for healthcare system and predicted various department operation are in parallel with their individual classification (Forestiero et al., 2018). For accessing operation and maintenance researchers reviewed big data analytics in healthcare (Galetsi et al., 2020). In many disease patient readmission required carried out using statistical modeling approaches for finding factors affecting early readmission but it is not easy to predict each specific event and has same characteristics for new patient (Gowsalya et al., 2014). Some researchers designed a specialised software system helping hospital for elderly patients readmission thus developing a ubiquitous environment for old-aged persons (Gravili et al. 2018). Researchers designed trustworthy system for heath analytics using big data for identification of predictor variable in readmission (Jin et al., 2016). Some worked on risk involved in prediction of patients readmission with chronic medical history (Kamble et al., 2018). For further assessment researchers worked on risk involved in prediction of patient's readmission with chronic medical history (Khanra et al., 2020). Utilization of need-based patient doctor connection researchers developed intelligent healthcare system using mobile computing thus accessing patient and doctor records in an online platform (Ma et al., 2018). Assessment of patient and doctor on call an online system was designed for trustworthy data processing of lab records, test results in healthcare analytics (Moutselos et al., 2018). Researchers developed application for online assessment of patient records by hospital administration sorted by doctor and department name (Navaz et. al. 2017). Authors studied using deep learning methodologies for finding pattern distribution and classification of healthcare datasets in severe requiring readmission for patients with comorbidities (Sabharwal et al., 2016). Researchers conducted a survey on persons with diabetes for need, application and characteristics of big data analytics in healthcare industry (Salomi et al., 2016) and designed a mobile application predicting patients requiring special treatment, attendant and special diet based on their past history through E-Commerce application (Wu et al., 2017). So implementing appropriate plans to prevent readmissions, identification of patients who are at a greater risk of hospitalization is very important. People with uncontrollable comorbidities often become acutely ill and enter into a cycle of hospital admission and readmissions. Patients with diabetes who are hospitalized are at greater risk of getting readmitted in comparison with patients without commodities (Jin et al., 2016). Besides this, intelligent systems based on specific patient subpopulation categorised by disease type are of more value than the models based on entire cohort. So, this work has been limited to diabetic patient readmission as diabetes is one of the most prevalent diseases and a major health hazard in developing countries like India as 17.1% adult population suffers from several heath issues as per ICMR data (Gravili et al., 2018).

RESEARCH METHODOLOGY

The research methodology is a conventional collection of different techniques for examining a certain problem. These practices are continuous in nature and help in the acquisition of new knowledge by modifying earlier knowledge. Research Methodology starts with interpretations about the events happening in surrounding world, developing myths or hypotheses by interrogating, how the certain the process takes place, usually makes way for predictions, validated using different statistical tests thus, generated from a controlled investigation which generate the empirical data thus adding on to the previous results., making our myths or hypotheses to be altered, refined, or rejected. Thus research the methodology used for designing an intelligent software system for readmission prediction uses a developmental design based on an incremental approach for imbalance learning using previous datasets evaluation using statistical measures. Using Machine Learning for accessing readmission of a patient using intelligent software system helps in reduction of medical cost thereby increasing the quality of health care in an optimal manner by formularizing the patient identification problem in a count of monthly discharges, assessing various steps involved in readmission risk prediction by exploring the Electronics Medical Records (EMR) of tests like Nerve Conduction Test (NCV), Electromyography (EMG), Magnetic resonance imaging (MRI) causing readmission related attributes, thereby extracting relevant features for predicting readmission of patients (Jin et al., 2016). Thereafter, applying Data Pre-Processing Techniques on readmissions data for efficiently prediction using machine-learning techniques and how can this prediction aid in reducing cost and improving the overall quality of health care in hospitals involved using optimal sets of patients who are expected to get readmission after immediate discharge of patients from an Indian hospital to study the attributes related to cause readmission of different patients by accessing the features that can be used in predicting readmissions of discharge patient with health issues within stipulated time by diagnosis and interventions from clinical notes to enhance predictor variables for the model using data mining techniques with the importance of each predictor variable with respect to its ability to predict readmissions by the generation of frequent patterns that inference readmission risk using various supervised learning algorithms in predicting the risk of readmissions and a best intelligent system is built and validated by statistical techniques and using cost-sensitive analysis on savings can be done if the model is implemented with the average the time-lapse between discharge and readmission corresponding to different diseases (Navaz et al., 2018). Thereby reducing and replacing missing values in the dataset and then normalizing the dataset values and on the normalized datasets relevant features influencing patient readmission are extracted using Feature Subset Selections and then overlapping these subsets to complete dataset in a bottom up manner without redundancy, after obtaining optimized dataset of relevant features then classification is done of identification of patient most likely to least likely for readmission assessment and after that model is evaluated on real hospital dataset.

Figure 5. Methodology adopted for data preprocessing

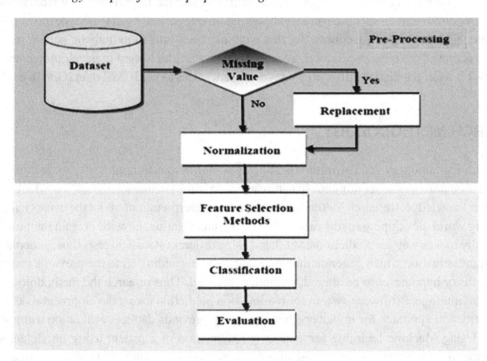

PROPOSED SOLUTIONS AND RECOMMENDATIONS

Designing intelligent software system by automated feature selection and using relevant features on Data Exploration using Data Collection, Acquire Domain Knowledge and Describing and Exploring datasets thus resolving class imbalance problem in an iterative manner by data pre-processing using Support Vector Machines defining class labels as risk-class and non-risk class directly to the features from the raw data, as constructed based on the previous history of the patient. So, most of the features extracted from individual patient admission records, but some features are aggregated across multiple admission records of the same patient and for multiple record using Discretization and frequency distribution on prediction modelling and evaluating model accuracy based on factors like Precision, Recall, AUC. Readmissions are acute, unplanned admissions to the hospital within a defined period of time from an initial admission. Readmission rates are a well-established health quality measure internationally as some readmissions that do occur are avoidable and if data is modelled correctly, groups of patients at high risk of readmission are identifiable. Hospital readmission is an important contributor to total medical expenditure and is an emerging indicator of quality of care. It is disruptive to patients and costly to healthcare systems. The objective of this research study was to develop a predictive risk model to identify patients with diabetes who are at high risk of hospital readmission in an Indian hospital. This is done by analysing key factors using machine learning methods and through retrospective analysis of patients' medical records of a reputed Indian hospital which impact the all-purpose readmission of a patient with diabetes within 30 days of discharge and comparing different classification models that predict readmission and evaluating the best model. In this research study, the problem of predicting the risk of readmission was framed as a binary classification problem and several available prediction models were developed and evaluated. This work explored a complex, high-dimensional clinical dataset (around 60,000 patient records) provided by an Indian Hospital towards identifying the risk factors related to readmission of patients with diabetes within 30 days of discharge. Total 58,625 inpatient admission records were explored from 1st July 2013 to 31st July 2015. Out of these, 9,381 records were diabetic patient encounters. It holds approximately 7,100 patients diagnosed with diabetes. Out of total 9,381 records, 1,211(12.9%) encounters were found as readmissions. Prediction of risk of hospital readmission is a complex task. Many factors influence this process and the outcome. There is currently a serious need for methods that can increase healthcare institutions' understanding of what is important in predicting readmission risk. This study contributed to the growing body of knowledge by proposing an architecture of hospital readmission prediction model and by identifying critical risk predictors, such as department, number of prior inpatient visits and length of stay in a hospital.

In this research study, the real-world hospital data of inpatients having diabetes as an existing condition in conjunction with other medical illnesses is analyzed. The objective was to build a predictive model to identify patients who have a higher likelihood of being readmitted. This study classifies the patients into two different risk groups of readmissions (Yes or No) within 30 days of discharge based on patients' characteristics using 2-year clinical and administrative data from an Indian Hospital. The dataset had information about patient socio-demographic characteristics, diagnosis, lab procedures, past history, medications and treatment given pertaining to a particular hospital admission. The prediction of readmissions is studied using different characteristics of the patients with diabetes. These characteristics are: Age, Gender, Admission Source, Department / Medical Specialty, Length of Stay, Number of inpatient visits, Number of lab procedures, Number of procedures, Number of diagnoses, Number of medications, HbA1c test result, Glucose serum test result, Fasting Glucose serum test result, Hemoglobin, Creatinine test result, Albumin test result, LDL/HDL ratio, Triglycerides test result, Hypertension, Renal test result, Diabetes medications, Retinopathy, Neuropathy, Diabetic foot, Troponin-I test result, Ketones test result, Clexane test result, Heart Problem, Gastropathy, Obesity, Potassium test result, Amylase test result, Lipase test result.

Figure 6. Prediction model for healthcare system

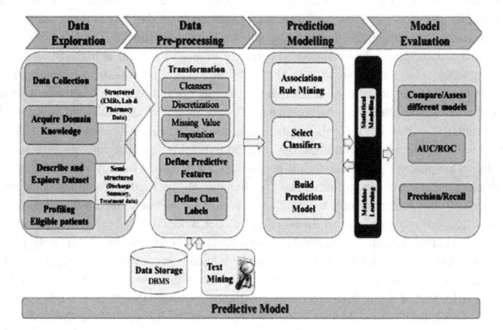

Dataset Used

National Health Systems Resource Centre, Ministry of Health and Family Welfare (MoHWF) of various districts in accordance to Primary Health Centre (PHC), Secondary and Tertiary Health Centre provided by specialized hospitals. The data set for this research was obtained from an Indian Hospital Ministry. Total 58,625 inpatient admission records were explored from 1st April 2016 to 31st December 2020. Out of these, 9,381 records were diabetic patient encounters which were considered for modeling purpose. Each admission record included demographic research (e.g. name, gender, age), clinical research (e.g., diagnosis, treatment, lab tests, medication data), administrative data (e.g. length of stay) and billing research (e.g. charge amount). After pre-processing, a subset of features was considered as shown in Table 1. Some of them are derived features known as aggregation of multiple datasets as presence of these features leads to a particular illness. Discretization and frequency distribution were done using Matlab tool with analysis of 9496 records and criteria was made for individual attribute. patterns using cost-sensitive formulation in the diagnosis, medications, lab test results and basic characteristics of patient related to readmissions, this model predicts a statistically problem solving using searching patterns for calculating annual savings with interventions are offered to high risk patients with interventions are offered to high risk patients.

In the proposed approach the hybrid algorithm based on PSO-MGA (Particle Swarm Optimization-Modified Genetic algorithm) is used, to improve the accuracy intelligent healthcare system estimation using feature selection by PSO-MGA for reducing noise and selecting relevant attributes.

Table 1. Ranking of relevant attributes for patients with comorbidities

Attributes	Criteria
Sugar level	1
Hemoglobin Level	1
Blood Pressure	1
Varicose Veins	2
Nerve Palsy Test: High Level / Low Level	3
Number of Surgery in last 5 years	4
Past History: Non-Union of factures	5
Gastroenteritis	5
Period of Stay in hospital	5

Feature Selection Using Hybrid MGA and PSO Algorithm

In this section, we proposed novel approach for Intelligent Readmission Risk Prediction Framework using Feature Selection using PSO-MGA for efficient categorization as class of patients to be readmitted and patients not to be readmitted. Wu et al. (2017) used healthcare data and categorize structured and unstructured datasets but with class imbalance problem. For resolving overtraining and class-imbalance problem extraction of relevant features is needed, for that a novel algorithm based on hybrid PSO-MGA is proposed, for obtaining best feature sets. For this dataset is loaded with kernel based fitness function defined and in an iteratively manner it is updated based on the best global function value of PSO or MGA and after best sets of feature are obtained. In this research study, the real-world hospital data of inpatients having diabetes as an existing condition in conjunction with other medical illnesses is analysed. The objective was to build a predictive model to identify patients who have a higher likelihood of being readmitted. This study classifies the patients into two different risk groups of readmission (Yes or No) within 30 days of discharge based on patients' characteristics using 2-year clinical and administrative data from an Indian Hospital. The dataset had information about patient socio-demographic characteristics, diagnosis, lab procedures, past history, medications and treatment given pertaining to a particular hospital admission. The prediction of readmissions is studied using different characteristics of the patients with diabetes. These characteristics are: Age, Gender, Admission Source, Department / Medical Specialty, Length of Stay, Number of inpatient visits, Number of lab procedures, Number of procedures, Number of diagnoses, Number of medications, HbA1c test result, Glucose serum test result, Fasting Glucose serum test result, Hemoglobin, Creatinine test result, Albumin test result, LDL/ HDL ratio, Triglycerides test result, Hypertension, Renal test result, Diabetes medications, Retinopathy, Neuropathy, Diabetic foot, Troponin-I test result, Ketones test result, Clexane test result, Heart Problem, Gastropathy, Obesity, Potassium test result, Amylase test result, Lipase test result. This study has assessed how various data pre-processing techniques such as feature selection, missing value imputation and class balancing techniques may impact the results of prediction modelling using readmission for patients with a diabetes diagnosis as the context for the analysis. Then, various predictive models like Logistic Regression, Naïve Bayes and Decision Tree were applied to this improved dataset (after pre-processing) to obtain risk of readmission predictions accuracy. The impact of different pre-processing choices was assessed on various performance metrics like Area under Curve (AUC), Precision, Recall and Accuracy. This study offers empirical evidence that most proposed models with selected pre-processing techniques significantly outperform the baseline methods (without any pre-processing) with respect to selected evaluation criteria. AUC is highly increased with the use of Oversampling technique if data is skewed on the class label. Recall was the biggest gainer with range increasing from (0.02 - 0.23) to (0.78 - 0.85) and there was also an increase in AUC from range (0.56 - 0.68) to (0.83 - 0.86) by using pre-processing approach. These observations conclude that it is indeed useful to apply pre-processing techniques to the data before creating a readmission prediction model for diabetic patients in Indian healthcare scenario. But there is a need to evaluate the medical relevance of the evaluation metric before the application and choice of the pre-processing techniques considered in this work because all evaluation metrics would not be expected to be of equal medical relevance. Thus, this study concludes that data pre-processing has a significant effect on hospital readmission predictive accuracy for patients with diabetes, with certain schemes proving inferior to competitive approaches. In addition, it is found that the impact of pre-processing schemes like feature selection, missing value imputation and balancing varies by various machine learning techniques and evaluation metrics. It signifies that there is a need of formulating different best practices to aid better results of a specific technique.

Predicting Hospital Readmission rates can increase the efficiency of initial treatment at hospitals which can save a lot of lives. This research study proposes an architecture of this prediction model and then explains each step in detail. It identified various risk factors using text mining techniques. Also, groups of consistently occurring factors, that inference readmission rates were revealed by associative rule mining. Out of total 9381 records, 1211(12.9%) encounters were found as readmissions. This study found that risk factors like hospital department where readmission happens, history of recent prior hospitalization and length of stay are strong predictors of readmission. Random forest was found to be the optimal classifier for this task using the evaluation metric Area under Precision-Recall curve (0.296). It then evaluates the classification accuracy using five different data mining classifiers – Naïve Bayesian, Logistic Regression, Random Forest, Adaboost and Neural Networks and the best classifier is chosen. The models were tested using ten-fold cross-validation, a technique that is one of the most popular techniques that allows generalization. Based on the findings of this study, it can be concluded that, for the given dataset, random forest classifier manifested the most accurate prediction of readmissions to the hospital within a 30-day time period for patients with diabetes using the evaluation metric Area under Precision-Recall curve. By mining hidden patterns in the diagnosis, medications, lab test results and basic characteristics of patient related to readmissions, this model finds a strong set of statistically significant implications or association rules. A ranked list of such rules can be instrumental for a doctor prior to diagnosis. As an additional safety check, the doctor can verify the prevalence (or lack of it) of these conditions to every patient, increasing the effectiveness of diagnosis and better medical decisions. It is widely argued that cost of readmission is a huge burden on health systems as well as patients. From the cost analysis, it is observed that a cost of INR 15.92 million can be saved for 9,381 instances of diabetic patient encounters over the period of 2 years. This indicates the potential of a significant amount of savings for any healthcare system especially for the developing countries like India. This work, first such study done from Indian Healthcare perspective, built a model to predict the risk of readmission within 30 days of discharge for diabetes. This study concludes that the model could be incorporated in healthcare institutions to witness its effectiveness. This model can be used by physicians to monitor the quality of inpatient care and reduce the readmission rate. Given the significant costs and public awareness of patient readmissions, the suggested readmission prediction model should be of great interest to departments of health in India, health and social services planners, and purchasers and providers of healthcare. The dataset analysed in this study was from a single hospital. This study can be conducted with a larger hospital sample size in rural and urban community settings in multiple states across India. This would allow determining if the readmission factors differ based on patient geographical location or if similar traits are observed nationwide. In addition, this would strengthen both urban and rural models

Figure 7. Depicts the working of proposed algorithm

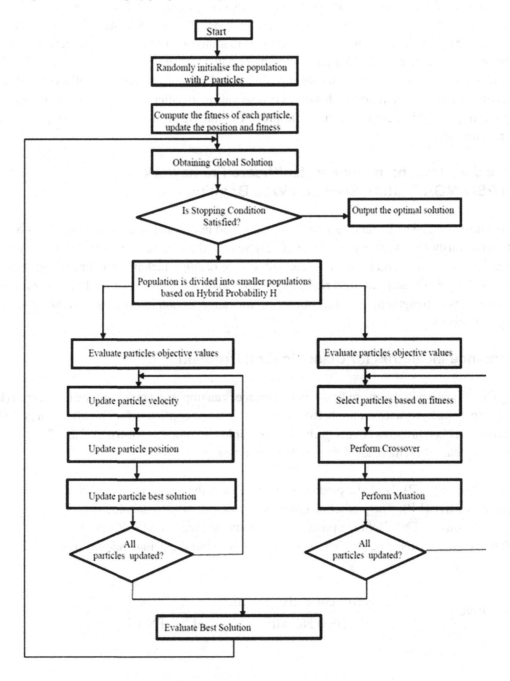

while assessing the importance of age categorization. This research study has only targeted patients with diabetes. Readmission prediction model needs to be generated for other key health conditions also such as Heart disease, Phenomena, kidney disease etc. in Indian Healthcare system. In the future studies, planned and unplanned (emergency) readmissions needs to be considered. Various other key features in the medical records, like family history (to find hereditary information), emotional status (depression), socioeconomic status, and lifestyle habits (exercise), smoking status and season of readmission need to be collected and analysed. It will be interesting to perform a more exhaustive exploration of additional features in the dataset and study their relevance towards predicting the risk of readmission. Living with diabetes is challenging and distressful. Diabetic patient's condition cannot be understood only from his with medical charts. There is a need to collect and analyse both subjective and objective patient information in order to fully understand the occurrence of readmission of patients with diabetes. Subjective data can be captured by interviewing patients or by conducting surveys which will enrich the depth of patient information. The conversation between doctor and patient can also be collected and analysed which could help to extract important features corresponding to patient's willpower and attitude by text-mining techniques. This information might improve the intelligent models to identify patients at high risk of readmission.

Proposed Approach: Intelligent Healthcare Framework Using PSO-MGA Feature Selection With Bagging

Firstly the unstructured and structure dataset is loaded and features are extracted using PSO-MGA, and for extracting further relevant features it iteratively scan and a new dataset with most relevant feature dataset is obtained. After obtaining most relevant feature bagging technique and avoiding overtraining in PSO-MGA hybrid algorithm, thus resolving class imbalance problem of readmission class or non-readmission class, strengthening feature subset optimization to obtain optimized value of feature sets with highest accuracy.

Performance Measures for Classification Problem

Dealing Classification Problem predictive performance is an important task with the F-measure (Babu et al., 2017). So, F-measure used for predictive performance using confusion for classification performance measurement. This represents counts of the four possible outcomes as shown in Table 2.

In a binary classifier, there are four possible outcomes:

- **True Positive (TP):** Both the prediction outcome and the actual value are true.
- **False Positive (FP):** The prediction outcome is true but the actual value is false.
- **True Negative (TN):** Both the prediction outcome and the actual value are false.
- **False Negative (FN):** the prediction outcome is false but the actual value is true.

$$\text{True Positive Rate}(t_p) = \frac{\text{Positive correctly classified}}{\text{Total Negative}} = \frac{TP + TN}{TP + TN + FP + FN} \tag{1}$$

Figure 8. Depict the working of hybrid algorithm

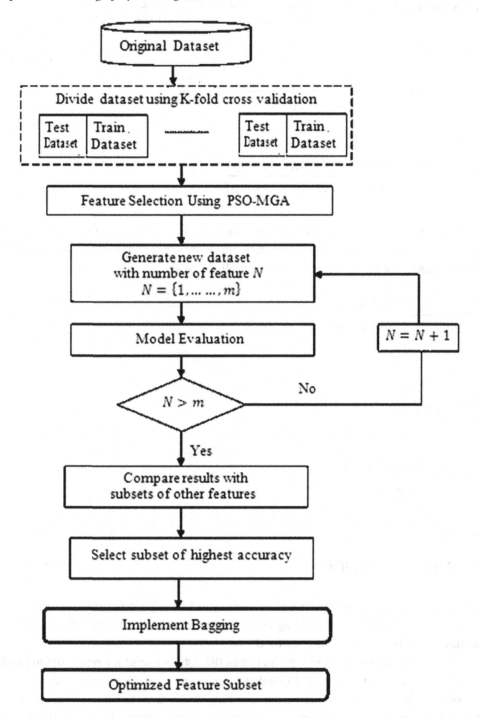

Table 2. Confusion matrix

	Predicted Positive	**Predicted Negative**
Actual Positive	True Positive (TP)	False Negative (FN)
Actual Negative	False Positive (FP)	True Negative (TN)

$$\text{True Negative Rate}(f_p) = \frac{\text{Negative correctly classified}}{\text{Total Negative}} = \frac{FP+FN}{TP+TN+FP+FN} \qquad (2)$$

$$\text{Sensitivity} = \text{recall} = \frac{\text{Total Positive classified}}{\text{Total samples}} = \frac{TP}{TP+FN} \qquad (3)$$

$$\text{Specificity} = \frac{\text{Total Negative classified}}{\text{Total samples}} = \frac{TN}{TP+FN} \qquad$$

F-measure is used for assessing the entire confusion matrix for evaluating a specific classifier as it properly takes into account all true and negative cases for interpretation. The Accuracy of classifiers defined as percentage of positively predicted over all the predicted values.

$$\text{Accuracy} = \frac{TP+TN}{TP+TN+FP+FN} \qquad (4)$$

$$\text{Precision} = \frac{TP}{TP+FP} \qquad (5)$$

$$F-\text{measure} = 2.\frac{\text{Precision.Recall}}{\text{Precision}+\text{Recall}} \qquad (6)$$

RESULT AND DISCUSSION

In this research, comprehensive experiment was conducted for exploring the basic characteristics of this problem; the effect of imbalanced learning and its interactions with data imbalance, type of classifier, input metrics and imbalanced learning method.

Based on above p-values removing imbalance in the data is useful for readmission prediction comparing with usual learning methods and imbalanced learning methods pairwise on the same base classifier, metrics and data sets From this we can compute the difference between predicting defects with and without an imbalanced learner for each data set as follows from the repeated measure design of the experiment in performance without imbalanced learning under differing levels of data imbalance causing negative effect.

Table 3. Feature analysis age on readmission

Feature Name	Total (9476)		Readmitted (1306)		Not Readmitted (10782)		
	Frequency	Percent	Frequency	Percent	Frequency	Percent	*p*-value
Age							
<= 25	32	0.3	5	0.4	27	0.3	
26 – 30	33	0.4	5	0.4	28	0.3	
31 – 35	66	0.7	4	0.3	62	0.8	
36 – 40	93	1	11	0.9	82	1	
41 – 45	252	2.7	37	3.1	215	2.6	
46 – 50	434	4.6	32	2.6	402	4.9	
51 – 55	916	9.8	1	10.7	786	9.6	
56 – 60	19	14	155	12.8	1154	14.1	0.012
61 – 65	1759	18.8	264	21.8	1495	18.3	
66 – 70	1760	18.8	216	17.8	1544	18.9	
71 – 75	1310	14	164	13.5	1146	14	
76 – 80	780	8.3	112	9.2	668	8.2	
81 – 85	447	4.8	56	4.6	391	4.8	
86 – 90	143	1.5	15	1.2	128	1.6	
91+	47	0.5	5	0.4	42	0.5	

Table 4. Feature analysis gender on readmission

Feature Name	Total (9476)		Readmitted (1306)		Not Readmitted (10782)		
	Frequency	Percent	Frequency	Percent	Frequency	Percent	*p*-value
Gender							
Female	3606	38.4	23	34.9	3183	39	.007
Male	5775	61.6	88	65.1	4987	61	

Table 5. Feature analysis admission source on readmission

Feature Name	Total (9476)		Readmitted (1306)		NotReadmitted (10782)		
	Frequency	Percent	Frequency	Percent	Frequency	Percent	*p*-value
Admission Source							
Emergency	3694	39.4	524	43.3	3170	38.8	.003
Planned	5687	60.6	687	56.7	5000	61.2	

Table 6. Feature analysis length of stay in days on readmission

Feature Name	Total (9476)		Readmitted (1306)		Not Readmitted (10782)		p-value
	Frequency	Percent	Frequency	Percent	Frequency	Percent	
Length of Stay in days							
1	1559	16.6	208	17.2	1351	16.5	
2	1509	16.1	176	14.5	1333	16.3	
3	1064	11.3	138	11.4	926	11.3	
4	822	8.8	94	7.8	728	8.9	
5	674	7.2	86	7.1	588	7.2	
6	528	5.6	75	6.2	453	5.5	
7	831	8.9	72	5.9	759	9.3	0.001
8	720	7.7	68	5.6	652	8	
9	373	4	41	3.4	332	4.1	
10	312	3.3	64	5.3	248	3	
11	209	2.2	39	3.2	170	2.1	
12	143	1.5	22	1.8	121	1.5	
13+	637	6.8	128	10.6	509	6.2	

Table 7. Feature analysis length of no. of inpatient visits on readmission

Feature Name	Total (9476)		Readmitted (1306)		Not Readmitted (10782)		p-value
	Frequency	Percent	Frequency	Percent	Frequency	Percent	
No. of Inpatient visits							
0	6928	73.9	676	55.8	6252	76.5	
1	1431	15.3	223	18.4	1208	14.8	
2	492	5.2	109	9	383	4.7	
3	225	2.4	82	6.8	143	1.8	
4	125	1.3	37	3.1	88	1.1	
5	65	0.7	22	1.8	43	0.5	0.001
6	34	0.4	16	1.3	18	0.2	
7	23	0.2	9	0.7	14	0.2	
8	12	0.1	4	0.3	8	0.1	
9	4	0.3	3	0.2	1	0.1	
10+	42	0.4	13	2.5	12	0.1	

Table 8. Feature analysis glucose serum test result visits on readmission

Feature Name	Total (9476)		Readmitted (1306)		Not Readmitted (10782)		
	Frequency	Percent	Frequency	Percent	Frequency	Percent	*p*-value
Glucose serum test result							
>200	845	9	87	7.2	758	9.3	
>300	355	3.3	41	3.4	264	3.2	
Normal	1927	20.5	226	18.7	1701	20.8	.0.17
None	6334	67.2	857	70.8	5447	66.7	

Table 9. Feature analysis HbA1c test result visits on readmission

Feature Name	Total (9476)		Readmitted (1306)		Not Readmitted (10782)		
	Frequency	Percent	Frequency	Percent	Frequency	Percent	*p*-value
HbA1c Test Result							
>6	391	4.2	41	3.4	350	4.3	
>7	1198	12.8	139	11.5	1059	13	
Normal	186	2	28	2.3	158	1.9	0.162
None	7606	81.1	1003	82.8	6603	80.8	

Table 10. Feature analysis HbA1c test result visits on readmission

Feature Name	Total (9476)		Readmitted (1306)		Not Readmitted (10782)		
	Frequency	Percent	Frequency	Percent	Frequency	Percent	*p*-value
Number of Diagnosis							
<= 1	117	1.2	12	1	105	1.3	
2	599	6.4	150	12.4	449	5.5	
3	1591	17	185	15.3	1406	17.2	
4	1207	12.9	135	11.1	1072	13.1	
5	1622	17.4	151	12.5	1479	18.1	
6	1395	14.9	144	11.9	1251	15.3	
7	1038	11.1	122	10.1	916	11.2	0.001
8	720	7.7	114	9.4	606	7.4	
9	445	4.7	73	6	372	4.6	
10	253	2.7	46	3.8	207	2.5	
11	137	1.5	28	2.3	109	1.3	
12	89	0.9	10	0.8	79	1	
13+	160	1.7	41	3.4	119	1.5	

Table 11. Feature analysis number of medications on readmission

Feature Name	Total (9476)		Readmitted (1306)		Not Readmitted (10782)		p-value
	Frequency	Percent	Frequency	Percent	Frequency	Percent	
Number of Medications							
<= 25	1399	14.9	199	16.4	1200	14.7	
26 - 50	26	28	346	25.3	2324	28.4	
51 - 75	1542	16.4	201	16.6	1341	16.4	
76 - 100	965	10.3	141	11.6	824	10.1	
101 - 125	1041	11.1	108	8.9	933	11.4	
126 - 150	685	7.3	76	6.3	609	7.5	0.001
151 - 175	360	3.8	56	4.6	304	3.7	
176 - 200	199	2.1	29	2.4	170	2.1	
201 - 225	137	1.5	19	1.6	118	1.4	
226 - 250	87	0.9	12	1	75	0.9	
251+	336	3.6	64	5.3	272	3.3	

Table 12. Feature analysis No. of lab procedures on readmission

Feature Name	Total (9476)		Readmitted (1306)		Not Readmitted (10782)		p-value
	Frequency	Percent	Frequency	Percent	Frequency	Percent	
No. of Lab procedures							
<= 25	1427	15.2	216	17.8	1306	14.8	
26 – 50	1129	12	122	10.1	1007	12.3	
51 – 75	1286	13.7	131	10.8	1155	14.1	
76 – 100	1248	13.3	110	9.1	1138	13.9	
101 – 125	1099	11.7	111	9.2	988	12.1	
126 – 150	784	8.4	102	8.4	682	8.3	0.001
151 – 175	575	6.1	73	6	502	6.1	
176 – 200	376	4	67	5.5	329	3.8	
201 – 225	293	3.1	46	3.8	247	3	
226 – 250	221	2.4	47	3.9	174	2.1	
251+	943	10.1	186	15.4	757	9.3	

CONCLUSION AND FUTURE WORK

In this research study, the real-world hospital data of beneficiaries under Ayushman Bharat Pradhan Mantri Jan Arogya Yojana (AB-PMJAY) having different comorbidities were analyzed and assessed with the objective to build an intelligent system helps in identification of patients who are prone of being readmitted. Thus among ten crores family approximately fifty crores members beneficiaries, this study classifies the patients into different risk groups of readmission as high, moderate, low, very low after discharge based on patients' characteristics using their previous clinical and lab test data of an Indian Hospital mainly finding patient demographic characteristics diving among clusters of patients suffering from similar illness and then using overlapping method for extracting repeated patients in two clusters using their diagnosis, lab reports, past history, medications used by them for specific period and treatment given to a particular class label admission. So, the prediction of readmissions is studied using different characteristics based on age as senior citizen patients prone to Sugar, Type II diabetes, gender specific, admission source as outdoor or indoor patient, department or medical specialty availed with length of stay and number of in-patient visits, number of lab procedures, number of diagnoses, number of medications, HbA1c test result, Triglycerides test result, Hypertension Glucose serum test result, Fasting Glucose serum test result, Hemoglobin, Creatinine test result, Albumin test result, LDL/HDL ratio, Renal test result, Diabetes medications, Retinopathy, Neuropathy, Diabetic foot, Troponin-I test result, Ketones test result, Clexane test result, Heart Problem, Gastropathy, Obesity, Potassium test result, Amylase test result, Lipase test result. This paper has assessed various feature selection techniques and proposed optimal solution by avoiding recursion in optimal subsets merger thereby avoiding class balancing that hampers accurate results of prediction modeling of readmission for patients. Based on this empirical study in predicting risk of readmission, the hospital readmission expense can significantly reduce which is greatly require for Indian healthcare system, further study can be conducted in rural and urban community settings in multiple states across India by designing a specialized healthcare system as this allows determining various readmission factors differ based on patient geographical location. Moreover, this would strengthen both urban and rural hospitalization based on age categorization with various health conditions also such as Heart disease, kidney disease etc. in emergency readmissions.

REFERENCES

Abdel-Basset, M., Chang, V., & Nabeeh, N. A. (2021). An intelligent framework using disruptive technologies for COVID-19 analysis. *Technological Forecasting and Social Change*, *163*, 163–175. doi:10.1016/j.techfore.2020.120431 PMID:33162617

Abdelrahman, M. (2020). Personality traits, risk perception, and protective behaviors of Arab residents of Qatar during the COVID-19 pandemic. *International Journal of Mental Health and Addiction*, 1–12. PMID:32837433

Babar, M. I., Jehanzeb, M., Ghazali, M., Jawawi, D. N., Sher, F., & Ghayyur, S. A. K. (2016, October). Big data survey in healthcare and a proposal for intelligent data diagnosis framework. In *2016 2nd IEEE International Conference on Computer and Communications (ICCC)*. IEEE Xplore. 10.1109/CompComm.2016.7924654

Babu, S. K., Vasavi, S., & Nagarjuna, K. (2017, January). Framework for Predictive Analytics as a Service using ensemble model. In *2017 IEEE 7th International Advance Computing Conference (IACC)*. IEEE Xplore. 10.1109/IACC.2017.0038

Bossen, C., & Piras, E. M. (2020). Introduction to the Special Issue on Information Infrastructures in Healthcare: Governance, Quality Improvement and Service Efficiency. *Computer Supported Cooperative Work, 29*(4), 381–386. doi:10.100710606-020-09381-1

Cheng, C. H., Kuo, Y. H., & Zhou, Z. (2018). Tracking nosocomial diseases at individual level with a real-time indoor positioning system. *Journal of Medical Systems, 42*(11), 1–21. doi:10.100710916-018-1085-4 PMID:30284042

De Silva, D., Burstein, F., Jelinek, H. F., & Stranieri, A. (2015). Addressing the complexities of big data analytics in healthcare: The diabetes screening case. *AJIS. Australasian Journal of Information Systems, 19*, 99–115. doi:10.3127/ajis.v19i0.1183

Forestiero, A., & Papuzzo, G. (2018, December). Distributed algorithm for big data analytics in healthcare. In *2018 IEEE/WIC/ACM International Conference on Web Intelligence (WI)*. IEEE Computer Society. 10.1109/WI.2018.00015

Galetsi, P., & Katsaliaki, K. (2020). A review of the literature on big data analytics in healthcare. *The Journal of the Operational Research Society, 71*(10), 1511–1529. doi:10.1080/01605682.2019.1630328

Gowsalya, M., Krushitha, K., & Valliyammai, C. (2014, December). Predicting the risk of readmission of diabetic patients using MapReduce. In *2014 Sixth International Conference on Advanced Computing (ICoAC)*. IEEE. 10.1109/ICoAC.2014.7229729

Gravili, G., Benvenuto, M., Avram, A., & Viola, C. (2018). The influence of the Digital Divide on Big Data generation within supply chain management. *International Journal of Logistics Management, 29*(2), 592–628. doi:10.1108/IJLM-06-2017-0175

Jin, Q., Wu, B., Nishimura, S., & Ogihara, A. (2016, August). Ubi-Liven: a human-centric safe and secure framework of ubiquitous living environments for the elderly. In *2016 International Conference on Advanced Cloud and Big Data (CBD)*. IEEE. 10.1109/CBD.2016.059

Kamble, S. S., Gunasekaran, A., Goswami, M., & Manda, J. (2018). A systematic perspective on the applications of big data analytics in healthcare management. *International Journal of Healthcare Management, 12*(3), 226–240. doi:10.1080/20479700.2018.1531606

Khanra, S., Dhir, A., Islam, A. N., & Mäntymäki, M. (2020). Big data analytics in healthcare: A systematic literature review. *Enterprise Information Systems, 14*(7), 878–912. doi:10.1080/17517575.2020.1812005

Ma, X., Wang, Z., Zhou, S., Wen, H., & Zhang, Y. (2018, June). Intelligent healthcare systems assisted by data analytics and mobile computing. In *2018 14th International Wireless Communications & Mobile Computing Conference (IWCMC)* (pp. 1317–1322). IEEE. doi:10.1109/IWCMC.2018.8450377

Moutselos, K., Kyriazis, D., Diamantopoulou, V., & Maglogiannis, I. (2018, December). Trustworthy data processing for health analytics tasks. In *2018 IEEE International Conference on Big Data (Big Data)*. IEEE. 10.1109/BigData.2018.8622449

Navaz, A. N., Serhani, M. A., Al-Qirim, N., & Gergely, M. (2018). Towards an efficient and Energy-Aware mobile big health data architecture. *Computer Methods and Programs in Biomedicine, 166*, 137–154. doi:10.1016/j.cmpb.2018.10.008 PMID:30415713

Sabharwal, S., Gupta, S., & Thirunavukkarasu, K. (2016, April). Insight of big data analytics in healthcare industry. In *2016 International Conference on Computing, Communication and Automation (ICCCA).* IEEE Xplore. 10.1109/CCAA.2016.7813696

Salomi, M., & Balamurugan, S. A. A. (2016). Need, application and characteristics of big data analytics in healthcare—A survey. *Indian Journal of Science and Technology, 9*(16), 1–5. doi:10.17485/ijst/2016/v9i16/87960

Wu, J., Li, H., Liu, L., & Zheng, H. (2017). Adoption of big data and analytics in mobile healthcare market: An economic perspective. *Electronic Commerce Research and Applications, 22*, 24–41. doi:10.1016/j.elerap.2017.02.002

KEY TERMS AND DEFINITIONS

Ayushman Bharat-National Health Protection Mission (AB-NHPM): Ayushman Bharat Yojana (ABY) is a central government-funded free healthcare coverage scheme. The scheme is focused on nearly 11 crore poor and vulnerable families in rural and urban India. It is the largest scheme of its kind in the world. ABY envisions a two-pronged, unified approach by both government and private hospitals, to provide a comprehensive healthcare on primary, secondary and tertiary levels. This is planned to be accomplished through Health and Wellness Centres (HWCs) and Pradhan Mantri Jan Arogya Yojana (PM-JAY).

Deep Learning: Deep learning is a subset of machine learning, which is essentially a neural network with three or more layers. These neural networks attempt to simulate the behavior of the human brain—albeit far from matching its ability—allowing it to "learn" from large amounts of data.

Machine Learning: Machine learning is a tool used in health care to help medical professionals care for patients and manage clinical data. It is an application of artificial intelligence, which involves programming computers to mimic how people think and learn.

Model Testing: In machine learning, model testing is referred to as the process where the performance of a fully trained model is evaluated on a testing set. The testing set consisting of a set of testing samples should be separated from the both training and validation sets, but it should follow the same probability distribution as the training set. Each testing sample has a known value of the target. Based on the comparison of the model's predicted value, and the known target, for each testing sample, the performance of the trained model can be measured. There are a number of statistical metrics that can be used to assess testing results including mean squared errors and receiver operating characteristics curves. The question of which one should be used is largely dependent on the type of models and the type of application. For a regression (Regression Analysis) model, the standard error of estimate is widely used.

Model Validation: It is a phase of machine learning that quantifies the ability of an ML or statistical model to produce predictions or outputs with enough fidelity to be used reliably to achieve business objectives.

Particle Swarm Optimization (PSO): It is an artificial intelligence (AI) technique that can be used to find approximate solutions to extremely difficult or impossible numeric maximization and minimization problems.

Support Vector Machine: A support vector machine (SVM) is a type of deep learning algorithm that performs supervised learning for classification or regression of data groups. In AI and machine learning, supervised learning systems provide both input and desired output data, which are labelled for classification.

Section 4
Artificial Intelligence in
Customer Support

Chapter 15
AI and Machine Learning Applications to Enhance Customer Support

Md Shamim Hossain

 https://orcid.org/0000-0003-1645-7470

Hajee Mohammad Danesh Science and Technology University, Bangladesh

Md. Mahafuzur Rahman

Hajee Mohammad Danesh Science and Technology University, Bangladesh

Abu Eyaz Abresham

Hajee Mohammad Danesh Science and Technology University, Bangladesh

Asif Jaied Pranto

Hajee Mohammad Danesh Science and Technology University, Bangladesh

Md Raisur Rahman

Hajee Mohammad Danesh Science and Technology University, Bangladesh

ABSTRACT

The aim of this study is to investigate the applications of machine learning (ML) and artificial intelligence (AI) techniques in customer support and to make recommendations for future research directions. Based on that, this study analyzed the articles linked to both AI and ML in customer service published on various scientific platforms using a systematic literature review methodology. The findings suggested that different types of AI and ML approaches are helpful for organizations in providing improved customer support and service for different sub-issues in different dimensions (integrated product service offerings, word of mouth, service excellence, and self-service technology) of customer support. The current study also provides businesses with helpful knowledge about how AI and ML technologies may be used to enhance customer service. Practitioners might also get advice from the current study on the need for further crucial measures and improvements.

DOI: 10.4018/978-1-6684-7105-0.ch015

INTRODUCTION

According to Martn et al. (2022), in this digital era, information is constantly received and processed everywhere, from a variety of sources, for a variety of purposes and industries. In this regard, machine learning (ML) and artificial intelligence (AI) are crucial in transforming raw data into usable predictions and recommendations to enhance domains such as corporate operations and citizens' overall lives. When brands combine analytics, artificial intelligence (AI), and machine learning, they are in a much better position to improve customer service at every touchpoint and build satisfying emotional connections (ML).

AI is a discipline of computer science that uses machine learning to swiftly draw conclusions from data patterns, providing computers with a platform to manage vast amounts of data (Hossain and Rahman, 2022). ML, on the other hand, gives computers the ability to learn how to learn by applying self-defining algorithms, as well as respond to desired needs or human behavior. And, without a doubt, these advancements are game changers for modern life and quick business judgments. AI is concerned with constructing intelligent machines that can think and act like humans, according to Haleem et al. (2022). It offers tremendous chances in a variety of businesses. The coming of AI has either worried or fascinated every industry mentioned. AI builds intelligent robots and systems that can think and react in the same way that people do. This technology has been named the "next step" in the industrial revolution. Most of today's problems are thought to be solved by AI and ML.

Machine learning enables systems to automatically learn from experience and improve without the need for explicit programming (Hossain et al., 2022). This may improve brand reputation, customer loyalty, and customer service while freeing up workers to focus on more challenging or valued tasks. A machine-learning model, for example, can be trained on previous client tickets to assist the customer. According to Syed et al. (2022), there are several applications of AI and ML in our daily lives that are growing over time in practically all industries. Self-driving cars, real-time machine translation, smartphones, and self-talking virtual personal assistants like Siri and Alexa, among other things, are instances of AI and ML that are making our lives easier than ever before. Artificial intelligence is employed in a variety of ways in today's culture. because of its adaptability and capacity to efficiently manage complex difficulties in a wide range of fields such as agriculture, e-commerce, navigation, chatbots, marketing, robotics, social media, and so on.

AI comes in a multitude of forms. AI can work alongside human support employees to tackle basic tasks, freeing them up to deal with more complex challenges (Hossain and Rahman, 2022). AI technology such as chatbots can swiftly understand voice triggers and provide relevant information and direction without the need for human workers. Another way AI is being integrated into customer service is through data collection and analysis (Hossain et al., 2022). AI may steer a user down a path that is in accordance with the organization's aims by deploying smart AI, intelligent email marketing, interactive web design, and other digital marketing services. ML, a subset of AI, is concerned with computer programs that retrieve data and utilize it to learn independently, according to Haleem et al. (2022). It gathers information from numerous sources, such as social media accounts, menus, online reviews, and websites. The information is then used by AI to create and deliver content that is relevant to the audience. Businesses may better utilize available data and reach out to potential customers with appealing advertising at more convenient times by incorporating AI into their marketing plan.

The aim of this study is to investigate the application of machine learning (ML) and artificial intelligence (AI) techniques in customer assistance and to make recommendations for future research directions. Therefore, the current study offers theoretical advancements and useful applications. It broadly responds to demands for study that have recently been made in the domain of consumer interaction with cutting-edge technologies, including AI. Thus, the current study is examined and explored using the abductive research methodology, a methodical strategy for developing new theories that draws on a variety of data gathering stages, including both theoretical and empirical research. The study is one of the first in terms of theoretical contributions to advance knowledge of how businesses might offer customer service through the use of AI and ML applications. Our research also contributes to our understanding of how users interact with services that use AI. By highlighting the significance of trust and perceived sacrifice, our proposed conceptual model contributes to a better understanding of AI-enabled customer support. The study's results can help businesses figure out how to use ML and AI to improve customer service.

LITERATURE REVIEW

AI and Machine Language for Customer Support

In order to process and analyze huge data streams and find any useful insights, machine learning is essential. Machine learning in customer service can assist agents with predictive analytics to recognize frequent queries and answers. Even items that an agent might have overlooked in the dialogue can be caught by the technology. Additionally, chatbots and other AI tools can be made to react to a situation based on past outcomes with the aid of machine learning, which will ultimately assist clients in self-serve problem solving. Brands are in a far better position to improve customer service experiences at every touchpoint and forge strong emotional connections by combining analytics, artificial intelligence (AI), and machine learning (ML). According to Dey and Lee (2021), Machine learning (ML) is one of the greatest contributors to this revolution. The task of a software engineer has now transformed from writing thousands of lines of code to training, retraining, testing, and maintaining a learning model. However, it is essential to realize that every advancement of technology comes with surprises and concerns, and AI is no exception. AI revolution is not at its inception any more. However, the means to ensuring safety, transparency, and level of fidelity of AI systems are still unclear.

Supervised learning is the types of machine learning in which machines are trained using well "labelled" training data, and on basis of that data, machines predict the output. The labelled data means some input data is already tagged with the correct output. In the real-world, supervised learning can be used for Risk Assessment, Image classification, Fraud Detection, spam filtering, etc. With the help of supervised learning, the model can predict the output on the basis of prior experiences. In supervised learning, we can have an exact idea about the classes of objects.

Unsupervised learning is a type of machine learning in which models are trained using unlabeled dataset and are allowed to act on that data without any supervision. Unsupervised learning is used for more complex tasks as compared to supervised learning because, in unsupervised learning, we don't have labeled input data. Unsupervised learning is preferable as it is easy to get unlabeled data in comparison to labeled data.

According to Wang and Biljecki (2022), Unsupervised learning (UL) has a successful track record of navigating the complexities of urban environments. As supervised learning's opposite, it finds patterns from inherent data structures without the aid of labels, which is thought to be the secret to producing actual AI-generated judgments. Reinforcement Learning is a feedback-based Machine learning technique in which an agent learns to behave in an environment by performing the actions and seeing the results of actions. For each good action, the agent gets positive feedback, and for each bad action, the agent gets negative feedback or penalty. From the above discussion, we can say that Reinforcement Learning is one of the most interesting and useful parts of Machine learning. In RL, the agent explores the environment by exploring it without any human intervention. It is the main learning algorithm that is used in Artificial Intelligence. But there are some cases where it should not be used, such as if you have enough data to solve the problem, then other ML algorithms can be used more efficiently. The main issue with the RL algorithm is that some of the parameters may affect the speed of the learning, such as delayed feedback. According to Delgado & Oyedele (2022), Reinforcement learning (RL), a machine learning (ML) paradigm, has been viewed as a strategy having the potential to simplify and expand the applicability of robots to many other industries besides the traditional ones, such as automotive and advanced manufacturing. Because RL may be used to teach robot behavior autonomously rather than precisely scripting high-dimensional robot movements step-by-step in a human manner, it is believed to be well-suited for robotic task planning and control. Furthermore, research suggests that by carefully modifying current RL implementations from other domains, RL approaches may be easily transferable to robots.

Machine learning in customer service can assist agents with predictive analytics to recognize frequent queries and answers. Even items that an agent might have overlooked in the dialogue can be caught by the technology. AI and ML and believes that the technologies will continue to grow and become routine across all verticals, with the democratization of analytics enabling data professionals to focus on more complex scenarios and making customer experience personalization the norm.

Current Issues in Providing Customer Support

Integrated Product Service Offering (IPSO)

A Product Service System (PSS), often referred to as an Integrated Product Service Offering (IPSO), is a collection of physical products, services, and systems that have been combined, optimized, and integrated from a life cycle viewpoint in connection to customer value (Nilsson & Lindahl, 2016). Additionally, the IPSO method assists providers in developing an offer that, from a life cycle viewpoint, best matches customer expectations while using the fewest resources and expenses as possible (Lindahl et al., 2014). Service is a key factor driving forece to increase profit, in addition to physical product. Services have grown in importance and played a big role in the significant shift in the global economy over the past few decades. By focusing on service offers, or "servitization," manufacturers improve their ability to compete. A specific research stream under this paradigm brings to mind product service systems (PSS), which combine products and services to provide value to the client (Tenucci & Supino, 2022). Increasing customer happiness, increasing ROI, customers' genuine requirements and demands, the proper product and service recommendations, customer complaint analysis, and developing customer loyalty are the primary challenges enterprises are now facing when implementing IPSO.

Word-of-mouth (WoM)

Information is spread through word of mouth from one person to another. Customer behavior decisions are heavily influenced by word-of-mouth communication (Iyer & Griffin, 2021). Customers who are dissatisfied or frustrated can seriously harm an organization's reputation by speaking poorly about its services to potential clients, yet the organization has no influence over WOM. Customers have several ways to spread their word of mouth in the age of social media and the internet (Hossain and Rahman, 2022). Organizations are currently having a lot of difficulty in the big data era determining the true sentiment of consumers (Hossain and Rahman, 2022), emotions of customers toward organizations, and the rates at which positive and negative emotions spread (Pashchenko et al., 2022). Organizations also struggle to detect negative emotions because they are harmful and spread quickly, as well as the empathy behavior of potential customers towards the online reviews (Hossain and Rahman, 2022).

Service Excellence (SE)

The ability of service providers to continuously meet and, on occasion, even exceed consumers' expectations is referred to as service excellence. Moreover, service excellence is defined as a company's ability to deliver high levels of customer satisfaction while maintaining high levels of service quality (Wirtz, 2019; Zhan et al., 2020). Johnston (2004) claims that service excellence consists of four essential components: keeping the promise, adding a personal touch, going above and above, and effectively handling issues and inquiries. Previous research demonstrates that customer perceptions of value, satisfaction, and intent to return are significantly impacted by the retail brand image (Padma and Wagenseil, 2018). The main challenges businesses face when providing customer support for achieving service excellence include optimizing logistical services, reduce cognitive load, simple customer feedback systems, complexity of the customer experience, handling irate customers, developing live chat systems, customer churn prediction, and challenges integrating various sources of customer data.

Self-Service Technology (SST)

The act of serving oneself, typically when making purchases, is known as self-service. Automated teller machines (ATMs), online banking, mobile scanners, and ticketing machines are just a few examples of self-service technologies (SSTs), which have become a distinct field of study, a source of competitive advantage for service providers, and an essential part of customers' daily lives (Vakulenko et al. 2019). New "elements" in the service industry and service science, like SST, which becomes a new tool for value generation, emerge as a result of new technology entering the market (Hsieh, 2005). SSTs are acknowledged as a source of value for the service provider as well as the customer (Vakulenko et al. 2019). The present challenges for providing good service through SSTs include automating the identification of consumer complaints, optimizing customer interactions, meeting customer expectations, controlling complex industrial processes and decision-making systems, capacity for problem-solving and offering expert support.

Applications of AI and ML in Customer Support

Every business encounter problem, but what matters more is how well they approach finding solutions. Problems with customer service must be resolved because they affect other business sectors. Businesses need to be more client-centered and connect their offerings with those that delight clients by successfully resolving their issues. The management practices of numerous businesses have experienced significant changes as a result of societal growth and the rapid advancement of scientific and technological knowledge (Wang, 2022). Making difficult decisions that either require a lot of manual labor and expense or are either too advanced for traditional programming is where artificial intelligence is very useful (Kler et al., 2022). For instance, artificial intelligence may be used to carry out data and workforce analytics, both of which are crucial components for organizations to work with in order to remain competitive and in a better position. Although the use of artificial intelligence in customer support is still in its early stages due to the ongoing advancement of this technology, businesses are utilizing it to enhance service quality and increase operational effectiveness. AI and ML have numerous applications in business. In order to help organizations better understand how to employ AI and machine learning, we have highlighted various applications in this study.

Customer Sentiment Analysis

According to Park et al. (2021), Machine learning can be used to analyze online reviews to determine customers' opinions of the products. Words used in reviews can convey positive or negative reactions, and grouping reviews might help readers understand the subjects they praise or criticize. Analyzing data to determine consumer sentiment is known as customer sentiment analysis (Hossain and Rahman, 2022a; Hossain and Rahman, 2022b; Hossain et al., 2022a; Hossain et al., 2022b). By taking the time to inquire, solve issues, and share both positive and negative experiences, customers can aid in the growth of a company. User-generated web content is growing as a result of social network users' increased interest in discussing different products and services on social media. Their social media reviews significantly affect customers' capacity to make sensible and ideal decisions when using services or buying goods. The majority of sentiment analysis approaches are based on machine learning and artificial intelligence techniques. Different kinds of sentiment analysis Models for sentiment analysis are created to identify and categorize a range of emotions, such as joy, surprise, interest, sadness, and rage. It is primarily divided into four types:

1. **Fine-Grained:** According to Bian et al. (2022), Fine-grained sentiment analysis often entails a number of core tasks, including sentiment element extraction, aspect-opinion pair (i.e., AOP) identification, and sentiment orientation analysis. The fine-grained type allows you to define the polarity of the text or interaction precisely. Polarity implies sentiments ranging from positive, negative, or neutral to very positive or very negative. Customer reviews and ratings are analyzed under this category. For example, considering the rating 1-10 implies that the rating 1-4 may denote a negative sentiment while a rating 5-10 shows a positive sentiment.

2. **Aspect-Based:** According to Gu et al. (2022), Aspect-based sentiment analysis aims to analyze the sentiment polarity of a given aspect. Aspect-based sentiment analysis goes a step further as it analyzes specific aspects that users discuss about a product, service, or idea. For example, let's say a customer gives a review for a laptop, stating, "The webcam seems to go on and off randomly". In this case, with aspect-based analysis, the laptop manufacturer can understand that the customer has made a 'negative' comment on the 'webcam' component of the laptop.

3. **Emotion Detection:** Emotion detection determines emotions such as joy, sadness, fear, worry, etc. (Hossain and Rahman, 2023). It uses lexicons (set of words and expressions) that identify specific emotions and machine learning-based classifiers. According to Pashchenko et al. (2022), Customers exhibit various emotions for various emotional characteristics, prompting them to assign various stars, As humans express feelings in various ways, ML-based emotion detection is preferred over lexicons. For example: "This phone is just insane". Such a review may confuse the sentiment analysis model as it may evoke two different sentiments. One may be entirely positive, while the

lexicon 'insane' may classify it as one denoting fear or panic. Thus, it may give inaccurate results if only lexicons are used. However, with ML-based detection, such a possibility is avoided.

4. **Intent Analysis:** Consumer intent is an essential variable that businesses must tap into while channeling their efforts to save time and money. Intent analysis helps accomplish this task by identifying user intent–whether the user is interested in purchasing a product or is just browsing the website without any intention of buying one. Consumers intending to buy the product can be tracked down and facilitated with targeted advertisements. Those who do not intend to purchase the product can be left alone, thereby saving the costs, efforts, and resources put into advertising.

AI and ML in Marketing

AI marketing uses artificial intelligence technologies to make automated decisions based on data collection, data analysis, and additional observations of audience or economic trends that may impact marketing efforts (Alarifi et al., 2023). AI is often used in digital marketing efforts where speed is essential. AI marketing tools use data and customer profiles to learn how to best communicate with customers, then serve them tailored messages at the right time without intervention from marketing team members, ensuring maximum efficiency. According to Haleem et al. (2022), the potential of artificial intelligence (AI) in marketing is enormous.AI is altering how businesses and customers communicate with one another. The type of business and the website's functionality have a big impact on how this technology is used (Hossain, 2023; Rahman and Hossain, 2022). Marketers may now give customers more of their attention and respond to their requirements immediately. Thanks to the data gathered and produced by its algorithms, AI enables them to swiftly decide what content to target customers with and which channel to use when.

According to Nan et al. (2022), Marketing refers to the business sales situation that is carried out by a company in response to the market. Marketing strategies in the context of machine learning are studied in the process of building a company for social development. Machine learning is diversified form, collecting data in various sources and forming a huge database. Its capacity is extensive, with different types of information content, carrying a huge amount of information. Machine learning has developed extremely fast in recent years, and its rich information value has led to more and more people to invest in the study of the value of machine learning and apply these technical tools to the development of various product industries. In this competitive and stimulating market environment, which occupies a pivotal position, marketing needs to be given top priority in response to the need to develop and enhance the competitiveness and sustainability of companies. Marketing is characterized by the relationship with customers, to maintain friendly relations to maintain old customers while strengthening the development of new customers. Understand the consumer tendencies of customers and consult their attitudes towards products.

AI Marketing Use Cases Include:

Data Analysis: Collecting and sifting through large amounts of marketing data from various campaigns and programs that would otherwise have to be sorted manually.

Natural Language Processing (NLP): Creating human-like language for content creation, customer service bots, experience personalization and more.

Media Buying: Predicting the most effective ad and media placements for a business in order to reach their target audience and maximize marketing strategy ROI.

Automated Decision-Making: AI marketing tools help a business to decide which marketing or business growth strategy they should use based on past data or outside data inputs.

Content Generation: According to Sharma et al. (2021), Unlike conventional data analytics software, AI can predict client behavior and is always learning from the data it analyzes. This enables businesses to deliver highly relevant content that enhances the consumer experience.

Real-time Personalization: Changing a customer's experience with a marketing asset such as a web page, social post or email to fit the customer's past preference to encourage a certain action such as clicking a link, signing up for something or buying a product.

AI and ML in Automobile Industry

Almost every stage of making a car involves the usage of artificial intelligence. Two examples of AI in the automotive industry are industrial robots constructing cars and autonomous vehicles employing machine learning and vision. AI is being used in the automotive industry to provide users with virtual assistants for better performance. For instance, the intelligent virtual assistant TeslaBot was just unveiled by Tesla. Self-driving cars are actively being developed by many businesses to improve the security and safety of your journey.

According to Kun et al. (2012), As driver aid systems, automotive navigation systems are becoming more common. Vendors continually work to improve route guiding by including new features into their platforms. The Internet of Things and autonomous driving, in particular, have continued to emerge and mature, causing many businesses, including Apple and Google, to start a deep expansion of future automotive technology. Hardware companies like Samsung are also developing components like autonomous driving as a result of the information technology industry's gradual disruption of industries like transportation and logistics. The automotive business has seen technology companies take an unprecedented interest, particularly in the field of automotive intelligence, and their presence has given the traditional automotive industry the impression that disruptive innovation is on the horizon. The coupling of automotive and information technology companies has become a trend, and the entry of large technology companies such as Neusoft and Huawei has made the Internet of Vehicles and the Internet of Things really get off the ground and gradually become a new growth point. Innovative automakers efficiently use data to deliver top-notch products and services. Artificial intelligence will be used by product designers and product development teams to uniquely personalize future car models to users' wants. Artificially intelligent (AI) driven robots help people produce cars by continuously learning skills like manufacturing and design. Additionally, automakers modify cutting-edge technologies in various car models in response to market preferences. In this method, resource utilization is enhanced through the automotive industry's use of machine learning and artificial intelligence. Implementing AI-driven technologies will undoubtedly add tremendous value to cars as time goes on. By utilizing this technology, output will grow, productivity will rise, and unique data will be gathered to create ever innovative driving experiences. AI would also keep transforming the auto sector, creating new opportunities and ensuring a higher rate of return on investment.

AI and ML in E-Commerce

E-commerce, also known as electronic commerce, refers to the exchange of goods and services as well as the transmission of money and data over an electronic network, most commonly the internet. These commercial transactions can be B2B (business-to-business), B2C (business-to-consumer), C2C (consumer to consumer) or C2B. Ecommerce marketing with AI and machine learning in Ecommerce is deriving important user insights from generated customer data based on specific data gathered from each online user. Online retailers use artificial intelligence in the e-commerce industry to provide chatbot services, analyze customer comments, and provide personalized services to online shoppers. Personalization and fraud prevention are the two most important AI applications in e-commerce. Accordiing to Pallathadka et al. (2021), With the main objective of designing standard, dependable product quality control methods and the search for new ways to reach and serve customers while maintaining low cost, AI has been used in the e-commerce and financial industries to achieve better customer experience, efficient supply chain management, improved operational efficiency, and reduced team size. Two of the most popular AI techniques are machine learning and deep learning. These models are used by people, companies, and government organizations to anticipate and learn from data.

1. Personalized Shopping:

According to Liu (2022), The need for information and services changes depending on the circumstances of each user, and those who utilize services that provide individualized information are not just accepted. E-commerce businesses can provide customers with a variety of options and, more crucially, can recommend product information that fits their wants and purchase habits, reducing the time it takes for users to find products that fulfill their demands. Additionally, businesses can leverage the user's personalized information recommendation service based on the user's information preferences and provide users with services that satisfy their wants for customized information. Users can be better served with information resources that fit their needs by studying how they utilize information. In the e-commerce sector, personalization involves modifying the buying experience to take into account each customer's unique demands, preferences, and tastes. Numerous online shops sell tens of thousands of items and receive a sizable number of regular consumers as a result. Large data sets may be processed by computers, allowing for real-time analytics and optimization. Artificial intelligence is used to generate personalized product recommendations that are based on past consumer behavior and lookalike customers. Websites that suggest things you might like based on prior purchases employ machine learning to look at your purchase history.

2. Fraud Prevention:

One of the most common scenarios in e-commerce fraud, called friendly fraud, is perpetrated by customers requesting groundless chargebacks for products they purchased and received. Friendly fraud accounts for up to 40% of the attacks experienced by online sellers. Next on the list, reported by over 30% of surveyed online merchants, are phishing and thieves testing whether stolen credit card numbers work. As the incidence of fraud has increased, fraud scenarios have become more elusive and varied. Every new e-commerce innovation, such as buy now pay later (BNPL) or peer-to-peer (P2P) payments, breeds new fraud scenarios. The diversity and constant evolution of fraud scenarios make them hard to detect with traditional technology and calls for more effective AI-based e-commerce fraud detection solutions.

According to Li (2022), AI technologies have exerted great potential and brought recent changes to the e-commerce industry. Millions of people's identification (ID) cards are stolen every year, but so far, there is no simple way to track down the thieves who stole them. A research team of foreign scholars has proposed a new fraud detection model (FDM) to trace the fraudster online within their few clicks of the mouse. Traditional lie detection includes face-to-face conversation and lie detectors that measure heart rate and skin electrical conduction. However, these methods lack remote control or simultaneous multiple people detection mechanisms. The new invention proposed by Italian researchers is a computer-based remote test method, which can identify fraud by measuring subjects' response time to true and false personal information. However, this method is limited and requires experimental researchers to know the truth before the test can be carried out smoothly. As this research has revealed, AI is constantly transforming the e-Commerce industry. Today, it's impacting how an eCommerce store features and sells products to its customers. By offering a highly personalized shopping experience with the help of virtual buying assistants, AI is improving the online shopping experience for both customers and retailers.

AI and ML in Robotics

A different field within artificial intelligence called robotics is used to research the development of intelligent robots and machines. Robotics, which contain mechanical construction, electrical components, and are programmable with programming languages, combine electrical engineering, mechanical engineering, and computer science and engineering. Despite the fact that robotics and artificial intelligence have distinct goals and uses, most people view robotics as a subset of AI. Robotic devices have a striking resemblance to people in appearance, and if given access to artificial intelligence (AI), they are also capable of performing like humans. According to Huanh et al. (2021), Owing to advances in mechanical engineering and computer science, especially artificial intelligence (AI) technologies, the use of robots has broadened from factories to complex human environments, providing services in numerous sectors. As a disruptive innovation, service robots have permeated hospitality and tourism areas such as hotels, restaurants, airports, museums, and tourist attractions. They perform tasks such as checking in, greeting guests, providing information, showing the way, cleaning, delivering items, cooking food, and maintaining social distance during pandemics. In robotics, artificial intelligence (AI) enables robots to carry out essential jobs with a human-like vision to find or identify distinct objects. Robots are now created using machine learning training. The computer vision model is trained using a vast number of datasets so that robotics can distinguish diverse things and behave in accordance with those recognitions with the desired outcomes.

According to Luo et al. (2021), Recently, information and communication technology has become increasingly important in determining consumer experiences and delivering service products. As numerous hospitality service providers combine human and robotic services, practitioners and academic researchers have become even more interested in how robots and artificial intelligence (AI) can enhance service delivery or consumer experiences. AI in robotics makes such machines more efficient with self-learning ability to recognize the new objects. However, currently, robotics is used at the industrial purpose and in various other fields to perform the various actions with the desired accuracy at higher efficiency, and better than humans. From handling the carton boxes at warehouses, robotics is performing the unbelievable actions making certain tasks easier. Right here we will discuss the application of AI robotics in various fields with types of training data used to train such AI models.

AI and ML in Chatbots

A *chatbot* is software that simulates human-like conversations with users via text messages on chat. According to Bilquise et al. (2022), Conversational technologies are transforming the landscape of human-machine interaction. Chatbots are increasingly being used in several domains to substitute human agents in performing tasks, answering questions, giving advice, and providing social and emotional support. According to Janssen et al. (2022), Due to significant advancements in machine learning (ML) and natural language processing (NLP), which have allowed for new types of chatbots, chatbots have recently grown more and more popular. Many businesses in a variety of industries have adopted chatbots as a result of the hoopla surrounding them, either to demonstrate their technological acumen or to simply provide a new way for customers to communicate with them.

The fastest-growing form of communication across all areas is chatbots. Organizations are making significant investments in this technology due to the numerous advantages of integrating chatbots in service and social disciplines. However, research suggests that people still feel uneasy communicating with chatbots and prefer speaking with a human person. Additionally, a review on the usability and user acceptance of chatbots reveals that consumers like natural communication over interactions that resemble those of machines and think that a human can comprehend them better. The study also shows that a successful integration and adoption of chatbots depends on user pleasure. To give a better experience and encourage consumers to use the technology, it is now imperative to increase user engagement and happiness with chatbot conversations. According to Sun et al. (2018), In the last few years, Artificial Intelligence (AI) and Natural Language Processing (NLP) technologies have been driving the development of chatbots to enable advanced conversational capabilities. Artificial intelligence (AI) and natural language processing (NLP) technologies have fueled the creation of chatbots in recent years, enabling more sophisticated conversational capabilities. In order to improve their performance in natural conversation, chatbots have advanced from employing pattern matching and rule-based models to AI-powered deep learning technologies. The development of chatbots that generate dynamic responses that do not already exist in the database has been made possible by advances in AI and NLP. This makes the discussion feel more natural. However, despite these advances, chatbot responses are frequently monotonous and repeated, which discourages and irritates users. Recent studies have proven that customers still prefer engaging with humans over chatbots despite the prevalence of chatbots in our daily lives. This reluctance is linked to chatbots' weak conversational abilities, which render the interaction artificial and lead to dissatisfaction and a breakdown in communication. Furthermore, if chatbots are given human-like interpersonal traits, end users might be more inclined to engage with them. Conversational agents are still a viable option for lowering operational expenses, despite the limitations of chatbot conversational abilities and high end-user expectations. The need to close the gap between customer expectations and chatbot technology has therefore become paramount for organizations. We selected three studies from around 1050 research articles on chatbots in customer service.

AI and ML in Navigation

The AI gets stronger the more robust the data is. Dynamic routing, a technique that enables AI navigation systems to genuinely predict how traffic will change and how the journey would be disrupted, however, enables this. Drivers and automated vehicles can navigate with caution thanks to dynamic routing. AI is essential for successful and efficient navigation, as well as for making sure the trip from point A to point B is as safe and enjoyable as possible. According to Duffany et al. (2010), GPS navigation systems choose the best route based on a shortest path algorithm by using map data that has been stored. This method is highly effective at getting you where you need to go in a fair amount of time, and it is fault tolerant in that it can immediately reroute in the event of a mistake.

The largest advantage of AI is its capacity to increase productivity and finish difficult jobs that are difficult for people to handle. In terms of navigation, this entails assessing current conditions with the best route recommendation that aids the driver in avoiding traffic and other road hazards. Drivers and automated vehicles can navigate with caution thanks to dynamic routing. However, creating the necessary AI models is not difficult. Data is what makes the distinction. For instance, TomTom needs enormous amounts of visual data to build high-definition maps that show street views. There is also a need for data on the same streets in a variety of environmental and meteorological situations to guarantee the navigation system is responsive. The maps will be more precise the more data there is. A crucial component of maintaining accurate and current digital maps is community involvement. It's imperative that automakers create navigation systems with an integrated community of individuals ready to contribute to the upkeep of accurate maps, or look for such systems. Drivers can post photographs of situations when reality doesn't match what has been recorded, such as road closures or road signs, via an app or interface that allows users to comment. This prompts cartographers to inspect and update the map as necessary.

Consumer mistrust is the obstacle to creating this community, though. Customers are less willing to provide their data as more people become aware that services like online mapping tools can frequently be sponsored by advertisements. How can we believe that these service providers will give us the fastest route when they are actually taking us on a diversion around one of their advertisers? Because of this, automakers must look for a navigation system that is not supported by advertisements.

As our transportation network continues to develop, AI navigation systems are in charge, providing greater responsiveness and precision. However, producers must first make sure a strong framework is in place. The most effective digital maps rely on precise information from numerous reliable sources. To guarantee AI-assisted navigation remains safe and effective, abstraction through AI modeling and crowdsourced maps will lessen the processing strain on systems.

AI and ML in Lifestyle

From voice assistants to smart appliances, artificial intelligence (AI) is all around us, and its influence on our lifestyle and work will continue to rise. Innovation in AI technologies is moving at lightning speed, and it's already being used in our homes and at work to automate a variety of tasks.

Image Recognition: The skill of identifying and analyzing photos to identify objects, places, people, or things viewable in one's natural environment is a subset of computer vision. The main objective is to view the objects similarly to how a human brain would see them. Emerging technologies powered by artificial intelligence (AI) have boosted expectations for patients' therapeutic outcomes, according to Susanto et al. (2022). One of the developments is the use of medical image recognition systems for screening, diagnosing, or classifying sickness risks. The sensitivity and specificity of disease diagnosis could be improved with the use of this technology. All of these things are what image recognition aims to identify and assess before making judgments based on the results. Contrarily, computer vision is a more general term that covers the methods for gathering, evaluating, and processing input from the real world for machines. Similar to how people do it, image recognition looks at each pixel in an image to extract pertinent information. AI cameras that have been educated in computer vision can find and identify a broad variety of objects.

Spam Filter: AI can also detect whether spam poses a hazard from malware. Malware is likely to reach your mailbox because not all spam emails are traps. Each incoming communication is scanned by AI spam filters, which flag any offensive content. With the aid of cognitive learning, it can identify malware warning indicators. Your inbox is immediately reported if a mail containing this harmful program is discovered there, and you are warned not to open it. Spam filtering is still a significant research issue, according to Lourés et al. (2022), since there is a desire and need to shield Internet users from the widespread distribution of garbage content. One of the most effective strategies for spam protection is based on text categorization methods employing ML techniques, despite the fact that various methods have been created to identify spam.

Recommendation System: Based on user data, an AI-powered recommendation system suggests products, services, and information. The user's past, the behaviors of other users who are similar to them, and their preferences, hobbies, and purchasing history are all collected by the recommendation system. AI-based recommender systems are very common and play a significant role in the current digital era. Nowadays, quick recommendations are more prevalent, especially with the practical and time-saving usage of artificial intelligence. They help the buyer quickly decide what they require in order to make a purchase. People become more devoted to the company as a result, and they are more likely to make more purchases there. In the end, these technologies serve as instruments to improve the user experience while increasing corporate productivity. Therefore, it is essential for your business to provide applicable advice if organizations want to maintain market dominance and satisfy customers' needs.

Zhanget et al. (2022) claim that recommender systems offer users individualized service support by anticipating their current preferences for specific products and learning about their past activities. In order to increase prediction accuracy and address data sparsity and cold start issues, recommender systems have naturally included artificial intelligence (AI), notably computational intelligence and machine learning methodologies and algorithms. This position paper thoroughly examines the fundamental methodology and widely used methods in recommender systems, as well as how AI may significantly advance the technological advancement and use of recommender systems.

AI and ML in Fuzzy Logic

A solution to dealing with complicated and changing real-world situations is fuzzy logic. It is employed to deal with a variety of problems, especially those pertaining to the management of intricate industrial processes, decision systems in general, and data compression and resolution. Fuzzy logic bases computing on "degrees of truth" as opposed to the traditional "true or false" (1 or 0) Boolean logic on which the modern computer is based. Fuzzy logic was first introduced in the 1960s by Lotfi Zadeh of the University of California, Berkeley. Kanwal et al. (2022) claim that process modeling, computer vision, deep learning, autonomous control systems, data mining, and data classification can all benefit from the use of fuzzy logic, a human-based reasoning system. A rule-based method for dividing up multidimensional data is fuzzy logic. It outputs precise fuzzy sets from imprecise table data. By classifying associated attributes via multidimensional partitioning, fuzzy classification not only protects privacy but also improves the usefulness of the data. Every hour, more data becomes easily accessible through social networking, claim Howells et al. (2017). Because much of this information relates to consumers' perceptions and attitudes of businesses, business intelligence gatherers in marketing are interested in it for customer relationship management and client retention. It will be possible to design, develop, and build social bots that can employ fuzzy logic and soft computing to analyze user comments in social media networks. With more programming, these social bots could interact with users, and well-designed social bots could disseminate advertising campaigns.

Fuzzy logic and fuzzy inference systems (FISs) have been recognized as suitable techniques for encoding and utilizing the essential cultural, social, and medical knowledge in the automated decision-making of SARs, according to Dell'Anna et al. (2022). In fact, the accessible and pertinent knowledge is frequently represented using linguistic phrases in circumstances that involve social assistance. A modification of classical logic called fuzzy logic takes into consideration the uncertainties that affect consumer judgment. It is widely used to tackle complex problems when the parameters are ambiguous or unclear. Fuzzy logic is used in investment software as well, and it can be used to interpret foggy or muddled trading signals.

AI and ML in Churn Prediction

Churn prediction is the practice of determining which customers, based on their usage of a product, are most likely to depart a company or cancel a service subscription. For many industries, particularly the telecommunications industry, customer churn is a serious problem. When a customer stops using the operator's service, they stop making money. One of the most effective methods to prevent customer turnover is to analyze customer behavior to determine the likelihood of churn. Customers are currently finding it difficult to keep their business in today's competitive markets, according to Mirabdolbaghi et al. (2022). Customer churn is a huge challenge for the sectors as a result. An effective churn prediction system is essential for achieving this. Churn prediction techniques are heavily based on artificial intelligence (AI) categorization algorithms, claim Mirabdolbaghi et al. (2022). High dimensionality and unbalanced datasets present challenges for these classification algorithms, making reliable churn prediction difficult. The amount of data available for research and the dataset's balance or unbalancedness have a significant impact on the effectiveness of several data mining techniques. The adoption of artificial intelligence (AI) and machine learning (ML) technology in recent years has enhanced firm performance, claim Banu et al. (2022). Forecasting customer attrition is a challenging issue in many corporate industries, particularly the telecoms sector. Telecommunications companies have started to build 76 models to reduce customer turnover at an earlier stage because it directly affects a company's overall revenue. Previous studies have shown that ML and AI models are good CCP solutions. Given the significance of managing customer retention in a variety of industries, including telecommunications, banking, insurance, and even online gaming, numerous studies on predicting customer churn and the variables driving it have been conducted. With machine learning and deep analysis for customer churn prediction, a business may increase customer retention rates, cut retention costs, and even protect future revenue from churning clients. A business can stop a lot of customers from leaving by employing customer churn models.

Neural Networks

A neural network is a set of algorithms that attempts to recognize underlying relationships in a batch of data using a technique similar to how the human brain works. According to Balemans et al. (2022), there has been an increase in interest in adapting AI components recently. This requires tailoring the components of an AI application to certain environmental constraints and features. As a result, the viability of pruning algorithms for network subtask specialization is investigated. A pre-trained network must be optimized for a subset of the job for which it was originally trained. This is what network specialization entails. AI and neural networks are increasingly being used in customer support. As a result of the COVID-19 pandemic, artificial intelligence (AI) and neural networks are now being used much more frequently in customer support. AI cannot function unless it is provided with the correct data. Neural networks are one of the most widely used deep learning approaches today. Furthermore, they are a hot topic of debate. Depending on the problems that businesses are aiming to tackle, neural networks are used in a variety of ways. According to Balemans et al. (2022), neural network specialization can be regarded as a sort of transfer learning because we start with a previously trained model and only seek to extract the knowledge required for the specialization. Pruning-based transfer learning has also been studied in the literature.

Natural Language Processing

Natural Language Processing is a type of AI that allows machines to understand and interpret human language rather than just read it (Hossain and Rahman, 2022). Machines can use NLP to understand written or spoken language and execute tasks such as speech recognition, sentiment analysis, and automatic text summarizing. Natural language processing (NLP) is a subfield of computer science that focuses on helping computers understand how humans write and speak. This is a difficult undertaking because of the large amount of unstructured data involved. According to Thessen et al. (2012), thanks to NLP, a computer can read (and presumably "understand") information from texts published in natural language, such as novels. We examine how modern NLP architectures are constructed, including a summary of the Apache Foundation's Unstructured Information Management Architecture, according to Nadkarni et al. (2011), and machine-learning methodologies that are being employed for varied NLP sub-problems.

Expert System

An expert system is a piece of computer software that uses artificial intelligence (AI) techniques to replicate the decision-making and behaviors of a person or group of people with expertise and experience in a specific field. Expert systems are frequently meant to supplement rather than replace human experts (Sahin et al., 2012). According to Aktepe et al. (2015), businesses can continue to operate efficiently as long as their customers are satisfied and loyal. Customer relationship management provides significant benefits to firms, notably in terms of boosting competitiveness. In order to attain these objectives, businesses must first identify and research their clients. In this sense, it is critical to communicate effectively with clients, to be loyal to them, and to be aware of changing market situations. In order to analyze this condition, customer pleasure and loyalty should be reliably measured utilizing a comprehensive technique. Customers are split into four basic categories in this study based on their degrees of satisfaction and loyalty, and they are analyzed using a novel method that employs group-based analysis and criteria. We use classification methods in WEKA programming software and loyalty in an equation modeling (SEM) study with LISREL tools to analyze the influence of each satisfaction and loyalty criterion in a satisfaction-loyalty matrix, bridging the gap between customer satisfaction and loyalty in a post-analysis study. The white goods industry is used to demonstrate how established conceptual understanding may be converted into experimental research. Four customer groups are evaluated using 15 criteria, and 200 consumers are interviewed face-to-face as part of an expert-designed satisfaction-loyalty study. As a result of the research, a strategy for grouping customers and criteria is established, which employs high performance classification approaches and structural models that match well. The findings are also evaluated in light of the techniques' outcomes for developing a tool to improve customer strategy.

It is an e-commerce recommender system that produces acceptable product recommendations, according to Walek and Fajmon (2023). The fuzzy expert system is used to generate the recommended product list after considering the various customer preferences and their online store behavior. The expert system considers several criteria, including the degree of resemblance to previously rated products, the coefficient previously purchased products, and the product's average rating. As a result, based on standard metrics, our proposed approach yields promising results (precision, recall, and F1-measure). The system produced results that exceeded 90%. In addition, as compared to traditional approaches, the technology offers better results. The main contribution is making a detailed hybrid system for making product suggestions in an online store. This system has been tested on a sample of real users and compared to traditional methods and the recommendation module of another online store.

Customer service, according to Andrade and Moazeni (2023), is the public face of a company and is critical to retaining and winning over customers. Self-service contact channels are used by organizations to expedite client interactions and reduce associated operating costs. Interacting with self-service customer care systems, on the other hand, has been identified as one of the most vexing aspects of a bad customer contact experience. Our research backs up the importance of a caller's location and demonstrates that there are considerable regional differences in the number, composition, and directions of important features. Our findings provide managers with a number of valuable insights that can be used to improve the customer contact process. Customized interactive voice response systems, for example, can be constructed using the findings of our feature selection research. Identifying calls that are likely to be transferred at any point might aid in workforce planning and hiring. Furthermore, the transfer rate is an important input variable for many call center management decision-making difficulties.

The fuzzy expert system for prioritizing heterogeneous consumers with different wants is provided in this paper by Mahmoum Gonbadi et al. (2019). It is therefore possible to reduce the average waiting time for a queuing system while increasing customer happiness, which is the cornerstone of all organizations. Every consumer has distinct characteristics and expectations, and each one expects the system to recognize his worth and provide the best service possible. Using a two-stage Mamdani fuzzy inference system, consumers were ranked based on Service Duration, Service Value, Customer Loyalty, Maximum Tolerance, and Waiting Time in this study (FIS).

For this purpose, a fantastic expert system that functions across multiple disciplines was developed. In order to assess and examine the effectiveness of the fuzzy prioritization system, the suggested model is compared to the First-In-First-Out (FIFO) and technique for ordering preferences by similarity to an ideal solution (TOPSIS) approaches for prioritizing consumers (FPS). The results of numerical experiments indicated the effectiveness of the proposed methodology in contrast to these two alternatives.

METHOD OF THE STUDY

The methodology of this study is explored and investigated utilizing abductive research methodology, a systematic approach to creating new theories based on a mix of many stages of the data collection process, including both theoretical and empirical research. The abductive approach was used to find

Figure 1. Number of researches published by different publishers on the application of AI and ML for customer support

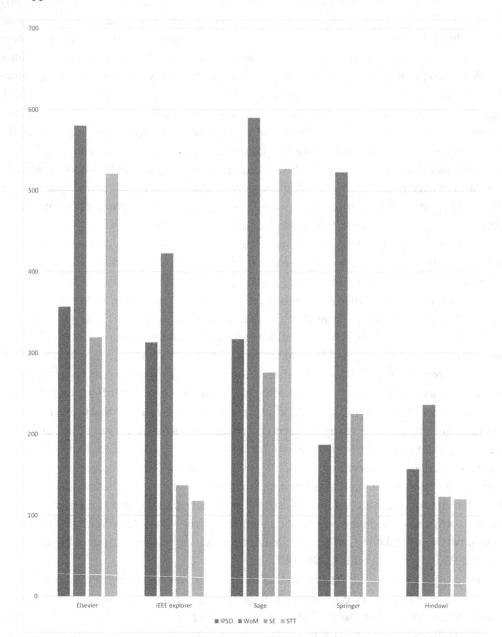

general ideas and principles before performing knowledge about the topic's current condition in order to avoid making assumptions about where the article should begin.

In this study project, a systematic approach is employed to gather data and carry out analysis. To understand the present uses of AI and ML in customer support, the data (published article) for this study was gathered from the Elsevier, IEEE explorer, Sage, Springer and Hindawi online platforms, where the data of customer support in relation to artificial intelligence and machine learning was taken. We specifically look for papers about how AI and ML are used for customer support, particularly in relation to integrated product service offerings (IPSO), word-of-mouth (WoM), service excellence (SE), and self-service technology (SST). We identified a total of 6186 papers; Figure 1 displays the number of studies published by various publishers on the use of AI and ML for various aspects of customer support-related problems.

FINDINGS

Approach to Customer Service Using AI and ML for Sustainable Development

According to the most recent studies (Hossain and Rahman, 2022; Pashchenko et al., 2022), firms could benefit from artificial intelligence and machine learning in a number of ways to improve customer service (presented in Table 1). Our systematic evaluation of the literature indicates that firms may utilize intent analysis methods to improve customer satisfaction, provide real-time personalization, develop customer loyalty, and use intent analysis approaches to forecast consumers' actual needs and desires. Additionally, we found that to offer the proper product and service recommendations, organizations may use content generation, recommendation systems, predictive models, and decision tree approaches; organizations may also use customer complaint prediction to analyze customer complaints.

Additionally, in the digital age, consumers have numerous chances to express themselves freely in any form of digital media, in addition to physically telling. Organizations can use different approaches of AI and ML for analysis of digital word of mouth, such as natural language processing and sentiment analysis for determining the true sentiment of consumers, emotion detection for analyzing the emotions of customers toward organizations, natural language processing and sentiment analysis to know the rates at which positive and negative emotions spread, natural language processing and emotion detection for detecting negative emotions because they are harmful and spread quickly, and customers' empathy behavior detection for detecting the empathy behavior of potential customers towards the online reviews.

Every organization wants to achieve service excellence. According to the prior studies, organizations may use different approaches of AI and ML to support customers to achieve service excellence, such as AI navigation systems for optimizing logistical services, data scraping and data extraction for minimizing the difficulty of unifying different sources of customer data, data analytics for optimizing logistic services, chatbots for developing easy and simple customer feedback systems, and reinforcement learning for reducing the complexity of the customer experience. Sentiment analysis, complaint prediction, managing complaints for handling irate customers, Cognitive systems and decision trees for reducing cognitive load, chatbots for developing live chat systems, and churn prediction for customer churn rate detection

Finally, to develop effective SSTs, organizations may use different approaches of AI and ML to support customers; for example, customer complaint classification for automating the identification of consumer complaints towards products and services, neural networks and chatbot for 24/7 customer support, intelligent optimization techniques and robotics for optimizing customer interactions, automotive navigation systems, personalized shopping, expert systems, and chatbots for better meeting customer expectations, Fuzzy logic and expert systems for controlling complex industrial processes and decision-making systems, Chatbots, decision trees, and neural networks for increasing the capacity for problem-solving, an expert system, and robotics for offering effective expert support

Table 1. Current issues in customer support and potential solutions using AI and ML

Areas of Customer Support	Current Issues	Solutions Through AI and ML
Integrated Product Service Offering (IPSO)	Increasing customer happiness	(i) Intent analysis
	Customers' genuine requirements and demands	(i) Real-time Personalization (ii) Intent analysis
	The proper product and service recommendations	(i) Content Generation (ii) Recommendation System (iii) Predictive models (iv) Decision tree
	Customer complaint analysis	(i) Customer complaint prediction
	Increasing ROI	(i) Media Buying
	Developing customer loyalty	(i) Intent analysis
Word-of-mouth (WoM)	Determining the true sentiment of consumers	(i) Natural Language Processing (ii) Sentiment analysis
	Emotions of customers toward organizations	(i) Emotion detection
	The rates at which positive and negative emotions spread	(i) Natural Language Processing (ii) Sentiment analysis
	Detect negative emotions because they are harmful and spread quickly	(i) Natural Language Processing (ii) Emotion detection
	Empathy behavior of potential customers towards the online reviews	(i) Customers' empathy behavior detection
Service excellence (SE)	optimizing logistical services	(i) AI navigation systems
	Difficulty of unifying different sources of customer data	(i) Data scraping (ii) Data extraction
	Optimizing logistic service	(i) Data Analytics
	simple customer feedback systems	(i) Chatbot
	complexity of the customer experience	(i) Reinforcement Learning
	Handling irate customers	(i) Sentiment analysis (ii) Complaint prediction (iii) Managing complaints
	Reduce cognitive load	(i) Cognitive system (ii) Decision tree
	Developing live chat systems	(i) Chatbot
	customer churn prediction	(ii) Churn prediction
SST	automating the identification of consumer complaints	(i) Customer complain classification
	24/7 Customer Support	(i) Neural networks (ii) Chatbot
	Optimizing customer interactions	(i) Intelligent optimization techniques (ii) Robotics
	Meeting customer expectations	(i) Automotive navigation systems (ii) Personalized Shopping (iii) Expert system (iv) Chatbots
	controlling complex industrial processes and decision-making systems	(i) Fuzzy logic (ii) Expert system
	Capacity for problem-solving	(i) Chatbot (ii) Decision tree (iii) Neural networks
	offering expert support	(i) Expert system (ii) Robotics

CONCLUSION

Artificial intelligence is currently widely used in customer service and is popular among the general public. Artificial intelligence customer service is currently universally accepted by consumers since it can provide customer help around the clock, has more unbiased and objective perspectives, and represents future development patterns. Customers' aversion to AI customer service is mostly owing to the fact that its quality, notably in the targeted, effective, and seamless parts, is significantly worse than that of manual customer service. Furthermore, if artificial intelligence customer service is unable to meet consumer demand, it is difficult to smoothly combine real-human customer service.

In this study, we evaluated the use of machine learning (ML) and artificial intelligence (AI) approaches in customer service and gave recommendations for future research initiatives. Based on that, this study used a systematic literature review methodology to assess publications related to both AI and ML in customer service published on multiple scientific platforms. Our findings revealed that different forms of AI and ML techniques can assist firms in improving customer support and service for distinct sub-issues of multiple customer support dimensions (integrated product and service offerings, word of mouth, service excellence, and self-service technology). As a result, we hope that our study will serve as a model for future research to advance understanding of AI and machine learning in customer support. It also identifies emerging themes that have the potential to make important theoretical and empirical contributions to the field of customer support and beyond.

Applications

Numerous theoretical and real-world applications stem from our study. First, as part of the study's essential theoretical applications, we conceptually created the various customer support dimensions in the modern era where massive amounts of data are being produced at a quick rate. Second, diverse features of the various dimensions of customer support are developed in the current study, which must make a significant contribution to the theories of online marketing, AI, and ML-based business fields, particularly marketing. Third, the study makes significant additions to the literature on customer services, consumer behavior, and AI and ML by categorizing several aspects of different customer support dimensions and offering various AI and ML methodologies under various aspects. Finally, based on our findings, businesses will be able to use the best kinds of AL and ML techniques to improve customer support and service.

Limitations and Future Research Directions

There are some limitations to our findings that should be taken into account in follow-up research. Our study focused exclusively on customer support provided by AI and machine learning. Therefore, by taking a wider view in future research, the outcomes might be enhanced. enhance customer service provided by artificial intelligence in all areas. While consumers' reluctance to artificial intelligence customer service is primarily due to the fact that it is currently of a lower caliber than traditional real-human customer service, they do not currently feel hostile toward the technology itself. As a result, there is a constant need for the sector to advance relevant technology completely and raise the standard of its services.

REFERENCES

Aktepe, A., Ersöz, S., & Toklu, B. (2015). Customer satisfaction and loyalty analysis with classification algorithms and Structural Equation Modeling. *Computers & Industrial Engineering*, *86*, 95–106. doi:10.1016/j.cie.2014.09.031

Alarifi, G., Rahman, M. F., & Hossain, M. S. (2023). Prediction and Analysis of Customer Complaints Using Machine Learning Techniques. [IJEBR]. *International Journal of E-Business Research*, *19*(1), 1–25. doi:10.4018/IJEBR.319716

Andrade, R., & Moazeni, S. (2023). Transfer rate prediction at self-service customer support platforms in insurance contact centers. *Expert Systems with Applications*, *212*, 118701. doi:10.1016/j.eswa.2022.118701

Balemans, D., Reiter, P., Steckel, J., & Hellinckx, P. (2022). Resource efficient AI: Exploring neural network pruning for task specialization. *Internet of Things*, *20*, 100599. doi:10.1016/j.iot.2022.100599

Balli, C., Guzel, M. S., Bostanci, E., & Mishra, A. (2022). Sentimental Analysis of Twitter Users from Turkish Content with Natural Language Processing. *Computational Intelligence and Neuroscience*, *20*(22), 23–45. doi:10.1155/2022/2455160 PMID:35432519

Bian, Y., Ye, R., Zhang, J., & Yan, X. (2022). Customer preference identification from hotel online reviews: A neural network based fine-grained sentiment analysis. *Computers & Industrial Engineering*, *172*, 108648. doi:10.1016/j.cie.2022.108648

Bilquise, G., Ibrahim, S., & Shaalan, K. (2022). Emotionally Intelligent Chatbots: A Systematic Literature Review. *Human Behavior and Emerging Technologies*, *2022*, 1–23. Advance online publication. doi:10.1155/2022/9601630

Delgado, J. M. D., & Oyedele, L. (2022). Robotics in construction: A critical review of the reinforcement learning and imitation learning paradigms. *Advanced Engineering Informatics*, *54*, 101787. doi:10.1016/j.aei.2022.101787

Dell'Anna, D., & Jamshidnejad, A. (2022). Evolving Fuzzy logic Systems for creative personalized Socially Assistive Robots. *Engineering Applications of Artificial Intelligence*, *114*, 105064. doi:10.1016/j.engappai.2022.105064

Dey, S., & Lee, S. W. (2021). Multilayered review of safety approaches for machine learning-based systems in the days of AI. *Journal of Systems and Software*, *176*, 110941. doi:10.1016/j.jss.2021.110941

Duffany, J. L. (2010, October). Artificial intelligence in GPS navigation systems. In *2010 2nd International Conference on Software Technology and Engineering* (Vol. 1, pp. V1-382). IEEE. 10.1109/ICSTE.2010.5608862

Faritha Banu, J., Neelakandan, S., Geetha, B. T., Selvalakshmi, V., Umadevi, A., & Martinson, E. O. (2022). Artificial Intelligence Based Customer Churn Prediction Model for Business Markets. *Computational Intelligence and Neuroscience*, *2022*, 1–14. Advance online publication. doi:10.1155/2022/1703696 PMID:36238670

Gu, T., Zhao, H., He, Z., Li, M., & Ying, D. (2022). Integrating external knowledge into aspect-based sentiment analysis using graph neural network. *Knowledge-Based Systems*, *110025*. Advance online publication. doi:10.1016/j.knosys.2022.110025

Haleem, A., Javaid, M., Qadri, M. A., Singh, R. P., & Suman, R. (2022). Artificial intelligence (AI) applications for marketing: A literature-based study. *International Journal of Intelligent Networks*. doi:10.1016/j.ijin.2022.08.005

Hossain, M. S., & Rahman, M. F. (2022a). Machine Learning and Artificial Intelligence: The New Move for Marketers. In J. Kaur, P. Jindal, & A. Singh (Eds.), *Developing Relationships, Personalization, and Data Herald in Marketing 5.0* (pp. 215–241). IGI Global., doi:10.4018/978-1-6684-4496-2.ch014

Hossain, M. S., & Rahman, M. F. (2022b). Sentiment Analysis and Review Rating Prediction of the Users of Bangladeshi Shopping Apps. In J. Kaur, P. Jindal, & A. Singh (Eds.), *Developing Relationships, Personalization, and Data Herald in Marketing 5.0* (pp. 33–56). IGI Global., doi:10.4018/978-1-6684-4496-2.ch002

Hossain, M. S., Rahman, M. F., & Uddin, M. K. (2022a). Analyzing and Predicting Learners' Sentiment toward Specialty schools using Machine Learning Techniques. In G. Trajkovski, M. Demeter, & H. Hayes (Eds.), *Applying Data Science and Learning Analytics Throughout a Learner's Lifespan*. IGI Global., doi:10.4018/978-1-7998-9644-9.ch007

Hossain, M. S., Uddin, M. K., Hossain, M. K., & Rahman, M. F. (2022b). User sentiment analysis and review rating prediction for the Blended Learning Platform app. In G. Trajkovski, M. Demeter, & H. Hayes (Eds.), *Applying Data Science and Learning Analytics Throughout a Learner's Lifespan*. IGI Global., doi:10.4018/978-1-7998-9644-9.ch006

Hossain, M. S., & Rahman, M. F. (2022). Detection of potential customers' empathy behavior towards customers' reviews. *Journal of Retailing and Consumer Services*, *65*, 102881. doi:10.1016/j.jretconser.2021.102881

Hossain, M. S., Rahman, M. F., Uddin, M. K., & Hossain, M. K. (2022). Customer sentiment analysis and prediction of halal restaurants using machine learning approaches. *Journal of Islamic Marketing*. Advance online publication. doi:10.1108/JIMA-04-2021-0125

Hossain, M. S., & Rahman, M. F. (2023). Detection of readers' emotional aspects and thumbs-up empathy reactions towards reviews of online travel agency apps, Journal of Hospitality and Tourism Insights. https://doi.org/10.1108/JHTI-10-2022-0487

Hossain, M. S. (2023). Behavioral Analytics of Consumer Complaints. In S. Nagaraj & K. Kumar (Eds.), *AI-Driven Intelligent Models for Business Excellence* (pp. 42–67). IGI Global., doi:10.4018/978-1-6684-4246-3.ch003

Howells, K., & Ertugan, A. (2017). Applying fuzzy logic for sentiment analysis of social media network data in marketing. *Procedia Computer Science*, *120*, 664–670. doi:10.1016/j.procs.2017.11.293

Huang, D., Chen, Q., Huang, J., Kong, S., & Li, Z. (2021). Customer-robot interactions: Understanding customer experience with service robots. *International Journal of Hospitality Management*, *99*, 103078. doi:10.1016/j.ijhm.2021.103078

Iyer, R., & Griffin, M. (2021). Modeling word-of-mouth usage: A replication. *Journal of Business Research, 126*, 512–523. doi:10.1016/j.jbusres.2019.12.027

Janssen, A., Cardona, D. R., Passlick, J., & Breitner, M. H. (2022). How to Make chatbots productive–A user-oriented implementation framework. *International Journal of Human-Computer Studies, 168*, 102921. doi:10.1016/j.ijhcs.2022.102921

Jin, P., Li, F., Li, X., Liu, Q., Liu, K., Ma, H., Dong, P., & Tang, S. (2022). Temporal Relation Extraction with Joint Semantic and Syntactic Attention. Computational Intelligence and Neuroscience. doi:10.1155/2022/5680971

Johnston, R. (2004). Towards a better understanding of service excellence. *Managing Service Quality, 14*(2/3), 129–133. doi:10.1108/09604520410528554

Kanwal, T., Attaullah, H., Anjum, A., Khan, A., & Jeon, G. (2022). *Fuzz-classification (p, l)-Angel: An enhanced hybrid artificial intelligence based fuzzy logic for multiple sensitive attributes against privacy breaches.* Digital Communications and Networks., doi:10.1016/j.dcan.2022.09.025

Kler, R., Elkady, G., Rane, K., Singh, A., Hossain, M. S., Malhotra, D., Ray, S., & Bhatia, K. K. (2022). Machine Learning and Artificial Intelligence in the Food Industry: A Sustainable Approach. *Journal of Food Quality, 2022*, 1–9. doi:10.1155/2022/8521236

Kun, A. L., Schmidt, A., Dey, A., & Boll, S. (2013). Automotive user interfaces and interactive applications in the car. *Personal and Ubiquitous Computing, 17*(5), 801–802. doi:10.100700779-012-0520-7

Li, J. (2022). E-Commerce Fraud Detection Model by Computer Artificial Intelligence Data Mining. *Computational Intelligence and Neuroscience, 2022*, 1–9. Advance online publication. doi:10.1155/2022/8783783 PMID:35586101

Lindahl, M., Sakao, T., & Carlsson, E. (2014). Actor's and system maps for Integrated Product Service Offerings - Practical experience from two companies. In *Procedia CIRP* (Vol. 16, pp. 320–325). Elsevier. doi:10.1016/j.procir.2014.01.030

Liu, L. (2022). e-Commerce Personalized Recommendation Based on Machine Learning Technology. *Mobile Information Systems, 2022*, 1–11. Advance online publication. doi:10.1155/2022/1761579

Luo, J. M., Vu, H. Q., Li, G., & Law, R. (2021). Understanding service attributes of robot hotels: A sentiment analysis of customer online reviews. *International Journal of Hospitality Management, 98*, 103032. doi:10.1016/j.ijhm.2021.103032

Lv, X., Zhang, G., Liu, J., & Li, J. (2022). The Innovation Ecological Model of Chinese Automotive Industry Based on Artificial Intelligence and Big Data Technology. *Mathematical Problems in Engineering, 2022*, 2022. doi:10.1155/2022/4328187

MahmoumGonbadi, A., Katebi, Y., & Doniavi, A. (2019). A generic two-stage fuzzy inference system for dynamic prioritization of customers. *Expert Systems with Applications, 131*, 240–253. doi:10.1016/j.eswa.2019.04.059

Martín, C., Langendoerfer, P., Zarrin, P. S., Díaz, M., & Rubio, B. (2022). Kafka-ML: Connecting the data stream with ML/AI frameworks. *Future Generation Computer Systems*, *126*, 15–33. doi:10.1016/j. future.2021.07.037

Nadkarni, P. M., Ohno-Machado, L., & Chapman, W. W. (2011). Natural language processing: An introduction. *Journal of the American Medical Informatics Association*, *18*(5), 544–551. doi:10.1136/ amiajnl-2011-000464 PMID:21846786

Nan, H., & Hu, M. (2022). Corporate Marketing Strategy Analysis with Machine Learning Algorithms. *Wireless Communications and Mobile Computing*, *2022*, 1–13. Advance online publication. doi:10.1155/2022/9450020

Nilsson, S., & Lindahl, M. (2016). A Literature Review to Understand the Requirements Specification's Role when Developing Integrated Product Service Offerings. In *Procedia CIRP* (Vol. 47, pp. 150–155). Elsevier B.V. doi:10.1016/j.procir.2016.03.225

Novo-Lourés, M., Ruano-Ordás, D., Pavón, R., Laza, R., Gómez-Meire, S., & Méndez, J. R. (2022). Enhancing representation in the context of multiple-channel spam filtering. *Information Processing & Management*, *59*(2), 102812. doi:10.1016/j.ipm.2021.102812

Padma, P., & Wagenseil, U. (2018). Retail service excellence: Antecedents and consequences. *International Journal of Retail & Distribution Management*, *46*(5), 422–441. doi:10.1108/IJRDM-09-2017-0189

Pallathadka, H., Ramirez-Asis, E. H., Loli-Poma, T. P., Kaliyaperumal, K., Ventayen, R. J. M., & Naved, M. (2021). Applications of artificial intelligence in business management, e-commerce and finance. *Materials Today: Proceedings*. Advance online publication. doi:10.1016/j.matpr.2021.06.419

Park, S., Cho, J., Park, K., & Shin, H. (2021). Customer sentiment analysis with more sensibility. *Engineering Applications of Artificial Intelligence*, *104*, 104356. doi:10.1016/j.engappai.2021.104356

Pashchenko, Y., Rahman, M. F., Hossain, M. S., Uddin, M. K., & Islam, T. (2022). Emotional and the normative aspects of customers' reviews. *Journal of Retailing and Consumer Services*, *68*, 103011. doi:10.1016/j.jretconser.2022.103011

Rahman, M. F., & Hossain, M. S. (2022). The impact of website quality on online compulsive buying behavior: Evidence from online shopping organizations. *South Asian Journal of Marketing*, *4*(1), 1–16. doi:10.1108/SAJM-03-2021-0038

Sahin, S., Tolun, M. R., & Hassanpour, R. (2012). Hybrid expert systems: A survey of current approaches and applications. *Expert Systems with Applications*, *39*(4), 4609–4617. doi:10.1016/j.eswa.2011.08.130

Sharma, R., Kumar, A., & Chuah, C. (2021). Turning the blackbox into a glassbox: An explainable machine learning approach for understanding hospitality customer. *International Journal of Information Management Data Insights*, *1*(2), 100050. doi:10.1016/j.jjimei.2021.100050

Sina Mirabdolbaghi, S. M., & Amiri, B. (2022). Model Optimization Analysis of Customer Churn Prediction Using Machine Learning Algorithms with Focus on Feature Reductions. *Discrete Dynamics in Nature and Society*, *2022*, 1–20. Advance online publication. doi:10.1155/2022/5134356

Sun, X., Chen, X., Pei, Z., & Ren, F. (2018, May). Emotional human machine conversation generation based on SeqGAN. In *2018 First Asian Conference on Affective Computing and Intelligent Interaction (ACII Asia)* (pp. 1-6). IEEE. 10.1109/ACIIAsia.2018.8470388

Susanto, A. P., Winarto, H., Fahira, A., Abdurrohman, H., Muharram, A. P., Widitha, U. R., Warman Efirianti, G. E., Eduard George, Y. A., & Tjoa, K. (2022). Building an artificial intelligence-powered medical image recognition smartphone application: What medical practitioners need to know. *Informatics in Medicine Unlocked, 101017*. Advance online publication. doi:10.1016/j.imu.2022.101017

Syed, F. I., AlShamsi, A., Dahaghi, A. K., & Neghabhan, S. (2020). *Application of ML & AI to model petrophysical and geo-mechanical properties of shale reservoirs–A systematic literature review.* Petroleum. doi:10.1016/j.petlm.2020.12.001

Tenucci, A., & Supino, E. (2020). Exploring the relationship between product-service system and profitability. *The Journal of Management and Governance, 24*(3), 563–585. doi:10.100710997-019-09490-0

Thessen, A. E., Cui, H., & Mozzherin, D. (2012). Applications of natural language processing in biodiversity science. *Advances in Bioinformatics, 2012*, 1–17. Advance online publication. doi:10.1155/2012/391574 PMID:22685456

Vakulenko, Y., Oghazi, P., & Hellström, D. (2019). Innovative framework for self-service kiosks: Integrating customer value knowledge. *Journal of Innovation and Knowledge, 4*(4), 262–268. doi:10.1016/j.jik.2019.06.001

Walek, B., & Fajmon, P. (2023). A hybrid recommender system for an online store using a fuzzy expert system. *Expert Systems with Applications, 212*, 118565. doi:10.1016/j.eswa.2022.118565

Wang, J., & Biljecki, F. (2022). Unsupervised machine learning in urban studies: A systematic review of applications. *Cities (London, England), 129*, 103925. doi:10.1016/j.cities.2022.103925

Wang, N. (2022). Application of DASH client optimization and artificial intelligence in the management and operation of big data tourism hotels. *Alexandria Engineering Journal, 61*(1), 81–90. doi:10.1016/j.aej.2021.04.080

Wirtz, J. (2019, June 15). Cost-effective service excellence in healthcare. *AMS Review.* doi:10.1007/s13162-019-00139-7

Zhan, X., Mu, Y., Hora, M., & Singhal, V. R. (2020). Service excellence and market value of a firm: An empirical investigation of winning service awards and stock market reaction. *International Journal of Production Research*, 1–17. doi:10.1080/00207543.2020.1759837

Zhang, Q., Lu, J., & Jin, Y. (2021). Artificial intelligence in recommender systems. *Complex & Intelligent Systems, 7*(1), 439–457. doi:10.100740747-020-00212-w

Chapter 16
Customer Face–Detecting Artificial Intelligence With People Search Social Site Algorithm for Product Encroachment in Supermarkets:
Business Development With Customer Perspective AI Technology

Napoleon D.
Bharathiar University, India

Gopal R.
Bharathiar University, India

ABSTRACT

This chapter explores the use of an artificial intelligence system-based product suggestion in supermarkets. This is a great way for supermarkets to increase their sales and profitability. The proposed preprocess is to take a picture of the customer at the entrance, and the AI algorithm does the facial recognition with people search in the social sites like Facebook, Amazon, Flipkart, etc. Thus, the result of the search will be classified as what the customer has recently searched for and what his or her favorite and frequent shopping items are get popped up as results. Supermarkets will hold a display board using that system and will automatically do a price slash for the customers' products, which are extracted from their social site data. This helps customers and supermarkets using this technology increase the sales, and the customers will have an opportunity to get preferred goods at a discounted price.

DOI: 10.4018/978-1-6684-7105-0.ch016

INTRODUCTION

Though the world is at our hands to buy anything people love to do shopping in supermarkets. AI and Machine Learning are the new technologies that have been changing the way we do customer support. AI and ML are used in customer support for a variety of purposes like call routing, chat bot management, and analytics. AI is also being used in analytics to provide insights on customer satisfaction, sentiment analysis, and predictive analytics. Thus, the supermarkets also still increasing and warming up their customers till date, Supermarkets are the large shops which holds the all-necessary goods of the people and there will be a security camera at the entrance itself. The use of Artificial Intelligence in customer support and analytics is a trend that is only growing (P Xu et al., 2013). The first use cases for AI in customer support and analytics were developed in the early 2000s. This happened by applying machine learning algorithms to help identify patterns that could be used to improve customer service and generate more accurate predictions.

AI has been used in Customer Support since the 1960s when it was first used as a means of automated call routing. In recent years, AI has been applied to provide more personalized customer service. This is done by analyzing data gathered from previous interactions with customers, their social media profiles, and other sources of data such as weather forecasts. AI is a tool, not a goal. It's a way to make our lives easier, but it's not the end-all-be-all of everything. AI is already being used by customer support and analytics teams in some companies to help them with their work. For example, AI can be used for chat bots that answer customer queries or for predictive analytics tools that can help you with business development. However, we should not see AI as the only solution to all of our problems. The use of Artificial Intelligence System based Product suggestion in Supermarkets is to help the customers to find the products they are looking for. The AI system provides an interactive shopping experience for the customers by suggesting products that are relevant to them based on their previous purchases. The increasing adoption of AI technology in the business world is changing the way companies do business. Businesses are now using customer perspective AI technology to understand their customers and develop products that will be a better fit for them. The information gathered through customer perspective AI technology helps businesses to understand what customers want, how they want it, and when they want it. This information can then be used to create a product that will be a better fit for the customer and help them stay loyal to the company. The customer perspective AI technology has a significant impact on the business development. It is used to identify customer preferred products and generate discount suggestions or combo offers. In the near future, AI will be able to take care of a lot of tasks that are currently handled by humans.

The role of technology in supermarkets. We will be looking at how it has been used to increase sales and customer satisfaction. Technology has been a huge part of the retail industry for quite some time now. From online shopping to apps that help you find your nearest supermarket, it is everywhere. But the use of technology in supermarkets is not just limited to finding them or checking what items are on sale today. In fact, there are many ways that it can be used to make your shopping experience easier and more enjoyable. One way that tech can help is by making sure that you always have everything you need when you get there. For example, if you have an app that tells you what items are on sale at your local store, then this could potentially (Lei Zhicheng et al., 2020). With the help of technology, supermarkets are able to provide better customer service and focus on providing fresh food. The customer experience has changed tremendously in supermarkets. With the help of technology, they are now able to provide customers with a more personalized shopping experience. For example, some supermarkets have implemented self-checkout points for customers that want to avoid the long queues at checkouts. This way, customers can scan their own items and pay for them without having to wait in line. The supermarket is one of the most important places for the customer to make their purchases. The store needs to be attractive, well-lit and clean. The store should also have a good variety of products so customers can find what they want. In this section, we will talk about how technology has been used in supermarkets to increase sales and improve customer satisfaction.

This system also helps store managers and consumers by providing a more efficient way of finding products. Store managers can focus on other tasks while letting the AI system do its job, while consumers can enjoy a more interactive shopping experience. The idea of Artificial Intelligence Systems based Product suggestion in Supermarkets is not a new one. It has been in the market for a while and is still being developed. The idea, when executed successfully, will be a great help to all the shoppers who visit supermarkets. The system will be able to provide an intelligent product suggestion based on the customer's previous purchase history. This will help customers find the right product they are looking for without having to search through products that they are not interested in or don't need. In this Chapter, the use of Artificial Intelligence System based Product suggestion in Supermarkets. Supermarkets are increasing their productivity by using AI-based product suggestions. This is done by analyzing the customer's previous purchase history and predicting what they might buy next. The supermarket could also use this data to suggest other products that customers might like based on their past purchase history. The AI system can also be used for inventory management, stock prediction and pricing optimization. This is a great way for supermarkets to increase their sales and profitability (Li Dan, 2020).

BACKGROUND

In the past few decades, supermarkets have evolved and changed to meet the needs of their customers. From providing more organic produce to more frequent deals, supermarkets have been able to stay competitive in their industry. In order for supermarkets to stay competitive in today's market, they must keep up with the demands of a new generation of consumers. This is where technology comes in. Supermarkets are now using tech such as apps and online shopping to provide a better customer experience and stay ahead of competition. The supermarket industry is facing a lot of challenges. The most recent one is the rise of online grocery shopping. Online grocery shopping is gaining popularity and supermarkets are being left behind. This has been happening because customers are looking for convenience and the ability to order food from their own homes which supermarkets cannot offer. Customers also want to avoid long lines, waiting in checkout lines and getting out of their cars in parking lots. One way that supermarkets have tried to combat this trend is by offering online grocery pickup services or drive-thru lanes for those who do not want to go inside the store but still need groceries quickly.

The disadvantages of supermarkets, first disadvantage is that supermarkets have a lack of variety in their products. This is because they are large and have to carry many products, so they can only carry a limited amount of each product (Xiao Shilong et al., 2020). The second disadvantage is that supermarkets are often crowded and noisy. This can be an issue for those with sensory sensitivities, such as people with autism or anxiety disorder. The third disadvantage is that supermarkets are expensive because they have to pay for the rent in their buildings and the cost of transportation for their food items. Supermarkets may not be perfect, but there are still advantages to them over other types of stores, such as convenience stores or grocery stores.

Supermarkets have been facing a lot of issues in recent years. They are struggling to keep up with the customer needs, and they are also having a hard time keeping up with the other competitors. Sales have been going down for supermarkets in the last few years. The reason for this is because customers are more willing to buy food from different places like restaurants or convenience stores. Another reason is because supermarkets seem to be lacking customer care and service (Sawyer, 2005). They often lack staff that can help customers find their way around the store or answer their questions about foods. Customers also complain about not being able to find what they want in the store, as well as not being able to find a good parking spot when they come into the store. These are all problems that need solving before supermarkets can start making a comeback and

Supermarket chains are facing a lot of issues these days. They are struggling with sales and customers are not happy with their services. There is an increased demand for online shopping which has resulted in the downfall of supermarkets. People nowadays prefer to shop online rather than going to a physical store and they want everything delivered to their doorstep, will provide information on the issues that supermarkets are facing and how they can solve these problems in order to be successful again (Althuizen et al., 2006).

Artificial Intelligence is a branch of computer science that deals with intelligent behavior, such as thinking, learning, and problem solving. Artificial Intelligence is a broad term that refers to the intelligence demonstrated by machines. Artificial Intelligence (AI) has been an interesting topic for many years now. AI has been used in many different industries including healthcare, military and transportation. It has also found its way into the business world where it is used for activities such as customer service and data analysis (Bitner et al., 2000). The most common way AI is applied to business is through machine learning and deep learning algorithms that are being used by software developers to create programs that can learn from experience without being explicitly programmed; this means they can recognize patterns in large datasets and learn from them to make decisions about future outcomes without having explicit instructions on how to do so.

PROBLEM DEFINITION

Supermarkets often face the problem of product encroachment, where customers put items from one section in another or don't pay for them at all. To combat this issue, the use of artificial intelligence (AI) with people search social site algorithm has been proposed. The proposed AI system would use customer face detection technology to identify individuals as they enter the supermarket. The system would then track these individuals as they move through the store, using machine learning algorithms to analyze their behavior and predict potential product encroachments. Additionally, the system would utilize a people search social site algorithm, which would scan social media platforms for mentions of the supermarket, its products, and related keywords. This data would be used to identify potential product encroachments that may have occurred outside of the store. The ultimate goal of this AI system is to reduce the occurrence of product encroachment in supermarkets, leading to increased revenue and decreased losses. However, the implementation of such a system raises questions about privacy concerns and the potential for false accusations, which must be carefully considered and addressed.

MAIN FOCUS OF THE CHAPTER

Our proposed preprocess is to take a picture of the customer at the entrance and the AI algorithm does the facial recognition with people search in the social sites like Facebook, Amazon, Flipkart, etc., The face of the customers is initially get captured using the security cameras in the entrance of the supermarkets and the recognition of face and cropping the background and the unwanted surroundings are made in the pre-processing stage. After the extraction of the face the people search algorithm will came into action to match the best social site websites like Instagram and Facebook. Once social media account was hocked up with the machine dataset then the desired customer linked amazon and flip kart account orders and the recent search will also get taken in to the dataset of product Encroachment list to suggest the customer to buy the product.

Thus, the result of the search will be classified as what the customer has recently searched for and what's his or her favorite and frequent shopping items are get popped up as results. And all the Supermarkets will hold an offer board or display board using those digital displays the system will automatically do a price slash for the customers indented products which are extracted from their social site data's. This helps the customers and the supermarkets as well because the both customer and seller are aiming to a profit in terms using this technology seller can increase the sales in order to maintain the sales growth rate and the customers also will have an opportunity to get their preferred goods at a discounted price. The discount calculator of the artificial intelligence system is a preprogrammed at the stage of the Stock order database and the purchase percentage rate.

When a product is not sold for a certain period of time this artificial intelligence system will pop up a best discount form the MRP price to the minimum margin price of the product and this will get displayed in the digital display of the supermarket to make the customers preference to the product even though there is no need of the product for the customers the price slash is a basic reason and make the customer intention to buy the product for the best price. This helps the seller form getting the products out the expiry stage and loss in purchase condition. This will free up time for employees to focus on other aspects of their jobs.

Face Detection AI is a technology that is used to detect and identify faces in digital images. It has been used for various purposes such as surveillance, security, and biometrics. The Face Detection AI can be used for product encroachment in store by linking the face with social sites and suggesting product as customer desire. A research team from the University of Southern California has recently developed an AI which can detect and identify customers in a supermarket. The system is able to detect customer faces as they walk around and then cross-reference them with social media profiles to find out what their interests are. This is done by linking the face with social sites and suggesting products as customer desire.

The algorithm makes use of a deep neural network for people search, which was initially designed for surveillance purposes. It's now being used for retail in order to provide customers with more personalized shopping experiences, while at the same time allowing stores to better understand their demographic make-up. Face recognition is not a new technology, but it has been used in some creative ways. This application of the technology can be seen in the supermarket, where customers have their face scanned with AI and linked to social media sites.

The algorithm then suggests products that are desired by the customer. This application of AI to customer service is advantageous for both the company and the customer. The company benefits from increased sales, and the customer is able to purchase more items, since they don't have to travel through aisles looking for what they want.

CUSTOMER FACE DETECTING ARTIFICIAL INTELLIGENCE

The customer face detecting artificial intelligence is a software that scans the faces of the customers and tries to identify them. This technology is used in various sectors of business such as banking, retail, and security. The main goal of this technology is to provide a personalized experience for each customer by remembering their preferences and making suggestions accordingly. The first use case of this technology was at Starbucks where it was used to detect if the customer had already purchased a drink in that store or not. This way the staff knew who had already bought coffee so they could make recommendations based on what they had previously consumed.

Figure 1. Customer face detection

Facial recognition is the most popular biometric technology that has been widely used in the past few years. It was first introduced in the late 1800s, but it wasn't until recently that it became a household name. Facial recognition technology is now being used to identify people who are walking down the street, as well as those who are on social media platforms like Facebook and Instagram. The facial recognition algorithm is an artificial intelligence-based face-detecting technology which can be used to detect faces in images or videos and then identify them based on a pre-trained facial profile. The algorithm works by analyzing pixels of an image or video frame and then comparing them with a pre-trained facial profile. Face detection is becoming more and more common in artificial intelligence. It is used for different purposes, from identifying a person's face in a photo to detecting emotions. A lot of companies are using this technology to create new products or improve existing ones. The most popular applications of this technology are discussed below:

- Facial recognition software that can identify people by their faces
- Customer service chat-bots that use facial expressions to detect emotions
- AI-based face recognition that can be used instead of passwords or PINs

Facial recognition is a type of biometric technology which uses the unique geometry of a person's face to identify them. It can be used in security, or identifying people in videos. The algorithm is based on the assumption that humans have similar facial features and the same distance between their eyes, nose and mouth.

The Face Detecting Algorithm has been developed by using deep learning techniques and machine learning algorithms. These algorithms are trained to detect faces from images and video frames obtained from cameras. The training data used for this algorithm mainly consists of face images taken under different conditions.

Most of the algorithms are used for the detection of human faces in still images. The algorithm detects the face by using a pre-trained neural network. The most popular algorithm is from Google which is called "FaceNet". It has been trained on over 1.6 million images and it has been carefully designed for real-time performance on mobile devices.

The Face Net is a system that captures images of people's faces and matches them against a database of known or suspected terrorists. The system is designed to help law enforcement agencies identify terrorists who might use disguises or wear masks.

Face Net is an AI-based surveillance camera that has the ability to recognize and match faces in real-time. It is able to match the images with a database of known or suspected terrorists and alert authorities if there is a match. The system can also be used for other purposes like matching images from security cameras, for example, to find missing persons or just for verification purposes.

Face recognition is one of the most popular biometric technologies that has been used in various ways. It can be used to identify people and also for authentication purposes.

There are three types of face recognition technologies:

1. **Face Net:** Face net is a technique which uses a network of cameras to capture images of faces in public places and then tries to match them with the records in their database. It is also called CCTV Camera or Closed-Circuit Television Network.
2. **Face Capturing Images:** These are the images captured by a camera and can be used for identification purposes. The captured images are then processed by an algorithm which matches it with the photo in the database. This algorithm is called face matching software.
3. **Face Recognizing Algorithms:** These algorithms are Face Net is a surveillance system that uses CCTV cameras to detect and recognize human faces.

The system is able to identify people in a crowd, or in public spaces by capturing their faces and matching them with the database of pre-registered faces, or with a database of people who have been previously captured on camera.

Face recognition software has been around for decades now and it has evolved into something even more powerful. The algorithm is based on the assumption that humans have similar facial features and the same distance between their eyes, nose and mouth. Face recognition algorithms can now be used for face matching purposes, where they are able to match two images of the same person.

PEOPLE SEARCH SOCIAL SITE ALGORITHM

Facebook, Instagram, Flipkart, and Amazon are the best examples of how people search has evolved over time. In this section we will talk about how these four companies have incorporated facial recognition in their social media accounts. The first company to use face matching was Facebook. In 2010 they introduced a feature that allowed users to upload profile pictures of friends and family members who were not on Facebook. This was done by matching the uploaded photo with other photos of the same person on Facebook and then suggesting potential matches to the user. The algorithm is based on a series of biometric measurements like skin color, shape of eyes and nose etc. In 2014, Instagram introduced a similar feature that allowed users to search for any user's profile by uploading their photo from their mobile phone's camera roll or from Instagram.

The popularity of social media has grown exponentially in recent years. It is a place where people go to share their thoughts, interests and life events with their friends and family. However, with the growth of social media comes the question of privacy and security. One major concern that many people have is that they are not always in control of who sees what they post on these sites. The people search algorithm makes sure that your profile picture matches your name, so it can be difficult for someone to take over your account without you noticing or for someone else to use your name on a different account without you knowing about it. Today, social networking is a part of our lives. We use it to connect with people, share our thoughts and opinions, and keep up with the latest news. The algorithms behind these sites are designed specifically to match people based on what they have in common.

In this section, I will be talking about the algorithms behind social sites and how they work to match people together based on what they have in common. The algorithm that powers search on social media sites is a complex algorithm. It's not so much about the content of the post, but more about the person posting it. The algorithm looks for profile pictures and name matches to find people. The social site similar picture matching algorithm is designed to find people with a similar appearance as someone you are looking for. This is not just based on facial recognition, but also on other factors like hair color, skin tone, eyeglasses, and clothing.

Name matching algorithms are designed to match a person's name with other people's names in order to find potential relatives or friends of that person. The customer preference prediction algorithm from Amazon and Flipkart is a system that predicts what products the customers will buy in the future. This system is based on data about what other customers have bought in the past. The customer purchase tracker from shopping sites such as Amazon and Flipkart, helps to analyze customer behavior by tracking their past purchases.

The purchase prediction algorithm from Amazon is based on the customer's previous purchase history. The prediction is based on a customer's purchasing habits and preferences, demographic information and other factors. This algorithm helps Amazon to predict what a customer will buy next. Flipkart also uses algorithms to predict customers' preferences in order to recommend products that are likely to be of interest to them. The algorithm takes into account the browsing and purchase history of each customer, as well as their demographic information and other factors such as time of day, location, device type etc. E-commerce websites track customers' browsing behavior using cookies or browser fingerprinting techniques in order to predict what they will buy next.

The purchase prediction algorithm is a machine learning technique that tries to predict what a customer will buy. This is done by mining the data of customer preferences, past purchases and other data points from the website. Amazon has been using this algorithm for years to build their own product recommendation engine, which recommends products based on customers' purchase habits. Amazon has also started using this algorithm for their advertising business.

Flipkart too uses this algorithm to recommend products to users who are browsing through their website. The company also uses it for its advertising business as well as for its mobile app and in-store kiosks. The most recent arrival in the market is E-commerce site – Shop-clues, which has built a predictive engine that helps them offer personalized recommendations based on the browsing. Online shopping tracking algorithms are not perfect. Different people have different shopping carts, and they also have different needs. The algorithm is only as good as the data it has been fed. More data would help the algorithm to be more accurate in predicting what a customer will buy next. The Cart analyzer is a software that helps online retailers by providing insights about shoppers' behaviors and preferences for products in their cart, which ultimately leads to better conversion rates. A shopping cart tracker is a software that tracks the items that a customer has selected for purchase in an online store. It helps the company to know which products are more popular and which ones less so, and what are the products that customers are not buying at all. This information can be used to improve marketing strategies and make better decisions about product placement and pricing. But there is one problem with this system: it can be hacked by hackers who want to steal credit card information from customers. They use scripts or bots to fill up customer's shopping carts without their knowledge, then they ask for credit card information when the customer goes to check out. The hacker then gets access to the customer's credit card number, expiration date, CVV code, name on credit card and all other data stored in the

Figure 2. People search social site algorithm

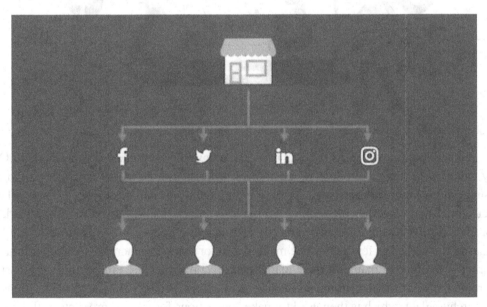

There are some companies that have developed face detection and matching algorithm that is being used to find people in social accounts. This algorithm is not new, it has been around for more than a decade. But it has now been improved to work on a larger scale and with a higher accuracy. This technique can be used for various purposes like finding the right person in an image, or finding the right person on social media platforms like Facebook, Instagram, Flipkart and Amazon.

PRODUCT ENCROACHMENT IN SUPERMARKETS
BY ARTIFICIAL INTELLIGENCE

This article aims to explore the role of Artificial Intelligence in the retail sector. It will also talk about how it is being used by retailers to improve their operations. The first use case of AI in retail is that it can be used for price slash technique. Retailers use this technique when they want to clear out their inventory and make room for new products. They do this by using big discounts or slashing prices on a particular product, which then creates a sense of urgency among consumers who may be looking for a bargain. In the second use case, Artificial Intelligence is being used by retailers to offer combo offers or bundled goods at discounted rates. This will increase sales and profit margins as people are more likely to buy two goods together than just one good on its own.

Figure 3. Product encroachment in supermarkets by artificial intelligence

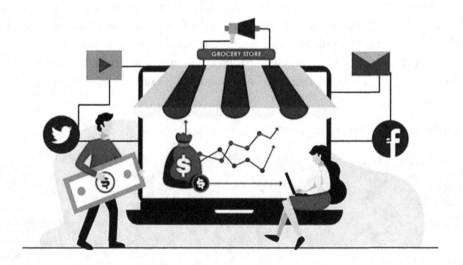

There are many ways in which AI is being used to increase the efficiency of supermarkets. One such way is by using AI to suggest products to customers. In this case, an algorithm can be used to make product suggestions for customers based on their individual tastes and preferences. This will not only help the customer find what they are looking for but also reduce the time spent in a supermarket.

The product encroachment in supermarkets by artificial intelligence is a phenomenon that has been steadily increasing in the last few years. The main reason for this is the increase in competition between various brands. In order to maintain their market share, companies are employing various strategies such as product suggestion algorithms and near expiry offers. Product suggestion algorithms rely on customer purchase data, which is then used to make suggestions for similar products to those that have been bought before.

Supermarket Combo offer algorithm also uses data from customers' purchase history, but instead of just making suggestions for similar products, it also suggests a specific combination of products that are not usually bought together but would make a good deal if added together.

Supermarket Strategies is a book written by Dr. Venkat Raghavan and Dr. Rajiv Dholakia. The book is about how to use pricing and product combo offers for maximum profit in the supermarket industry. It also discusses price margin fixing algorithms, which are used to identify the optimal prices of products in the store and how to fix them at that level.

In this section, we will learn more about Supermarket Strategies techniques, AI Algorithms and Product combo offers with Price margin fixing algorithms. Supermarkets are playing a huge role in shaping the future of retail. They are using AI algorithms to provide personalized shopping experiences to their customers.

The future of retail is all about personalized shopping experiences, and supermarkets are at the forefront of this change. Supermarkets use AI algorithms to offer personalized product combo offers and price margin fixing for their customers by analyzing their buying patterns and preferences. Supermarkets are using AI algorithms to keep prices low and make their products more attractive to customers.

Supermarket strategies techniques have evolved over time to keep up with the changing times. In the past, supermarkets used to compete with each other by making their prices high. Nowadays, they are competing on price margin fixing algorithms and product combo offers.

The use of AI algorithms by supermarkets is not new, but it has increased in recent years as retailers have been investing in these technologies. The benefits of these technologies are numerous - they help retailers predict customer demand, optimize inventory levels and manage prices more effectively.

The supermarket industry is facing a lot of problems and the current strategies are not enough to fix them. Supermarkets are struggling with product combo offers and price margin fixing algorithms.

Supermarket Strategies Techniques:

- Product combo offers
- Price margin fixing algorithms
- Struggles in supermarket strategies
- Difficulties in supermarket strategies

In the age of e-commerce, supermarkets are struggling to keep up with their competitors. This is not only because they have to compete with the convenience of online shopping, but also because they have to deal with the issue of low margins and price fixing algorithms.

QUALITATIVE AND QUANTITATIVE ANALYSES

Customer face detecting artificial intelligence (AI) technology has the potential to revolutionize the way supermarkets monitor product encroachment and prevent theft. This technology uses algorithms to analyze customer faces and detect suspicious behavior, such as hiding products or attempting to steal them. To evaluate the effectiveness of this technology, both qualitative and quantitative analyses can be performed.

A qualitative analysis would involve gathering feedback from customers and store employees to evaluate their perceptions of the technology. This could be done through surveys, interviews, or focus groups. Some potential questions to ask might include:

- How comfortable do you feel with this technology being used in the store?
- Do you feel that this technology makes the store feel safer?

- Have you ever seen someone caught using this technology? If so, what was your reaction?
- Do you think this technology has improved the store's ability to prevent theft?

The responses to these questions can provide valuable insights into how the technology is perceived by different stakeholders and whether it is achieving its intended goals.

A quantitative analysis would involve gathering data on the effectiveness of the technology in preventing product encroachment and theft. This could be done by comparing the number of incidents before and after the technology was implemented. Some potential metrics to track might include:

- The number of products reported missing each month.
- The number of incidents of product encroachment caught on camera each month.
- The number of incidents where the technology was able to prevent theft.

By tracking these metrics over time, it will be possible to evaluate whether the technology is having a measurable impact on preventing theft in the store.

People Search Social Site Algorithm

Another important factor to consider is the algorithm used by the technology to detect suspicious behavior. One potential approach is to use a "people search social site algorithm," which can analyze facial features to identify specific individuals who may have a history of theft or suspicious behavior. This algorithm could be trained on data from social media sites, law enforcement databases, or other sources to improve its accuracy.

In conclusion, qualitative and quantitative analyses are important tools for evaluating the effectiveness of customer face detecting AI technology for preventing product encroachment in supermarkets. By gathering feedback from customers and employees and tracking key metrics over time, it is possible to determine whether the technology is achieving its intended goals and making the store a safer place for everyone. Additionally, the use of a people search social site algorithm can improve the accuracy of the technology and increase its effectiveness in preventing theft.

Product Combo Offers

Supermarkets are now using AI to create their own product combo offers. This is a great example of how AI can be used in the retail industry. The technology behind these offers is called "product bundling" and it has been around for decades. The first use of this technology was by the airline industry when they started offering passengers two tickets for the price of one. However, it wasn't until recently that retailers began using this new technology to offer customers discounts on specific products if they buy more than one at a time. This new use of AI will help retailers better compete with online shopping giants like Amazon, who have been able to offer customers deals and discounts for years without having to pay for store upkeep or employees' salaries. AI is being used to create product combo offers for supermarkets. It does this by looking at a customer's purchase history and suggesting products that might interest them.

Price Margin Fixing Algorithms

Price margin fixing algorithms are a type of algorithm that helps to fix the price margins for products in supermarkets. These algorithms are important because they help to keep prices competitive. The first supermarket that implemented this technology was Tesco. They started using these algorithms in order to offer more competitive prices and stay ahead of the competition. This helped them to increase their revenues by 3%.

Price margin fixing algorithms are a way to ensure that the supermarkets make a profit. They are usually done by a computer that is programmed to search for the best deals in order to offer the best price possible. This is how price-margin fixing algorithms work:

- The algorithm searches for the lowest prices on products and services, and then uses these prices as reference points when determining what price to charge.
- It can also be used to analyze competitors' pricing strategy and adjust accordingly.
- It can also be used for promotional purposes, such as offering discounts or other incentives at certain times of year or on certain days of the week.

Struggles in Supermarket Strategies

Supermarket Strategies, a consulting firm that advises retailers on their digital strategies, has faced many struggles in the past few years. They have been using technology to help them with their business, but they have not seen the success they were hoping for. The company has had a hard time adapting to how quickly technology is changing. They can't keep up with all of the new developments and this is causing them to fall behind in the market.

Difficulties in Supermarket Strategies

The Difficulties in Supermarket Strategies technology approach is difficult to implement because of the lack of human resources and a lack of understanding of the new technology. The Difficulties in Supermarket Strategies technology approach is difficult to implement because it requires a lot of human resources and a lot of understanding on how the new technology works.

The difficulties in Supermarket Strategies are not just limited to these two issues, but also include problems in product combo offers and difficulty in price margin fixing algorithms.

Supermarket Strategies techniques are facing a lot of problems. The market is changing, and the supermarkets need to adapt to the new demands.

Product combo offers are struggling with not being able to compete with other offers in the market. Price margin fixing algorithms have a difficult time trying to fix prices for their products and adjust them at different times of the day.

Artificial Intelligence (AI) is a type of technology that makes machines function in a way that is similar to human intelligence. In the past few years, there has been an increase in the use of AI in different sectors such as healthcare, education and retail. One of the most recent applications of AI is in supermarkets. Supermarkets are using AI to make product suggestions, display boards and offers. These technologies help improve customer experience and increase revenue for supermarkets.

SOLUTIONS AND RECOMMENDATIONS

In the future, supermarkets will be more like a shopping mall. Customers can get everything they need from a single store and have it delivered to their doorstep. The first step in this process is to make sure that customers can find everything on the shelves that they need. This is where technology comes in, as it can be used to help customers find what they are looking for by using voice assistants or augmented reality systems. In the future, supermarkets will be more like a shopping mall with all of the latest technology available to help customers find what they want and get it delivered right at their doorstep.

The artificial intelligence system is a set of computer programs that can think and act like humans. They can be used to make decisions and solve problems. The customer face detection is when the camera detects the person's face and automatically captures it. This is a way for companies to provide better service because they save time by not having to search for the customer's information. Finally, product listing with price is when an artificial intelligent system automatically generates a product listing with the price of an item.

The artificial intelligence system is used to detect the customer's face and also it is used to generate the product listing with price. The artificial intelligence system is really smart. It can detect the customer face that appears on the screen and use the information to generate a product listing with price. This new system is really powerful. It can also detect the customer face, and then it will list all of the products in this store, as well as their prices.

Supermarkets are now using AI solution to get a better understanding of their customers. This helps them to come up with a strategy that not only attracts new customers but also retain the old ones. AI is being used for many things in the retail industry. It is used for customer service and marketing. But one of the most important areas where it has been used is in supply chain management. It helps retailers to manage inventory and plan deliveries more efficiently, which improves customer experience and reduces costs at the same time.

TECHNICAL BRIEFING

Customer Face Detecting Artificial Intelligence (AI) with the help of People Search Social Site Algorithm is a cutting-edge technology that allows supermarkets to detect and prevent product encroachment. This technology combines computer vision and machine learning techniques to analyze and identify customers who are attempting to encroach on products. The AI system is equipped with cameras that are strategically placed around the supermarket. These cameras capture images of the customers as they move through the store. The system then uses computer vision algorithms to identify the faces of the customers and track their movements.

In addition to facial recognition, the AI system is also integrated with People Search Social Site Algorithm. This algorithm allows the system to search social media platforms to gather additional information about the customers, such as their demographics, interests, and shopping behavior. This information is then used to enhance the accuracy of the product encroachment detection system.

The AI system is capable of detecting when a customer is reaching for a product that is not in their designated area. For example, if a customer is in the beverage aisle and attempts to grab a bag of chips, the system will detect this and alert store employees. The system can also detect when a customer is attempting to remove a product from its packaging or when a customer is attempting to conceal a product in their bag or clothing. The AI system is designed to be highly accurate and reliable, with a low rate of false positives. This means that the system is able to detect genuine cases of product encroachment while minimizing the number of false alarms.

Customer Face Detecting AI with the help of People Search Social Site Algorithm is a powerful tool for supermarkets to prevent product encroachment and enhance their security measures. With its advanced computer vision and machine learning capabilities, this technology is sure to become an integral part of supermarket operations in the near future.

FUTURE RESEARCH DIRECTIONS

The research areas like business developments, business associates and the sellers who are seeking to sell their product at their best price and keep the sales in a growth rate will be much more benefitted with this idea and the researcher in the field of artificial intelligence and face analysis are seeking a boom in their field and has an huge scope in these research areas where the future goods selling business deals with the computer intelligence and the researchers are playing a vital role in this fields. AI solutions for supermarkets are expected to be more and more prevalent in the future.

In order for AI to be able to provide an accurate prediction of what a customer will want to buy, it needs to have access to a lot of data. It also needs to be able to process that data quickly and accurately.

The use of AI in the supermarket is still in its nascent stage. However, it has been predicted that AI will be used in all areas of the supermarket industry.

The future research directions are to focus on the following:

- Implementing AI based solutions to improve customer experience
- Creating a better shopping experience with the help of AI and VR technology
- Using predictive analytics to predict customer behavior and needs

ETHICAL AND LEGAL ISSUES

The use of customer face detecting artificial intelligence (AI) with the help of people search social site algorithm for product encroachment in supermarkets raises several ethical and legal issues that must be carefully considered. One ethical concern is the potential invasion of customers' privacy. By using facial recognition technology, supermarkets may be able to identify and track individual customers without their knowledge or consent. This raises questions about whether customers have a reasonable expectation of privacy when shopping in a public space and whether supermarkets have the right to collect and use this information without customers' explicit consent. Another ethical issue is the potential for discrimination. Facial recognition technology has been shown to be less accurate in identifying individuals with darker skin tones and women, which raises concerns about the potential for discrimination against these groups. If supermarkets use this technology to monitor customers' behavior or to make decisions about promotions or product placement, this could lead to unfair treatment of certain customers based on their race or gender. There are also legal issues that must be considered. For example, there are currently no federal laws in the United States that regulate the use of facial recognition technology in public spaces, although some states and cities have passed their own laws. In addition, the use of facial recognition technology may be subject to existing laws such as the Fair Credit Reporting Act, which regulates the collection and use of consumer information by credit reporting agencies. Finally, there is the issue of data security. If supermarkets collect and store customers' facial recognition data, they must ensure that this data is protected from unauthorized access or use. This includes implementing strong security measures to prevent data breaches and ensuring that customers are informed about how their data is being collected, used, and protected. In summary, the use of customer face detecting artificial intelligence with the help of people search social site algorithm for product encroachment in supermarkets raises several ethical and legal issues that must be carefully considered. Supermarkets must ensure that they are using this technology in a way that respects customers' privacy and civil rights, and that they are taking appropriate steps to protect customers' data from misuse or unauthorized access.

CONCLUSION

Using the AI Technology customer face detection done and matching function occurs with the social site like Amazon, Facebook, Flipkart, etc., to pick out the customer preferred products and flashing the best discount price for the goods in the supermarket digital display boards. This helps the seller form getting the products out the expiry stage and loss in purchase condition. As this chapter makes a far best move in the business and customer relationship management using the Artificial intelligence system and this chapter influence the inventors to develop a product-based technology with this advanced technology concepts and the software too. There are a lot of supermarket chains that are struggling to keep up with the demand for food. One of the ways to solve this problem is to use AI as a solution. AI can be used in various ways in supermarkets. It can be used as an assistant in identifying and solving problems, it can also be used as a tool to help customers find their way around the store, or it can even be used by store managers in order to keep track of inventory and sales. And this chapter will help the researchers somehow in the area of facial analysis, data scientist, and business development teams also. This chapter mainly focus on the Artificial intelligence system which works independently with the customer face detection and the automatic data collection of the desired customer and finally product listing with price also done with the artificial intelligent system which are more advanced and practically possible with the full effort of the described methodology. The only hassle of the data collection is the sorting data form the social sites with the permission of the social sites and the customers too. And the Social sites will also get benefited with this approach and the chapter is not fetching any privacy data other than the product or the goods which customer intended to search and likely to purchase in the online stores like amazon and flip kart so this chapter has a huge scope in future.

NOTE

This research received no specific grant from any funding agency in the public, commercial, or not-for-profit sectors.

REFERENCES

Althuizen, N. A. P., & Wierenga, B. (2006). Deploying Analogical Reasoning as a Decision Support and Understanding the Predictive Accuracy of Customer Churn Models. *Journal of Marketing Research*, *43*, 204–211. doi:10.1509/jmkr.43.2.204

Berry, L. L. (1983). Relationship marketing. In L. L. Berry, G. L. Shostack, & G. D. Upah (Eds.), *Emerging Perspectives on Services Marketing* (pp. 25–28). American Marketing Association.

Bitner, M. J., Brown, S. W., & Meuter, M. L. (2000). Technology infusion in service encounters. *Journal of the Academy of Marketing Science*, *28*(1), 138–149. doi:10.1177/0092070300281013

Bradlow, E. T., Gangwar, M., Kopalle, P., & Voleti, S. (2017). The role of big data and predictive analytics in retailing. *Journal of Retailing*, *93*(1), 79–95. doi:10.1016/j.jretai.2016.12.004

Dan, L. (2020). Research on the application and key technology of artificial intelligence in China Unicom's customer service system. Computer Knowledge and Technology, 16(26), 176-177.

Dwyer, R. F., Schurr, P. H., & Oh, S. (1987). Developing Buyer-Seller Relationships. *Journal of Marketing*, *51*(April), 11–27. doi:10.1177/002224298705100202

Dysart, J. (1999). Email marketing grows up: A primer for the new millennium. *Networker (Washington, D.C.)*, *3*(4), 40–41. doi:10.1145/323409.328686

Gaskell, A. (2016, Apr. 14). Why AI Should Augment, And Not Replace, Staff. *Forbes*.

Lei, Z., Tong, L., Wu, J., & Jie, Y. (2020). Tencent intelligent customer service human-machine collaboration practice. Artificial Intelligence, 3, 106-113.

Sawyer, S., & Tapia, A. (2005). The sociotechnical nature of mobile computing work:Evidence from a study of policing in the United States. *International Journal of Technology and Human Interaction*, *1*(3), 1–14. doi:10.4018/jthi.2005070101

Xiao, S., & Sen, Z. (2020). Research and design of urban rail transit intelligent customer service system. *Technological Innovation and Application*, *3*, 87–88.

Xu, P., & Sarikaya, R. (2013). Convolutional neural network based triangular CRF for joint intent detection and slot filling. *Automatic Speech Recognition and Understanding (ASRU) IEEE Workshop*, 78-83. 10.1109/ASRU.2013.6707709

Chapter 17

User Sentiment Prediction and Analysis for Payment App Reviews Using Supervised and Unsupervised Machine Learning Approaches

Md Shamim Hossain

ⓘ https://orcid.org/0000-0003-1645-7470

Hajee Mohammad Danesh Science and Technology University, Bangladesh

Omdev Dahiya

Lovely Professional University, India

Md Abdullah Al Noman

ⓘ https://orcid.org/0000-0002-1377-7113

Hajee Mohammad Danesh Science and Technology University, Bangladesh

ABSTRACT

Businesses must be aware of customer sentiment in order to provide the best customer service. Instead of using cash or a credit card, a user can use a payment app on a mobile device to pay for a variety of services and digital or physical goods, which is becoming increasingly popular around the world. The goal of this study is to evaluate and predict user sentiment for payment apps using supervised and unsupervised machine learning (ML) approaches. For the study's data, Google Play Store reviews of the PayPal and Google Pay apps were gathered. Following cleaning, the filtered summary sentences were assessed for positive, neutral, or negative feelings using two unsupervised and five supervised machine learning approaches. According to the findings of the current study, the majority of customer reviews for payment apps were positive, with the average number of words with negative sentiment being higher. Furthermore, recent research found that, while all ML approaches can correctly classify review text into sentiment classes, logistic regression outperforms them in terms of accuracy.

DOI: 10.4018/978-1-6684-7105-0.ch017

INTRODUCTION

Since the first handheld mobile phone was introduced in 1973, phone technology has experienced the fastest growth of any technology (Wiese and Humbani, 2019). As the number of mobile devices increases, people are increasingly using various mobile apps, including mobile payment apps, for their daily needs (Hossain and Rahman, 2023). In recent years, mobile payment technology has significantly advanced, and the widespread use of third-party mobile payment systems in mobile apps has been encouraged by the rapid rise of smartphones.

Compared to traditional payment channels such as credit cards, third-party in-app payment transactions are completed more conveniently within mobile apps (Hossain and Rahman, 2023). By bypassing the need to open another app or web browser, users can pay their bills immediately. Third-party cashiers are eager to offer this functionality to popular Android and iOS apps to enable in-app payments, helping these apps to employ their mobile payment services (Yang et al., 2019).

In today's digital age, information is readily shared among users and can greatly impact how others perceive events (Hossain et al., 2021; Alarifi et al., 2023; Hossain, 2023). It is therefore imperative to comprehend the general consensus (Daudert, 2021). Web 2.0 has given rise to forums, blogs, and online social medias, providing individuals with a platform to discuss and share their ideas on a wide range of topics, including expressing their opinions on products, discussing current events, or sharing political views. User data from such platforms is used in numerous applications, such as organizational survey analysis, recommendation systems, and political campaign planning (Dang et al., 2020). Data is the lifeblood of an organization, and data-driven decisions are crucial for maintaining competitiveness. However, manually collecting and analyzing vast amounts of data is a daunting task (Aslam et al., 2020). Fortunately, modern technology allows for efficient collection and investigation of massive amounts of online data, through the use of artificial intelligence (AI). For instance, in this project, we employed ML programming, a subset of AI, to gather and examine data from 224,281 reviews.

User reviews are a valuable resource for businesses as they provide consumer feedback on goods or services used by individuals in the form of comments. Reviews are typically posted on a business's website or platforms of third-party, such as the Google Play Store (Hossain and Rahman, 2023). Dwidienawati et al. (2020) noted that user reviews support the decisions and increase assurance in the individual making them. Wang et al. (2021) further showed that growing the number and quality of reviews can enhance a business's effectiveness. Chevalier and Mayzlin (2006) found that consumer internet assessments have a significant influence on the sales of goods and services. Therefore, businesses should take note of user reviews and utilize them to improve their offerings, enhance customer satisfaction, and ultimately improve their bottom line.

The utilization of smartphone applications has witnessed a notable upsurge in recent years. (Hossain and Rahman, 2023). Mobile apps have made routine tasks and jobs more convenient, leading to an increase in app downloads from app stores and the number of smartphones worldwide (Triantafyllou et al., 2020; Hassan et al., 2017). One unique feature of mobile app stores like the Google Play Store is the ability for developers to receive user feedback through reviews. The Google Play Store is a digital distribution system that offers various digital goods, such as movies, software, e-books, and music. Mobile apps can be downloaded and updated automatically or manually through the Google Play store (McIlroy et al., 2015). The app store offers both free and paid applications, with paid apps requiring purchase before use.

Manual categorization of app reviews can be a time-consuming and critical task for developers. Therefore, automated categorization of app reviews can be beneficial, especially in addressing issues quickly.

Aslam et al. (2020) emphasized how ratings and reviews provide developers with valuable information about the user experience, complaints, feature requests, and overall rating of the app, enabling them to monitor and improve their apps. Like other online retailers, customers often read reviews before downloading an app. Studies have shown that ratings and reviews are associated with increased downloads and sales, with stable ratings associated with higher downloads and sales (Martens and Maalej, 2019; Finkelstein et al., 2017). Furthermore, mobile app reviews on platforms like the Google Play Store are becoming increasingly essential for app developers to gain insights into users' experiences with their products. The automated categorization of app reviews can help developers manage and enhance their apps more effectively, while ratings and reviews play a crucial role in driving app downloads and sales.

The process of classifying user reviews of apps to extract relevant information for software development is a challenging and complex task. It involves text preprocessing, feature extraction, and machine learning techniques to effectively categorize reviews. Manual review reading is not practical, especially for popular apps with a high number of reviews (Aslam et al., 2020; Hossain and Rahman, 2022a; Maalej et al., 2016). Previous research has proposed automated methods for feature engineering that can group reviews based on ratings or general topics (Aslam et al., 2020; Maalej et al., 2016; Triantafyllou et al., 2020; Hossain and Rahman 2022b). User evaluations are crucial for app developers and users to make informed decisions regarding apps. However, no research has been conducted on evaluating payment apps. Therefore, this study aims to use unsupervised and supervised machine learning methods to analyze reviews of payment apps and predict users' feelings about these apps.

LITERATURE REVIEW

Sentiment analysis (SA) is a rapidly growing field of study due to the exponential increase in digital information (Hossain and Rahman, 2022a; Hossain and Rahman, 2022b; Hossain et al., 2022a; Hossain et al., 2022b). According to Kumar et al. (2020), SA is a critical instrument for artificial intelligence to extract emotional evidence from large datasets. Sentiment analysis aims to identify whether opinions stated in texts are optimistic, unbiased, or undesirable (Daudert, 2021), and it has become a powerful technique for understanding people's attitudes with numerous applications (Dang et al., 2020). Feizollah et al. (2019) explain how natural language processing (NLP) techniques are used in the procedure of sentiment analysis to evaluate text and determine the representation of emotions in texts.

The popularity of sentiment analysis has been on the rise in recent times in analyzing user feedback in various fields using machine learning techniques (Hossain et al., 2022). It has been utilized to examine data from different domains such as education, drugs, and transportation services (Ali et al., 2020; Kastrati et al., 2020). Sentiment analysis is a subfield of natural language processing that categorizes the polarity of attitudes in text as positive, negative, or neutral (Amin et al., 2019). On the other hand, assessment theory, a subfield of psychology, aims to explain why people feel a certain way. Sentiment analysis involves extracting emotions, ideas, and sentiments from text, and it has numerous applications, including consumer satisfaction and political ideas (Mäntylä et al., 2018). Nasukawa and Yi (2003) are credited with introducing the term "sentiment analysis," which refers to the identification of a consumer's review text's subjective polarity and strength or the writer's attitude. The term encompasses different subjects, including subjectivity classification, emotion classification, and opinion identification. Ravi & Ravi (2015) discussed several aspects of sentiment categorization, including polarity determination and ambiguity resolution. With the internet's ability to access vast amounts of opinionated data and its diverse applications in daily life, sentiment analysis has become increasingly popular in recent times (Garay et al., 2019).

Appraisal theory, which is rooted in Systemic Functional Linguistics (SFL), has been explored by investigators like Martin and White (2005) and Barcena et al. (2020). This theory is concerned with how language is used to express positive or negative evaluations and categorizes interpersonal offers and propositions based on attitudes and emotions. According to this theory, emotions arise from our assessments of events, which may differ among individuals. Scherer et al. (2001) suggest that our assessment of a situation causes an emotional response. Appraisal theory distinguishes between numerous kinds of appraising statements and examines the choices that writers and speakers make, as mirrored in the SFL vocabulary and syntax of evaluative writing. While the syntax can be difficult to comprehend, local grammar can be used to analyze it by describing how words and phrases appear randomly in a text and are expressed in various ways. The appraisal theory informs readers of the writer or speaker's attitudes and emotions toward people and things, making it a concept of interpersonal meaning that facilitates interpersonal connections. Scholars such as Widyaningrum et al. (2019), Hossain and Rahman (2022a), and Read and Carroll (2012) have utilized this theory to explain language interaction. Although appraisal theory has been used to examine reviewers' feelings, it has not yet been employed to evaluate users' sentiments when they post reviews on payment apps.

The analysis of online reviews is a popular method for sentiment analysis (SA) to quickly gauge public opinion. This approach is commonly used to assess people's views on specific items or places, such as hotels. Machine learning (ML) technology is used in SA to automatically analyze reviews, enabling the rapid delivery of information. In recent years, polarity detection-based machine learning techniques have become popular in SA research (Han et al., 2018). There are two primary types of learning techniques used in SA: supervised learning and lexicon-based learning (Jurek et al., 2015; Saif et al., 2016). However, research on user sentiment regarding payment apps is limited, despite the use of customer reviews in several recent studies to evaluate customer sentiment (Luo and Xu, 2021; Mostafa, 2018; Feizollah et al., 2019). This study utilized five supervised learning approaches to predict user sentiment and two unsupervised learning methods based on a lexicon to determine user sentiment in mobile payment apps.

THEORETICAL FRAMEWORK AND HYPOTHESES DEVELOPMENT

Theoretical Framework

The majority of people believe that ratings offer a numerical representation of textual emotions with distinct valences (Hossain and Rahman, 2022). To evaluate the overall tone of a review, sentiment analysis can be used. However, factors like the product category and review length can affect how accurately an approach captures the genuine sentiment of a customer (Hossain and Rahman, 2022b; Al-Natour and Turetken, 2020). Reviews left by users in internet forums can be useful for those interested in learning about other people's experiences with specific products or services (Hossain and Rahman, 2022b; Chiou et al., 2014). Lately, Hossain and Rahman (2022a) found a relationship between the length of a customer review and its emotion class for financial consumers' evaluations on social media. Various strategies or procedures can be used to classify emotions (Hossain et al., 2022). A novel word weighting method was proposed by Deng et al. (2014) based on the phrase's value for expressing mood and the text's importance (Hossain and Rahman, 2022b). This method can appropriately weigh words while

Figure 1. Theoretical framework

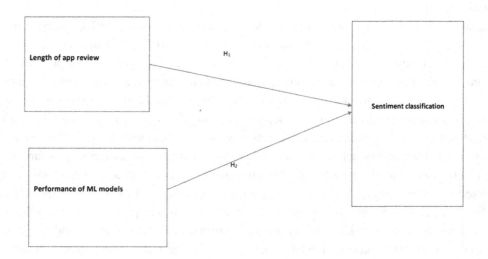

fully utilizing the available marking data. Although insurance reviews have not been studied, several studies (Pang et al., 2019; Hossain et al., 2022; Gul et al., 2021) have revealed that different machine learning (ML) models can beat others for various types of reviews in different sectors. In this study, we investigate if there is a association between the length of payment app reviews and different attitudes. Furthermore, we anticipate that different ML models will perform differently in classifying consumer sentiment (as presented in Figure 1).

Hypotheses Development

The Relationship Between Review Text Length and Customer Sentiment

In today's market, clients are confronted with a massive array of options, leading to an overload of information that can make it difficult to make informed decisions. According to the cognitive load concept, individuals have a limited capacity to comprehend and process information (Hossain and Rahman, 2022a; Pashchenko et al., 2022). Consequently, consumers are more likely to attempt to lessen the time they spend to make purchasing decisions (Hossain et al., 2022; Hu et al., 2014). This is where user reviews come into play, as they can help to accelerate decision-making and improve consumer purchasing behavior (Ha and Hoch, 1989). Buyers often turn to feedback and associated ratings to gather information about other people's perceptions or sentiments when making purchasing decisions, as it can help to cut down on the time and money they spend (Hossain and Rahman, 2022a). For businesses, customer review ratings can provide valuable insights into how their products and services are perceived by consumers. However, it is important to note that clients are more disposed to displaying harmful emotions, such as rage and despair, when consuming (Zeelenberg and Pieters, 2004). A customer who has had a negative experience is more likely to share it with someone else by leaving a negative comment. Interestingly, research has shown that negative experiences have more power than positive ones when it comes to focusing and influencing consumer behavior (Fors et al., 2016; Corns, 2018; Baumeister et al., 2001).

Negative experiences are often given more weight and influence than positive experiences, leading to a phenomenon known as the "negativity bias" or "negativity effect" (Lee et al., 2009). Besides, strongly negative response has a bigger effect on brand perception compared to slightly critical or overwhelmingly positive evaluations (Lee et al., 2009). This can have significant consequences for businesses, as negative reviews can impact their bottom line. Research by Ghasemaghaei et al. (2018) using a panel dataset of customer evaluations for insurance of house, car, and life from January 2012 to December 2015, found that content of longer review was linked to poorer customer ratings. This suggests that negative evaluations are more likely to be lengthier than positive comments in the form of online user reviews (Hossain and Rahman, 2022b). Moreover, studies have shown that undesirable emotions are more likely to lead to longer written exchanges in online reviews, supporting the theory that negative emotions drive verbal exchanges in face-to-face interactions (Rodrguez-Hidalgo et al., 2015). This finding suggests that individuals who have had a undesirable experience with a good or service are more likely to share their feelings and experiences with others, which can have significant consequences for businesses. Thus, user reviews have become an integral part of the consumer decision-making process, as they can provide valuable insights into how products and services are perceived by consumers. However, businesses need to be aware of the negativity bias and the impact that negative reviews can have on their bottom line. They should strive to address negative feedback promptly and effectively to mitigate any potential damage to their brand's reputation. In the current study, we examined the association between review text length and sentiment polarity using lexical-based techniques. As a consequence, we suggested the following supposition for reviews of payment applications:

H1: Negative sentiment will be linked to longer review text.

Performance of ML Models in Classifying Customers' Reviews

Sentiment analysis has been extensively implemented in various fields such as marketing, customer service, and social media analysis to determine the sentiment of a particular text. In particular, supervised learning has been a popular approach for sentiment analysis due to its high efficiency and precision. One of the most commonly used supervised learning procedures for sentiment analysis is Support Vector Machines (SVM). Gul, Alpaslan, and Emiroglu (2021) found that SVM exhibited the uppermost classification accuracy. Similarly, Hossain et al. (2021) developed a sentiment classification system based on SVM that assigned values to particular phrases and terms and then combined them to create a model for text categorization. Their system showed promising results in accurately classifying the sentiment of the text. In the domain of movie reviews, Pang, Lee, and Vithyanathan (2019) compared the effectiveness of different supervised machine learning techniques for sentiment classification such as Naive Bayes, Maximum Entropy Classification, and SVM. They found that the SVM approach outperformed the other approaches while the Naive Bayes method performed the worst. Another study by Ye, Zhang, and Law (2009) used a controlled tool on traveler review websites to identify sentiment in customer evaluations. Their findings revealed that SVM outperformed the Naive Bayes approach in accurately classifying the sentiment of the text. Overall, SVM has been demonstrated to be an effective approach for sentiment analysis in various domains. Its high efficiency and precision make it a popular choice for sentiment analysis tasks. However, it is important to note that the effectiveness of SVM may vary depending on the specific domain and the nature of the text being analyzed. According to Hossain et al. (2022), SVM provides the following advantages.

(1) Extreme overfitting resistance. (2) It can fit quite large feature spaces. (3) It supports knowledge prediction and is quite good at extracting sentiments from huge Twitter datasets.

Therefore, we put out the following proposition for payment app reviews:

H2: When categorized user evaluations of payment apps, the SVM approach outperformed the other approaches.

METHOD

The current study utilized the Play store of Google, a digital distribution online service managed and created by Google, to collect user reviews of payment applications. This official app store provides access to apps made with the Android software development kit (SDK) and distributed for approved devices running Android and Chrome OS. Online reviews have been shown to significantly influence customer purchase decisions (Hossain and Rahman, 2022a; von Helversen et al., 2018), and app users can rate and review any mobile app on a five-star scale based on their personal experiences in the Google Play store.

In this study, the researchers chose two popular payment services, PayPal and Google Pay, and collected all the English reviews for these services using the Google-play-scraper Python tool. The collected data included the reviewers' names, review dates, and number of likes. After cleaning the data by removing punctuation, missing values, and stopwords, the TF-IDF vectorizer was implemented to convert the text into a mathematical depiction. The AFINN Sentiment and VADER Sentiment tools of intrinsic Python programming were used to analyze the sentiment of the reviews based on the rating given by the reviewer. The sentiment scores ranged from -1 for negative emotions (1 and 2 stars) to 0 for neutral sentiment (3 stars) and 1 for positive sentiment (4 and 5 stars). To predict users' views about payment applications, five machine learning models were used, including SVC, random forest classifier, k-neighbors classifier, logistic regression, and decision tree classifier. The performance of these models was assessed using several metrics, including accuracy, recall, precision, R squared, and F1-Score. The study's findings were analyzed using Python scripts in a Jupyter notebook that loaded necessary machine learning packages such as seaborn, pandas, Afinn, wordcloud, googletrans, and vaderSentiment.

RESULTS AND DISCUSSION

Figure 2 demonstrated that a total of 2,24,281 evaluations of two payment applications (PayPal and Google Pay) were gathered for the current study. Figure 3 showed the wordcloud of the collected reviews towards payment apps. In Table 1, the number of user reviews for each app in proportion to the rating was displayed. Positive reviews received ratings of 4 and 5, neutral reviews received 3, while negative reviews received ratings of 1 and 2. The study shows that, generally, 49.05% of reviewers have a favorable impression of payment apps, 45.13% have a bad opinion, and only 5.82% have a neutral opinion of apps (shown in Table 2 and Figure 4). Additionally, the current study revealed that users have more negative opinions of the Google Pay applications than of PayPal. Out of the 1,46,464 reviews on PayPal, 65.82% had positive emotions, 29.53% had negative sentiment, and only 4.65% had neutral feelings. In contrast, out of the 77,817 reviews on Google Pay, only 17.48% had positive sentiment, 74.51% had negative sentiment, and 8.016% had neutral sentiment (presented in Table 2)

Table 1. The number of reviews for each app in proportion to the rating

Score	Apps		Total
	Google Pay	PayPal	
1	50114	36657	86771
2	7865	6590	14455
3	6238	6809	13047
4	5000	11955	16955
5	8600	84453	93053
Total	77817	146464	224281

Figure 2. Number of reviews towards each app

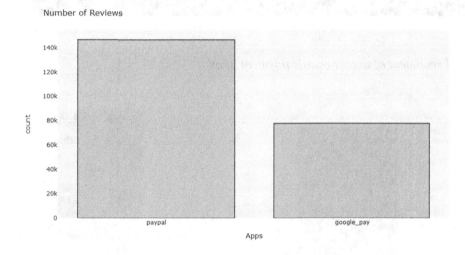

Using the function, def word count (text string), we also calculated the average number of words for each sentiment type in the review text, and we discovered that negative sentiment had 37.71 words, neutral sentiment had 30.96 words, and positive sentiment had just 14.07 words (presented in Table 3). In light of the association we've seen between lengthier review content and negative emotions, we may accept hypothesis H1, which predicts that negative sentiment would be associated with longer review text. This proposes that unhappy users of apps are more likely than satisfied users to share their opinions

Table 2. With a percentage of positive (1), neutral (0), and negative (-1) sentiment toward each app

Apps	Sentiment			Total
	-1	0	1	
Google Pay	57979 (74.51%)	6238 (8.016%)	13600 (17.48%)	77817
PayPal	43247 (29.53%)	6809 (4.65%)	96408 (65.82%)	146464
Total	101226 (45.13%)	13047 (5.82%)	110008 (49.05%)	224281

Figure 3. Wordcloud

Figure 4. Overall sentiment of users towards payment apps

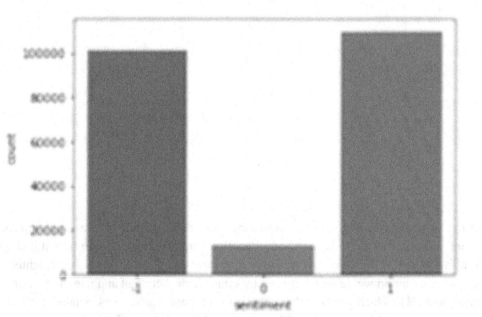

Table 3. The average scores for each sentiment class for word count, AFINN, and VADER

	word_count	afinn_score	vader_neg	vader_neu	vader_pos	vader_compound
sentiment						
-1	37.70714	-1.55126	0.133694	0.791302	0.075003	-0.21063
0	30.95869	0.885644	0.088931	0.788783	0.122279	0.101574
1	14.0744	2.861819	0.025864	0.591077	0.38306	0.550184

Table 4. The average scores for each app for word count, AFINN, and VADER

	word_count	afinn_score	vader_neg	vader_neu	vader_pos	vader_compound
Apps						
Google Pay	37.69996	-0.59203	0.123455	0.757848	0.118695	-0.07256
PayPal	19.35969	1.470798	0.054157	0.658463	0.28738	0.315266

with others and write longer reviews on the Google Play Store. Additionally, the current study found that Google Pay users write longer average reviews than PayPal users (presented in Table 4). Additionally, Tables 3 and 4 included the average Afinn and Vader scores for each sentiment class and app, respectively.

The study revealed the lowest Afinn score to be -40 (Table 5) and the highest 70 (Table 6), with the average Afinn score for negative emotion being -1.55, neutral sentiment being 0.89, and positive sentiment being 2.86 (Table 3). Table 3 further revealed that the average Vader compound score for positive emotion was 0.55 and for neutral and negative sentiment respectively, it was 0.01 and 0.10. According to Table 4, the average Afinn scores for Google Pay and PayPal were -0.59 and 1.47, respectively, while the average Vader Compound Scores were -0.07 and 0.32, respectively.

Additionally, Tables 5 and 6 reveal, respectively, the top 10 unfavorable and favorable review messages (The present study displayed only a single line extracted from each text, rather than the entire text). The whole review text may also be revealed using the iloc [] function of machine learning algorithm. Table 5 revealed that 6 evaluations of PayPal and 4 reviews of Google Pay were among the top 10 unfavorable comments. Table 6 further revealed that just 3 reviews of PayPal and 7 reviews of Google Pay were found in the top ten favorable reviews.

Table 5. Top 10 negative reviews

	Apps	Content	afinn_score
119341	PayPal	PayPal sucks there app sucks the customer service sucks even more their products suck website su...	-40
8065	PayPal	u dont back the seller and your fees are ridiculously high find a different service if you can.....	-32
174009	Google Pay	This app has three fatal flaws that took it from getting a 5-star to a 1-star review: -- It uses...	-30
205361	Google Pay	Really dirty app..i forgot my upi pin. When I am trying to get upi pin it is asking me to enter ...	-30
72036	PayPal	Worst, incredibly awful, deceiving, thief, stupid, annoying disastrous, highly non recommendable...	-29
181272	Google Pay	worst app.. i could not add my bank account only.. it's been showing your bank is busy i hate th...	-29
13122	PayPal	A warning to all sellers that want to use PayPal as a platform for transcations. PayPal will alw...	-28
223011	Google Pay	Don't use Google pay. It's fake app.3 times my payment get stuck. Suffered loss of money because...	-28
142876	PayPal	Fraud! Fraud! Fraud! Its worst company...dont ever go for this company they are fraud... they wi...	-28
67069	PayPal	Close too damn near 1 hour and I still haven't been able to log into my account. 4x I called the...	-27

Table 6. Top 10 positive reviews

	Apps	Content	afinn_score
157712	Google Pay	one of the good app for BHIM UPI transactions but not the best app. why we need to use GPay, if ...	29
170343	Google Pay	Unlike the other payment apps, the app looks less cluttered. Would like to see other used cases....	29
210225	Google Pay	Good Very useful, easy to use feeling happy to use thanks for creating this useful app .Very int...	29
158433	Google Pay	The payment Plateform is awesome. And the other person typing see feature is just amazing. The n...	29
11497	PayPal	I love PayPal it's been the most useful and easiest app I ever downloaded and especially for all...	30
32732	PayPal	I greatly appreciate mobile PayPal. It makes doing business and transactions. So much easier for...	32
158278	Google Pay	I don't understand the logic behind a random winner in scratch cards. Google needs to understand...	33
146925	Google Pay	Its good. Being good. Its pleasure to use with this. I am so happy while I am usimg thi app Its ...	34
24370	PayPal	Amazing I loved j t. Best time ever I loved it thank you so much PayPal you the best no one's be...	42
167403	Google Pay	Keeps me thinking New games added lots of fun! The game gets better every week there are many co...	70

The outcomes presented in Table 7 specify that all five machine learning models were able to successfully identify user reviews of PayPal and Google Pay. However, the logistic regression model outperformed the other models in terms of accuracy, validity, completeness of data, influence efficacy, and mean squared error. This means that the logistic regression model provided the most accurate and reliable results when it comes to classifying user app reviews. The accuracy scores of the decision tree classifier, SVC, logistic regression, random forest classifier, and k-neighbors classifier were 88.197, 88.279, 86.107, 67.186, and 79.865, respectively. The logistic regression model had the highest accuracy score among all models allowing us to reject the H2 hypothesis. The validity of the results was also measured using the ratio of true positives to all positives, which showed that the logistic regression model had the highest validity with a score of 0.856. In terms of recall scores, the decision tree classifier, SVC, logistic regression, random forest classifier, and k-neighbors classifier had scores of 0.882, 0.883, 0.861, 0.672, and 0.799, respectively. This indicates that the logistic regression model had the highest recall score, meaning it was able to correctly identify the most positive and negative reviews. The F1 scores for the SVC, logistic regression, random forest, k-neighbors, and decision tree classifier models were 0.857, 0.860, 0.836, 0.647, and 0.795, respectively. The logistic regression model had the second-highest F1 score, indicating that it had a good balance between precision and recall. Finally, the logistic regression model had the lowest mean squared error of 0.289, which means that it was the most accurate model when it came to classifying user app reviews. Overall, the results suggest that the logistic regression model is the best model for predicting users' views about payment applications based on their reviews.

Table 7. Performance of different models

Models	accuracy_score	Precision	Recall	F-Measure	mean_squared_error	r2_score
SVM	88.197	0.852	0.882	0.857	0.296	0.685
Logistic_Regression	88.279	0.856	0.883	0.860	0.289	0.692
Random_Forest_Classifier	86.107	0.831	0.861	0.836	0.380	0.595
K_Neighbors_Classifier	67.186	0.650	0.672	0.647	1.134	-0.206
Decision_Tree_Classifier	79.865	0.792	0.799	0.795	0.525	0.442

APPLICATIONS

Reviews have the ability to influence both purchase decisions and a company's reputation. Customer happiness and the likelihood that they would interact with the business are both influenced by customer evaluations. The emotions of its consumers must thus be considered by app developers. Accurate methods for evaluating and distinguishing viewpoints are essential since there is so much user-generated information. Users have the ability to make snap judgments on whether or not to install apps, and app developers may benefit greatly from understanding users' psychological perspectives. By providing a foundation of knowledge on the tone of payment app evaluations, our research will be useful to both payment app developers and customers. The professionals will also greatly benefit from this research. Business sentiment analysis applications are difficult to ignore. Workplace sentiment monitoring has the power to alter how companies run. The capacity to gain insightful knowledge from unstructured data is crucial for a data-driven firm to prosper. In the internet age of today, when businesses are dealing with data overload, businesses may have amassed a significant amount of client feedback (which does not always equal better or deeper insights). Manual evaluation of it without prejudice or errors is still challenging. In light of this, our research may be beneficial to a number of businesses in addition to payment applications.

In our study, we found that dissatisfied customers are less likely to provide positive ratings and lengthy reviews, indicating a higher tendency to express their frustrations to others. Therefore, app developers may want to focus on analyzing longer reviews to identify the reasons for customer dissatisfaction when dealing with a large number of complaints. This will enable them to respond to criticism more quickly, minimizing potential harm to their business. We also found that logistic regression had the highest accuracy score in predicting user sentiment for payment applications. This suggests that online payment companies could use logistic regression to obtain the best outcomes when analyzing customer behavior towards their products and services. Understanding consumer behavior is becoming increasingly important for companies to succeed in today's competitive business environment. By working in a fast-paced environment, companies can develop new strategies. These findings could benefit not only app developers but also service industries such as banking and tourism. Moreover, the results could be modified and applied to a variety of other problems. In conclusion, the study's results highlight the importance of analyzing longer reviews to identify customer dissatisfaction, as well as the use of logistic regression for predicting user sentiment in payment applications. The findings could help businesses to enhance their services and stay ahead of their competition in the rapidly evolving digital landscape.

CONCLUSION

Sentiment analysis is a powerful tool that can be used to gain valuable insights into customer sentiment and improve products and services accordingly. For app development, user reviews can be a particularly valuable source of information, but manually categorizing each review is impractical. Machine learning techniques, such as the ones employed in this study, can be used to automate the categorization and analysis of user reviews. The authors of this study focused on how sentiment analysis can be used to differentiate between words and product ratings in two popular payment apps, Google Pay and PayPal. By collecting and analyzing user reviews from the Google Play Store and using techniques such as TF-IDF vectorization and AFINN and VADER sentiment analysis, the authors were able to train and evaluate several machine learning models for classifying app reviews. The results showed that logistic regression performed the best in terms of accuracy, validity, completeness of data, and influence efficacy, making it the most suitable model for classifying user app reviews. The study found that the majority of evaluations of payment applications appeared to be favorable, and that consumers had a more positive perception of PayPal compared to Google Pay. Only 4.65% of the 146,464 evaluations on PayPal had neutral thoughts, while 65.82% were good and 29.53% were negative. On the other hand, just 17.48% of the 77,817 evaluations on Google Pay were good, 74.51% were negative, and 8.016% were indifferent. In addition, the study utilized five supervised ML models, all of which were effective in recognizing user reviews. However, logistic regression delivered the best results in terms of accuracy, precision, recall, F-measure, R2 score, and mean squared error. Overall, this study highlights the importance of sentiment analysis in app development and demonstrates how machine learning techniques can be used to automate the categorization and analysis of user reviews. By leveraging these techniques, organizations can gain valuable insights into customer sentiment and improve their products and services accordingly. Future research could further explore the effectiveness of different machine learning algorithms for sentiment analysis, and could also examine the use of sentiment analysis in other domains beyond app development.

The present study, though informative, has some limitations that must be acknowledged. Firstly, the study employed a limited dataset, which may have impacted the accuracy of the findings. In order to establish the generalizability of the results, future research should be conducted across multiple platforms such as the Apple App Store, Galaxy Store, and others. Further research could compile and compare information on payment applications from various sources to enhance the validity of the findings. Secondly, the sentiment analysis and prediction techniques employed in this research were based on traditional supervised and unsupervised machine learning procedures. To obtain more dependable outcomes, deep learning models should be utilized in future studies. Additionally, aspect-level sentiment analysis could improve the accuracy of future studies, allowing for the identification of specific aspects that users like or dislike. For example, users' preferences regarding payment conveniences, payment fees, and pre-existing conditions could be examined in detail. Finally, although the current study used evaluations of two international payment apps, it may not accurately reflect the overall user opinion towards payment apps. This is because certain countries like Bangladesh do not allow PayPal, and some countries may have their own preferred payment applications. For instance, Ali Pay and WeChat are the most widely used payment apps in China. A future study could explore consumer attitudes towards local payment applications in such countries to provide a more comprehensive picture of user behavior towards payment apps. In summary, although the present study provides valuable insights into user sentiment towards payment applications, there are opportunities for improvement. Conducting research across multiple platforms, utilizing deep learning models, and employing aspect-level sentiment analysis could enhance the accuracy and reliability of future studies. Additionally, examining local payment applications in countries where international payment apps are not available could provide a more comprehensive understanding of user behavior towards payment apps.

REFERENCES

Alarifi, G., Rahman, M. F., & Hossain, M. S. (2023). Prediction and Analysis of Customer Complaints Using Machine Learning Techniques. [IJEBR]. *International Journal of E-Business Research*, *19*(1), 1–25. doi:10.4018/IJEBR.319716

Ali, S., Wang, G., & Riaz, S. (2020). Aspect based sentiment analysis of ridesharing platform reviews for kansei engineering. *IEEE Access : Practical Innovations, Open Solutions*, *8*, 173186–173196. doi:10.1109/ACCESS.2020.3025823

Amin, A., Hossain, I., Akther, A., & Alam, K. M. (2019). Bengali VADER: A Sentiment Analysis Approach Using Modified VADER. *2019 International Conference on Electrical, Computer and Communication Engineering (ECCE)*. 10.1109/ECACE.2019.8679144

Aslam, N., Ramay, W. Y., Kewen, X., & Sarwar, N. (2020). Convolutional Neural Network Based Classification of App Reviews. *IEEE Access : Practical Innovations, Open Solutions*, *8*, 1–1. doi:10.1109/ACCESS.2020.3029634

Barcena, E., Read, T., & Sedano, B. (2020). An Approximation to Inclusive Language in LMOOCs Based on Appraisal Theory. *Open Linguistics*, *6*(1), 38–67. doi:10.1515/opli-2020-0003

Basiri, M. E., Abdar, M., Cifci, M. A., Nemati, S., & Acharya, U. R. (2020). A novel method for sentiment classification of drug reviews using fusion of deep and machine learning techniques. *Knowledge-Based Systems*, *198*, 105949. Advance online publication. doi:10.1016/j.knosys.2020.105949

Bhaumik, U., & Yadav, D. K. (2021). Sentiment Analysis Using Twitter. In J. K. Mandal, I. Mukherjee, S. Bakshi, S. Chatterji, & P. K. Sa (Eds.), *Computational Intelligence and Machine Learning. Advances in Intelligent Systems and Computing* (Vol. 1276). Springer. doi:10.1007/978-981-15-8610-1_7

Chevalier, J. A., & Mayzlin, D. (2006). The Effect of Word of Mouth on Sales: Online Book Reviews. *JMR, Journal of Marketing Research*, *43*(3), 345–354. doi:10.1509/jmkr.43.3.345

Chiou, J. S., Hsiao, C. C., & Su, F. Y. (2014). Whose online reviews have the most influences on consumers in cultural offerings? Professional vs consumer commentators. *Internet Research*, *24*(3), 353–368. doi:10.1108/IntR-03-2013-0046

Dang, N. C., Moreno-García, M. N., & De la Prieta, F. (2020). Sentiment analysis based on deep learning: A comparative study. *Electronics (Switzerland)*, *9*(3), 483. Advance online publication. doi:10.3390/electronics9030483

Daudert, T. (2021). Exploiting textual and relationship information for fine-grained financial sentiment analysis. *Knowledge-Based Systems*, *230*, 107389. Advance online publication. doi:10.1016/j.knosys.2021.107389

Deng, Z. H., Luo, K. H., & Yu, H. L. (2014). A study of supervised term weighting scheme for sentiment analysis. *Expert Systems with Applications*, *41*(7), 3506–3513. doi:10.1016/j.eswa.2013.10.056

Dwidienawati, D., Tjahjana, D., Abdinagoro, S. B., Gandasari, D., & Munawaroh. (2020). Customer review or influencer endorsement: Which one influences purchase intention more? *Heliyon*, *6*(11), e05543. Advance online publication. doi:10.1016/j.heliyon.2020.e05543 PMID:33294687

Finkelstein, A., Harman, M., Jia, Y., Martin, W., Sarro, F., & Zhang, Y. (2017). Investigating the relationship between price, rating, and popularity in the Blackberry World App Store. *Information and Software Technology*, *87*, 119–139. doi:10.1016/j.infsof.2017.03.002

Fors Brandebo, M., Nilsson, S., & Larsson, G. (2016). Leadership: Is bad stronger than good? *Leadership and Organization Development Journal*, *37*(6), 690–710. doi:10.1108/LODJ-09-2014-0191

Fors Brandebo, M., Nilsson, S., & Larsson, G. (2016). Leadership: Is bad stronger than good? *Leadership and Organization Development Journal*, *37*(6), 690–710. doi:10.1108/LODJ-09-2014-0191

Garay, J., Yap, R., & Sabellano, M. J. (2019). An analysis on the insights of the anti-vaccine movement from social media posts using k-means clustering algorithm and VADER sentiment analyzer. *IOP Conference Series. Materials Science and Engineering*, *482*, 012043. doi:10.1088/1757-899X/482/1/012043

Ghasemaghaei, M., Eslami, S. P., Deal, K., & Hassanein, K. (2018). Reviews' length and sentiment as correlates of online reviews' ratings. *Internet Research*, *28*(3), 544–563. doi:10.1108/IntR-12-2016-0394

Gul, E., Alpaslan, N., & Emiroglu, M. E. (2021). Robust optimization of SVM hyper-parameters for spillway type selection. *Ain Shams Engineering Journal*, *12*(3), 2413–2423. doi:10.1016/j.asej.2020.10.022

Gul, E., Alpaslan, N., & Emiroglu, M. E. (2021). Robust optimization of SVM hyper-parameters for spillway type selection. *Ain Shams Engineering Journal*, *12*(3), 2413–2423. Advance online publication. doi:10.1016/j.asej.2020.10.022

Ha, Y.-W., & Hoch, S. J. (1989). Ambiguity, Processing Strategy, and Advertising-Evidence Interactions. *The Journal of Consumer Research*, *16*(3), 354. doi:10.1086/209221

Halliday, M. A. K., & Matthiessen, C. M. I. M. (2004). *An Introduction to Functional Grammar* (3rd ed.). Edward Arnold.

Han, H., Zhang, Y., Zhang, J., Yang, J., & Zou, X. (2018). Improving the performance of lexicon-based review sentiment analysis method by reducing additional introduced sentiment bias. *PLoS One*, *13*(8), e0202523. Advance online publication. doi:10.1371/journal.pone.0202523 PMID:30142154

Hassan, S., Tantithamthavorn, C., Bezemer, C.-P., & Hassan, A. E. (2017). Studying the dialogue between users and developers of free apps in the Google Play Store. *Empirical Software Engineering*, *23*(3), 1275–1312. doi:10.100710664-017-9538-9

Hossain, M. S., & Rahman, M. F. (2022a). Detection of potential customers' empathy behavior towards customers' reviews. *Journal of Retailing and Consumer Services*, *65*, 102881. doi:10.1016/j.jretconser.2021.102881

Hossain, M. S., & Rahman, M. F. (2022b). *Customer Sentiment Analysis and Prediction of Insurance Products' Reviews Using Machine Learning Approaches*. FIIB Business Review., doi:10.1177/23197145221115793

Hossain, M. S., & Rahman, M. F. (2022a). Machine Learning and Artificial Intelligence: The New Move for Marketers. In J. Kaur, P. Jindal, & A. Singh (Eds.), *Developing Relationships, Personalization, and Data Herald in Marketing 5.0* (pp. 215–241). IGI Global., doi:10.4018/978-1-6684-4496-2.ch014

Hossain, M. S., & Rahman, M. F. (2022b). Sentiment Analysis and Review Rating Prediction of the Users of Bangladeshi Shopping Apps. In J. Kaur, P. Jindal, & A. Singh (Eds.), *Developing Relationships, Personalization, and Data Herald in Marketing 5.0* (pp. 33–56). IGI Global., doi:10.4018/978-1-6684-4496-2.ch002

Hossain, M. S., Rahman, M. F., & Uddin, M. K. (2022a). Analyzing and Predicting Learners' Sentiment toward Specialty schools using Machine Learning Techniques. In G. Trajkovski, M. Demeter, & H. Hayes (Eds.), *Applying Data Science and Learning Analytics Throughout a Learner's Lifespan*. IGI Global., doi:10.4018/978-1-7998-9644-9.ch007

Hossain, M. S., Uddin, M. K., Hossain, M. K., & Rahman, M. F. (2022b). User sentiment analysis and review rating prediction for the Blended Learning Platform app. In G. Trajkovski, M. Demeter, & H. Hayes (Eds.), *Applying Data Science and Learning Analytics Throughout a Learner's Lifespan*. IGI Global., doi:10.4018/978-1-7998-9644-9.ch006

Hossain, M. S. (2023). Behavioral Analytics of Consumer Complaints. In S. Nagaraj & K. Kumar (Eds.), *AI-Driven Intelligent Models for Business Excellence* (pp. 42–67). IGI Global., https://doi.org/10.4018/978-1-6684-4246-3.ch003.

Hossain, M. S. and Rahman, M. F (2023). Detection of readers' emotional aspects and thumbs-up empathy reactions towards reviews of online travel agency apps, Journal of Hospitality and Tourism Insights. https://doi.org/ doi:10.1108/JHTI-10-2022-0487

Hossain, M. S., & Rahman, M. F (2023). Detection of readers' emotional aspects and thumbs-up empathy reactions towards reviews of online travel agency apps. *Journal of Hospitality and Tourism Insights*. doi:10.1108/JHTI-10-2022-0487

Hossain, M. S., Rahman, M. F., Uddin, M. K. & Hossain, M. K. (2022). Customer sentiment analysis and prediction of halal restaurants using machine learning approaches. *Journal of Islamic Marketing*. doi:10.1108/JIMA-04-2021-0125

Hossain, M. S., Rahman, M. F., & Zhou, X. (2021). Impact of customers' interpersonal interactions in social commerce on customer relationship management performance. *Journal of Contemporary Marketing Science*, *4*(1), 161–181. doi:10.1108/JCMARS-12-2020-0050

Jurek, A., Mulvenna, M. D., & Bi, Y. (2015). Improved lexicon-based sentiment analysis for social media analytics. *Security Informatics*, *4*(1), 9. Advance online publication. doi:10.118613388-015-0024-x

Kanna, P. R., & Pandiaraja, P. (2019). An Efficient Sentiment Analysis Approach for Product Review using Turney Algorithm. In *Procedia Computer Science* (Vol. 165, pp. 356–362). Elsevier B.V. doi:10.1016/j.procs.2020.01.038

Kastrati, Z., Imran, A. S., & Kurti, A. (2020). Weakly Supervised Framework for Aspect-Based Sentiment Analysis on Students' Reviews of MOOCs. *IEEE Access : Practical Innovations, Open Solutions*, *8*, 106799–106810. doi:10.1109/ACCESS.2020.3000739

Kim, J. C., & Chung, K. Y. (2020). Knowledge expansion of metadata using script mining analysis in multimedia recommendation. *Multimedia Tools and Applications*. Advance online publication. doi:10.100711042-020-08774-0

Lee, M., Rodgers, S., & Kim, M. (2009). Effects of valence and extremity of eWOM on attitude toward the brand and website. *Journal of Current Issues and Research in Advertising*, *31*(2), 1–11. doi:10.1080/10641734.2009.10505262

Luo, Y., & Xu, X. (2021). Comparative study of deep learning models for analyzing online restaurant reviews in the era of the COVID-19 pandemic. *International Journal of Hospitality Management*, *94*, 102849. Advance online publication. doi:10.1016/j.ijhm.2020.102849 PMID:34785843

Maalej, W., Kurtanović, Z., Nabil, H., & Stanik, C. (2016). On the automatic classification of app reviews. *Requirements Engineering*, *21*(3), 311–331. doi:10.100700766-016-0251-9

Machová, K., Mikula, M., Gao, X., & Mach, M. (2020). Lexicon-based sentiment analysis using particle swarm optimization. *Electronics (Switzerland)*, *9*(8), 1–22. doi:10.3390/electronics9081317

Mäntylä, M. V., Graziotin, D., & Kuutila, M. (2018). The evolution of sentiment analysis—A review of research topics, venues, and top cited papers. *Computer Science Review*, *27*, 16–32. doi:10.1016/j.cosrev.2017.10.002

Martens, D., & Maalej, W. (2019). Towards understanding and detecting fake reviews in app stores. *Empirical Software Engineering*, *24*(6), 3316–3355. doi:10.100710664-019-09706-9

Martin, J. R., & White, P. R. R. (2005). *The Language of Evaluation: Appraisal in English. The Language of Evaluation: Appraisal in English.* Palgrave Macmillan. doi:10.1057/9780230511910

McIlroy, S., Ali, N., & Hassan, A. E. (2015). Fresh apps: An empirical study of frequently-updated mobile apps in the Google play store. *Empirical Software Engineering*, *21*(3), 1346–1370. doi:10.100710664-015-9388-2

Miao, Q., Li, Q., & Zeng, D. (2010). Fine-grained opinion mining by integrating multiple review sources. *Journal of the American Society for Information Science and Technology*, *61*(11), 2288–2299. doi:10.1002/asi.21400

Mostafa, M. M. (2018). Mining and mapping halal food consumers: A geo-located Twitter opinion polarity analysis. *Journal of Food Products Marketing*, *24*(7), 858–879. doi:10.1080/10454446.2017.1418695

Mostafa, M. M. (2019). Clustering halal food consumers: A Twitter sentiment analysis. *International Journal of Market Research*, *61*(3), 320–337. doi:10.1177/1470785318771451

Mostafa, M. M. (2020). Global halal food discourse on social media: A text mining approach. *Journal of International Communication*, *26*(2), 211–237. doi:10.1080/13216597.2020.1795702

Mujahid, M., Lee, E., Rustam, F., Washington, P. B., Ullah, S., Reshi, A. A., & Ashraf, I. (2021). Sentiment analysis and topic modeling on tweets about online education during covid-19. *Applied Sciences (Switzerland)*, *11*(18), 8438. Advance online publication. doi:10.3390/app11188438

Mullen, T., & Collier, N. (2004). Sentiment Analysis using Support Vector Machines with Diverse Information Sources. In D. Lin & D. Wu (Eds.), *Proceedings of EMNLP 2004* (pp. 412–418). Association for Computational Linguistics. http://research.nii.ac.jp/~collier/papers/emnlp2004.pdf

Nasukawa, T., & Yi, J. (2003). Sentiment analysis: Capturing favorability using natural language processing. In *Proceedings of the 2nd International Conference on Knowledge Capture, K-CAP 2003* (pp. 70–77). Association for Computing Machinery, Inc. 10.1145/945645.945658

Nemes, L., & Kiss, A. (2021). Prediction of stock values changes using sentiment analysis of stock news headlines. *Journal of Information and Telecommunication*, *5*(3), 375–394. doi:10.1080/24751839.2021.1874252

Oliveira, N., Cortez, P., & Areal, N. (2016). Stock market sentiment lexicon acquisition using microblogging data and statistical measures. *Decision Support Systems*, *85*, 62–73. doi:10.1016/j.dss.2016.02.013

Pak, A., & Paroubek, P. (2010). Twitter as a corpus for sentiment analysis and opinion mining. In *Proceedings of the 7th International Conference on Language Resources and Evaluation, LREC 2010* (pp. 1320–1326). European Language Resources Association (ELRA). 10.17148/IJARCCE.2016.51274

Pang, B., & Lee, L. (2008). Opinion mining and sentiment analysis. *Foundations and Trends in Information Retrieval*, *2*(1–2), 1–135. doi:10.1561/1500000011

Pang, B., Lee, L., & Vithyanathan, S. (2019). Thumbs up? Sentiment Classification using Machine Learning Techniques. *Proceedings of the Institution of Civil Engineers - Transport, 172*(2), 122–122.

Pano, T., & Kashef, R. (2020). A Complete VADER-Based Sentiment Analysis of Bitcoin (BTC) Tweets during the Era of COVID-19. *Big Data and Cognitive Computing*, *4*(4), 33. Advance online publication. doi:10.3390/bdcc4040033

Pashchenko, Y., Rahman, M. F., Hossain, M. S., Uddin, M. K., & Islam, T. (2022). Emotional and the normative aspects of customers' reviews. *Journal of Retailing and Consumer Services*, *68*, 103011. doi:10.1016/j.jretconser.2022.103011

Preethi, P. G., Uma, V., & Kumar, A. (2015). Temporal sentiment analysis and causal rules extraction from tweets for event prediction. In *Procedia Computer Science* (Vol. 48, pp. 84–89). Elsevier B.V. doi:10.1016/j.procs.2015.04.154

Ravi, K., & Ravi, V. (2015). A survey on opinion mining and sentiment analysis: Tasks, approaches and applications. *Knowledge-Based Systems*, *89*, 14–46. doi:10.1016/j.knosys.2015.06.015

Rodríguez-Hidalgo, C. T., Tan, E. S. H., & Verlegh, P. W. J. (2015). The social sharing of emotion (SSE) in online social networks: A case study in Live Journal. *Computers in Human Behavior*, *52*, 364–372. doi:10.1016/j.chb.2015.05.009

Saif, H., He, Y., Fernandez, M., & Alani, H. (2016). Contextual semantics for sentiment analysis of Twitter. *Information Processing & Management*, *52*(1), 5–19. doi:10.1016/j.ipm.2015.01.005

Scherer, K. R., Schorr, A., & Johnstone, T. (Eds.). (2001). *Appraisal processes in emotion: Theory, methods, research*. Oxford University Press.

Sigirci, I. O., Ozgur, H., Oluk, A., Uz, H., Cetiner, E., Oktay, H. U., & Erdemir, K. (2020). Sentiment Analysis of Turkish Reviews on Google Play Store. *2020 5th International Conference on Computer Science and Engineering (UBMK)*. doi:10.1109/ubmk50275.2020.921

Tan, M. J., & Guan, C. H. (2021). Are people happier in locations of high property value? Spatial temporal analytics of activity frequency, public sentiment and housing price using twitter data. *Applied Geography (Sevenoaks, England), 132*, 102474. Advance online publication. doi:10.1016/j.apgeog.2021.102474

Triantafyllou, I., Drivas, I. C., & Giannakopoulos, G. (2020). How to utilize my app reviews? A novel topics extraction machine learning schema for strategic business purposes. *Entropy (Basel, Switzerland), 22*(11), 1–21. doi:10.3390/e22111310 PMID:33287075

Vashishtha, S., & Susan, S. (2020). Fuzzy Interpretation of Word Polarity Scores for Unsupervised Sentiment Analysis. In *2020 11th International Conference on Computing, Communication and Networking Technologies, ICCCNT 2020*. Institute of Electrical and Electronics Engineers Inc. 10.1109/ICCCNT49239.2020.9225646

Wang, Y., Kim, J., & Kim, J. (2021). The financial impact of online customer reviews in the restaurant industry: A moderating effect of brand equity. *International Journal of Hospitality Management, 95*, 102895. Advance online publication. doi:10.1016/j.ijhm.2021.102895

Widyaningrum, P., Ruldeviyani, Y., & Dharayani, R. (2019). Sentiment analysis to assess the community's enthusiasm towards the development chatbot using an appraisal theory. In *Procedia Computer Science, 161, 723–730*. Elsevier B.V. doi:10.1016/j.procs.2019.11.176

Wiese, M., & Humbani, M. (2019). Exploring technology readiness for mobile payment app users. *International Review of Retail, Distribution and Consumer Research,* ●●●, 1–20. doi:10.1080/09593969.2019.1626260

Yang, L., Li, Y., Wang, J., & Sherratt, R. S. (2020). Sentiment Analysis for E-Commerce Product Reviews in Chinese Based on Sentiment Lexicon and Deep Learning. *IEEE Access : Practical Innovations, Open Solutions, 8*, 23522–23530. doi:10.1109/ACCESS.2020.2969854

Yang, W., Li, J., Zhang, Y., & Gu, D. (2019). Security analysis of third-party in-app payment in mobile applications. *Journal of Information Security and Applications, 48*, 102358. doi:10.1016/j.jisa.2019.102358

Yue, L., Chen, W., Li, X., Zuo, W., & Yin, M. (2019). A survey of sentiment analysis in social media. *Knowledge and Information Systems, 60*(2), 617–663. doi:10.100710115-018-1236-4

Zeelenberg, M., & Pieters, R. (2004). Beyond valence in learner dissatisfaction: A review and new findings on behavioral responses to regret and disappointment in failed services. *Journal of Business Research, 57*(4), 445–455. doi:10.1016/S0148-2963(02)00278-3

KEY TERMS AND DEFINITIONS

Machine Learning: An area of artificial intelligence (AI) that includes the creation of algorithms and models that can learn from and anticipate or make choices based on data.

Mobile Apps: Software programs that operate on mobile devices like smartphones, tablets, and smartwatches. These apps are designed to offer users a variety of features and capabilities, such as entertainment, productivity, communication, and usefulness.

Payment Apps: Software applications designed to enable users to send or receive money electronically using their mobile devices. These apps provide a convenient and secure way for users to make payments, transfer funds, and manage their finances on-the-go.

Sentiment Analysis: Involves using natural language processing (NLP) techniques to determine the sentiment of a given text as positive, negative, or neutral. This can be useful in understanding how people feel about a particular product, service, or topic, and can be used to inform business decisions, marketing strategies, and customer service improvements.

Sentiment: Refers to the emotion or attitude expressed in a particular piece of text, such as a review, comment, or social media post.

Smartphone: A mobile computer device that combines mobile phone and computing operations into a single device.

User Reviews: Feedback and comments given by users or customers of a product or service, usually in written or numerical form.

Chapter 18
Sequence Graph–Based Query Auto–Suggestion (SGQAS)

Soumya George

iD https://orcid.org/0000-0002-7256-7677

St. George's College Aruvithura, India

ABSTRACT

Query autosuggestion or auto-completion is a query prediction service that returns suggested queries for text-based queries when users type in the search box. It is a search-assistant feature of almost all search engines that helps users complete the queries without typing the entire search query. The process of query auto-suggestion typically involves analyzing the user's partial query and generating a list of suggestions based on factors such as popular search terms, the user's search history, and the search context. The suggestions are then displayed to the user in real-time, often in a drop-down menu or other interface types, allowing them to select and refine their search query easily. This chapter proposes a content-based query auto-suggestion using a graph-based word sequence representation of documents using a knowledge graph. It uses the whole sequence of all entered query terms to retrieve the names of all nodes connected to the end node of the entered path sequence of query terms to provide user suggestion queries.

INTRODUCTION

In recent years, search engines have become an integral part of our daily lives. We use them to find information on just about anything, from the latest news to products to purchase. As a result, search engines have been developed to be more user-friendly and efficient, with a range of features to help users find what they are looking for quickly and easily. One such feature is autosuggestion.

Web search engines facilitate easier search and retrieval of information from the world wide web. The existence of a search engine depends on its ability to satisfy users by suggesting relevant documents according to their queries. The user-friendliness of the search engine interface also plays a major role in the selection of a search engine by users. Query Autosuggestion, also known as query auto-completion is a search-assistant facility provided by almost all search engines to help users with different query

DOI: 10.4018/978-1-6684-7105-0.ch018

suggestions as they type in the search box (Tahery, 2020). Searching lengthy keywords is a tedious task for users. Also, it may lead to many typos or grammatical errors. The partial query entered by the user will be compared against a set of target strings stored to find suitable matches to complete the query and will be suggested to the user. Users can select a completion string from the list of suggestions with a single click without having to type the entire query. It enhances search by saving user time without having to type the full query. Figure 1 shows the query auto-suggestion facility of Google that retrieves a list of candidate substrings to complete the query.

Figure 1. Google query auto-suggestion example

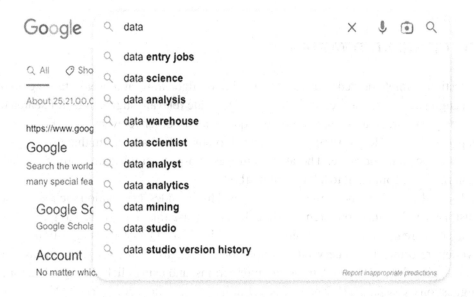

Some search engines use the prefix-matching method to complete the query, while others depend on both prefix matching and postfix matching. The main advantages of Query Auto-Suggestion Systems include a reduction in the number of keystrokes to complete the user query. It also improves the quality of user queries by reducing the number of typo errors by suggesting completion queries beforehand. (Krishnan, 2021).

Search queries are of 3 types. They are:

1. Navigational search queries
2. Informational search queries
3. Transactional search queries

Navigational search queries intend to find a particular website or webpage like 'YouTube', 'Facebook' etc. by navigating through a URL. Informational search queries are normal queries with the intent to find a particular information search or need that expects relevant documents as results. Transactional search queries may include 'buy', 'purchase' etc. to do a transaction like purchasing a product or shopping for items, etc.

The sequence structure or the word order of contents plays a major role in finding suggestion queries based on user search patterns. Graph-based representation of contents can easily capture the sequence structure of contents. Knowledge graphs like Neo4j become increasingly popular in this field because of the capability to easily create nodes and edges and the enhanced feature to add properties on both nodes and edges. This chapter proposes a Sequence Graph-based Query Auto-Suggestion, SGQAS, which helps to predict the completion queries based on the keyword prefix sequence of user-entered queries. This is an extension of the previous work on graph-based index representation of all documents in the documents pool using a knowledge graph that captures the sequence or word order of terms of each sentence of each document using the Word Sequence Graph (WSG) model (George, 2017).

REVIEW OF RELATED WORKS

Autosuggestion is implemented using a combination of algorithms and user data. The algorithms used by search engines analyze user search behavior to generate relevant suggestions for search queries. This includes analyzing previous searches, popular queries, and other relevant data. For example, in their research paper, Cho and Roy (2016) proposed an auto-suggestion algorithm that uses click-through data to improve suggestion relevance. The algorithm was shown to significantly improve the accuracy of suggestion rankings compared to a baseline method.

User data is also used to generate autosuggestions. This includes information such as the user's location, search history, and language preferences. Search engines use this information to generate personalized suggestions that are tailored to each user's needs and interests. Query autosuggestion in search engines includes query reformulation, query auto-completion, personalized query suggestion based on user intent and social tagging data, user perceptions and interactions, and using click-through data for personalized query suggestion (Kousha, 2021; Zhang, 2021; Laitinen, 2021; Roy, 2020; Yu, 2020; Jansen, 2010; Kim, 2019). In their research paper, Peetz et al. (2019) investigated the effect of using personalized data on the performance of auto-suggestion algorithms. They found that incorporating personalized data can improve the relevance of suggestions, especially for queries with low frequency. A survey of query auto-suggestions in search engines is done (Huang, 2019) and a study on the effects of query autosuggestions and user experience in the search process is conducted (Park, 2017; Shen, 2016).

Query autosuggestion adopts context-aware, location-aware, time-sensitive, and logs-based approaches to predict suggestion queries. Context-sensitive query auto-completion depends on the context of recent user-entered queries or past queries to predict suggestions for user queries (Bar-Yossef, 2011; Schmidt, 2016; Hu, 2018). A Nearestcompletion algorithm is proposed by Bar-Yossef (2011) that suggests queries based on recent user queries. Context-sensitive predictions fail when the frequency of recent queries is very low. As a solution, a semantic similarity approach that first converts terms into entities of a knowledge base and suggests queries based on cosine similarity is proposed (Schmidt, 2016). A similar approach using a knowledge base is proposed (Hu, 2018) that suggests queries based on query logs and corpus statistics. Another approach is time-sensitive query auto-completion. A temporal query auto-completion is proposed (Shokouhi, 2012) that uses time-sensitive features to predict queries.

A hybrid model that uses both temporal and personalized aspects to predict completion queries that first capture query suggestions based on popular trends and then re-rank them based on past search behavior is narrated (Cai, 2014). A similar approach using a regression model for long-tail prefixes is described in (Cai, 2016). Query auto-completion using a neural language model for unseen prefixes, not in query logs or recent searches is proposed by (Park, 2017). A combination of semantic, context-aware, time-sensitive approaches to predict suggestion queries using a deep learning method based on a recurrent neural network model is described in (Tahery, 2022). Location-sensitive query autosuggestion uses demographic features that rely on user location to predict suggestions. This method is proposed in Jiang (2018) and uses both recent queries and location preference to suggest queries.

One approach to improving auto-suggestion algorithms is to incorporate machine learning techniques. For example, in their research paper, Yin et al. (2016) proposed a machine learning-based auto-suggestion algorithm that uses neural networks to predict query suggestions. The algorithm was shown to outperform several baseline methods in terms of both accuracy and efficiency.

Today, graph databases conquer the big data world of databases, and graph-based index creation of documents become popular (George, 2015). The authors proposed a sub-graph-based query auto-completion framework, AUTOG (Yi, 2017) that uses initial query and user preference in combination to predict suggestion queries using frequent subgraphs. In Peipei (2020), the authors present a GFocus framework for graph query suggestions by presenting a visual or graphical user interface to users. Graph searches use either cipher or SPARQL queries to search in graph databases. A SPARQL-based query auto-completion method on a large knowledge graph is detailed in Bast (2022) to assist users in completing complex SPARQL queries.

TYPES OF QUERY AUTOSUGGESTION

There are mainly two types of query autosuggestion techniques used in search engines:

Real-Time Autosuggestion

Real-time autosuggestion is the most commonly used technique in search engines. It works by predicting the user's search query as they type. The search engine provides suggestions based on the user's query, and these suggestions are updated in real-time as the user types. This type of autosuggestion is fast and accurate and is used by most popular search engines like Google, Bing, and Yahoo.

Static Autosuggestion

Static autosuggestion is another type of query autosuggestion that works by providing a predefined list of suggestions to the user. These suggestions are displayed as the user types and are not updated in real time. This type of autosuggestion is used by some search engines that do not have the infrastructure to support real-time autosuggestion.

HOW QUERY AUTOSUGGESTION WORKS

Query autosuggestion works by predicting the user's search query based on what they have typed. This prediction is based on various factors, including the user's search history, the popularity of the search query, and the relevance of the search query to the user's previous search queries. When the user types in a search query, the search engine's algorithm compares the query to its database of search queries and suggests the most relevant ones. The suggestions are updated in real-time as the user types, making it easier for them to find what they are looking for.

HISTORY OF AUTOSUGGESTION IN SEARCH ENGINES

Autosuggestion has been used in search engines since the early 2000s. The first major search engine to implement this feature was Google, which introduced its "Google Suggest" feature in 2008. This feature was designed to help users find what they were looking for more quickly and efficiently by providing suggestions based on previous searches, popular queries, and other relevant data.

Following the success of Google Suggest, other search engines began to implement their own versions of autosuggestion. For example, Bing introduced its "Instant Answers" feature in 2009, which provided relevant suggestions and answers as users typed their search queries. Yahoo also implemented a similar feature, called "Search Assist," in 2010.

COMPARISON OF QUERY AUTO-SUGGESTION OF DIFFERENT SEARCH ENGINES

The auto-suggestion feature of search engines can be a helpful tool for users, as it provides suggestions for commonly searched terms related to their query. The query auto-suggestion algorithms used by different search engines are proprietary and not publicly disclosed. Here is a comparison of the query auto-suggestion features of different popular search engines:

Google

Google's auto-suggestion feature is arguably the most widely used and comprehensive among search engines. It provides multiple suggestions as the user types, with real-time updates as they add or removes words from their query. Additionally, Google's auto-suggestions are personalized based on the user's search history and location. Google's auto-suggestion feature is highly regarded for its speed and comprehensiveness (Sullivan, 2015). The suggestions are displayed in real-time and are personalized based on the user's search history and location (Google, n.d.). Google's auto-suggestion algorithm is based on machine learning and natural language processing techniques, such as neural networks and word embeddings (Google, n.d.). It uses various sources of data, including the user's search history and real-time search data, to generate suggestions.

Bing

Bing's auto-suggestion feature is similar in speed and functionality to Google's (Mack, 2020). However, it does not offer personalized suggestions, but does display related searches and questions (Microsoft, n.d.). Bing's auto-suggestion algorithm is also based on machine learning techniques, including deep neural networks and decision trees

Yahoo

Yahoo's auto-suggestion feature is also similar to Bing's, but may be less accurate and comprehensive than Google and Bing (Brinkmann, 2013). It provides related searches and questions, but does not offer personalized suggestions (Yahoo, n.d.). Yahoo's auto-suggestion algorithm uses machine learning techniques such as Bayesian networks and decision trees, as well as collaborative filtering to generate suggestions.

Duckduckgo

DuckDuckGo's auto-suggestion feature prioritizes user privacy and does not personalize suggestions based on search history or location (DuckDuckGo, n.d.). While it may not be as comprehensive as other search engines, it does provide relevant and accurate suggestions for common searches (Friedman, 2015). It uses machine learning techniques such as neural networks and decision trees to generate suggestions.

Overall, Google and Bing offer the most comprehensive and personalized auto-suggestion features, while DuckDuckGo and Yahoo offer decent suggestions without personalized features. Ultimately, the choice of search engine and its auto-suggestion feature will depend on the user's needs and preferences. Each search engine's auto-suggestion algorithm uses a combination of machine learning and natural language processing techniques, as well as various sources of data, to generate suggestions.

QUERY AUTO-SUGGESTION ALGORITHMS: REVIEW

There are various query auto-suggestion algorithms used by search engines, including the following:

Prefix-Based Algorithm

This algorithm suggests completions to the user's query based on the user's input prefix. For example, if a user types "y", the algorithm might suggest "Year" or "Yeast".

Statistical Language Model Algorithm

This algorithm suggests completions based on the statistical likelihood of a query given the user's input so far. For example, if a user types "Christmas n", the algorithm might suggest "Christmas night" because it is statistically likely that a user searching for "Christmas n" around December 25th might be searching for events related to Christmas.

Collaborative Filtering Algorithm

This algorithm suggests completions based on the search queries of other users who have entered similar queries in the past. For example, if a user types "data m", the algorithm might suggest "data mining" because other users who have entered "data m" in the past have also searched for data mining.

Neural Network-Based Algorithm

This algorithm suggests completions based on a neural network trained on a large corpus of search queries. For example, Google uses a neural network-based algorithm for its auto-suggestions (Yin et al., 2016).

Hybrid Algorithms

Many auto-suggestion algorithms are a combination of the above methods, incorporating multiple sources of data and algorithms to generate suggestions.

WORD SEQUENCE GRAPH (WSG) REPRESENTATION OF DOCUMENTS

A Word Sequence Graph (WSG) is a directed graph, $G = (V, E)$, where V is the set of vertices that represent either document nodes or unique term nodes appearing in each document, and E is the set of edges that captures the various relationships to identify document contents (George, 2017, 2019). A WSG conversion of documents is shown in Figure 2. Tika's AutoDetect Parser is used to parse all types of files into plain .txt files which are then split into sentences using PTBTokenizer and then extract words keeping the sentence structure to capture the sequence to represent as a sequence of word graph model.

Figure 2. Word sequence graph (WSG) representation

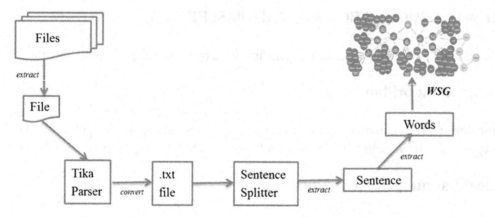

Pseudocode for creating WSG representation of document index is given in Algorithm 1. Nodes will be created for each unique document and term in the entire content pool with a unique 'id' for document and term nodes. Sentences representing document contents were connected using the 'contents/next_seq'

relationship with the first non-stop word of each sentence by the 'contents' relationship and the remaining terms in sequence by the 'next_seq' relationship capturing sentence no as 'sentence' property, 'seqid' property to identify the document to which the sentence belongs and the word order of each sentence by incrementing the 'id' property of the relationship by 1 in each next relationship that belongs to the same sentence of the same document and other properties in the relationship. All non-stop words and special symbols in between will be concatenated into one string with space in between and stored as a 'stop_word' property in the edge connecting start and end terms. Common stop words and symbols set in the English language are stored in 'stop_words' and 'symb_set' respectively which can be sued to identify stop words and symbols in the contents. All words will be converted to lowercase, but at the same time, the original case of each term will be stored as a 'case' property too. A special node called 'ter_node' will be added as an end node for all sentences that terminate with stop word terms or symbols. WSG representation and database representation of the sentence outlined in the box is given in Figure 3.

The proposed sequence graph-based representation captures the sequence of the contents by preserving term order and sentence order by using different properties like seqid, sentence, etc. without eliminating stop words or symbols or punctuations, but efficiently.

SGQAS: SEQUENCE GRAPH-BASED QUERY AUTO-SUGGESTION

One of the important applications of Word Sequence Graph representation of documents is the Content-based query auto-suggestion and completion. It is one of the important features every search engine user expects when they search for some query. It helps the user by providing different query suggestions to complete rather than typing the entire query based on the query terms entered. WSG representation facilitates this task easier since the sequence of each sentence of each document is well represented as a graph of sequence nodes.

The proposed method SGQAS suggests query completions by considering the whole sequence of all entered query terms entered by the user to capture the same sequence sentences in the graph and then retrieve the name of all nodes connected to the end node of this sequence path that gets updated iteratively for each new keystroke. Since the stop words and symbols are not represented as term nodes in the graph and are concatenated together at the time of document indexing, the same steps should be followed at the time of query parsing too to find the matching sequence path in the graph. The pseudocode for the query auto-suggestion is given in Algorithm 2.

Algorithm 1. Word Sequence Graph (WSG) Construction

Require:

i) G_{i-1}: Cumulative graph up to document d_{i-1}

   or G_0: initial state when no documents were processed.

ii)   stop_words: List of commonly used stop words.

iii) symb_set: List of commonly used punctuation marks in a sentence.

1: begin

2: *d* ← Next Document to be processed

3: *stop_word* ← Empty string { Concatenated stop word string between two non-stop words in a sentence}

4: Create a document node, *d* that stores the details of the file including a unique id, file name, type, etc.

5: *seqid* ← *id* of document, *d*

6: for each sentence *s* in *d* do

7: *id* ← 0 { *relationship id incremented by 1 for each edge connecting keys in a sequence, to identify*

8: *the sequence of connected terms in a sentence }*

9: for each term *t* ϵ *s* do

10: $v ← t$; v_p ← previous non-stop word { initially set to '*Null*' for each sentence *s*};

11: *prev* ← case of v_p, *case* ← case of current word { initially set to 'N' };

12: *rel_type* ← '**contents**' { if v_p is null } or '**next_seq**' {if v_p is not null}

13: if v ϵ *stop_words* or v ϵ *symb_set*

14: Append v to *stop_word* without space, if v ϵ *symb_set* or *stop_word* is empty, else with space {no space needed before punctuation marks }

15: if v is the last word in *s* then

16: if a term node with the name, '*ter_node*' not exists, then

17: Create a node, *n* with the name, '*ter_node*' to detect the end of sentence, *s*

18: else

19: Connect the previous node v_p to node *n* using an edge of type *rel_type* with properties like *seqid*, *id*, *stop_word*(the concatenated stop word string between v_p & *t*), and other optional parameters based on document type like chapter no:, the sentence no: or verse, etc.

20: end if

21: else

22: go to step 7 { until the next non-stop word }

23: end if

24: else

25: increment *relid* by 1

26: Find the case of v a *U, S,* or *N* for upper case, sentence case, and lower case or no case respectively

27: if *case* = *U* or *S* then

28: Convert v lowercase

29: end if

30: if a term node with the name as v not exists, then

31: Create a node, *n* with name, v, and *node type*: *word*

32: else

33: Connect the previous node, v_p to node *n* using an edge of type *rel_type* with properties like s*eqid*, *id*, *stop_word*(the concatenated stop word string between v_p & *t*), and other optional parameters like the *case* or based on document type like chapter no:, the sentence no: or verse, etc.

34: end if

35: $v_p = v$;

36: Clear the string, ***stop_word***
37: end if
38: end for
39: end for
40: end

The first step is to separate the user-entered query, 'q' into a term list and stop word list, stop_word list in sequence order by concatenating stop words in between each unique term. This is the same step done during the document indexing time. Next step is to find all matching paths, '*p*' in the graph where the sequence of node names representing *term = term* list of entered query and stop word property in *edges = stop_word* list formed from the query. A path in a graph is a sequence of connected nodes with their associated edges. In the graph, only one node will be created for each unique term. So different terms of different sentences of different documents get connected in the graph. So all the matching paths are not valid.

Figure 3. WSG representation of a sentence

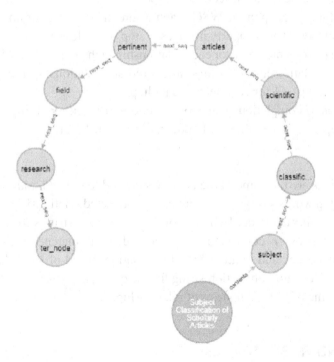

We need to check whether the matching paths belong to the same sentence of the same document. To check this, we can utilize the 'seqid' property that represents the document to which the path belongs and the 'id' property of the relationship to capture the sequence of connected relationships, and the 'sentence' property to check whether all nodes and edges belong to the same sentence. The 'id' property will be incremented by 1 for the next-next relationship of the term nodes belonging to the same sentence of the same document. So, the matching path will be the one with the same 'seqid', same sentence no, 'sentence', and relationship id incremented by 1 in each next relationship in the sequence. After a matching path is found, the next step is to find the autosuggestion strings to recommend for the user.

Algorithm 2. Search Query Auto-Suggestion

Require:

i)   Query Substring, q: Entered substring of query
ii)   stop_words: List of commonly used stop words.
iii) symb_set: List of commonly used punctuation marks in a sentence.
   1: begin
   2: Separate query q into two lists, term list and stop_word list to store nonstop word terms in the sequence and concatenated stop-word strings at the beginning or between two nonstop words or at the end of the query in sequence respectively.
   3: Find all matching paths, p in the WSG graph where the sequence of node names = term list and sequence of stop_word property in edges = stop_word list in order with same seqid and relationship id incremented by 1 for each relationship in the sequence of the path, for each path, p.
   4: Find matching relationship, r having same seqid and relationship id = (relationship id of last relationship of p) +1 for each matched path, p.
   5: Retrieve the auto-completion string for the query, q as either stop_word string, if present in relationship r, or name of the end node, n of relationship, r.
   6: end

The candidate strings are the name of the nodes connected to the end node of all matched paths, '*p*' or the concatenated stop words strings, if present in the connected relationship '*r*' between the end node of '*p*' and the newly connected node. Hence to find all candidate strings to recommend for users, we need to find all relationships, '*r*' connected to the end node of all matched paths '*p*' with same 'seqid', same sentence no, 'sentence', and relationship id = (relationship id of last relationship of p) +1. The final step is to retrieve the auto-completion string for the query, *q* as either stop_word string, if present in relationship *r*, or name of the end node, n of relationship, *r*.

EVALUATION AND RESULTS

Since this is an extension of the previous works (George, 2017, 2019), a sequence graph-based index of around 1900 documents is already there.

The Neo4j graph database is used to build the graph-based index. Neo4j is a graph database management system that is designed to store and manage data as graphs. Graph databases are a type of NoSQL database that use a graph data model to represent and store data. In a graph database, data is represented as nodes and edges, which are connected to each other in a network. Nodes represent entities or objects, while edges represent the relationships between them. This allows for complex data structures to be modeled and queried more efficiently than in traditional relational databases. Neo4j is a popular graph database that is used in a variety of applications, including social networking, recommendation systems, fraud detection, and network analysis. It is designed to be highly scalable and reliable, with built-in features such as clustering and replication for high availability. Neo4j supports the Cypher query language, which is a declarative language for querying and updating graph data. It also provides a range of APIs and drivers for integrating with other applications and tools. Overall, Neo4j is a powerful tool for managing and querying complex graph data, and is widely used in industries such as finance, healthcare, and e-commerce.

Tika's autodetect parser is used to convert the documents to .txt file and it is a feature of the Apache Tika framework that allows for automatic detection and extraction of metadata and text content from a variety of file formats. Tika is a content detection and analysis framework that provides a set of parsers for extracting text and metadata from different types of files, such as PDFs, Microsoft Office documents, HTML pages, and more. The autodetect parser is a special parser that can automatically identify the file format and select the appropriate parser to use for extracting content and metadata. This feature is particularly useful when dealing with large collections of files with mixed formats, as it eliminates the need to manually select the appropriate parser for each file. It also makes it easier to handle new file formats that may not be supported by existing parsers. To use Tika's autodetect parser, simply create an instance of the Tika parser and pass the file to be parsed as a parameter. The autodetect parser will then automatically detect the file format and use the appropriate parser to extract the content and metadata.

CERMINE (Content ExtRactor and MINEr) is used to extract the contents of scientific articles and it is an open-source Java library for extracting bibliographic information and structured content from scholarly articles in PDF format. CERMINE is designed to identify the structure of scholarly articles, including sections, paragraphs, and citations. It can automatically detect and extract metadata, such as the title, author, abstract, and references, as well as structured content, such as tables and figures. CERMINE uses machine learning algorithms to analyze the layout and structure of PDF documents, and can be trained on specific document types or domains. It also supports a range of output formats, including BibTeX, MODS, and TEI. One of the key advantages of CERMINE is its ability to handle a wide range of document formats, including those with complex layouts and multiple columns. It is also highly accurate, with a reported precision of up to 95% for extracting metadata. CERMINE is available as a standalone library, as well as a RESTful web service that can be used to extract content from PDFs on the fly. It is widely used in the digital libraries and scholarly publishing communities, and has been integrated into a number of open-source tools and platforms.

Stanford PTBTokenizer is the tokenizer used to split the text into tokens and it is designed according to the Penn Treebank tokenization conventions. It is part of the Stanford CoreNLP toolkit, a set of natural language processing tools developed by the Stanford Natural Language Processing Group. The Penn Treebank tokenization conventions define a set of rules for splitting text into tokens, including handling punctuation, contractions, and other common linguistic features. The PTBTokenizer follows these conventions to produce a standardized set of tokens that can be used for further analysis, such as part-of-speech tagging or parsing. The PTBTokenizer is written in Java and can be easily integrated into Java-based applications. It provides a range of options for customizing the tokenization process, such as specifying how to handle numeric values, URLs, and email addresses. One of the key advantages of the

PTBTokenizer is its accuracy and consistency, which is important for tasks such as information retrieval or sentiment analysis, where small variations in tokenization can have a significant impact on results.

The entire application is built in Java. Java is a high-level, object-oriented programming language that was developed by Sun Microsystems in the mid-1990s. It is widely used for developing a wide range of applications, including desktop, web, and mobile applications, as well as enterprise-level software and embedded systems. Java is designed to be platform-independent, which means that Java code can be run on any system that has a Java Virtual Machine (JVM) installed, without the need for recompilation. This feature makes Java highly portable and flexible and has contributed to its popularity among developers. Java is known for its robustness, security, and scalability, which has made it a popular choice for developing large-scale applications in a variety of industries, including finance, healthcare, and e-commerce. It also has a large and active developer community, which has contributed to the development of a wide range of libraries, frameworks, and tools for working with Java.

To evaluate the work, the user query is searched in this index to suggest completion queries. An example of query auto-suggestion for the query "partial order relation and poset" with suggestion queries in each iteration that gets updated with each keystroke is given in Figure 4. The suggestion queries will get updated on each keystroke. Users can choose the completion string from the suggested list by selecting the preferred one and by either pressing the tab key or by pressing the enter key. It gives accurate suggestions based on user-entered query prefix sequences if such a sequence exists in the graph.

BENEFITS OF AUTOSUGGESTION:

Autosuggestion offers several benefits for search engine users, including:

1. **Time-Saving:** Autosuggestion can save users time by providing quick and relevant suggestions for search queries. This can be especially helpful for long or complex search queries.
2. **Spelling Correction:** Autosuggestion can help users find what they are looking for more accurately by offering spelling corrections and related searches.
3. **Personalization:** Autosuggestion can generate personalized suggestions based on a user's search history, location, and language preferences. This can improve the accuracy and relevance of search results.
4. **Discoverability:** Autosuggestion can help users discover new content that they may not have otherwise found. By providing relevant suggestions, users can explore new topics and find new sources of information.
5. **Improves User Experience:** Query autosuggestion enhances the user experience by providing users with relevant suggestions for their search queries. This feature makes it easier for users to find what they are looking for and reduces the frustration associated with not finding relevant search results.
6. **Increases Search Engine Traffic:** Query autosuggestion can increase search engine traffic by helping users find more relevant search results. This feature can also encourage users to explore other search queries related to their initial query, which can result in increased search engine traffic.

Figure 4. Auto suggestion example for the query "partial order relation and poset" at each iteration (a, b, c, d)

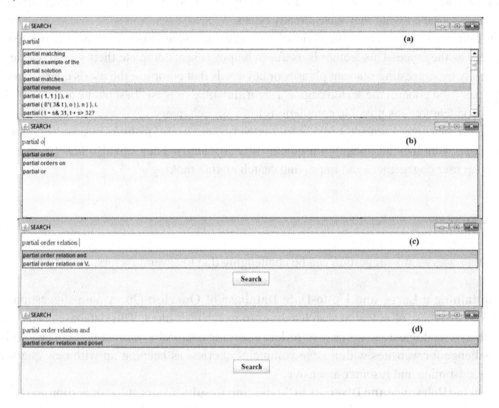

LIMITATIONS OF AUTOSUGGESTION

While autosuggestion offers many benefits, there are also some limitations to this feature. These include:

1. **Limited Scope:** Autosuggestion is limited to the search engine's database, which means that it may not provide suggestions for all possible search queries.
2. **Privacy Concerns:** Autosuggestion relies on user data to generate personalized suggestions. This can raise privacy concerns for some users, who may not want their search behavior to be tracked.
3. **Over-Reliance:** Autosuggestion can lead to over-reliance on the search engine, with users relying too heavily on the suggestions provided rather than exploring other search options.
4. **Bias:** Autosuggestion can be influenced by factors such as user location and search history, which can lead to bias in the suggestions provided.

DIFFERENCE BETWEEN QUERY AUTOSUGGESTION AND QUERY AUTO-COMPLETION

Query autosuggestion and query auto-completion are two related features in search engines that serve slightly different purposes. Query autosuggestion is a feature in search engines that predicts and suggests search queries to the user based on what they have typed so far. This feature is useful in helping users find what they are looking for quickly and efficiently, and it saves them time by suggesting relevant search queries based on what they have already typed.

On the other hand, query auto-completion is a feature that suggests possible completions to the user's search query as they type. This feature is useful in helping users complete their search queries quickly and efficiently by suggesting relevant phrases or keywords that complete the user's query. For example, if a user types "best phone," the search engine's algorithm may suggest "best phone under 15000 rupees" or "best phone features" as possible completions to the search query.

Both query autosuggestion and query auto-completion are useful features in search engines that can help users find what they are looking for quickly and efficiently. They can also benefit search engines by increasing user engagement and improving search engine rankings.

CHALLENGES

Implementing query auto-suggestion can be challenging due to several factors, including:

1. **Maintaining a Large and Up-to-Date Database of Queries:** Query auto-suggestion relies on having a database of potential search queries to match user input. This database needs to be comprehensive and updated regularly to reflect changing user behavior and preferences. This can be a challenge for websites with a large volume of queries, as keeping up with new queries can be time-consuming and resource-intensive.
2. **Balancing Relevance and Diversity in Suggestion Results:** Query auto-suggestion needs to provide suggestions that are relevant to user input, but also diverse enough to provide options that may not have been considered. Finding the right balance between relevance and diversity can be challenging, as it requires analyzing user behavior and preferences to provide personalized suggestions.
3. **Addressing Privacy Concerns:** Users may be uncomfortable with their search queries being stored and used to provide suggestions. This can be a challenge for websites that want to implement query auto-suggestion while also respecting user privacy. To address this challenge, websites need to provide transparent privacy policies and give users the option to opt-out of the feature.
4. **Handling Misspellings and Incomplete Queries:** Users may make spelling mistakes or enter incomplete queries, which can be challenging for query auto-suggestion systems to handle. These errors can lead to inaccurate or irrelevant suggestions, which can harm the user experience.
5. **Dealing With Ambiguous Queries:** Some search queries can be ambiguous, meaning they could have multiple interpretations. Query auto-suggestion systems need to be able to identify the user's intent and provide suggestions accordingly. This can be challenging, as it requires analyzing the context and user behavior to determine the most likely interpretation.
6. **Supporting Multiple Languages:** Query auto-suggestion systems need to be able to support multiple languages, which can be challenging as each language has its own unique syntax, grammar, and vocabulary. This requires a comprehensive understanding of each language and the ability to analyze user input accurately.

Overall, implementing query auto-suggestion can be challenging due to the need to maintain a large database of queries, balance relevance and diversity in suggestion results, and address privacy concerns.

However, these challenges can be overcome with the right algorithms, techniques, and processes, leading to a better user experience and increased engagement on the website.

CONCLUSION

Query auto-suggestion is one of the demanding needs of almost all search engine users that helps them to complete the query with different suggestions rather than typing a complete query. This chapter proposes a Sequence Graph-based Query Auto-Suggestion, SGQAS, that suggests queries based on entered query term sequences given by the user using a Word Sequence Graph-based, WSG representation of documents. Experimental evaluation shows that it gives accurate suggestions based on user-entered query prefix sequences if such a sequence exists in the graph.

ACKNOWLEDGMENT

I sincerely thank my guide, Dr. Sudheep Elayidom, Professor, Division of Engineering, SOE, CUSAT, and my co-guide Dr. T Santhankrishnan, Scientist-F, DRDO, NPOL, Kakkanad for their valuable suggestions and corrections.

REFERENCES

Bar-Yossef, Z. &. (2011, March). Context-sensitive query auto-completion. *Proceedings of the 20th International Conference on World Wide Web*, 107-116. 10.1145/1963405.1963424

Bast, H. K. (2022, October). Efficient and Effective SPARQL Autocompletion on Very Large Knowledge Graphs. In *Proceedings of the 31st ACM International Conference on Information & Knowledge Management* (pp. 2893-2902). 10.1145/3511808.3557093

Brinkmann, M. (2013, September 16). *A look at Yahoo's search suggestions.* Ghacks Technology News. https://www.ghacks.net/2013/09/16/a-look-at-yahoos-search-suggestions/

Cai, F. L. (2014, November). Time-sensitive personalized query auto-completion. In *Proceedings of the 23rd ACM international conference on conference on information and knowledge management* (pp. pp. 1599-1608). 10.1145/2661829.2661921

Cai, F. L., Liang, S., & de Rijke, M. (2016). Prefix-adaptive and time-sensitive personalized query auto completion. *IEEE Transactions on Knowledge and Data Engineering*, 28(9), 2452–2466. doi:10.1109/TKDE.2016.2568179

Cho, H., & Roy, S. B. (2016). Incorporating click-through data in query auto-completion. In *Proceedings of the 25th International Conference on World Wide Web* (pp. 699-709). Academic Press.

DuckDuckGo. (n.d.). *Instant answers.* https://duckduckgo.com/features/instant-answers/

Friedman, L. (2015, February 17). *DuckDuckGo CEO: We don't store any personal information*. ABC News. https://abcnews.go.com/Business/duckduckgo-ceo-store-personal-information/story?id=28907092

George, S. E. (2015). A Study on Applicability of Graph Databases in Big Data Analysis. *International Journal of Advanced Research Trends in Engineering and Technology*.

George, S. E. (2017). A novel sequence graph representation for searching and retrieving sequences of long text in the domain of information retrieval. *Int. J. Sci. Res. Comput. Sci. Eng. Inf. Technol*, 2(5).

George, S. E. (2019). Knowledge Graph Based Subject Classification of Scholarly Articles. *Journal of Advanced Research in Dynamical and Control Systems*, 11(2), 1763–1766.

Google. (n.d.). *Get suggestions for your search terms*. https://support.google.com/websearch/answer/106230?hl=en

Hu, Y. X. (2018, March). Context-sensitive query auto-completion with knowledge base. In *The 10th forum on data engineering and information management. The 16th annual meeting of database society of Japan* (pp. 4-6). Awara.

Huang, J. C. (2019). Query auto-suggestion in search engines: A survey. *Information Processing & Management*, 56(2), 315–332.

Jansen, B. J. (2010). An examination of searcher's perceptions of and interactions with query auto-suggestions. *Journal of the American Society for Information Science and Technology*, 61(4), 716–732.

Jiang, D. C. (2018, August). Location-sensitive personalized query auto-completion. In *10th International Conference on Intelligent Human-Machine Systems and Cybernetics (IHMSC)* (vol. 1, pp. 15-19). IEEE.

Kim, S. W. (2019). Improving query suggestion based on personalized search history. *Journal of Convergence*, 10(5), 17–23.

Kousha, K. (2021). Query reformulation for web search: A systematic review. *Information Processing & Management*, 58(2), 102522.

Krishnan. U. (2021). *Methods for Evaluating Query Auto Completion Systems* [Doctoral dissertation]. University of Melbourne.

Laitinen, A. T. (2021). Using click-through data for personalized query suggestion. *Journal of Information Science*, 47(4), 499–515.

Mack, E. (2020, February 28). *How to use Bing's search suggestions*. Lifewire. https://www.lifewire.com/use-bing-search-suggestions-3973291

Microsoft. (n.d.). *Bing search help*. https://www.microsoft.com/en-us/bing/search-help

Park, D. H. (2017, August). A neural language model for query auto-completion. In *Proceedings of the 40th International ACM SIGIR Conference on Research and Development in Information Retrieval* (pp. 1189-1192). 10.1145/3077136.3080758

Park, J. (2017). A study on the effects of search suggest on the search process and user experience. *Journal of Information Science Theory and Practice, 5*(1), 6–19.

Peetz, M. H., Myllärniemi, V., & Oulasvirta, A. (2019). Investigating the effect of user modeling on query auto-completion performance. In *Proceedings of the 2019 Conference on Human Information Interaction and Retrieval* (pp. 235-244). Academic Press.

Peipei, Y. I. (2020). Gfocus: User focus-based graph query autocompletion. *IEEE Transactions on Knowledge and Data Engineering*.

Roy, A. (2020). An adaptive approach for query suggestion based on user's intent. *Journal of Intelligent Information Systems, 54*(1), 77–102.

Schmidt, A. H. (2016, July). Context-sensitive auto-completion for searching with entities and categories. *Proceedings of the 39th International ACM SIGIR conference on Research and Development in Information.* 10.1145/2911451.2911461

Shen, H. L. (2016). A study on personalized query suggestion based on user search intent. *Neurocomputing, 173*, 855–864.

Shokouhi, M. (2012, August). Time-sensitive query auto-completion. In *Proceedings of the 35th international ACM SIGIR conference on Research and development in information retrieval* (pp. 601-610). 10.1145/2348283.2348364

Sullivan, D. (2015, April 22). *Google Instant is dead. Long live Google Instant!* Search Engine Land. https://searchengineland.com/google-instant-is-dead-long-live-google-instant-219553

Tahery, S., & Farzi, S. (2020). Customized query auto-completion and suggestion—A review. *Information Systems, 87*, 101415. doi:10.1016/j.is.2019.101415

Tahery, S., & Farzi, S. (2022). TIPS: Time-aware Personalised Semantic-based query auto-completion. *Journal of Information Science, 48*(4), 524–543. doi:10.1177/0165551520968690

Yahoo. (n.d.). *Search help.* https://help.yahoo.com/kb/search-for-desktop/SLN2217.html

Yi, P. C., Choi, B., Bhowmick, S. S., & Xu, J. (2017). AutoG: A visual query autocompletion framework for graph databases. *The VLDB Journal, 26*(3), 347–372. doi:10.100700778-017-0454-9

Yin, J., Zhou, K., Li, Y., Li, X., Wang, F., & Lu, J. (2016). Auto-completion with recurrent neural networks. In *Proceedings of the 25th ACM International on Conference on Information and Knowledge Management* (pp. 55-64). ACM.

Yu, S. G. (2020). Personalized query suggestion based on social tagging data. *Journal of Intelligent Information Systems, 54*(1), 103–125.

Zhang, Y. (2021). A survey on query auto-completion in search engines. *Journal of the Association for Information Science and Technology, 72*(4), 397–411.

KEY TERMS AND DEFINITIONS

CERMINE: An open-source library for extracting metadata and references from scholarly articles in PDF format using machine learning and computer vision techniques.

Java: A high-level, object-oriented programming language that is designed to be platform-independent, portable, and secure, used for developing a wide range of applications from desktop to web and mobile.

Neo4j: A highly scalable graph database management system designed to efficiently store, manage, and query highly connected data using the graph data model.

Search Engine: A search engine is a software system that enables users to search and retrieve information from a database or the internet based on specific keywords or phrases.

SGQAS, Sequence Graph-Based Query Auto-Suggestion: Query auto-suggestion for Word Sequence Graph-based indexed document collection.

Stanford PTB Tokenizer: A natural language processing tool that segments text into individual words, punctuation marks, and other tokens, based on the Penn Treebank standard for syntactic annotation.

Tika's AutoDetect Parser: A component that automatically identifies and applies the appropriate parser to extract content and metadata from a wide range of file formats without the need for manual specification.

WSG, Word Sequence Graph: Indexing documents in a graph in sequence order of terms of each sentence.

Compilation of References

Abadi, M., Barham, P., Chen, J., Chen, Z., Davis, A., Dean, J., Devin, M., Ghemawat, S., Irving, G., & Isard, M. (2016). TensorFlow: A System for Large-Scale Machine Learning. In *12th USENIX Symposium on Operating Systems Design and Implementation (OSDI 16)* (pp. 265-283). USENIX.

Abadi, M., Agarwal, A., Barham, P., Brevdo, E., & Zheng, X. (2016). *TensorFlow: large-Scale Machine Learning on Heterogeneous Distributed Systems.* https://einvoice1.gst.gov.in/

Abdel-Basset, M., Chang, V., & Nabeeh, N. A. (2021). An intelligent framework using disruptive technologies for COVID-19 analysis. *Technological Forecasting and Social Change, 163*, 163–175. doi:10.1016/j.techfore.2020.120431 PMID:33162617

Abdelrahman, M. (2020). Personality traits, risk perception, and protective behaviors of Arab residents of Qatar during the COVID-19 pandemic. *International Journal of Mental Health and Addiction*, 1–12. PMID:32837433

Abrishami, S., Kumar, P., & Nienaber, W. (2017). Smart stores: A scalable foot traffic collection and prediction system. In *Industrial Conference on Data Mining*. Springer. 10.1007/978-3-319-62701-4_9

Adam, M., Bonch, D., Fisher, D., Klemmer, S., McFarland, D., Noor, M., . . . Campbell, J. (2020). *Flipped Classroom Field Guide.* https://www.coursera.org/lecture/university-teaching/flipped-learning-rKwAE

Adler, M. (1942). In defence of the philosophy of education. In N. Henry (Ed.), *The Fortyfirst Yearbook of the National Society for the Study of Education* (pp. 197–249). Public School Publishing Company.

Adler, M. (1984). *The Paideia Program.* Institute of Philosophical Research.

Adnan & Akbar. (2019). An analytical study of information extraction from unstructured and multidimensional big data. *J. Big Data, 6*(1), 1–38. doi:10.1186/S40537019-0254-8

Adomavicius, G., & Tuzhilin, A. (2010). Context-aware recommender systems. In *Recommender systems handbook* (pp. 217–253). Springer US.

Aela, A., Kenne, J. P., & Mintsa, H. (2022). Adaptive neural Network and Nonlinear Electrohydraulic active suspension control system. *Journal of Vibration and Control, 28*(3-4), 243–259. doi:10.1177/1077546320975979

Agarwal, A., Dekel, O., & Xiao, L. (2010). Optimal algorithms for online convex optimization with multi-point bandit feedback. *Proceedings of the annual Conference on Learning Theory.*

Aggarwal, C. C. (2018). *Neural Networks and Deep Learning.* Springer International Publishing AG.

Agudo-Peregrina, A., Iglesias-Pradas, S., Conde-González, M., & Hernández-García, A. (2014). Can we predict success from log data in VLEs? Classification of interactions for learning analytics and their relation with performance in VLE-supported F2F and online learning. *Computers in Human Behavior*, *31*, 542–550. doi:10.1016/j.chb.2013.05.031

Ahmed, F., & Kabir, M. H. (2012) Directional ternary pattern (DTP) for facial expression recognition. In *IEEE International Conference on Consumer Electronics* (pp. 265-266). 10.1109/ICCE.2012.6161859

Ahmed, M. I., Hazlina, M. Y., & Rashid, M. (2016). Mathematical Modeling and Control of Active Suspension System for a Quarter Car Railway vehicle. *Malaysian Journal of Mathematical Sciences*, *10*, 227–241.

Aishwarya, Rao, Kumari, Mishra,& Rashmi. (2020). Food demand prediction using machine learning. *International Research Journal of Engineering and Technology*, *07*, 3672–3675.

Aktepe, A., Ersöz, S., & Toklu, B. (2015). Customer satisfaction and loyalty analysis with classification algorithms and Structural Equation Modeling. *Computers & Industrial Engineering*, *86*, 95–106. doi:10.1016/j.cie.2014.09.031

Alarifi, G., Rahman, M. F., & Hossain, M. S. (2023). Prediction and Analysis of Customer Complaints Using Machine Learning Techniques. [IJEBR]. *International Journal of E-Business Research*, *19*(1), 1–25. doi:10.4018/IJEBR.319716

Alboukaey, N., Joukhadar, A., & Ghneim, N. (2020). Dynamic behavior-based churn prediction in mobile telecom. *Expert Systems with Applications*, *162*, 113779. doi:10.1016/j.eswa.2020.113779

Ali, S., Wang, G., & Riaz, S. (2020). Aspect based sentiment analysis of ridesharing platform reviews for kansei engineering. *IEEE Access : Practical Innovations, Open Solutions*, *8*, 173186–173196. doi:10.1109/ACCESS.2020.3025823

Alpaydin, E. (2016). *Machine learning: the new AI (The MIT press essential knowledge series)*. The MIT Press.

Al-Saqqa, S., Al-Naymat, G., & Awajan, A. (2018). A large-scale sentiment data classification for online reviews under apache spark. *Procedia Computer Science*, *141*, 183–189. doi:10.1016/j.procs.2018.10.166

Althuizen, N. A. P., & Wierenga, B. (2006). Deploying Analogical Reasoning as a Decision Support and Understanding the Predictive Accuracy of Customer Churn Models. *Journal of Marketing Research*, *43*, 204–211. doi:10.1509/jmkr.43.2.204

Amin, A., Hossain, I., Akther, A., & Alam, K. M. (2019). Bengali VADER: A Sentiment Analysis Approach Using Modified VADER. *2019 International Conference on Electrical, Computer and Communication Engineering (ECCE)*. 10.1109/ECACE.2019.8679144

Ananatachaisilp, P., & Lin, Z. (2017). Fractional order PID control of rotor suspension by active magnetic bearings. In actuators. *Multidisciplinary Digital Publishing Institute*, *6*(1), 4.

Andrade, R., & Moazeni, S. (2023). Transfer rate prediction at self-service customer support platforms in insurance contact centers. *Expert Systems with Applications*, *212*, 118701. doi:10.1016/j.eswa.2022.118701

Anh, N. (2020). Control an Active Suspension System using PID and LQR Controller. *International Journal and Production Engineering Research and Development, 10*(3), 7003-12.

Anita, P., & Kumar, V. (2016). Customer engagement: the construct, antecedents, and consequences. *Journal of the Academy of Marketing Science*, 294-316.

Apache HBase. (n.d.). *Apache HBase™ Home*. https://hbase.apache.org/

Apache Kafka. (n.d.). https://kafka.apache.org/

Applegard, M., & Wellstead, a. P. (1995). Active suspension: Same Background. *IEEE Proceedings-Control theory and Application, 14*(2), 123-128.

Arenas, G., & Coulibaly, S. (2022). *A New Dawn for Global Value Chain Participation in the Philippines*. Academic Press.

Arkansas Plant Disease Database. (n.d.). https://www.uaex.edu/yard-garden/resource-library/diseases/

Arnaud, D. B., Vijay, V., & Yean, S. B. (2020, August 20). Artificial Intelligence and Marketing: Pitfalls and Opportunities. *Journal of Interactive Marketing*, *51*, 91–105. doi:10.1016/j.intmar.2020.04.007

Arora, S., Bindra, S., Singh, S., & Nassa, V. N. (2022). Prediction of Credit card defaults through data analysis and machine learning techniques. *Materials Today: Proceedings*, *51*(part 1), 110–117. doi:10.1016/j.matpr.2021.04.588

Aslam, N., Ramay, W. Y., Kewen, X., & Sarwar, N. (2020). Convolutional Neural Network Based Classification of App Reviews. *IEEE Access : Practical Innovations, Open Solutions*, *8*, 1–1. doi:10.1109/ACCESS.2020.3029634

Attaran, M., & Deb, P. (2018). Machine learning: The new 'big thing' for competitive advantage. *International Journal of Knowledge Engineering and Data Mining.*, *5*(4), 277–305. doi:10.1504/IJKEDM.2018.095523

Awad, M., & Khanna, R. (2015). Support vector regression. In *Efficient Learning Machines* (pp. 67–80). Springer. doi:10.1007/978-1-4302-5990-9_4

Babar, M. I., Jehanzeb, M., Ghazali, M., Jawawi, D. N., Sher, F., & Ghayyur, S. A. K. (2016, October). Big data survey in healthcare and a proposal for intelligent data diagnosis framework. In *2016 2nd IEEE International Conference on Computer and Communications (ICCC)*. IEEE Xplore. 10.1109/CompComm.2016.7924654

Babu, S. K., Vasavi, S., & Nagarjuna, K. (2017, January). Framework for Predictive Analytics as a Service using ensemble model. In *2017 IEEE 7th International Advance Computing Conference (IACC)*. IEEE Xplore. 10.1109/IACC.2017.0038

Baghersad, M., Zobel, C. W., Lowry, P. B., & Chatterjee, S. (2022). The roles of prior experience and the location on the severity of supply chain disruptions. *International Journal of Production Research*, *60*(16), 5051–5070. doi:10.1080/00207543.2021.1948136

Bakharia, A., Corrin, L., de Barba, P., Kennedy, G., Gašević, D., Mulder, R., ... Lockyer, L. (2016). A Conceptual Framework linking Learning Design with Learning Analytics. In *Proceedings of the Sixth International Conference on Learning Analytics & Knowledge (LAK '16)* (pp. 25-29). New York: ACM. 10.1145/2883851.2883944

Balemans, D., Reiter, P., Steckel, J., & Hellinckx, P. (2022). Resource efficient AI: Exploring neural network pruning for task specialization. *Internet of Things*, *20*, 100599. doi:10.1016/j.iot.2022.100599

Balli, C., Guzel, M. S., Bostanci, E., & Mishra, A. (2022). Sentimental Analysis of Twitter Users from Turkish Content with Natural Language Processing. *Computational Intelligence and Neuroscience*, *20*(22), 23–45. doi:10.1155/2022/2455160 PMID:35432519

Barcena, E., Read, T., & Sedano, B. (2020). An Approximation to Inclusive Language in LMOOCs Based on Appraisal Theory. *Open Linguistics*, *6*(1), 38–67. doi:10.1515/opli-2020-0003

Barr, A. J., & Ray, A. J. (1996). Control of an active suspension using fuzzy logic. *Proceedings IEEE the International Fuzzy Systems, 1*, 42-48.

Barreno, M., Nelson, B., Joseph, A. D., & Doug Tygar, J. (2010). The security of machine learning. *Machine Learning*, *81*(2), 121–148. doi:10.100710994-010-5188-5

Bar-Yossef, Z. &. (2011, March). Context-sensitive query auto-completion. *Proceedings of the 20th International Conference on World Wide Web*, 107-116. 10.1145/1963405.1963424

Basiri, M. E., Abdar, M., Cifci, M. A., Nemati, S., & Acharya, U. R. (2020). A novel method for sentiment classification of drug reviews using fusion of deep and machine learning techniques. *Knowledge-Based Systems*, *198*, 105949. Advance online publication. doi:10.1016/j.knosys.2020.105949

Basso, B., Ritchie, J. T., Pierce, F. J., Braga, R. P., & Jones, J. W. (2001, May). Spatial validation of crop models for precision agriculture. *Agricultural Systems*, *68*(2), 97–112. doi:10.1016/S0308-521X(00)00063-9

Bast, H. K. (2022, October). Efficient and Effective SPARQL Autocompletion on Very Large Knowledge Graphs. In *Proceedings of the 31st ACM International Conference on Information & Knowledge Management* (pp. 2893-2902). 10.1145/3511808.3557093

Bates, A. (2015). *Teaching in a Digital Age: Guidelines for Designing Teaching and Learning*. Tony Bates Associates Ltd.

Batra, G., Nolde, K., Santhanam, N., & Vrijen, R. (2018). *Right product, right time, right location: Quantifying the semiconductor supply chain*. McKinsey & Company.

Bayne, S. (2015). Teacherbot: Interventions in automated teaching. *Teaching in Higher Education*, *20*(4), 455–467. doi:10.1080/13562517.2015.1020783

Belhumeur, P. N., Hespanda, J., & Kiregeman, D. (1997, July). Eigenfaces vs. Fisherfaces: Recognition Using Class Specific Linear Projection. *IEEE Transactions on Pattern Analysis and Machine Intelligence*, *19*(7), 711–720. doi:10.1109/34.598228

Bennett, K. P., & Mangasarian, O. L. (1993). Bilinear separation of two sets in n-space. *Computational Optimization and Applications*, *2*(3), 207–227. doi:10.1007/BF01299449

Benson, P. J., & Perrett, D. I. (1991). Perception and recognition of photographic quality facial caricatures: Implications for the recognition of natural images. *The European Journal of Cognitive Psychology*, *3*(1), 105–135. doi:10.1080/09541449108406222

Berg, C. (2005). Factors Related to Observed Attitude Change Toward Learning Chemistry Among University Students. *Chemistry Education Research and Practice*, *6*(1), 1–18. doi:10.1039/B4RP90001D

Berry, L. L. (1983). Relationship marketing. In L. L. Berry, G. L. Shostack, & G. D. Upah (Eds.), *Emerging Perspectives on Services Marketing* (pp. 25–28). American Marketing Association.

Bhaumik, U., & Yadav, D. K. (2021). Sentiment Analysis Using Twitter. In J. K. Mandal, I. Mukherjee, S. Bakshi, S. Chatterji, & P. K. Sa (Eds.), *Computational Intelligence and Machine Learning. Advances in Intelligent Systems and Computing* (Vol. 1276). Springer. doi:10.1007/978-981-15-8610-1_7

Bhoomi NBSS&LUP Geo Portal. (n.d.). https://www.nbsslup.in/bhoomi/

Bian, Y., Ye, R., Zhang, J., & Yan, X. (2022). Customer preference identification from hotel online reviews: A neural network based fine-grained sentiment analysis. *Computers & Industrial Engineering*, *172*, 108648. doi:10.1016/j.cie.2022.108648

Biggs, J. (1996). Enhancing teaching through constructive alignment. *Higher Education*, *32*(3), 347–364. doi:10.1007/BF00138871

Bilquise, G., Ibrahim, S., & Shaalan, K. (2022). Emotionally Intelligent Chatbots: A Systematic Literature Review. *Human Behavior and Emerging Technologies*, *2022*, 1–23. Advance online publication. doi:10.1155/2022/9601630

Birkenkrahe, M., & Kjellin, H. (2015). Improving Student Interaction and Engagement in the Flipped Classroom. In *Proceedings of the 14th European Conference on e-Learning (ECEL 2015)* (pp. 73-79). Curran Associates, Inc. doi:978-1-5108-1431-8

Bisong, E. (2019). *Building machine learning and deep learning models on Google cloud platform: A comprehensive guide for beginners*. Apress. doi:10.1007/978-1-4842-4470-8

Bitner, M. J., Brown, S. W., & Meuter, M. L. (2000). Technology infusion in service encounters. *Journal of the Academy of Marketing Science*, *28*(1), 138–149. doi:10.1177/0092070300281013

Black, P. E. (2007, December). Revisiting the Thornthwaite and Mather water balance. *Journal of the American Water Resources Association*, *43*(6), 1604–1605. doi:10.1111/j.1752-1688.2007.00132.x

Bloom, B. (1956). *A taxonomy of educational objectives*. Longman, Green & Co.

Blumberg, P. (2013). *Assessing and Improving Your Teaching : Strategies and Rubrics for Faculty Growth and Student Learning*. Jossey-Bass Higher and Adult Education Series.

Bobzien, S. (2006). Stoic Logic. In M. de Grazia & S. Wells (Eds.), *Cambridge Companions Online* (pp. 85–123). doi:10.1017/CCOL0521650941

Boldyguin, G. (2013). On The Meaning of the Word "Philosophy"(on History of the Word). *Journal of Siberian Federal University*, *11*, 1599–1609.

Bossen, C., & Piras, E. M. (2020). Introduction to the Special Issue on Information Infrastructures in Healthcare: Governance, Quality Improvement and Service Efficiency. *Computer Supported Cooperative Work*, *29*(4), 381–386. doi:10.100710606-020-09381-1

Boyapati, S.N., & Mummidi, R. (2020). *Predicting sales using Machine Learning Techniques*. Academic Press.

Boyd, S., & Vandenberghe, L. (2004). *Convex Optimization*. Cambridge University Press. doi:10.1017/CBO9780511804441

Bradlow, E. T., Gangwar, M., Kopalle, P., & Voleti, S. (2017). The role of big data and predictive analytics in retailing. *Journal of Retailing*, *93*(1), 79–95. doi:10.1016/j.jretai.2016.12.004

Bramer, M. (2007). *Principles of data mining* (Vol. 180). Springer.

Brinkmann, M. (2013, September 16). *A look at Yahoo's search suggestions*. Ghacks Technology News. https://www.ghacks.net/2013/09/16/a-look-at-yahoos-search-suggestions/

Brooke, C., & Frazer, E. (Eds.). (2013). *Ideas of Education: Philosophy and Politics from Plato to Dewey*. Routledge, ProQuest Ebook Central. doi:10.4324/9780203817544

Brownly, J. (2021). A Gentle Introduction to Stochastic Optimization Algorithms. *Optimization*.

Bruce, V., Hanna, E., Dench, N., Healy, P., & Burton, A. M. (1992). The importance of 'mass' in line drawings of faces. *Applied Cognitive Psychology*, *6*(7), 619–628. doi:10.1002/acp.2350060705

Bruff, D. (2019). *Intentional Tech: Principles to Guide the Use of Educational Technology in College Teaching (Teaching and Learning in Higher Education)* (1st ed.). West Virginia University Press.

Butler, J. (1968). *Four philososophies add their practice in education and religion*. Harper & Row Publishers, Inc.

Cai, F. L. (2014, November). Time-sensitive personalized query auto-completion. In *Proceedings of the 23rd ACM international conference on conference on information and knowledge management* (pp. pp. 1599-1608). 10.1145/2661829.2661921

Cai, F. L., Liang, S., & de Rijke, M. (2016). Prefix-adaptive and time-sensitive personalized query auto completion. *IEEE Transactions on Knowledge and Data Engineering*, *28*(9), 2452–2466. doi:10.1109/TKDE.2016.2568179

Center for Teaching and Learning (CTL). (2013). *Strategy for Teaching and Learning 2014 - 2018.* Retrieved from University of Stellenbosch: www.sun.ac.za/ctl

Cerezo, R., Sanchez-Santill, M., Paule-Ruiz, M., & Núnez, J. (2016). Students' LMS interaction patterns and their relationship with achievement: A case study in higher education. *Computers & Education, 96*, 42–54. doi:10.1016/j.compedu.2016.02.006

Chang, C. C., & Lin, C. J. (2011). LIBSVM: A library for support vector machines. *ACM Transactions on Intelligent Systems and Technology, 2*(3), 27.

Chen, T., He, T., Benesty, M., & Khotilvoich, V. (2019). *xgboost: eXtreme Gradient Boosting.* R package version 0.82.1

Chen, F., Nielsen, C. P., Wu, J., & Chen, X. (2022). Examining socio-spatial differentiation under housing reform and its implications for mobility in urban China. *Habitat International, 119*, 102498. doi:10.1016/j.habitatint.2021.102498

Cheng, C. H., Kuo, Y. H., & Zhou, Z. (2018). Tracking nosocomial diseases at individual level with a real-time indoor positioning system. *Journal of Medical Systems, 42*(11), 1–21. doi:10.100710916-018-1085-4 PMID:30284042

Chen, L., Liao, H., Ko, M., Lin, J., & Yu, G. (2000). A New Lda Based Face Recognition System which Can Solve the Small Sample Size Problem. *Pattern Recognition, 33*(10), 1713–1726. doi:10.1016/S0031-3203(99)00139-9

Chen, T., Yin, H., Chen, H., Wu, L., Wang, H., Zhou, X., & Li, X. (2018). Tada: Trend alignment with dual-attention multi-task recurrent neural networks for sales prediction. In *2018 IEEE International Conference on Data Mining (ICDM).* IEEE. 10.1109/ICDM.2018.00020

Cherfi, A., Kaouther, N., & Ferchichi, A. (2018). Very fast C4. 5 decision tree algorithm. *Applied Artificial Intelligence, 32*(2), 119–137. doi:10.1080/08839514.2018.1447479

Chevalier, J. A., & Mayzlin, D. (2006). The Effect of Word of Mouth on Sales: Online Book Reviews. *JMR, Journal of Marketing Research, 43*(3), 345–354. doi:10.1509/jmkr.43.3.345

Chiou, J. S., Hsiao, C. C., & Su, F. Y. (2014). Whose online reviews have the most influences on consumers in cultural offerings? Professional vs consumer commentators. *Internet Research, 24*(3), 353–368. doi:10.1108/IntR-03-2013-0046

Cho, H., & Roy, S. B. (2016). Incorporating click-through data in query auto-completion. In *Proceedings of the 25th International Conference on World Wide Web* (pp. 699-709). Academic Press.

Choudhury, T., Kumar, V., & Nigam, D. (2015). An innovative and automatic lung and oral cancer classification using soft computing techniques. *International Journal of Computer Science & Mobile Computing, 4*(12), 313–323.

Choudhury, T., Kumar, V., & Nigam, D. (2015). Intelligent classification & clustering of lung & oral cancer through decision tree & genetic algorithm. *International Journal of Advanced Research in Computer Science and Software Engineering, 5*(12), 501–510.

Ciba, Z., Abghour, N., Moussaid, K., Omri, A. E., & Rida, M. (2018). A novel Architecture Combined with Optimal Parameters for Back-Propagation Neural Network Applied to Anomaly Network Instrusion Detection. *Computers & Security, 75*, 36–58. doi:10.1016/j.cose.2018.01.023

Claypo, N., & Jaiyen, S. (2015). Opinion mining for thai restaurant reviews using K-Means clustering and MRF feature selection. In *2015 7th International Conference on Knowledge and Smart Technology (KST).* IEEE. 10.1109/KST.2015.7051469

Cline, B., Niculescu, R. S., Huffman, D., & Deckel, B. (2017). Predictive maintenance applications for machine learning. In *2017 annual reliability and maintainability symposium (RAMS)* (pp. 1-7). IEEE. 10.1109/RAM.2017.7889679

Cottingham, J. (2020). *Western Philosophy: An Anthology* (3rd ed.). Blackwell Publishing.

Dan, L. (2020). Research on the application and key technology of artificial intelligence in China Unicom's customer service system. Computer Knowledge and Technology, 16(26), 176-177.

Dang, N. C., Moreno-García, M. N., & De la Prieta, F. (2020). Sentiment analysis based on deep learning: A comparative study. *Electronics (Switzerland)*, *9*(3), 483. Advance online publication. doi:10.3390/electronics9030483

Dan, H., & Sun, W. (2018). Nonlinear output feedback finite-time control for vehicle active suspension systems. *IEEE Transaction on Industrial Information*, *15*(4), 2073–2082.

Daudert, T. (2021). Exploiting textual and relationship information for fine-grained financial sentiment analysis. *Knowledge-Based Systems*, *230*, 107389. Advance online publication. doi:10.1016/j.knosys.2021.107389

Davenport, T., Guha, A., Grewal, D., & Bressgott, T. (2020). How artificial intelligence will change the future of marketing. *Journal of the Academy of Marketing Science, 48*(1), 24-42.

De Martini, F. (2021). *Supply chains and disruptive events: An inventory management system perspective*. Academic Press.

De Raadt, M. (2021). *Progress Bar*. Retrieved 7 7, 2021, from Moodle: https://moodle.org/plugins/block_progress

De Silva, D., Burstein, F., Jelinek, H. F., & Stranieri, A. (2015). Addressing the complexities of big data analytics in healthcare: The diabetes screening case. *AJIS. Australasian Journal of Information Systems*, *19*, 99–115. doi:10.3127/ajis.v19i0.1183

Delgado, J. M. D., & Oyedele, L. (2022). Robotics in construction: A critical review of the reinforcement learning and imitation learning paradigms. *Advanced Engineering Informatics*, *54*, 101787. doi:10.1016/j.aei.2022.101787

Delgado, M., & Mills, K. G. (2020). The supply chain economy: A new industry categorization for understanding innovation in services. *Research Policy*, *49*(8), 104039. doi:10.1016/j.respol.2020.104039

Dell'Anna, D., & Jamshidnejad, A. (2022). Evolving Fuzzy logic Systems for creative personalized Socially Assistive Robots. *Engineering Applications of Artificial Intelligence*, *114*, 105064. doi:10.1016/j.engappai.2022.105064

Deng, Z. H., Luo, K. H., & Yu, H. L. (2014). A study of supervised term weighting scheme for sentiment analysis. *Expert Systems with Applications*, *41*(7), 3506–3513. doi:10.1016/j.eswa.2013.10.056

Devlin, K. (1997). *Goodbye, Descartes*. John Wiley and Sons, Inc.

Dewey, J. (1938). *Experience and education*. Macmillan.

Dey, S., & Lee, S. W. (2021). Multilayered review of safety approaches for machine learning-based systems in the days of AI. *Journal of Systems and Software*, *176*, 110941. doi:10.1016/j.jss.2021.110941

Dhaoui, C., Webster, C. M., & Tan, L. P. (2017, September 11). Social media sentiment analysis: Lexicon versus machine learning. *Journal of Consumer Marketing*, *34*(6), 480–488. doi:10.1108/JCM-03-2017-2141

Dolan, E., & More, J. (2002). Benchmarking optimization software with performance profiles. *Mathematical Programming*, *91*(2), 201–213. doi:10.1007101070100263

Doshi, R., Apthorpe, N., & Feamster, N. (2018). Machine learning ddos detection for consumer internet of things devices. In *2018 IEEE Security and Privacy Workshops (SPW)* (pp. 29-35). IEEE.

Drachsler, H., & Kalz, M. (2016). The MOOC and learning analytics innovation cycle (MOLAC): A reflective summary of ongoing research and its challenges. *Journal of Computer Assisted Learning*, *32*(3), 281–290. doi:10.1111/jcal.12135

DuckDuckGo. (n.d.). *Instant answers.* https://duckduckgo.com/features/instant-answers/

Duffany, J. L. (2010, October). Artificial intelligence in GPS navigation systems. In *2010 2nd International Conference on Software Technology and Engineering* (Vol. 1, pp. V1-382). IEEE. 10.1109/ICSTE.2010.5608862

Dunaway, M. (2011). Connectivism Learning theory and pedagogical practice for networked information landscapes. *Emerald Insight, 39*(4), 675–685.

Dutta, S., Pramanik, S., & Bandyopadhyay, S. K. (2021). S. K. (2021) "Prediction of Weight Gain during COVID-19 for Avoiding Complication in Health. *International Journal of Medical Science and Current Research, 4*(3), 1042–1052.

Dwidienawati, D., Tjahjana, D., Abdinagoro, S. B., Gandasari, D., & Munawaroh. (2020). Customer review or influencer endorsement: Which one influences purchase intention more? *Heliyon, 6*(11), e05543. Advance online publication. doi:10.1016/j.heliyon.2020.e05543 PMID:33294687

Dwyer, R. F., Schurr, P. H., & Oh, S. (1987). Developing Buyer-Seller Relationships. *Journal of Marketing, 51*(April), 11–27. doi:10.1177/002224298705100202

Dysart, J. (1999). Email marketing grows up: A primer for the new millennium. *Networker (Washington, D.C.), 3*(4), 40–41. doi:10.1145/323409.328686

Eleonora, P., & Alessandro, G. (2018). Shopping as a "networked experience": An emerging framework in the retail industry. *International Journal of Retail & Distribution Management, 46*(7), 690–704. Advance online publication. doi:10.1108/IJRDM-01-2018-0024

Emmanuel, M., & Taiwo, O. S. (2020). The implications of artificial intelligence on the digital marketing of financial services to vulnerable customers. *Australasian Marketing Journal, 29*(3). Advance online publication. 10.1016%2Fj.ausmj.2020.05.003

Enfield, J. (2013). Looking at the impact of the flipped classroom model of instruction on undergraduate multimedia students at CSUN. *TechTrends, 57*(6), 14–27. doi:10.100711528-013-0698-1

Engle, R. F., & Russell, J. R. (1997). Forecasting the frequency of changes in quoted foreign exchange prices with the autoregressive conditional duration model. *Journal of Empirical Finance, 4*(2-3), 187–212. doi:10.1016/S0927-5398(97)00006-6

Enss, C. (1993, February). Integrating separate and connected knowing: The experiential learning model. *Teaching of Psychology, 20*(1), 7–13. doi:10.120715328023top2001_2

Erjavec, J., & Thompson, R. (2014). *Automotive technology a systems approach.* Ongage Learning.

Esmaeilian, B., Sarkis, J., Lewis, K., & Behdad, S. (2020). Blockchain for the future of sustainable supply chain management in Industry 4.0. *Resources, Conservation and Recycling, 163*, 105064. doi:10.1016/j.resconrec.2020.105064

Ezenkwu, C. P., & Ozuomba, S. (2015). *Application of K-Means Algorithm for Efficient Customer Segmentation: A Strategy for Targeted Customer Services.* Academic Press.

Ezenkwu, C. P., Ozuomba, S., & Kalu, C. (2015). Application of K-Means algorithm for efficient customer segmentation: A strategy for targeted customer services. *International Journal of Advanced Research in Artificial Intelligence, 4*(10), 40–44.

Fabregas, A. C. (2019). Decision Tree Algorithm Applied in Suitability Assessment of Temporary Crops Based on Agrometeorological Forecasts. *Indian Journal of Science and Technology, 12*(26), 1–7. doi:10.17485/ijst/2019/v12i26/145096

Faritha Banu, J., Neelakandan, S., Geetha, B. T., Selvalakshmi, V., Umadevi, A., & Martinson, E. O. (2022). Artificial Intelligence Based Customer Churn Prediction Model for Business Markets. *Computational Intelligence and Neuroscience*, *2022*, 1–14. Advance online publication. doi:10.1155/2022/1703696 PMID:36238670

Fayyad, U. M., Reina, C., & Bradley, P. S. (1998, August). Initialization of Iterative Refinement Clustering Algorithms. In KDD (pp. 194-198). Academic Press.

Feldman, M. A. (1998). *Computing with Structured Neural Networks*. Academic Press.

Fellani, M. A., & Gabaj, A. (2015). PID Controller Deign for Two Tanks Liquid Level Control System Using MATLAB. *Iranian Journal of Electrical and Computer Engineering*, *5*(3), 436.

Finkelstein, A., Harman, M., Jia, Y., Martin, W., Sarro, F., & Zhang, Y. (2017). Investigating the relationship between price, rating, and popularity in the Blackberry World App Store. *Information and Software Technology*, *87*, 119–139. doi:10.1016/j.infsof.2017.03.002

Fitzpatrick, T., & Mues, C. (2021). How can Lenders prosper? Comparing machine learning approaches to identify profitable Peer-to-Peer loan investments. *European Journal of Operational Research*, *294*(2), 711–722. doi:10.1016/j.ejor.2021.01.047

Flaxman, A. D., Kalai, A. T., & McHanan, H. B. (2005). Online convex optimization in the bandit setting: gradient descent without a gradient. *ACM-SIAM Symposium on Discrete Algorithms (SODA)*.

Flumerfelt, S., & Green, G. (2013). Using Lean in the Flipped Classroom for At Risk Students. *Journal of Educational Technology & Society*, *16*(1), 356–366.

Forestiero, A., & Papuzzo, G. (2018, December). Distributed algorithm for big data analytics in healthcare. In *2018 IEEE/WIC/ACM International Conference on Web Intelligence (WI)*. IEEE Computer Society. 10.1109/WI.2018.00015

Fors Brandebo, M., Nilsson, S., & Larsson, G. (2016). Leadership: Is bad stronger than good? *Leadership and Organization Development Journal*, *37*(6), 690–710. doi:10.1108/LODJ-09-2014-0191

Foster, S. T., & Gardner, J. W. (2022). *Managing quality: Integrating the supply chain*. John Wiley & Sons.

Fraley, C., & Raftery, A. E. (2002). Model-based clustering, discriminant analysis, and density estimation. *Journal of the American Statistical Association*, *97*(458), 611–631. doi:10.1198/016214502760047131

Francis, H., & Kusiak, A. (2017). Prediction of engine demand with a data-driven approach. *Procedia Computer Science*, *103*, 28–35. doi:10.1016/j.procs.2017.01.005

Friedman, L. (2015, February 17). *DuckDuckGo CEO: We don't store any personal information*. ABC News. https://abcnews.go.com/Business/duckduckgo-ceo-store-personal-information/story?id=28907092

Fung, G. M., & Mangasarian, O. (2004). A Feature Selection Newton Method for Support Vector Machine Classification. *Computational Optimization and Applications*, *28*(2), 185–202. doi:10.1023/B:COAP.0000026884.66338.df

Galetsi, P., & Katsaliaki, K. (2020). A review of the literature on big data analytics in healthcare. *The Journal of the Operational Research Society*, *71*(10), 1511–1529. doi:10.1080/01605682.2019.1630328

Ganga, E., & Maphalala, M. (2016). Contributions of Constructivism to Teaching and Learning. In Teaching and Learning Strategies in South Africa (pp. 43 - 54). Cheriton House, UK: Cengage.

Garay, J., Yap, R., & Sabellano, M. J. (2019). An analysis on the insights of the anti-vaccine movement from social media posts using k-means clustering algorithm and VADER sentiment analyzer. *IOP Conference Series. Materials Science and Engineering*, *482*, 012043. doi:10.1088/1757-899X/482/1/012043

Gaskell, A. (2016, Apr. 14). Why AI Should Augment, And Not Replace, Staff. *Forbes*.

George, S. E. (2015). A Study on Applicability of Graph Databases in Big Data Analysis. *International Journal of Advanced Research Trends in Engineering and Technology*.

George, S. E. (2017). A novel sequence graph representation for searching and retrieving sequences of long text in the domain of information retrieval. *Int. J. Sci. Res. Comput. Sci. Eng. Inf. Technol*, *2*(5).

George, S. E. (2019). Knowledge Graph Based Subject Classification of Scholarly Articles. *Journal of Advanced Research in Dynamical and Control Systems*, *11*(2), 1763–1766.

Ghasemaghaei, M., Eslami, S. P., Deal, K., & Hassanein, K. (2018). Reviews' length and sentiment as correlates of online reviews' ratings. *Internet Research*, *28*(3), 544–563. doi:10.1108/IntR-12-2016-0394

Ghazaly, N. M., Ahmed, A. E., Ali, A. S., & El-Jaber, G. (2016). H^∞ Control of An Active Suspension System for a Quarter Car Model. *International Journal of Vehicle Structures and System*, *8*(1). Advance online publication. doi:10.4273/ijvss.8.1.07

Gibbs, G. (1988). *Learning by Doing: A Guide to Teaching and Learning Methods*. Oxford Further Education Unit.

Goel, E., & Abhilasha, E. (2017). Random Forest: A Review. *International Journal of Advanced Research in Computer Science and Software Engineering*, *7*(1), 251–257. doi:10.23956/ijarcsse/V7I1/01113

Goldie, J. (2016). Connectivism: A knowledge learning theory for the digital age? *Medical Teacher*, *38*(10), 1064–1069. doi:10.3109/0142159X.2016.1173661 PMID:27128290

Google. (n.d.). *Get suggestions for your search terms*. https://support.google.com/websearch/answer/106230?hl=en

Gouda, S. K., & Saranga, H. (2018). Sustainable supply chains for supply chain sustainability: Impact of sustainability efforts on supply chain risk. *International Journal of Production Research*, *56*(17), 5820–5835. doi:10.1080/00207543.2018.1456695

Gouravaraju, S., Narayan, J., Sauer, R. A., & Gautam, S. S. (2023). A Bayesian regularization-backpropagation neural network model for peeling computations. *The Journal of Adhesion*, *99*(1), 92–115. doi:10.1080/00218464.2021.2001335

Gowsalya, M., Krushitha, K., & Valliyammai, C. (2014, December). Predicting the risk of readmission of diabetic patients using MapReduce. In *2014 Sixth International Conference on Advanced Computing (ICoAC)*. IEEE. 10.1109/ICoAC.2014.7229729

Gowtham, K. J. (2022). A Study of Cellular neural networks with new vertex-edge topological indices. *Int. J. Open Problems Compt. Math*, *15*(3), 115–133.

Gravili, G., Benvenuto, M., Avram, A., & Viola, C. (2018). The influence of the Digital Divide on Big Data generation within supply chain management. *International Journal of Logistics Management*, *29*(2), 592–628. doi:10.1108/IJLM-06-2017-0175

Greller, W., & Drachsler, H. (2012). Translating Learning into Numbers: A Generic Framework for Learning Analytics. *Journal of Educational Technology & Society*, *15*(3), 42–57.

Grollberg, D. (1989). *Genetic algorithms in search, optimization, and machine learning*. Addison-Wesley.

Gul, E., Alpaslan, N., & Emiroglu, M. E. (2021). Robust optimization of SVM hyper-parameters for spillway type selection. *Ain Shams Engineering Journal*, *12*(3), 2413–2423. doi:10.1016/j.asej.2020.10.022

Gupta, S., Vijarania, M., & Udbhav, M. (2023). A Machine Learning Approach for Predicting Price of Used Cars and Power Demand Forecasting to Conserve Non-renewable Energy Sources. In *Renewable Energy Optimization, Planning and Control: Proceedings of ICRTE 2022* (pp. 301-310). Singapore: Springer Nature Singapore. 10.1007/978-981-19-8963-6_27

Gu, T., Zhao, H., He, Z., Li, M., & Ying, D. (2022). Integrating external knowledge into aspect-based sentiment analysis using graph neural network. *Knowledge-Based Systems*, *110025*. Advance online publication. doi:10.1016/j.knosys.2022.110025

Haleem, A., Javaid, M., Qadri, M. A., Singh, R. P., & Suman, R. (2022). Artificial intelligence (AI) applications for marketing: A literature-based study. *International Journal of Intelligent Networks*. doi:10.1016/j.ijin.2022.08.005

Halliday, M. A. K., & Matthiessen, C. M. I. M. (2004). *An Introduction to Functional Grammar* (3rd ed.). Edward Arnold.

Hammoodi, S. J., Flayyih, K. S., & Hamad, A. (2020). Design and implementation Speed Control System of DC Motor Based PID Control and MATLAB/SIMULINK. *International Journal of Power Electronic and Drive Systems*, *11*(1), 127. doi:10.11591/ijpeds.v11.i1.pp127-134

Hamza, A., & Yahia, N. (2023). Artificial Nearal Networks Controller of Active Suspension for Ambulance based on ISO Standards. Proceedings of Institution of Mechanical Enginners, Part D. *Journal of Automobile*, *237*(1), 34–37. doi:10.1177/09544070221075456

Han, H., Zhang, Y., Zhang, J., Yang, J., & Zou, X. (2018). Improving the performance of lexicon-based review sentiment analysis method by reducing additional introduced sentiment bias. *PLoS One*, *13*(8), e0202523. Advance online publication. doi:10.1371/journal.pone.0202523 PMID:30142154

Hansen, C., Emin, V., Wasson, B., Mor, Y., & Rodriguez-Triana, M. (2013). *Towards an Integrated Model of Teacher Inquiry into Student Learning, Learning Design and Learning Analytics*. Paphos, Cyprus: EC-TEL 2013 - 8th European Conference, on Technology Enhanced Learning. doi:10.1007/978-3-642-40814-4 73

Harmon, D., & Jones, T. (2005). *Elementary Education: A Reference Handbook (Contemporary Education Issues)* (1st ed.). ABC-CLIO.

Harper, R. (1955). *Significance of Existence and Recognition for Education. In 54th Yearbook of the National Society for the Study of Education*. University of Chicago Press.

Hassan, S., Tantithamthavorn, C., Bezemer, C.-P., & Hassan, A. E. (2017). Studying the dialogue between users and developers of free apps in the Google Play Store. *Empirical Software Engineering*, *23*(3), 1275–1312. doi:10.100710664-017-9538-9

Hastie, T., Tibshirani, R., & Friedman, J. (2009). *"The Elements of Statistical Learning", Data Mining, Inference, and Prediction* (2nd ed.). Springer Science & Business Media.

Ha, Y.-W., & Hoch, S. J. (1989). Ambiguity, Processing Strategy, and Advertising-Evidence Interactions. *The Journal of Consumer Research*, *16*(3), 354. doi:10.1086/209221

Hebb, D. O. (1993). *The organization of behavior*. John Wiley & Sons.

Herrero, J. M., Blasco, X., Martinez, M., & Salcedo, J. V. (2002). Optimal pid tuning with genetic algorithms for nonlinear process models. *IF1AC Proceedings, 35*(1), 31-36.

Holmberg, M., & Halldén, P. (2018). *Machine Learning for Restaurant Sales Forecast.* Academic Press.

Home Page. (n.d.). https://www.krishimaratavahini.kar.nic.in/department.aspx

Hossain, M. S. and Rahman, M. F (2023). Detection of readers' emotional aspects and thumbs-up empathy reactions towards reviews of online travel agency apps, Journal of Hospitality and Tourism Insights. https://doi.org/ doi:10.1108/JHTI-10-2022-0487

Hossain, M. S., & Rahman, M. F. (2023). Detection of readers' emotional aspects and thumbs-up empathy reactions towards reviews of online travel agency apps, Journal of Hospitality and Tourism Insights. https://doi.org/10.1108/JHTI-10-2022-0487

Hossain, F. T., Hossain, M. I., & Nawshin, S. (2017). *Machine learning based class level prediction of restaurant reviews. In 2017 IEEE Region 10 Humanitarian Technology Conference (R10-HTC).* IEEE. doi:10.1109/R10-HTC.2017.8288989

Hossain, M. S. (2023). Behavioral Analytics of Consumer Complaints. In S. Nagaraj & K. Kumar (Eds.), *AI-Driven Intelligent Models for Business Excellence* (pp. 42–67). IGI Global., doi:10.4018/978-1-6684-4246-3.ch003

Hossain, M. S., & Rahman, M. F. (2022). Detection of potential customers' empathy behavior towards customers' reviews. *Journal of Retailing and Consumer Services, 65,* 102881. doi:10.1016/j.jretconser.2021.102881

Hossain, M. S., & Rahman, M. F. (2022a). Machine Learning and Artificial Intelligence: The New Move for Marketers. In J. Kaur, P. Jindal, & A. Singh (Eds.), *Developing Relationships, Personalization, and Data Herald in Marketing 5.0* (pp. 215–241). IGI Global., doi:10.4018/978-1-6684-4496-2.ch014

Hossain, M. S., & Rahman, M. F. (2022b). *Customer Sentiment Analysis and Prediction of Insurance Products' Reviews Using Machine Learning Approaches.* FIIB Business Review., doi:10.1177/23197145221115793

Hossain, M. S., & Rahman, M. F. (2022b). Sentiment Analysis and Review Rating Prediction of the Users of Bangladeshi Shopping Apps. In J. Kaur, P. Jindal, & A. Singh (Eds.), *Developing Relationships, Personalization, and Data Herald in Marketing 5.0* (pp. 33–56). IGI Global., doi:10.4018/978-1-6684-4496-2.ch002

Hossain, M. S., Rahman, M. F., & Uddin, M. K. (2022a). Analyzing and Predicting Learners' Sentiment toward Specialty schools using Machine Learning Techniques. In G. Trajkovski, M. Demeter, & H. Hayes (Eds.), *Applying Data Science and Learning Analytics Throughout a Learner's Lifespan.* IGI Global., doi:10.4018/978-1-7998-9644-9.ch007

Hossain, M. S., Rahman, M. F., Uddin, M. K., & Hossain, M. K. (2022). Customer sentiment analysis and prediction of halal restaurants using machine learning approaches. *Journal of Islamic Marketing.* Advance online publication. doi:10.1108/JIMA-04-2021-0125

Hossain, M. S., Rahman, M. F., & Zhou, X. (2021). Impact of customers' interpersonal interactions in social commerce on customer relationship management performance. *Journal of Contemporary Marketing Science, 4*(1), 161–181. doi:10.1108/JCMARS-12-2020-0050

Hossain, M. S., Uddin, M. K., Hossain, M. K., & Rahman, M. F. (2022b). User sentiment analysis and review rating prediction for the Blended Learning Platform app. In G. Trajkovski, M. Demeter, & H. Hayes (Eds.), *Applying Data Science and Learning Analytics Throughout a Learner's Lifespan.* IGI Global., doi:10.4018/978-1-7998-9644-9.ch006

Howells, K., & Ertugan, A. (2017). Applying fuzzy logic for sentiment analysis of social media network data in marketing. *Procedia Computer Science, 120,* 664–670. doi:10.1016/j.procs.2017.11.293

Hsu, D. (2015). Comparison of integrated clustering methods for accurate and stable prediction of building energy consumption data. *Applied Energy, 160,* 153-163.

Hu, Y. X. (2018, March). Context-sensitive query auto-completion with knowledge base. In *The 10th forum on data engineering and information management. The 16th annual meeting of database society of Japan* (pp. 4-6). Awara.

Huang, D., Chen, Q., Huang, J., Kong, S., & Li, Z. (2021). Customer-robot interactions: Understanding customer experience with service robots. *International Journal of Hospitality Management, 99*, 103078. doi:10.1016/j.ijhm.2021.103078

Huang, G. B., & Siew, C. K. (2005). Extreme learning machine with randomly assigned RBF kernels. *Int J Inf Technol, 11*(1), 16–24.

Huang, G. B., Zhou, H., Ding, X., & Zhang, R. (2012). Extreme learning machine for regression and multiclass classification. Part B. *IEEE Transactions on Systems, Man, and Cybernetics, 42*(2), 513–529. doi:10.1109/TSMCB.2011.2168604 PMID:21984515

Huang, J. C. (2019). Query auto-suggestion in search engines: A survey. *Information Processing & Management, 56*(2), 315–332.

Huang, S., Jiau, M., & Liu, Y. (2019, March). An Ant Path-Oriented Carpooling Allocation Approach to Optimize the Carpool Service Problem With Time Windows. *IEEE Systems Journal, 13*(1), 994–1005. doi:10.1109/JSYST.2018.2795255

Huang, Y., Na, J., Wu, X., Liu, X., & Guo, Y. (2015). Adaptive control of nonlinear uncertain active suspension system with prescribed performance. *ISA Transactions, 54*, 145–155. doi:10.1016/j.isatra.2014.05.025 PMID:25034649

Hull, K. (2002). Eros and Education: The Role of Desire in Teaching and Learning. *The NEA Higher Education Journal*, 19 - 32.

Hutchins, R. (1945). *The Higher Learning in America*. Transaction Publishers.

Ignatius, O., Obinalv, C. E., & Evboglai, a. M. (2016). Modeling Design and Simulation of Active suspension system PID Controller Using automated Tuning Technique. *Network and Complex Systems, 6*, 11-15.

Ijaz, M. U. (2021). Analysis of Clustering Algorithms for Mall. *International Journal of Wireless Communications and Mobile Computing, 8*(2), 39.

IMD. (n.d.). https://mausam.imd.gov.in/

Ioffe, S., & Szegedy, C. (2015). Batch normalization: accelerating deep network training by reducing internal covariate shift. *ICML'15: Proceedings of the 32nd International Conference on International Conference on Machine Learning, 37*, 448–456.

Islam, M. G. C., & Jin, S. (2019). An Overview of Neural Network. *American Journal of Neural Networks and Applications, 5*(1), 7–11. doi:10.11648/j.ajnna.20190501.12

İşlek, İ., & Öğüdücü, Ş. G. (2015). A retail demand forecasting model based on data mining techniques. In *2015 IEEE 24th International Symposium on Industrial Electronics (ISIE)*. IEEE. 10.1109/ISIE.2015.7281443

Iyer, R., & Griffin, M. (2021). Modeling word-of-mouth usage: A replication. *Journal of Business Research, 126*, 512–523. doi:10.1016/j.jbusres.2019.12.027

Izadkhah, A., Nouri, K., & Nikoobin, A. (2020). Proportional Integral Derivative Control of Fractional-Order for a Quarter Car System. *Ram. J. Phys, 65*, 103.

Jaarsma, A., Kinaschuk, K., & Xing, L. (2016). Kierkegaard, Despair and the Possibility of Education: Teaching Existentialism Existentially. *Studies in Philosophy and Education, 35*(5), 445–461. doi:10.100711217-015-9488-x

Jabid, T., Kabir, M. H., & Chae, O. (2010). Robust facial expression recognition based on local directional pattern. *ETRI Journal*, *32*(5), 784–794. doi:10.4218/etrij.10.1510.0132

Jain, A. K. (2010). Data clustering: 50 years beyond K-means. *Pattern Recognition Letters*, *31*(8), 651–666. doi:10.1016/j.patrec.2009.09.011

James, G., Witten, D., Hastie, T., & Tibshirani, R. (2013). *An Introduction to Statistical Learning* (Vol. 112). Springer. doi:10.1007/978-1-4614-7138-7

Jansen, B. J. (2010). An examination of searcher's perceptions of and interactions with query auto-suggestions. *Journal of the American Society for Information Science and Technology*, *61*(4), 716–732.

Janssen, A., Cardona, D. R., Passlick, J., & Breitner, M. H. (2022). How to Make chatbots productive–A user-oriented implementation framework. *International Journal of Human-Computer Studies*, *168*, 102921. doi:10.1016/j.ijhcs.2022.102921

Jayachitra, A., & Vinodha, R. (2015). Genetic algorithm based PID controller tuning approach for continuous stirred tank reactor. *Advances in Artificial Intelligence*, *2014*, 9–9.

Jayasingh, R. (2022). Speckle noise removal by SORAMA segmentation in Digital Image Processing to facilitate precise robotic surgery. *International Journal of Reliable and Quality E-Healthcare*, *11*(1), 1–19. Advance online publication. doi:10.4018/IJRQEH.295083

Jiang, D. C. (2018, August). Location-sensitive personalized query auto-completion. In *10th International Conference on Intelligent Human-Machine Systems and Cybernetics (IHMSC)* (vol. 1, pp. 15-19). IEEE.

Jin, P., Li, F., Li, X., Liu, Q., Liu, K., Ma, H., Dong, P., & Tang, S. (2022). Temporal Relation Extraction with Joint Semantic and Syntactic Attention. Computational Intelligence and Neuroscience. doi:10.1155/2022/5680971

Jin, Q., Wu, B., Nishimura, S., & Ogihara, A. (2016, August). Ubi-Liven: a human-centric safe and secure framework of ubiquitous living environments for the elderly. In *2016 International Conference on Advanced Cloud and Big Data (CBD)*. IEEE. 10.1109/CBD.2016.059

Johnston, R. (2004). Towards a better understanding of service excellence. *Managing Service Quality*, *14*(2/3), 129–133. doi:10.1108/09604520410528554

Jordan, M. I., & Mitchell, T. M. (2015). Machine learning: Trends, perspectives, and prospects. *Sci (NY)*, *349*(6245), 255–260. doi:10.1126cience.aaa8415 PMID:26185243

Joudhav, A. M., & Vadnajacharya. (2012). Performance Verification of PID Controller in an Interconnected Power System Using Particle Swarm Optimization. *Energy Procedia*, *14*, 2075–2080. doi:10.1016/j.egypro.2011.12.1210

Jovanović, J., Gašević, D., Dawson, S., Pardo, A., & Mirriahi, N. (2016a). Learning Analytics to Unveil Learning Strategies in a Flipped Classroom. *The Internet and Higher Education*, *33*, 74–85. doi:10.1016/j.iheduc.2017.02.001

Jowett, B. (2016). *The Dialogues of Plato, Volumes 1 - 3*. Eternal Sun Books.

Jun-yi, C., Jin, L., & Bing, A. C. (2005). Optimization of fractional-order pid controllers based on genetic algorithms. *International conference on machine learning and cybernetics*, *9*, 5686-5689.

Jurek, A., Mulvenna, M. D., & Bi, Y. (2015). Improved lexicon-based sentiment analysis for social media analytics. *Security Informatics*, *4*(1), 9. Advance online publication. doi:10.118613388-015-0024-x

Kamble, S. S., Gunasekaran, A., Goswami, M., & Manda, J. (2018). A systematic perspective on the applications of big data analytics in healthcare management. *International Journal of Healthcare Management*, *12*(3), 226–240. doi:10.1080/20479700.2018.1531606

Kanna, P. R., & Pandiaraja, P. (2019). An Efficient Sentiment Analysis Approach for Product Review using Turney Algorithm. In *Procedia Computer Science* (Vol. 165, pp. 356–362). Elsevier B.V. doi:10.1016/j.procs.2020.01.038

Kanungo, T., Mount, D. M., Netanyahu, N. S., Piatko, C. D., Silverman, R., & Wu, A. Y. (2002). An efficient k-means clustering algorithm: Analysis and implementation. *IEEE Transactions on Pattern Analysis and Machine Intelligence*, *24*(7), 881–892. doi:10.1109/TPAMI.2002.1017616

Kanwal, T., Attaullah, H., Anjum, A., Khan, A., & Jeon, G. (2022). *Fuzz-classification (p, l)-Angel: An enhanced hybrid artificial intelligence based fuzzy logic for multiple sensitive attributes against privacy breaches*. Digital Communications and Networks., doi:10.1016/j.dcan.2022.09.025

Karimi, Karami, & Keshavarz. (2018). Climate change and agriculture: Impacts and adaptive responses in Iran. *Journal of Integrative Agriculture*, *17*(1), 1–15. . doi:10.1016/S2095-3119(17)61794-5

Karna, A., & Gibert, K. (2022). Automatic identification of the number of clusters in hierarchical clustering. *Neural Computing & Applications*, *34*(1), 119–134. doi:10.100700521-021-05873-3

Kashem, S., Nagarajah, R., & Eklesabi, M. (2018). *Vehicle Suspension System and Electromagnetic Damper*. doi:10.1007/978-981-10-5478-5

Kastrati, Z., Imran, A. S., & Kurti, A. (2020). Weakly Supervised Framework for Aspect-Based Sentiment Analysis on Students' Reviews of MOOCs. *IEEE Access : Practical Innovations, Open Solutions*, *8*, 106799–106810. doi:10.1109/ACCESS.2020.3000739

Kebdy, J., & Russell, E. (1995). Particle Swarm Optimization. *Proceedings of ICNN95-International Conference on Neural Networks, 4*.

Kelleher, J. D., Mac Namee, B., & D'arcy, A. (2020). *Fundamentals of machine learning for predictive data analytics: algorithms, worked examples, and case studies*. MIT Press.

Kettani, O., Ramdani, F., & Tadili, B. (2014). An agglomerative clustering method for large data sets. *International Journal of Computers and Applications*, *92*(14).

Kevin, L. (2017). *Mark Cuban Says This Is Where the World's First Trillion-aires Will Emerge*. https://fortune.com/2017/03/14/mark-cuban-sxsw-first-trillionaire-ai/

Khanra, S., Dhir, A., Islam, A. N., & Mäntymäki, M. (2020). Big data analytics in healthcare: A systematic literature review. *Enterprise Information Systems*, *14*(7), 878–912. doi:10.1080/17517575.2020.1812005

Khoza, L. (2018). Reflection: Usage of the Learning Management System at the Faculty of Military Science. In *International Conference on e-Learning* (pp. 161-170). Kidmore End: Academic Conferences International Limited.

Khoza, L., & Van Zyl, G. (2015). Disparity: Threat or opportunity to distance education throughput at the South African Military Academy. *Scientia Militaria. South African Journal of Military Studies*, *43*(2), 151–173. doi:10.5787/43-2-1128

Kim, J. C., & Chung, K. Y. (2020). Knowledge expansion of metadata using script mining analysis in multimedia recommendation. *Multimedia Tools and Applications*. Advance online publication. doi:10.100711042-020-08774-0

Kim, S. W. (2019). Improving query suggestion based on personalized search history. *Journal of Convergence*, *10*(5), 17–23.

Kirillov, N., Fadeeva, V., & Fadeev, V. (2016). Modern philosophy of education. *Web of Conferences, 28*. 10.1051hsconf/20162801034

Kirsch, R. A. (1971). Computer determination of the constituent structure of biological images. *Computers and Biomedical Research, an International Journal, 4*(3), 315–328. doi:10.1016/0010-4809(71)90034-6 PMID:5562571

Kler, R., Elkady, G., Rane, K., Singh, A., Hossain, M. S., Malhotra, D., Ray, S., & Bhatia, K. K. (2022). Machine Learning and Artificial Intelligence in the Food Industry: A Sustainable Approach. *Journal of Food Quality, 2022*, 1–9. doi:10.1155/2022/8521236

Knight, S. (2020). Augmenting Assessment with Learning Analytics. In M. Bearman, P. Dawson, R. Ajjawi, J. Tai, & D. Boud (Eds.), *Re-imagining University Assessment in a Digital World. The Enabling Power of Assessment* (Vol. 7). Springer. doi:10.1007/978-3-030-41956-1_10

Kolb, A., & Kolb, D. (2005). Learning Styles and Learning Spaces: Enhancing Experiential Learning in Higher Education. *Academy of Management Learning & Education, 4*(2), 193–212. doi:10.5465/amle.2005.17268566

Kop, R. (2011). The challenges to connectivist learning on open online networks: Learning experiences during a massive open online course. *International Review of Research in Open and Distance Learning, 12*(3), 19. doi:10.19173/irrodl.v12i3.882

Kousha, K. (2021). Query reformulation for web search: A systematic review. *Information Processing & Management, 58*(2), 102522.

KPMG. (2022). *Global Semiconductor industry outlook 2022*. KPMG.

Kramer, O. (2017). *Genetic algorithms, genetic algorithm essential*. Springer.

Krishnan. U. (2021). *Methods for Evaluating Query Auto Completion Systems* [Doctoral dissertation]. University of Melbourne.

Kshetri, N. (2014, July). The emerging role of Big Data in key development issues: Opportunities, challenges, and concerns. *Big Data & Society, 1*(2). Advance online publication. doi:10.1177/2053951714564227

Kulkarni, A., Bhandari, D., & Bhoite, S. (2019). Restaurants Rating Prediction using Machine Learning Algorithms. *International Journal of Computer Applications Technology and Research, 8*(9), 375-378.

Kumar, K. V., Kumari, P., Rao, M., & Mohapatra, D. P. (2022). Metaheuristic feature selection for software fault prediction. *Journal of Information & Optimization Sciences, 43*(5), 1013–1020. doi:10.1080/02522667.2022.2103301

Kumar, L., kumar, P., Satyajeet, & Narang, D. (2018). Tuning of fractional-order controllers using evolutionary optimization for pid tuned synchronous generator excitation system. *IFAC-PapersOnLine, 51*(4), 859–864. doi:10.1016/j.ifacol.2018.06.121

Kumar, V. K., Sharma, P. D., Rout, P., Vanit, A., Rao, M., & Mohapatra, D. (2022). Effect on Feature selection in Software Fault Prediction. In D. Mishra, R. Buyya, P. Mohapatra, & S. Patnaik (Eds.), *Intelligent and Cloud Computing. Smart Innovation, Systems and Technologies* (Vol. 286). Springer. doi:10.1007/978-981-16-9873-6_44

Kun, A. L., Schmidt, A., Dey, A., & Boll, S. (2013). Automotive user interfaces and interactive applications in the car. *Personal and Ubiquitous Computing, 17*(5), 801–802. doi:10.100700779-012-0520-7

Kushwaha, D. Y., & Prajapati, D. (2008). *Customer segmentation using K-means algorithm*. 8th Semester Student of B. tech in Computer Science and Engineering.

Kutiel, G. (2017). Approximation Algorithms for the Maximum Carpool Matching Problem. In P. Weil (Ed.), Lecture Notes in Computer Science: Vol. 10304. *Computer Science – Theory and Applications. CSR 2017*. Springer. doi:10.1007/978-3-319-58747-9_19

Lage, M., Platt, G., & Tregua, M. (2000). Inverting the classroom: A gateway to creating an inclusive learning environment. *The Journal of Economic Education*, *31*(1), 30–43. doi:10.1080/00220480009596759

Laitinen, A. T. (2021). Using click-through data for personalized query suggestion. *Journal of Information Science*, *47*(4), 499–515.

Lalwani, P., Mishra, M. K., Chadha, J. S., & Sethi, P. (2022). Customer churn prediction system: A machine learning approach. *Computing*, *104*(2), 271–294. doi:10.100700607-021-00908-y

Lasek, A., Cercone, N., & Saunders, J. (2016). Restaurant sales and customer demand forecasting: Literature survey and categorization of methods. In *Smart City 360* (pp. 479–491). Springer. doi:10.1007/978-3-319-33681-7_40

Latha, K., Rajinikanth, V., & Surekha, P. (2013). Pso-based PID Controller Design for a Class of Stable and Unstable Systems. *International Scholarly Research Notices*.

Laurillard, D. (2013b). *The teacher as action researcher: Building Pedagogical Patterns for Learning and Technology*. Routledge.

Ledesma, S., Ibarra-Manzano, M. A., Cabal-Yepez, E., Almanza-Ojeda, D. L., & Avina-Cervantes, J. G. (2018). Analysis of data sets with learning conflicts for machine learning. *IEEE Access : Practical Innovations, Open Solutions*, *6*, 45062–45070. doi:10.1109/ACCESS.2018.2865135

Lee, M., Rodgers, S., & Kim, M. (2009). Effects of valence and extremity of eWOM on attitude toward the brand and website. *Journal of Current Issues and Research in Advertising*, *31*(2), 1–11. doi:10.1080/10641734.2009.10505262

Lei, Z., Tong, L., Wu, J., & Jie, Y. (2020). Tencent intelligent customer service human-machine collaboration practice. Artificial Intelligence, 3, 106-113.

Lemley, J., Bazrafkan, S., & Corcoran, P. (2017, March 15). Deep Learning for Consumer Devices and Services: Pushing the limits for machine learning, artificial intelligence, and computer vision. *IEEE Consumer Electronics Magazine.*, *6*(2), 48–56. doi:10.1109/MCE.2016.2640698

Liang, Y. J., & Wu, S. L. (2013). Optimal vibration control for tracked vehicle suspension systems. *Mathematical Problems in Engineering*, *2013*, 1–7. doi:10.1155/2013/178354

Libório, M. P., Martinuci, O., Machado, A. M. C., Lyrio, R. M., & Bernardes, P. (2022). Time–Space Analysis of Multidimensional Phenomena: A Composite Indicator of Social Exclusion Through k-Means. *Social Indicators Research*, *159*(2), 569–591. doi:10.100711205-021-02763-y

Li, J. (2022). E-Commerce Fraud Detection Model by Computer Artificial Intelligence Data Mining. *Computational Intelligence and Neuroscience*, *2022*, 1–9. Advance online publication. doi:10.1155/2022/8783783 PMID:35586101

Lin, Tsai, & Yu. (2012). A Review Of Deterministic Optimization Methods in Engineering and Management. Mathematical Problems in Engineering.

Linda, D. (2019). Developing business customer engagement through social media engagement-platforms: An integrative S-D logic/RBV-informed model. *Industrial Marketing Management*, *81*, 89–98. Advance online publication. doi:10.1016/j.indmarman.2017.11.016

Lindahl, M., Sakao, T., & Carlsson, E. (2014). Actor's and system maps for Integrated Product Service Offerings - Practical experience from two companies. In *Procedia CIRP* (Vol. 16, pp. 320–325). Elsevier. doi:10.1016/j.procir.2014.01.030

Lin, J. S., & Kanellakopoulos, I. (1997). Nonlineardesign of active suspension. *IEEE Control Systems Magazine*, 45–59.

Liu, L. (2022). e-Commerce Personalized Recommendation Based on Machine Learning Technology. *Mobile Information Systems, 2022*, 1–11. Advance online publication. doi:10.1155/2022/1761579

Liu, L., Zhu, C., Liu, Y. J., Wang, R., & Tong, S. (2022). Performance Improvement of active susepnsion Constrained system via Neural Networks and Learning System. *IEEE Transactions on Neural Networks and Learning Systems*.

Liu, X., & Ichise, R. (2017). Food sales prediction with meteorological data—a case study of a japanese chain supermarket. In *International Conference on Data Mining and Big Data*. Springer. 10.1007/978-3-319-61845-6_10

Liu, Y. J., Zeng, Q., Tong, S., Chen, C. L. P., & Liu, L. (2019). Adaptive Neural Network Control for Active Suspension Systems with Time-Varying Vertical Displacement and Speed Constraints. *IEEE Transactions on Industrial Electronics, 66*(12), 9458–9466. doi:10.1109/TIE.2019.2893847

Livingstone, J. D. (2008). *Artificial Neural Networks Methods and Applications*. Humana Press.

Livingston, M., McClain, B., & DeSpain, B. (1995). Assessing the consistency between teachers' philosophies and educational goals. *Education, 116*(1), 124.

Lokers, R., Knapen, R., Janssen, S., van Randen, Y., & Jansen, J. (2016, October). Analysis of Big Data technologies for use in agro-environmental science. *Environmental Modelling & Software, 84*, 494–504. doi:10.1016/j.envsoft.2016.07.017

Lund, S., Manyika, J., Woetzel, J., Bughin, J., & Krishnan, M. (2019). *Globalization in transition: The future of trade and value chains*. Academic Press.

Luo, J. M., Vu, H. Q., Li, G., & Law, R. (2021). Understanding service attributes of robot hotels: A sentiment analysis of customer online reviews. *International Journal of Hospitality Management, 98*, 103032. doi:10.1016/j.ijhm.2021.103032

Luo, Y., & Xu, X. (2021). Comparative study of deep learning models for analyzing online restaurant reviews in the era of the COVID-19 pandemic. *International Journal of Hospitality Management, 94*, 102849. Advance online publication. doi:10.1016/j.ijhm.2020.102849 PMID:34785843

Lu, X., Shankar, D., Gugnani, S., & Panda, D. K. D. K. (2016). High-performance design of apache spark with RDMA and its benefits on various workloads. *Proc. - 2016 IEEE Int. Conf. Big Data*, 253–262. doi:10.1109/BigData.2016.7840611

Lv, X., Zhang, G., Liu, J., & Li, J. (2022). The Innovation Ecological Model of Chinese Automotive Industry Based on Artificial Intelligence and Big Data Technology. *Mathematical Problems in Engineering, 2022*, 2022. doi:10.1155/2022/4328187

Lyons, M., Akamatsu, S., Kamachi, M., & Gyoba, J. (1998). Coding facial expressions with gabor wavelets. *Third IEEE International Conference on Automatic Face and Gesture Recognition*, 200-205. 10.1109/AFGR.1998.670949

Ma, C., & Hori, Y. (2004). Fractional order control and its application of PI/SUP/SPL alpha //d. *Proceedings of the 4th International power electronics and motion control conference*, 1477-1482.

Maalej, W., Kurtanović, Z., Nabil, H., & Stanik, C. (2016). On the automatic classification of app reviews. *Requirements Engineering, 21*(3), 311–331. doi:10.100700766-016-0251-9

Machan, T. (2011). Truth in Philosophy. *Libertarian Papers, Academic OneFile, 3*. Retrieved 07 22, 2019, from http://link.galegroup.com/apps/doc/A280387350/AONE?u=27uos&sid=AONE&xid=201e249e

Machová, K., Mikula, M., Gao, X., & Mach, M. (2020). Lexicon-based sentiment analysis using particle swarm optimization. *Electronics (Switzerland), 9*(8), 1–22. doi:10.3390/electronics9081317

Mack, E. (2020, February 28). *How to use Bing's search suggestions*. Lifewire. https://www.lifewire.com/use-bing-search-suggestions-3973291

Madhani, P. M. (2019). Strategic supply chain management for enhancing competitive advantages: Developing business value added framework. *International Journal of Value Chain Management, 10*(4), 316–338. doi:10.1504/IJVCM.2019.103270

MahmoumGonbadi, A., Katebi, Y., & Doniavi, A. (2019). A generic two-stage fuzzy inference system for dynamic prioritization of customers. *Expert Systems with Applications, 131*, 240–253. doi:10.1016/j.eswa.2019.04.059

Mäntylä, M. V., Graziotin, D., & Kuutila, M. (2018). The evolution of sentiment analysis—A review of research topics, venues, and top cited papers. *Computer Science Review, 27*, 16–32. doi:10.1016/j.cosrev.2017.10.002

Marcondes, F. S., Durães, D., Gonçalves, F., Fonseca, J., Machado, J., & Novais, P. (2021). In-Vehicle Violence Detection in Carpooling: A Brief Survey Towards a General Surveillance System. In *Distributed Computing and Artificial Intelligence, 17th International Conference. DCAI 2020. Advances in Intelligent Systems and Computing* (vol. 1237). Springer. 10.1007/978-3-030-53036-5_23

Maritain, J. (1938). *True humanism.* Charles Scribner's Sons.

Maroufpoor, S., & Bozorg-Haddad, O. (2020). Stochastic optimization. Handbook of Probabilistic Models.

Marr, B. (2019). *Artificial intelligence in practice: How 50 successful companies used AI and machine learning to solve problems.* John Wiley & Sons.

Marrs, H., & Benton, S. (2009). Relationships between Separate and Connected Knowing and Approaches to Learning. *Sex Roles, 60*(1-2), 57–66. doi:10.100711199-008-9510-7

Martens, D., & Maalej, W. (2019). Towards understanding and detecting fake reviews in app stores. *Empirical Software Engineering, 24*(6), 3316–3355. doi:10.100710664-019-09706-9

Martín, C., Langendoerfer, P., Zarrin, P. S., Díaz, M., & Rubio, B. (2022). Kafka-ML: Connecting the data stream with ML/AI frameworks. *Future Generation Computer Systems, 126*, 15–33. doi:10.1016/j.future.2021.07.037

Martinez, A. M., & Benavente, R. (1998). *The AR Face Database.* CVC Technical Report #24.

Martin, J. R., & White, P. R. R. (2005). *The Language of Evaluation: Appraisal in English. The Language of Evaluation: Appraisal in English.* Palgrave Macmillan. doi:10.1057/9780230511910

Matsumoto, D. (2009). *The Cambridge dictionary of psychology.* Cambridge University Press.

Ma, X., Wang, Z., Zhou, S., Wen, H., & Zhang, Y. (2018, June). Intelligent healthcare systems assisted by data analytics and mobile computing. In *2018 14th International Wireless Communications & Mobile Computing Conference (IWCMC)* (pp. 1317–1322). IEEE. doi:10.1109/IWCMC.2018.8450377

McEwan, H. (2011). Narrative Reflection in the Philosophy of Teaching: Genealogies and Portraits. *Journal of Philosophy of Education, 45*(1), 125–140. doi:10.1111/j.1467-9752.2010.00783.x

McIlroy, S., Ali, N., & Hassan, A. E. (2015). Fresh apps: An empirical study of frequently-updated mobile apps in the Google play store. *Empirical Software Engineering, 21*(3), 1346–1370. doi:10.100710664-015-9388-2

McKinsey. (2018). *Right product, right time, and right location: Quantifying the semiconductor supply chain.* Author.

McKinsey. (2022). *How Semiconductors makers can turn a talent challenge into competitive advantage.* Author.

McPherran, M. (2013). Socrates, Plato, erôs, and liberal education. In C. Brooke, E. Frazer, C. Brooke, & E. Frazer (Eds.), *Ideas of Education: Philosophy and Politics from Plato to Dewey* (pp. 6–19). Routledge.

Means, B. e. (2009). *Evaluation of Evidence-Based Practices in Online Learning: A Meta-Analysis and Review of Online Learning Studies Washington.* US Department of Education.

Meng, X. H., & Baoye, S. (2007). Fast genetic algorithms are used for pid parameters optimization. In *International conference on automation and logistics*. IEEE. 10.1109/ICAL.2007.4338930

Messer, K., Matas, J., Kittler, J., Luettin, J., & Maitre, G. (1999). XM2VTSDB: the Extended of M2VTS Database. *Proceedings of International Conference on Audio- and Video-Based Person Authentication*, 72-77.

Meulstee, P., & Pechenizkiy, M. (2008). Food sales prediction: "If only it knew what we know". In *2008 IEEE International Conference on Data Mining Workshops*. IEEE. 10.1109/ICDMW.2008.128

Meyer, W., Moore, C., & Viljoen, H. (1989). *Personality Theories - from Freud to Frankl*. Lexicon.

Miao, Q., Li, Q., & Zeng, D. (2010). Fine-grained opinion mining by integrating multiple review sources. *Journal of the American Society for Information Science and Technology*, *61*(11), 2288–2299. doi:10.1002/asi.21400

Microsoft. (n.d.). *Bing search help*. https://www.microsoft.com/en-us/bing/search-help

Mikalef, Pappas, Krogstie, & Giannakos. (2017). Big data analytics capabilities: a systematic literature review and research agenda. *Inf. Syst. E-bus. Manag., 16*(3), 547–578. . doi:10.1007/s10257-017-0362-y

Miller, T. (2019). Explanation in artificial intelligence: Insights from the social sciences. *Artificial Intelligence*, *267*, 1–38. Advance online publication. doi:10.1016/j.artint.2018.07.007

Mirriahi, N., & Lorenzo Vigentini, L. (2017). Analytics of Learner Video Use. In C. Lang, G. Siemens, A. Wise, & D. Gasevic (Eds.), *Handbook of Learning Analytics* (pp. 251–267). Society for Learning Analytics Research. doi:10.18608/hla17.022

Mitsos, A., Najman, J., & Kevrekidis, I. G. (2018). Optimal deterministic algorithm generation. *Journal of Global Optimization*, *71*(4), 891–913. doi:10.100710898-018-0611-8

MJ & IM. (2022). *Hybrid filter and wrapper methods based feature selection for crop recommendation*. . doi:10.1109/ICESIC53714.2022.9783542

Moghaddam, B., & Pentland, A. (1997, July). Probabilistic Visual Learning for Object Recognition. *IEEE Transactions on Pattern Analysis and Machine Intelligence*, *19*(7), 696–710. doi:10.1109/34.598227

Mohammadi, Y., & Ganjefar, S. (2017). Quarter Car Active Suspension system: Minimum time controller design using singular perturbation method. *International Journal of Control, Automation, and Systems*, *15*(6), 2538–2550. doi:10.100712555-016-0608-3

Mohammad, S., & Nastaran, H. (2021). How human users engage with consumer robots? A dual model of psychological ownership and trust to explain post-adoption behaviours. *Computers in Human Behavior*, *117*, 106660. Advance online publication. doi:10.1016/j.chb.2020.106660

Mohebbanaaz, K., Kumari, L. V. R., & Sai, Y. P. (2022). Classification of ECG beats using optimized decision tree and adaptive boosted optimized decision tree. *SIViP*, *16*(3), 695–703. doi:10.100711760-021-02009-x

Moore, A. (2001). *K-means and Hierarchical Clustering*. Academic Press.

Mostafa, M. M. (2018). Mining and mapping halal food consumers: A geo-located Twitter opinion polarity analysis. *Journal of Food Products Marketing*, *24*(7), 858–879. doi:10.1080/10454446.2017.1418695

Mostafa, M. M. (2019). Clustering halal food consumers: A Twitter sentiment analysis. *International Journal of Market Research*, *61*(3), 320–337. doi:10.1177/1470785318771451

Mostafa, M. M. (2020). Global halal food discourse on social media: A text mining approach. *Journal of International Communication, 26*(2), 211–237. doi:10.1080/13216597.2020.1795702

Mouleeswaran, S. (2012). *Design and Development of PID Controller-Based Active Suspension System for Automobiles. PID Controller Design Approaches: Theory, Tuning and Application to Frontier Areas.* BoD–Books on Demand.

Moutselos, K., Kyriazis, D., Diamantopoulou, V., & Maglogiannis, I. (2018, December). Trustworthy data processing for health analytics tasks. In *2018 IEEE International Conference on Big Data (Big Data).* IEEE. 10.1109/BigData.2018.8622449

Moynat, O., Volden, J., & Sahakian, M. (2022). How do COVID-19 lockdown practices relate to sustainable well-being? Lessons from Oslo and Geneva. *Sustainability: Science, Practice and Policy, 18*(1), 309–324.

Mujahid, M., Lee, E., Rustam, F., Washington, P. B., Ullah, S., Reshi, A. A., & Ashraf, I. (2021). Sentiment analysis and topic modeling on tweets about online education during covid-19. *Applied Sciences (Switzerland), 11*(18), 8438. Advance online publication. doi:10.3390/app11188438

Mullen, T., & Collier, N. (2004). Sentiment Analysis using Support Vector Machines with Diverse Information Sources. In D. Lin & D. Wu (Eds.), *Proceedings of EMNLP 2004* (pp. 412–418). Association for Computational Linguistics. http://research.nii.ac.jp/~collier/papers/emnlp2004.pdf

Mykel & Kochenderfer. (2019). *Algorithms for Optimization.* The MIT Press. Available: https://edubookpdf.com/computer/algorithms-for-optimization-the-mit-press.html

Nadkarni, P. M., Ohno-Machado, L., & Chapman, W. W. (2011). Natural language processing: An introduction. *Journal of the American Medical Informatics Association, 18*(5), 544–551. doi:10.1136/amiajnl-2011-000464 PMID:21846786

Nagy, R. (2016). Tracking and visualizing student effort: Evolution of a practical analytics tool for staff and student engagement. *Journal of Learning Analytics, 3*(2), 165–193. doi:10.18608/jla.2016.32.8

Naidu, L. G. K., Ramamurthy, V., & Challa, O. (2006). *Soil suitability criteria for major crops.* National Bureau of Soil Survey and Land Usage Planning. http://krishikosh.egranth.ac.in/displaybitstream?handle=1/2034266

Nan, H., & Hu, M. (2022). Corporate Marketing Strategy Analysis with Machine Learning Algorithms. *Wireless Communications and Mobile Computing, 2022,* 1–13. Advance online publication. doi:10.1155/2022/9450020

Nasukawa, T., & Yi, J. (2003). Sentiment analysis: Capturing favorability using natural language processing. In *Proceedings of the 2nd International Conference on Knowledge Capture, K-CAP 2003* (pp. 70–77). Association for Computing Machinery, Inc. 10.1145/945645.945658

Navaz, A. N., Serhani, M. A., Al-Qirim, N., & Gergely, M. (2018). Towards an efficient and Energy-Aware mobile big health data architecture. *Computer Methods and Programs in Biomedicine, 166,* 137–154. doi:10.1016/j.cmpb.2018.10.008 PMID:30415713

Naz, N. A., Shoaib, U., & Shahzad Sarfraz, M. (2018). A review on customer churn prediction data mining modeling techniques. *Indian Journal of Science and Technology, 11*(27), 1–27. doi:10.17485/ijst/2018/v11i27/121478

Nemes, L., & Kiss, A. (2021). Prediction of stock values changes using sentiment analysis of stock news headlines. *Journal of Information and Telecommunication, 5*(3), 375–394. doi:10.1080/24751839.2021.1874252

Nemhauser, G., & Wolsey, L. (1999). *Integer and Combinatorial Optimization.* Wiley.

Nikolaev & Jacobson. (2011). Using Markov chains to analyze the effectiveness of local search algorithms. *Discrete Optimization, 8*(2), 160-173.

Nilsson, S., & Lindahl, M. (2016). A Literature Review to Understand the Requirements Specification's Role when Developing Integrated Product Service Offerings. In *Procedia CIRP* (Vol. 47, pp. 150–155). Elsevier B.V. doi:10.1016/j.procir.2016.03.225

Nise, N. S. (2020). *Control System Engineering*. John Wiley and Sons.

Nitesh, M., & Chawla, A. (2021). *Semiconductors Supply Chain Model*. https://www.google.com/url?sa=t&rct=j&q=&esrc=s&source=web&cd=&cad=rja&uact=8&ved=2ahUKEwi_jcPT5LX9AhVkRmwGHY47CZEQFnoECAkQAQ&url=https%3A%2F%2Fwww.birlasoft.com%2Farticles%2Fdigital-supply-chain-resilience-semiconductor-industry&usg=AOvVaw1NrCRKJ-n2XHOo-nbJxjUK

Noel, C., & Kieran, C. (2020). Normalising the "new normal": Changing tech-driven work practices under pandemic time pressure. *International Journal of Information Management, 55*, 102186. Advance online publication. doi:10.1016/j.ijinfomgt.2020.102186 PMID:32836643

Novo-Lourés, M., Ruano-Ordás, D., Pavón, R., Laza, R., Gómez-Meire, S., & Méndez, J. R. (2022). Enhancing representation in the context of multiple-channel spam filtering. *Information Processing & Management, 59*(2), 102812. doi:10.1016/j.ipm.2021.102812

Ojala, T., Pietikainen, M., & Maenpaa, T. (2002). Multiresolution gray-scale and rotation invariant texture classification with local binary patterns. *IEEE Transactions on Pattern Analysis and Machine Intelligence, 24*(7), 971–987. doi:10.1109/TPAMI.2002.1017623

Ojansivu, V., & Heikkilä, J. (2008). Blur insensitive texture classification using local phase quantization. *International conference on image and signal processing*, 236–243. 10.1007/978-3-540-69905-7_27

Oliveira, N., Cortez, P., & Areal, N. (2016). Stock market sentiment lexicon acquisition using microblogging data and statistical measures. *Decision Support Systems, 85*, 62–73. doi:10.1016/j.dss.2016.02.013

Omidire, M. (2017). Contributions of Cognitive Theories to Teaching and Learning Strategies. In M. Maphalana (Ed.), Teaching and Learning Startegies in South Africa (pp. 27 - 42). Cheriton House, UK: Cengage.

Ongaro, E. (2017). *Philosophy and Public Administration: An Introduction*. Northampton, MA: Edward Elgar Publishing Limited, ProQuest Ebook Central. Retrieved July 22, 2019, from https://ebookcentral.proquest.com/lib/sun/detail.action?docID=4980439

Open Government Data (OGD) Platform India. (n.d.). https://data.gov.in/

Osman, A. M. S. (2019, February). A novel big data analytics framework for smart cities. *Future Generation Computer Systems, 91*, 620–633. doi:10.1016/j.future.2018.06.046

Ozan, Ş. (2018, September). A case study on customer segmentation by using machine learning methods. In *2018 International Conference on Artificial Intelligence and Data Processing (IDAP)* (pp. 1-6). IEEE. 10.1109/IDAP.2018.8620892

Padma, P., & Wagenseil, U. (2018). Retail service excellence: Antecedents and consequences. *International Journal of Retail & Distribution Management, 46*(5), 422–441. doi:10.1108/IJRDM-09-2017-0189

Pak, A., & Paroubek, P. (2010). Twitter as a corpus for sentiment analysis and opinion mining. In *Proceedings of the 7th International Conference on Language Resources and Evaluation, LREC 2010* (pp. 1320–1326). European Language Resources Association (ELRA). 10.17148/IJARCCE.2016.51274

Palimkar, P., Bajaj, V., Mal, A. K., Shaw, R. N., & Ghosh, A. (2022). Unique Action Identifier by Using Magnetometer, Accelerometer and Gyroscope: KNN Approach. In M. Bianchini, V. Piuri, S. Das, & R. N. Shaw (Eds.), *Advanced Computing and Intelligent Technologies. Lecture Notes in Networks and Systems* (Vol. 218). Springer. doi:10.1007/978-981-16-2164-2_48

Pallathadka, H., Ramirez-Asis, E. H., Loli-Poma, T. P., Kaliyaperumal, K., Ventayen, R. J. M., & Naved, M. (2021). Applications of artificial intelligence in business management, e-commerce and finance. *Materials Today: Proceedings*. Advance online publication. doi:10.1016/j.matpr.2021.06.419

Pamina. (2019). Inferring machine learning based parameter estimation for telecom churn prediction. In *International Conference on Computational Vision and Bio Inspired Computing* (pp. 257-267). Springer.

Pandula, F., & Antonio, V. (2011). *Tuning Rules for Optimal PID and Fractional- Order PID Control.* Academic Press.

Pang, B., Lee, L., & Vithyanathan, S. (2019). Thumbs up? Sentiment Classification using Machine Learning Techniques. *Proceedings of the Institution of Civil Engineers - Transport, 172*(2), 122–122.

Pang, B., & Lee, L. (2008). Opinion mining and sentiment analysis. *Foundations and Trends in Information Retrieval, 2*(1–2), 1–135. doi:10.1561/1500000011

Pano, T., & Kashef, R. (2020). A Complete VADER-Based Sentiment Analysis of Bitcoin (BTC) Tweets during the Era of COVID-19. *Big Data and Cognitive Computing, 4*(4), 33. Advance online publication. doi:10.3390/bdcc4040033

Pardo, A., & Kloos, C. D. (2011). Stepping out of the box: Towards analytics outside the learning management system. In *Proceedings of the 1st International Conference on Learning Analytics and Knowledge* (pp. 163–167). New York, NY: ACM. 10.1145/2090116.2090142

Park, D. H. (2017, August). A neural language model for query auto-completion. In *Proceedings of the 40th International ACM SIGIR Conference on Research and Development in Information Retrieval* (pp. 1189-1192). 10.1145/3077136.3080758

Park, C., & Heo, W. (2020). Review of the changing electricity industry value chain in the ICT convergence era. *Journal of Cleaner Production, 258*, 120743. doi:10.1016/j.jclepro.2020.120743

Park, J. (2017). A study on the effects of search suggest on the search process and user experience. *Journal of Information Science Theory and Practice, 5*(1), 6–19.

Park, S., Cho, J., Park, K., & Shin, H. (2021). Customer sentiment analysis with more sensibility. *Engineering Applications of Artificial Intelligence, 104*, 104356. doi:10.1016/j.engappai.2021.104356

Pashchenko, Y., Rahman, M. F., Hossain, M. S., Uddin, M. K., & Islam, T. (2022). Emotional and the normative aspects of customers' reviews. *Journal of Retailing and Consumer Services, 68*, 103011. doi:10.1016/j.jretconser.2022.103011

Patel, D., Modi, R., & Sarvakar, K. (2014). A comparative study of clustering data mining: Techniques and research challenges. *International Journal of Latest Technology in Engineering, Management & Applied Sciences, 3*(9), 67–70.

Patrick, S., Idaumghar, L., & Julien, A. L. (2016). *Swarm Intelligence-Based Optimization.* Berlin: Springer International Publishing AG.

Patzig, G. (1968). What is an Aristotelian Syllogism? In *Aristotle's Theory of the Syllogism. Synthese Library (Monographs on Epistemology, Logic, Methodology, Philosophy of Science, Sociology of Science and of Knowledge, and on the Mathematical Methods of Social and Behavioral Sciences)* (Vol. 16). Springer. doi:10.1007/978-94-017-0787-9_1

Pavlyshenko, B. (2018). Using stacking approaches for machine learning models. In *2018 IEEE Second International Conference on Data Stream Mining & Processing (DSMP)* (pp. 255-258). IEEE. 10.1109/DSMP.2018.8478522

Peetz, M. H., Myllärniemi, V., & Oulasvirta, A. (2019). Investigating the effect of user modeling on query auto-completion performance. In *Proceedings of the 2019 Conference on Human Information Interaction and Retrieval* (pp. 235-244). Academic Press.

Peipei, Y. I. (2020). Gfocus: User focus-based graph query autocompletion. *IEEE Transactions on Knowledge and Data Engineering*.

Phillips, R., Maor, D., Preston, G., & Cumming-Potvin, W. (2012). Exploring Learning Analytics as Indicators of Study Behaviour. In T. Amiel, & B. Wilson (Ed.), *Proceedings of EdMedia 2012—World Conference on Educational Media and Technology* (pp. 286-286). Association for the Advancement of Computing in Education (AACE).

Pidstrigach, J., & Reich, S. (2022). Affine-Invariant Ensemble Transform Methods for Logistic Regression. *Foundations of Computational Mathematics*. Advance online publication. doi:10.100710208-022-09550-2

Pondlubny. (1998). *Fractional differential equations*. Academic Press.

Popat, S. K., & Emmanuel, M. (2014). Review and comparative study of clustering techniques. *International Journal of Computer Science and Information Technologies*, *5*(1), 805–812.

Potharaju, S. P., Sreedevi, M., & Amiripalli, S. S. (2019). An ensemble feature selection framework of sonar targets using symmetrical uncertainty and multi-layer perceptron (su-mlp). In *Cognitive Informatics and Soft Computing: Proceeding of CISC 2017* (pp. 247-256). Springer Singapore.

Potharaju, S. P., & Sreedevi, M. (2017). A Novel Clustering Based Candidate Feature Selection Framework Using Correlation Coefficient for Improving Classification Performance. *Journal of Engineering Science & Technology Review*, *10*(6), 38–43. doi:10.25103/jestr.106.06

Potharaju, S. P., Sreedevi, M., Ande, V. K., & Tirandasu, R. K. (2019). Data mining approach for accelerating the classification accuracy of cardiotocography. *Clinical Epidemiology and Global Health*, *7*(2), 160–164. doi:10.1016/j.cegh.2018.03.004

Power, E. (1990). *Philosophy of education*. Waveland Press.

Power, E. (1996). *Educational philosophy: A history from the ancient world to modern America*. Garland Publishing, Inc.

Pramanik, S., Sagayam, K. M., & Jena, O. P. (2021) Machine Learning Frameworks in Cancer Detection. ICCSRE 2021.

Pramanik, S., Galety, M. G., Samanta, D., & Joseph, N. P. (2022). Data Mining Approaches for Decision Support Systems. *3rd International Conference on Emerging Technologies in Data Mining and Information Security*.

Pramanik, S., & Ghosh, R. (2020). Intelligent Agent Facilitated e-Commerce. *Turkish Journal of Computer and Mathematics Education*, *11*(2), 906–913.

Pramanik, S., & Suresh Raja, S. (2020). A Secured Image Steganography using Genetic Algorithm. *Advances in Mathematics: Scientific Journal*, *9*(7), 4533–4541.

Preethi, P. G., Uma, V., & Kumar, A. (2015). Temporal sentiment analysis and causal rules extraction from tweets for event prediction. In *Procedia Computer Science* (Vol. 48, pp. 84–89). Elsevier B.V. doi:10.1016/j.procs.2015.04.154

Pring, R. (2013). John Dewey: Saviour of American education or worse than Hitler? In C. Brooke & E. Frazer (Eds.), *Ideas of Education: Philosophy and Politics from Plato to Dewey* (pp. 267–284). Routledge.

Pudumalar, S., Ramanujam, E., Rajashree, R. H., Kavya, C., Kiruthika, T., & Nisha, J. (2017). Crop recommendation system for precision agriculture. *2016 8th International Conference on Advanced Computing, ICoAC 2016*, 32–36. 10.1109/ICoAC.2017.7951740

Raghu, N. C., & Praveen, G. (2022, March 29). Emerging trends in digital transformation: A bibliometric analysis. *Benchmarking*, *29*(4), 1069–1112. Advance online publication. doi:10.1108/BIJ-01-2021-0009

Rahman, M. F., & Hossain, M. S. (2022). The impact of website quality on online compulsive buying behavior: Evidence from online shopping organizations. *South Asian Journal of Marketing*, *4*(1), 1–16. doi:10.1108/SAJM-03-2021-0038

Rajasshrie, P., Brijesh, S., & Yogesh, K. D. (2020). Shopping intention at AI-powered automated retail stores (AIPARS). *Journal of Retailing and Consumer Services*, *57*, 102207. Advance online publication. doi:10.1016/j.jretconser.2020.102207

Rajkhowa, B. (n.d.). *Impact of Artificial Intelligence on Customer Experience*. Retrieved from: https://www.ijrte.org/wp-content/uploads/papers/v9i2/B3727079220.pdf

Raju, N. R., & Reddy, P. (2016). Robustness Study of Fractional Order PID Controller Optimized by Particle Swarm Optimization in AVR System. *Iranian Journal of Electrical and Computer Engineering*, *6*, 2033–2040.

Rameshwar, D. (2020, August). Big data analytics and artificial intelligence pathway to operational performance under the effects of entrepreneurial orientation and environmental dynamism: A study of manufacturing organisations. *International Journal of Production Economics*, *226*, 107599. Advance online publication. doi:10.1016/j.ijpe.2019.107599

Rao, P., Pollayi, H., & Rao, M. (2022). Machine Learning based design of reinforced concrete shear walls subjected to earthquakes. *Journal of Physics: Conference Series*, *2327*(1), 4. doi:10.1088/1742-6596/2327/1/012068

Raouf, A. (2021). Demystifying the effects of perceived risk and fear on customer engagement, co-creation and revisit intention during COVID-19: A protection motivation theory approach. *Journal of Destination Marketing & Management*, *20*, 100564. Advance online publication. doi:10.1016/j.jdmm.2021.100564

Rastogi, M., Vijarania, D., & Goel, D. (2022). *Role of Machine Learning in Healthcare Sector*. Neha.

Ravenscroft, A. (2011). Dialogue and Connectivism: A New Approach to Understanding and Promoting Dialogue-Rich Networked Learning. *International Review of Research in Open and Distance Learning*, *12*(3), 139. doi:10.19173/irrodl.v12i3.934

Ravi, K., & Ravi, V. (2015). A survey on opinion mining and sentiment analysis: Tasks, approaches and applications. *Knowledge-Based Systems*, *89*, 14–46. doi:10.1016/j.knosys.2015.06.015

Recognition. (n.d.). In *Advanced Multimedia and Ubiquitous Engineering*. Springer.

Reza, F. M., & Abbs, A. N. (2011). *On fractional-order pid design. Application of matlab in science and engineering*. Intech Open.

Riccardo, P., James, K., & Tim, B. (2017). *Particle Swarm Optimization Intelligence*. Academic Press.

Riduan, A. F., Tamaldin, N., Sudrajat, A., & Ahmad, A. F. (2018). Review on active suspension system. *SHS Web of Conferences, 54*.

Rifkin, R., & Klautau, A. (2004). Defences of one-vs-all classification. *Journal of Machine Learning Research*, *5*(Jan), 101–141.

Robert, P. C. (2002, November). Precision agriculture: A challenge for crop nutrition management. *Plant and Soil, 247*(1), 143–149. doi:10.1023/A:1021171514148

Robinson, G. S. (1977, October 1). Edge detection by compass gradient masks. *Computer Graphics and Image Processing, 6*(5), 492–501. doi:10.1016/S0146-664X(77)80024-5

Rodríguez-Hidalgo, C. T., Tan, E. S. H., & Verlegh, P. W. J. (2015). The social sharing of emotion (SSE) in online social networks: A case study in Live Journal. *Computers in Human Behavior, 52*, 364–372. doi:10.1016/j.chb.2015.05.009

Rogers, C. (1951). *Client Centred Therapy*. Hachette.

Roll, I., & Winne, P. H. (2015). Understanding, evaluating, and supporting self-regulated learning using learning analytics. *Journal of Learning Analytics, 2*(1), 7–12. doi:10.18608/jla.2015.21.2

Rousseau, J.-J. (1979). *Emile: Or, On education*. Basic Book.

Rousu, J., Saunders, C., Szedmak, S., & Shawe-Taylor, J. (2006). Kernel-based learning of Hierarchical multilabel classification models. *Journal of Machine Learning Research, 7*, 1601–1626.

Roy, A. (2020). An adaptive approach for query suggestion based on user's intent. *Journal of Intelligent Information Systems, 54*(1), 77–102.

SA Military Academy. (2019). *Annual Performance Plan 2019. Saldanha, RSA*. SA Military Academy.

Sabharwal, S., Gupta, S., & Thirunavukkarasu, K. (2016, April). Insight of big data analytics in healthcare industry. In *2016 International Conference on Computing, Communication and Automation (ICCCA)*. IEEE Xplore. 10.1109/CCAA.2016.7813696

Sadker, D., & Zittleman, K. (2016). *Teacher-Centered Philosophies. Teachers, Schools, and Society: A Brief Introduction to Education*. McGraw Hill.

Sahin, S., Tolun, M. R., & Hassanpour, R. (2012). Hybrid expert systems: A survey of current approaches and applications. *Expert Systems with Applications, 39*(4), 4609–4617. doi:10.1016/j.eswa.2011.08.130

Saif, H., He, Y., Fernandez, M., & Alani, H. (2016). Contextual semantics for sentiment analysis of Twitter. *Information Processing & Management, 52*(1), 5–19. doi:10.1016/j.ipm.2015.01.005

Saintilan, D., & Shelley, M. J. (2013). Active suspension and their non-linear models. *Competes Rendus Physique, 4*(6), 497-517.

Sajana, T., Rani, C. S., & Narayana, K. V. (2016). A survey on clustering techniques for big data mining. *Indian Journal of Science and Technology, 9*(3), 1–12. doi:10.17485/ijst/2016/v9i3/75971

Salomi, M., & Balamurugan, S. A. A. (2016). Need, application and characteristics of big data analytics in healthcare—A survey. *Indian Journal of Science and Technology, 9*(16), 1–5. doi:10.17485/ijst/2016/v9i16/87960

Sameh, A.-N., & Ozgur, T. (2020). A comparative assessment of sentiment analysis and star ratings for consumer reviews. *International Journal of Information Management, 54*, 102132. Advance online publication. doi:10.1016/j.ijinfomgt.2020.102132

Santhana Lakshmi, V., & Bavishna, A. (2020). Analyzing the Restaurant data to Predict the Best Mode of Income. *Sustainable Humanosphere, 16*, 270–277.

Sari, J. N., Nugroho, L. E., Ferdiana, R., & Santosa, P. I. (2016). Review on customer segmentation technique on ecommerce. *Advanced Science Letters, 22*(10), 3018–3022. doi:10.1166/asl.2016.7985

Satre, J. (1956). *Being and nothingness* (H. Barnes, Trans.). Philosophical Library.

Sawyer, S., & Tapia, A. (2005). The sociotechnical nature of mobile computing work:Evidence from a study of policing in the United States. *International Journal of Technology and Human Interaction, 1*(3), 1–14. doi:10.4018/jthi.2005070101

Scherer, K. R., Schorr, A., & Johnstone, T. (Eds.). (2001). *Appraisal processes in emotion: Theory, methods, research.* Oxford University Press.

Schmidt, A. H. (2016, July). Context-sensitive auto-completion for searching with entities and categories. *Proceedings of the 39th International ACM SIGIR conference on Research and Development in Information.* 10.1145/2911451.2911461

Schulz, F., Ebbecke, M., Gillmann, M., Adrian, B., Agne, S., & Dengel, A. (2009). Seizing the Treasure: Transferring Knowledge in Invoice Analysis. *2009 10th International Conference on Document Analysis and Recognition*, 848-852. 10.1109/ICDAR.2009.47

Sculley, D. (2010, April). Web-scale k-means clustering. In *Proceedings of the 19th international conference on world wide web* (pp. 1177-1178). 10.1145/1772690.1772862

Seber, G. A. F., & Lee, A. J. (2003). *Linear Regression Analysis.* Wiley Series. doi:10.1002/9780471722199

Selim, S. Z., & Ismail, M. A. (1984). K-means-type algorithms: A generalized convergence theorem and characterization of local optimality. *IEEE Transactions on Pattern Analysis and Machine Intelligence, PAMI-6*(1), 81–87. doi:10.1109/TPAMI.1984.4767478 PMID:21869168

Sharma, R., Kumar, A., & Chuah, C. (2021). Turning the blackbox into a glassbox: An explainable machine learning approach for understanding hospitality customer. *International Journal of Information Management Data Insights, 1*(2), 100050. doi:10.1016/j.jjimei.2021.100050

Shen, H. L. (2016). A study on personalized query suggestion based on user search intent. *Neurocomputing, 173*, 855–864.

Sherly Alphonse, A., & Dharma, D. (2017a). Enhanced Gabor (E-Gabor), Hypersphere-based normalization and Pearson General Kernel-based discriminant analysis for dimension reduction and classification of facial emotions. *Expert Systems With Applications, 90*, 127-45.

Sherly Alphonse, A., & Dharma, D. (2017b). Novel directional patterns and a Generalized Supervised Dimension Reduction System (GSDRS) for facial emotion recognition. *Multimedia Tools and Applications*, 1-34.

Sherly Alphonse, A., & Dharma, D. (2017c). A novel Monogenic Directional Pattern (MDP) and pseudo-Voigt kernel for facilitating the identification of facial emotions. *Elsevier International Journal of Visual Communication and Image Representation, 49*, 457-470.

Sherly Alphonse, A., & Starvin, M.S. (2019). A novel Maximum and Minimum Response-based Gabor (MMRG) Feature Extraction method for Facial Expression Recognition. *Springer Multimedia Tools and Applications*.

Sheth, J. (2020). Impact of Covid-19 on consumer behavior: Will the old habits return or die? *Journal of Business Research, 117*, 280–283. Advance online publication. doi:10.1016/j.jbusres.2020.05.059 PMID:32536735

Shi, A. M., Oliveares, A., & Rosseel, A. Y. (2020). Assessing fit in Ordinal Factor Analysis Models: SRMR vs RMSEA Structural Equation Modeling. *A Multidisciplinary Journal, 27*(1), 1-15.

Shivaswamy, P. K., Bhattacharyya, C., & Smola, A. J. (2006). Second order cone programming approaches for handling missing and uncertain data. *Journal of Machine Learning Research, 7*, 1283–1314.

Shokouhi, M. (2012, August). Time-sensitive query auto-completion. In *Proceedings of the 35th international ACM SIGIR conference on Research and development in information retrieval* (pp. 601-610). 10.1145/2348283.2348364

Shreshth, T., Shikhar, T., Rakesh, T., & Sukhpal, S. G. (2020). Predicting the growth and trend of COVID-19 pandemic using machine learning and cloud computing. *Internet of Things*, *11*, 100222. Advance online publication. doi:10.1016/j. iot.2020.100222

Shu-Hui, C. (2020). Co-creating social media agility to build strong customer-firm relationships. *Industrial Marketing Management*, *84*, 202–211. Advance online publication. doi:10.1016/j.indmarman.2019.06.012

Sigirci, I. O., Ozgur, H., Oluk, A., Uz, H., Cetiner, E., Oktay, H. U., & Erdemir, K. (2020). Sentiment Analysis of Turkish Reviews on Google Play Store. *2020 5th International Conference on Computer Science and Engineering (UBMK)*. doi:10.1109/ubmk50275.2020.921

Sina Mirabdolbaghi, S. M., & Amiri, B. (2022). Model Optimization Analysis of Customer Churn Prediction Using Machine Learning Algorithms with Focus on Feature Reductions. *Discrete Dynamics in Nature and Society*, *2022*, 1–20. Advance online publication. doi:10.1155/2022/5134356

Slavin. (2016). Climate and famines: A historical reassessment. *Wiley Interdisciplinary Reviews: Climate Change*, *7*(3), 433–447. doi:10.1002/wcc.395

Snekha, C. S., & Birok, R. (2013). Real Time Object Tracking Using Different Mean Shift Techniques–a Review. *International Journal of Soft Computing and Engineering*.

Song, Yu., Wang, Y., & Ye, X. (2023). Loan Default Prediction using a credit rating-specific and multi-objective ensemble learning scheme. Information Sciences, 629, 599-617.

Soni, N., Sharma, E. K., Singh, N., & Kapoor, A. (2019). Impact of Artificial Intelligence on Businesses: From Research, Innovation, Market Deployment to Future Shifts in Business Models. *Journal of Business Research*.

SparkA. (n.d.). https://runawayhorse001.github.io/LearningApacheSpark/setup. html

Spedding, E. (2010). Advancement of Learning. In *The Works of Francis Bacon* (pp. 1857–1870). London: Bartleby. com. Retrieved 6 11, 2019, from https://www.bartleby.com/br/193.html

Strang, K. (2017). Beyond engagement analytics: Which online mixed-data factors predict student learning outcomes? *Education and Information Technologies*, *22*(3), 917–937. doi:10.100710639-016-9464-2

SU. (2017). *SU strategy for teaching and learning 2017-2021*. Retrieved Oct 6, 2021, from https://www.sun.ac.za/english/learning-teaching/ctl/Documents/SU%20TL%20Strategy.pdf

Sullivan, D. (2015, April 22). *Google Instant is dead. Long live Google Instant!* Search Engine Land. https://searchengineland.com/google-instant-is-dead-long-live-google-instant-219553

Sullivan, E. (2022). Understanding from machine learning models. *The British Journal for the Philosophy of Science*.

Sun, S., Cao, Z., Zhu, H., & Zhao, J. (2019). A Survey of Optimization Methods form a Machine Learning Perspective. *IEEE Transactions on Cybernetics*, *50*(8), 3668–3681. doi:10.1109/TCYB.2019.2950779 PMID:31751262

Sun, W., Zhao, Y., & Li, J., L. Z. (2014). Active suspension control with frequency band constraints and actuator input delay. *IEEE Transactions on Industrial Electronics*, *59*(01), 530–537.

Sun, X., Chen, X., Pei, Z., & Ren, F. (2018, May). Emotional human machine conversation generation based on Seq-GAN. In *2018 First Asian Conference on Affective Computing and Intelligent Interaction (ACII Asia)* (pp. 1-6). IEEE. 10.1109/ACIIAsia.2018.8470388

Susanto, A. P., Winarto, H., Fahira, A., Abdurrohman, H., Muharram, A. P., Widitha, U. R., Warman Efirianti, G. E., Eduard George, Y. A., & Tjoa, K. (2022). Building an artificial intelligence-powered medical image recognition smartphone application: What medical practitioners need to know. *Informatics in Medicine Unlocked, 101017*. Advance online publication. doi:10.1016/j.imu.2022.101017

Suvritsra, Nowozin, & Wright. (2011). Optimization for Machine Learning. MIT Press.

Suykens, J. A., & Vandewalle, J. (1999). Least squares support vector machine classifiers. *Neural Processing Letters*, *9*(3), 293–300. doi:10.1023/A:1018628609742

Suzuki, K. (Ed.). (2013). *Artificial Neural Networks. Architecture and applications*. B.D. Books on Demand.

Syed, F. I., AlShamsi, A., Dahaghi, A. K., & Neghabhan, S. (2020). *Application of ML & AI to model petrophysical and geo-mechanical properties of shale reservoirs–A systematic literature review*. Petroleum. doi:10.1016/j.petlm.2020.12.001

Tabane, R. (2016). Contributions of Behaviourist Theories to Teaching and Learning. In M. Maphalala (Ed.), Teaching and Learning Strategies in South Africa (pp. 13 - 26). Cheriton House: Cengage.

Tahery, S., & Farzi, S. (2020). Customized query auto-completion and suggestion—A review. *Information Systems*, *87*, 101415. doi:10.1016/j.is.2019.101415

Tahery, S., & Farzi, S. (2022). TIPS: Time-aware Personalised Semantic-based query auto-completion. *Journal of Information Science*, *48*(4), 524–543. doi:10.1177/0165551520968690

Tandon, A. R. (2011). Genetic algorithm-based parameter tuning of PID controller for a composition control system. *International Journal of Engineering Science and Technology*, *3*(8), 6705–6711.

Tandon, B., & Randeep, K. (2011). Genetic algorithm-based parameters tuning of pid controller for a composition control system. *International Journal of Engineering Science and Technology*, *3*(8), 6707–6771.

Tang, P., Qiu, W., Huang, Z., Chen, S., Yan, M., Lian, H., & Li, Z. (2020). Anomaly Detection in electronic invoice systems based on machine learning. *Information Sciences*, *535*, 172–186. doi:10.1016/j.ins.2020.03.089

Tang, X., & Wang, X. (2002). *Face photo recognition using sketch*. Image Processing.

Tan, M. J., & Guan, C. H. (2021). Are people happier in locations of high property value? Spatial temporal analytics of activity frequency, public sentiment and housing price using twitter data. *Applied Geography (Sevenoaks, England)*, *132*, 102474. Advance online publication. doi:10.1016/j.apgeog.2021.102474

Tan, X., & Triggs, B. (2010). Enhanced local texture feature sets for face recognition under difficult lighting conditions. *IEEE Transactions on Image Processing*, *19*(6), 1635–1650. doi:10.1109/TIP.2010.2042645 PMID:20172829

Taylor, P., & Maor, D. (2000). Assessing the efficacy of online teaching with the Constructivist On-Line Learning Environment Survey. In A. Herrmann, & M. Kulski (Ed.), *Flexible Futures in Tertiary Teaching. Proceedings of the 9th Annual Teaching Learning Forum.* Curtin University of Technology.

Te, Y.-F., Müller, D., Wyder, S., & Pramono, D. (2018). Predicting the growth of restaurants using web data. *Economic and Social Development (Book of Proceedings), 237*.

Tenucci, A., & Supino, E. (2020). Exploring the relationship between product-service system and profitability. *The Journal of Management and Governance*, *24*(3), 563–585. doi:10.100710997-019-09490-0

Thakur, R., & Workman, L. (2016). Customer portfolio management (CPM) for improved customer relationship management (CRM): Are your customers platinum, gold, silver, or bronze? *Journal of Business Research*, *69*(10), 4095–4102. doi:10.1016/j.jbusres.2016.03.042

Thessen, A. E., Cui, H., & Mozzherin, D. (2012). Applications of natural language processing in biodiversity science. *Advances in Bioinformatics*, *2012*, 1–17. Advance online publication. doi:10.1155/2012/391574 PMID:22685456

Tien, N. H., Anh, D. B. H., & Thuc, T. D. (2019). *Global supply chain and logistics management. Dehli.* Academic Publications.

Tikmani, J., Tiwari, S., & Khedkar, S. (2015). An Approach to Customer Classification using k-means. *International Journal of Innovative Research in Computer and Communication Engineering*, *3*(11).

Tran, T. H., & Hoang, N. D. (2016). Predicting Colonization Growth of Algae on Mortar Surface with Artificial Neural Network. *Journal of Computing in Civil Engineering*, *30*(6), 04016030. doi:10.1061/(ASCE)CP.1943-5487.0000599

Triantafyllou, I., Drivas, I. C., & Giannakopoulos, G. (2020). How to utilize my app reviews? A novel topics extraction machine learning schema for strategic business purposes. *Entropy (Basel, Switzerland)*, *22*(11), 1–21. doi:10.3390/e22111310 PMID:33287075

Triguero, I., Galar, M., Merino, D., Maillo, J., Bustince, H., & Herrera, F. (2016). Evolutionary undersampling for extremely imbalanced big data classification under apache spark. *2016 IEEE Congr. Evol. Comput. CEC 2016*, 640–647. 10.1109/CEC.2016.7743853

Trinh, C., Huynh, B., Bidaki, M., Rahmani, A. M., Hosseinzadeh, M., & Masdari, M. (2022). Optimized fuzzy clustering using moth-flame optimization algorithm in wireless sensor networks. *Artificial Intelligence Review*, *55*(3), 1915–1945. doi:10.100710462-021-09957-3

Trivedi, A., Rai, P., DuVall, S. L., & Daumé, H. III. (2010, October). Exploiting tag and word correlations for improved webpage clustering. In *Proceedings of the 2nd international workshop on Search and mining user-generated contents* (pp. 3-12). 10.1145/1871985.1871989

Tseng, H. E., & Hrovat, D. (2015). State of the art survey: Active and semi-active suspension control. *Vehicle System Dynamics*, *53*(7), 1034–1062. doi:10.1080/00423114.2015.1037313

Tsoumakas, G. (2019). A survey of machine learning techniques for food sales prediction. *Artificial Intelligence Review*, *52*(1), 441–447. doi:10.100710462-018-9637-z

TurnIip, A., & Panggbean, J. H. (2020). Hybrid controller design-based magneto-rheological damper lookup table for quarter car suspension. *Int. J. Artif Intell, 18*(1), 193-206.

Ullah, I., Kim, C. M., Heo, J. S., & Han, Y.-H. (2022). An Energy-efficient Data Collection Scheme by Mobile Element based on Markov Decision Process for Wireless Sensor Networks. *Wireless Personal Communications*, *123*(3), 2283–2299. doi:10.100711277-021-09241-1

Ullah, Raza, B., Malik, A. K., Imran, M., Islam, S. U., & Kim, S. W. (2019). A churn prediction model using random forest: Analysis of machine learning techniques for churn prediction and factor identification in the telecom sector. *IEEE Access : Practical Innovations, Open Solutions*, *7*, 60134–60149. doi:10.1109/ACCESS.2019.2914999

Ulsoy, A. G., Deng, H., & Calanakci, A. M. (2012). *Active Suspension, Automotive control systems.* Academic Press.

Vakulenko, Y., Oghazi, P., & Hellström, D. (2019). Innovative framework for self-service kiosks: Integrating customer value knowledge. *Journal of Innovation and Knowledge*, *4*(4), 262–268. doi:10.1016/j.jik.2019.06.001

Vangie, B. (n.d.). What is customer experience. *Webopedia*. https://www.webopedia.com/TERM/C/customer_experience.html

Vapnik, V. (2013). *The Nature of Statistical Learning Theory*. Springer Science & Business Media.

Vartak, M., & Madden, S. (2018). Modeldb: Opportunities and challenges in managing machine learning models. *IEEE Data Eng. Bull.*, *41*(4), 16–25.

Vashishtha, S., & Susan, S. (2020). Fuzzy Interpretation of Word Polarity Scores for Unsupervised Sentiment Analysis. In *2020 11th International Conference on Computing, Communication and Networking Technologies, ICCCNT 2020*. Institute of Electrical and Electronics Engineers Inc. 10.1109/ICCCNT49239.2020.9225646

Veerachamy, R., & Ramar, R. (2021, March). Agricultural Irrigation Recommendation and Alert (AIRA) system using optimization and machine learning in Hadoop for sustainable agriculture. *Environmental Science and Pollution Research International*, *2021*, 1–20. doi:10.100711356-021-13248-3 PMID:33788091

Venhovens, K. P. T., & der, a. A. (1995). *Delft active suspension (DAS)*. Academic Press.

Vijarania, M., Udbhav, M., Gupta, S., Kumar, R., & Agarwal, A. (2023). Global Cost of Living in Different Geographical Areas Using the Concept of NLP. In Handbook of Research on Applications of AI, Digital Twin, and Internet of Things for Sustainable Development (pp. 419-436). IGI Global. doi:10.4018/978-1-6684-6821-0.ch024

Vijarania, M., Gambhir, A., Sehrawat, D., & Gupta, S. (2022). Prediction of Movie Success Using Sentimental Analysis and Data Mining. In *Applications of Computational Science in Artificial Intelligence* (pp. 174–189). IGI Global. doi:10.4018/978-1-7998-9012-6.ch008

Vincent, O.R., & Folorunso, O. (2009). A descriptive algorithm for sobel image edge detection. In *Proceedings of Informing Science & IT Education Conference (InSITE)* (Vol. 40, pp. 97-107). California: Informing Science Institute.

Vivek, S. (2018). *Clustering algorithms for customer segmentation*. Academic Press.

Walek, B., & Fajmon, P. (2023). A hybrid recommender system for an online store using a fuzzy expert system. *Expert Systems with Applications*, *212*, 118565. doi:10.1016/j.eswa.2022.118565

Wang, H., Lu, Y., Tian, Y., & Christov, N. (2020). Fuzzy Sliding mode Based Active Disturbance Rejection Control for Active Engineers. Part D. *Journal of Automobile Engineering*, *234*(2-3), 449–457. doi:10.1177/0954407019860626

Wang, J., & Biljecki, F. (2022). Unsupervised machine learning in urban studies: A systematic review of applications. *Cities (London, England)*, *129*, 103925. doi:10.1016/j.cities.2022.103925

Wang, L. (2020). *PID Control System Design and Automatic Tuning Using MATLAB/SIMULINK*. John Wily and Sons. doi:10.1002/9781119469414

Wang, N. (2022). Application of DASH client optimization and artificial intelligence in the management and operation of big data tourism hotels. *Alexandria Engineering Journal*, *61*(1), 81–90. doi:10.1016/j.aej.2021.04.080

Wang, X., & Tang, X. (2004a). Dual-Space Linear Discriminant Analysis for Face Recognition. *Proc. IEEE Int'l Conf. Computer Vision and Pattern Recognition*.

Wang, X., & Tang, X. (2004b). Random Sampling Lda for Face Recognition. *Proc. IEEE Int'l Conf. Computer Vision and Pattern Recognition*.

Wang, X., & Tang, X. (2006). Random Sampling for Subspace Face Recognition. *International Journal of Computer Vision*, *70*(1), 91–104. doi:10.100711263-006-8098-z

Wang, X., & Tang, X. (2009). *Face Photo-Sketch Synthesis and Recognition. In IEEE Transactions on Pattern Analysis and Machine Intelligence* (Vol. 31). PAMI.

Wang, Y., Kim, J., & Kim, J. (2021). The financial impact of online customer reviews in the restaurant industry: A moderating effect of brand equity. *International Journal of Hospitality Management, 95*, 102895. Advance online publication. doi:10.1016/j.ijhm.2021.102895

Wang, Z., Xie, P., Lai, C., Chen, X., Wu, X., Zeng, Z., & Li, J. (2017, January). Spatiotemporal variability of reference evapotranspiration and contributing climatic factors in China during 1961–2013. *Journal of Hydrology (Amsterdam), 544*, 97–108. doi:10.1016/j.jhydrol.2016.11.021

Weinberger, K. Q., Blitzer, J., & Saul, L. K. (2006). Distance metric learning for large margin nearest neighbor classification. *Advances in Neural Information Processing Systems*, 1473–1480.

Widyaningrum, P., Ruldeviyani, Y., & Dharayani, R. (2019). Sentiment analysis to assess the community's enthusiasm towards the development chatbot using an appraisal theory. In *Procedia Computer Science, 161, 723–730.* Elsevier B.V. doi:10.1016/j.procs.2019.11.176

Wiese, M., & Humbani, M. (2019). Exploring technology readiness for mobile payment app users. *International Review of Retail, Distribution and Consumer Research*, ●●●, 1–20. doi:10.1080/09593969.2019.1626260

Windler, K., Jüttner, U., Michel, S., Maklan, S., & Macdonald, E. K. (2017). Identifying the right solution customers: A managerial methodology. *Industrial Marketing Management, 60*, 173–186. doi:10.1016/j.indmarman.2016.03.004

Winne, P. H. (2017). A cognitive and metacognitive analysis of self-regulated learning. In P. Alexander, D. Schunk, & J. Greene (Eds.), *Handbook of selfregulation of learning and performance* (pp. 15–32). Routledge. doi:10.4324/9781315697048-3

Winston, P. H. (1992). *Artificial Intelligence Addison.* Westely Longman Publishing Co, Inc.

Wirtz, J. (2019, June 15). Cost-effective service excellence in healthcare. *AMS Review.* doi:10.1007/s13162-019-00139-7

Wise, A., & Vytasek, J. (2017). Learning Analytics Implementation. In C. Lang, G. Siemens, A. Wise, & D. Gasevic (Eds.), Handbook of Learning Analytics (pp. 151 - 160). New York: Society of Learning Analytics Research. doi:10.18608/hla17

Wise, A., Vytasek, J., Hausknecht, S., & Zhao, Y. (2016). Developing Learning Analytics Design Knowledge in the "Middle Space": The Student Tuning Model and Align Design Framework for Learning Analytics Use. *Online Learning, 20*(2), 155–182. doi:10.24059/olj.v20i2.783

Wiskott, L., Fellous, J., Kruger, N., & Malsburg, C. (1997, July). Face Recognition by Elastic Bunch Graph Matching. *IEEE Transactions on Pattern Analysis and Machine Intelligence, 19*(7), 775–779. doi:10.1109/34.598235

Wolfert, S., Ge, L., Verdouw, C., & Bogaardt, M. J. (2017). Big Data in Smart Farming – A review. *Agricultural Systems, 153*, 69–80. doi:10.1016/j.agsy.2017.01.023

World Bank Open Data. (n.d.). https://data.worldbank.org/

Wu, J., Li, H., Liu, L., & Zheng, H. (2017). Adoption of big data and analytics in mobile healthcare market: An economic perspective. *Electronic Commerce Research and Applications, 22*, 24–41. doi:10.1016/j.elerap.2017.02.002

Xia, L., Hyunju, S., & Alvin, C. (2021, March). Examining the impact of luxury brand's social media marketing on customer engagement: Using big data analytics and natural language processing. *Journal of Business Research, 125*, 815–826. Advance online publication. doi:10.1016/j.jbusres.2019.04.042

Xiao, S., & Sen, Z. (2020). Research and design of urban rail transit intelligent customer service system. *Technological Innovation and Application, 3*, 87–88.

Xin, H., & Den, Z. (n.d.). *Research on Artificial Intelligence Customer Service on Consumer Attitude and Its Impact during Online Shopping*. Academic Press.

Xu, P., & Sarikaya, R. (2013). Convolutional neural network based triangular CRF for joint intent detection and slot filling. *Automatic Speech Recognition and Understanding (ASRU) IEEE Workshop*, 78-83. 10.1109/ASRU.2013.6707709

Xu, H., Lai, J. G., Yu, Z. H., & Liu, J. Y. (2013). Based on neural network PID controller design and simulation. *Advanced Materials Research, 756*, 514–517. doi:10.4028/www.scientific.net/AMR.756-759.514

Yahoo. (n.d.). *Search help*. https://help.yahoo.com/kb/search-for-desktop/SLN2217.html

Yang, L., Li, Y., Wang, J., & Sherratt, R. S. (2020). Sentiment Analysis for E-Commerce Product Reviews in Chinese Based on Sentiment Lexicon and Deep Learning. *IEEE Access : Practical Innovations, Open Solutions, 8*, 23522–23530. doi:10.1109/ACCESS.2020.2969854

Yang, W., Li, J., Zhang, Y., & Gu, D. (2019). Security analysis of third-party in-app payment in mobile applications. *Journal of Information Security and Applications, 48*, 102358. doi:10.1016/j.jisa.2019.102358

Yin, J., Zhou, K., Li, Y., Li, X., Wang, F., & Lu, J. (2016). Auto-completion with recurrent neural networks. In *Proceedings of the 25th ACM International on Conference on Information and Knowledge Management* (pp. 55-64). ACM.

Yi, P. C., Choi, B., Bhowmick, S. S., & Xu, J. (2017). AutoG: A visual query autocompletion framework for graph databases. *The VLDB Journal, 26*(3), 347–372. doi:10.100700778-017-0454-9

Yogesh, K. D., Elvira, I. D., Laurie, H., & Jamie, C. (2021). Setting the future of digital and social media marketing research: Perspectives and research propositions. *International Journal of Information Management, 59*, 102168. Advance online publication. doi:10.1016/j.ijinfomgt.2020.102168

You, J. (2016). Identifying significant indicators using LMS data to predict course achievement in online learning. *Internet and Higher Education, 29*, 23–30. doi:10.1016/j.iheduc.2015.11.003

Yue, L., Chen, W., Li, X., Zuo, W., & Yin, M. (2019). A survey of sentiment analysis in social media. *Knowledge and Information Systems, 60*(2), 617–663. doi:10.100710115-018-1236-4

Yu, S. G. (2020). Personalized query suggestion based on social tagging data. *Journal of Intelligent Information Systems, 54*(1), 103–125.

Zamfir, V. A., Carabas, M., Carabas, C., & Tapus, N. (2019). Systems monitoring and big data analysis using the elasticsearch system. *Proc. - 2019 22nd Int. Conf. Control Syst. Comput. Sci. CSCS*, 188–193. 10.1109/CSCS.2019.00039

Zannin, L. (2020). Combining multiple probability predictions in the presence of class imbalance to discriminate between potential bad and good borrowers in peer-to-peer lending market. *Journal of Behavioral and Experimental Finance, 25*, 100272. doi:10.1016/j.jbef.2020.100272

Zeelenberg, M., & Pieters, R. (2004). Beyond valence in learner dissatisfaction: A review and new findings on behavioral responses to regret and disappointment in failed services. *Journal of Business Research, 57*(4), 445–455. doi:10.1016/S0148-2963(02)00278-3

Zha, J., Nguyen, V., Su, B., Jiao, R. et al., "Performance of the Seat Suspension System Using Negative Stiffness Structure on Improving the Driver's Ride Comfort," SAE Int. J. Veh. Dyn., Stab., and NVH 6(2):135-146, 2022, https://doi.org/ doi:10.4271/10-06-02-0009

Zhang, Q., Lu, J., & Jin, Y. (2021). Artificial intelligence in recommender systems. *Complex & Intelligent Systems, 7*(1), 439–457. doi:10.100740747-020-00212-w

Zhang, Y. (2021). A survey on query auto-completion in search engines. *Journal of the Association for Information Science and Technology*, 72(4), 397–411.

Zhan, X., Mu, Y., Hora, M., & Singhal, V. R. (2020). Service excellence and market value of a firm: An empirical investigation of winning service awards and stock market reaction. *International Journal of Production Research*, 1–17. doi:10.1080/00207543.2020.1759837

Zhao, L., Zeng, Z., Wang, Z., & Ji, C. (n.d.). PID control of vehicle active suspension based on particle Swarm optimization. Journal of Physics: Conference Series, 1748(3). doi:10.1088/1742-6596/1748/3/032028

Žliobaite, I., Bakker, J., & Pechenizkiy, M. (2009). Towards context aware food sales prediction. In *2009 IEEE International Conference on Data Mining Workshops*. IEEE. 10.1109/ICDMW.2009.60

About the Contributors

Md. Shamim Hossain is an accomplished academic and researcher in the field of marketing, with a research focus on the applications of machine learning in marketing, operations management, online business, e-marketing, self-service technologies (SSTs), e-commerce, m-banking, online customer behavior, and other areas of business. He received his Ph.D. in Business Management from the University of International Business and Economics (UIBE) in Beijing, China, and is currently an Associate Professor in the Department of Marketing at Hajee Mohammad Danesh Science and Technology University (HSTU) in Bangladesh. Dr. Hossain has published numerous research papers in prestigious journals, including the Journal of Retailing and Consumer Services, the Economic Analysis and Policy, the Journal of Food Quality, the Discrete Dynamics in Nature and Society, the Journal of Sport Psychology, the Journal of Hospitality and Tourism Insights, the Journal of Islamic Marketing, the FIIB Business Review, the Economic Research-Ekonomska Istraivanja, and the International Journal of Engineering Business Management. He has also contributed book chapters to several high-quality textbooks published by IGI-Global in the United States. In addition to his research work, Dr. Hossain is a dedicated teacher and has taught a variety of courses in marketing at HSTU. He is highly regarded for his engaging teaching style and his ability to make complex marketing concepts accessible and interesting. Dr. Hossain is a pioneer in the field of machine learning-based marketing and is actively engaged in research related to this area.

Ree Chan Ho, Ph.D., is an associate professor at Taylor's University, Malaysia. Dr Ho has extensive academic leadership and research experience. His current and previous academic portfolio includes the dean, head of the department, director of postgraduate programs, stream coordinator, etc. Prior to his academic career, Dr. Ho worked in the capacity of regional manager for the development of corporate enterprise systems, particularly in the areas of enterprise, finance, and real estate. He serves as the editorial advisory board member and acts as a regular reviewer for several indexed journals. His current research interests include business innovation and technology, online business, artificial intelligence, immersive live streaming, fintech, social commerce, big data analytics, etc.

Goran Trajkovski, Ph.D., is a lifelong learner with a passion for innovation in higher education and technology. With over 30 years of experience in leadership roles at institutions such as Western Governors University, Visa Inc., and Marian University, Dr. Trajkovski has designed and launched numerous academic products in the computing and business disciplines for institutions across the United States. With interests spanning from data-driven decision making to curriculum and customer learning experience design and development, Dr. Trajkovski has published over 300 works, including research papers and books, on topics such as diversity in IT education, cognitive and developmental robotics, and learning analytics. His contributions to the field have been recognized by numerous professional organizations. He remains committed to helping students and colleagues succeed in their academic and professional pursuits.

* * *

Abu Eyaz Abresham is an undergraduate studying in the department of marketing at Hajee Moham-mad Danesh Science and Technology University (HSTU). Abresham's research focuses on artificial intelligence, machine learning in marketing, e-marketing and online shopping.

Manu Banga is a Ph.D. in CSE with specialization AIML from Amity University Uttar Pradesh Noida having 10 years of teaching experience, published more than 15 papers in SCI & Scopus Journals and communicated 6 books with 2 patents awarded.

Anuja Bokhare is working as Assistant Professor in the department of Computer Science at Sym-biosis Institute of Computer Studies and Research, Pune, Maharashtra India. She has completed PhD in computer Studies from Symbiosis International (Deemed University). Also received M.Phil. (Computer Science) at Y.C.M.O.U, Nasik, India. Shehas 20 years of experience in the field of academics. Her research interest includes applications of fuzzy logic, artificial neural network, machine learning, deep neural network and software Engineering. She had published 22 research papers in international journal and conferences along with one book in her account.

Kingshuk Chatterjee, Asst. Prof, obtained his B.Sc.(H) from Asutosh College, B.Tech and M.Tech from Department of Computer Science and Engineering, University of Calcutta, PhD in Computer Science from Indian Statistical Institute, Kolkata. He is teaching Data Structure, Algorithms and Database Man-agement systems. His current research interests are automata theory, complexity theory and algorithms.

Kesavaraja D. has completed his B.E. (CSE) from Jayaraj Annapackiam CSI College of Engineer-ing, Nazareth under Anna University Chennai in 2005, M.E (CSE) from Manonmaniam Sundaranar University, Tirunelveli in 2010 and Ph.D. (I&CE) from Anna University, Chennai in April 2019. He is a co-author of a book titled "Fundamentals of Computing and Programming" and "Fundamentals of LaTeX Programming". He is currently working as an Associate Professor, Department of CSE, Dr.Sivanthi Aditanar College of Engineering, Tiruchendur. He has 14 years and 1 month of Teaching Experience. He received SAP Award of Excellence from IIT Bombay and Outstanding Reviewer Award from Elsevier. He has published many National and International Journal and conference papers. He has served as a reviewer for scientific journals such as Springer, Elsevier, IET, T&F and Technical Programme Committee Member for International Conferences. He has guided a student R&D Project Sponsored by IE (I), Kolkatta and TNSCST. His research interests include Cloud Computing, Internet of Things and Blockchain.

Omdev Dahiya is working as an Assistant Professor in the Department of Computer Science & Engineering, Lovely Professional University, Phagwara, Punjab, India. His research areas include Data Mining, Artificial Intelligence, Machine Learning, the Internet of Things, and Software Engineering.

He has more than 20 publications in SCI/Scopus indexed journals and conferences, 1 Patent granted (International) and 2 patents published (National).

Paramita Dey, Assistant Professor, obtained her B.Tech from Kalyani Government Engineering College, M.Tech from Department of Radiophysics & Electronics, University of Calcutta, and Ph.D in Computer Science from Jadavpur University, Kolkata. She is teaching Computer network, System security and Advanced Architecture. Her current research interests are Social network analysis, Distributed and Cloud computing, Machine learning and Big data analytics.

Soumya George is an Asst. Professor at St. George's College, Aruvithura. She completed her Ph. D in Computer Science from Cochin University of Science and Technology. Her research areas of interest include data mining, information retrieval, etc. She had many journal publications to her credit.

Ankur Gupta has received the B.Tech and M.Tech in Computer Science and Engineering from Ganga Institute of Technology and Management, Kablana affiliated with Maharshi Dayanand University, Rohtak in 2015 and 2017. He is an Assistant Professor in the Department of Computer Science and Engineering at Vaish College of Engineering, Rohtak, and has been working there since January 2019. He has many publications in various reputed national/ international conferences, journals, and online book chapter contributions (Indexed by SCIE, Scopus, ESCI, ACM, DBLP, etc). He is doing research in the field of cloud computing, data security & machine learning. His research work in M.Tech was based on biometric security in cloud computing.

Swati Gupta is currently working as Associate Professor in Department of Computer Science in KR Mangalam University, Gurugram. Her area of research are Database, Data Mining, Machine Learning and Artificial Intelligence. Prior to her appointment at KRMU, she was working in Amity University, Gurugram. Dr. Swati has received her undergraduate as well as her postgraduate degree in the field of computer science and her PhD is in field of Database and Data Mining. She has published a large number of papers in reputed Journals, conferences and books chapter.

Raj Gurram is innovative, Result Oriented Professional and Strategic leader with a history of success working in multiple industries. He has expertise in Enterprise Data Architecture, Data Lake, Data Migration, Data Integration, Data Quality, Master Data Management, Data Governance, Data Modeling and Data Warehousing. Complex problem solving, simplifying the legacy business systems & processes through creative solutions, re-structuring the complete support organizations to fit the next gen landscape are some of proven abilities.

Madhuri J. is working as Assistant Professor in Department of Computer Science and Engineering. She received her BE and MTech degree from Visvesvaraya Technological University. She is pursuing her research in the field of Machine Learning and Big Data Analytics. Her areas of interest include remote sensing and Artificial Intelligence.

Nitin Kumar is a BSc (Data Science) student of K R Mangalam University Gurugram. He has good experience in machine learning, deep learning projects. He has published few papers in international conferences and book chapters.

Rohit Kumar is a BSc (Data Science) student of K R Mangalam University Gurugram. He has good experience in machine learning, deep learning projects. He has published few papers in international conferences and book chapters.

XeChung Leow Nelvin expertise lies in research methodology and data analysis using multiple software. His research interests are marketing, smart mobility, and travel behavior modeling.

Indiramma M. is currently working as Professor in Computer Science and Engineering Department. She is also a coordinator for Industry Institute Interaction Cell (IIIC) at BMS College of Engineering. Dr. Indiramma M received the BE degree in Computer science and Engineering from Mysore University, India. She received the ME degree in Computer science and Engineering from Bangalore University, India. Also She received the Ph.D. degree in Computer Science and Engineering from Visvesvaraya Technological University (VTU), Belguam, India. Her research interests and area are Big Data Analytics, Artificial Intelligence, Machine learning, and Cloud Computing.

Md Abdullah Al Noman has completed his B.B.A major in finance degree from the Department of Finance and Banking at Hajee Mohammad Danesh Science and Technology University, Dinajpur, Bangladesh. In the field of research, he shows deep enthusiasm for exploring new business ideas and opportunities. His research activities have primarily been related to customer satisfaction, e-payment, customer sentiment analysis, and marketing. He has written some articles on his research area mentioned above and participated in two research conferences to present his research paper, like International Conference on Business and Economic Challenges. He is always very sincere and interested in research-related matters.

Sabyasachi Pramanik is a Professional IEEE member. He obtained a PhD in Computer Science and Engineering from the Sri Satya Sai University of Technology and Medical Sciences, Bhopal, India. Presently, he is an Associate Professor, Department of Computer Science and Engineering, Haldia Institute of Technology, India. He has many publications in various reputed international conferences, journals, and online book chapter contributions (Indexed by SCIE, Scopus, ESCI, etc). He is doing research in the field of Artificial Intelligence, Data Privacy, Cybersecurity, Network Security, and Machine Learning. He is also serving as the editorial board member of many international journals. He is a reviewer of journal articles from IEEE, Springer, Elsevier, Inderscience, IET, and IGI Global. He has reviewed many conference papers, has been a keynote speaker, session chair and has been a technical program committee member in many international conferences. He has authored a book on Wireless Sensor Network. He has edited 8 books from IGI Global, CRC Press EAI/Springer and Scrivener-Wiley Publications.

Asif Jaied Pranto is a student at Hajee Mohammad Danesh Science and Technology University pursuing a Bachelor of Business Administration (BBA) in the marketing department. Machine learning, internet marketing, mobile banking, service marketing, e-banking, and e-commerce are among his research interests.

André Pretorius's research was conducted during his studies as masters student at the University of Stellenbosch and approved for publication by the Dean of the Faculty of Military Science.

Gopal R. has completed B.C.A., M.Sc., M.Phil., and pursuing Ph.D. in Computer Science in the Department of Computer Science Bharathiar University. Done publication of 3 Papers in Scopus, 4 papers in UGC and peer-reviewed journals, 2 papers communicated in SCI journal, 2 book chapters communicated, 1 self-published book and presented papers in 15 national & international conferences, attended 12 FDP Faculty Development Programs, 7 workshops, 11 seminars and webinars and also participated in various technical symposiums and completed certification courses. I was acted as a Project Fellow for the duration of 2 years which was funded by MHRD in Bharathiar University and also as a dedicated candidate I was chosen for the post of Secretary in UG and Department Chairman in PG.

Md. Mahafuzur Rahman is a student of the Bachelor of Business Administration (BBA) in marketing at Hajee Mohammad Danesh Science and Technology University. His research interests include customer satisfaction, internet marketing, service marketing, e-banking, and e-commerce.

Md Raisur Rahman is a student at Hajee Mohammad Danesh Science and Technology University pursuing a Bachelor of Business Administration (BBA) in the marketing department. Customer satisfaction, internet marketing, service marketing, e-banking, and e-commerce are among his research interests.

Madhuri Rao is currently working as an Assistant Professor at Symbiosis Institute of Computer Studies & Research, Symbiosis International Deemed University, India. She has obtained her Doctoral Degree in the year 2022 from the Biju Patnaik University of Technology and her work was essentially on sensor network. She acquired her Post Graduate Degree in Master of Computer Science & Engineering from Bharath University in 2008 and her Graduate Degree of Bachelor of Engineering in Computer Science in the year 2005. She has more than 10 years of teaching and research experience with 2 years of Industrial experience as Application Engineer at Slash Support Private India Limited. She is also the recipient of Best Research Scholar Award of BPUT in the year 2019 sponsored by TEQIP-III. He research interest are distributed systems, cloud computing, IoT, Software engineering and Machine Learning.

Naveen Saharan is working as a Data Scientist who believes in keeping up to date by acquiring new skills and continuous learning with an IT experience of over 11 years in Automotive, Retail, insurance and finance domain. He has experience in all the phases of Analytics and Machine Learning project from Model building, Model Validation, deployment, Model Serving and Model Monitoring He has hands on experience in building ML solution for Customer Analytics and involved in building of recommender System, Chatbots, Big data Solution designing for batch and real time analytics.

S M Nazmuz Sakib was birthed in Dinajpur, Bangladesh on the 16th of April in 2001. He achieved his Primary School Certificate (PSC) from Cotton Research Station School, Sreepur, Gazipur and after several months of studying Class 6 in Alhaz Dhanai Bepari Memorial High School, Sreepur, Gazipur, he relocated to Jashore. He accomplished his Junior School Certificate (JSC) from Jagodishpur Mirzapur Ismail Secondary School, Jagodishour, Chaowgacha, Jashore, and his Secondary School Certificate (SSC) from A. K. High School And College, Dhania, Dhaka-1236. He obtained his Higher Secondary Certificate (HSC) from Chowgacha Government College, Chowgacha, Jashore. He received a BSc in Business Studies, earning a CGPA of 4 out of 4 (1st class 1st) with 97.06% marks from School of Business and Trade, an online business school situated in Switzerland. He completed an MBA in Human Resources from International MBA Institute, an online business institute in Switzerland. Currently, he is in the final year of the LLB(Hon's) program at Dhaka International University, Dhaka, Bangladesh. He has accomplished several CPD verified advanced diploma and diploma programs, such as a diploma in Human Resources (HR), Web Design, Manufacturing - Productive Management with Fundamental Tools, ISO Standards - Integrated Management System (IMS), Effective Human Resource Administration, and Training of Trainers. Additionally, he completed advanced diplomas in Tourism and Hospitality Management, Modelling and Analytics for Supply Chain Management, Production and Operation Management, Principles of Industrial Engineering, and has obtained certifications such as TESOL from Arizona State University, TEFL from Teacher Record, Scrum Master Professional Certificate. Additionally, he completed advanced diplomas in Tourism and Hospitality Management, Modelling and Analytics for Supply Chain Management, Production and Operation Management, Principles of Industrial Engineering, and has obtained certifications such as TESOL from Arizona State University, TEFL from Teacher Record, Scrum Master Professional Certificate(SMPC®), Google IT Support Certificate, Google Data Analytics Certificate, and IBM New Collar: Customer Engagement Specialist credential.

Yuvraj Sharma has overall 7+ years' experience in different data related roles. He primarily works on managing and analyzing large amounts of data to solve key business-related problems. He ensures that maximum value generated from the data. He involved in identifying and managing data cleanup projects to improve data accuracy and enhance transparency of data. Provided support for Supply Chain projects by extracting requested data and providing analysis work when required. Yuvraj obtained post graduate in IT & Finance and completed his B-tech in Computer Science Engineering from Rajasthan Technical University.

A. Sherly Alphonse has received her B.E degree from Manonmaniam Sundaranar university, India and M.E from Anna University, India. She has five years teaching experience in various prestigious institutions. She is a reviewer of various international journals. She completed her full time Ph.D at Anna University, Chennai, India. Her research interest includes image processing and facial expression analysis.

Meenu Vijarania received her B.Tech degree in Information Technology from MDU university, Haryana in 2005 and M.Tech (I.T) degree from GGSIPU, New Delhi in 2007. She has 8 years of experience in teaching. Since 2011 she is working at Amity University Haryana as faculty in Computer Science Department and Completed PhD in the field of Wireless Ad-hoc Network. Her research area include topics of Wireless Networks and Genetic Algorithm.

Index

A

Absolute Error 205, 209, 221-222, 225
Accuracy 6, 8, 10, 12, 37, 51-52, 80, 107, 110, 117, 159, 183-185, 188, 194, 196-197, 204-209, 211, 220, 225, 239-240, 243, 245, 256-257, 262, 265, 272, 276, 279-280, 283-286, 288, 290, 309, 312, 333, 336, 338, 341-342, 347-348, 352-355, 364-365, 374
Advance Technology 1, 161
AFINN and VADER Sentiment Algorithms 342
AI Algorithm 325, 329
AI and Machine Learning 49, 89, 298, 300, 305, 308, 319, 326
Algorithms 2, 6-9, 12, 14, 45, 47, 80-81, 83, 88, 90-94, 96-97, 100, 108-111, 113-122, 124-126, 128, 138-140, 145, 154, 156-157, 159, 165-166, 170, 172, 174, 179, 181, 183, 188, 193, 196-197, 202-203, 205, 207-211, 218, 220-226, 229, 231, 233, 236-237, 241, 245-247, 251, 255-256, 258, 260, 263, 265, 267, 270, 274, 280, 282, 301, 303, 306, 312-314, 320, 323, 326, 328, 331-335, 337-338, 342, 354, 361, 364-368, 373, 377
Analysis 2-3, 5, 9, 11-12, 16-17, 25, 27, 34-35, 37, 40-41, 44-46, 54-55, 59, 63, 70, 73, 79-80, 88, 90-94, 97-98, 101, 104-105, 107, 109-111, 115, 117-118, 122, 125, 131, 134, 153, 158, 163, 166, 174, 176, 181, 196, 198-200, 204-205, 207-209, 211-213, 215-216, 218, 220-223, 225-226, 228-230, 232-233, 246-251, 254-255, 272-274, 279, 282-286, 291-295, 297, 301, 303, 305-306, 313-314, 316-317, 320-323, 326, 328, 335-336, 339-340, 342-345, 347, 353-361, 373-374, 378
Artificial Intelligence (AI) 1-4, 7, 10, 13-14, 16, 18, 31, 34, 36-40, 43-49, 52-53, 57, 82-83, 85-87, 89, 111, 128, 137, 159, 226, 273, 298, 300-312, 314, 316-321, 323-329, 334-341, 343, 361
Artificial Neural Networks (ANN) 128, 159
Ayushman Bharat-National Health Protection Mission

(AB-NHPM) 297

B

Bagging 118, 262-263, 276, 288
Big Data 2, 4, 7, 9, 31, 33-35, 54-55, 84-85, 92, 110, 115, 208, 224, 227-233, 245-247, 277-281, 295-297, 304, 322, 324, 341, 359, 365, 378
Body Motion 159
Brand Anthropomorphism 17, 21, 23, 28-29, 31, 36

C

CERMINE 373, 380
Churn 1-16, 115, 181, 304, 313, 317, 320, 323, 341
Class Imbalance 12, 274, 276, 282, 285, 288
Clearance Due Date Prediction 248, 252, 257
Cluster Technique 90
Clustering 8, 90-101, 105, 107-111, 115, 117-118, 122, 161, 163, 165, 174-177, 179-182, 205-206, 208, 224, 233, 279, 356, 358, 373
Combined Local Directional Pattern 183, 187
Commodities 276, 281
Computer Science 80, 109-110, 120, 181, 202, 223-225, 273, 301, 309, 314, 321, 328, 357-360
Contextual Commerce 17-23, 25-29, 36
Correlation 3, 110, 172, 203, 208, 213, 225, 236, 258, 265
Crop Recommendation 227, 231, 234, 236, 240, 242, 245-246
Customer Data of Restaurant (CDR) Dataset 225
Customer Demographics 220, 225
Customer Experience 5, 23, 43, 46, 49, 80-84, 86-87, 89, 303-304, 308, 317, 321, 326-327, 337-339
Customer Feedback 39, 115, 220, 225, 304, 317
Customer Service 3, 5-6, 46, 80-83, 86-89, 115, 207, 300-304, 306, 310, 315, 317, 319, 326, 328-329, 331, 338, 341-342, 347, 361
Customer Support Analytics 113-114, 125

D

Data Cleaning 212, 225

Data Pre-Processing 203, 207-208, 220, 225, 248, 281-282, 285-286

Dataset 6-8, 10-13, 37, 49, 90, 93, 96-100, 105-106, 109, 116, 118-119, 123-124, 162-163, 165-166, 170-171, 174, 176, 179, 187, 190, 193-194, 196-198, 203, 205, 207-210, 212-213, 220-221, 223, 225-226, 231-232, 235-236, 241, 243, 250-258, 261-265, 267, 271-273, 276, 282-288, 302, 313, 329, 347, 354

Decision Tree 7-9, 12, 109, 162, 166, 169-170, 181, 207, 221, 225, 236, 242-246, 248, 251, 261-263, 265-266, 268, 273, 285, 317, 348, 352

Deep Learning 8-9, 14, 18, 20, 23, 31, 33, 85, 89, 115, 155, 202, 218, 220, 223, 225, 247, 281, 297-298, 308, 310, 312, 314, 328, 331, 354-355, 358, 360, 365

Deep Learning Models 14, 218, 220, 225, 247, 354, 358

Di Pattern 183

Discount Slasher 325

E

E-Commerce 31-36, 39, 47-49, 84-85, 88, 114-115, 125, 181, 281, 301, 307-309, 315, 322-323, 332-333, 335, 360, 373-374

Economic Conditions 220, 225

Effort Expectancy 17, 19, 21-22, 27-28, 34-36

Elasticsearch 227, 233-234, 240, 242, 245, 247

Enhance Customer Support 300

Ensemble Learning 8, 12, 118, 205, 225, 274

Extreme Gradient Boosting (XG Boost) 225

Extreme Learning Machine 183, 187, 193, 199

F

Face Detection 325, 328-330, 333, 338, 340

Facilitating Conditions 19, 21, 23, 27-28, 34, 36

Feature Selection 110, 126, 165, 207, 224, 236, 246, 248, 251, 257, 265, 273-274, 276, 280, 282, 284-286, 288, 295, 315

Features Selection 220-221, 225

G

Genetic Algorithms (GA) 128

Grab Community 325

Gradient Boosting 119, 203, 208, 222, 225, 263, 273

Gradient Descent Algorithm 237, 241

I

Information Technology 31, 34, 161, 202, 225, 228, 307

Integrated Product Service Offerings 300, 317, 322-323

IoT 3, 13, 55, 115, 160, 232, 249, 320

J

Java 10, 233, 373-374, 380

K

Kafka 227, 231-233, 236, 240-241, 245

Kart Analyzer 325

K-Fold Cross Validation 221, 225

K-Mean Clustering 90, 206

Knowledge Graph 362, 364-365, 378

L

Learning Analytics 56-57, 74-79, 276, 321, 357

LightGBM 218, 221-223, 225

Linear Regression 117-118, 172-174, 207-208, 210, 221, 225, 248, 250-252, 254, 261, 265-267, 273-274

Location 4, 14-15, 44, 46, 167, 207-209, 211, 220, 225-226, 231, 234, 240, 242, 245, 252, 287, 295, 315, 332, 364-367, 374-375

Logistic Regression 2, 6-9, 12-14, 16, 117-119, 162, 181, 206, 209, 249, 285-286, 342, 348, 352-354

Long Short-Term Memory (LSTM) Neural Network 226

M

Machine Learning (ML) 1-4, 7-14, 16, 57, 80, 83-86, 88, 116, 122, 125, 159, 234, 240, 250, 297, 300-307, 309-313, 316-319, 323-324, 326, 342-343, 345-347, 354

Machine Learning Algorithms 2, 7-8, 14, 81, 88, 113-114, 116, 118, 125, 183, 202, 205, 208, 218, 220-226, 233, 236, 241, 256, 323, 326, 328, 331, 354, 373

Machine Learning Approaches 94, 114, 125, 207, 209, 221-222, 250, 272-273, 321, 342, 357

Mall Customers 90

Mathematical Programming 113, 122, 126

Mean Squared Error (MSE) 226, 239, 265

Mobile Apps 277, 343, 358, 361

Mode of Payment 213, 226

Model Testing 86, 297

Model Validation 297

N

Neo4j 364, 372-373, 380
Normalization 11, 126, 173, 199, 203, 220, 225-226

O

Online Shopping 18, 31, 34, 37, 39, 48-49, 89, 309, 323, 326-328, 333, 335-336
Optimization Techniques 113-116, 125, 241, 317
Order Wise Sales Summary (OSS) Dataset 226

P

Particle Swarm Optimization (PSO) 142, 298
Payment Apps 342-345, 348, 350, 354-355, 361
Pedagogy 56-57, 68-69, 72-73
People Search 325, 328-329, 332-333, 336, 338-340
Performance Expectancy 19, 21-22, 27-28, 30-31, 34-36
Predictive Analysis 254
Pre-Order 213-214, 226
Product Picker 325
Public Holidays and Weekend Impact on Sales 226

Q

Query Auto-Completion 362, 364-365, 375-379
Query Autosuggestion 362, 364-366, 374-376

R

Random Forest 2, 6, 8-9, 12, 16, 118, 206-209, 218, 223, 248, 251-252, 254, 261-263, 265, 267, 269-270, 273, 286, 348, 352
Rapid Miner 90
Readmission 276-277, 279-283, 285-288, 290-296
Ride Comfort 130-131, 146-147, 154, 159
Road Handling 130-131, 159
Root Mean Square Error (RMSE) 226

S

Sales 19, 22, 33, 40, 47, 49, 53, 81, 88, 202-205, 207-209, 211-213, 215-218, 220-226, 261, 306, 325-329, 334, 339-340, 343-344, 355
Sales Predication 202-203
Sales Prediction 202-203, 209, 224, 226
Search Engine 362, 365-367, 369, 374-377, 379-380
Seasonal Trends 220, 226
Self-Efficacy 36, 38, 71

Self-Service Technology 300, 304, 317, 319
Semiconductor Supply Chain 1-7, 9-11, 13-15
Sentiment 2, 7, 44, 47, 55, 80, 88, 97, 208, 220, 223, 225, 304-305, 314, 317, 320-323, 326, 342, 344-351, 353-361, 374
Sentiment Analysis 2, 55, 80, 88, 97, 208, 220, 225, 305, 314, 317, 320-323, 326, 342, 344-345, 347, 353-361, 374
Sentiment Prediction 342
Sequence Graph-Based Query Auto-Suggestion (SGQAS) 362, 364, 369, 377, 380
Service Excellence 300, 304, 317, 319, 322-324
Smart Carpooling 160, 180
Smartphone 324, 343, 361
Social Influence 19, 21-23, 27-28, 30, 32, 36
Social Media Platforms 36-39, 41, 47, 328, 330, 333, 338
Spark 8, 208, 223, 227-228, 231-233, 236, 240-241, 245-247
Standardization 161, 203, 226
Stanford PTB Tokenizer 380
Supervised Learning 91, 113, 116-118, 162, 169, 172, 208, 282, 298, 302, 345, 347
Support Vector Machine 9, 117, 126, 166, 200, 207-210, 276, 298
Support Vector Regression 221-223, 226
Suspension Travel 159

T

TensorFlow 203, 223, 226, 272-273
Two Degrees of Freedom 159

U

Unsupervised Learning 85, 91, 96-98, 100, 116-118, 163, 174, 205, 272, 302, 345
User Reviews 343-344, 346-348, 352, 354, 361
UTAUT 17-23, 28-29, 31-32, 34-35

W

Weather Forecasting 203, 226
Weather Impact on Sales 226
Word of Mouth 300, 303-304, 317, 319, 355
Word Sequence Graph 362, 364, 368-369, 380
WSG, Word Sequence Graph 380

X

XGBoost 8-9, 12, 119, 248, 251-252, 254, 263-265, 267-268, 273

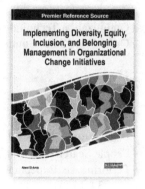

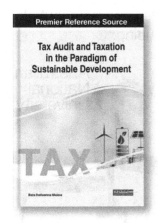   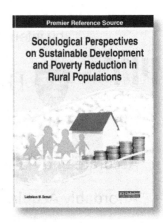